Sri Subuddipradayi
may you be able
understand & rem
this material.
—Freedom

M000105741

Science of Light

Foundations of Vedic Astrology

श्रीः

Science of Light

ज्योतिर्विद्या

Foundations of Vedic Astrology

वेदाङ्गज्योतिषप्रदीपिका

By
Freedom Tobias Cole

First Edition 2012
Science of Light, Volume II
ISBN-10: 098501220X
ISBN-13: 978-0-9850122-0-5

Copyright ©2012 Freedom Tobias Cole

Trademark SN 85-419,496

All rights reserved. No part of this publication may be reproduced, stored in a retrieval system or transmitted in any form or by any means electronic or mechanical, without the copyright owner's prior written consent.

Published by Science of Light LLC.

Nevada City, CA

Science of Light

www.ScienceofLight.net

Introduction

Vedic Astrology is a beautiful, ancient science of self-discovery which teaches us how life works, how we fit into the bigger picture, our purpose for being here, and the goal of our lives. This study and practice enriches our own life and enables us to help other people enrich theirs, giving guidance in all matters of life, from career to love to health. As a teacher of yoga and āyurveda, I am amazed at the profound perspectives offered by understanding this often complex, yet always inspiring science.

I traveled all over the world to study with many Western and Indian teachers before meeting an Indian Guru who was able to answer any question I asked about this science. Sitting in classes with his advanced students literally made my head spin; sometimes I had to hold onto the seat of my chair. The way my brain processed information and viewed reality shifted - it was a change in my own consciousness from knowing that everything in the universe is connected, to understanding how it is all connected.

This book lays a firm foundation to expand the awareness toward the higher teachings of Vedic astrology. Many books aim to help a person read their chart and the charts of others; that important component is also taught in this book, but a deeper layer of astrological information is also presented here. It is by setting a proper foundation that the fully empowered flower of intuition will bloom. A technical understanding forms the roots, and it is the strength of the roots that show the might of the tree.

I have spent the last few years researching more advanced topics in Vedic Astrology, but have felt the lack of proper foundations limiting the audience of such research. This book attempts to create an honest, well-rounded understanding of Vedic astrological principles. I plan to follow this edition with two more books, completing the full set of tools a person will need to have a holistic approach and comprehension as a qualified Vedic Astrologer. This book is Vedic Astrology 101. Each chapter here could be a whole book in and of itself, but my goal is to make sure a person has the overall view of the field of this science.

I offer this book for students of Vedic Astrology to find the gems without wandering around for years looking for the mines. I have used the ancient text of Mahārṣi Parāśara, the grandfather of Indian astrology, as a basis for this book. His text is a gold mine filled with endless gems, and this book elucidates the secrets found therein. The systematic study of this text will open the doorway to the ancient science of light.

Dedication

This book is dedicated to my Paramguru, Kaśinath Rath. He has made the secret science of Jyotiṣa accessible to people everywhere with the grace of our Paramparaguru Śri Acyutānanda Dasa.

Vṛṣabhaṁ carṣaṇīnāṁ viśvarūpamadābhyam।
Bṛhaspatiṁ vareṇyam।। 3।62।6

Auṁ Śrīṁ Dhlīṁ Jyotirbrahmāya Namaḥ

Acknowledgements

I give thanks to my Jyotiṣa guru Pandit Sanjay Rath and my Sanskrit guru Vāgīśa Śāstri. I may sound like a know something, but in front of them I am a little child, and without them, I would be a sinking fool in the sea of jñāna. I want to thank Mark Dyczkowski for his small suggestions that opened a hundred doors. And I acknowledge the above three teachers who have shown me that there is a reason to devote one's life to study. I would like to acknowledge my senior guru brothers, Zoran Radosavljevic and Visti Larsen for their clarifications when I have needed them. I also want to thank my students who support me in so many ways and for reminding me of the value of my work. A special thanks to Alexandra Epple for her help in editing.

I am just a student who believes he is good at writing and explaining things. Please forgive me for any mistakes in the present text. I fall at the feet of the Śūnya Guru, Mahāpuruṣa Acyutānanda, who teaches that absolute humility is the way to learn.

ॐ

गणानां त्वा गणपतिं हवामहे कविं कवीनामुपमश्रवस्तमम्
ज्येष्ठराजं ब्रह्मणां ब्रह्मणस् पत आ नः शृणवन्नूतिभिः सीद सादनम्

Gaṇānāṁ tvā gaṇapatiṁ havāmahe kaviṁ kavīnāmupamaśravastamam
Jyeṣṭharājaṁ brahmaṇāṁ brahmaṇas pata ā naḥ śṛṇvannūtibhiḥ sīda sādanam

Note on the First Edition

Volume II expects one to be familiar with the terminology taught in volume I of *Science of Light*. These two books go together. This book can also be read on its own by one educated in Vedic Astrology. If the terminology of this book is too advanced, one is advised to review the introductory volume. There is an online course that goes chapter by chapter through volume I and II at www.ScienceOfLight.net. Various additional materials can also be found there. Pandit Sanjay Rath offers a five year Parāśara course. The material covered here is introductory to the information covered in that course and therefore complimentary.

The first edition is not as grammatically correct as I would like. Being that a large percentage of my audience doesn't have English as their first language anyway, I have put my emphasis into the content. My writing falls into a void between two worlds. There are astrology books meant for the masses written in simple language and without Sanskrit. Then there are well edited Sanskrit filled university texts that will only speak of such subjects as if they are the outdated beliefs held by people of the past. The future holds a new era, which has germinated and is bursting forth. This book speaks to the new era, which is a realm where this ancient knowledge will be researched and held to a professional level.

Comments can be sent to:

Freedom Cole
P.O.Box 2665
Nevada City, CA 95959 USA
freedomfamily@gmail.com

Preface

The first volume of *Science of Light* focused on teaching the primary components of Vedic astrology with the intent to have students able to read a chart, have access to traditional scriptures and know how to deepen their knowledge with experience. The second volume goes deeper into the philosophical foundations of Vedic astrology. Deepening our underlying understanding strengthens our foundations and creates a context for more advanced techniques.

Our individual reality is created by the thought structures and language we have. The more language we have, and the deeper we understand it, the broader we can approach the world and the deeper our astrology will go. The first volume shifted the individual reality into an interconnected whole and the second volume goes into the structure and functioning of that holistic framework. Proper understanding of this reference point allows one to unlimit themselves and their vision.

Chapter 1: Process of Creation

The first chapter of the second volume is a translation of the first chapter of *Bṛhat Paraśara Horā Śastra* (BPHS) on creation. All important Vedic texts start with the creation for reasons explained in the chapter, but the level of this information was too much for the first volume where the student would have been confronted with very advanced Vedic philosophy too soon. Vedic astrology gives a holistic view of reality, but we must expand to that vantage point. So the first volume starts with introducing the Vedic arena and its organization, and after making it through that text, one is more prepared to learn this deeper level.

One's interpretations are guaranteed to be biased according to one's perspective; therefore the perspective must be purified. We must deepen our perception of the universe and perceive from a clear vantage point. Sāṁkhya philosophy is ruled by the Moon as it relates to our *perception* of reality and its purification. Understanding the emanation of the universe opens the doorway to becoming a Seer of Reality (*tattva-darṣinī*). This first chapter is difficult for the average person, but I ask students to read it the best they can. There are certain concepts taught there that will be elaborated on later, such as the nature of Time, the guṇas and the elements. This chapter lays the framework in which the other concepts will rest within.

Translating this chapter has strengthened my faith in Ṛṣi Parāśara and that this text was truly a transmission from his lineage. It was only relatively recently that these types of texts were written down. Verses of the Ṛgveda have stayed unchanged in time and transmission, but other śāstras have undergone a change in grammar to fit the time they were actually put into written form. Getting lost in dating Sanskrit words and grammar takes huge efforts away from the primary task of understanding the transmission of knowledge. I have attempted to balance between scholarly dating/explication based on ideology present in the text, and the intent of the knowledge being transmitted. The result is a balance between the realms of scholastic interpretations and faith in the knowledge, while avoiding fundamentalist beliefs on either side.

Chapter 2: Time

Some aspects of this chapter are high philosophy, and may not be easy to read for that reason, but the student is encouraged to read it and at least let these chapters digest in the unconscious. To truly be a Vedic astrologer one needs to understand the Vedic paradigm, otherwise it is western astrology with Vedic techniques. The concepts in these chapters have greater implications for how we perceive creation and time, and therefore how we look at human existence.

The first chapter briefly talks about the creation. We now exist in time and this must be explained. If one can follow the philosophy of Time and its movement of the guṇas from the creation chapter to this chapter, the profundity of Parāśara is beautifully broadened. Everything in Vedic astrology is based upon time, as things happen in time, at the right time. The chapter is divided into two sections. The first section begins with looking at the Vedic perception of Time; through the Vedas, Upaniṣads, Āgamas and Purāṇas which aims to give us a sense of how Parāśara may have conceived of time. There is a certain stress on getting the astrologer to think in the traditional Vedic sense about Time- to realize the powerful force which Time is.

The second section focuses on the breakdown of the units of empirical time. These time units should be understood by a Vedic astrologer to deepen their understanding of the mathematics of Jyotiṣa and the mysticism which is based upon the numbers related to these units. The student of Vedic Astrology must be familiar with the basic workings of Vedic time keeping (the calendar), on a larger scale than just the days pañcaṅga. This is just an introduction presenting the lunar and solar workings of the calendar with the calculation of months, intercalary months and relevant variations. Then we look at the larger time units to see how both the quantumly small and galacticly large units of time existed in the ancient world.

Chapter 3: Naisargika Daśā

After studying time in the external world, we take a look at time in the internal world; getting practical. The chapter starts with a brief look at the types of daśā that exist; the differences and the applications to give a general framework for the multitude of daśās. The intention is to help give a cognitive place to put all the multiple daśās that will be presented as we go along so they do not become overwhelming.

Then the chapter focuses on natural time (naisargika graha daśā), which is a daśā that precedes all others, and is therefore foundational to interpreting other daśās successfully. It is a very basic daśā that is so simple, you really should have learned it first, but it is almost too simple to learn first, so we learn something that has a wide utility, then we refine our understanding with something that runs underneath.

This daśā is 'time' according to the internal biological clock of the human being, a clock that ticks basically the same for everyone. Since this daśā was used in all places from India to Greece, I have added some additional cross cultural references. The mind is ripe from mediating on time and is ready to see it even more deeply. From the perspective of daśā, I show how we can utilize more than one and use this to compliment what we already know. My guru, Pandit Sanjay Rath thinks in about ten daśās a minute, like a watch that you can see the parts inside moving. As our astrological knowledge grows we must become aware of the multiple cogs of time always at work.

Then the chapter looks at two methods of progressing through the houses. We briefly look at naisargika bhāva daśā which is taught by Ṛṣi Jaimini, just to give an understanding of a natural house progression. Then we have a basic introduction to the Sudarśana Cakra according to the *Sudarśana-cakra-phala-adhyāya* of Parāśara.

Chapter 4: Guṇas

In the first part of this chapter, I go deeper into understanding the guṇas, quoting from various texts to help deeper one's understanding. Then we look at Parāśara's teachings in the *Sattva-ādi-guṇa-phala-adhyāya*, which is based on the relationship of the guṇas and time. This section shows the practical application of some of the expounded philosophy of time/guṇas. The deeper import is to show the power of Time and how an astrologer works within it. The astrologer is reading the flow of Time. To understand that is to appreciate what we see as astrologers. In the process, I have taken this space to elaborate the general understanding of the guṇas and how they impact an individual's nature as well as profession.

When something has sattva it is *sāttvika*, when something has rajas it is *rājasika*, and that which has tamas is *tāmasika*. In Hindi, the 'a' at the end is dropped. And in unscholarly English transliteration people have used the 'c' at the end instead of a 'k': sattvic, rajasic, tamasic. We will use the proper Sanskrit transliteration of these words.

Chapter 5: Five Elements

The next chapter focuses on the five elements. Volume one intended to insure that a student could understand the general qualities of each of the five elements. Here we take a deeper look at the elements, how they came to be, and the related tanmātrā and indriya.

Parāśara does not follow the non-theistic *Sāṅkhya Kārikā* and its system of dividing the ahaṅkāra, but follows a standard theistic Sāṅkhya found in other texts. This was explained in the chapter on creation. Here we start with a general overview of the attributes of the five elements, and then go into the philosophy of their role in creation/perception to be able to understand their function more holistically. Then I get a small soapbox moment discussing the difference between the five elements in Vedic science compared to modern western science. The deities of the elements are briefly mentioned here as utilization will be discussed elsewhere.

Then we look at the elemental qualities of an individual according to Parāśara in the *Pañca-mahābhūta-phala-adhyāya*. I have added a small introduction to Svara Śāstra which is a Saṁhitā science that involves Yoga, Tantra and Jyotiṣa. There is only mention of what pertains directly to the study of the five elements. A deeper study is important for use in praśna and muhūrta, and will be discussed there. We also look at the Kulākula Cakra since it directly pertains to the elements and helps elucidate their interaction. I have referenced what I feel is important. Students who have these texts available should take the time to check some of these references and become familiar with the root texts.

Chapter 6: Circumstances of Birth

An astrologer looks at a **birth** chart, so birth is definitely an important phenomena to understand. The chapter on circumstances of birth is centered around the *Sūtikā-adhyāya* which is found in some versions of BPHS and not others. Was it lost in one version or found in the other? Comparing the chapter order and topics to other texts (conception, birth circumstances, bālāṛṣṭā), it is traditional to put this topic in this place and so I have accepted it. I have also supplemented with techniques given in *Janma-kāla-lakṣaṇa-adhyāya* of Varāhmihira's Bṛhat Jātaka and texts which elaborate Varāhmihira's teaching.

This chapter starts with an overview of some debated issues associated with birth, such as conception and birth time. On the topic of embyological development, I have used the Āyurvedic texts where they are accurate and supplemented this with modern understandings where needed. I agree with many of the arguments of Rahul Peter Das that we need to be accurate and not accomodating with the ancient medical texts. But I do use the word *śoṇita* to refer to the *strī-bīja* for its conceptual purposes, as Vedic science accepts the use of inference. After the philosophical foundation is given, there is an analysis of the general birth circumstance techniques, making them practical and showing the general principles that can be applied in other situations. There is a small excerpt from a Nāḍī text to show how these techniques were actually used in a traditional reading. I have also included a small section on choosing a name in this chapter since it is a circumstance of birth. The major classics do not give much information on choosing a name, but there are many traditional teachings which are mentioned here.

Chapter 7: Special Ascendants

The chapter on special ascendants (*Viśeṣa-lagna-adhyāya*) is given in the second volume of this introductory book while Parāśara in BPHS gives the calculations in the very beginning right after the calculation of planetary position. His focus was more on teaching the mathamatical calculation so that the information needed to create a complete chart would be present. For the first three special ascendants, Parāśara gives no teaching about how to interpret them. In this chapter, we learn the mathematical calculations according to Parāśara and the interpretation of the special ascendants according to tradition with a few verses from the *Jaimini Upadeśa Sūtras*. I have waited until signs, planets, aspects, strengths and timing were understood first to introduce these special points of a chart. Traditionally a student does calculations for a few years (or a decade) and then starts to learn about interpretation. In this way, the calculations are traditionally given in the very beginning.

These calculations teach a principle of time according to the birth time from Sunrise. In the version of BPHS available to us, the bhāva lagna, horā lagna, and ghaṭīkā lagna are taught in one chapter with the varṇada lagna and the varṇada daśā. I have not gone into the daśā but just focused on the special ascendants. I add calculations and information here on the Śrī lagna which is mentioned by Parāśara in the *Daśā-adhyāya*, but do not go into calculation or use of sudaśā. I also include the prāṇapada lagna here while Parāśara has put it in the end of the *Graha-guṇa-svarūpa-adhyāya*and the *Aprakāśa-graha-phala-adhyāya* with the aprakāśa grahas. I have tried to have one chapter that gives a general idea about the various special ascendants; the conceptual framework for their calculations and practial usage of both their positions and using them as a lagna (seeing placements from them). Their usage brings a new level of deeper refined vision to the astrological chart.

Chapter 8: Nārāyaṇa daśā

It is very important to have a good understanding of daśā based on rāśi, not just planets. In the naisargika chapter we introduced some rāśi periods, but they were calculated based primarily on the houses instead of an actual rāśi calculation. Here we learn a method of timing to begin understanding the realm of rāśi daśā; to use both with other daśā and alone for its own specific type of prediction. A Venus daśā will have a different impact in a seventh house Sagittarius daśā than in a tenth house Pisces daśā. The right rāśi daśā will also make it easier to see certain things like moving home or getting a raise at work.

Rāśī daśās are taught by Parāśara, but are not used in the Varāhamihira line of texts. The uneducated consider using rāśi daśā as a "Jaimini" technique, and I have already spoken much about this misnomer. I clearly indicate the references for rāśi daśā calculation in this chapter and request practitioners to be educated about this aspect of Parāśara.

Cara daśā is the first rāśi daśā given by Parāśara in the *Daśā-adhyāya* (v.155 -167). There are different variations of Cara daśā from different traditions and teachers. Many, like B.V. Raman, K.N.Rao, and P.S. Sastri, use their interpretation of Nīlakaṇṭha. Others, like Sri Iranganti Rangacharya, use the rules given by Jaimini. Our tradition uses a few verses from Jaimini to do a form of Cara daśā called *rāśi-pada-krama daśā* in South India, or as *Nārāyaṇa daśā* in East India.

All aspects of the calculation of Nārāyaṇa daśā are found in Parāśara in either the *Daśā-adhyāya* or the *Antardaśā-adhyāya* and the references have been given. Which calculations to utilize and and how to utilize them has variation in different traditions. I have given the variation which has been given according to the tradition I am educated within and have given the interpretation of the daśā accordingly. A basic level of interpretation is given based on a direct translation of the *Carādi-daśā-phala-adhyāya*. In this way, everything is directly referenced from Parāśara.

Most of the chapters in this book and the previous could be whole books in themselves. Sometimes even small sections of chapters are material that could take an entire book to understand fully. The goal of this text is to give a vast overview to provide a framework for a proper perspective to learn within. This requires being explicit sometimes and brief other times, particulary when the information is readily available. Pandit Sanjay Rath, who is a master of this daśā, has written an entire book on this topic. Therefore, I give just a brief lesson to begin working with this daśā: what is the daśā, why is it used, how to calculate it, and how to interpret it in rāśi and other vargas.

Chapter 9: Āyurjyotiṣa

Āyurjyotiṣa has two main branches: health (*daiva-cikitsā*) covered in the first section of this chapter and longevity calculation (*āyurdāya*) covered in the second section. Āyurjyotiṣa is basically its own division of Jyotiṣa which can be translated as medical astrology. You can't read a chapter in a book and expect to know a science which takes many years to learn. But at the same time you need a foundation on which to begin learning, to understand where your darkness is and where you need to grow. I first learned Āyurveda from a small class in a Yoga Āśram which landed me a few years in Āyurveda school, where I had a small class in medical astrology that landed me in the field of Jyotiṣa. In this way, introductions are important to bring the knowledge into our awareness so that we can expand it. This chapter lays down some bare bone fundamentals, for the beginner to understand what Āyurjyotiṣa is (beyond new age books to find your doṣa). A proper study should include many examples to fully understand the numerous variations of application and exceptions.

The first section on daiva-cikitsā focuses on explaining the causes of disease and how to perceive and remove them astrologically. A small summary of the elements of Āyurveda ensure one is talking in Vedic language and not western medical language. Then we discuss differentiating the level at which a disease is being caused according to the three bodies and five kośas. The second section on āyurdāya focuses on the basic principles of longevity and an introduction to āyurdaśās which are used for timing disease and death. After study of this chapter, those who wish to go in depth into Āyurjyotiṣa have the basic tools and vocabulary to proceed on that path. Those who find it too complex at least are aware of the approach to health in the Vedic paradigm.

Chapter 10: Bhādhakādi

This chapter focuses on designations that a planet acquires through special positions: the māraka, ghātaka, and bādhaka planets. It works to give both a very specific definition of each of these terms as well as give a general definition of the terms based upon their function. Mārakas kill you, ghātakas hurt you and bādhakas obstruct you. The chapter goes into understanding these special significations and the special remedial measures for them.

The information for the māraka section comes from the *Māraka-bheda-adhyāya* of BPHS and remedial measures are based on the *Viśeṣa-nakṣatra-daśa-phala-adhyāya*. Ghātaka is not studied in depth here but only mentioned in reference to its special significations. Bādhaka is first mentioned in the *Carādi-daśā-phala-adhyāya* by Parāśara. More details and remedial measures are based on *Praśna Mārga* and the teachings of Pandit Sanjay Rath. There are three calculations for bādhaka in *Praśna Mārga*; here we focus on the one mentioned by Parāśara which is related to Aquarius (called the vāyu bādhaka). It is more masculine and relates to blockages in finances, health and such, compared to the jala bādhaka (related to Scorpio) which is more feminine, like the menstrual cycle, and blocks emotions and relationships.

The intention here has been to give a clear definition of the terms and how they are used. At the same time there is a lose connotation given to the terms so they can be used in varied other ways in other situations. This conceptual understanding benefits learning future techniques to not get stuck on simple definitions. One needs a hard definition to begin with, to ground an idea into the material world. Then by understanding the conceptual purpose one can be more fluid with other techniques as well as give more room for the intuition to work. The mind understands the clear definition, but the ātmā understands the ātmā. Ātmā means essence; a jīvātmā is an individual's essence (known as the soul). The essence on any technique is its ātmā, and this must be understood to work with it on the higher intuitive level.

When studying the darker energies of the māraka and bādhaka one should ensure to protect oneself from their energy by chanting the Mṛtyuñjaya mantra when studying mārakas, as well as the appropriate mantra associated with the various types of bādhaka when studying them. Often when we study things in depth, they come alive in our life, and we want to insure we are protected from these energies.

Chapter 11: Curses

Bhartṛhari says that "In this world no comprehension is possible except as accompanied by speech; all knowledge shines by means of speech... It is speech that binds all knowledge of arts and crafts; everything, when it is produced, is differentiated through it."[2] In our art and science of astrology, we have to distinguish the meaning of 'curse'. When I started researching the sanskrit word *śāpa* I was hoping to find another translation than 'curse' but after researching I found that it really did seem like the best word, so I just opened the meaning of the word in English a little.

The chapter is based on the *Pūrva-janma-śāpa-dyotana-adhyāya,* which is Śiva talking to Pārvati. The first section describes what a curse is and how to see it in a chart. It offers the first level of letting go of the energy of a curse from the practice of forgiveness. The second section goes into powerful remedial measures that are available to everyone: donation. To understand a curse and to create the proper energetic balance to that karma is key to be an astrologer who will give results in people's lives.

The third section introduces mūla daśā, which is used to time blessings and curses. In 1999, Sanjay Rath said, "Lagna Kendrādi Graha Daśā, also known as the Mūla Daśā, is one of the very important daśā systems of Vedic astrology. It is a sister daśā or derivative of the viṁśottarī daśā and is fundamental to Jyotiṣa. Although this had been known for quite some time, to my knowledge this would be the first time that this secret of the tradition is being revealed in print." This section is a summary of what has already been taught by Sanjay Rath with added references and translations to root one in the tradition of this daśā.

Chapter 12: Remedies

There are three remedy sections for Saturn, Rāhu and Ketu. I have not covered Mars in this section and look forward to that in the next volume. The malefics covered here are tamas, malefic and asura (demon). Mars is tamas and malefic but he is a sura graha (deva), which gives him a different remedial approach.

[2] Vākyapadīya, I.123-125

As stated in many places prior to these chapters, this tradition teaches to focus on the sattva nature that you want to cultivate, not the tamas nature you want to remove. For example, you can focus on getting rid of *poverty*, or you can focus on becoming *prosperous*. Both would seem to lead to the same place, but one keeps poverty in the consciousness and the other clears the space and fills it with prosperity. The approach we take towards the planetary energies is to focus on the positive: the dirt of Saturn is removed by the cleanliness of Viṣṇu, the poverty of Saturn is removed by abundance of Sūrya, the suffering of Saturn is removed by conquering of Rudra.

All of the gods are a personification of the essentials in reality (*tattva*), or you could say that, 'reality is the personification of the essential reality of the gods'. From Parāśara's teachings as a whole we can understand that the perception of the Supreme is non-dual in nature and in this created world dualistic practices do lead to their desired effects. Therefore we remove duality from our perception of god yet utilize it in daily practice.

This chapter is more advanced in that one also needs a foundation in the practice of Veda and Tantra to fully utilize all the information, which requires a living teacher. This cannot be given in a chapter, but for those with a proper background, this chapter will fully empower one with effective remedial measures. The final section ends with the states of consciousness invoked by Ketu, which guide our lives to the highest.

This book has many techniques, but more important than any technique, it teaches how to be an astrologer. It has the fundamental Vedic philosophy that is required to practice Vedic Astrology from the heart, as a spiritual aspirant. This book is a journey of spiritual evolution that an astrologer passes through to understand the nature of reality and to help guide people's lives with this information.

Freedom Tobias Cole
19 September 2012
Nevada City, California

पराशर उवाच

Parāśara uvāca

Parāśara said:

अविकाराय शुद्धाय नित्याय परमात्मने ।
सदैकरूपरूपाय विष्णवे सर्वजिष्णवे ॥१॥

avikārāya śuddhāya nityāya paramātmane|
sadaikarūparūpāya viṣṇave sarvajiṣṇave||1||

Praises to the Unchangeable, Pure,
Eternal, Supreme Essence,
To the One True Form in all forms,
All-pervasive, All-victorious,

नमो हिरण्यगर्भाय हरये शङ्कराय च ।
वासुदेवाय ताराय सर्गस्थित्यन्तकारिणे ॥२॥

namo hiraṇyagarbhāya haraye śaṅkarāya ca|
vāsudevāya tārāya sargasthityantakāriṇe||2||

To the Golden Egg (Brahmā), Hari, Śaṅkara,
The beginning, the existence, and the end, and
To Vāsudeva, the One who helps us Cross over,

एकानेकस्वरूपाय स्थूलसूक्ष्मात्मने नमः ।
अव्यक्तव्यक्तरूपाय विष्णवे मुक्तिहेतवे ॥३॥

ekānekasvarūpāya sthūlasūkṣmātmane namaḥ|
avyaktavyaktarūpāya viṣṇave muktihetave||3||

To the one whose own condition is One and many,
Whose nature is gross and subtle.
Praises to the All-pervasive,
Unmanifest and Manifest (the cause and the creation),
The means of liberation,

सर्गस्थितिविनाशानां जगतोऽस्य जगन्मयः ।
मूलभूतो नमस्तस्मै विष्णवे परमात्मने ॥४॥

sargasthitivināśānāṁ jagato'sya jaganmayaḥ|
mūlabhūto namastasmai viṣṇave paramātmane||4||

The creator, sustainer, and destroyer of the world, and
That which the world is made of,
The Root of Existence,
The All-pervasive, Supreme Essence.

-Viṣṇu Purāṇa, I.2.1-4

Table of Contents

Introduction i
Dedication iii
Acknowledgements iv
Present Edition vi
Preface vii

Chapter One: Creation

Process of creation 2
Śakti 10
Saṅkarṣaṇa 14
Pradyumna 15
Aniruddha 17
Auṁ and the Levels of Speech 18
Sonic Theory 19
Primary Elements of Perception 20
Theistic Sāṅkhya 22

Chapter Two: Time

Time 30
Vedas: The Eternally Turning Wheel 30
Pāñcarātras Āgama and Purāṇas 32
Time as the Destroyer 36
Units of Time 39
Ghaṭīkās, Vighaṭikās and Muhūrta 41
Ahorātra 42
Aṅgular units 43
Śiśumāra the Celestial Dolphin 45
Kāla-Pratijñā 45
Yāmas, Kalās, Etc. 46
Vedic Calendrical Systems 50
Synodic Month (Lunation) 50
Solar Year 51
Interaction of Solar and Lunar Months 52
Intercalary Month (Adhika Māsa) 53
Beginning of the Year (Varṣa-Praveśa) 54
Other Calendrical Systems 55
Seasons (Ṛtu) 56
Sunrise (Sūryotthāna) 58

Metonic Cycle (Brahmā-Cakra). 59
Draconic Month and Year 61
Time of Eclipse (Vimardārdha) 62
Path of the Eclipse (Chhedyaka) 63
Saros Cycle (Grahaṇa-Parivartana) 63
Bṛhaspati-Saṁvatsara Cakra 65
Rhythm of Time. 69
Relativity of Time 69
Large Units of Time 71
Caturyuga. 72

Chapter Three: Naisargika Dasha

Types of Timing. 78
Naisargika-Graha Daśā 80
Moon Daśā: Infancy 82
Mars Daśā: Toddlerhood 83
Mercury Daśā: Childhood 85
Venus Daśā: Adolescence 86
Jupiter Daśā: Family Life 86
Sun Daśā: Golden Years 87
Saturn Daśā: Old Age 87
Basic Interpretation. 89
Antardaśā 91
Antardaśa Calculation 91
Integrating Interpretation 94
Natural Antardaśā 95
Naisargika Bhāva Daśā. 97
Sudarśana Cakra 99
Calculation of Daśā 100
Interpretation. 101

Chapter Four: Guṇas

The Guṇas of Material Nature. 106
Relativity of the Guṇas. 113
Guṇa and Gaze 121
Guṇa Determination. 122
Guṇa Relationships. 125

Chapter Five: Five Elements

Five Elements. 132
Tanmātrās. 136
Philosophical Variations 137
Indriya. 139
Sensory Perception 141
The System of the Five Elements in the Modern World 143

Deities Associated with Pañcatattva 146
Planets and Tattvas 147
Svara Śāstra (Science of Breath) 155
Kālacakra Elements 157
Kulākula Cakra 158
Piṇḍa-Brahmāṇḍa Tattva 159

Chapter Six: Birth Circumstances

Life 162
Conception Chart Calculation 165
Creating the Perfect Child 166
The Months of Pregnancy 167
Birth and Birth-time 170
Birth and Death 174
Casting the Chart 175
Circumstances of Birth 177
Location 180
Nāḍī Text Examples 183
Nurses in the Room 185
The Dīpa 188
Pain to Mother 189
Absence of Father 192
Adoption Combinations 195
Birth Marks and Body Markings 196
Naming 198

Chapter Seven: Special Ascendants

Special Ascendants 207
Bhāva Lagna 207
Bhāva Cakra and Bhāva-Calita Cakra 208
Bhāva Lagna Interpretation 213
Horā Lagna 214
Horā Lagna in Houses 216
Second House from Horā Lagna 218
Dhana Yogada 219
Ghaṭīkā Lagna 220
Rājya Yogada 222
Mahāyogada 222
Varṇada Lagna 224
Varṇada Lagna Interpretation 226
Tithyaṁśa 227
Śrī Lagna 228
Interpretation of Śrī Lagna 230
Prāṇapada Lagna 231
Prāṇapada Calculation 232
House placement 234
Navāṁśa Prāṇapada Lagna 238

Chapter Eight: Narayana Dasha

Nārāyaṇa Daśā 240
Calculation of Nārāyaṇa Daśā 242
Strength Rules 243
Progression of the Daśā 244
Length of the Daśā 245
Antardaśā Calculations 246
Calculation Example 246
Interpretation 249
Daśā Results 252
Pāka and Bhoga 254
Transits 256
Bādhaka 257
Antardaśā 258
Varga Nārāyaṇa 261

Chapter Nine: Āyurjyotiṣa

Āyurjyotiṣa 266
I. Daiva-Cikitsā 266
Basic Causes of Disease 267
Kāla Pariṇāma 267
Prajñāparādha 269
Asātmyendriyārtha 270
Components of Āyurveda 272
Āyurveda 272
Tri-Doṣa 273
Constitution: Prakṛti 274
The Twenty Attributes 277
Agni 278
Dhātus 280
Nidāna: Āyurvedic Pathology 281
Timing Disease 283
Ṣaṣṭāṁśa (Kaulakas) 283
Āyurvedic Remedy 284
Science of Taste: Rasa 286
Inherited Disease: Ādibala-Pravṛtta 288
Soul Level Disease: Svāṁśa 288
The Three Bodies (Tri-Śarīra) 290
The Five Fields: Pañca-Kośas 291
Treatment 293
Internal Medicine and Longevity 296
II. Āyurdāya 298
Lifespans 299
Method of Three Pairs 306
Āyurdāya Yogas 307

Nature of Death 311
Śūla Daśā 311
Calculation of Śūla Daśā 311
Calculation of Brahmā, Rudra and Maheśvara 313
Brahmā Planet 313
Rudra 313
Maheśvara Planet 314

Chapter Ten: Badhakādi

I. Māraka 318
Other Mārakas 321
Prosperity 323
Daśā 324
Remedies for Mārakas 325
Mrtyunjaya Mantra 325
Mahā-mṛtyuñjaya Mantra 326
Mrtyunjaya Bija 326
II. Bādhakasthāna and Bādhakeśa 328
Anger of the Deity: Devatā-bādhaka 332
Anger of the Serpents: Sarpa-bādhaka 336
Anger of the Ancestors: Pitṛ-bādhaka 339
Anger of Spirits: Preta-bādhaka 340
Cursed Speech: Jihvā Doṣa 341
Blocked Perception: Dṛṣṭi-bādhaka 342
Black Magic: Abhicāra 344

Chapter Eleven: Curses

Curses 348
Curses in the Chart 350
Forgiveness 353
Understanding Curse Combinations 356
Who, What, Where 363
The Curse of Lord Rāma 366
Free from a Curse (Śāpa-mukti) 368
Mechanics of Donation 372
Technicalities of Donation 374
The Transient Nature of Time 380
Timing Results of Curses 382
Mūla Daśā 383
Mūla Daśā Calculation 386
Example of Śrī Rāma 388
Example of Cursed Divorce 391
Levels of the Mūla Daśā 393

Chapter Twelve: Remedial Measures

I. Saturn Mantras 396
Saturn Afflicting Health 398
Saturn Transiting Lagna 399
Maraṇa-Kāraka-Sthāna Saturn 400
Strengthening Saturn 400
Pacification: Saturn Gāyatrī 400
Saturn Conjunct the Moon 401
Preta Yoga 403
Sadhe-Sati 403
Rudra Chamakam 406
II. Rāhu Remedial Measures 409
Rāhu and Moon 411
Ucca and Nīca Rāhu 413
Rāhu in Lagna 413
Rāhu Transiting Lagna 414
Maraṇa-Kāraka-Sthāna Rāhu 414
Strenghtening Rāhu 415
Pacification: Rāhu Gāyatrī 415
Solar Eclipse 416
Agni- Stambhana Yoga 417
Guru-Candala Yoga 418
Sarpa Ruling the Directions 419
Karkotaka Yoga: Rahu and Mercury 419
Mahāpadma Yoga: Rāhu and Venus 420
Preta Badhaka 420
Kālasarpa Yoga 421
III. Ketu Remedial Measures 423
Dhūmāvatī 424
Pacification: Ketu Gāyatrī 425
Ketu Śānti: Spiritual Remedies 425
Six Aspects of Surrender 425
The Sun and Moon 426
Mars 428
Mercury 429
Jupiter 430
Venus 432
Saturn 432
Conclusion 435

Appendix 437
References 442

Chapter 1

The Process of Creation

ॐ
क्षेतक्षेत्रज्ञयोर् एवम्
अन्तरं ज्ञानचक्षुषा
भूतप्रकृतिमोक्षं च
ये विदुर् यान्ति ते परम्
kṣetakṣetrajñayor evam
antaraṁ jñānacakṣuṣā
bhūtaprakṛtimokṣaṁ ca
ye vidur yānti te param
Those who know the distinction with the eye of knowledge
Between the field (body/mind) and the knower of the field
And about liberation from material nature
They go to the Supreme (*param*).
-Bhagavad Gītā XIII.34

The Process of Creation

Sṛṣṭi means the creation of the world or 'the emanation of existence'. *Krama* is a step by step process, and *kathana* is the narration of a story. Therefore the first chapter (*adhyāya*) of Bṛihat Parāśara Horā Śāstra is called the "Story of The Process of the Emanation of Existence". It is the first chapter, not because it is beginner material. It is the first chapter because traditional texts always began with a chapter on how we ended up being here. Some texts give elaborate genetic lineages and time cycles. Even the Old Testament begins with the creation of the world. Parāśara's terminology in explaining the creation relates to the Bhāgavata philosophy found in the group of texts called the Pāñcarātra Āgama, which will help elaborate the deeper meaning of his verses.

Parāśara's grandfather was the great Vedic Sage Vasiṣṭha. According to tradition, the time of the great sages (*Ṛṣi*) was Satya Yuga which was a time when people would live for centuries. Parāśara lived during Dvāpara Yuga, a time where the consciousness on the earth was becoming more dense. His son Veda Vyāsa lived during the transition between Dvāpara to Kali Yuga. This is important to understand in order to understand the time frame of his ideology. He lived in a period where traditional Vedic thought and practice was slowly transitioning to what is now modern Hinduism. The Pāñcharātra were the texts of the Bhāgavatas (those who believe in the multiplicity of a singlular divinity) and teach a philosophy that existed during the transition from Vedic religion to what is now present day Vaiṣṇavism.

The fundamental principles of creation are important for us to understand the guṇas, the tattvas, how we interact with divinity, and most important- how we actually exist. It is therefore important to understand the essence referenced in the ancient terminology and get the deeper insight that is being offered. At the level of perception through the individual mind (*manas*) time is linear, at the level of the individual soul (*jīvātman*) time is cyclical. At the level of the Supreme (*Paramātman)* time is only Now: all-present beingness. At the manas level of perception, the creation is something that has *happened*, at the ātman level it is that which is *happening*- creating the present perception of reality. At the level of the highest (*Param*)- creation exists as a heartbeat exists in a human; It Is - *Tat Sat*. Happened, happening, Is[2]. Creation is explained as a process at the level of the mind for intellectual understanding, but must be realized in deep meditation by those who want to know the nature of the true Self for full utility. This is the first chapter but it is also the final understanding from which all principles of life and our perception through Jyotiṣa arise. It is a map to liberation because when you have a map to get to a place, that same map also shows how to return. This is why the story of creation begins most of the ancient texts.

[2] In actuality, there are no tenses (which refer to time) to accurately use words at the final level.

But even before the story of creation begins, the ancient texts start with the question of the student to the teacher. If not for the transmission of knowledge, how would we have any *words* to guide us to this place and let us speak of it. It is the Guru that guides and our guide here is the Ṛṣi Parāśara.

अथैकदा मुनिश्रेष्ठं त्रिकालज्ञं पराशरम्।
पप्रच्छोपेत्य मैत्रेयः प्रणिपत्य कृताञ्जलिः ॥ १ ॥

athaikadā (now) muniśreṣṭhaṁ (superior/most excellent/best sage) trikālajñaṁ (knower of the three times) parāśaram (Parāśara), papracchopetya (approached) maitreyaḥ, praṇipatya (bowing down at the feet in submission/reverence, obeisance) kṛtāñjaliḥ (palms together in reverence)| | 1| |

Now the distinguished sage Parāśara who could see the past, present and future was approached by Maitreya, fully giving obeisance with folded hands.

भगवन् परमं पुण्यं गुह्यं वेदाङ्गमुत्तमम्।
त्रिस्कन्धं ज्यौतिषं होरा गणितं संहितेति च ॥ २ ॥

bhagavan (venerable, holy, illustious, god, saint) paramaṁ (highest, primary) puṇyaṁ (virtous) guhyaṁ (concealed, mystic) vedāṅgamuttamam (the best Vedāṅga), triskandhaṁ (three branches) jyautiṣaṁ (Vedic astrology) horā (astrology) gaṇitaṁ (astronomy) saṁhiteti (omenology) ca (and)| | 2| |

Oh great, virtous, mystic sage, Jyotiṣa is the best limb of the Vedas
having three branches of Horā, Gaṇita, and Saṁhita.

एतेष्वपि त्रिषु श्रेष्ठा होरेति श्रूयते मुने।
त्वत्तस्तां श्रोतुमिच्छामि कृपया वद मे प्रभो ॥ ३ ॥

eteṣvapi triṣu (among the three) śreṣṭhā (best) horeti (astrology) śrūyate (heard) mune (the sage) tvattaḥ-tāṁ (that from you) śrotum-icchāmi (I wish to hear) kṛpayā (please) vada me (tell me) prabho (origination, appear)| | 3| |

Among these three, the sages say Horā is superior, I want to hear about this from you, and if you are inclined, please tell me about the origination.

कथं सृष्टिरियं जाता जगतश्च लयः कथम्।
खस्थानां भूस्थितानां च सम्बन्धं वद विस्तरात्॥ ४ ॥

kathaṁ (where from) sṛṣṭiḥ (creation) iyaṁ (this) jātā (has been done, became) jagataḥ (of the world) ca (and) layaḥ (dissapearance, dissolution) katham (where from, how), khasthānāṁ (stationed in the sky) bhūsthitānāṁ (living beings) ca (and) sambandhaṁ (connection) vada (speak) vistarāt (extensively)| | 4| |

From where has the world come to be, and how does it end,
Please speak elaborately about the relationship between
the heavenly bodies and living beings.

In the *Ahirbudhnya Saṁhitā*, the sage Bharadvāja asks similar questions to the sage Durvāsas. He replies, "When the passions of the inner organs have been stopped through austerities, one has a desire to contemplate upon the *Highest Principle.*" (1.16) He then tells a story of Nārada asking Śiva similar questions and the answers reveal the same material about creation presented by Parāśara. In Bṛhat Parāśara Horā Śāstra, Parāśara answers Maitreya,

साधु पृष्टं त्वया विप्र लोकानुग्रहकारिणा ।
अथाहं परमं ब्रह्म तच्छक्तिं भारतीं पुनः ॥ ५ ॥
सूर्यं नत्वा ग्रहपतिं जगदुत्पत्तिकारणम् ।
वक्ष्यामि वेदनयनं यथा ब्रह्मामुखाच्छ्रुतम् ॥ ६ ॥

sādhu (honorable) pṛṣṭaṁ (query) tvayā (given by thee) vipra (Brahman) lokānugrahakāriṇā (act for welfare of the world), athāhaṁ (now I) paramaṁ brahma (supreme creator) tat-śaktiṁ (his śakti) bhāratīṁ (the word, Saraswatī) punaḥ (again, further, moreover) | | 5 | | sūrya (Sun-god) natvā (bow- and) grahapatiṁ (lord of the planets) jagadutpattikāraṇam (universe-produce, producing an effect- reason, cause, instrument)|vakṣyāmi (I shall narrate) vedanayanaṁ (directing, eye- veda) yathā (as) brahmā-mukhāt-śrutam (heard from the mouth of Brahmā)| | 6| |

You have an honorable question for the welfare of the world,
Now, bowing to the Parabrahma, his power the Word, and
The Sun, lord of the grahas, who causes the universe to produce it effects,
I will speak about the Eye of the Vedas (*veda-nayana*) as heard from the mouth of Brahmā.

Parāśara acknowledges his student's question and prays to the Supreme creator. Brahmā is the rajas form of the divinity; here the Parabrahma is all forms of the divinity. This is seen in the *Guru Vandanā* where Brahmā, Viṣṇu and Mahādeva *(Śiva)* are worshiped as gurus and then the Parabrahma,[3] which includes them all, is worshipped. He is worshipped with his śakti, Bhārātī. Vāgīśa Śāstrī has taught that this is a name of Sarasvatī when placed with Brahmā but when it is placed with Parabrahma it represents the word (*vāc*) which is divinity as sound (*śabda-brahma*) which creates the manifestation. Parabrahma resides in the crown center (*sahasrāra-chakra*) while the Śabdabrahma is the Kuṇḍalinī residing in the root center (*mūlādhāra-chakra*) at the base of the spine.

Then the lord of the planets, Sūrya, is worshipped as the creative instrument producing the universe. The Sun is the producer of time and the continually moving reality /universe. This creator aspect of the Sun is also seen in the Gāyatrī mantra where the Sun is called *Savitṛ*, which literally means the producer of the creation. In this way when Brahmā, the creator, is indicted as a remedy in Jyotiṣa the Sun is worshipped with the Gāyatrī mantra.

[3] Brahmā, Viṣṇu and Śiva are worshipped in the masculine gender while the Parabrahma is in the neuter for emphasis.

This is the speech of a great Ṛṣi, with a vast understanding. Parāśara invokes the blessings of these energies and then proceeds to teach the eye of the Vedas which is the eye or guiding light of knowledge. He indicates this is a divine science (heard from the mouth of the creator). This is called the śāstra-āvatara, or the story of how the teaching incarnated into the physical realm: Parāśara heard from Brahmā and gave the teaching to Maitreya. Parāśara begins first by giving some clauses to qualities of a student before preceeding.

शान्ताय गुरुभक्ताय सर्वदा सत्यवादिने ।
आस्तिकाय प्रदतव्यं ततः श्रेयो ह्यवाप्स्यति ॥ ७ ॥

śāntāya (peaceful, tranquil, passions subdued) gurubhaktāya (respects the guru) sarvadā (at all times) satyavādine (speaks the truth)।āstikāya (faithful, one who believes in that which exists, believes in god) pradatavyaṁ (these are to be taught, given) tataḥ (thereupon) śreyo (excellent, fortunate) hi (certainly) avāpsyati (you will obtain)।। 7।।

You will certainly get good results to teach this to one who is peaceful,
Respects their teacher, speaks the truth at all times,
And believes in a higher power (*āstika*).

न देयं परशिष्याय नास्तिकाय शठाय वा ।
दत्ते प्रतिदिनं दुःखं जायते नात्र संशयः ॥ ८ ॥

na deyaṁ (not proper for a gift/giving) paraśiṣyāya (better or worse than- to become the pupil of) nāstikāya (non-believer, atheist) śaṭhāya (deceitful) vā (or), datte (gives) pratidinaṁ (daily, day by day) duḥkhaṁ (suffering) jāyate (bringing forth) nātra (not here) saṁśayaḥ (doubt)।। 8।।

There is no doubt, it will cause an increase in suffering to impart this science to
an unfit student, who has no faith (*nāstika*), and is deceitful.

Parāśara acknowledges Maitreya's question and gives him first the basic prerequisites of a student learning astrology and spirituality. The student must be peaceful (have a clean heart/fourth house), speak the truth (good second house) and honor the elders (beneficial ninth house). Students who are atheist (*nāstika*)- thereby not believing in the soul and the laws of karma and being disrespectful to elders end up causing a headache to the teachers of the science imparted by the sages. Students who have negative intentions will use the knowledge incorrectly and thereby ruin astrology in the eyes of the people and create bad karma for the student as well as the teacher who gave them the knowledge to cause the harm they perform.

A student of astrology should live a sacred life and work to be a fit vessel for the Jyotir Vidyā (the Science of Light). After this clarification, Parāśara gives the teaching of the creation; from the absolute, to the formation of consciousness, to the manifestation of the material world in a few short ślokas that are filled with various conceptual realities.

1. List the qualities of a good student and a student to be avoided. Compare this to the list given by Varāhamihira.

2. Find a few examples in real life of teachers who have had good relationships with their students and teachers who have had negative relationships with their students. What factors created the positive situation and what factors created negative situations.

एकोऽव्यक्तात्मको विष्णुरनादिः प्रभुरीश्वरः ।
शुद्धसत्त्वो जगत्स्वामी निर्गुणस्त्रिगुणान्वितः ॥ ९ ॥
संसारकारकः श्रीमान्निमित्तात्मा प्रतापवान् ।

Eko (chief, primary, one) avyakta (the imperceptible, the unmanifest which evolves all things, the primary productive principle) ātmako (forms the nature of) viṣṇur (Viṣṇu- the all pervasisve) anādiḥ (having no beginning, eternal) prabhur (much existence, powerful, master) īśvaraḥ (controller, lord, the supreme soul), śuddha-sattvo (cleansed, clear, pure-balance, breathing, living) jagatsvāmī (lord of the world, controlling that which does not stop) nirguṇaù (who has no guṇas, without attributes- formless absolute) triguṇa (three guṇa) anvitaḥ (endowed with) ||9||Saṁsāra (cycle of births and deaths-passage of transmigration) kārakaḥ (the doer of) śrīmān (endowed with prosperity, beauty or Śrī) nimitta (reason, efficient cause, motive) ātmā (soul, self) pratāpavān (one having great heat, much energy/glory/splendour), |10a|

That One, Unmanifest, Eternal, All-pervasive powerful lord,
The pure essence, and master of the universe (*jagatsvāmī*),
Is both the formless [Absolute] (*nirguṇa*),
And endowed with form (*tri-guṇa*). ||9||
The maker of saṁsāra,
The efficient cause accompanied by Śrī,
Splendorous,

The verse is not talking about a limited form of god with a specific function, but refers to the One Being (*Ekam*) who is called by many names.[4] And the many epithets are for the purpose of clearly defining the reference point as the Supreme Being.

Ahirbudhnya Saṁhitā (2.32) says the transcendent Brahman is called Eternal or Endless (*ananta*) because there exists no measure of it (*mitya-abhāva*). It says (2.29) that the transcendent One, also known as *Nārāyaṇa*, is called Avyakta because he has no individuality (*avyakti*) related to form or mode. Many other similar names are given to the Highest Principle, but the Ahirbudhnya Saṁhitā adds that these names are close to the essence of the Supreme but cannot describe it completely, they are used to *imply* that Principle (2.40).

[4] Ṛgveda1.164.46 *ekaṁ sad viprā bahudhā vadantya…*

एकांशेन जगत्सर्वं सृजत्यवति लीलया ॥ १० ॥

ekāṁśena (his one part) jagat-sarva (whole world)
sṛjati-avati (creates, produces, emits), līlayā (sport, past time, easily, mere appearance).

From one quarter of himself he creates the whole universe playfully || 10b||

Why did the One become many? The view being shared by Parāśara is that the world is the Lord's play, and therefore called a *līlā*. Interpretating this from a nondualist internal perspective (*adhyātma*), there is only One, a single being, and the play is the game that there is more than one. The unity becomes diverse multiplicity. The One manifests the perception of the entire world playfully (*līlay*ā). A play or a game is not real- it is a mere appearance with created rules for the game to be played, or a script for the play to act out. From a dualist perspective the divine lord creates the world populated by individual souls as a play, and participates in it as a pastime. Either perspective takes the view that the creation is done playfully (*līlayā*), implying that the world is created with joy and not suffering.

Parāśara states that everything manifests from only one quarter of the Supreme. The 'true nature' is more vast than the part which is manifest. What we see is just a small part of what really is. That Beingness that creates (*sṛjati*) the whole universe (*sarva-jagat*) is often called the *Puruṣa* which can be translated as the cosmic being, or the one whose beingness/ body becomes the whole universe. It is translated as the *Supreme Personality of Godhead* by A.C.B.Prabhupāda. It is translated as *Spirit* by Winthrop Sargeant. Here the term will remain as Puruṣa with the understanding that it represents that consciousness which is the foundation of all consciousness and the existence of everything.

In the *Puruṣa Sūktam* (Ṛgveda 10.90) the Puruṣa is desribed as all that is and is to be *and more.* He is the head, eyes, hands, feet etc. of all beings (that which enlivens and acts through all beings) and he is that which is *beyond even that.*

> एतावानस्य महिमातो ज्यायांश्च पूरुषः ।
> पादोऽस्य विश्वा भूतानि त्रिपादस्यामृतं दिवि ।३।
> The Puruṣa is great (*jyāya*) and much greater than this; all beings are one-fourth of him; his other three-fourths are immortal (*amṛta*), abiding in heaven. (Ṛgveda 10.90.3)
>
> त्रिपादूर्ध्व उदैत्पुरुषः पादोऽस्येहाऽऽभवात्पुनः ।
> ततो विष्वङ्व्यक्रामत्साशनानशने अभि । ४ ।
> Three-fourths of the Puruṣa are ascended; the other fourth remains in this world proceeding repeatedly into diversified forms of all animate and inanimate creation" (10.90.4)

The manifest one quarter from which the universe is created is the world in the cycles of birth and death (*saṁsāra*) where the soul, bound by the guṇas, evolves with karma. The pure consciousness is that which everything is made of in this appearance of the world (*līlā*). It is the multitude of eyes which are perceiving this reality.

The unmanifesting three-fourths of the Puruṣa is immortal

(*a-mṛta*), and is sometimes called pure matter (*śudha tattva*). It is immortal (undying) because it is never born. It is that consciousness/beingness that is *'even greater than this'*.

त्रिपादं तस्य देवस्य ह्यमृतं तत्त्वदर्शिनः ।
विदन्ति तत्प्रमाणं च सप्रधानं तथैकपात् ॥ ११ ॥

tripādaṁ (three parts/three quarters) tasya (from that) devasya (god) hyamṛtaṁ (indeed-nectar, immortal) tattva (essence, reality) darśinaḥ (seen, known, perceived), vidanti (they know) tatpramāṇam (that-measure/ judge/to cause correct perception) ca sapradhānaṁ (with-the chief, principle evolute/prakṛti/root matter/primary originator) tatha (because/that) ekapāt (one part) || 11||

The other three quarters of him are unchanging (*amṛta*) and known by the seers of reality by proper perception of the root matter (*Pradhāna*) of the one part.

These three parts are immortal (*tri-pādasya-amṛta*). Paraśara says this unchanging essence (*amṛta tattva*) is known to those who understand what the universe is made of and can therefore discern the creation from the chief evolver. When one refines the mind through meditation and the knowledge of the creation one understands or discerns (*pramāṇa*) what is the created and what is beyond the creation. Most people are lost in their attachment to the created universe and do not even have a desire to meditate on that which is beyond.

Ahirbudhnya Saṁhitā speaks of the amṛta tattva and says that "When the good and bad [karmas] that have been collected through many lives are totally destroyed, when the net of predispositions is cut off with the sword of correct knowledge (2.41), and when the three guṇas cease to work, It can be experienced naturally. We cannot express It directly and clearly by means of words such as "It is this" (2.42)". The other three parts (*tripād-vibhūti*) are transcendant and known as the Parama Padam- the highest place, the highest heaven (śrī-vaikuṇṭha), or the great void (*parama-vyoman*). This concept is the key teaching Parāśara is giving to the Jyotiṣī and must be understood much more deeply.

It is not that which is creating matter, it is uncreated. It is silent, beyond thoughts and their seeds, beyond that which is going to be created, it is beyond the beyond, and called by different names in different traditions as it is beyond name. This divine silence (*aśabda-brahma*) is pure stillness. It is not an understanding, nor an experience, as it is beyond mind and soul. The Maitrī Upaniṣad calls it non-thought hidden underneath of thought. Meditation upon that highest essence clears all thoughts, burns all karmas and makes the being clear to perceive with a divine eye. It is not something far away, it permeates everything.

From the perspective of modern science, the pure matter of the three parts (*amṛta-tattva*) is called dark energy. The unmanifest half of the one quarter (*avyakta*) is called dark matter. Only a small percentage of the universe is actually manifest stars and planets (*vyakta*).

व्यक्ताव्यक्तात्मको विष्णुर्वासुदेवस्तु गीयते ।

vyaktāvyakta (perceived and not perceived) ātmakaḥ (forms the nature of)
viṣṇurvāsudevastu gīyate (praised, addressed)

The All-pervasive one who is both manifest and
unmanifest is called Vāsudeva| | 12a| |

Parāśara first spoke about the All-pervasive, then divided it into four parts. The four parts as a whole are called Nārāyaṇa.Three fourths are beyond comprehension. The fourth portion of the All-pervasive that proceeds repeatedly into various forms of the animate and inanimate world is called Vāsudeva. Vāsudeva is again divided into two parts: the manifest *(vyakta)* and the unmanifest potential *(avyakta)* that is coming into manifestation.

The unmanifest portion of Vāsudeva is defined as the perfect balance of the guṇas therefore it is peaceful *(śānta)* like a waveless ocean or a cloudless sky. The imbalance or mixture of the guṇas is the manifestation of the world.

The Pāñcarātra understanding is that Vāsudeva is both transcendental and accesible to mankind, in this way god/goddess is totally beyond everything, but has the power to incarnate for the benefit of the creation. There is both the transcendant divinity *(nirguṇa Brahman)* and the tangible form *(saguṇa)* deity for the individual to interact with in their life. Vāsudeva denotes that divine being which forms the universe from himself and resides in the hearts of all beings. The Ahirbudhnya Saṁhitā (2.28) says he is called Vāsudeva because he resides in all creatures *(samastabhūta-vāsin)*. When a human being thinks of god, this is what they can think of. Vāsudeva is the conceivable divinity.

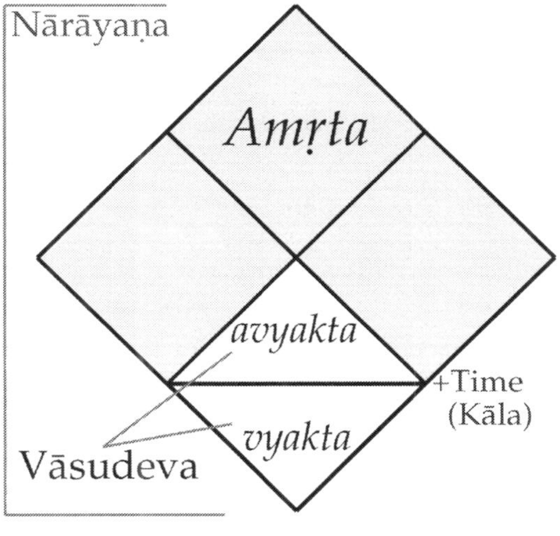

This manifest-unmanifest portion, called Vāsudeva, is composed of three primal elements: Puruṣa, Prakṛti, and Time. Time turns to separate Prakṛti from Puruṣa, and manifests the unmanifest. Parāśara teaches a trinity, not a duality, which creates the religious divisions of Viṣṇu, Śakti and Śiva.

3. What are the percetanges of the divisions of the primal principles? What do scientists say about the percentage of *dark energy* and *dark matter* in the universe?

4. What is Vāsudeva composed of?

5. What is the trinity of creation taught by Parāśara?

Vāsudeva has Śakti, though there is only one not two, or two sides to one coin. His Śakti is not different than him, as moonlight to the Moon, or sesame oil in the seed. These are all just analogies to mark the non-difference of the One who is both god and goddess, as wet cannot be different to water, or water to wet. Though different qualities of the same thing can also be called as different Śaktis.

यद्व्यक्तात्मको विष्णुः शक्तितद्वयसमन्वितः ॥ १२ ॥
व्यक्तात्मकस्त्रिभिर्युक्तः कथ्यतेऽनन्तशक्तिमान् ।

yadavyaktātmako (that not- manifest nature) viṣṇuḥ (All-pervasive) śaktita (powers) dvaya (two-fold, double) samanvitaḥ (possesed of) vyaktātma (the perceptible-manifest nature) kas (moves/ approaches) tri (three) bhiryuktaḥ (joined) kathyate (spoken about, mentioned) 'nanta (endless, boundless) śaktimān (one possessed of power),

The unmanifest nature possesses two powers. || 12b||
The manifest nature is united with three powers,
And is said to possess unlimited power (*ananta-śaktimān*) || 13a||

The unmanifest contains two Śaktis (sattva and rajas) while the manifest has three Śaktis (sattva, rajas and tamas). The final addition of the tamas śakti creates the visibly *manifest* world. The first two Śaktis relate to the Puruṣa and Prakṛti, while the third śakti relates to Time (*Kāla*). In this way, Kālī, who is the tamas śakti and the female personification of Time, manifests the material world.

Śrī-śakti (sattva) is the conscious guide behind everything and impells Time to turn. Time agitates (*kṣoba/ceṣṭā*) the guṇas and causes them to change proportion which leads to the creation of the universe. The form of god as Time is without limit (*na-anta*), and creates the uninterrupted cycles of creation, preservation and destruction. God (*brahman*) is called Anantam in the Upaniṣads to indicate his limitlessness beyond space and time.

Parāśara calls the All-pervasive as *Ananta-śaktimān* which means the One with infinite śakti or boundless powers, or it can also be interpreted as the *One with Infinite Goddesses.* Śakti is a word meaning power. It is the power of anything and is personified as a female consort. For example, the Sun has two Śaktis (two consorts), the power to shine and the power to make shadows. *Ananta-śaktimān* is indicating that the three mentioned Śaktis are only a specific aspect of the Supreme's power, and that there are many more aspects besides what is being discussed. In this way, Vāsudeva in his unmanifest-manifest form is not limited to only these three Śaktis. But for the purpose of understanding the creation we see that there are two primary Śaktis in the unmanifest and the addition of the tamas Śakti creates the physical world. It is tamas that creates the five elements and all that composes the physical world. It is the tamas Śakti that creates the consciousness of the material world.

सत्त्वप्रधाना श्रीशक्तिर्भूशक्तिश्च रजोगुणा ॥ १३ ॥
शक्तिस्तृतीया या प्रोक्ता नीलाख्या ध्वान्तरूपिणी ।

sattvapradhānā (the pure/balanced-root matter/ primary principle/ superior) śrīśaktiḥ (power of Śrī) bhūśaktiśca (power of Bhū) rajoguṇā, śaktistṛtīyā (the third power) yā (who is) proktā (called) nīlā (dark-blue) khyā (called, praised) dhvānta (dark, veiled, covered) rūpiṇī (female form).

Śrī Śakti relates to the primal guṇa of Sattva,
Bhū Śakti relates to Rajas guṇa || 13b||
Nīla Śakti, who is called the form of the dark-goddess, relates to Tamas guṇa. || 14a||

Prakṛti is the root matter (*pradhāna*) which is the unmanifest (*avyakta*) substance of manifestation. It is the *first principle* or the *unevolved matter* of creation which is composed of the guṇas. Śrī-śakti relates to the sattva guṇa of Prakṛti. Śrī-śakti is the power of sattva, the action of sattva. Śrī-śakti is also called the *krīya śakti* or the active power of Nārāyaṇa (God's creative potency). Puruṣa is stillness, the impetus to move is Śakti. Śrī-śakti is the impetus for all creation and therefore the supreme goddess.

Bhū-śakti is the power of rajas, the power of becoming, the creatrice. The Śri-śakti becomes Bhū-śakti as soon as her desire is set in motion.

Nīla-śakti is the power of tamas. She is also called *sākṣāt śakti* or the power to make manifest to the senses. Parāśara calls Nīla Śakti the *dvānta* form, this can mean the dark form or the form that veils our consciousness. In the Pāñcarātra, the tamas form of Śakti is called Mahāmāyā. She is the one who is covering the truth of our true nature in the manifestation of the material world (*avidyā*). Nīla-śakti becomes the ideological foundation for Kālī and *Mahāvidyā* worship. She is the mother giving form to our reality and changing it (destroying it) as Time.

The fourth quarter of Nārāyaṇa, called Vāsudeva, is motivated or impelled (*prerita*) into the creation process by Śrī-śakti. God and Goddess relate as being and becoming (*bhāvodbhāvātmaka*). Śrī-śakti is Vāsudeva's *will-to-be*. Bhū-śakti is the power of creating, and Nīla-śakti is the manifestation. The one original Śakti takes on different names in her different roles according to her actions.

The goddess Durga is a form representing the Śrī-śakti. In the *Devī-Saptaśatī*, which is the story of Durga, all goddesses are seen to manifest from her. This is explained in the secret chapters (*Rahasya-traya*) as the single Krīyā-śakti (as the supreme goddess) creating all other śaktis from herself. Relative to the Nīla-śakti, the *Devī-Saptaśatī* says She permeates her brilliance (*tejas*) filling the unbroken void (*śūnyaṁ tadkhilaṁ*), and that which is darkness (*tamas*) becomes her dark form. In this way, we understand the evolution of the guṇas and their śaktis from the Śri-śakti.

वासुदेवश्चतुर्थोऽभूच्छ्रीशक्त्या प्रेरितो यदा ॥ १४ ॥
संकर्षणश्च प्रद्युम्नोऽनिरुद्ध इति मूर्तिधृक् ।
तमःशक्त्याऽन्विता विष्णुर्देवः संकर्षणाभिधः ॥ १५ ॥
प्रद्युम्नो रजसा शक्त्याऽनिरुद्धः सत्त्वया युतः ।

vāsudevaścaturthaḥ (the fourth of Vāsudeva) abhūta śrī-śaktyā (Śrī-śakti) preritaḥ (becomes impelled,incite, directed) yadā (when, at that time), saṅkarṣaṇaśca pradyumno'niruddha iti (in this manner) mūrti (embodiment, manifestation, incarnation) dhṛk (carry, hold, maintain, support), tamaḥśaktyā'nvitā (accompanied, conjoined, endowed with tamas śakti) viṣṇurdevaḥ (lord Viṣṇu, the all-pervasive god) saṅkarṣaṇa abhidhaḥ (named), pradyumno rajasā śaktyā'niruddhaḥ sattvayā yutaḥ (combined, connected, conjoining, united)

When the fourth quarter [called] Vāsudeva becomes directed by Śrī Śakti, || 14b||
It takes the form of Saṅkarṣaṇa, Pradyumna, and Aniruddha.
The All-pervasive lord accompanied by Tamas Śakti is called Saṅkarṣaṇa|| 15||
Pradyumna is accompanied by Rajas Śakti
And Aniruddha is accompanied by Sattva Śakti || 16a||

Here Parāśara introduces the *supporting manifestations* of Vāsudeva, called the vyūhas: Saṅkarṣaṇa, Pradyumna, and Aniruddha. The vyūhas are states of Vāsudeva, aspects of the Perceiver (*Puruṣa*). Puruṣa is consciousness and these forms represent different levels of consciousness taken on by Puruṣa: deep sleep (*suṣupti*), dream (*svapna*) and waking (*jagrat*).

The Śaktis are the natures of Prakṛti while the vyūhas are states (*avasthā*) of the Puruṣa. They are non-phenomenal (*aprākṛti*) and consist only of pure consciousness. The physical guṇas do not apply to the vyūhas but are created by them, as jaggery comes from the juice of sugar cane. Sattva comes from the densification of Saṅkarṣaṇa, Rajas comes from the densification of Pradyumna and Tamas comes from Aniruddha. These guṇas then apply to the creation (*Prakṛti*). Time turns these principles and the guṇas mix to manifest the creation.

At the first level of creation Saṅkarṣana (that which condenses to sattva) conjoins the tamas-śakti. The most refined level of consciousness is limited by tamas in order to create the individual consciousness (*jīvātman*). It separates the consciousness to give it individuality and the power to desire/will.

Pradyumna (essence of rajas) conjoins the rajas-śakti to create the mind which gives the individual the power to know. The rajas joins the rajas to create the catalyst between the soul (*jīvātman*) and the material world. It manifests the seeds of the individual consciousness into a material reality.

Aniruddha (essence of tamas) conjoins the sattva-śakti to bring life to material consciousness which creates the individual sense of I. This allows one to interact with the material world and gives the individual the power to act. The mixing of these three states of consciousness with the three guṇas brings about the creation of the root attributes (25 tattvas) which compose the manifest world.

महान्‌ संकर्षणाज्जातः प्रद्युम्नाद्यदहंकृतिः ॥ १६ ॥
अनिरुद्धात्‌ स्वयं जातो ब्रह्माहंकारमूर्तिधृक्‌ ।
सर्वेषु सर्वशक्तिश्च स्वशक्त्याऽधिकया युतः ॥ १७ ॥

mahān (the great one, cosmic intelligence) saṅkarṣaṇāj jātaḥ (Saṅkarṣaṇa propelled the birth, caused to be born) pradyumnād (from Pradyumna) yad (who, which) ahaṅkṛtiḥ (I-doer, the sense of I-doing, that created by the I), aniruddhāt (from Aniruddha) svayaṁ (one's self, of one's own accord) jātaḥ (brought into existence, arisen, born) brahmā (creator) ahaṅkāra (I-ness, I-maker) mūrti (form, manifestation, embodiment, incarnation) dhṛk (maintaining, supporting), sarveṣu (all-delivery, all-child-bearing) sarvaśaktiśca (power of accomplishing all) svaśaktyā'dhikayā (own strength, own ability- abundant, superior) yutaḥ (combined) || 17||

Saṅkarṣaṇa propelled the birth of the individual soul,
Pradyumna is the cause of the present mind || 16b||
Aniruddha is the supporting manifestation of ahaṅkara (sense of I), the creator.
Each has all the powers of accomplishing (*śakti*) but
acts according to the predominant śakti|| 17||

Saṅkarṣaṇa manifests the soul (*jīvātman*), Pradyumna manifest the mind (*manas*), and Aniruddha creates the I-sense (*ahaṅkara*) which is like Brahmā the creator of the world. It is like Brahmā because through it all the elements of material existence manifest: the elements and indriyas- or the things we experience and that which we experience them with.

We will take a deeper look at each of these vyūhas, the states of consciousness that they represent and the levels of sound associated with each of these states. This will give a better understanding of the creation and the functions of the soul, mind and material realms from a Vaidika-Tāntrika perspective.

Saṅkarṣaṇa	**Pradyumna**	**Aniruddha**
Sattva + Tamas	Rajas + Rajas	Tamas + Sattva
Jīvātman	Manas	Ahaṅkāra

Saṅkarṣaṇa

Parāśara says that the *Saṅkarṣaṇa-vyūha* propelled the creation of the individual soul.[5] What is the soul? The *Bṛhadāranyaka-Upaniṣad* gives the definition as "that prāṇa to which in dreamless sleep (*suṣupti*) and death all our conscious functions return in order to go forth from it once more in awakening and birth respectively". The *jīvātma* is the individual soul or life force (*prāṇa*) that gives a being their individual nature in existence.

The jīvātma is that which incarnates from body to body in various lives. It is where the kārmik seeds are stored and therefore the seed of all deeds. The Vedas teach that the world came into existence from a seed of desire. The soul is made into its own entity which is the individual seed of desire that exists within everyone. Within the twelve petaled heart chakra is an eight-petaled lotus holding the energies of eight colors of desire related to the planets. One of them becomes predominant in each of us and becomes the Ātmakāraka in the birth chart, indicating the nature of our soul's desires in this life.

Desire creates and reproduces, and the original supreme desire replicates its nature in all things. All soul manifestations reproduce; plants spread their seeds into the wind, females have eggs and males have sperm. These represent the physical manifestion of the seed of desire to manifest. In the soul itself there are constant seeds being released which bubble up into the consiousness to become thoughts.

Saṅkarṣaṇa is the personification of the suṣupti state of consciousness which when limited by the tamas-śakti creates the jīvātma; the limited consciousness that makes you an individual through various incarnations. Parāśara says that Saṅkarṣaṇa 'caused the birth' (*jāta*) of the soul. The *Viṣvaksena Saṁhitā* elaborates on the topic and says that Saṅkarṣaṇa governs the state of the individual soul (*jīvatattva*) by separating (*vivic*) it from Nature (*Prakṛti*). Therefore Saṅkarṣaṇa is the form of the divine which fashions the individual souls from the unitative principle. Similar to when in classical Sāṅkhya there was the Mahat emanating from the division of Puruṣa and Prakṛti, here it is explained that it is Saṅkarṣaṇa that divides or creates that which is the conscious principle *in the creation*.

The word *saṅkarṣaṇa* literally means *drawing out* or *extracting*. It was the name given to Balarāma because mythology says he was pulled out of his mother's womb. In this way, Saṅkarṣaṇa is that which pulls us out from the One (supreme womb) and gives the soul its individuality or personal consciousness. Through this there is the ability to perceive name (and form) creating the first level of duality. And when this perceived duality exists then discrimination (*viveka*) exists and the form of the vyūha *becomes* Pradyumna.

[5] The soul is called *mahān* (the great principle) by Parāśara and *jīva* in most texts.

Pradyumna

Saṅkarṣaṇa is characterized by the initial appearance of creative activity (*unmeṣa*), or literally the opening of the eyes of consciousness. Pradyumna is the moment in subtle time that duality is created between Puruṣa and Prakṛti. Pradyumna rules the creation of the mind (*manas*); or the individualized knowing. The *Mahābhārata* says Pradyumna is the mind of all creatures, while the *Viṣvaksena Saṁhitā* says that he is the nature of the mental realm (*manomaya*).

Many cultures in their religion or shamanism speak of multiple layers or densities of reality. The **causal realm** is the existent essence of things perceived by highly evolved yogis in meditation or in yoga nidra. It is said only prāṇa is manifest there and so the knower resides there only in the form of prāṇa (or that prāṇa which is one's ātman). The state of consciousness associated with this realm is called suṣupti, which means deep sleep. It is where our consciousness goes in deep sleep or death as it is the level of the soul.

The **subtle realm** is the mental realm where beings exist in dreams or astral travel. This is perceived by those with clarity of the subtle body, control over their dreams, or siddhis which involve movement in the astral realm. One is not limited by physical manifest space and movement happens by the volition of the internal organs (mind, intelligence, etc).

Then the **physical realm** is perceived by all people. All realms exist within the physical state, while the subtle realm is unrestricted by the physical manifestation and the causal realm is unrestricted by mental impressions. Yogis aim to retain full awareness in each of these states of consciousness to be able to perceive the supreme which is "all states *and more*."

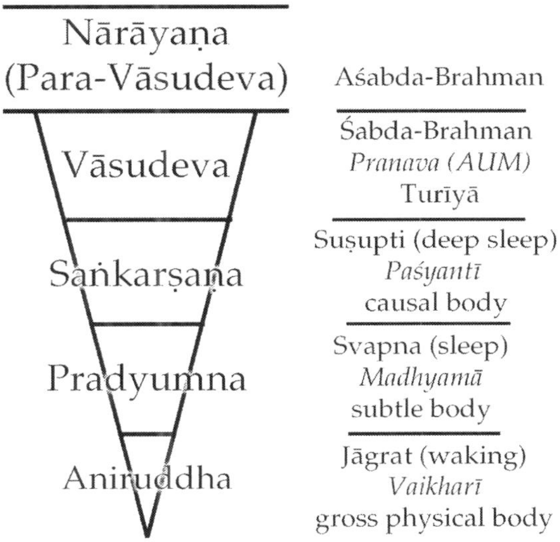

The vyūhas are the deification of these realms called the levels of consciousness (*avasthā-traya*) in the Vaidik tradition. Vāsudeva-vyūha relates to the *Turīyā* state- unitative aware consciousness which contains all states and is beyond them (*śūnyamaya*). Saṅkarṣaṇa relates to the consciousness of the causal realm (*suṣupti)*, the level of deep sleep or the causal realm (*sūkṣmāya*). Pradyumna relates to *svapna*, the level of dream, subtle body, or the realm of the mind (*manomaya*). Aniruddha relates to the most physical state of *jāgrat-* the physical state consciousness of wakefullness. The vyūhas are the puruṣa, the perceiver, in these realms while prakṛti perceived through them is the phenomenal aspect of these realms.

The diagram of the states of consciousness is called the Viśākha-yūpa and is found in the oldest Pāñcarātra texts. A yūpa is a pole which a sacrificed animal is tied to. Viśākha means branch, and the pole or pillar is divided into the states of consciousness. All created beings are tied to this pole as it is the root consciousness or mode of perception that composes the indivual being. It is these apects of consciousness that we bring our awareness to.

Pradyumna is the perceiver at the level of the mental reality. The realm of the mind exists because of the mode of perception. The mind is made of rajas, it is the catalyst between the soul and the material reality. The seeds of the soul arise and the mind choses which to receive and give life to.

The mind is moving, giving the impetus for the soul to spill forth its desires as the sexual act invokes the sperm to come forth and move their genetic material forward. But only one sperm makes it to the egg to generate life, and in this way, the mind is chosing which of the seeds given forth from the soul to give life to. When you have made a wrong choice, you always know that you knew the right choice. Various impressions had come to the mind but you chose to follow a particular thought, not always the right one. The mind is the catalyst, bringing life to the seed impressions of the soul. We have natural tendencies to chose the same seed impressions time and again. By using mantra, we guide the mind to chose the proper seeds, to chose the impressions we wish to manifest. The mind needs structure and guidance. By understanding the flaws of the mind we can chose the correct mantras to insure the mind is chosing the thoughts which insure the individual's highest potential. The mind is the interface between the soul and the material world, mantras work by guiding the mind to take the right direction.

The desires of the soul are seen from the situation of the Ātmakāraka in the rāśi and the placements from it in the navāṁśa. In this way, when the AK is in the navāṁśa lagna it is a rājayoga as the desires of the soul line up with the abilities of the individual. The story indicated by the Ātmakāraka' s placement is sure to happen as the soul will continue to send seed impressions into the mind until its desire gets fulfilled.

The mind is seen from the situation of the Moon and the placements from it. When the Moon is involved in or aspecting a combination it is said that it is sure to happen as the mind will follow those thoughts and actions that will lead to that circumstance.

As when a sperm meets an egg a new creation begins, so does the seed of desire go through the mind to pierce into the material world. As the sperm and egg become one, then divide into two, then four, then 16 and onwards expanding, the material world also develops. Our own material creative potential is a reflection of the internal spiritual-mental creative potential as well as the external divine creative potential to manifest the world. If one is thinking in terms of material reality (neutrinos, atoms, or chemicals) this might seem strange, but it is illuminating when one understands that consciousness is the root of creation, and everything is a perception affected by the *perceiver*.

Vāsudeva is the transcendental state which is called pure knowledge. Saṅkarṣaṇa is the state of suṣupti which generates the causal realm where the soul exists. Pradyumna is the state of svapna which generates the subtle realm where the jīva distinguishes between the subjective and objective frames of reference. Aniruddha projects the world of multiplicity and differentiations.

Aniruddha

Aniruddha takes over the creation of Pradyumna in gross time evolving out manifest matter which gives the soul opportunity to grow. Aniruddha is the vyūha which gives birth to the I-sense (*ahaṅkāra*) by mixing with the sattva-śakti who is the I-hood of the Puruṣa.

Parāśara calls this form the *Brahmā-ahaṅkāra* as it functions to create the material world. The ahaṅkāra itself then takes on three attributes relative to each of the three guṇa which create the manifest world and sets the stage for the laws of karma to work. Aniruddha thereby bestows upon men the fruits of their karma.

6. Draw a diagram of the three states of consciousness and the three śaktis and then show how they mix and what they create. Define each of these factors.

7. The *Māṇḍūkya Upaniṣad* (12 verses) was written by the sage Manduka who came from a family of linguists. Read about Auṁ and the states of consciousness in the *Māṇḍūkya Upaniṣad* and show your notes.

Auṁ and the Levels of Speech

The Maitrī Upaniṣad (VI.3) says, "There are two forms of brahman, the shaped and the unshaped. What is shaped is the unreal. What is unshaped is the real; it is brahman: it is light. What is light is the Sun. This is Auṁ. It became the self. It divided itself into three. Auṁ is three elements. Through them, all this is woven on it as warp and weft."

The Auṁ is three letters and candra-bindu yet is still only one syllable. There are three states and one beyond containing them, but they are all just one state individuated by its functions, all just one divinity. The *Ahirbudhnya Saṁhitā* (chapter 51) gives six stages of Auṁ. A is Aniruddha or the waking state, U is Pradyumna or the dreaming state, and M is Saṅkarṣana or the suṣupti state. Then the echo of the ardha-mātra is Vāsudeva, the lingering nasal sound is his Śakti and finally the silence observed after the pronunciation of the syllable is the All-pervasive highest Brahman.

The Maitrī Upaniṣad (VI.5) speaks of the sound body of Auṁ and says that the feminine, masculine and neuter are its gender-body, Brahmā, Rudra and Viṣṇu are its overlord-body, the Ṛg, Yajur and Samaveda are its knowledge-body, Bhūr, Bhuvaḥ and Svaḥ are its world-body. Past, present and future are its time-body… Intelligence (*buddhi*), mind (*manas*) and the I-sense (*ahaṅkāra*) are its consciousness-body (*cetanavati*).

Terminology changes in the various scriptures but the basic conceptual realities stay the same. In this verse we see the Auṁ and its relationship to the consciousness/sentience (*cetana*) is the same as in the Upaniṣads. Auṁ is called the pranava, it is god as sound (*śabda-brahman*). It comes forth from the silence and creates, divides into the three and establishes the three worlds. This is called the sonic creation or the sound body of the creative being, and as above, so below.

Sonic Theory

In the ancient world, the scripture was considered to create reality. As reality is perceived through concepts and language, the scripture gives particular conceptions and language in which you alter your individual understanding of reality. Thinking requires language/speech (*vac*). All thought has linguistic form; therefore thinking cannot exist independently of words/sound (*śabda*). Bhratṛhari used the terms *consciousness* and the *word* interchangeably. As reality is created by the perceiving consciousness, everything is made of the words and sounds which we learn.

Each level of consciousness has a level of sound/word associated with it. Auṁ relates to Vāsudeva; Patañjali called it Īśvara. The suṣupti relates to *paśyantī* speech which is the level of speech which contains all things, the entire concept and reality of that which is communicated. The svapna relates to *madhyamā* speech which is the sounds you hear in a dream, or the thought construct in the mind. The jāgrat relates to the *vaikarī* speech which is gross audible sound that comes in sound waves which strike the ear through the medium of air.

Three Primary Elements of Perceiving

Within the comprehension of sound there are three primary elements to perceiving. The first is the sound or word (*śabda*) which denotes an object. Then there is the mental apprehension (*pratyaya*) of the meaning of the word, connecting the sound to the object. For example, if I say 'chair', you have the apprehension that I mean something you sit upon (an image of a chair is created in the mind). Then there is the actual object (*artha*) denoted by the word. The consciousness has pratyaya (apprehension) of artha (objects) and names those objects by śabda (word).

At the level of Auṁ these three elements are one and not distinct. Auṁ is the all and everything of the divine: the sound, apprehension and the object. It is sound as divinity (*śabda-brahman*). In the causal body of the Paśyantī they are co-related; the word has color and form. The word/sound *is* what it sounds like. Paśyantī is the level of seed-sounds (*bījas*) for meditation.

In the subtle realm of madhyama, the śabda (word) and the pratyaya (apprehension) become distinct. In the mind, when you say a word it brings to mind a certain concept. In a dream, to think of an object (which is to be conscious of its sound/word) is to make it present, there is not a separation between the pratyaya and the artha. In the physical realm of the vaikhari (articulate speech), the śabda, pratyaya, and the artha are all distinct. In the *Yoga Sūtras* of Patañjali (3.17) it is stated that to meditate (*saṁyama*) on these three distinctions gives the knowledge of the sounds made by all living beings (*sarva bhūta ruta jñāna*). By meditation on these distinctions we hear the 'deeper intention' and understand the sound made by any creature.

Time is different at each of these levels of sound which changes its quality. In the vaikharī, language has grammatical sequence as there is gross time, in mental discourse (*madhyama*) there is a trace of sequence, but in the paśyantī there is no sequence as it is a very different level of time.

At the causal level of paśyantī the sound is like a seed containing everything that will soon grow. In the subtle level of madhyama, the logical relation of the word to its meaning sprouts itself into an impression (*saṁskara*). The distinction between the object indicated and the sound denoting it is discernable in the form of an impression that grows into thoughts and feelings. These sounds then become the audible speech of a human being, or in the case of the Puruṣa become the material reality.

In an individual, speech will start as an all-inclusive conception, or the energy of an idea in the paśyantī speech coming from the soul (what is desired to be said). This is understood by the mind and takes the form of a thought sound (*madhyamā*) in the mind. Then it is spoken through the mouth of an individual as the words (*vaikharī*) in which they choose to express an idea. In this way, a person has certain speech to express what the soul intends. This is interpreted by the mind and formed into thoughts which may be true to the original intention or not. Then this intention is formed into words according to the nature and culture of an individual and spoken. In the levels of speech there is what is meant, what is understood and what is stated. A highly conscious individual learns to express the intentions of the soul directly, and to hear the true intention of others.

The Bhagavad Gītā (2.69) says, "What is night for all beings is the time of awakening for the one with a controlled mind; and the time of awakening for all beings is night for the one who sees (*paśyataḥ*)." The normal waking state is the most dense and limited, while the suṣupti resides closest to the Supreme. This state is experienced in deep meditation or yoga nidra. One who hears the causal speech (*paśyantī*) is one who can see (*paśyataḥ*).

In the waking consciousness (*jagrat*), the material world is the most fully manifested, but consciousness is the most limited. In the suṣupti, the material world is less manifest but the consciousness is more vast or expansive. This gives us two triangles, Puruṣa going upwards and Prakṛti going downwards, which when put together create a six pointed star.

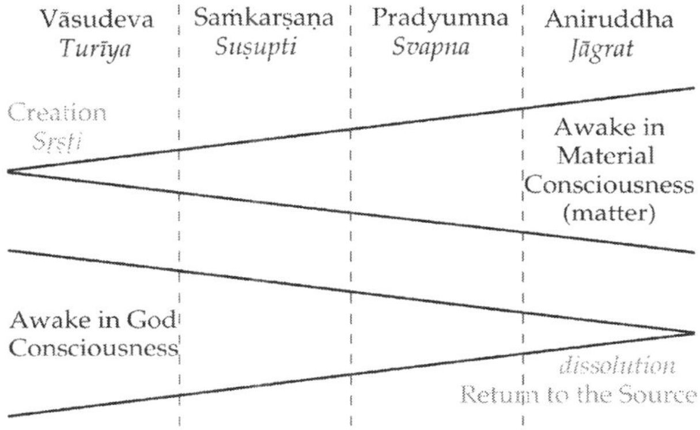

On the level of practice, a Jyotiṣī works to see more than can be seen by normal consciousness and is therefore always working on expanding awareness. Through yogic practices one refines the mind to be aware of more subtle levels. Patañjali gives five ways that the veils of consciousness are removed in the *Yoga Sūtras* (4.1). He says that accomplishment (*siddhi*) is attained through 1) previous life karma (*janma*), or 2) herbs (*oṣadhi*), or 3) mantras, or 4) training the senses/personal growth/austerities (*tapaḥ*), or 5) yoga and meditation (*samādhi*).

For our own spiritual growth, it is important to understand the construction of reality and trace it backwards to remove the veils over our consciousness. The more subtle our own consciousness becomes the better we are able to see the real nature of an individual and to help them on all levels of being.

Knowledge changes the way we perceive, and the constructs which we can place our understanding within. Intellectual knowledge is only half-knowledge. Therefore the levels of consciousness need to be experienced through meditation.

As astrologers we need to have a deeper understanding of the levels of being and Time. The supreme form of Time turns and separates Puruṣa and Prakṛti which leads to the manifestation of the causal realm and the individual soul. Then subtle time turns and leads to the creation of the mental realm. Finally the material time turns and manifests waking consciousness, the I-sense and the physical world. Time urges the vyūhas and the śaktis to mix and create. For this reason, Kālī, the personification of the power of Time, is the mother creatice as well as the destroyer.

The world is a manifestation of consciousness, therefore consciousness must be understood to understand creation. The Puruṣa takes four modes of awareness; that which is all encompassing, the causal, subtle and physical/awake. From this last mode (*jāgrat*), conjoined with Śrī-śakti, the ahaṅkāra is born and manifests in three ways according to each of the guṇas.

अहंकारस्त्रिधा भूत्वा सर्वमेतदविस्तरात् ।
सात्त्विको राजसश्चैव तामसश्चेदहंकृतिः ॥ १८ ॥

ahaṅkārastridhā (I-sense has 3 parts) bhūtvā (and become) sarvametadavistarāt (all-this-expansion, becoming large, spreading), sāttviko rājasaścaiva tāmasaśced ahaṅkṛtiḥ || 18||

The ahaṅkāra (I-sense) has three aspects from which all things become,
these are Sattva, Rajas and Tamas ahaṅkāra.

देवा वैकारिकाज्जातास्तैजसादिन्द्रियाणि ।
तामसाच्चैव भूतानि खादीनि स्वस्वशक्तिभिः ॥ १९ ॥

devāḥ (heavenly, divine, sense organs) vaikārikāt (sattva-ahaṅkāra) jātāḥ (arisen) taijasād (rajas-ahaṅkāra) indriyāṇi (senses, sense organs), tāmasāt caiva ((from tamas) bhūtāni (is produced) khādīni (space, etc) svasvaśaktibhiḥ (with their respective śakti/powers)|| 19||

From the sattva-ahaṅkāra (*vaikārika*) the devas arise,
From the rajas-ahaṅkāra (*taijasa*) the sense organs (*indriya*) arise,
From the tamas-ahaṅkāra (*tāmasa*) the earth, etc are produced,
each with their respective powers.

The ahaṅkāra takes on the mode of the three guṇas and is called accordingly as *vaikārika* for the sattva, *taijasa* for the rajas, and *tāmasa* (or *bhūtādi)* for the tamas ahaṅkāra. From *taijasa* the 10 sense organs[6] are created and through *vaikārika* the devas of each of these arise. From tamas the manifest creation comes into existence through the five elements.

The elements then have their own evolution as Śrīmad Bhāgavatam [3.26.32] explains; the tamas-ahaṅkāra (*tāmasāt*) impells the divine energy (*bhagavat-virya*) to transform into the subtle element of sound (*śabda-tanmātra*). And from that was impelled the space element (*ākāśa*) and from that the sense of hearing (*śrotram*) and then the ear (*śabda-gam*). Then through the impulse of time (*kāla-gatyā*) the tanmātra of *touch* evolved, then sight, taste and smell. There are some differences in opinion as to how the factors (*tattvas*) came

6 Parāśara repeats this in the Viṣṇu Purāṇa I.2.45 indicating the texts are by the same tradition.

about (whether it was time or some other śakti) but the primary correlations of the subtle elements, gross elements, and sense organs remains the same in all traditions: Sound-Space- Hearing- Ear.

Ahaṅkāra (I-sense)			
Bhūtādi (tamas-ahaṅkāra)		Taijasa (rajas-ahaṅkāra)	
Tanmātra & Bhūta		Karma-Indriya	Jñāna-Indriya
Sound(*śabda*)	Space (*ākāśa*)	Speech (*vāc*)	Ear/hearing (*śrota*)
Touch (*sparśa*)	Air (*vāyu*)	Hand (*pāṇī*)	Skin/feeling (*tvac*)
Sight (*rūpa*)	Fire (*agni*)	Feet (*pāda*)	Eyes/seeing (*cakṣus*)
Taste (*rasa*)	Water (*jala*)	Urethra (*upastha*)	Tongue/tasting (*jihva*)
Smell (*gandha*)	Earth (*pṛthvi*)	Anus (*pāyu*)	Nose/smelling (*nāsikā*)

The 10 sensory organs each have a devā[7] associated with them (also called adhidevatā, or overlords[8]), which arises at the same time as the sensory organ. Though there are eleven devatā as the mind is the eleventh organ ruled by the Moon (*Candra*).[9] The manifest Puruṣa is the cosmic being who is made up of all these devatā.

Vaikārika (sattva-ahaṅkāra)			
Karma-Indriya		Jñāna-Indriya	
Speech/ vocal organ (*vāc*)	Agni	Ear/hearing (*śrota*)	Diśa
Hand/ handling organ (*pāṇī*)	Indra	Skin/feeling (*tvac*)	Virāja/Vāyu
Feet/ locomotive organ (*pāda*)	Hari	Eyes/seeing (*cakṣus*)	Sūrya
Urethra/generating organ (*upastha*)	Āpas	Tongue/tasting (*jihva*)	Āpas/Varuṇa
Anus/ evacuation organ (*pāyu*)	Mṛtyu	Nose/smelling (*nāsikā*)	Bhūmi/Vāyu

All these devatās reside in the Cosmic Being but are lifeless without the perceiver (*kṣetra-jña*).[10] Therefore these organs are the tools of the inner being. One is not to identify themselves with them but to identify with the inner being who *perceives* their actions. The mind is the organ which registers the sensory information and is therefore an aspect of the sensory organs, its state changes according to the stimuli given to it through the senses. The ahaṅkāra seeks to identify the self with the mind, elements and the sensory organs but the nature of oneself is actually that consciousness which perceives these attributes. Therefore it is called kṣetra (the place of existing)- jña (knower), or the one who knows the place of existing.

7 Sāmkhya-Pravachana-Sūtram II.21. For discussion about the relationship of the devatā to indriya see Sinha, p.252-255.

8 Suśruṭa-Saṁhitā, Śārīrasthāna I.7 (III.I. 9), Suśruta lists Vayū for skin, Āpas for tongue, Pṛthvī for smell, Mitra for anus, and Prajāpati for the sexual organ.

9 Viṣṇu Purāṇa, I.2.46, *ekādaśa manaścātra devā vaikārikāḥ smṛtāḥ|tvak cakṣurnāsikā jihvā śrotramatra ca pañcamam||*

10 Śrīmad Bhāgavatam, 3.26.70, *cittena hṛdayaṁ caityaḥ kṣetra-jñaḥ prāviśad yadā virāṭ tadaiva puruṣaḥ salilād datiṣṭhata||*

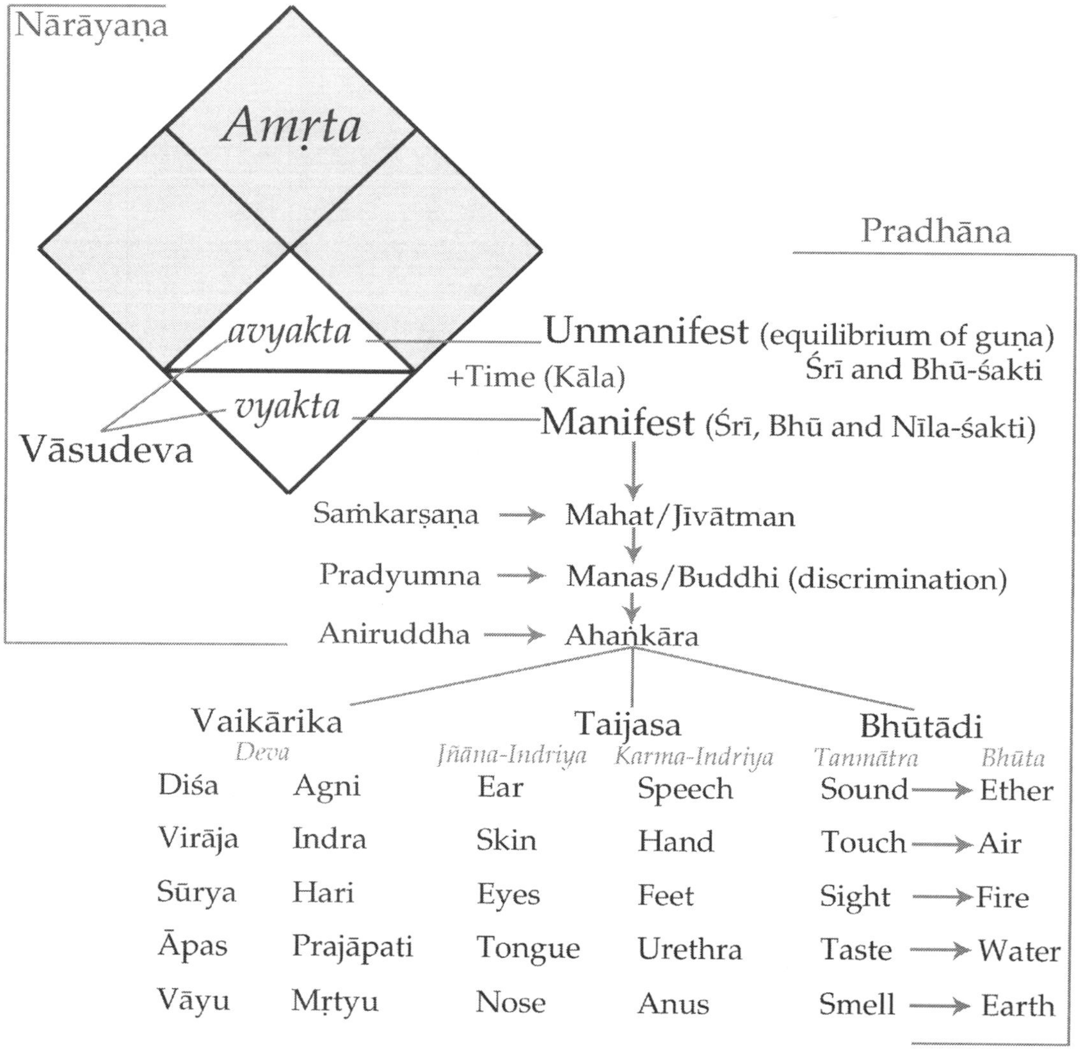

11. How does the division of the ahaṅkāra guṇas of Parāśara's teaching vary from that of *Sāṅkhya Kārikā* and that of the *Lakṣmī Tantra*?

12. For Āyurvedic practioners: what is the system of Sāṅkhya used by *Caraka Saṁhitā* and *Suśruṭa Saṁhitā* (found in the Śārīrasthānam chapter)?

This level of creation precedes the question of creationism versus evolution. This process of emanation focuses on the state of the Perceiver and the elements through which it perceives. Whether humans were created by god instantly or evolved over millions of years, the *guiding principle* to our present material state are the elements (*tattvas*). These elements create the types of bodies the perceiver utilizes. Therefore all living beings develop some way to communicate, feel, see, taste and smell. This is a view of emanation based on the densification of consciousness into matter which forms the foundation of Vedic and Hindu thought.

The relationships such as Sound, Space, Speech, and Hearing or Touch, Air, Hand, Skin are an important part of Vedic science. Their relationship reveals the reason why massage (touch) has the ability to pacify vāta (vāyu in the body), the reason ringing a bell (sound) in worship clears the space (ākāśa), or why astrologers use Agni mantras to improve their predictive powers (sight). These correlations are the logic that is applied in many techniques in Āyurveda, Yoga and Jyotiṣa.

The process of explaining the 25 elements (*tattvas*) that compose the creation is called *Sāṅkhya*, which means enumerating, to catalog or list. Sāṅkhya is one of the six orthodox view points (*darśanas*) of the Vedas. It is a system of enumerating the primary principles of creation. There are various schools of Sāṅkhya found in the Indian scriptures, and some individuals argue about correctness of one or another. These systems are intended to give *distinctions* in which to create a context to explain the nature of reality. They are not a final truth, but a way of percieving creation and giving distinctions (*viveka*) with which to discuss and understand the functions and processes of reality. Truth is not something that is taught in a 25 point system, truth is something that is experienced. The framework of Sāṅkhya is meant to give distinctions in reality in order to help the mind perceive the experience of truth, and interact consciously with the world.

Sāṅkhya is one of the official views (*darśanas*) of Vedic philosophy and there are two main types of Sāṅkhya: theistic (*āstika*) and non-theistic (*nir-Iśvara*). The Sāṅkhya of the *Sāṅkhya Kārikā* says that an eternal, self-caused god cannot be proven by the normal methods of proof, perception, inference, and testimony. It therefore gives the verdict of 'not proven' which is *nir-Iśvara*. It does not deny god which is atheist (*nāstika*).

Parāśara, the Pāñcarātra, and the Purāṇas present a theistic Sāṅkhya which has the process of creation guided by a higher power. Both āstika and nir-Iśvara are accepted views, while nāstika is not. The Puruṣa is the stable consciousness that perceives. This Puruṣa watches the manifestation as the individual watches a movie or a play.

The first stage of creation (*śuddha-sṛṣṭi*) is the manifestation of enumerated factors (25 tattvas) from the Puruṣa creating the root prakṛti (*Pradhāna*). Time is a mixing element. The second part of creation is the mixing of all these tattvas to become compounds. They come together and create the *cosmic egg* which is defined as containing the entire universe within it (or the body of the universe). At the transition from the first stage to the second stage of creation the trinity of Brahmā, Śiva, and Viṣṇu come into being to create, preserve and transform the created reality, coupled with their respective śakti.

श्रीशक्त्या सहितो विष्णुः सदा पाति जगत्त्रयम्।
भूशक्त्या सृजते ब्रह्मा नीलशक्त्या शिवोऽत्ति हि ॥ २० ॥

śrīśaktyā (Śrī-śakti) sahito (conjoined, associated with) viṣṇuḥ (Viṣṇu) sadā (always, ever, continually) pāti (lord) jagattrayam (three worlds), bhūśaktyā (Bhū-śakti) sṛjate (producing, creating) brahmā nīlaśaktyā (nīla-śakti) śivo'tti (Śiva) hi (indeed)|| 20||

The All-pervasive lord conjoined Śrī-śakti becomes lord of the three worlds (*Viṣṇu*),
Conjoined Bhū-śakti he is Brahmā, the creator,
Conjoined Nīla-śakti he is Śiva.

Brahma, Śiva, and Viṣṇu are here stated to be the same deity just taking different roles according to the union of the three types of śakti. The teaching of a single deity with many names according to their role is repeated by Parāśara in the Viṣṇu Purāṇa.[11] Therefore, Parāśara does not favor or disfavor worship of Viṣṇu, Śiva or Śakti but utilizes the form of the deity for its functional utility.

The final manifestations of Brahmā, Śiva and Viṣṇu as personifications of the guṇas relate to the created reality (*vyakta*). These are the trinity that show up as characters in various Hindu myths; they are a mode of the Supreme as are all other deities. The unmanifest (*avyakta*) Supreme is called differently by various traditions (whether the person worships Viṣṇu, Śiva, or Śakti). Sometimes the Supreme is called *Mahāviṣṇu* or *Sada-Śiva* to differentiate the limited form from the Supreme form. Sometimes in scriptures there is no differentiation in name used and one needs to utilize the context to know if the passage is refering to the manifest mode of Viṣṇu or Śiva who has qualities within the creation, or the Viṣṇu/Śiva as the unlimited Supreme. An example of this can be seen in the Mahābhārata where Mārkaṇḍeya describes the Supreme (called by him as Nārāyaṇa) and says that the whole universe and all gods are Him (3.188.6). In the list of his names, Brahmā, Viṣṇu and Śiva are all mentioned. In this way, an astrologer should not be attached to name, but should understand the quality of name (*nāma tattva*) and use it properly.

Sāṅkhya teaches that by having an understanding of the tattvas of creation one knows what is *not* Puruṣa. This knowledge allows us to remove ourselves from the false identification that we are the aspect of our being that is the limited material world. It allows us to focus our attention on the true perceiver.

Parāśara says that the immortal (*amṛta*) can be known by those who have proper discrimination (*pramāṇa*) of the root matter (*pradhāna*) or those that can differentiate the changing from the unchanging. The teaching of Kapila in the Śrīmad Bhāgavatam (3.26.72) is that the mind should stay focused on the supreme soul (*pratyak-ātmān*) in one's being, bound by Yoga (*yoga-pravṛttya*), devotion (*bhāktya*), with detachment (*viraktya*), knowledge (*jñāna*), and practice of proper discrimination (*vivecya*). Ignorance is bondage

[11] Viṣṇu Purāṇa I.2.64-68, II.11.12-14

caused by misidentification of one's self with the limited tattvas of creation. One's *true nature* is that of the unlimited nature of Puruṣa.

Some religious views hold that in the proper identification with the true nature of Puruṣa the soul lives eternally in the Amṛta, while other religious views hold that the soul dissolves and becomes One with the Puruṣa. Be clear that this is a personal religious *belief* about the nature of the soul and separate from our discussion.

The important understanding for an astrologer is that the true nature of the soul is the perceiver beyond the limitations of the manifest creation. One needs proper identification of oneself with the *awareness* perceiving the manifestation and to not *identify* oneself as the elements of creation. This knowledge purifies the mind of the individual by creating non-attachment (*vairāgya*), allowing one's bias to fall away. This leads to the individual in a material body becoming unaffected by guṇas of material nature (*prakṛti*). One releases the thought of being the performer of actions (*akartṛtva*), remaining unchanging (*avikārāt*) just as the Sun remains aloof from its reflection on water.

The soul lives in the manifest creation, bound by the guṇas and the rules of cause and effect. The soul is therefore bound to the karmas created with the tattvas of creation. Remedial measures are based upon balancing karma which is encoded as proportions of these tattva compounds and states of consciousness. The astrologer understands the elements of creation and utilizes them to achieve the four goals of life remembering that the true soul is beyond this.

Chapter 2

Time

The cyclic recurrence of the sunset and dawn
daily serves to measure life's decay,
but burdened with his mundane tasks,
man does not grasp time's movement;
seeing old age and pain and death,
he does not experience terror.
Drunk on the heady wine of delusion,
the world is mad in oblivion.

-Sanskrit Poems of Bhartṛhari

Time

The manifest world is created and it exists within Time. Time is the force impelling events forward (*kalana*) and is measured by change (*pariṇām*). There are three different levels of time; the supreme level of Time as a deity who motivates creation, subtle time creating the building blocks of reality and perception, and empirical time that is perceived in units.

Sound creates notes according to its frequency while light takes on color based on frequency. These frequencies are the number of waves in a portion of time. Therefore, the universe is not just made of sound, but sound frequencies, which are sound regulated by time. Time takes on qualities such as guṇas, sound, color, etc., which lead to experience and emotion. Daśā is the quality of time being experienced at a particular level.

Parāśara says that the zodiac is Viṣṇu's *Kālarūpa;* his manifestation as 'Time'.[2] The *time* of birth dictates the position of planets, which indicates the karma of the individual. The time determines the unfoldment of events (via daśā) in an individual's life. From the astrologer's perspective, Time controls everything, and the study of astrology is the study of god as Time (*kālapuruṣa*). The birth chart is just a picture of time, and the astrologer is the one trained to read this time. Therefore, we must understand the nature of Time.

Vedas: The Eternally Turning Wheel

In the Ṛgveda, the natural law of the universe is called Ṛta. It is the way things are, the truth of how things work, the higher truth, or divine law. In the universe, everything has a time and a place; something is in line with the divine law when it is in the proper time and place. The seasons are called *ṛtu,* a fixed order or rule, they are the times of year during which certain actions are to be performed in certain ways. The word 'ṛtu' also means a right time (*ṛtva*), or the proper time for an action. When a woman ovulates it is also called the ṛtu, as it is the proper time to conceive. The seasons come in their proper order at their proper time. They govern the proper time to plant and the proper time to harvest. They govern the rituals and the actions of human life- all things exist and are guided by the proper time. And all things are in divine alignment (*Ṛta*) when they happen at the right time in the right place. The Ṛgveda symbolized Ṛta with solar images[3] since the Sun was the most regular (*ṛtviya*) element of time.

The order of the seasons is made by the movement of the Sun (or our movement around the Sun). The Sun is creating day and night, the months, seasons and years, which keep a steady and constant reality. The priest is called a *ṛtvij,* or one who knows

---

[2] Bṛhat Parāśara Horā Śāstra, Rāśi-svarūpa-adyāya, *yadavyaktātmako viṣṇuḥ kālarupo janārdanaḥ | tasyāṅgāni nibodha tvaṁ kramānmeṣādirāśyaḥ* || 2||

[3] Johnson, *Poetry and Speculation of the Ṛg Veda,* p. 82

the appropriate times to do ritual (*yajña*), or who does ritual regularly. The Sun is the significator of dharma; that which is the right action performed by the appropriate person at the appropriate time.

The Sun is therefore the king, controlling the time of everything.[4] The Ṛgveda says that the Sun promotes order (*Ṛta*) and has subdued disorder (*anṛta*), and in this way he is the incomprehensible god (*acitta brahman*).[5] He is represented as a wheel indicating the order of the world in which humans live (*cakraṁ ṛtasya*). Śaunaka's *Bṛhad-devatā* says the Sun is the cause of creation and destruction, of the animate and inanimate, and the past, present and future. The Sun is the Creator (*Prajāpati*), the eternal Spirit (*Brahman*) which is imperishable (*akṣaram*).[6] The Sun is called the form of god that can be seen with the eyes (*pratyakṣa-devatā*).

The wheel of the Sun, seasons and cosmic law are the symbolic expressions of time. Time is a flow, a rhythm,[7] and there are seven rhythms of the Ṛgveda like the seven colors/rays which are the seven horses that pull the chariot of the Sun across the sky. Time works like a wheel that spins in cycles moving forward around an unchanging axle. Everything ages, deteriorates and goes away, but the axle of time continues, unchanging, undecaying (*ajara*). This is basically the modern saying that "everything changes except change itself". Change is the measurement of Time, therefore everything changes except Time who makes everything change.

In the Vedas, Time is perceived as a wheel (*chakra*) with a center and axle.[8] The wheel moves and everything changes but the axle, which makes everything move, remains the same. The Sun ripens everything on earth by means of days, nights, half-months, months, seasons and years.[9] The Sun rising and setting is the chakra of Time. It brings decay (*jarā*) to everything else, yet it is Time which is undecaying (*ajara*) at the axis. The Atharvaveda says that Time is Brahman, the father of Prajāpati (the creator).[10]

Everything that exists or will exist is in Time.[11] The Atharvaveda directly addresses Time (*Kāla*) as God 'seen in many different forms'.[12] Time produced all existence, the Sun

---

[4] Bṛhat Parāśara Horā Śāstra, Sṛṣṭi-krama-kathana-adhyāya,v.6

[5] Ṛg Veda 1.152.3-5, Wheel of order (*cakrām ṛtasya*).

[6] Śaunaka's Bṛhad-devatā, 1.61-62

[7] Dandekar, R.N. Ṛta in the Ṛgveda, p.2 (article in *Traividyam* edited by Mukherji). "Vedic man saw definite order and harmony, regular pattern and scheme, and constancy and rhythm behind the flux".

[8] This is seen in the Asyavāmīya of Dīrghatamas (1.164), Kāla Sūkta of the Atharvaveda (XIX.53-54), and Atharvaveda (X.VIII.4), see also commentary by Singh, S.P. Life and Vision of Vedic Seers. P. 91-116

[9] Śatapatha Brāhmaṇa X.4.2.19

[10] Atharvaveda, XIX.53.2

[11] Atharvaveda, Kāla Sūkta, XIX.53.5

[12] Atharvaveda, Kāla Sūkta, XIX.53.3, see also Achar, B.N. Narahari. Journal of Vedic Studies Vol. 4 (1998)

burns in Time, the entire world is in Time, Time gives the eyes the power to see.[13] Time is not considered a phenomenon that you may or may not pay attention to, it is the cause of the world, and the whole world is situated within time and works according to it. He is the lord of all (*sarvasyeśvara*).[14] Time is the cause/the driver (*iṣita*) and the creator (*jātaṁ*), and therefore the foundation (*pratiṣṭhita*). Time is the Divine Spirit (*Brahman*), the power of existence (*bhūtva vibharti*), the supreme being (*parameṣṭhinam*).[15]

Time is God. The Sun is God.[16] And there are the twelve Ādityas, and Agni who are also God. The clock has so many pieces to make it work, but it is One clock. One needs to understand the concept of God from a Vedic viewpoint. The early indologists used to argue whether the word Ṛta was an adjective or a subject. They defined the word as truth, either as in both the simple meaning of the word as well as a magically active cosmic power.[17] The Vedas say all these different realities are really one divine truth, *eka sat*, one reality. The Upaniṣads say that the Time, the Sun, Viṣṇu, Prajāpati, "he is all these, the lord, the witness, who shines in yonder circle."[18] There are different frequencies of the Supreme, and we need to listen to all of them to understand the song of the divine. The Vedic seers were Ṛṣis with expanded consciousness. These concepts need to be meditated upon for the nature of Time and its manifestations to be able to reveal the Supreme.

Pāñcarātras Āgama and Purāṇas

In the Pāñcarātra āgama philosophy, Time is an integral aspect of the Supreme.[19] Time is symbolized by the lotus (*paṅkaja*) which did not grow from mud (*paṅka*),[20] but which comes forth from Nārāyaṇa's navel. Nārāyaṇa lies asleep with his consort Lakṣmī and in the lotus growing from his navel sits the 'self-born' Brahmā who creates the world. This symbolizes the transcendent one with his Śakti impelling the creation with the power of time. [21]

Classical Sāṅkhya (of the *Kārikā* and *Sūtra*) has only two primary principles to start with, but in Pāñcarātra philosophy there are three principles: Puruṣa, Prakṛti, and Kāla (soul, matter, and time). The principle of Time (*kālamaya tattva*) impels the universe, separating Puruṣa and Prakṛti in creation, manifesting their effects and uniting

[13] Atharvaveda, Kāla Sūkta, XIX.53.6
[14] Atharvaveda, Kāla Sūkta, XIX.53.8
[15] Atharvaveda, Kāla Sūkta, XIX.53.9
[16] Maitrāyaṇa Upaniṣad, VI.16
[17] Chauhan, D.V. Understanding Ṛgveda, p. 77
[18] Maitrāyaṇa Upaniṣad, VI.16
[19] Viṣṇu Purāṇa, I.3.6 *kāla-svarūpaṁ viṣṇośca yanmayoktaṁ tavānagha* |
[20] Lakṣmī Tantra, 5.22 The lotus is made of Time (*kālamaya*).
[21] Nārāyaṇa is asleep representing the inactive aspect of the Supreme beyond action- as the Śāṅkhya concept of the Puruṣa. Lakṣmī by his side represents the Kriyā Śakti impelling the creation as the lord's will. The lotus is Time and Brahmā is the cosmic being (or Puruṣa) who is creating the manifest world.

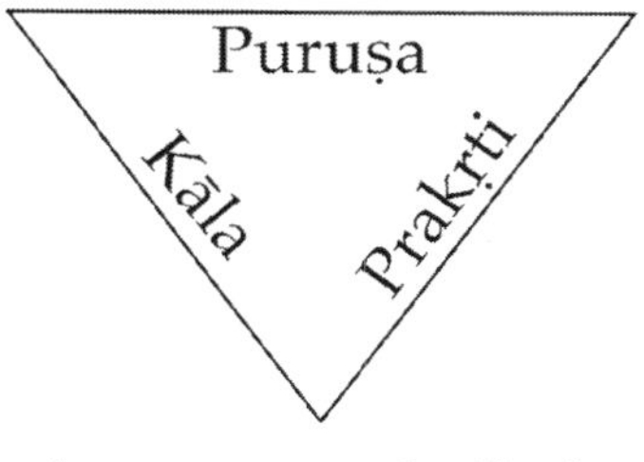

them in dissolution.[22] In this way, the Atharvaveda calls Time the first or chief (*prathama*) deva.[23] Time churns and Prakṛti manifests from Puruṣa. Prakṛti transforms herself like water and clay, while the Puruṣa undergoes no transformation though is the cause by its beingness. Time ripens both principles, bringing forth the Avyakta [the unmanifest composed of the cosmic being, the three guṇas in equilibrium, and Time]. From these elements come the Vyakta- the manifestation. The Viṣṇu Purāṇa says that the wise call [1] the Puruṣa (the cosmic being), [2] Avyakta/Pradhāna (unmanifest matter), [3] Vyakta (matter) and [4] Kāla (time) as the four aspects of the Supreme which cause the manifest world.[24]

In the Upaniṣads, there is a differentiation made between transcendental time and gross time. Gross time is called the time with parts (*sakala kāla*) and the other is the non-time (*akāla*) without parts. That which is prior to the sun is the Timeless (*a-kāla*) without parts (*a-kala*). But that which begins with the sun is Time, which has parts.[25]

Ahirbudhnya Saṁhitā breaks Time down into three levels. [1] Gross time (*sthūla kāla*) can be divided into seconds, minutes, etc. [2] Subtle time (*sūkṣma kāla*) arising from niyati in the unmanifest (*mūla-prakṛti*) and directs the elements (*tattvas*). [3] Transcendent time (*paraḥ kāla*) moves the activities of the vyūhas (or drives the subtle aspects of consciousness).[26] The Supreme Divinity (*Nārāyaṇa*) is beyond Time. It is said that Time cooks all things, but is excelled by him in whom time is cooked. In this way, all three levels of existence (jāgrat, svapna, and suṣupti) have a quality of Time associated with them, except the Turīyā state which is beyond. When the Supreme desires creation, the transcendental Time (*paraḥ kāla*) begins the creation process.

Time urges forth the entire creation in an orderly manner.[27] From the four aspects of the Supreme, the great tattva called Mahat (cosmic intelligence) manifests having three parts: judgment (*buddhi*), life (*prāṇa*), and (empirical) time (*kāla*)- relating to its sattva, rajas, and tamas aspects. Time at this level of manifestation is gross time which is measured in increments. This form of Time is not just what we perceive but it is that with which we do perceive.[28] These three aspects [thought (*buddhi*), breath (*prāṇa*), and time (*kāla*)] cannot happen without each other. To breathe is the movement of prāṇa. Thought is the movement of prāṇa -when a yogi stops the thoughts -the breath stops with it. That

[22] Ahirbhudhnya Saṁhitā VII.3, and Viṣṇu Purāṇa I.2.24-27
[23] Atharvaveda, Kāla Sūkta, XIX.53.2
[24] Lakṣmī Tantra 17.41-43, and Viṣṇu Purāṇa I.2.15-17
[25] Maitrāyaṇa Upaniṣad, VI.15
[26] Ahirbhudhnya Saṁhitā, LIII.11-12. Schrader, p.77
[27] Ahirbudhnya Saṁhitā 6.52. Also see BPHS, Sṛṣṭi-Krama-Kathana-Adhyāya,v.6
[28] Schrader, Introduction to Pāñcarātra, p.83

movement of mind/prāṇa is time which is calculated and divisional.[29]

In Pāñcarātra philosophy, the elements of Creation manifest and then the soul enters into the creation. When the souls descend from the higher realms, the creative womb [of the *bhuti śakti*] has two things it uses to develop the souls for material existence- Time and the guṇas. *Niyati* is the subtle aspect of Time which governs/limits everything or is the controller of everything (*sarva-niyāmaka*).[30] Niyati literally means the fixed order of things, necessity, destiny, and is sometimes personified as a goddess. It is the aspect of Time which moves according to one's fate, which is the fructification of one's own karma. Good and bad times, the time for success or the time for failure are one's own karma which will be brought about according to the right time.

Time is not just quantitative but gives birth to the qualities, it brings them about originally and controls when they arise individually in one's life. The soul first descends into Niyati.[31] The regulating power (*niyama-bhāvita*) of Niyati, the subtle aspect of Time, brings about whatever form one may have, whatever actions one may do, and whatever true nature (*svabhāvaka*) one may have.[32] In this way, the subtle aspect of Time determines the abilities, inclinations, and intellectual capacity of the individual according to one's karma. One's entire past (*sañcita karma*) is not present, just that which will be experienced in this life (*prārabdha*). This can be understood deeper when one contemplates the relationship between the time of birth, the position of the stars and the nature of an individual being. The past karma chosen for experience in this life is according to Niyati and is seen in the birth chart with special importance to the navāṁśa (D9) and ṣaṣṭyāṁśa (D60).

The aspect of time, arising from Niyati, is its ripening (*pācanam*) form, which has the nature of driving everything onwards (*kalanātmaka*). It makes everything happen at the right time, or at the proper season. It impels everything, according to Time, just as the bank of a river controls the stream. It takes the skill from one life, the bad karma from another and the debt to someone and then organizes all to unfold. Step by step according to Time the soul determines which karma it will experience and then manifests its body made of guṇas.[33]

---

29 Bṛhad-Araṇyaka Upaniṣad I.4.3

30 Ahirbudhnya Saṁhitā, VI.45-46

31 From one perspective the soul descends from the higher realms into Niyati according to the will of Sudarśana (*kriyā śakti*). From another perspective, the perceived individuality created by Saṅkarṣana is guided or limited by its karmas in Niyati. According to Advaita, time is just an illusion of the mind, and so this can be seen as the process of limitation by Māyā/Prakṛti. Suśruṭa-Saṁhitā, Śārīrasthāna I.11, calls niyati one of the six aspects of prakṛti known by those with wide vision.

32 Ahirbudhnya Saṁhitā, VI.48

33 Ahirbudhnya Saṁhitā, VI.49-53

In Nyāya philosophy, it is said that time (*kāla*) is not manifested by *adhvā* (space, distance) but by *kriyā* (action, work, doing). [34] Time impels action. Time creates space.[35] When the first separation of Puruṣa and Prakṛti happens this *is* transcendent Time. The movement requires time to exist, and the movement *is* its existence. Then the subtle unmanifest aspects of reality are acted upon or moved by subtle time, changed in subtle time. Those movements are the existence of subtle time. The manifestation of a gross universe happens through gross time. Jāgrat is born from svapna through gross time. Each state of consciousness is therefore created by the modification of time. In the dream realm (*svapna*), the mental impressions are moving forward according to subtle time (*niyati*), which unfolds the images one needs to digest and integrate at that moment. Huge amounts can happen in a small amount of time, and in irregular procession. These experiences being limited by dense time units, which control the length of experience and its 'logical' order, create the awake state (*jāgrat*).

Time is manifested by action and impels actions. As long as there is a "doer", one will exist in time. The second was originally defined as 1/86400th of the average time required for the earth to complete one rotation on its axis. But since this is not a stable length of time with the proper accuracy for high-precision scientific work, the atomic clock uses the time of a certain transition of the caesium atom. There is no connection to space in either calculation, both relate to change (movement) which is action.

Transcendent time brings forth the guṇas which turn everything and generate actions. This guides subtle time to manifest which guṇas your soul will experience in material manifestation from your karma. This guides which daśā systems will control gross time to manifest your experience of life. Time then has two functions: permission (*abhyanujña*), and prevention (*pratibandha*).[36] Something appears because time allows its cause to be effective, or a thing does not appear because time doesn't allow its cause to be effective.

What manifests in life is based upon our desires, which are seeds. Time brings the season for these desires to sprout and grow. Just as fire cooks (*pācana*) food to make it ready to eat, time is that which matures us. Lakṣmī Tantra says the various latent impressions (*vāsanā*) stored in the psyche (*antaḥkaraṇa*) torment embodied beings during a particular time.[37] Time takes us to our destiny in the same way an acorn will become a tree. Depending on the soil they are planted in, the acorns will be small shrubs or great trees. It

[34] Vātsyāyana, Nyāya Bhāṣya II.39, translated by Pannikkhar, Raimon "Kālaśakti: The Power of Time" in *Concepts of Time*, edited by Vatsyayan, Kapila. This concept can be compared with the Kantian concept of Time which puts the manifestation of time within space.

[35] Stephen Hawking, *The Grand Design*, p.133-134 "once we add the the effects of quantum theory to the theory of relativity, in extreme cases warpage can occur to such a great extent that time behaves like another dimension of space."

[36] Vākyapadīya III

[37] Lakṣmī Tantra 17.52

is our desires arising from past tendencies (*saṁskāra*) which give rise to our actions. Those actions become our tendencies which give rise to new desires. Turned onward by Time, the cycle of action, tendency and desire continues.

Certain flowers bloom in the spring and others in the summer. One time period you have a certain desired goal and the next it changes. Time influences what we want and when we want it. That wheel is turning on its eternal axis, constantly changing everything. The only constant is the axis which continues to turn, the wheel of Time with 360 spokes (degrees of the Sun). The Sun rises and sets every day. Only when the soul returns to the highest realm is one no longer tossed about by the waves of time (*kāla-kallola-saṅkulam*).[38]

The *Mahābhārata* says, "Time, exerting his irresistible strength, cooks all creatures, with the aid of his ladle constituted by months and seasons, the Sun for his fire, and days and nights for his fuel. The man possessed of true vision, beholding this world to be only the field of action, should do good acts."[39]

Time as the Destroyer

Time transforms us, ages us; it forces us onward with or without choice. Time makes us rise up in life, propels us forward and takes us to our death like Yama controlling us (he is personified as having a noose around your neck). Time (*kāla*) is the impeller (*kalana*), who makes everything happen; he makes us grow weak and forget all we know, cuts off the lifespan, and finally removes our consciousness.[40] Everything we have is about to be taken away. We will all loose everything and die.... in Time. Death is just an outfit of Time, which he puts on to not be underdressed for the occasion. Time is the great destroyer taking us to our death- who is our death. Death is when your *Time has come*, or when your *time has run out*.

Time is valuable, so valuable that we take it away as a punishment. The judicial system tries to rectify other's misdeeds by taking away an individual's time. Can karma be rectified by taking away personal time? Jail is bondage, where one has their time taken, they are *doing time*. Every moment we are alive is a moment of time that we have. And that time is limited, limited by time itself. Āyus is one's allotted lifespan; therefore it means 'health' or the 'duration of life'.

The wheel of the nakṣatras gives birth to the daśā system which activates the results of our individual as well as collective karmas. That wheel of time urges us onwards and guides our actions, like water in the banks of a stream. That wheel of time gives us the zodiac (*bha-chakra*), as well as the wheel of existence (*bhava-chakra*), also called saṁsāra.

[38] Ahirbhudhnya Saṁhitā, VI.29
[39] Mahābhārata, Śanti Parva CCCXXII
[40] Lakṣmī Tantra 17.51

Everything in the manifest world is mortal; bound to death (*mṛtyubandhu*), being moved by the wheel of Time.

The *Babaji Gorakhvani* says that time is like a grinding wheel, crushing everything. In a grinding wheel the grains closest to the center do not get crushed. Therefore Gorakhnath says one should chant the divine Name and be close to the center.[41] That center, which is the immortal turning axis. The Śvetāśvatara Upaniṣad says, the soul (*haṁsa*) circles around the wheel of creation (*brahma-cakra*) confused, thinking its inner spirit and the turner of the wheel are different. When it is inspired by *That*, it experiences its immortality (*amṛtatva*).

Sometimes we have great moments of inspiration and clarity and then the next day happens, and the next day, and then you remember that you *had* a great moment of clarity. The power of Time's movement (*kālagatā śaktī*) is Kālī who drives everything onward.[42] Kālī is the dark form of the Mother who represents the *power of Time*. She brings everything into existence, impels it forward, allows its own nature to manifest and then takes it back into herself. Nothing can ever stop; she is pushing it all forward. Even if you wanted that great moment to last, she *covers* it up.

Her husband is Śiva and in this regard he is known as *Mahākāla*, Great-Time. He stops for no one and crushes everyone. Young or beautiful, wise or rich, he doesn't care; he crushes everybody in his wheel of time (*kālacakra*). Śiva takes on various aspects to represent his destructive forces. In his fierce destructive (*ugra*) form he is called *Bhairava*[43] because he is terrifying (*bhīṣaṇa*). Bhairava is also called *Kālarāja* because he has the luster of the god of death.[44] Śiva in his fierce forms represents the destructive forces of time, his power (*Śaktī*) is represented as the dark mother, fierce, hungry, and violent; Time eating everything.

Śiva is white and Kālī is black, the white day and black night.[45] There is no night without day and no day without night.[46] The day is male and the night female (JB II.434). The day-night (*aho-ratra*) are the procreators (*sarvaṁ prajana*) of everything (JB II.287), they are the mother and the father (JB I.50). Their dance together is imperishable Time, the days and nights are endless and these two while rolling on obtain everything.[47]

---

41 Babaji Gorakhvani, and Praśna Upaniṣad 6.6

42 Ahirbudhnya Saṁhitā IV.48

43 The Bhairava form of Śiva, which represents the awake perception, is so destructive because it destroys all the illusions that bind us down into limited nature.

44 ŚivaPurāṇa Śatarudra Saṁhitā, Chapter 8

45 Ṛgveda VI.9.1 *ahaś ca kṛṣṇam ahar arjunaṁ ca*

46 Jaiminīya Brāhmaṇa I.207 *na vai rātryā ṛte'har na rātrir ṛte'hnaḥ*

47 Jaiminīya Brāhmaṇa III.357 *ete ha va aparyante yad ahorātre| ye te vā idaṁ parivartamāne sarvam āpnutaḥ||*

They toss, day and night,
like a pair of dice
and move men like pawns-
'Time' plays a frenzied game with Kālī,
his partner in destruction.[48]

The Sun and Moon play with each other in the heavens, and toss day and night like a pair of dice, as a game that almost makes one forget the ever-present death that Time is churning. Life and everything in it, is so fragile, that at any moment you can lose it. At the throw of the dice, it's over.

The Sun is symbolized time. The deity of the Sun is Śiva, as he is the burning heat that destroys the worlds. Time consumes (*pratapanti*) everything, like the radiance (*bhāsa*) of the Sun[49]. The Sun gives life *and* it destroys all things, beats upon them, takes away their color, ages them, and returns them to elements. This cruel form (*ugrarūpa*) of the Sun is Time. He shines, does penance, causes pain, cooks, and burns it all away (*pratap*).

In the Mahābhārata, it says Śiva, as Time slays all people.[50] His mouth is like *Kālāgni-Rudra* the form of Śiva as fire who destroys everything at the end of a kalpa (*pralaya*). Even the most powerful warriors or those who have the power to live hundreds of years are devoured by the mouth of Time. 'As herbs are pulverized into a powder, they are crushed (*cūrṇana*) in the teeth of Time.'[51]

In the Bhagavad Gītā, Arjuna received a divine eye (*divyacakṣu*) and was then able to see Kṛṣṇa's supreme form (*parama rūpa*).[52] He gets a vision of the lord of all (*viśveśvara*), whose form is the universe (*viśvarūpa*). Arjuna sees all he knows being devoured in the mouth of the all-pervasive One, and is told "I am Time, the great destruction of the world". In the vision of God's greatest all-encompassing form, he names himself as Time (*Kāla*).

One can begin the study of Time with the prayer that Arjuna spoke to Kṛṣṇa in his form of the Universe.[53] This prayer asked the Primeval One (*ādyaṁ*) to reveal both mental understanding (*vijñātum*) of Time and the intuitive understanding (*prajñā*) of how it works/moves all things forward (*pravṛttim*).

> Namo'stu te, most excellent of gods, have mercy and tell me about thy fierce form, Original One, I wish to understand thee, I do not comprehend your workings (XI.31).

---

48 Miller, Barbara Stoler, trans. *The Hermit and the Love-Thief: Sanskrit Poems of Bhartrihari and Bilhaṇa*. V.171.
49 Bhagavad Gītā XI.30
50 Sutton, *Religious Doctrines of Mahābhārata*, p.194
51 Bhagavad Gītā XI.25-27
52 Bhagavad Gītā XI.8-32
53 Bhagavad Gītā XI.31 *ākhyāhi me ko bhavānugrarūpo namo›stu te devavara prasīda* | *vijñātumicchāmi bhavantamādyaṁ nahi prajānāmi tava pravṛttim* ||

Units of Time

The science of time which has units is called kālajñāna or ahorātra vidyā[54], and in the west it is called horology. Most cultures have based their time cycles on years that are familiar to the human mind, with the thought of thousands of years being large. The Vedic units of time go from a truṭi (1/1,000,000 of a second) to periods of trillions of years. These units of time were called illogical by medieval Indian Astronomers, but are now very fitting in modern physics. These time units (large and small) have been transmitted (blindly repeated) down through the millennia and directly relate to a civilization (or consciousness) more advanced than our own.

Varāhamihira said a competent astrologer should know how to calculate the starting and ending times of a yuga, year, seasons, month, fortnight, day, night, yāma, muhūrta, nāḍīka, prāṇa, and a truṭi.[55] They should be able to calculate planetary motions, retrogrades, speeds, the calendar, solstices, eclipses, and the length of the day. One should be able to calculate longitude and latitude for a place from Ujjain and be able to find the nakṣatras and constellations in the sky. And an astrologer should be able to teach this to a learned person.

With modern computers, to learn all the mathematical calculations might be in excess of the average person's interest, but one should still understand the principles behind these elements. The third eye (Jupiter) is a balance between the logical (Sun) and intuitive (Moon) aspects of the mind, and these elements help our own practice and understanding of the techniques we utilize.

You may not logically understand how a few mathematical rules and calculations will change how you read a chart. But astrological charts are just a way of Time being perceived. The numbers, math and divisions are a way of opening your mind to Time, changing the way your mind works, the way your mind perceives, the awareness you have of a moment and your interaction with reality. Regular time, doing mathematical calculations and observations of the stars is extremely beneficial for opening you to astral energies that are beyond logical comprehension,[56] and this will benefit how you read a chart.

---

54 *Kālajñāna* in the Vedāṅga Jyotiṣam I.2, *Ahorātravidyā* in the Bhagavad Gītā VIII.17

55 The Sūrya Siddhānta (I.10-11) says there are gross (*sthūla*) and subtle (*sūkṣma*) divisions of time. That which begins with prāṇas are with form (*mūrta*) and that which begins with truṭi do not have form (*amūrta*). The truṭi is about 1/1,000,000 of a second.

56 A negative example of this is the physical state happening to Stephen Hawking, the man who has understanding (*prajña*) of black holes. The effect of his disease on the mind-body connection (or disembodiment) is directly related to the relation of black holes to the disembodiment of matter in the universe.

Units

The level of timelessness, or all-present-now, is a spiritual state of experiential reality. It is a state to be achieved, to enter in spiritual moments. It is eternal, transcendental, and dimensionless, which is the focus of spiritual practice. Here we focus on temporal time which is imminent and has quantitative and qualitative dimensions of chronology.

Parāśara's Units of Time	
15 Nimeṣas	= 1 Kāṣṭhā-kalā
30 Kāṣṭhā-kalā	=1 Muhūrta
30 Muhūrtas	= 1 Ahorātra
30 Ahorātra	=1 Māsa
6 Māsa	=1 Ayana
2 Ayana	= 1 Year

Parāśara says to Maitreya, "I have already declared to you that Time is a form of Viṣṇu, hear now how it is applied to measure the duration of Brahmā, and of all other living beings, as well as the inanimate creation like the mountains, oceans, and the like".[57]

The base time unit is equivalent to 4 seconds. It is called either a prāṇa which is a breath, or a nimeṣa which is the time between blinking the eye. Another school also uses the paramāṇu (a moment).[58]

Six prāṇa create a vighaṭikā composed of 24 seconds.[59] There are 60 vighaṭikās in a ghaṭikā (that is 1440 seconds[60]), and 60 ghaṭīkās in a day (like 60 minutes in an hour).

24 seconds	**24 minutes**
Vighaṭ*ikā*	Ghaṭīkā
Vikalā	Daṇḍa
Vināḍī	Nāḍī*kā*
Vināḍī*ka*	Naligais
Pala[1]	Ghari
Lita	Daṇḍa

In India there is always more than one way to name the month. In the same way, there are a few different systems of dividing the basic increments of time found in different traditions as well as different names for the same units in different regions of India. Below is a chart of vighaṭikās and ghaṭīkās and all the various terminology they are given.

A ghaṭa is a large earthen water-jar that has a hole in the bottom. When filled with water it takes exactly 24 minutes to leak out, similar to an hour glass with sand. Calculations allowed the timekeepers to determine how long the day/night difference was, based on how much water was left at the end of the day.

---

57 Viṣṇu Purāṇa, Chapter III.6-7

58 For a discussion of the variation in the Purāṇas see the notes on III.22 of the Viṣṇu Purāṇa translated by Wilson.

59 Between a prāṇa and muhūrta different traditions (as seen in groups of Purāṇas) have their own systems of dividing time. We will utilize the Sūrya Siddhānta instead of the Purāṇas. The order given by Parāśara in Viṣṇu Purāṇa is listed on the table on the previous page as a sample of the variation, but will not be utilized as it is a non-standard system.

60 The 24 hour day has 1440 minutes.

Ghaṭīkās, Vighaṭikās and Muhūrta

Traditionally in India, time was recorded as ghaṭīkās and vighaṭis past sunrise. In the present time, I often see Indian charts where I need to calculate this into hours and minutes to create a natal chart. This system is becoming rarer, and one may never see a chart of this nature, but one should be able to convert these times in case such a situation arises, or in case one finds such dating records while doing research.

Some of the ancient units of time are more for philosophy than general usage.[61] A few ancient units of time we need to have good understanding of are the vighaṭikā, ghaṭikā and muhūrta. Two ghaṭīkās compose a muhūrta. The ghaṭikā relates to the amount of change between the *ahas* (12 hours of daylight) and the *tidal constituent*; which is presently about 12 hours 25 minutes. A Muhūrta relates therefore to the tidal change over an entire day. The motion is longer than the earth day because the Moon orbits in the same direction the Earth spins, and this changes the tides by about 24 minutes semi-diurnally and 48 minutes diurnally. The day is divided into 15 muhūrtas[62] in the day and 15 at night making 30 in the ahorātra similar to 30 degrees in a sign, or 30 days in a month.

Muhūrtas are the basic unit of time to choose auspicious events within. Śāstras list the qualities of the daily muhūrtas and the daily ghaṭīkās. There is a Vedic ritual which uses 10,800 bricks relating to 10,800 muhūrtas in a year (used in the five year yuga system). In qualities, the muhūrtas relate to Jupiter like the months, and the ghaṭīkās relate to Venus like the pakṣas.

In older or more traditional Indian charts the time will be given in ghaṭīkās and vighaṭikās. This will need to be translated into hours and minutes. One ghaṭīkā is 24 minutes and one vighaṭikā is 24 seconds. The time is changed to hours and minutes and then added to the time of Sunrise for the location the person was born.

Exercises:

1. Change 38 ghaṭīkās and 13 vighaṭikās on January 21st to hours and minutes for Boston, Massachusetts and then for Mexico City.

2. Change your own birth time into ghaṭīkās and vighaṭikās.

[61] A quick look at Vedic atomic units of time: a nimeṣa is composed of 3 lava, which is composed of 3 vedhas (prativipalas), which is composed of 100 truṭi (4.44 miliseconds). A truṭi is the time needed to integrate 3 trasareṇus which is the combination of 6 celestial atoms.

[62] Viṣṇu Purāṇa, II.8.55-63

Ahorātra

Units of Time		
Prāṇa	Respiration (same as a nimeṣa)	4 seconds
Vighaṭi*ka*	6 prāṇa	24 seconds
Ghaṭī*ka*	60 vighaṭikā or 360 prāṇa	24 minutes
Muhūrta	2 ghaṭīkā or 720 prāṇa	48 minutes
Horā	1/24th of the day or 900 prāṇa	60 minutes or 1 hour
Ahas	30 ghaṭīkā or 60 muhūrta or 10,800 prāṇa[2]	12 hour day-light
Ahorātra	60 vighaṭikā or 30 muhūrta or 21,600 prāṇa[3]	1 day or 24 hours

The day (*vāra*) is divided into two sections; day (*ahas*) and night (*rātri*). In this way, the twenty-four hour day is referred to as *ahorātra*.

Horā comes from the word *Aho-rātra* which means day-night (of 24 hours). The last syllable of the first word and the first syllable of the second word become Horā. Horā means an hour (60 minutes) because it is about one horā (15°) of the Sun's movement that creates an hour. Jyotiṣa is also called horā śāstra- the science of day-night (*horā*). It is the movement of the Sun (perceived from Earth) that gives us the day and night cycle.[63] The movement of the Sun allows us to perceive the movement of time via the day-night cycle as the in and out breath of a human is moved by time.

Rātri means night, it can be taken as ***ra*** (light) and ***tri*** (protection). The night is the protection of the light. The night balances the day's heat, as the male and female energies balance each other, like hot-cold, or hard-soft. The day-night is a representation of the two opposites that creates the universe- from the level of Puruṣa-Prakṛti to the negative-positive wire in an electric circuit. The day-night (*horā*) is similar to the Taoist yin-yang symbology.

Day-night represents the Sun and the Moon- our left and right eyes. It is a dual concept- not a trinity as the three guṇas. Though the day can be seen as rajas and the night as tamas- there is no sattva outside. The sattva is the balancing of the right solar channel (*Piṅgalā*) and the left lunar channel (*Iḍā*) and moving into the central channel inside the body. As the yin-yang symbol is composed of black and white and has the two in perfect balance representing sattva.

Day-night is time passing, and all things arise and pass through time. The day and night create whatever has happened and whatever is going to happen.[64] Time creates the universe by imbalance of guṇas. Horā is the science of the Kāla Puruṣa- the body of time and its effect on life. In order for a battery to work there must be more positive charge than negative- when the two are in balance- energy does not move between the two poles and the battery has no energy. Imbalance creates movement. Great Time imbalances the

[63] Atharvaveda XIII.2.3 calls the Sun to be the creator of the days and nights

[64] Jaiminīya Brāhmaṇa I.207, day and night create whatever has happened and whatever is going to happen.

energy between Puruṣa and Prakṛti which causes creation and the manifestation of the universe. Time is shifting that balance constantly with the Moon entering different phases relative to its angle from the Sun, creating the whole pañcāṅga.

Aṅgular units

Aṅgular Terminology		
1 sign	1 rāśi	
30 degrees	30 bhāga	30°
60 arc minutes	60 kalā	60′
60 arc seconds	60 vikalā	60″

Angular units are the measurements of the arc of a circle or in our case the arc across the ecliptic. The numerical significance of angular measures is the same in Western and Vedic astronomy. There are a few different naming systems, but the most common is that degrees are called *bhāgas* (or *aṁśas*), minutes of arc are called *kalā* and seconds of arc are called *vikalā*. There are 30 degrees in a sign (*rāśi*), 60 arc minutes in a degree and 60 arc seconds in an arc minute.

Equivalents of Arc and Time	
360°	24 hours
15°	1 hour
1°	4 minutes
0° 15′	1 minute
0° 01′	4 seconds
0° 0′ 15″	1 second

There are 360 degrees in a 24 hour day. That makes 30 degrees (or a rāśi) in two hours and 15 degrees in an hour. An hour ***is*** 15 degrees of arc by its very definition. There are 4 minutes of time in one degree, and 15 seconds of arc in one minute of time. In one kalā (a minute of arc) there are 4 seconds. This is the same unit as a *nimeṣa* or a *prāṇa*, giving a base unit that is the same between the sidereal time and angular time. The human breath (a *prāṇa* of 4 seconds) creates the *vikalā* and 6 breaths creates the *vighaṭikā*. There are 60 breaths in one degree.

The *angula*r units are integrated into the human being in more than one way. A 360 degree circle not only has the benefit of many integers for mathematical calculations, but it also has an easy observational benefit. When the index finger (*aṅgulī*) is held to the sky at arm's length its end tip is approximately a degree. This will be the same for any age or size as the finger should be proportional to the length of the arm. One eye will need to be closed as you look at your *aṇgula* (finger distance[65]) against the sky. When this is held up to the full Moon, one will notice that the Moon is covered by half of your finger, giving it the proportion of half a degree.

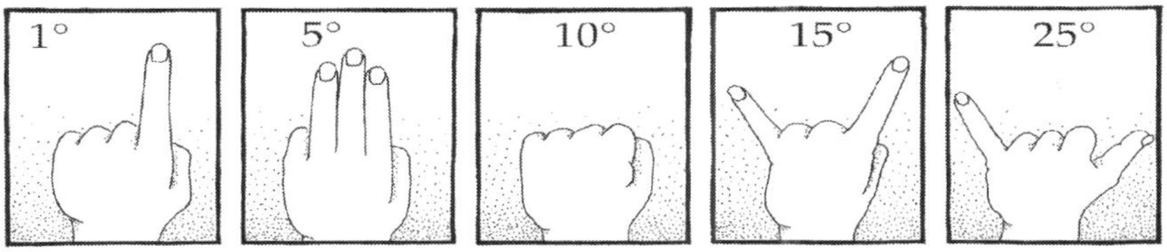

[65] The thumb can be referred to as *aṇgula* (masculine) and the fingers are *aṅgulī* (feminine). The thumb is considered the husband and the four fingers are his wives. The thumb is also called *aṅguṣṭha* or that which gives the fingers grounding, or a place to be situated within like a husband to his wives. The thumb is what allows the fingers to pick things up and manipulate them like humans can do. The unit of space created by the finger is called an *aṅgula*. This creates an angular measure and is the source for the Latin word angulus (English- angle).

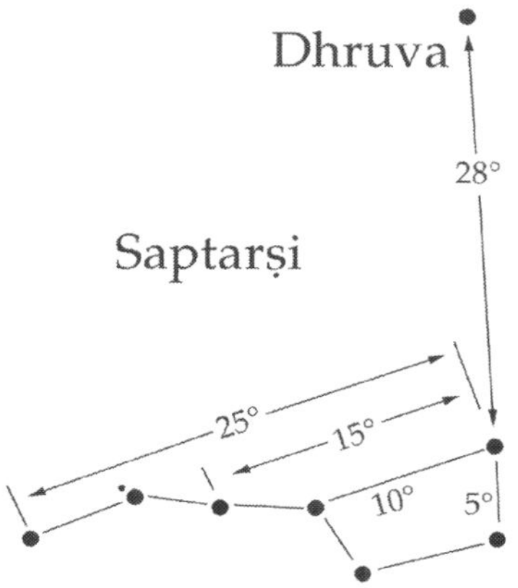

This method is approximate but good enough for the average star-gazer. The knuckles of the fist are about 10 degrees across, and the hand span from the open thumb to the small finger is about 25 degrees. The little dipper is about 25 degrees wide. The ecliptic can easily be divided into drekkaṇas (10°), or the position of the Moon noted at sunset with this simple method of observational astronomy.

Ṛkṣa-vibhāvana means the watching of the stars, or star gazing.[66] The Big Dipper (*saptarṣi maṇḍala*) is composed of seven (*sapta*) Vedic sages (*ṛṣi*). There are seven different groups of seven sages. The present seven are Marīci, Vasiṣṭha (who sits with his wife Arundhatī), Aṅgiras, Atri, Pulastya, Pulaha, and Kratu. The Big Dipper has a bowl about 10 degrees3 wide, and the entire ladle is 25 degrees. From Kratu to Dhruva[67] is about 28 degrees.

Star	Ṛṣi[4]	Ṛṣi's Wife (Śaktī)
Dubhe	Kratu	Kriyā (action, work)
Merak	Pulaha	Gati (going, path)
Phacda	Pulastya	Havirbhū (place of sacrafice)
Megrez	Atri	Anasūya (no envy)
Alioth	Aṅgiras	Śraddhā (faith)
Mizar	Vasiṣṭha	Arundhatī (metaphor)
Alkaid	Marīci	Kalā (fine art, ingenuity)

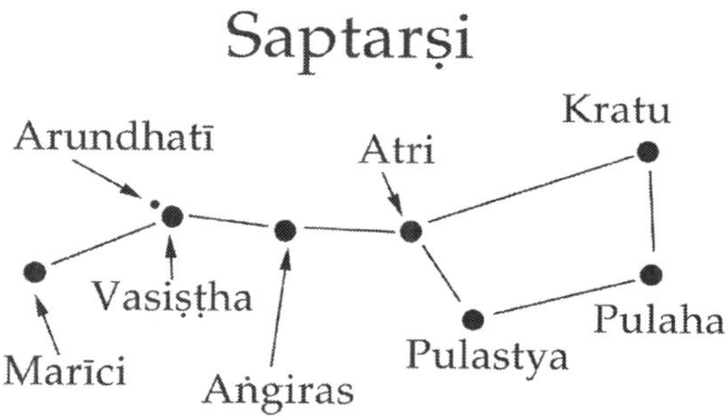

The Big Dipper/Great Bear is called the *Saptarṣi* (*Ṛkṣas*) or the Ṛkṣa[68] (the bear). Both of the English names correlate in Sanskrit; the term Big Dipper relates to the ladle of the seven ṛṣi as they pour ghee in their fire sacrafice. Ṛkṣa means bear but takes a dual meaning- since the constellation of the Bear is a central feature of the sky, it also means a constellation or nakṣatra. It is like calling all products after the name brand in the modern day world. Ṛkṣapati can literally mean lord of the bears or the lord of a nakṣatra.

---

[66] Strict astronomical observation was called *vedha*, which can mean "hitting on the mark". There were individual's whose full time job was observation and calculation of exact stellar degrees so that Vedic rituals could be done at the proper time.

[67] Dhruva is the pole star who discusses sādhana with the Saptarṣis in Viṣṇu Purāṇa I.11.55. He worships Viṣṇu in the form of hiraṇyagarbha-puruṣa-pradhāna-avyakta with *Auṁ namo vāsudevāya shuddha-jñāna-svarūpine*.

[68] Ṛkṣa is not the same root as *ṛk* (verse) of the Ṛgveda which comes from the sandhi of *ṛc*. But they both share the same *ṛ* dhātu. *Ṛkṣa* is masculine for bear (or sign), *Ṛkṣam* is neuter for constellation and *Ṛkṣas* is plural for sages (*ṛṣi*). The Greek word for bear is *arktos*, the Latin is *Ursus*, the Avestan is *aresho*; all have a similar root. See also Witzel, Michael, *The Pleiades and the Bears viewed from Inside the Vedic Texts*. IV. The Seven Ṛṣi and Thompson, *The Cosmology of the Bhāgavata Purāṇa*, p. 80.

Śiśumāra the Celestial Dolphin[69]

The pole star (*Dhruva*) never sets, rises or moves, because it is directly in line with the celestial pole on which the Earth spins. The constellations in this area are called circumpolar as they revolve around the pole star but do not rise or set. The Saptarṣi and the celestial Dolphin (*Śiśumāra*) are circumpolar, always present in the night sky. The Śiśumāra is considered an incarnation of Time and was born as the son of the Śarvarī (the star-spangled sky) and Doṣa (the darkness of night).[70]

The Śiśumāra constellation is presently known as Draco.[71] In Egypt this constellation was associated with a goddess who was symbolized by the hieroglyph for the Hippopotamus. In Babylonia it was associated with the half of Tiamat that made heaven. In India it is associated with Viṣṇu in the form of a Dolphin. It is said that the view of it at night frees one from whatever sin has been committed during the day.

Draco (*Śiśumāra*) is a constellation that winds around the little dipper and is composed of 14 stars. Śāstra says that Dharma is the head, Brahmā is the upper jaw, yajña the lower jaw, Viṣṇu is the heart, saṁvatsara the genitals, the Āśvins the front legs, Mitra and Varuṇa the hind legs, Agni is the first stem of the tail, then Indra, Prajāpati and Dhurva. When you watch this constellation over time it is like a dolphin swimming, and it was used by ancient sailors as a guide in the sea.

All the Vedic sages and gods are also stars in the sky. In Greek mythology there is a story of how someone became placed in the stars, but in Vedic mythology their manifestation on Earth is a reflection of their existence in the heavens.

Study of the stars will bring into perspective other systems of time caused by the universe we live in. For example, during the Vedic period, the star Thuban was the polestar (4800 years ago), now it is Polaris. The *Vedāṅga Jyotiṣam* stresses the observation of the sky.[72] It is particularly concerned with the calendar not becoming misaligned because people read tables of planetary motion and ignore the sky. Studying the sky brings all kinds of other knowledge and alignment.

Kāla-Pratijñā

A good astrologer should at some point take a vow (*pratijñā*) to give up (for one year or other fixed period) the daily news, TV, and the newspaper which only keep one farther away from focusing on your true nature. One should take that same rajas time and use it to focus on natural time; calculate the tithis, full moons, and movement of the stars.

[69] Viṣṇu Purāṇa. II.8.93-100, II.9.1, II.9.24-25
[70] Bhagavata Purāṇa 6.6.14
[71] Some have associated the Dolphin with Makara but then it would not be circumpolar as indicated.
[72] VedāṅgaJyotiṣam, v.41

Watch each planet and pay attention when it changes signs to see their placement in the stars. Use aṅgulas to find the beginning and ending of signs at the moment the Moon is changing. Study the ocean's movement and the placement of the Moon in the sky. Pay attention to the rising sign, when it changes, and how this relates to the Sun's position and the time of Sunrise.

Calculate the hours and their lords during the day and notice differences externally when they change: subjects discussed, people visiting, project focus, etc. And also be aware of internal changes of breath, sensitivity, volatility, emotions, etc., according to the hours, ascendants, days, and planetary movements. Give up the rajas phenomena in your life and make time to become aware of natural time and its effect on the internal and external environment. Study and integrate all these facets of time into your awareness so they become tools of perception.

An astrologer should practice a few simple visualizations on the space-time indicators around us. Visualize the size of the planets and the solar system, and the galaxy. Visualize the motions of these bodies. Be aware of the spaciousness between everything and mediate upon that.

Yāmas, Kalās, Etc.

Yāmas are a period of 3 hours or an 8th of the day. It is taken as 4 quarters of the day and four quarters of the night. They are similar to the English unit of time called a 'watch'. They are also called *praharas,* which comes from the root 'to beat'. It relates to the fact that in many places a gong or bell would be struck at the change of every 3 hours to mark the day and night similar to church bells ringing on the hour. When a baby was born in the night, a person could calculate that they were born just past the third watch of the night which would mean between midnight and 3 AM. The praharin was the 'watchman' who would announce the hours by ringing the bell.

These times are used in praśna, for spiritual practice and for timing remedial measures (as they relate to the Sun being in the eight directions of the bhāvas). In the science of dream interpretation (*svapna śāstra*), the praśna chart made to interpret a dream is generally done for dreams in the last prahara. Dreams in the first prahara are generally considered the rehashing of daily activities, the second prahara is subconscious issues of the individual and the third prahara has the possibility of prophetic meaning.

The chart below breaks time down into various increments. The ayana can be seen as 3 seasons (or 2 depending on location) or 6 months, as well as 12 pakṣas, 180 days or half of a year. Time is meant to be perceived in this way, in various increments that can mutually relate. An individual has two hands or a hand has five digits or a hand has 14 joints (5 independently moving and 9 dependent). In this way, the *Vedāṅga Jyotiṣam* says that the Creator is the Saṁvatsara whose body has limbs composed of the day, season, ayana, and month.[73]

Kalā	Eighths of the day and Eighths of the night	1.5 hours
Yāma	Quarters of the day and Quarters of the day	3 hours or 45 degrees of arc
Diva-ṛtu	Third of day and Third of night	4 hours or 60 degrees of arc
Ahorātra	8 Yāma or 16 kalā or 30 muhūrta or 60 vighaṭikā	1 tropical day (about 24 hours)
Pakṣa	½ month (ardhamāsa)	About 15 days
Māsa	2 pakṣas (lunar) or 30 degrees of Sun (Solar)	About 30 days
Ṛtu	2 solar māsa, 4.5 nakṣatra	1/6 of the year
Ayana	3 ṛtu, 6 māsa, 12 pakṣas	180 solar days, ½ year, 4320 hours
Varṣa	2 ayana, or 6 ṛtu, 12 māsa, or 24 pakṣa 10,800 mūhurta	360 (365) days, 8640 hours

The term *kalā* has a few different connotations depending on context, and a few different equations depending on tradition.[74] In general, kalā means a sixteenth part, and here refers to the day divided into 16 parts of 1½ hours each. The day has eight parts and the night has eight parts each lorded by all the planets (except for Ketu). The rulership of these kalās is according to the planets ruling the directions of the Kālachakra.

The aṣṭapadma-kālachakra is an 8 petaled lotus diagram. Each padma is connected to a graha in an order specific to the kālachakra. The first kalā (1½ hours) of the day will be ruled by the lord of the day. The second kalā will be ruled by the planet second to it in the kālachakra in a clockwise direction.

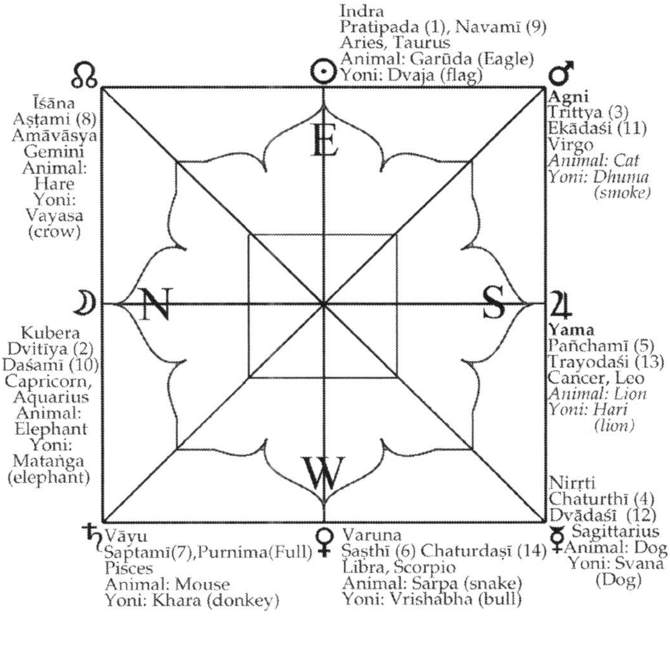

For example, on Saturday, the first kalā will be Śanikalā, the second Candrakalā, the third will be Rāhukalā. If Śanikalā runs from 6 AM till

[73] Vedāṅga Jyotiṣam I.1

[74] Kalā is also a minute of arc in angular time, a pakṣa divided into 16 parts instead of 15 (16 digits of the Moon), 1/900 of a day (1.6 minutes or 24 prāṇas), or 1/1800 of a day (.8 minutes or 48 seconds), depending on tradition and context. Kalā literally can mean a digit or unit, and it is these digits which makes up kāla.

7:30, Candrakalā will run from 7:30 till 9AM, which places Rāhukalā between 9AM and 10:30 on Saturday. Many Indian Pañcāṅgas just list the times of *Rāhukalā* for each day of the week since this is considered the most inauspicious kalā of the day. It is not beneficial to do any good works, but the best time to do pūjā or other remedial measures. The chart below is for quick reference and to insure you are calculating correctly, but it is easiest to simply remember the planets lording the kālachakra.

	Sunday	Monday	Tuesday	Wed	Thursday	Friday	Saturday
6:00-7:30	Sun	Moon	Mars	Mercury	Jupiter	Venus	Saturn
7:30-9:00	Mars	Rāhu	Jupiter	Venus	Mercury	Saturn	Moon
9:00-10:30	Jupiter	Sun	Mercury	Saturn	Venus	Moon	Rāhu
10:30-12:00	Mercury	Mars	Venus	Moon	Saturn	Rāhu	Sun
12:00- 1:30	Venus	Jupiter	Saturn	Rāhu	Moon	Sun	Mars
1.30- 3:00	Saturn	Mercury	Moon	Sun	Rāhu	Mars	Jupiter
3:00-4:30	Moon	Venus	Rāhu	Mars	Sun	Jupiter	Mercury
4:30- 6:00	Rāhu	Saturn	Sun	Jupiter	Mars	Mercury	Venus

The Sun had two children that are connected to time. The eldest is Yama Dharmarāja, who was born from his wife Sūnya. As Yama upholds Dharma his time is calculated from Sunrise. The other son was Kāla born from Chhāyā, the shadow of his wife. Kāla was not interested in following his father and so does not depend on Sunrise. A kalā starts at 6 AM no matter when the Sun rises.[75]

The kalās of the night are also ruled in the same way except starting at the fifth planet in the kālachakra from the day lord. On Saturday, the first 1½ hours after 6 PM will be Maṅgalakalā, the next will be Gurukalā. In this way, the evening starts opposite the day lord on the kālachakra as if it was the setting of the day. On Monday, the last 1½ hours of the day (4:30-6) is Śanikalā, at 6 PM will become Gurukalā.

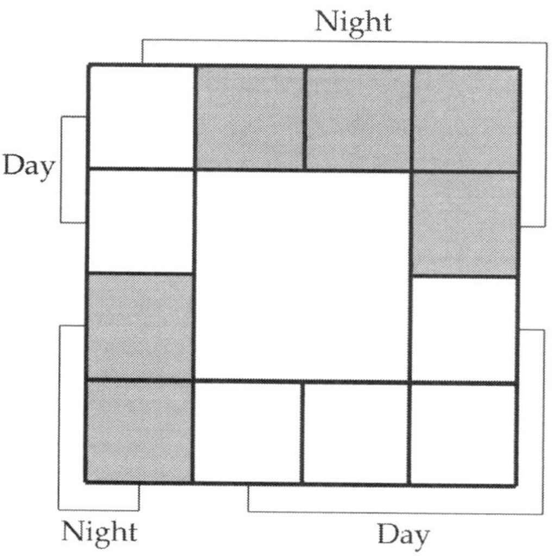

The best time to do a weekly pūjā to a planet is on the day of the sign lord, at the kalā of the planet. So if one has Moon in Aries, the best time for that individual's weekly Candra

[75] There are also kāla-horās and yama-horās. A kāla-horā starts at 6 AM no matter what, it is like the clock that has numbers irrelative to the cycle of the Sun. This is important for civil purposes to insure that everyone is using the same hour. The yama-horā starts at sunrise, and has 12 hours in the day and 12 at night. Its size is lengthened or shortened depending on the length of the day. The yama-horā is often utilized in praveśa charts.

remedy is on Tuesday at Candrakalā (1:30-3:00). If Jupiter is in Capricorn then weekly Guru upāya can be done on Saturday from 1:30 to 3:00.

This timing can also involve the evening (though need not) if the day and night signs are taken into account. If the Sun is in the Mercury's night sign, Gemini, then the upāya can be done Wednesday night at 7:30 to 9PM. If the Sun was in Virgo, Mercury's day sign, then it would be better to do a pūjā on Wednesday afternoon during 1:30 to 3 PM. This can be followed in many cases except when the time is late in the night. For example, if Venus was in Gemini, it would have its best time on Wednesday night during 1:30 to 3AM. As one would be unlikely to employ a priest (*pujārī*) at this time or do other upāyas like feeding the poor etc. then it would be better to use the day timing as next best. This timing is used for weekly pūjās to remove the negative effects of planets.

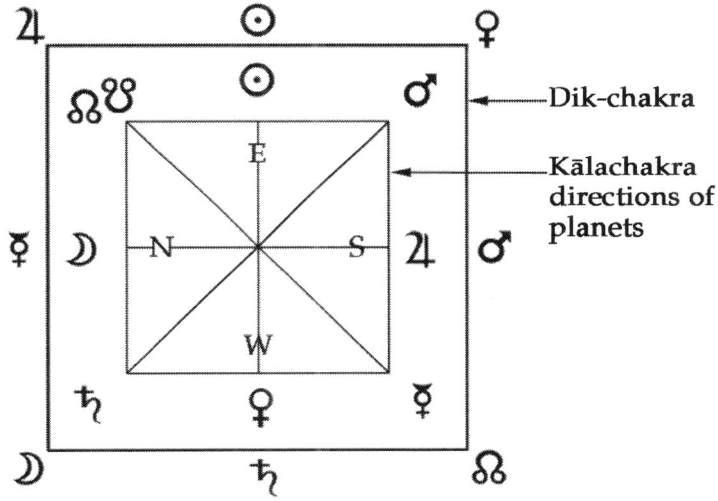

Each padma of the kālachakra is connected to a direction which is ruled by a graha (without Ketu). The corresponding direction lords (*digīśa*) are different in the kālachakra than the dik-cakra. You can see how they overlap in the diagram. Kālachakra is a destructive energy and it will destroy the negativities of the planet. If an individual is in Venus daśā and is moving, it is very beneficial to move to the South-eastern direction according to the lord of the direction (*digīśa*). If one moved to the western direction (the kālacakra direction of Venus) they would have great troubles. In the daśā of a well placed planet, a person will naturally move in the right direction, or get a job in a beneficial direction. When the daśā lord is negatively placed then the individual will naturally go in the wrong direction. Therefore one should be aware that the direction of the kālachakra is for destructive (*nidhana*) purposes, or it will cause suffering. In the case of remedial measures, we are trying to remove the defect of a planet, which relates to the defect of that frequency within us. It is therefore efficient to perform a remedy at this time.

Why leave your house for worship if the temple is closed? The Kālachakra is turning and She is dancing. The kalā is a doorway in which a specific energy can be accessed. When the doorway is open specific change can actually happen. Find the specific Rāhukalā for your chart and use that time to remove your delusions. An astrologer must have clarity or all this is just entertainment.

Vedic Calendrical Systems

The basic astronomical cycles are the **day** (based on the rotation of the Earth on its axis), the **month** (based on the revolution of the Moon around the Earth), and the **year** (based on the movement of the Earth around the Sun). It would seem easy to calculate a calendar but the complexity arises because the year is not made of an integral number of days or an integral number of months. Different cultures have had very different calendars and ways of rectifying this. Even in India, throughout the millenniums there have been various systems utilized.

Day	dina, vāra, ahorātra
Month	māsa
Year	varṣa, abda saṁvatsara

To understand the basics of the Vedic calendar we must understand the calculation of lunar months and solar years, which have within them solar months and lunar years. The solar months are considered the *hinges* which the *doors* of the lunar months move upon. What is a door without hinges or hinges without a door? They work together to create a solar-luni calendar which integrates the Sun and Moon, male and female, Śiva and Śakti.

Synodic Month (Lunation)

The Sun gains 1 degree a day, while the Moon gains 13 degrees a day, they are both moving. The quickly moving Moon is chasing the slow and steady moving Sun. The Synodic month is the period in which the Moon gains one complete revolution over the apparent or visible motion of the Sun. It is when the Moon gains 360 degrees over the Sun (not just moves 360 degrees in the zodiac). The moment of New Moon (*amāvāsyā*) is the moment when the Sun and Moon have the same longitude.

The time from one New Moon to the next New Moon is approximately 29.5 days, according to *Sūrya Siddhānta* it is 29.530587946 days. Modern calculation is 29.530588853 which is the same for the first six decimal places, though it is getting longer by a little less than a fiftieth of a second per century. The ancient Vedic astronomers calculated the length of the lunation to nine decimal places to insure precision of calculations over thousands of years. The modern and Vedic difference would amount to a variation of about 1 hour and 11 minutes in 5,000 years.

The *mean* New Moon occurs every 29.530587946 days (29 days, 12 hours, 44 minutes, 3 seconds) but the *actual* New Moon does not recur at exactly this interval. The mean motion is the average motion which is a constant, while the actual or true motion is what is actually happening and has fluctuations. The Moon may be fast or slow according to its elliptical motion at the time of becoming new and this *anomaly* needs to be taken into consideration.[76]

[76] This irregularity (or anomaly) is called *eccentricity* of orbit and the correction to be applied to it is called

The anomaly is based upon the anomalistic month of 27.5546 days (according to the *Sūrya Siddhānta*) where the Moon will repeat its pace according to its position. The siddhāntas gives charts of the Moon's anomaly for precise calculation of the exact moment of new moon. In 1600 A.D. the Vedic Astronomer Gaṇeśa Daivajña added a correction raising the annual increase of the Moon's anomaly 2 seconds and decreasing the length of the anomalistic month from 27.5546 to 27. 55459797. The precision is needed to calculate the new Moon which also needs to take into account the anomaly of the Sun's pace (the earth's elliptical motion around the Sun).

The moment of amāvāsyā marks the beginning of the lunar month and the end of the previous month, this calculation is called *amānta* months (which is used in most places in India today). There is an ancient system called *Pūrṇimānta* months which calculates the months from full moon to full moon, which is no longer in use in most of India.

Solar Year:

The solar year is based upon the Sun's 365 day motion through the zodiac as perceived from earth. There are two types of solar years; the tropical year and the sidereal year. It is their difference which creates the *ayanāṁśa*.

The tropical year is the period of time from one vernal equinox to the next which according to modern calculations is 365.2422408 days, though the tropical year is getting shorter by a half second every century.[77] The utility of the tropical solar year is for starting the seasons at the same time every year. The Gregorian calendar is presently based upon the Sun's motion only and therefore utilizes the tropical year.

The sidereal year is the period of time wherein the Sun passes through all twelve signs of the zodiac and returns to 0 degrees Aries (*meṣa saṅkrānti*). The length of the solar year according to the *Sūrya Siddhānta* is 365.258756484 days; modern data lists it as 365.256363051 days. The anomalistic solar year takes into account the difference of speed of the Sun at different times of the year when the Sun is farthest and nearest to the earth. This varying pace is needed for calculation of the exact point of new moon and the precise time of sunrise. The Vedic calendar utilizes the sidereal solar year (with the correction for the Sun's anomaly) as it is based upon the location of the luminaries during the new Moon and at Sunrise.

the *equation of the center*. The mean and actual positions are the same at 0° (perigee) and at 360° (apogee).

[77] The synodic month, the tropical year, even the second which creates a minute/hour/day are gradual changing length over long periods of time. Modern science wants to lock us into one fixed length which they need for science, but we should be aware of the subtle variation over time and continue to utilize the natural time and its divisions.

Interaction of Solar and Lunar Months

A *solar month* is based upon the motion of the Sun through each of its signs, and is related to the energy of the Sun.[78] As the sidereal solar year begins with Meṣa saṅkrānti, this is also the first solar month. The second month begins with 0 degrees of Taurus (*vṛṣabha saṅkrānti*). As the Sun's motion varies, a solar month will have either 29, 30 or 31 days.

Saṅkrānti is the time while the Sun is within its zero degree, and the solar month starts the moment it enters. Even though this is clear, the actual day the month begins has different variations in different parts of the country. The moment of saṅkrānti is the same all over India but the corresponding month for *civil* purposes is not the same all over India. For example, some use the day that the Sun is in its 0 degree at sunrise, while others will use the day if the Sun enters 0 degrees before Sunset. Other parts will take the day even if it changes signs in the night time. There are a few other rules in different parts of the country which can often change which day is considered the first day of the solar month. In this way, there is a large amount of variation within different regions of India, which creates a hard time calling something standard and actually being proper. So we can generalize that the saṅkrānti is the first day of the solar month, though we must understand that detailed calculations will have variations according to tradition. These variations are also found in the naming of the solar months.

The solar months are considered the *hinges* and the lunar months are the *doors* of the Vedic calendar. The lunar month which began with a New Moon has its name determined by that New Moon occurring before a particular saṅkrānti. Vedic and Hindu rituals, festivals and vratas are determined according to the lunar month (the door) but that door is determined based upon the solar month (the hinge which opens the door).

In the table below you will notice that the month of Caitra (lunar New Year) begins at the New Moon *before* Meṣa Saṅkrānti (in the previous solar year), while the next month (Vaiśākha) begins in the New Moon before Vṛṣabha sankrānti.

	Lunar Month	**Saṅkrānti**	**Approximation**
1	Caitra	Meṣa	March-April
2	Vaiśākha	Vṛiṣabha	April-May
3	Jyeṣṭha	Mithuna	May-June
4	Āśāḍha	Karka	June-July
5	Śrāvaṇa	Siṁha	July-August
6	Bhādrapada	Kanyā	August-September
7	Āśvina	Tulā	September-Oct
8	Kārttika	Vṛścika	October- Nov
9	Mārgaśirṣa	Dhanus	November- Dec
10	Pauṣa	Makara	December- January
11	Māgha	Kumbha	January- February
12	Phalguna	Mīna	February-March

[78] Jaiminīya Brāhmaṇa II.77

It is therefore the solar year beginning with Aries which determines the entire lunar year. There is western belief that rāśis were imported to India, yet ancient calendar texts such as the *Vedāṅga Jyotiṣam* utilize saṅkrāntis and the mutual relation of solar and lunar months,[79] which require a 30 degree solar sign. It is also the solar year which determines the intercalary months which allows the lunar years to have consistency. In general new moons and saṅkrāntis occur alternately; therefore each door has its own hinge. There may occasionally be two new moons within one solar month and in this case they will both take the same name. The first month is *Adhika* (additional, abundant, intercalated) and the second month is *Nija* (innate, native). Adhika months ordinarily occur once every three years. Therefore in a year there could be an adhika Śrāvaṇa and a nija Śrāvaṇa.

Once or twice a century there is a lunar month which begins and ends without a solar month beginning or ending in between and this lunar month is suppressed. It is said there is no hinge for the door to turn on. This suppressed month is called a lost month (*kṣaya māsa*). Only the three months of Mārgaśirṣa, Pauṣa, and Māgha can be kṣaya because they are the three lunar months that turn on 29 days each.

The Ṛgveda says the Sun and Moon move proceeding and following each other, because of Māyā, like two children playing round the sacrifice.[80] Time is seen according to the Sun's movement because it is steady and constant each year. While the lunar months move all over the place like the emotions constantly fluctuating. The Vedic calendar keeps stability with the Sun, like an individual keeps centered with the ātma. The individual happenings are guided by the Moon, like the emotions fluctuating across the mind.

Intercalary Month (Adhika Māsa)

The kṣaya month happens only once or twice a century as an astronomical rule. The intercalary month happens about once every three years. It is the key for keeping the solar and lunar cycles in harmony and thereby allowing a functional luni-solar calendar.

We shall calculate the first six years of Kali Yuga to see the actual functioning of the intercalary month. According to *Sūrya Siddhānta,* Kali Yuga began on midnight between the 17th and 18th of February 3102 B.C. (Caitra Pratipad). At the end of the first sidereal year and beginning of the second, 12 synodic months had passed and 10.891701134 days of the next lunation. At the end of the second year, 12 synodic months had passed and 21.783402268 days of the next lunation. By the next year there were 12 lunations plus 32.6751034 days. This is actually 32.6751034 days so we subtract a lunation of 29.530587946 days which is therefore 13 lunations and 3.144515454 days of the next lunation.

79 Mishra, Suresh Chandra. *Vedanga Jyotisham*, p. 33
80 Ṛgveda 10.85.18

Kali Yuga	B.C.E.	First New Moon in that Year	Synodic months in that Year
0	3102	Absolute beginning of the year	12 lunations and 10. 891701134 days
1	3103	18.638886812 days into year	12 lunations and 21.783402266 days
2	3104	7.74719 days into year	*13 lunations* and 3.144515454 days
3	3105	26.386072492 days into year	12 lunations and 14.036216586 days
4	3106	15.49437136 days into year	12 lunations and 24.927917722 days
5	3107	4.60335 days into year	*13 lunations* and 6.28903091 days

Again we can see that since there were 10.891701134 days of the next lunation in the previous solar year the next New Moon starts 18.638886812 days into year (not 29.530587946 days as the previous year which began on the New Moon). Each year the New Moon will start 18.638886812 days later. At the end of the second year we have 18.638886812 days multiplied by 2 which is 37.277773624 days. This amount of time is more than one lunation, therefore we subtract 29.530587946 and have thirteen lunations with the next New Moon happening 7.747185678 days into the month.

Beginning of the Year (Varṣa-Praveśa)

There are various beginnings of the year (*varṣa-praveśa*) for various purposes just as there are various types of years for different purposes: the calendar year for dating, the civil (*sāvana*) year for government related work, the seasonal (tropical) year for agriculture, lunar year for festivals, the fiscal year for financial books and taxes, the academic year for education, etc. The astronomical New Year is Meṣa sankrānti. The lunar New Year is the New Moon before that, Caitra Pratipad, called the door to the year.[81] Dīpāvali, the New Moon of Āśvina, is the fiscal New Year (similar to April 15th in the USA).

Makara Saṅkrānti is the New Year for many dating systems, and shares the same astronomical roots as the Gregorian New Year. Makara Saṅkrānti is generally in the middle of January and marks the *Dakṣiṇāyana*- the Sun moving towards the Southern Hemisphere (relating to the Winter Solstice and the lengthening of the days). Karka Saṅkrānti is approximately the middle of July and it is not celebrated because it marks the Sun moving towards the Northern Hemisphere, the start of *Uttarāyaṇa* (relating to the Summer Solstice) where the days get shorter and the nights longer.

[81] Śatapatha Brāhmaṇa XI.1.1.1 Prajāpati is the year, the dark Moon is its gate, the Moon is the gate's bolt.

The Solar calendar has been used for civil purposes (work days, government planning, business), while the lunar calendar and tithis are used for religious purposes. The lunar months utilize tithis, while the solar month utilizes days of the week. The overall calendar is luni-solar because it is regulated by the movements of the Moon but it is made to fit in the divisions of the Solar year. The *National Calendar of India* is prepared by the India Meteorological Department and published annually in *The Indian Astronomical Ephemeris*.

Other Calendrical Systems

Luni-solar calendars are used by the Hindus, Buddhists, Tibetans, Chinese, Mongolians, Koreans, and Hebrews. The Japanese used a luni-solar calendar till 1873. The Babylonian calendar (derived from the Sumerian calendar), the Greek Calendar, the pre-Islamic calendar, and the pre-Christian Germanic calendar were all luni-solar.

The Islamic calendar is completely lunar and has no relation to the position or movement of the Sun. The twelve lunar months regress through the seasons over a cycle repeating every 33 years. The month begins with the first visibility of the crescent Moon after conjunction, though a lunar calendar of approximation is used for civil purposes in Muslim countries (a fifth of the world's population).

The Hebrew calendar is luni-solar and was originally observational based upon the first sighting of the crescent Moon but in the fourth century AD it became a fixed-arithmetic luni-solar calendar. The names of the months were adopted from the Babylonian names. The Hebrew calendar uses the 19 year *Metonic cycle* with 12 common years and 7 intercalary years (which are 3, 6, 8, 11, 14, 17 and 19th year of the Metonic cycle). The Hebrew day and month starts at sunset because this is when there was the first sighting of the crescent Moon.

The ancient Egyptian calendar was totally solar, made of twelve thirty day months with 5 intercalated days at the end of the year. The solar calendar was important for them to be aware of the flooding Nile. The calendar did rotate through the seasons over a 1460 year period that was tracked by the helical rising of Sirius (it moved about 1 day every 4 years). Their weeks were 10 days long and based upon the 36 drekkaṇa (zodiac divided into ten degree sections). The weeks matched the rising of the stars associated with the week's zodiac division, and they also kept time through the night with this division of the stars.

The West used the Julian calendar which replaced the Roman calendar in 46 B.C. It was introduced by Julius Caesar according to the astronomer Sosigenes of Alexandria. Some say Caesar shackled the months to the solar year as the Hellenic calendar was luni-solar. But the intercalation was manipulated for political purposes, like not inserting a month when opposition was in power and putting too many intercalary months when supporters were in power. The Julian calendar used a 365.25 day sidereal solar year with a leap day every four years, which creates an excess of .00776 days, and thereby over long periods of time misaligns itself with the seasons. In A.D. 1582, Pope Gregory dropped out 10 days to rectify this thereby creating the Gregorian calendar. The modern western calendar now uses the tropical solar year along with the leap year to avoid such a recurrence. From its foundation one can see that it was originally based upon a luni-solar calendar but has become a tropical solar calendar in its present state. The variance in the days of the month originally corresponded to the anomaly of the Sun and its motion through the signs of the zodiac. The Gregorian calendar has presently become the internationally accepted *civil calendar*.

Seasons (Ṛtu)

Vasanta	Spring	March-May
Grīṣma	Summer	May- July
Varṣa	Rainy	July-September
Śarad	Autumn	Sept-November
Hemanta	Winter	Nov-January
Śiśira	Cool	January-March

There are different ways to divide the year into seasons (*ṛtu*). The seasons are actually what is happening on the Earth and therefore very important for agriculture. The tropical zodiac stays in alignment with the seasons. The Sanskrit name for the tropical zodiac literally means "with the solstice" (*sāyana*). The Western year has four seasons divided by the equinoxes (*viṣuva*) and solstices (*ayana*). The spring Equinox is called *Mahāviṣuva* and is the head of the personified year,[82] like the sign of Aries. The Ṛgveda talks about the tropical zodiac (*viṣṇu cakra*) and says "with four times ninety marks, Viṣṇu sets in motion moving forces like a turning wheel."[83] The equinox and solstices divide the year into 4 portions of 90 degrees each. The benefit of the Gregorian calendar is that it was made to stay constantly aligned to the ayanas, so the seasons will remain the same every year.

There have been different seasons used throughout India, but the standard is to divide the year into six seasons of two months each.[84] Seasons will vary according to a location and must be understood accordingly when used in astrological techniques. India presently uses the seasons according to the sidereal zodiac (*nārayāna cakra*), giving a season to every two signs (60 degrees of the Sun's motion).

It takes 72 years for the precession (*ayanāṁśa*) to move one degree of the zodiac. It takes 2,160 years for the ayanāṁśa to move through one sign. It takes 4,320 years for the precession to make it through two signs (or one ṛtu). It takes approximately 25,920 years for the Vernal equinox to make a complete revolution. These time phases will shift the

[82] Śatapatha Brāhmaṇa SB XII.1.4.2

[83] *caturbhiḥ sākaṁ navatiṁ ca nāmabhiścakraṁ na vṛttaṁ vyatīnravīvipat |bṛhaccarīro vimimāna ṛkvabhiryuvākumāraḥ pratyetyāhavam || Ṛgveda I.155.6*

[84] Keith & Macdonell, Vedic Index Vol I, p. 110-111 discusses the various number of ṛtu throughout Vedic literature.

sidereal zodiac (the stars in the sky) from the seasons (tropical zodiac), and need various corrections in the calendar.

In the Gregorian calendar, Christmas is celebrated on December 25th. This was originally the day related to the winter solstice in the old Julian calendar. First the Julian calendar became out of sync with the solstices and when the Gregorian calendar was adopted they did not take the actual reason for the date into consideration. Therefore Christmas which directly has its roots in the celebration of the solstice is celebrated 4 days late.

The Indian solar zodiac used to be more mutable, but became much more fixed after Greek influence. Presently, Makara Saṅkrānti (January 14th) is still celebrated as the beginning of the Sun's northern course (winter solstice) which actually happens December 21st.[85]

The English New Year was also originally on the Spring Equinox, March 21st, but when this was changed, the English still collected taxes on the out of sync date which is why taxes are done in April. There are many other dates in the modern calendar that have their reasoning based upon calendars that became out of sync and had originally been connected to the solstices, equinoxes and seasons. This has been a standard issue in many cultures and calendars.

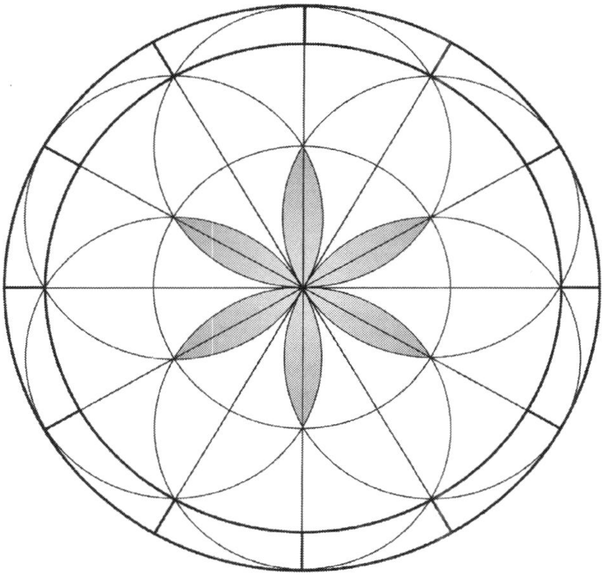

[85] Viṣṇu Purāṇa II.8.26-30, 62-62, 68-70 clearly indicates the link between the seasons and the ayanas

Sunrise (Sūryotthāna)

The calculation of sunrise is taken for granted when it shows up on the computer generated astrological chart. The moment of sunrise changes according to longitude and latitude which means that each place should have its own pañcāṅga. This being quite complex, Indian astronomers overcame this by calculating the pañcāṅgas for an imaginary island that took the longitude of Ujjain (75° 46′ 6″ East of Greenwich) and the latitude of the Equator. This island called *Laṅkā* (though not the actual island of Śrī Laṅkā) was used by ancient Indian astronomers like the present day use of the Royal Observatory in Greenwich, London. From Laṅkā all adjustments and corrections were calculated for one's location.

Local sunrise requires a correction for (1) terrestrial longitude, (2) equation of time, and (3) Sun's tropical longitude. The terrestrial longitude takes into account that the sun does not rise at 6 AM at all places. The equation of time takes into account that the Sun does not move equally throughout the year. The third correction takes into account that the Sun does not move along the equator but along the ecliptic and therefore moves throughout the seasons of the year.

The **center** of the Sun's disk is truly on the eastern horizon
The **tip** of the Sun's disk is truly on the eastern horizon
The **tip** of the Sun's disk appears to be on the eastern horizon
The **center** of the Sun's disk appears to be on the eastern horizon

Modern astronomers (or your software) presently use the *mean solar time* of GMT and make corrections from this simplifying your calculations of time. Though, while the Sun rises, what is the actual astronomical moment that is considered Sunrise? Most software will give you four choices, and according to your definition of Sunrise there will be a slight variation on the longitudes of special lagnas and upagrahas. The choice of Sunrise/Sunset definition is given in most programs under preferences.

The primary definition of sunrise is the moment when the upper edge of the Sun appears above the horizon. Sunrise and sunset calculated from the leading and trailing edges of the Sun makes the day longer. The center of the Sun's disk is used to determine the longitude of the Sun and other planets. Though, when calculating from the center, the Sun has already risen or not yet completely risen and for the end of the day not fully set. There is a difference of about 4 minutes (10 vighaṭikās) from the rise of the upper limb to the center of the Sun.

True sunrise and apparent sunrise are based on *atmospheric refraction* which is when light from a celestial body travels from the vacuum of space into the Earth's atmosphere the path of the light is bent due to refraction. Because the light is bent in the atmosphere the Sun can be seen while still below the horizon. This effect causes apparent sunrise which is earlier than actual sunrise, yet it is what the naked eye would observe. Many believe this is what the Ṛṣis would have started their day with; the first *rays* of the Sun on the horizon. This is therefore utilized as the time to start yajñas. It is used by many for Jyotiṣa purposes as it was used by Varāhamihira.

Utthāna is the act of standing up or rising. Sūryotthāna means the Sun rises, appears, bursts forward, or is resurrected. When the first rays are seen many start their Gāyatrī mantra. When the lower limb (bottom) of the Sun has risen it is then time to perform the Ādity-Hṛdaya Stotra.

Metonic Cycle (Brahmā-Cakra)

235 lunar months	29.53059 days	6939.68865 days
19 tropical years	365.2425 days	6939.6075 days

There are a few other cycles that interact with the normal luni-solar calculations that a good astrologer should be aware of. If a New Moon starts on the beginning of the year, it will take 235 lunar months (19 years) till the New Moon starts again at the beginning of the year. This is an approximation rounded to 6,940 days with an error of 2 hours each cycle (one full day every 219 years). This is related to the number of years in Saturn's viṁśottarī daśā. This cycle was recorded and therefore named after the Greek astronomer Meton of Athens in 432 B.C. and is used by calendar makers. In general, adhika months happen seven times in this nineteen year cycle.

0	0		15	13.81		30	27.61		45	11.89
1	***18.64***		16	2.92		31	16.72		46	1.00
2	7.75		17	21.56		32	5.83		47	19.64
3	26.39		18	10.66		33	24.47		48	8.75
4	15.49		19	29.3		34	13.58		49	27.39
5	*4.60*		20	***18.41***		35	2.69		50	16.5
6	23.24		21	7.52		36	21.33		51	5.6
7	12.35		22	26.16		37	10.44		52	24.24
8	1.46		23	15.27		38	29.07		53	13.35
9	20.1		24	*4.38*		39	***18.18***		54	2.46
10	9.21		25	23.01		40	7.29		55	21.1
11	27.84		26	12.12		41	25.93		56	10.21
12	16.95		27	1.23		42	15.04		57	28.85
13	6.06		28	19.87		43	*4.15*		58	***17.95***
14	24.7		29	8.98		44	22.79		59	7.06

The Metonic Cycle was the basis of the Greek calendar and is retained in the Hebrew calendar. The cycle is an approximation and still needs rectification over large periods of time, as it is not an exact orbital resonance. The cycle can be viewed in the table below according to the time of the first New Moon in a solar year (this is the same chart as used in adhika māsa example with additional years). The chart begins with 0 Kali Yuga, and one can see the

19 year cycles having a very close return to the same number, minus 2 hours.

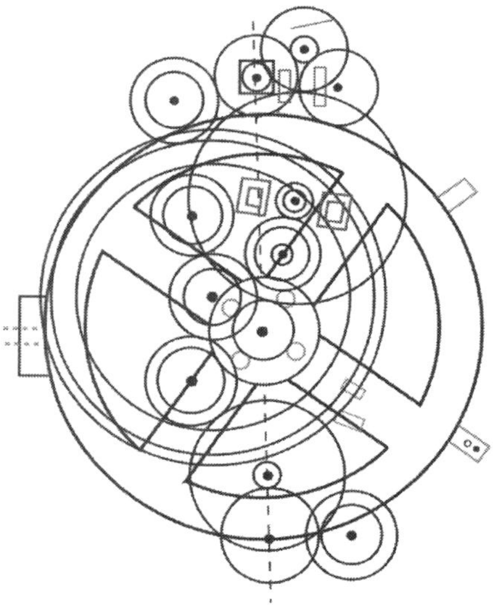

The *Antikythera Mechanism* was an astronomical analog calculator designed to calculate astronomical positions and is one of the world's oldest known geared devices. It was found off the Greek coast on a ship wreck from the first century B.C. The calculator showed the motion of the Sun and Moon (the anomaly in the Moon's angular velocity), the lunar phases, and planetary motion. It has dials for both the 19 year Metonic cycles, the 76 year Callipic cycles (containing 4 metonic cycles), and Draconic cycles. It must have been an astrologer's best friend in the ancient world. Early Greek and Indian texts reference many complicated machines like this that were looked at by modern scholars with skeptism. Such geared mechanisms were not thought to appear till the 12th century. The Antikythera Mechanism has made modern science change its understanding of the evolution of machines in history by over a millenium. The precision of the Antikythera Mechanism shows that it could not have been a one of a kind and that the technology had evolved a number of years previous to 150 B.C.

Ancient India also had instruments of this type. We now know that the measurement of the islands (*dvīpas*) given surrounding Mount Meru in the Purāṇas is equivalent to the size to make cogs for a machine of this nature. Formerly they had been called incorrect calculations of the distance to the Sun and Moon, etc. But now it is seen that they would have created a device which would have the ability to calculate the proper motion of the planets and stars.

Draconic Month and Year

The *Draconic month* (also called a nodical month) is the time for the Moon to make two successive passes of the ecliptic plane and return to the same node. In others words, just as the month becoming conjunct with the Sun creates a synodic month, the Moon becoming conjunct with Rāhu creates the nodical month. The time it takes the Moon to return to Rāhu takes 27.212220 days (27d 5h 5min 35.8s). The difference between a synodic month and a draconic month is approximately 2⅓ days.

Month	Synodic	Anomalistic	Sidereal	Tropical	Draconic
1994-2000	29.530588853	27.55454988	27.321662	27.321582	27.212220817

A *semester* is an eclipse season. It is the time it takes the Sun to go from one node to the other node, which takes about 177.18 days or 6 synodic months (±1). This is the time period between possible eclipses. These indicate whether the eclipse will relate to the significations of Rāhu or to the significations Ketu.

A *draconic year* is the time it takes the Sun to complete one revolution with regard to Rāhu. This is also called an eclipse year (or an ecliptic year) and takes 346.620075883 days (346 d 14 h 52 min 54 s). The Vedic calculation had 13 months of 27 tithis which created 351 tithis (346-347 solar days) to calculate the draconic year.[86]

A *nodal period* (*Rāhu-Bhagaṇa*) is the 18.612815932 year period that the plane of the moon's orbit precesses the zodiac (which we locate as the period of Rāhu through the zodiac). This period of time also relates to a *tidal cycle* where there is an 18.6 year tidal oscillation.

These eclipse time periods create the *Sun-Moon-Rāhu Cakra* in Vedic Astrology. And they can be interpreted outwardly in transit for mundane events, in one's natal chart for general events and with a special technique to time daily events.[87] The Sun's position always shows what rises or is activated. When the Sun transits Rāhu you can find out about your enemies or that which is hidden. The Moon's transit over Rāhu has the power to destroy illusion. In a daily chart it is called Dakṣiṇāmūrti hour, because the effects of Rāhu are destroyed. A ritual practice is to take Prasād with the name of Viṣṇu at this hour. Rāhu's transit over the Sun will show a time when you are vulnerable in your life, it is where Rāhu can take your light, your vitality, or your wealth. When Rāhu transits over your Moon, it can take your prāṇas or hurt your health in obscure ways.

86 Iyengar, *Connection Between Vedāṅga Jyotiṣa and other Vedic Literature*, p.361-2.

87 Sun-Moon-Rāhu Cakra in Praśna Mārga, p.165, and Sarvachintamani, p.26.

Time of Eclipse (Vimardārdha)

The globe (*gola*) which becomes the cause of eclipsing another body is called the *chhādaka* (the obscuring object).[88] This will cause different magnitudes of an eclipse according to the anomaly of the Moon from the Earth and the exact alignment of luminaries with the ecliptic. The map which shows the projection of the eclipse is called the *chhedyaka*. The time from the apparent conjunction till the end of the eclipse is called *vimardārdha* (the measure of obscuration/devastation). The time of complete eclipse is called *nimīlana* or the closing of the eyes. The luminary's emergence from the eclipse is called *Unmīlana* or the opening of the eyes. This is symbolic of igonorance obscuring (*chhādaka*) the mind which doesn't know its true nature. One first shuts their eyes (*nimīlana*) to meditate in order to destroy the world (or attachment to it). Then after realization one opens the eyes (*unmīlana*) to percieve divinity everywhere. The end of the eclipse is called the *mokṣa*, when the luminary is free from the *grahaṇa*.

The New Moon is the conjunction of the Sun and Moon and therefore their union. Śiva's night is kṛṣṇa caturdaśī, when the consciousness is about to disappear into the emptiness (*śūnya*). He is meditating on the void, and ready to merge with it. The New Moon is Kālī, the dark mother from which everything came yet is now being completely consumed. She is a mother who loves all her children, a mother who is hungry for bringing everyone home. She is the undifferentiating consciousness, where no duality can reside. Her place is beyond thought, which is why the Moon is dark, empty, and unseen.

The Full Moon is Lakṣmī, the complete Śrī Śakti in all abundant forms. No mother cannot be found and worshipped in her. The Full Moon is the opposition of the Sun and Moon; they stand apart in full view like a husband and wife at a special event. Viṣṇu and Lakṣmī live in the world with complete devotion for each other. They represent the balance of all creation, the appreciation of life, and celebration of love.

Sectarianism is a disease of the mind which likes to separate things. The astrologer should be beyond these types of limited perceptions. Viṣṇu washes you like a Mother, and Śiva burns you like a father. Śiva is solar and his path (and Śakti) is the New Moon. Viṣṇu is lunar and his path (and Śakti) is the Full Moon. In either place, only full or new, an eclipse can happen. Realization is possible. The solar eclipse only happens on the New Moon, and the lunar eclipse only happens on the Full Moon.

The solar eclipse has the power of completely awakened perception, the burning of any illusion of separate self. It is absolute vision, not even one to see one, just One awareness. Rāmana Maharṣi was born during a solar eclipse. The Lunar eclipse has the power of complete surrender, the falling away of any illusion of separate self. It is the washing away of any self made desires, and having only One presence that moves all

88 Ṛṣi Atri observes an eclipse in Ṛgveda 5.40.

things. Chaitanya Mahāprabhu was born during a lunar eclipse. Philosophies may say various things, but in the energy of an eclipse, there is nothing to hold onto. One who grasps for the impermanent is lost and suffers. The one who stations themselves in the Unchanging reaches the Supreme Abode (*paramaṁ padam*).

Path of the Eclipse (Chhedyaka)

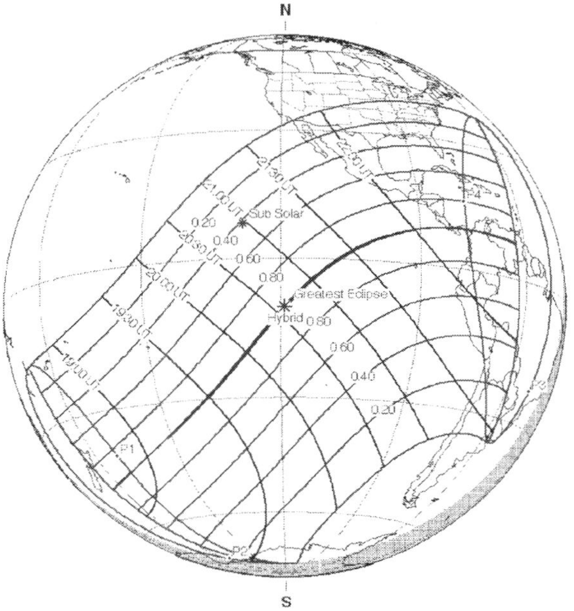

The path of an eclipse will show political upheavals in the areas of visibility. This path is mapped out to show where the eclipse will be visible, at what time, and in what magnitude. Various calculations based on the length of the eclipse indicate the time frame for the results of the eclipse to manifest in this region.

From 878 to 1715 A.D. the city of London, the capital of the British Empire, did not see an eclipse. This gave the British a period of 837 years to gain political strength.[89] The path of other eclipsed planets can also be utilized to show disturbances related to the elements they rule. For example, the Tsumani, experienced in Southeastern Asia in 2005, fell along the same path as the eclipse of the planet Venus.[90]

Saros Cycle (Grahaṇa-Parivartana)

Eclipses occur repeatedly in certain intervals of time; this is called the *grahaṇa parivartana* or the revolution of eclipses. In modern astronomy it is called the *Saros cycle*, or an *eclipse cycle*. It is the period after which the pattern of lunar and solar eclipses repeats. The periodicity of the eclipses is 18 years and 11.3 days (or 18 years, 11 days, and 8 hours), and is closely related to the number of years in Rāhu's viṁśottarī daśā.

In the Vedas this time period is called the 3339 deities that drink the nectar of the Moon.[91] The deities were related to the pitṛs who drank the nectar of the Moon during the

---

[89] Rath, Sanjay, Jyotish News, October 2001

[90] Prabhakaran, Sanjay, *Venus Eclipse on 8 June 2004*

[91] Ṛgveda 3.9.9, 10.52.6, Brahmāṇḍa Purāṇa I.23.61-69. See R.N. Iyengar, *Eclipse Period Number 3339 In The Ṛgveda*.

waning tithis.[92] The Ancient Babylonian astronomer's left many cuneiform clay tablets with detailed observations of these eclipse cycles.[93] Therefore this cycle was known throughout the ancient world.

223 synodic months	6,585.321 days
242 draconic months	6,585.357 days
239 anomalistic months	6,585.537 days

The eclipse cycle is related to three periodicities of the lunar orbit: the synodic month, the draconic month, and the anomalistic month. The Moon needs to be either new or full for an eclipse which relates to the synodic month. The magnitude and duration of the eclipse is caused by the distance of the Moon from the Earth which relates to the anomalistic month. And whether the Moon is conjunct or opposite Rāhu relates to the draconic month. When these three align there is an eclipse of similar magnitude and duration. The Saros cycle approximation (with an error of about 51 minutes) brings these three periodicities into alignment; the Moon will have the same phase, be at the same node, and have the same distance from Earth.

Taking the date of an eclipse and adding one Saros to it will indicate a nearly identical eclipse. As the Saros is a third of a day longer the eclipse will occur 8 hours later in the day. After three Saros cycles, the eclipse will be nearly the same in this regard, as the movement will add up to 24 hours and then the eclipse will repeat at the same time of the day. The *Triple Saros* takes 54 years and 1 month (or almost 19,756 full days) and was called an *exeligmos* (turn of the wheel) by the Greeks.

There are also 8 year cycles with 99 lunar months used by the Greeks, an 84 year cycles with 1039 lunar months used by the Romans, a 532 year cycle relating the Metonic cycle integrated with a 28 year cycle used by the Romans. There is the 90 year cycle (*Graha-parivṛtti*) used in South India, composed of 1 solar revolution, 15 of Mars, 22 of Mercury, 11 of Jupiter, 5 of Venus, and 29 of Saturn. There are many others, but these have less relevance for the general practice of astrology. The most relevant have been mentioned and one will come across these in general practice. For example, when an eclipse is calculated by NASA, they will list the saros cycle. These cycles can be studied and the changes in society, politics and other aspects of life can be noticed.

[92] 371 tithis in the solar year (according to the *Vedāṅga Jyotiṣa*) multiplied by 18 years is 6,678 tithis which half is 3,339 waning tithis.

[93] Aaboe, A. *Saros Cycle Dates and Related Babylonian Astronomical Texts*.

Bṛhaspati-Saṁvatsara Cakra

The saṁvatsara (or *bārhaspatya saṁvatsara*) usually refers to a year based upon Jupiter's transit of a sign which takes almost the same time as a solar year. The Jupiter years, also called *Jovian years*, each have a name within a sixty year cycle. The numerology of this cycle is composed of 12, 30, 60, 120, 800 and 43,200 year cycles.

The average daily motion of Jupiter is 5 kalās (minutes) and therefore takes 12 years to complete a revolution of the zodiac. The average daily motion of Saturn is 2 kalās, therefore takes approximately 30 years (or 29.5) to cover the zodiac. These two numbers directly relate to the number of months in a year (Sun/Jupiter) and the number of days in a synodic month (Moon/Saturn). These two planets are linked by these numbers, as Jupiter moves 30 degrees a year (1 sign) and Saturn moves about 12 degrees a year (2:5 ratio).

1	Prabhava	31	Hemalamba
2	Vibhava	32	Vilamba
3	Śukla	33	Vikāri
4	Pramodhuta	34	Śārvari
5	Prajāpati	35	Plava
6	Āngirasa	36	Śubhakṛt
7	Śrīmukha	37	Sobhana
8	Bhāva	38	Krodhi
9	Yuva	39	Visvāvasa
10	Dhātṛ	40	Parabhava
11	Īśvara	41	Plavaṅga
12	Bahudhānya	42	Kīlaka
13	Pramāthi	43	Saumya
14	Vikrama	44	Sādhāraṇa
15	Vṛṣa	45	Virodhakṛt
16	Citrabhānu	46	Paridhāvi
17	Subhānu	47	Pramādīcha
18	Tāraṇa	48	Ānanda
19	Pārthiva	49	Rākṣasa
20	Vyaya	50	Anala (Nala)
21	Sarvajit	51	Piṅgala
22	Sarvadhari	52	Kālayukta
23	Virodhi	53	Siddhārthi
24	Vikṛta	54	Raudra
25	Khara	55	Durmati
26	Nandana	56	Dundubhi
27	Vijaya	57	Rudhirodgāri
28	Jaya	58	Raktākṣa
29	Manmatha	59	Krodhana
30	Durmukha	60	Kṣaya (Akṣaya)

Every twenty years Saturn and Jupiter will have a conjunction, and every 60 years that conjunction will return to the same sign. This is the basic saṁvatsara cycle with each of the sixty years of Jupiter's cycle receives its own name. These years can be used for the prediction of individual nature as well as for yearly agricultural and economic prediction.[94]

In India there are three main ways (in different areas) that Jovian years have been calculated.[95] In northern India, they give the name according to the Jovian year expired at the beginning of the solar year. In this calculation it is possible to have a kṣaya Jovian year. In Eastern India, they use Jovian year actually completed at the actual moment one is dealing with.

[94] The interpretations of saṁvatsaras are given in *Brihat Saṁhita*, *Jātaka Pārijata*, as well as *Mānasāgari*.

[95] This variation is discussed in detail by Sewell and Dikshit, p. 32-39

In Southern India, it is merely a solar year with sixty names (no relation to Jupiter). In this way, the word saṁvatsara can also mean a year in general usage and would often be called a saṁvat (in texts like the Śatapata Brahmaṇa the word saṁvatsara is defined as a year).

The Jovian year is also sometimes named for the rāśi it is in, sometimes after the lunar month associated with the rāśi, and sometimes it is calculated according to the helical rising of Jupiter (his reappearance after conjunction with the Sun). There is the calculation that starts from Jupiter entering Māgha nakṣatra (which at one time was the winter solstice). There are also other variations.

In the Vedic period these 60 years were divided into 12 five year *yugas*. The yugas were sometimes given 366 day years,[96] or 360 days each and corrected with an extra month twice a yuga (every five ayanas). The five years of the Yuga[97] were named *Saṁvatsara, Parivartsara, Idvatsara, Anuvatsara, Vatsara,* with the intercalations named as *Aṁhasaspati* and *Saṁsarpa*. The 5 year yuga contains 60 solar months within making the 60 year cycle divided into periods of 60 month sections. This ancient calendar of 60 years divided into 12 groups of five shares common roots with the Chinese zodiacal calendar, where a 60 year cycle is composed of 12 animals of five elements each.

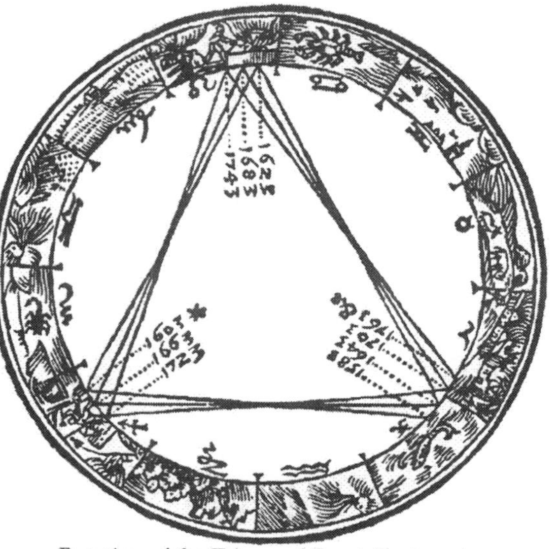

Rotation of the Trigon of Great Conjunctions drawn by Johannes Kepler

The sixty year cycle has three 20 year periods relating to the conjunctions of Jupiter and Saturn. The first 20 years relate to Brahmā, the middle 20 to Viṣṇu, and the last 20 years to Śiva according to the guṇa of the sign in which the conjunction occurs within. According to the named saṁvatsaras, the first twenty from Prabhava to Vyaya correlate to Brahmā, Sarjajit to Parabhava to Viṣṇu, and the last twenty to Śiva.

Every twenty years (19.859), Saturn and Jupiter will have a conjunction at about 123 degrees apart (approximately ninth from the previous conjunction). Every 60 years (59.577) that conjunction will return to the same sign. If a conjunction happened

96 Five sidereal years is 1826.2819 days and 62 synodic months is 1830.8965 days. So they were averaged to 1830 which is divisible by five to be 366 days, which is then divisible by 2 for 183 days in an ayana or by 6 to have 61 days in a ṛtu.

97 Viṣṇu Purāṇa, II.8.67

in Aries, the next will happen in Sagittarius, then Leo, and then back to Aries after 60 years. In this way, the conjunctions will move in trines of the same element creating a triangle in the zodiac. This triangle relates to Śakti and is utilized in various tantric techniques for showing where Śakti resides in a chart.[98] Saturn is Kālī and Jupiter is Tara.

The 60 year cycle advances 9 degrees (8.93°) every 60 years.[99] In this way the triangle can be seen as moving forward in the zodiac. This movement of triangles (*śakti-parivartana*) was called the "Rotation of the Trigon of Great Conjunctions" in the West. The cycle will stay in one elemental trine for about 200 years, when it will enter the next element. When this cycle changes elements it was thought to show great change, especially when moving over gaṇḍāntas (water to fire).

The cycle will move through the elements every 800 years (794.37 years or 40 conjunctions) returning to within .93° of the starting point, and completely through the zodiac in 2400 years (800 X 3).[100] Completely means the triangle completely turns, not just the corner returns to the trine.

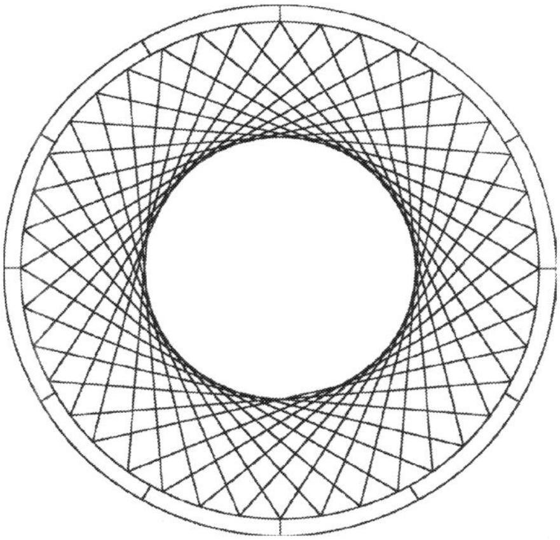

This 1° discrepancy creates a larger cycle in which the exact degree returns in 288,000 years (800 X 360). In Satya Yuga there are 6 of these cycles, in Tretā Yuga there are 4.5, in Dvāpara there are 3, and in Kali Yuga there are 1.5 which gives a total of 15 of the grand 288,000 year cycles in a Mahāyuga.

The 20 year cycle is used for predicting short-term historical events, the first 10 years are ruled by Jupiter and the second 10 are ruled by Saturn. The 60 year cycle is used for the prediction of politics and economics. The 200 year cycles is used for predicting changes in governments or dynasties, and the larger 800 year cycle is used to see the rise and fall of civilizations (or religious history). Predictions are made according to the chart at the time of the exact conjunction. The lagna of this will vary over the globe which indicates different results for different parts of the world.

There has been some historical research done on the rise and fall of dynasties in China that have been correlated to a cycle falling between 808 and 779 years which directly supports the mean cycle of 800 years, as well as the 200 year cycles.[101] Many Sasanian and Arab works, that are still available, are written on the history of the world and these

[98] This is foundation for the calculation of the śakti rāśi and trikoṇa daśā.

[99] The 9 degrees and the 9 conjunctions form a nine pointed star.

[100] The Polestar (*Dhruva*) always appears in the same position in the night sky. Different stars have occupied the position during different periods which last 2,400 years. The polestar is presently Polaris, next it will be Vega.

[101] DeVore, Nicholas. *Encyclopedia of Astrology*, P.74-76, the research historical investigator Dr. J. S. Lee.

conjunctions.[102] The ancient world histories were composed based upon these conjunctions starting the cycles from the beginning of Kali Yuga or for Arabic astrologers from the Flood (which was astrologically the same date[103]). Historians agree that the calculation of the present date A.D. as the birth of Jesus is incorrect since Herod the Great died in 4 B.C. Many astronomers link the triple conjunction of Jupiter and Saturn in 7 B.C. to the Star of Bethlehem, indicating this to be a more likely date.[104]

Below is a table of over 40 Jupiter-Saturn conjunctions so one can study to understand the movement of these two planets in an 800 year time frame. One can see the 60 year cycle in Gemini going from July 25, 1265 to June 01, 1325 to April 09, 1385. One can see the 800 year cycle from September 21, 1246 to October 31, 2040. One should notice the elemental trine cycle, the irregularity in the transition to another element, the variation caused by retrogressions, and the similar but not exact return to the original cycle. The table is listed in tropical positions.

NOV 08, 1186	12LI04	JAN 31, 1524	09PI14	NOV 28, 1901	14CP00
APR 16, 1206	25TA46	SEP 18, 1544	28SC05	SEP 10, 1921	26VI36
MAR 05, 1226	02AQ58	AUG 25, 1563	29CA10	AUG 08, 1940	14TA27
SEP 21, 1246	**19LI07**	MAY 03, 1583	20PI11	OCT 20, 1940	12TA28R
JUL 25, 1265	*09GE42*	DEC 18, 1603	08SA19	FEB 15, 1941	09TA07
DEC 31, 1285	08AQ02	JUL 16, 1623	06LE36	FEB 19, 1961	25CP12
DEC 25, 1305	00SC49	FEB 24, 1643	25PI07	DEC 31, 1980	09LI30
APR 20, 1306	28LI05R	OCT 16, 1663	12SA58	MAR 04, 1981	08LI06R
JUL 19, 1306	26LI01	OCT 24, 1682	19LE09	JUL 24, 1981	04LI56
JUN 01, 1325	*17GE53*	FEB 09, 1683	16LE43R	MAY 28, 2000	22TA43
MAR 24, 1345	19AQ01	MAY 18, 1683	14LE30	DEC 21, 2020	00AQ29
OCT 25, 1365	07SC01	MAY 21, 1702	06AR36	**OCT 31, 2040**	**17LI56**
APR 09, 1385	*25GE54*	JAN 05, 1723	23SA19	APR 07, 2060	00GE46
JAN 16, 1405	23AQ46	AUG 30, 1742	27LE09	MAR 15, 2080	11AQ52
FEB 14, 1425	17SC18	MAR 18, 1762	12AR21	SEP 18, 2100	25LI32
MAR 18, 1425	16SC33R	NOV 05, 1782	28SAG07	JUL 15, 2119	14GE52
AUG 26, 1425	12SC40	JUL 17, 1802	05VI08	JAN 14, 2140	17AQ05
JUL 14, 1444	08CA57	JUN 19, 1821	24AR39	DEC 21, 2159	07SC59
APR 08, 1464	04PI35	JAN 26, 1842	08CP54	MAY 28, 2179	23GE03
NOV 18, 1484	23SC11	OCT 21, 1861	18VI22	APR 07, 2199	28AQ19
MAY 25, 1504	16CA25	APR 18, 1881	01TA36	OCT 31, 2219	14SC42

[102] The Sasanian and Arab astrologers wrote books with titles like the *Great Book of Conjunctions*, the *Book Concerning the Judgements of the Conjunctions*, the *Book of Ascensions of Caliphs and Knowledge of the Ascension of Each King*, the *Book Concerning the Conjunctions and Religions and Faiths*, the *Book of Conjunctions and Revolutions of Years of the World*, all based on the Saturn-Jupiter conjunctions. For a discussion on these texts see Pingree, David, *From Astral Omens to Astrology* From Babylon to Bīkāner, p.42-45, 56-60, 63-66.

[103] Based upon Abū-Ma'shar, according to Pingree, *From Astral Omens to Astrology From Babylon to Bīkāner*, p. 53-54.

[104] Harper, David, The Calendar, p. 8

Rhythm of Time

The human mind has a tendency to become limited in small periods of time. You have to eat, get into the shower to get to work, find a parking space. The mind is working on a very limited focus (while it is not day dreaming). An astrologer must expand and develop the capacity to perceive the rhythmical processes which happen over long periods of time.

One should meditate on time in its greater rhythm. Sitting for meditation, one first becomes aware of the body and breath. After being grounded and centered, one becomes aware of the last hour, of the last hours, and then of the entire day, seeing it as a whole. All the activities and associated emotions are one day. Then take into awareness the entire week, all the days of the week and see them as one, slowing expanding the memory of the entire month, and associating the Moon's movement. Be aware of all the projects, events and activities and see them as a holistic period of time. The month becomes a season, then an ayana, and then a year. Visualize the Earth and Sun's movement along with all the events of this time. Expand the perceiving memory to the period of the current daśā and then the entire life. Then include the larger movements of time and the changes of culture and civilization on the planet. Include the visualizations of the movements of the eclipse cycles, Saturn and Jupiter movements, as well as the movement of the ayanāṁśa through the nakṣatras. At each level sit and observe the rhythms of time, as if you were listening to a piece of music. Practice seeing large periods of time as a whole, as songs at a concert.

Relativity of Time

Time is not the same to all beings in all places, even the same time units can stretch or shrink. From a modern physics perspective this is shown by Einstein's General Theory of Relativity, and modern quantum physics is showing there are many other things that induce space-time distortion. In myths from around the world we see space-time distortion in situations where an individual will enter another realm and return to the land of humans to find that a day or two had been a few hundred years.

In different planes of existence (*lokas*) time has a different pace relative to the one in which we experience. In the higher lokas time broadens and in the lower lokas time condenses similar to the concept of "gravitational time dilation." This dilation is seen within our own plane of existence when clocks which are far from massive bodies (higher gravitational potentials) run faster. Clocks that are closer to massive bodies (lower gravitational potentials) run slower. Time dilation is as valid on the astral realms as in the physical realms, as well as the past compared to the future.

As reality is a manifestation of consciousness, we have the ability to understand this within our own consciousness. When we mentally enter the lower realms of emotional suffering, time seems to slow down and pass more slowly. When we enter the higher realms of joy we perceive that time speeds up and moves more quickly. The hour of fun felt like only a few minutes, and the few minutes of pain felt like hours. In this way, in the lower realms many things can happen in a small amount of time. In the deva realms, one breath of 4 seconds is equal to 24 minutes passing on the human plane, (1 prāṇa=1 ghaṭīkā).

The Sun divides days and nights of both humans and devas. An Ahorātra (day-night) is a day to a human, while two ayana (*dakṣiṇāyana and uttarāyaṇa*) is a year to the devas (*divya-varṣa*).[105] In this way, one day for humans is equated to one year for the devas. This can be seen on the poles of the Earth where a day is half a year long and a night is half a year long.

One day for humans is equated to one month for the departed ancestors (*pitṛs*). A ahorātra relates to the two pakṣas of the Moon. The sukla pakṣa is the day and the kṛṣṇa pakṣa is the night in the realm of the ancestors. Śrāddha is often done once a month which is a way of feeding the departed ancestor their once a day offering. This is most often done on the New Moon which is the waking time in the pitṛ-loka.

Reckoning among the Pitṛs			Reckoning among the Devas	
1 synodic month	Day for pitṛs		1 sidereal year	Day for the devas
2.5 years (30 lunations) or 900 human days	Month for pitṛs (30 pitṛ days)		30 years or 10800 human days	Month of the devas (30 divya-varṣa)
30 years (360 lunations) or 10800 human days	Year of pitṛs (12 pitṛ months)		360 human years or 129,600 days	Divine Year (12 divya-māsa)
Lifespan is 100 pitṛ years (36,000 lunations) = 1,080,000 human days or 3,000 human years			Lifespan is 100 divya-varṣa = 36,000 human years	

In astrology, these time periods are used for timing events. For example, the Sun will progress one degree each year. The foundation of the western technique of progressed charts is based upon this reckoning of time. In the navāṁśa, the Sun is progressed one entire sign for each completed year of an individual's life (from its natal placement). This is used to time learning new skills (transit of the fifth house), getting married (transit of the seventh house) or meeting a teacher (transit of the ninth house).

[105] The year of the devas or a divine year (*divya-varṣa*) is a standard unit equalling 360 years utilized in Purāṇas and Siddhāntas when discussing units of time.

Large Units of Time

There is always a debate about whether time is linear or cyclic. The western approach has always been linear, the world was created and it is evolving and will eventually end. The Purāṇas focus on much larger cycles where the universe goes through regular creation and destruction cycles. At the same time no creation is exactly the same, it is like a season where the cycles have a qualitative recurrence. On a small scale- this can be seen in the cycles of months and years that keep a cyclic time but each year things are different, the planets are in different places and if they were ever to be in an almost similar space the ayanāṁśa (our position in the solar system and universe) would have changed. Therefore we have the Greek saying of Herakleitos, "you cannot step into the same river twice." The channel of water remains- as do the years and months- but it is never the same river, never the same Time. Yet the river is still there, so in this way cyclic and linear time exist side by side within each other.

The movement of an atom needs extremely small measurements, while the age of the universe needs extremely large units of time. Why would sages thousands of years ago need to use these types of numbers is dumbfounding to modern science, as a child that is sure it knows how to do things better than its father. The existence of these units represents an advanced concept of time and understanding of the universe. Modern science thinks that big machines lead to better results, but they actually lead to lack of human ability, as the invention of the calculator has diminished the ability of a modern person to do math in their head. We live in a conscious universe, fully aware. The power of the aware mind does not have boundaries.

Parāśara says that he will discuss the larger time cycles to understand the existence of insentient creations like mountains and oceans. Commentators from the 1800's called the number calculations of the Hindu texts as fanciful and showing of the Hindu's wild imagination. Now that science has began to measure the life of stars in billions of years and to study the age of our universe, the numbers no longer seem to far from reality.

In the *Ahirbudhnya Saṁhitā*, the sage is asked, "How long is the creation a milk giving cow taking any shape she wishes and how long is she *adhenu* a cow giving no milk (not flourishing)?" The units of time are mentioned when discussing the timing of the creation and dissolution. They use larger units of time which are measured in divine years (equal to 360 human years).

The Yugas are big cycles of time. They are not ending any day in your lifetime, or your 7th generation's lifetime. But as astrologers (*ahorātra-vidas*) we must understand them as it is our dharma to hold this knowledge of both the small and large cycles of the universe and contemplate their meaning.

Caturyuga

The four (*catur*) yuga are the four ages of mankind relating to the four stations of Dharma in the world ages. The four yuga together (also called a *Mahāyuga*) are composed of 12,000 *divine years* which are divided into 4 proportional divisions (4:3:2:1). Each period has a tenth portion of itself as an entry and also as an exit of its daśā. So for Kali Yuga which is composed of a thousand divine years, there is a Saṇdhi of 100 years entry and a hundred year exit Saṇdhi which makes a total of 1,200 divine years. There are 360 human years in a divine year which means that Kali Yuga is 432 thousand years long. In these calculations the number 432 thousand and 4.32 million become important.

Yuga	Composition	Entry & Exit		Length	Human Years
Satya	4,000	+400	+400	4,800	1,728,000
Tretā	3,000	+300	+300	3,600	1,296,000
Dvāpara	2,000	+200	+200	2,400	864,000
Kali	1,000	+100	+100	1,200	432,000
			Total	12,000	4,320,000 (4.32 million)

Some authorities' say that the present Kali Yuga began when Kṛṣṇa left the Earth plane (*Bhādrapada 13*), this is an approximation not an astronomical calculation.[106] The Siddhāntas and the ancient Vedic astronomers have said that Kali Yuga began on midnight between the Julian 17th and 18th of February (or Gregorian 23rd January) 3102 B.C. (this is also called 0 K.Y.). This was Caitra pratipad tithi (a kṣaya tithi that year).

The Mahāyuga (four yugas together) are 12,000 divine years. 1,000 such Mahāyugas are called a day of Brahmā (*kalpa*), and another 1,000 are the night of Brahmā. During the day of Brahmā everything is manifested and during the night of Brahmā everything is dissolved back to the unmanifest. During the day of Brahmā there are 14 Manvantara (manu-antardaśā) which are each equal to 71 Mahāyuga.

	Divine Years	Human Years
Caturyuga (*Mahāyuga*)	12,000	4.32 million
Manvantara	71 mahayugas	306,720,000
Brahmā Day (*Kalpa*)	14 Manvantaras	4.32 billion

In the Bhagavad Gītā, Kṛṣṇa says that those who know that Brahmā's day is a thousand yugas and that his night ends in a thousand yugas are the day-night knowing men (*ahorātra-vidas*).[107] This is another term for a horā-śāstri, one who has mastered the science of horā, or astrology. The Gītā says it is they who know about the large cycles of creation and

[106] Kṛṣṇa was born June 24nd, 3227 B.C. This Gregorian based date is calculated by putting the planetary positions of Śrī Kṛṣṇa's chart (given in Śāstra) into Sri Jyoti Star software and searching 10,000 years ahead and behind our own date for that chart. This is the only time that chart occurred in that 20,000 year time period.

[107] Bhagavad Gītā VIII.16-21

dissolution. During the day of Brahmā all manifestations (*sarva vyakta*) come forth from the unmanifest (*avyakta*) and return to the unmanifest when night returns. And this continues again and again. In comparison to this, Śrī Kṛṣṇa refers to a higher level of primordial unmanifest (*avyakta sanātana*) which is not a place of coming and going, but the eternal/unbroken unmanifest (*akṣara avyakta*) which is the supreme goal (*paramāṁ-gatim*). This akṣara avyakta is praised by the Ṛṣis of the Ṛgveda.

Brahmā dina	1000 caturyuga	1 kalpa	4.32 billion human years
Brahmā ahorātra	2000 caturyuga	2 kalpa	8.64 billion human years
Brahmā month	30 Brahmā days	60 kalpa	259.2 billion human years
Brahmā year	12 Brahmā months	360 Brahmā days	3.1104 trillion human years
Parārddham	50 Brahmā years	½ Mahākalpa	
Param	100 Brahmā years	1 Mahākalpa	311.04 trillion human years

When Brahmā manifests, the creation lasts for 4.32 billion years (which is close to the scientific age of the Sun and Earth - 4.57 billion years). It is said that in the same way as the results of the seasons recur in a periodical manner, the circumstances repeat themselves each yuga, again and again.[108] In the Vedas, the kalpa is described as a bull. The cosmic bull has four horns, three feet, two heads and seven hands.[109] The seven hands represent the number of zeroes in 4,320,000,000 and the other numbers correspond accordingly.

720 kalpa or 360 Brahmā ahorātra make a Brahmā year. Brahmā's life is equal to 100 Brahmā years which is called a *Para*. Within the Para, the universe is dissolved (*pralaya*) 36,000 times after which it is completely withdrawn (*Mahāpralaya*) and then born anew. Present science believes that the solar system is about 4.6 billion years old, and the universe is about 14 billion years old, though all dating is arguable.

There are many New Age opinions about the Yugas and various other calculations[110] given that could put us in any yuga you would like. But the above method is the standard as taught by most Purāṇas, Siddhāntas and agreed upon by the ancient Vedic astronomers like Āryabhaṭa.

Many nineteenth century commentators, with Newtonian ideas in their head, called these large numbers fanciful. But these large numbers indicate a concept of time being much bigger than ourselves, and are now quite relevant to the actual age of the universe. If these terms are taken as units (the yuga, mahāyuga, kalpa, and param) then they are basically a sexigesimal number system similar to our giga, mega, tetra decimal system. Just as 311,040,000,000,000 can be written as 311.04 trillion years, it can also be written as

[108] Viṣṇu Purāṇa I.5.59-60

[109] *catvāri śṛṅgā trayo asya pādā dve śīrṣe sapta hastāso asya | tridhā baddho vṛṣabho roravīti maho devo martyām ā viveśa* || Ṛgveda IV.58.3

[110] The calculations of Śrī Yukteśvar do not take the yugas as divine years which makes the entire yuga only 12,000 human years. He relates it to the precession which is 25, 920 years and to the solar systems revolution around the galactic center, but this has been discovered to take approximately 230 million years (closer to the time of a Manvantara).

1.00 mahākalpa. The galactic year may be 230 million years or 0.8 Manvantara. The Earth and all the planets are spinning about their axis and about the Sun, and the solar system is spinning about the galactic center, and the galaxy is also moving, and galaxies all spin. Time is cyclic, it has a circular motion, and the Vedic astronomers used the 360 divine years to calculate it.

Time is relative, and the life of the universe may seem long to a human, as a day would seem long to a fly. But to Brahmā, the entire Universe is only a lifetime, and the Galaxy we know of is only a day to him. From the large perspective, the worlds swiftly flow into the mouth of Time like moths to a blazing flame.[111] The cycles of creation and destruction flow by like a day when you are busy.

In a conscious Universe, creation and destruction are like the waking and sleeping of a human being. In sleep, your consciousness is withdrawn from the external world, all sound or sensation leaves and your awareness recedes to the mental realms. In death (*mahāpralaya*) your entire body and mind are destroyed and your consciousness withdrawals back into the causal body (*kāraṇa śarīra*). In a similar way, the small cycles below relate to the large cycles above. Matter is only perceived as dense because of the tamas guṇa. We live in a conscious Universe, fully aware.

From the perspective of the mind attached to the sensory reality, the emanation of the world happened at the beginning of time and is slowly evolving forward in a linear progression. From a higher perspective, time is happening in a cyclic fashion again and again through different ages of the creation and destruction of the universe. From the highest level, the emanation is just now, just happening at every moment. In pratyāhāra (withdrawal of the senses) the yogin perceives the cessation of the external world created by the five elements. In deep meditation the yogin can perceive the emanation and follow the course back to the source; follow it back to a place that was never disturbed by the movement of Time. As a dream world is created in an instant, and dissolves in the moment of awakening, the yogin realizes the nature of the material world through meditation.

There are many variations regarding calculations that an astrologer must use astronomy to decide. For instance should one use a 360 day year for Viṁśottarī daśā or a sidereal year? In order to answer these types of questions for yourself, you should understand some astronomy, cycles of time and their interactions. This small text cannot describe everything, but foundations allow one to make logical deductions. Viṁśottarī is 120 years duration, if you calculate the days according to solar years of 365 days you will get 43831 days in the cycle. If we use 360 days to a year we get 43,200 days in the viṁśottarī daśā cycle. Understanding the general cycles and their numerology will make your thinking more clear and give parameters to work within.

---

[111] Bhagavad Gītā XI.29

Conclusion

On a material level, Kāla-Puruṣa manifests as the movement of the luminaries and the stars of the sky. Maitrāyaṇa Upaniṣad (VI.16) says that "the time that has a body *is* the ocean of creatures. Resting in it is the Sun (*Savitṛ*) from whom the Moon, stars, planets, year, etc. are produced. From them comes all this here, whatever is seen in this world, fair or foul. So God (*Brahman*) has the Sun as its Self, therefore one should worship the Sun under the name of Time".

This Time with parts works through its limbs: the days, months, seasons and ayanas.[112] The increments of time make the manifestation of the embodied (*mūrta*) time. In this way, we cannot separate the divisions of time from this Creator (*Prajāpati*) who is made of the year (*saṁvatsara*).[113] The full moon days are the breaths of the year.[114] The śukla pakṣa days are the inhaling and the kṛṣṇa pakṣa days are the exhaling of Prajāpati.[115] The day-nights are the bones of Prajāpati.[116] The hours ticking on the clock are the form of Time that is manifesting our daily lives.

The Vedas say that some look at the Father with five parts and 12 forms (*saṁvatsara*) as abiding in the far off heavens and others say he is the clear-seeing one (the Sun) who abides below in the seven wheels (revolutions of the seven graha) that has six spokes (divisions of the year into ṛtu).[117] Time is a wheel that keeps moving around its eternal axis, a wheel divided into increments of various time units. We need to merge our sense of time and god and the intervals of time with the manifestation of the reality we know.

The Purāṇic stories of creation say Brahmā (the grandfather) manifests everything from his emotions or body. From his anger (Mars) was born Rudra. Feeling disgust (Rāhu), the hairs on his head fell off and created the serpents. From his vital energy (Sun) were created the birds, from his breast (Moon) were created the sheep, from the hairs on his body (Mercury) sprang herbs, roots and fruits.[118] These stories are not about a creator

[112] Vedāṅga Jyotiṣam I.1 *pañcasaṁvatsaramayaṁ yugādhyakṣaṁ prajāpatim| dinartvayanamāsāṅgaṁ praṇamya sirasā suciḥ||*

[113] Maitrāyaṇa Upaniṣad, VI.15, The form of Time with parts is the year: for all creatures are born from the year; once born here, they live by the year and in the year they meet their end. So the year is Prajapati, Time, food, the nest of Brahman, and the Self.

[114] Jaiminīya Brāhmaṇa II.396

[115] Jaiminīya Brāhmaṇa II.394

[116] Śatapatha Brāhmaṇa X.1.1.2

[117] *pañcapādaṁ pitaraṁ dvādaśākṛtiṁ diva āhuḥ pare ardhe purīṣiṇam| atheme anya upare vicakṣaṇaṁ saptacakre ṣaḷara āhurarpitam||* I.164.12 This is a translation that agrees with the Vedāṅga Jyotiṣam and the earliest Vedic Calendrical systems.

[118] The frequencies related to a material manifestation, which are the metaphorical building blocks of all astrological interpretations, are abundant in all Vedic literature. In classical times to say a person is ruled by the Sun or ruled by Jupiter, or connected to the lion was similar to telling a psychiatrist that a patient has bi-polar disorder. There was a clear understanding of the frequencies represented in these namings, and hence the power of speech to indicate reality.

god in a material sense; Vedic sages did not take this literally, as that is not how Vedic scripture has ever been written. The universe is a manifestation of consciousness and everything has its frequencies relating to various emotions or activities. From his anger Rudra was born, or the frequency of anger and heat that can destroy is the force we name (*vācam*) as Rudra. From the strength of his arms were created the warrior caste as the arms represent strength and power as well as control. This is all metaphorical to indicate the qualities of the things in our reality. Everything in our reality is manifest consciousness with perceived form and its frequencies or qualities are communicated to each other through metaphor.

The various gods exist as forces of the divine. Being a metaphor does not mean they are not real, it means that their form has meaning representative of their energy.

In Arjuna's divine vision of Time, the Supreme (*viśvarūpa*) was revealed as *one* single complete universe yet divided in many ways.[119] This primeval Puruṣa[120] divided the universe of himself. For one to perceive the entire universe as this form is the *Yoga of the Universal Form*. So not only is the creation from the one body of the Supreme taught, but the yoga of *seeing* everything *as* the divine body.

The Śatapatha Brāhmaṇa (XII.2) says that the year is Man and describes the parts of the year as the bodily parts of the Cosmic Man. The Jaiminīya Brāhmaṇa (II.60) says that one should know that they are identical with the year and that the year is established in oneself. The year is born and established from and on a person knowing this. Time makes the world move and brings forth all that is present, which is our own body and life.

This manifest world is moving forward, impelled by its own aspect of Time, unfolding everything like water to a seed. Time takes visible manifestation and name in individual increments, it becomes tangible in division. First we become aware of these increments and their interaction with our lives. We work to see the divinity in the flow of time that moves the universe. Then we realize the true nature of time and who we are. The Maitrāyaṇa Upaniṣad (VI.15) says,

Time ripens all beings
In the great Self.
But the one who knows in what
Time is ripened, knows the Veda.

[119] Bhagavad Gītā XI.13
[120] Bhagavad Gītā XI.18

Chapter 3

Naisargika Dasha

Time cooks up all created beings and
Time brings dissolution to everything born.
Time sits up fully awake when all else is asleep, therefore,
Time is unconquerable. (108.7)
Time makes the semen flow and
Time makes the fetus grow inside the womb.
Time generates the creation again and again and Time destroys it all. (108.8)
Time is unseen and eternal and conceived as two-fold;
Gross Time is comprehended by movement/change and
Subtle Time is that which is within (*antareṇa*) the change. (108.9)

-Garuḍa Purāṇa

Naisargika Daśā

Creation unfolded impelled by Time, and everything exists within a Universe unfolding in time. Therefore Time pushes forth the creation, growth, results, and destruction of the happenings in our life. The Vedic Ṛṣis have given hundreds of ways to perceive time; therefore the quality of time needs to be understood by an astrologer. There are methods for timing the fluctuations of the mind, for timing material events in life, for timing death and destruction. There are internal clocks and external transits. Every human lives in a wheel of Time (*kālacakra*) that spins its various cogs activating the various karmas in our lives.

The zodiac is called the Kāla-Puruṣa or the supreme person manifest as Time. The zodiac is not created by the stars but the division of the stars according to the motions of the Sun and the Moon. The mathematical geometries of the sky, of time, continue to divide and create various systems of energetic qualities. Hours, minutes, seconds are numerical divisions in the outer world. Time divides the outside, as well as dividing our *individual* lives into various periods that express our life. Time controls the thinking of living beings and gives the individual their results of dharma and wealth.[2] The Sanskrit word for 'result' is *phala* which also means fruit. Sage Parāśara often uses the terminology that a result will be given when the time is ripe. As time ripens the fruit on a tree to be ready, so time ripens our karma to give results. At different times we focus on different goals, we think and desire different things.

Life has many facets, and therefore there are many methods used to determine the ripe time of a person's life. A competent astrologer has multiple techniques to catch the intricacies of life's enfoldment. Different charts will require different daśā systems, and discrimination in their application. Besides daśās, planets have their maturity ages and maturing houses which ignite the relationships they have in the chart. Transits are also a simple method which gives accurate results and must be integrated into any daśā being applied.

Types of Timing

There are many varieties of daśās. In general they will either indicate a *planet* that is giving results or a *rāśi* that is giving results. There are daśā that utilize *graha* periods and those which utilize *rāśi* periods. There are graha daśā that are calculated from the nakṣatra (janma, lagna, or fifth) like viṁśottari daśā and its variations, or tribhagi daśā, or yogini daśa. There are rāśi daśā calculated from the nakṣatra like kālacakra daśā.

[2] Mahābhārata XIII.150.2 *kāla evātra kālena nigrahānugrahau dadat| buddhimāviśya bhūtānāṁ dharmārṭheṣu pravartate||*

There are daśā that are calculated based upon houses in the rāśi or placements of planets or special lagnas. Nārāyaṇa daśā starts from the stronger of the first or seventh house and shows us the cicumstances and directions in our life. Lagna-kendradi-rāśi daśā starts from the lagna and its kendras and shows how our personality impacts life and how life impacts our personality. Ātmkāraka-kendrādi-rāśi daśā starts from the ātmakāraka and is used to time spiritual experiences. Dṛg daśā starts from the ninth house and is used to time dharma and spirituality. Sudaśā is calculated from the Śrī lagna and is used to time finances. Trikoṇa daśā shows where the śakti is activated in a chart. It shows what rāja yogas are becoming active and also which forms of śakti are active at different times.

These are all *phalita daśā* which means they show time periods of 'bearing fruit' or giving results in the world. There is another broad group of daśās called *āyurdaśās*, which are used particularly for health and timing disease and death. These are the śūla daśā, niryana-sūla daśā, brahmā daśā, sthira daśā, navāṁśa daśā and the paryāya daśās which are used to see suffering, disease and death. The varṇada daśā shows health relative to your work life or the health of your business. The maṇḍūka daśā is more about the health of countries than the health of individuals.

Each type of daśā has advantages and disadvantages. In the nakṣatra daśās there are some fine-tuned predictions available. There is also a difference of opinion about the definition of the length of years; whether it is a numerical year of 360 days or a natural year of 365 days. The difference of opinion in the ayaṇāṁśa can also create a few days to sometimes over a few months variation in daśā. Rāśi daśās do not have such a large variable for error, since many are determined with basic calculations. The variability with those daśās is found in rules for calculation, such as in mūla daśā whether to calculate from lagna or the stronger of lagna, Sun and Moon, or options such as starting the antardaśā from the same sign or the sign lord. These variables are determined according to one's tradition as well as through time tested wisdom.

Then there is the broad range of natural (*naisargika*) timing methods where planets mature at a certain age; the same for everybody (though activating different placements). There are natural planetary time periods such as naisargika-graha daśā. There are a few natural progressions of houses that mature with age such as the naisargika-bhāva daśā, or natural order of houses getting activated with time such as Cakra daśā and Sudarśana Cakra daśā in their simplifications and complexities.

And then there are transits which have a general cycle which is like a maturity such as a Saturn return (29 ½ years) or a nodal return (18 years), and these relate to a specific situation according to the individual's chart, such as Saturn transiting the Moon. The transit of Saturn and Jupiter are affecting the year. The transit of Sun, Mars, Venus and Mercury are affecting the month. The lunar transit is influencing the day. Transits are a simple method which give accurate results and must be integrated into any daśā being applied.[3] The daśā lords are controlling circumstances according to their nature, either manifesting or obstructing certain events. Transits operate on these events by increasing or decreasing the force and extent of the situation.[4] The use of transits should be well integrated with daśās to give the best results.

There are reasons with pros and cons for using each daśā. In general they will all work if you understand them and are well trained how they work, when they work and what they will indicate. A competent astrologer should have a handle on at least one of each category, and slowly get to know the other daśās after having refined their predictions with experience. There are many complications to getting accurate results, but the work is a fruitful one.

This chapter focuses on understanding the naisargika daśās; both the naisargika-graha daśā and the naisargika-bhāva daśās. These daśā lay a foundation for the energy being active in a chart, almost like the weather of the day. If the schedule says there will be a ball game and nature says it will rain, then the game is cancelled. If the schedule doesn't have a game planned but the weather is just so nice, there may be an unofficial game anyway. In this way, the naisargika daśā has the power to alter results indicated by other daśā.

Ptolemy says that 'when predicting the results of a chart, first we have to consider the cultural conditions of an individual. Just as we don't expect a straight haired, white person to be born in Ethiopia or a curly haired, black person born in Germany, or a literate person to be born in Ethiopia or Germany and an illiterate person born in Greece, we should also consider the time divisions of life'. Ptolemy says 'one should not predict things in an infant that can only be done in manhood or procreation to one who is too old. One should instead predict circumstances appropriate by observing the period of life'.[5]

Naisargika-Graha Daśā

Something inside, a biological clock, makes you mature, go from a child to an adult, and soon from a middle aged person to an elderly person. Naisargika daśā is time according to the internal biological clock of the human being, a clock that ticks at basically the same rate for everyone. Naisargika daśā is one of the most basic underlying daśās utilized to understand a person's condition in life. It is so basic it should be utilized before even looking at viṁśottarī daśā, to help understand the life situation before making any predictions.

---

3 The conjunction of natal planets and transit planets remains the same whether using tropical or sidereal systems. Therefore, many of the complications with calculating accurate daśās are not an issue.

4 Ptolemy, Tetrabiblos IV.10

5 Ptolemy, Tetrabiblos IV.10

The natural life periods are ruled by a particular planet, showing the focus of human development during those years. Each stage of life relates to a planet which indicates the quality of development in that stage of life. Parāśara mentions the natural periods of life in the Āyurdāya chapter,[6]

अथ विप्र निसर्गायुः खेटानां कथयाम्यहम् ।
चन्द्रारज्ञसितेज्यार्कशनीनां क्रमशोब्दका ॥ १६ ॥

atha vipra nisargāyuḥ kheṭānāṁ kathayāmyaham |
candrārajñasitejyārkaśanīnāṁ kramaśobdakā || 16||

Now, I will explain the natural longevity (*nisargāyu*) of the planets:
Moon (*Candra*), Mars (*Āra*), Mercury (*Jña*), Venus (*Sita*), Jupiter (*Ijya*),
Sun (*Arka*), and Saturn (*Śani*), in that order of years.

एकद्वयंकनखा धृत्यः कृतिः पंचाशदेव हि ।
जन्मकालात् क्रमाज् ज्ञेया दशाश्चैता निसर्गजाः ॥ १७ ॥

ekadvayaṅkanakhā dhṛtyaḥ kṛtiḥ pañcāśadeva hi |
janmakālāt kramāj jñeyā daśāścaitā nisargajāḥ || 17||

One, two, nine (*aṅka*), twenty (*nakhā*), eighteen (*dhṛti*), twenty (*kṛti*), and fifty.
These are known as the natural periods starting from the time of birth.

Naisargika		Age
Moon	1	0-1
Mars	2	1-3
Mercury	9	3-12
Venus	20	12- 32
Jupiter	18	32-50
Sun	20	50-70
Saturn	50	70-120

Infancy is ruled by the Moon (the time of breast-feeding), toddlerhood is ruled by Mars (the time of growing the teeth), childhood by Mercury (which is the time of learning one's lessons).[7] Adolescence, which begins with puberty and the desire for sexual intercourse, is ruled by Venus. Family life is ruled by Jupiter, the golden years are ruled by the Sun, and old age is ruled by Saturn.[8] Varāhamihira and related texts include lagna daśā following Saturn.[9]

6 Bṛhat Parāśara Horā Śāstra, Āyurdāya-adhyāya v.16-17, Sārāvalī 40.20, and Jātaka Pārijāta V.2 mention these years, but in this context it is used as a nitya āyurdāya (*naisargāyus*) when Moon is stronger than Sun and Lagna. It is taught as a phalita daśā in Bṛhat Jātaka VIII.9, Horā-Sāra VIII.9 and Sārāvalī 41.21.

7 Yavanajātaka 39. 1-5

8 Ptolemy mentions in the *Tetrabiblos (IV.10)* a naisargika daśā in the known order of the planets Moon (0-4), Mercury (5-14), Venus (15-22), Sun (23-41), Mars (42-56), Jupiter (57-68), Saturn (69-end of life).

9 Varāhamihira, Bṛhat *Jātaka* VIII.9, *lagnadaśā śubheti yavanā necchanti kecit tathā.* Varāhamihira states that the Greeks consider this a beneficial daśā but others disagree. The lagna is not used for antardaśās nor will the lagna daśā come till after the age of 120, so there is little reason to discuss it relative to naisargika daśā.

Moon Daśā: Infancy

In the womb, the nervous system develops and the embryo moves according to involuntary reflexes. At birth, control of movement is very limited. Purposeful voluntary movements develop in the first year after birth. Each month, the infant has more and more control; from lifting its head, to being able to roll from its back onto its stomach, to grabbing, or crawling. This first year, is a process of becoming embodied from head to toe.

The infant develops their senses and the understanding of sensory information in the first year. These senses are born limited; a newborn infant can see about 8 to 12 inches (which is enough to see the face of their mother while breastfeeding). The mind (Moon) interacts with the world through the senses; the senses are the interface of the individual with the material reality.

During this time infants cannot do anything for themselves; it is a time that requires constant nurturing. They are protected by the mother, and live primarily off of breast milk. The infant and mother are so intensely identified with each other that they are unaware of their separate existence.

From a Vedic astrological perspective, you cannot separate the emotional psychology (Moon) of the individual from the first year of their life (Moon). The Moon (and fourth house) indicates the first year circumstances and the Moon (and fourth house) indicates the emotional psychology of the individual.

The strength or afflictions to the Moon will indicate challenges at this time. When the Moon and Sun are severely afflicted this can even indicate infant death (*sadyoriṣṭa*). The aspects of malefics to the Moon will indicate health or development issues that may need attention during the first year. For example, Mars associating with the Moon will indicate problems from rashes and fevers, or Saturn associating will give slow development. When the navāṁśa lagna is Scorpio, the debilitation of the Moon, problems getting breast milk are indicated. In this way, an astrologer can understand the natural development during the first year of life.

The nature of the Moon becomes apparent from the moment of birth. Both attachment and repulsion are innate predispositions of the Moon and are apparent in all infants wherever they are born, even in children born deaf and blind from birth who differentiate familiar people and strangers by smell. Likes and dislikes will be present from birth, though awareness of these will depend on the awareness of the parents/guardians.

There is a belief among the scientific community that the situation of the first year of a child reflects on them for the rest of their life: "It is clear from the work of Jared Diamond (The Third Chimpanzee), and the work of Jean Liedloff (The Continuum Concept), and the work of Thomas Lewis, Fari Amini and Richard Lannon, M.D. (A General Theory of Love) that birthing and rearing of the child for the first year or so is critical to the remainder of the child's life for reasons Freud never even dreamed of."[10] There is plenty of evidence to support this belief, but from a Vedic perspective we look at it from a slightly different angle. The nature of the individual's Moon will reveal itself in the first year. It's not that the environment is imposing itself on the mind, the mind is manifesting the nature of itself in its environment. We can see that an afflicted Moon will have a hard time in the first year of life. The nature of the affliction will show itself in the environment, and this will reflect in the person's thinking later in life. For example, an amāvāsya Moon indicates financial suffering in the parents, which makes the individual struggle with feelings of lack later. Any planet with the Moon will show its indications in some way in the first year of life.

Mars Daśā: Toddlerhood

At approximately the age of one a child starts to walk; they are no longer an infant. Some children will walk a little earlier and some a little later, but the standard is when the child turns one and begins Mars naisargika daśā. If Mars is weak or afflicted the child will be delayed in walking. This will also indicate other issues during the period of Mars and its indications in the chart. Early walking will indicate that Mars is very prominent.

Mars is the kāraka for the third house of parākrama, which indicates how an individual goes about getting things in their life. At this stage the child learns about their will and how to get what they desire. The interaction with siblings will alter this learning and is seen in the argalā of the third and eleventh house (from lagna and ārūḍha lagna). The child is also highly aware of how the parents and other role models act during this period and they directly copy this action. Children learn by imitation, so discipline is best done by example. The parent is the natural authority (Sun/Moon) in the child's life, so it is the parents job to be worthy of imitating and avoid exposing the young child to media which is disrespectful of life. Instead of telling a child not to act a certain way, it is better to show them the right way to act. Children will imitate.

Logic and reasoning do not develop until the second half of Mercury naisargika daśā, so reasoning with your child will get them stuck in their head instead of their heart. Discipline is best done with rhythm (Sun). Consistency and routine is the best way to discipline the mind. At the young age, this starts with eating, napping, and evening rituals being at the same *time* every day. As we grow older, the routine evolves but the rhythm of a schedule grounds our body and mind bringing better health and mental balance. During the period of Mars, the child learns to regulate their body and their actions.

Gender consciousness and an awareness of the opposite sex develop during this

[10] Blanton, *Radical Parenting*. p77

period. Carl Jung says the female toddler identifies with the mother and contrasts herself to the father, while the male toddler contrasts himself to the mother and compares himself to the father. The child will start performing actions according to its understanding of gender roles and will refine these within their play groups.

Children at this age are known for their high level of activity, but the lack of full understanding to play cautiously. This has been called the 'terrible twos' because of the excess activity and lessons of dealing with frustration. In general, Mars has problems with paying attention, this is how accidents happen. During this daśā, the toddler learns to be aware of what they are doing and to apply proper sensitivity to their actions.

In the third year (age 2-3) there is the first awakening of the I-sense. The child becomes an individual and parents must learn to deal with another person being present. In this way, the 'terrible twos' are a time for learning about *boundaries* of the individual and others, and how they relate to on another.

In Moon daśā, the baby's consciousness is connected to the body but surrounding it. The consciousness is manifesting in the material realm but still transitioning from the level of Turiya (Vāsudeva). The infant is in all states of consciousness (auṁ). At this stage, the child hears speech on the level of the frequency it contains, they sense/know what is around them.

Control of the body spreads from the head downwards; first eye control, then holding up the head (neck). Then the arms and spine and the ability to roll over, followed by crawling (hips/knees) and then walking (feet). At each of these stages there is a change in the densification of consciousness that is embodied and a slow manifestation of the awake consciousness (*turīya-jagrat*).

After walking has been accomplished, the next stage (from age 1 to 2) is the development of the first level of talking. At first, speech is an expression of pure desire as the suṣupti level of consciousness. The child says 'mama' as a whole concept, as the level of paśyantī speech, there is no thinking as the word contains everything in it. There is no separation between the child and that which is spoken, everything is still co-related.

Then naming develops which shows the development of the ability to form concepts about an external world that is separate from the individual, though there is not a clear boundary between internal and external yet. The child is living in a dream reality which relates to the svapna level of consciousness. Words invoke the reality of what they represent to the child. Sequences of words develop slowly showing the subtle time of the svapna level, but real individuation is not yet complete.

In the third year (from age 2 to 3) thinking develops. Thinking and conscious memory happens only with language. In the third year, sequential memory (time) and localized memory (space) develop. The jagrat level of consciousness manifests in the development of the sense of self (*ahaṅkāra*). The child starts to use the word "I" and clearly differentiates themselves from others, which creates their boundaries.

Consciousness develops in time; thinking happens in time, with breath. Cogitation (*kalpanā*) is time itself.[11] In this way, consciousness/speech/thinking develop in the child as they develop in the creation of the material world. The Tantras divide each of these states into sub-periods as well. The level of the Jagrat develops through Jagrat-turīya, Jagat-suṣuptī, Jagrat-svapna, and Jagrat-Jagrat which develop the nature of the conscious being. The average individual is aware of only the jagrat-jagrat while the yogin becomes aware of finer and finer levels of consciousness and traces awareness back through them. All sixteen levels of consciousness are present always in the incarnated conscious being.

Mercury Daśā: Childhood

At the age of three a child is aware and *thinking*. They can start actively learning and playing constructively with other children. Most child-care services, such as pre-schools, start caring for the child when Mercury daśā starts. The previous daśā was learning how to use the body and speech on a physical level, but the Mercury daśā takes the learning to a refined mental level of understanding. Physical skills are refined and educational learning is focused on giving the foundation from which any higher learning will stand upon.

During the Mars period, the child wants to play with other children, but they are not ready to accomplish tasks by themselves. As a police officer or soldier (Mars) works within the regulations of a higher authority, so does the child need to be with an elder authority during that phase. In the Mercury period, the child begins to develop independence (*svatantra*). They can accomplish tasks on their own and enjoy doing so. Mercury is the planet of imitation (*anukaraṇa*), and rules theatre and acting. The child interacts with the world and plays in a world of fantasy.

If Mercury is weak or afflicted there will be learning difficulties at this time, inability to accomplish work independently, and communication problems. Mercury rules communication skills. Speech is seen from the second house, the second from AL and the second from Mercury. When these are malefic then there is harsh speech. When Saturn is conjunct or aspecting Mercury, then speech develops slowly. Fine skills, dancing, yoga, and Gaṇeśa pūjā are taught at this age to strengthen Mercury and aid development of the mind.

[11] Dyczkowski, Mark. *Manthānabhairavatantram*, vol. 1, p.399.

Mercury is a neuter planet, and represents the time when children do not focus on their sexuality, they are pre-sexual. Boys and girls can be mixed with no problems during this time. Mercury daśā lasts till puberty begins. Puberty initiation rites found in most cultures help individuals cross from Mercury to Venus daśā.

Venus Daśā: Adolescence

Venus naisargika daśā relates to when puberty starts and sexual differentiation begins. It runs twenty years, from age 12 to 32. The first half relates to physical development, while the second half relates to relationship development (marriage).

When puberty starts, the hormones develop a male or female both physically as well as mentally. Attraction to the opposite sex develops and interaction between male and female becomes a prominent aspect of life. Venus rules the reproductive organs and their development relates to the planet's condition. Some children hit puberty early and others extremely late. Both indicate a problem with Venus.

Mercury daśā represents general study that is foundation for everyone. Venus represents likes and dislikes and it is in Venus daśā that we chose which areas of study we will focus on for career life. The strength of Mercury and Venus are important for one's education in the material world. The strength of Venus and Jupiter are important for professional success.

Venus indicates one's sense of love; to self and to others. Venus indicates an individual's ability to have a healthy relationship and to show affection in a healthy way. The period of Venus is the proper time for an individual to find their spouse and get married. If Venus is afflicted this may not happen, or if it does the marriage may not last. In this way, if Venus is afflicted, one should be much more particular when doing marriage compatibility. Venus placed in the 6th or 8th house of the navāṁśa will tend to delay marriage or cause problems, and in the 12th house may altogether remove the desire to get married or shorten marriage longevity. Malefics in the Upapada lagna will also tend to make an individual remain unmarried. Some astrologers recommend that an individual with a cursed Venus should not get married until after Venus daśā ends and Jupiter begins.

Jupiter Daśā: Family Life

Jupiter daśā starts at age 32 and lasts for 18 years. Previous to this period the focus was on education and enjoying married life. In this stage, the focus becomes the children and having a stable family life. While Venus is a stage in which personal pleasure can be a focus, this is lost in the dharma of living in the world with a family. The marriage is not about personal pleasure but about creating a healthy home for the children. One must take the role to represent the proper dharma as a role model for the next generation.

During Venus, one should have acquired their college education and also their first jobs. In Jupiter, one is stepping into more prominent roles in the workplace, and beginning to live their personal dharma. With more financial prosperity one can support the aspects of life that are important to them; charities, schools, religious institutions, etc. In this period there is an active role about maintaining family and society.

Physically, the metabolism changes and extra weight is easy to gain. The body has reached its fullest growth and begins to decline towards the end of this daśā.

Sun Daśā: Golden Years

The years of the Sun (50-75) are called the golden years, as one has achieved the wisdom of a long life, the comfort of financial stability, and if they have lived healthy, they still have energy to truly appreciate life. In modern society, retirement is accepted around age 65. For a business owner, at the age of 50, the children can be stepping in and running the business. In western society, the business is often not transferred until the parent dies, but in traditional society, it is passed along so the rajas of business can belong to the young. The elders have better things to focus on, like learning spiritual teachings (scriptures, astrology, metaphysics), doing yoga, traveling to mystic places, etc. The cultivation of the soul and its knowledge (*ātmajñāna*) becomes the focus during this time. If the Sun is weak or afflicted, or other non-spiritual combinations exist in the chart, the individual may chose to play golf and go on cruises instead of spiritual pursuits, which can lead to a lost sense of self in later years.

More important than retiring from work is the ability to have time with the grandchildren, to be a guiding light for the future. In traditional societies the entire family is a unit: the self (lagna), the child (5th house), and the parent (9th house). This trine turns through the various generations establishing dharma. Jupiter had represented a support of dharma in the community, while the Sun works for the greater dharma of the world.

Saturn Daśā: Old Age

In Saturn daśā the body is in decay. In Sun daśā, it was manageable, but in Saturn daśā organs stop working properly, limbs slowly lose their capacity, and everything slows down. In Sun daśā it was still possible to keep up with the young, but Saturn limits everyone. The skin dries out and becomes thinner. All the signs of age are present in the body and are in the awareness as a regular part of life.

Ptolemy says 'Saturn, moving in the last sphere, regulates the final old age. He is cold and obstructs the mental movements, the appetites and enjoyments; rendering one stupid and dull, in conformity with the dullness of his own motion'. In this way, disease, suffering and eventually death are the natural indications of Saturn. The pleasures of the world do not have the same value. This is the time to give up desires and illusions of the material world (*moha*) and focus on the spiritual path. A natural unattachment (*vairāgya*) develops. The individual has lived through all the other natural daśā and has seen a complete life.

The female yogin, Sulabha, teaches about unattachment in the Mahābhārata (CCCXXI). On answering who she is to King Janaka, she elaborates about the tattvas of the universe which then compose a human and says that we are all given a body by Prakṛti. She elaborates the stages from conception to birth, and infancy to old age and states that in each stage the form presented changes. The elements of the body are constantly changing and cells are being born and dying in a successive condition that is so minute it cannot be marked as the changes in a flame of a burning lamp cannot be marked. And as the changes don't stop, moving onwards like the rapid movement of a strong bull, which body can a creature be attached to? Individuals in duality see their body as their own body and their soul as their own soul. Why is it that you don't see your body and soul in the body and soul of others?

In this way, in the last daśā of Saturn, one has moved through all the stages of life and seen themselves in many different forms in this one life. The attachment to form is no longer relevant to those who dedicate themselves to spirituality in the last phase. The individual is a manifestation of the universe both physically and mentally, and realizing the essential nature is the focus of Saturn daśā.

These stages are natural to all humans and take only subtle variation according to place and culture. Carl Jung says that whenever phenomena are found to be characteristic of all human communities, it is an expression of an archetype of the collective unconscious. He describes the life stages very similar to the Vedic and Greek views and shows that these are apparent in all human communities known to anthropology and therefore are expressions of the archetypes of shared human consciousness. As Time unfolds consciousness in the beginning of creation, so does Time unfold the natural biological clock which determines how we use our consciousness throughout life; 'All this is Time'.[12] All other daśā are operating within this natural time (*naisargika daśā*).

[12] Śatapatha Brāhmaṇa XI.1.2.12, XIV.3.2.22 *sarvaṁ vai saṁvatsaraḥ*

Basic Interpretation

Naisargika daśā is very easy to interpret as the basic significations are according to the naisargika kārakas, or natural significations of the planets. Venus is love, Mercury is learning, and Saturn is suffering. The time periods of the planets relate to these significations. Strength is taken into account to understand the level those significations will manifest, but house lordship, aspects and such temporal significations are not *prominently* utilized. In this way, it is much simpler than viṁśottarī daśā, though it is looking at a different aspects of life. The kārakas of the planets as well as their associations (*sambandha*) play an important role.

Venus daśā is the time period of love and relationship and in this daśā any period or transit indicating relationship is highly likely to give results. Occasionally people have childhood 'crushes' when they are younger than this (before puberty). This happens when Mercury has a sambandha with Venus, and then the significations of Venus will be seen in the naisargika daśā of Mercury. When Jupiter daśā starts, there is more focus on dharma and social roles. If Venus, the kāraka of love and relationship, has no sambandha with Jupiter then there is little care about love and relationship in the Jupiter naisargika daśā. If an individual has no strong sexual or relationship yogas they will not be interested in getting a relationship during this time. If they are in a relationship, they will shift their focus to significations related to Jupiter and the planets it associates with and partners may feel a lack of passion in the relationship. If Jupiter has a sambandha with Venus then there will continue to be a strong focus on love and relationship during the period from age 30 to 50. In this way, periods and transits that indicate relationship in a Jupiter naisargika daśā with Jupiter having no Venus association are less likely to give the result of relationship. Remedies can be done to bring more Venus energy into the life if the person desires a relationship. If Jupiter is conjunct or aspecting Venus, or in a Venus sign or navāṁśa then there would still be plenty of natural Venus energy to ignite relationship.

If the Sun has no relationship to Venus, then there is a shift in the relationship arena as well. People in relationship will feel a shift away from sexuality. In the West people are conditioned to not want to lose their sexual passion, but lack of a Venus sambandha with the Sun can let it go away and then it is considered a problem. In other cultures, where sexuality is supposed to stop at this age it is considered great. In those cultures, if Venus does have a sambandha with the Sun, then there are problems as the person still seeks love and relationship after the age of 50. The relationship of Saturn and Venus will do the same thing. People that get married in their eighties generally have this sambandha. Someone without a relationship of Sun and Venus will think they are over relationship till they turn seventy and then all of a sudden they start looking at the opposite sex again. The tough situation arises when someone who is 56 and has no Sun Venus relationship in their chart asks you when they will find a partner in their life. Maybe they have a Venus Saturn connection and you can insure them that there will be a partner by their side in old age. Otherwise, they will have to do remedies to bring Venus into their life.

When there is no Venus sambandha during a naisargika daśā and the individual is seeking relationship, they will often face obstacles to find one. It is like swimming upstream, it is possible, but a lot of work. When an individual is in a relationship and a new naisargika daśā takes place which has no Venus sambandha then the individual feels they have lost the passion in their relationship. In this case, it is important to help the person transition into another focus. Often the individual may think it is their partner and leave the relationship, or they may resort to chemical drugs to artificially enhance sexual appetite. In these cases, the individual can do best to redirect their mind to the significations of the naisargika daśā lord and/or the significations of the planets it has sambandha with. For example, if a married man enters Jupiter daśā and there is no sambandha with Venus then the passion lessens in his life. If Jupiter is conjunct Mercury or in the sign of Mercury the individual can focus their energy on education, teaching, writing, or other Mercury related activities. In cases where the individual is not interested in shifting their focus, then Tāntric remedies can be used to help them achieve their goals or to help change their mind (depending on the planet being activated).

The Skanda Purāṇa teaches the naisargika years to indicate the past life origination of our suffering.[13] When a child is between birth and 4 years of age, their suffering relates to the negative karma of the mother (*matṛ doṣa*) and remedial measures are to be done by the mother at this time. This may seem like putting a lot of responsibility on the mother, but if a child is suffering, the mother is also going to suffer, so there is shared karma between the two being played out.

Between the ages of 4 and 12, the karma relates to the father (*pitṛ doṣa*) and remedial measures are to be done by the father. Issues that afflict the child between 12 and 20 relate to negative karma done as a child in the previous life. Suffering between the years of 20 and 32 relate to the bad actions done against the spouse, while suffering during 32-50 relates to negative actions done towards society. Suffering during the 50-70 time period indicate negative karma towards elders or children in the past life. Suffering after 70 is natural, but is worse if one has negative karma against teachers. Just as suffering during these times indicates negative karma from that time period in our last life, blessings during these time periods also relate to good karma we have done during these time periods, or good karma that the parent has done.

[13] Skanda Purāṇa, Bṛhaspati Niti Śāstra as taught by Pandit Sanjay Rath

Antardaśā

The mahādaśā are based on natural human development. They are also called phases (*dāya*) of life. Each phase is again broken down into smaller phases (*antardaśā*) which show more detailed events related to that phase of life. In this way, the antardaśā are used as a *phalita daśā* and help in predictions.

Interpreting the mahādaśā of the naisargika graha is very simple. It is based on the basic significations of the planet and that phase of life. The antardaśā can be used similarly but more emphasis is given to the situation of the planets in the individual chart as the antardaśā are calculated from their placements. When using antardaśā there are more specific rules according to a phalita daśā.

Antardaśa Calculation

The order of the antardaśā is based on a general rule: The planets in kendra exercise their influence in the first part of life, those in the succedent (*paṇapara*) in middle age and those in cadent (*āpoklima*) in old age. In each group the order of precedence is determined according to their strengths. By this method, one can understand the condition in the three parts of life.[14] The antardaśā is first furnished by the strongest planet in kendra (1, 4, 7 & 10 houses) to the mahādaśā lord, then the next strongest. After all the planets in kendra are utilized then planets in paṇapara (2, 5, 8 & 11 houses) will indicate the daśā, and finally the planets in āpoklima (3, 6, 9, 12 houses). The standard rules for how to determine kendrādi daśās in this way are given by Parāśara in the Daśā-adhyāya[15] and Antardaśā-adhyāya.

The length of the naisargika antardaśā is taught by Paraśāra in the Antaradaśā-adhyāya.[16] This is also clarified by Kalyāṇa Varmā of the 10th century in the Antardaśā-phala-adhyāya of *Sārāvalī*.[17] The planets are given a fractional weightage based upon placement from the daśā lord. This gives a proportional variation to the length of the antardaśā in each of the different mahādaśā.

The antardaśā are calculated from the mahādaśā lord, which makes them change order in each daśā (as the kendra are different from each lord). In this way the daśā lord becomes the temporary lagna and indicates how you perceive things through the various phases of life.

[14] Yavanajātaka 1.94-95, Bṛhajjātaka VIII.1-2, Sārāvalī of Kalyāṇa Varmā 41.3-5

[15] Bṛhat Parāśara Horā Śāstra, Daśa-adhyāya v.175-176, 200-202. explained more in the mūla daśā section.

[16] Bṛhat Parāśara Horā Śāstra, Antaradaśā-adhyāya v.13-16

[17] Yavanajātaka 41.2-4, Sārāvalī of Kalyāṇa Varmā 42.1-4, also Horā Makarand 10.4-7.

The house placement from the daśā lord will indicate a percentage to calculate the length of antardaśā of planets. The daśā lord[18] gets a percentage of 1, and planets conjunct the daśā lord get a percentage of ½. The third and tenth houses from the daśā lord get a percentage of ¾, the trines get a 1/3 percentage, while the fourth and eighth houses get a percentage of ¼. The seventh house from the daśā lord is given a 1/7 percentage, and the 2nd, 12th, and 6th, 11th houses have a percentage of 1.

This proportional length of the daśā also gives a special level of interpretation based on those proportions which cannot be used in the normal kendrādi calculations (as seen in mūla daśā). The antardaśā of planets in the second and twelfth house from the daśā lord will bring a financial focus (in a good way if they are benefics). The antardaśā of planets in the third show a struggle to achieve something, and in the tenth will indicate a need to work. Planets in the fourth and eighth will relate to the fourth and eighth house aspect of Mars and protection. The fifth and ninth house planets will relate to the beneficence of Jupiter's aspects; the fifth showing planning based on one's own intelligence and the ninth showing decisions being made based on traditions and society. The antardaśā of planets in the sixth and eleventh can show punishment if they are malefics.

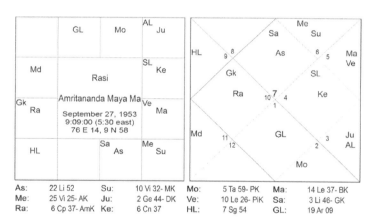

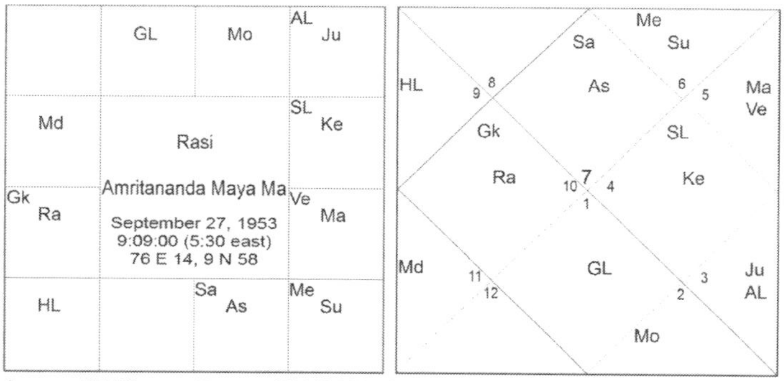

As:	22 Li 52	Su:	10 Vi 32- MK	Mo:	5 Ta 59- PK	Ma:	14 Le 37- BK
Me:	25 Vi 25- AK	Ju:	2 Ge 44- DK	Ve:	10 Le 26- PiK	Sa:	3 Li 46- GK
Ra:	6 Cp 37- AmK	Ke:	6 Cn 37	HL:	7 Sg 54	GL:	19 Ar 09

Jupiter Antardaśā (18 yrs)		
Mercury	¼	01- 00- 14
Jupiter	1	04- 01- 25
Sun	¼	01- 00- 14
Saturn	1/3	01- 04- 18
Moon	1	04- 01- 25
Venus	¾	03- 01- 12
Mars	¾	03- 01- 12

We will work out the calculations on the chart of Amritananda Maya Ma for the mahādaśā and the antardaśā of Jupiter. Jupiter antardaśā has a weight of 1. Moon in the twelfth has the weight of one. Mars and Venus in the third are ¾. Saturn is 1/3, and Mercury and Sun are ¼. Rāhu and Ketu do not have antardaśā here. This ratio is multiplied by the number of months in the daśā (12 X 18 = 216) to give a percentage length (the multiplier) which is then used to calculate the antardaśā:

[18] There is difference in opinion about whether the daśā lord has a daśā or not, therefore software gives you an option to choose to use the daśā lord or not. I use the daśā lord with normal strength rules in the examples.

$\frac{1}{1}+\frac{1}{1}+\frac{3}{4}+\frac{3}{4}+\frac{1}{3}+\frac{1}{4}+\frac{1}{4}=\frac{52}{12}$ $\frac{12}{52}$ X 216 months = 49.8462 months (4yr- 01m- 25d)

Mahādaśā			Jupiter Antardaśā		
Year	**Month**	**Day**	**Year**	**Month**	**Day**
1953	09	27 Moon	1985	09	27 Mercury
+ 01	00	00	+ 01	00	14
1954	09	27 Mars	1986	10	11 Sun
+ 02	00	00	+ 01	00	14
1956	09	27 Merc	1987	10	25 Jupiter
+ 09	00	00	+ 04	01	25
1965	09	27 Venus	1991	12	20 Saturn
+ 20	00	00	+ 01	04	18
1985	09	27 Jupiter	1993	05	08 Mars
+ 18	00	00	+ 03	01	12
2003	09	27 Sun	1996	06	20 Venus
+ 20	00	00	+ 03	01	12
2023	09	27 Saturn	1999	08	02 Moon
+ 50	00	00	+ 04	01	25
2073	09	27	2003	09	27 [Sun]

The simple way to check your math, is that when you add up all the antardaśā they should end exactly when the next mahādaśā is supposed to begin.

The first antardaśā is the strongest planet in kendra from Jupiter, which is exalted Mercury. Then the next strongest is Sun (as it is conjunct an ucca graha) followed by Jupiter (a single planet). Then the strongest planet in paṇapara (2, 5, 8 & 11) from the daśā lord is Saturn as it is the only planet. The strongest planet in āpoklima (3, 6, 9 & 12) is Mars, then Venus, then Moon (as a single planet).

From Jupiter, Mercury is in the fourth house relating to protection. As it is in the twelfth it can show protection of foreign ventures or of the books of spiritual organizations. The next antardaśā is of Jupiter himself showing Jupiter beginning to give his full potential in the ninth house of dharma and pilgrimage. The next antardaśā is the twelfth house Sun which is fourth from Jupiter, indicating again the protection of spiritual teachings going abroad. It shows some setback as the Sun is MKS. Then Mahāpuruṣa Saturn antardaśā is fifth from Jupiter showing planning and steps taken to insure the growth of her organization. Moon is placed twelfth from Saturn in the eighth house indicating in the Moon antardaśā large financial investments for beneficial causes related to the people (Moon) who are suffering (MKS).

We can do a very simple analysis of the Jupiter naisargika mahādaśā for Pandit Sanjay Rath. In the Jupiter mahādaśā and Jupiter antardaśā (1995-08-08) he wrote two of his most important books: *Jaimini Upadeśa Sūtras* and *Crux of Vedic Astrology*. With the passing of his guru, he began to teach astrology publicly. In Mars antardaśā (1999-05-03) Pandit Sanjay Rath worked for the government of India in the department of defense. In the Sun antardaśā (1999-11-17) he first had a small side business with his father and left both that business and his government position to teach Jyotiṣa full time. Jupiter-Sun also produced *Remedies in Vedic Astrology*.

In Venus antardaśā (2001-02-12) his first marriage broke. In Saturn antardaśā (2002-05-14) he dealt with some financial issues of becoming a full time astrologer. He had to change the organization he created and had to battle false accusations. In Mercury antardaśā (2006-02-09) he was remarried and started teaching Jyotiṣa in a new way; with powerpoints and online recorded sessions. In Moon antardaśā (2009-11-10) his living and work situation became very stable and he was able to fully focus on research, writing and teaching.

Integrating Interpretation

The first level of interpretation is very simple and based upon naisargika significations. In the antardaśā of Venus, relationship or marriage is most likely. In the antardaśā of Jupiter, spiritual study or interest is more likely. These antardaśā show what is naturally on the individuals mind and in their life. It is not as specific as other daśās and is best used in combinations with them.

For example, an unmarried older man is asking when he will meet someone special. First see the naisargika daśā to see when things will naturally and easily be available in his life, then study the viṁśottarī (or special daśā) to see when a relationship period overlaps with the naturally indicated time. Then find a time when the transits are also supporting relationship. If these all align then you can surely predict a relationship in that period. If only two of these indications are present then it is a less likely prediction, and if only one is present then there is a small chance of the situation taking place. By learning to use multiple daśās and transits together, one will be able to increase their accuracy of prediction.

In this way, predictions about children, work, education and the natural happenings of life can be seen. Naisargika daśā is a foundational daśā to use before looking at another daśā to see the situation a person is in. It is very clear that we treat a baby differently than a toddler and a toddler different than a teenager. And you would not make the same prediction for them as you would for someone who is in their fifties. In this way, naisargika daśā gives a clear way to tailor the way you give advice to different age groups.

Varāhamihira and the Greeks used the Naisargika daśā as a phalita daśā to give accurate predictions. The situation of the antaradaśā lord are taken into account for this. In the *Tetrabiblos* (IV.10), Ptolemy says 'the natural significations attributable to the various times of life are subject to the place/culture of the people. The particular periods (antardaśā) calculated according to the particulars of the individual's chart are subject to place/culture and also the peculiarities of the individual's chart. These must be determined from the various ascendants, from the whole of them and not from any single one only, similar to the calculation of the duration of the life.' For example, Ptolemy states, 'reading the chart from the rising ascendant we see events that affect the body, travelling, or change of residence. From the part of Fortune we see incidents that affect the substance of wealth. From the Moon we see actions of the mind, marriage, and cohabitation, while from the Sun we see dignities and glory, and from the mid-heaven we see employment, friendship and the possession of children. Therefore, a single planet, benefic or malefic, will not possess sole dominion, as many conflicting events frequently occur in the same period. A person may be ill in health but well in finances, or struggle with finances but beget many children. Situations affect the body, mind, career position, finances which are not all good or bad for all of them unless benefics or malefics line up completely to do so,' which Ptolemy says 'is rare as human nature is generally moderate not extreme'.

Ptolemy says 'the various ascendants must, therefore, be separately distinguished in the mode before pointed out and the planet's position from them taken into consideration'. This is a good rule to remember for viṁśottarī daśā as well.

Natural Antardaśā

There is another system of natural antardaśā in which the years are assigned the same to everyone.[19] In this way, it is similar to planetary maturities, yet the results are judged according the mahādaśā that the antardaśā are within. In this system the house lordships, etc. are not taken into account, it is just the general naisargika indications of the planet relative to the phases of life. This is not prominently used, but I have given an example of Venus naisargika daśā in the chart below, just to give an understanding of the system. Venus rules the age of twelve, Saturn the age of thirteen, and the Sun rules the age of fourteen, etc. I have a great interest in this area but it needs more practical research and correlation to the planetary ages of maturity.

Venus Naisargika Antardaśā			
12	Venus	19, 20	Lagna
13	Saturn	21, 22	Saturn
14	Sun	23, 24	Sun
15	Moon	25, 26	Moon
16	Mars	27, 28	Mars
17	Mercury	29, 30	Mercury
18	Jupiter	31, 32	Jupiter

[19] Sanjay Rath, *Crux of Vedic Astrology* (Sagar Publications), and the Naisargika Daśā handout, Tenth International Symposium on Vedic Astrology in Sedona AZ, 2003.

The maturity of planets has a primary maturity and also secondary maturity.[20] For example, the primary maturity of the Sun is between 21 and 22 years of age. There is also a secondary maturity at 48 and another at age 70. The table below lists these years.

Sun	21,22	48	70
Moon	23,24	5	49
Mars	27,28	10	39
Mercury	31,32	20	54
Jupiter	30,34	24	56
Venus	25,26	6	52
Saturn	35,36	39	82
Rāhu	41,42		
Ketu	45,46		

There is also another set of natural cycles given by the transits of the planets as they are moving through the sky during our life. One can take into account the larger planetary returns. Jupiter has a twelve year cycle creating a Jupiter return (or transit) every 12, 24, 36, and 48 years.

Saturn has a cycle of 29.5 years which gives a cycle of 30, 60, and 90. Rāhu has an 18 year cycle giving a nodal cycle at 18, 36, 54, and 72 years. The nodal cycle can also be divided in half to represent the half nodal return and create twelve 9 year cycles. Those that use Uranus[21] which returns at 84 (two cycles of 42) will also see some results in that year. These are naturally occurring events that happen in every chart, though natural cycles are always modified by the individual chart.

Practice Exercises

1. Calculate the naisargika daśā of your chart and one other. Then calculate the antardaśā of the present daśā and the one before it. See how it correlates to the general events taking place.

2. Lay out the viṁśottarī daśā next to the naisargika to see their interaction. See when malefic periods line up and when benefic times line up.

3. Note these six times: when Jupiter transited directly over the lagna and its opposite point, when Saturn went over the Moon and through the lagna, when Rahu went over the Sun and through the seventh house.

4. Take all these three groups of time and see what lines up and how it affected the events of your life. Do this with one other chart.

5. If you get frustrated at any point, remember Albert Einstein, "Do not worry about your difficulties in Mathematics. I can assure you mine are still greater."[22]

[20] Sanjay Rath, Crux of Vedic Astrology (Sagar Publications).
[21] See Thompson, *The Cosmology o the Bhāgavata Purāṇa*, p. 19-46, 92-107, (with special attention to p.93-94).
[22] Letter to high school student Barbara Lee Wilson (7 January 1943), Einstein Archives 42-606

Naisargika Bhāva Daśā

The houses have a natural time of maturing which is often called *bhāva daśā*. This is based on the understanding of the *Jaimini Sūtras*. It is a very general daśā which is seen for the time of life a yoga will most likely fructify.

Jaimini says that a yoga in the 2nd and 4th house will fructify early in life [3.1.10]. This is extended to include the 7th house from them, so the 2nd, 4th, 8th and 10th give results early in life.

Planets in the 1st, 7th, and 9th will fructify late in life [3.1.9]. This is extended to the seventh from the ninth, so 1st, 3rd, 7th and 9th are seen to give fruit late in life. The other houses (5th, 6th, 11th and 12th) are middle life.

Early	2,4,8,10
Middle	5,6,11,12
Late	1,7,9,3

The specific sequence to these houses within that phase of life is based on maṇḍūka gati (frog movement) and the goal of self-actualization. The first daśā starts with the fourth house of mother. The first experiences are those in the home and with the mother. Then maṇḍūka gati towards the lagna takes one to the second house of the close family (*kuṭumba*). Maṇḍūka gati is the frog jump, so from the fourth, over the third and landing in the second. The direction is towards the lagna or towards self-actualization; nature wants us to know ourselves. The frog does not jump over the lagna so it goes to the seventh house from it: the 8th house relating to the transformation of going out on one's own; becoming an adult. Then maṇḍūka gati towards the lagna gives the next daśā in the tenth house of career. These first 36 years of life are roughly divided into these four houses, which can roughly be given about 9 years each; this is a standard rule with a bhāva daśā.[23]

Then maṇḍūka gati towards the lagna lands in the 12th house. This age (36-45) is where the life is often re-evaluated to try to understand the purpose of why one is here- it is a step of looking at your life from being slightly outside of it. To not jump over the lagna, the next jump is to the 7th house, which is the 6th house. This is the middle of the 108 years of life, and the next house starts with the fifth house. And then goes seventh from there to the 11th house.

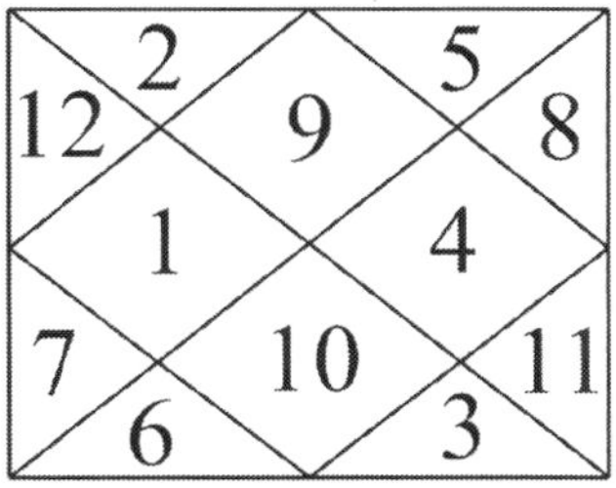

In the last phase of life (72-108) the maṇḍūka gati moves towards the lagna and gives the daśā of the lagna. Then it moves to the 7th from it which is the seventh house. Then maṇḍūka gati towards the lagna gives the ninth house daśā. And the final daśā is the third house which is seventh from the ninth. The third house is 8th from the 8th which relates to the ending of life. These daśā are used to see the likely time a combination will give

[23] If longevity calculations indicate middle life, then the years can be taken to eight per house, and if short life is indicated then the years are taken to seven.

results in life. As a bhāva daśā it shows when circumstances (the area of life) support the event. It is used along with other daśā just as the naisargika graha daśā. Things need to line up with the other daśā and the more they line up, the more likely they are to happen.

The daśā of nine years can be divided into three parts. The first portion gives more the results of the house/sign. The middle portion gives the results of the lord, and the last portion gives the results of the planets in the sign and their aspects. This is a standard way to interpret rāśi daśā. The benefic results are more likely in the beginning of the daśā and the malefic results are more likely at the end of the daśā.

The naisargika bhāva daśā is calculated using Rāhu's maṇḍūka gati. Rāhu indicates that which we desire and our actions towards the fulfillment that desire. The naisargika bhāva daśā therefore indicates the likely time for the fructification of the yogas that help one achieve their desires in life.

There is another way to progress through the signs in a linear zodiacal manner to indicate the unfolding of life's experiences. In this daśā, the first house relates to the first year, the second house relates to the second year, and so on. The forward zodiacal movement (*parivṛtti*) is related to Saturn (Brahmā) and indicates naisargika results of the houses and the planets placed therein.

The first twelve years (first twelve houses) are like layers of an onion. They stay with us, build us, and make us who we are being. The experiences that happen in the first twelve years create the perspective in which we view the reality we live in. If Saturn is in the second house, there is an experience of lack in the second year. If Mars is in the fifth house, there is an experience of frustration or anger in the fifth year that shapes how one relates to their life. The next cycle through these houses, is built upon the original layers already present and attracts reflections of these experiences.

When this natural zodiacal (*parivṛtti*) unfoldment of the chart is seen from the lagna, Moon and Sun at the same time it indicates the multiple levels of where events affect us on the body, mind and soul levels of being. This daśā is called Sudarśana Cakra daśā and is seen in a special cakra.

Sudarśana Cakra

Parāśara teaches the Sudarśana Cakra as secret superior knowledge (*rahasyaṁ jñānam-uttamam*) taught by Brahmā for the welfare of the world.[24] A triple circle is divided by twelve. The inner circle has the planets placed from lagna. The second circle has the Moon placed above the lagna and the planets placed therefrom. Then the Sun is put in the final circle above the Moon and the planets placed therefrom. In this way, every house of the cakra will have three signs [v.5-6]. The first house, the Sun and Moon all get combined and the planets are seen from all of them.

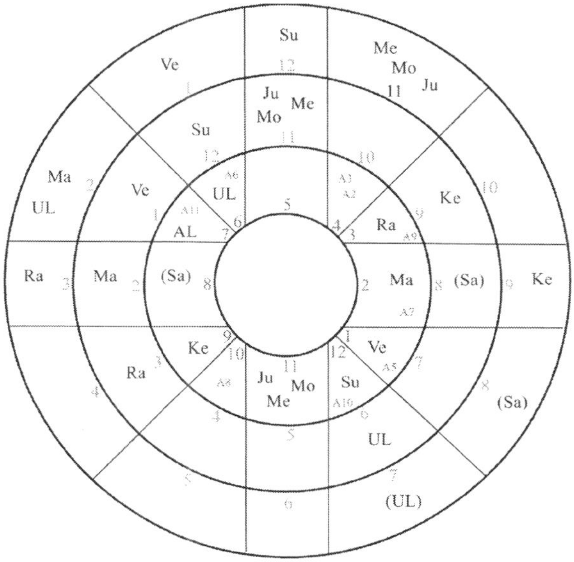

All the ārūḍhas are calculated in the first circle. Tradition teaches that the upapada (A12) from lagna shows how you give in this world. The Candra-upapada is added to the lunar circle; this is the ārūḍha of the twelfth from the Moon. The Sūrya-upapada is added to the outer circle. These will show giving on the level of the body, mind and soul.

Parāśara says to first analyze the benefic and malefic nature of the planets, adding that malefic planets in their own sign or exaltation are not to be treated as inauspicious [7-9]. The results of the combined houses depend on the occupation and aspects to that house. The aspect and presence of a benefic in a house or its own lord will make a house prosper. The aspect and presence of malefics will cause loss or decrease (*hāni*) in that area of life [10].

Therefore if benefics are in a house that area of life will prosper. If there are malefics in a house, that area of life will suffer. If there are both, then results we be according to whichever benefic or malefic are more in number, and if equal number then whichever is stronger will predominate. If there are no planets then take into account aspects. If by chance there are no aspects take into account the significations of the sign lords [11-14].

Parāśara teaches that the benefic and malefic nature of the planets should be studied in the saḍvargas (six divisional charts). Planets in benefic or own signs and exaltation make it give good results. Planets in enemy or cruel signs and debilitation will give negative results [15-16].

[24] Bṛhat Parāśara Horā Śāstra, Sudarśana-cakra-phala-adhyāya, v.1

In the example chart of Cesar Chávez, he was born in a Jupiter viṁśottarī daśā and entered Saturn at the age of four. His parents started to have financial hardships because of the depression. They lost their home in his 11th year (with Rāhu and Ketu), and moved to California in his 12th year. In his 15th year (4th house daśā) his father had an accident and he dropped out of school to work in the fields. Here we see the line-up of Saturn, Mars and Rāhu destroying his childhood education. He joined the Navy in his 17th year (6th house daśā). After he entered Mercury vimśottarī daśā, he began his Unionizing career. He became the organizer for the CSO in the daśā of the second house containing his Sun from Moon. He became the CSO's national director in the daśā of the 8th house containing the Sun from Lagna. The Ketu viṁśottarī daśā started and the next daśā of the 8th house imprisoned him by the government for challenging an injunction on a boycott. In this way, we see how the Sudarśana Cakra is helping to indicate results.

Calculation of Daśā

The first year of life starts in the first house, and at the birthday moves to the second house. Each year progresses through one house, and repeats at the age of 13, then again at age 25. The house of the mahādaśā becomes the ascendant for that year and the rest of the chart is read from there. So in the 28th year, the mahādaśā is coming from the 4th house from lagna-Sun-Moon. The fifth house will be seen for second house significations for that year, the 8th house will be seen for 5th house significations for that year, etc.

The antardaśā will be given to one house for each month of the year. So the first month of the year will be the same house as the mahādaśā, the second month will be the second from that house, and so on. Then starting from the house of t he antardaśā, the twelve houses can again be divided into 2½ days for calculating the pratyantardaśā. And for a deeper fine tuning the śūkṣmadaśā can divide the houses into 5 hours from the pratyantardaśā house [21-23].

	Degree	Bālādi Avasthā
a	0-6	Infant (*bāla*)
ī	6-12	Youth (*kumara*)
u	12-18	Adolescent (*yuva*)
e	18-24	Adult (*vridha*)
o	24-30	Old (*mṛta*)

Pañca Svara daśā and Sandhya daśā are used along with the Sudarśana Cakra to indicate the variations every twelve years. They help indicate the difference between year 12, 24, 36, etc. Pañca svara daśā[25] relates to the five primary vowels; a, ī, u, e, o. Each of these vowels, in order, correspond to one of the five bālādi avasthā: infant (*bāla*), youth (*kumara*), adolescent (*yuva*), adult (*vridha*), old (*mṛta*). Depending on the first vowel in the name, one of these avasthā will be activated for twelve years. After which the next cycle of the Sudarśana Cakra will commence with the proceeding avasthā. The planets with the same avasthā will be

[25] Bṛhat Parāśara Horā Śāstra, Daśā-adhyāya, v.191-194, 204

activated and others will act within that state. The first letter of the name will not only start the cycle but it will show which planets are more strongly guiding the mind.

In this way, the name Priya has the Sanskrit sound 'I' as the first vowel, which is in youth avasthā. Planets in the youth avasthā will become strong. On the thirteenth year, the planets in adolescence will become more prominent, followed by planets in adult on the third cycle of the Sudarśana cakra. If there is a name change, the daśā cycle will become that of the new name for twelve years, and the cycle will continue onwards from that new name vowel. If Priya changed her name to Rudraṇī at age 20, then she enters an adult phase till age 32. In this way, Sudarśana daśā can be further refined.

Interpretation

Sudarśana Cakra can be analyzed on many levels. The first is a simple way of observing patterns happening in the individual's life. For example, an individual who has an afflicted dark Moon in the 12th house was suicidal at the age of 12 and then had a very hard time at the age of 24 and again experienced suicidal tendencies and deep depression at the age of 36. Each time it was slightly different but the general darkness was experienced deeply at these times. In this way, we can see how some planets are repetitively being activated every twelve years. In this way, we can predict another episode happening in her 48th year. Using the chart in this simple way, we see the planets being activated by the years of the Sudarśana Cakra, but they will give results according to their house placement from the lagna. In this way, houses are in the same year, not the same house.

The Sudarśana Cakra can be used for longevity calculations (*āyurdāya*) under the age of 24. The first cycle of 12 (*bālāriṣṭa*) will show health issues in the first part of life according to indications from the lagna and Moon. The second cycle (*janmariṣṭa*) will show health issues from the lagna and Sun. Health issues will happen at the age indicated by the afflicted house. Getting over severe issues can also be seen in the year when the house containing benefics, which give relief from an affliction, are activated.

The Sudarśana Cakra can be used for spiritual purposes. The first level is called sucakra, the second level is called vicakra and the third level is called mahācakra, while together they are the Sudarśana Cakra held by Viṣṇu. The lagna upapada shows how we get close to our spouse /children/family, the Candra upapada shows how we get close to community/society, and the Sūrya upapada shows how we get close to god/universe. They are the three steps of Viṣṇu to come near to him and make everything god's family. When the lagna UL is active it shows a debt needed to be paid to the spouse or family (*ṛṣi-ṛṇa*). When the Candra UL is activated it shows a debt that needs to be paid to the community in service (*pitṛ-ṛṇa*). When the Sūrya UL is activated, it shows a debt needed to be paid to the devas (*deva-ṛṇa*). Understanding these debts will help one understand why certain things are happening and the area of service to help the situations in life flow better.

First we can see the results of the houses being activated. Then for more qualitative analysis of the daśā we can read it as a rāśi daśā. In this way, Parāśara then repeats some of the general rules for specific interpretation of a rāśi daśā [24-26]. The results of the daśā are to be seen *from* the daśā rāśi.

> Benefics in trines, angles and 8th house give good results.
> The houses of Rāhu and Ketu suffer loss.
> A house with many malefics is destroyed.
> Benefics give good results in all houses except the 6th and 12th.
> Malefics give good results in the 3rd, 6th and 11th houses.

Benefics give excellent results when in a trine or angle from the daśā rāśi; that house's significations will prosper. If the mahādaśā is of the fourth house, then a benefic in the eighth and twelfth house from lagna will give good results in that daśā, as they are in the 5th and 9th (trines) from the fourth house. For example, a child is likely in the period of the mahādaśā in the ninth from Jupiter, because the fifth from the daśā rāśi is a benefic like Jupiter. The house with Rāhu and that with many malefics lining up will give negative results in that area of life. Benefics will make everything prosper and in the sixth and twelfth they make your enemies and secret enemies prosper which isn't good. In business, this would mean that your competition may outdo you, or in legal situations that the opponent will win. Malefics in the third, sixth and eleventh give the energy (*parākrama*) to accomplish things and overcome obstacles. Reading these significations from the daśā rāśi will give a qualitative nature of the daśā.

Maitreya asks Parāśara, "When we can make predictions from the Sudarśana Cakra, why do other sages teach results from the lagna?" Parāśara says that if the Sun or Moon (or both) are in the lagna then one should just read the chart from the lagna. Only when all these three points are in different houses is one to use the Sudarśana Cakra [18-20]. The Sudarśana Cakra takes into account the houses from lagna, the Moon, and the Sun. When we use the house progression technique then we are to see the houses from each of these, therefore we combine them. There are other daśās that start from the stronger of the Lagna, Sun *or* Moon, but this daśā progression is read from all three together, unless two line up which will naturally make them more prominent.

Conclusion

The sages have taught that there is nothing outside the year[26] or the year is everything.[27] Time is turning and manifesting everything we experience. The years are manifesting the nature of our thoughts, and the nature of the choices we make. On an external level the years are manifesting the quality of the yearly harvest, the prices of food and resources, and the political situations of the world. Understanding the natural progression of the yearly cycles of an individual will help understand where the individual is in their life and set a strong foundation for using all other daśās which will aid an astrologer's ability to make accurate predictions.

We looked at three natural daśās. Naisargika graha daśā shows the planets ruling the natural biological maturity of an individual. This shows the natural clock revealing the physical situation and consciousness that will come with those time periods. Its use will be like gold when you are accustomed to it. Naisargika bhāva daśā shows the very broad time periods when various yogas may fructify in life. It is not used much because of its broadness, but it will help add in factors when trying to make a tough Judgment. Sudarśana Cakra daśā shows the yearly unfolding of the chart, house by house. It is a daśā that takes some time to understand, but by being aware of it, you can begin observing its results. These are ways to see time naturally moving in the chart, or to watch time growing us; taking us to where we are going.

In the Mahābhārata, Bhīṣma teaches that the followers of Saṅkhya attain liberation by watching the "courses of seasons, the fading of years, of months, of fortnights, and of days, beholding directly the waxing and the waning of the Moon, seeing the rising and the ebbing of the seas, and the diminution of wealth and its increase once more, and the separation of united objects, the lapse of Yugas, the destruction of mountains, the drying up of rivers, the starting of lineages and their deterioration occurring repeatedly, beholding the birth, decrepitude, death, and sorrows of creatures, knowing truly the faults attaching to the body and the sorrows to which human beings are subject, and the alternation to which the bodies of creatures are subject, and understanding all the faults that attach to their own souls, and also all the inauspicious faults that attach to their own bodies."[28]

By watching the transitory nature of all things in Time, we learn to not be attached to that which will go away. We then begin the search for that which is beyond the transitory world. Unless we unattach ourselves to the transitory (*prakṛti*) we will not be able to find

[26] Jaiminīya Brāhmaṇa II.335, 339, 341, 346, 353, 355, 361 *na hi kiñcana bahiḥ saṁvatsarāt asti*

[27] Śatapatha Brāhmaṇa XI.1.2.12, XIV.3.2.22 *Sarvaṁ vai saṁvatsaraḥ*, XIII.4.1.5, XIII.5.1.4, XIII.5.3.11 *Sarvaṁ saṁvatsaraḥ*, SB XII.8.2.36 *idaṁ sarvaṁ saṁvatsaraḥ*, and Jaiminīya Brāhmaṇa I.27, II.334 *saṁvatsaro vā idaṁ sarvam*

[28] Mahābhārata, Śānti Parva CCCII

the unchanging which is beyond (*puruṣa*). By understanding these cycles of time an astrologer has the ability to see the transitory nature of the world and the hand of a greater power at work. The ability to differentiate the field (*kṣetra*), which is the transitory world, from the knower of the field (*kṣetrajña*) is considered true knowledge (*jñāna*).[29]

[29] Bhagavad Gītā XIII.2

Chapter 4

Gunas

"When the observer (*draṣṭā*) perceives nothing
other than the guṇas as the doer,
and knows that which is higher than the guṇas,
he approaches the Supreme Being.
That one attains the Supreme Being (*madbhāva*).
-Bhagavad Gītā (XIV.19)"

The Guṇas of Material Nature

"Tamo-guṇa people have nothing to do. Rajo-guṇa people have too much to do. Sattva people have the right amount of work to do. That is the difference. Sattva guṇa is those people who have a perfect 24 hours. That is the perfect day. God has made the correct day for us. Have you ever heard someone say that? No. The day you hear someone say that, know that he is in perfect sattva guṇa. The correlation of time and the guṇas is very important because time is what is running us. Time is our controller. We are totally controlled by time. Time alone is the boss. So like this all these planets cause us to have different gunas."[2]

Time separates Puruṣa and Prakṛti and therefore gives birth to the guṇas which create the world. The movement of Time disturbed the balance of the Supreme and led to the creation of the manifest world.The Mahābhārata says that 'in the same way as men can light thousands of lamps from but a single lamp, Prakṛti, by modification of the guṇas, multiplies into thousands of existent objects from the Puruṣa'.[3] Prakṛti is the three guṇas, not a separate entity containing the guṇas.[4] All things in the universe are made from Prakṛti (the guṇas) and therefore nothing is without guṇa.

Tamas is heaviness densifying into thefive elements to create the physical nature of things. Rajas is the fast moving creative energy of life which, according to Parāśara, creates the indriyas that allow us to interact with the world. Sattva is balanced, sustaining energy which gives consciousness to all things. These three attributes create the manifest world and are needed for the creation, sustenance, and transformation of all activities in life.

Rajas	Sattva	Tamas
Creative, quick/rushed, greedy, desire filled, Not enough time in the day	Sustaining, balanced, high consciousness, truthful, clear, Perfect amount of time	Destructive, dull, slow, thoughtless, unconscious, Boredom,
Venus, Mercury	Sun, Moon, Jupiter	Mars, Saturn, *nodes*

The planets relate to the three guṇas. The sattvic planets (Sun, Moon and Jupiter) sustain life and bring harmonious benefit to one's life. The Sun provides resources and is regular and dependable. The Moon supports and nourishes life. And Jupiter shows the proper use of our intelligence which includes proper use of energy, resources, learning, children and fulfilling our dharma to make the world a better place.

---

[2] Rath, Sanjay. Opening lecture 0016

[3] Mahābhārata , Book 12, Śānti Parva CCCXIV

[4] Vedānta Pañcadaśī of Śrī Vidyaranya Svami I.15, and Sāṅkhya Kārikā 11,and Sāṅkhya-Pravachana SūtraVI.39 *sattvādīnāṁ-atat-dharma-tvaṁ tat-rūpa-tvāt,*

The rajas planets use energy to bring creativity into our life. Venus has creative energy through living beings, in love, sex, and sensory enjoyment. Mercury has creative energy through material things like business, business products, information, books, magazines, etc. Most issues that people have are around these two areas of life (relationship and work) as this is the rajas that is running the mind amuck.

The tamas planets transform life by removing the old and making room for the new. Mars just follows orders (without contemplation). He breaks the material world and makes/engineers new objects. Saturn uses time, aging and disease to finish the life span and allow for rebirth. Saturn makes us forget, he makes us lazy, and he makes us uncaring so that the negative things in the world are possible to happen.

An important differentiation is made in the physical plane of the five elements. The pṛthvī (earth) and jala (water) represent tamas; tejas (fire) and vāyu (air) represent the rajas guṇa. While on the subtle plane, the earth (Mercury) and water (Venus) represent rajas and the air (Saturn) and fire (Mars) represent tamas guṇa. The rājasika planets move the tamas elements, and the tāmasika planets move the rajas elements. Only Jupiter who represents the ākāśa is both sattva in his nature and in his element.

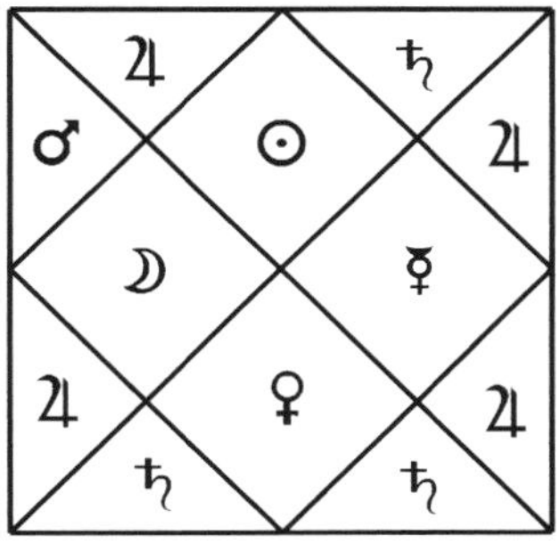

The inner (*antara*) planets, situated between the Earth and the Sun [Sun, Moon, Venus and Mercury], are sattva and rajas in nature. As inner planets (*antargrahas*), they significate the kendra of the chart. The lagna is signified by Sun, the fourth house by the Moon, the seventh house by Venus, and the tenth house by Mercury. The outer (*bāhya*) planets, which are those that move slower than the Sun, are Mars, Jupiter, and Saturn. These planets are sattva and tamas. Therefore, rajas is inside and fast, and tamas is outside and slow, while sattva is on both sides. The outer planets (*bāhyagrahas*) significate all houses other than kendra. Jupiter is the bhāva kāraka of the 2nd, 5th, 9th and 11th, Mars is the kāraka of the 3rd house, and Saturn is the bhāva kāraka of the 6th, 8th, and 12th houses.

The deepening of our understanding of the guṇas is very important to deepen our practice of astrology in both predictions as well as in giving proper remedial measures. First, we understand how the guṇas create reality, then how they work in the external world and then how they are perceived within a human being. One can contemplate the various indications of the guṇas discussed here. One can meditate upon them and bring a deep natural intelligence about the guṇas within themselves.

The Mahābhārata gives a list of qualities which springs from each guṇa:[5]

Sattva	Rajas	Tamas
Patience, joy, prosperity, satisfaction, brightness of all faculties, happiness, purity, health, contentment, faith, liberality, compassion, forgiveness, firmness, benevolence, equanimity, truth, keeping obligations, mildness, modesty, calmness, external purity, simplicity, observance of obligatory practices, dispassionateness, fearlessness of heart, disregard for good and evil in present and past acts, appropriation of objects only when obtained by gift, the absence of lust, regard for the interests of others, compassion for all creatures	Pride of personal beauty, assertion of lordship, war, disinclination to give, absence of compassion, enjoyment and enduring of happiness and misery, pleasure in speaking ill of others, indulgence in quarrels and disputes of every kind, arrogance, discourtesy, anxiety, indulgence in hostilities, sorrow, appropriation of what belongs to others, shamelessness, crookedness, disunions, roughness, lust, wrath, pride, assertion of superiority, malice, and slander	Confusion of judgment, obscuration of every faculty, darkness (death) and blind darkness (wrath), greediness in respect to all kinds of food, ceaseless appetite for both food and drink, taking pleasure in scents and robes and sports and beds and seats and sleep during the day,slander and all kinds of acts proceeding from heedlessness, taking pleasure from ignorance, and aversion for every kind of religion

The guṇa of the mind is determined based upon an individual's repeated actions. If certain actions are constantly repeated then it shows this guṇa is predominant.[6] No one is in only one guṇa all the time, but there is a predominant quality of action. Therefore if a pure and sāttvika doctor, who lives a balanced life, has a tāmasika food item once a week, it will not make him tāmasika. In the same way, if a tāmasika individual goes to temple occasionally it will not mean they are sāttvika. That which is the standard action of the individual is the guṇa they are within.

Suśruta says those whose minds are strong and sāttvika are not easily imbalanced by their environment; they control themselves. Those whose minds are rājasika will need the help of others to support them in balance and those who are tāmasika don't even try to stay in balance.[7]

Strength	Indication
sahaja bala	natal Moon
kālaja bala	daśā, age, season
yuktikṛta bala	lagna, lagneśa

Within the chart, there are three factors indicating the strength and guṇa of the mind.[8] The *sahaja bala* is the natural constitutional guṇa of the mind given at birth, which is indicated by the natal Moon. The

[5] Mahābhārata , Book 12, Śanti Parva CCCXIV
[6] Caraka Saṁhitā, Sūtrasthāna VIII.6
[7] Suśruta Saṁhitā, Sūtrasthāna XXXV.37-38
[8] Caraka Saṁhitā, Sūtrasthāna XI.36

kālaja bala is the temporal state of guṇa indicated by the individual's present daśā, age and season. The kālaja bala will change according to the guṇa of the planet presiding over the daśā period and this will vary in different parts of the life according to the type of daśā being utilized. And then there is the *yuktikṛta bala* which is the guṇa acquired by the choices one makes in daily life, which is indicated by the lagna and lagneśa.

The Bhagavad Gītā (XVI) first explains the two paths of humans; those which aim for the light (*dāivīm*) and those which walk towards the darkness (*āsurīm*). Then the Bhagavad Gītā (XVII and XVIII) gives a lengthy discussion on the various qualities of the three guṇas. Here is an abbreviatedsection listing the attributes concerning the guṇas:

Sattva	Rajas	Tamas
Foods promoting life, truth, strength, health, happiness and satisfaction that are pleasant tasting, smooth, firm, and hearty. (17.8)	Foods that are pungent, sour, salty, excessively hot, harsh, and burning. Foods that cause pain, sorrow and disease. (17.9)	Foods that are stale, tasteless, putrid, and left-over. Food that has impurities within it. (17.10)
Prayer or sacrifice which is done according to scriptures, with offerings and done without thought of reward. (17.11)	Prayer or sacrifice offered with view of the reward or out of hypocrisy. (17.12)	Prayer or sacrifice without faith, disregarding scripture, without offerings, not using traditional prayers (*mantra*), and without donation. (17.13)
A gift given only with the thought "to be given" to a worthy person at the proper time and place. (17.20)	A gift given drudgingly, with aim of compensation, thinking about what one will get. (17.21)	A gift given with contempt, without paying respects, to an unworthy person, at the wrong time or place. (17.22)
Knowledge that sees the One in all beings; sees the undivided in the divided. (18.20)	Knowledge which separates different kinds among all beings. (18.21)	Knowledge attached to one object of action without concern for motive, and with small or no real purpose.(18.22)
Action which is controlled, free of attachment, performed without liking or disliking, and without desiring fruit. (18.23)	Action done with desires, with much effort and selfishness. (18.24)	Action undertaken because of delusion, disregarding consequences and loss or injury to others, as well as one's own strength. (18.25)
Action done because it is one's duty, in a disciplined manner, unattached to getting something from it. (18.9)	Not performing one's duty merely because it's difficult or fear of physical discomfort. (18.8)	Not performing one's duty because of delusion (*moha*), [seeing others as separate and not part of a whole]. (18.7)
Released of attachment, free from talk of self, steadfast, with perseverance, and unperturbed by success or failure. (18.26)	Passionate, desiring fruits of action (*karmaphala*), greedy, violent-natured, impure, and filled with joy or sorrow. (18.27)	Undisciplined, vulgar, stubborn, deceitful, lazy, depressed, and procrastinating. (18.28)
Firmness/resolution which holds the mind, prāṇa and sense functions focused. (18.33)	Firmness/steadfastness which clings to dharma, kāma, and artha with the desire to get something. (18.34)	Firmness that does not remove sleeping too much, fear, grief, depression and conceit. (18.35)
Understanding when to act and when not to act, what is to be done and what is not to be done, what is to be feared and what is not to be feared. (18.30)	Understanding which distinguishes incorrectly between right and wrong, what is to be done and what is not to be done. (18.31)	Unclear understanding, imagines right to be wrong and things are mixed up. (18.32)

The Bhagavad Gītā talks about the three qualities of austerities (*tapasya*) which are self-disciplines for personal and spiritual growth. The Gītā lists three types of sāttvika tapasya related to the body, mind and soul. The tapasya of the body (XVII.14) is cleanliness (*śāucam*), honesty/directness/straightness (*ārjava*), continence (*brahmacarya*), and non-violence (*ahiṁsa*), as well as reverencing god (*deva*), priests (*dvija*), teachers and the wise. The tapas of speech/soul (XVII.15) is using words that do not cause distress, truthfulness (*satya*), agreeableness, and recitation [of sacred texts]. The tapas of the mind (XVII.16) is mental tranquility or clarity, gentleness (*saumya-tva*), quietness (*mauna*), self-control, and purity of being. These may sound simple, but to stay vigilant in day to day life and hold oneself constantly to this level of integrity is hard work. These self-disciplines purify the body, mind and soul and allow us to grow personally and spiritually, which brings sattva into one's being.

Self-disciplines	
Body	cleanliness, honesty, brahmacarya, non-violence, reverencing god, priests, teachers and the wise
Mind	mental tranquility, gentleness, quietness, self-control, and purity of being.
Soul	using words that do not cause distress, truthfulness, agreeableness, and recitation [of sacred texts].

Self-disciplines, which are for the sake of being respected, honored or done with hypocrisy, are rājasika (XVII.18). An example of hypocrisy is the priest that denounces sexuality but has a girlfriend or worse on the side. It is not having the girlfriend that is theprimary issue, but it is acting like one is self-disciplined about it and not truly upholding it, which is deceitful (*dambha*). Trying to be austere is noble, but there is nothing wrong with being humble about when we fail. Humility, which is an austerity, is more beneficialfor the spiritual path than deceit for the sake of honor and respect. The desire to look good in the eyes of others, which compromises our truth, is rājasika. What is achieved in a false way is called unsteady (*cala*) and impermanent (*adhruva*) as the facade will be seen through at some point in time (most likely in a negative Saturn transit).

Self-disciplines which are done with deluded, confused, or foolish (*mūḍha*) notions of the self,or torturing [oneself], or with the aim of destroying another are tāmasika. Self-disciplines which have no logical sense, or are done to make oneself better than another, or are done with no understanding are tāmasika. There are various physically painful practices which are more masochistic than spiritual, and they do not treat the body as a temple which has been given to one nor do they appreciate the being inside. A desire for self-mortification or self-annihilation is not the same as a desire for merging into the Supreme (which is a Supreme love). There are also various self-disciplines that can be done to gain special powers (*siddhi*) and be better than someone else, or to hurt someone, or to get what you want unfairly or without another's consent. Tapasya for this purpose is done with a very gross intention and filled with desire that generates lots of karma and another birth filled with weak or cursed planets. Curses are caused by Mars, Saturn and Rāhu; the tāmasika planets. It is tāmasika actions from our past births that make us suffer the most in this life.

The practice of the sāttvika self-disciplines will increase our sattva, giving us greater clarity and allowing us to make the decisions that guide ourselves and others in the highest path. Sattva is something that all people aspire to, from deep within. But not everyone is a saint. Every person is in the place that they are in for a reason, and understanding this isimportant for sattva in our own mind. Considering another 'wrong' is tāmasika, and wanting to change another is rājasika. The Gītā (III.26) says we should not disturb others about the way they live but help them enjoy (*joṣa*) their life while living our own life in a disciplined way. In this way, we accept people as they are and don't focus *outwardly* on them, but focus *inwardly* on our own self. By living a life of sattva, we inspire others with who we are, not by looking down on them or trying to make them change.

To blame others is tāmasika, while taking responsibility for one's situation is sattva. Iyengar explains this according to the doctrine of yoga and says, "For a wrong done by others, men demand justice; while for that done by themselves they plead for mercy and forgiveness. The yogi, on the other hand, believes that for a wrong done by himself, there should be justice, while for that done by another there should be forgiveness. He knows and teaches others how to live. Always striving to perfect himself, he shows them by his love and compassion how to improve themselves."[9] We must be filled with compassion, and understand that others are where they are right now because of karma, and they are being moved by the guṇas of that karma.

As astrologers we can see the state and fluctuation of the guṇas in the chart and through the daśās. The Gītā (III.27) says that "In all cases, actions are performed by the guṇas of material nature". The guṇas are ruling the mind and the mind is making choices on how to act. Therefore, we must be aware to not be attached to the guṇas, or to let them cloud our vision, but to see the person for the divine that is within them.

The divine spark is the same (*sama*) in everyone and not more or less. Śrī Acyutānanda Dāsa teaches that as astrologers, we need to focus on that divinity inside of ourselves and others. He teaches that when giving a consultation to a person, we must first see the lord (*bhagavan*) in their heart. Then we can begin the reading; after we have recognized the divinity in them. The Gītā says, that which is 'undivided' is divided, it is the light of lights,[10] and seated in the hearts of all beings (XIII.16-17).One who sees (*paśyati*) the Supreme Lord (*parameśvaram*) alike in all beings, not perishing when they perish, truly sees (*paśyati*) (XIII.27). As astrologers (*jyotiṣi*) we aim to see (*paśyati*) the light (*jyoti*) of lights (*jyotiṣa*).

9 Iyengar, B.K.S. p.32
10 Bhagavad Gītā XIII.17 *Jyotiṣāṁ api taj jyotis*

Those who have incomplete knowledge are deluded (*mūḍha*) by the guṇas of material nature (*prakṛti*) and are attached to the actions of the guṇas, the one who 'knows the whole' should not disturb others (III.29).We must have love and acceptance of people as they are so we can truly see them and allow them to feel heard.

This does not mean one should allow oppression or abuse of another being. B.K.S Iyengar speaking about ahiṁsa says, "The yogi opposes the evil in the wrong-doer, but not the wrong-doer. He prescribes penance not punishment for a wrong done. Opposition to evil and love for the wrong-doer can live side by side. A drunkard's wife whilst loving him may still oppose his habit. Opposition without love leads to violence; loving the wrong-doer without opposing the evil in him is folly and leads to misery. The yogi knows that to love a person whilst fighting the evil in him is the right course to follow. The battle is won because he fights it with love." In this way, love and acceptance does not mean inaction (which would be tāmasika). But it does mean we must focus on our own practice, accept people as they are and see the divine in them. By respecting someone at that level, we open the doorway for them to grow, and invite them into the sattva that we ourselves have attained. At the same time we remember that the guṇas make everything happen.

Relativity of the Guṇas

Yājñavalkya says that sometimes rajas is seen existing with sattva, tamas existing with rajas, tamas with sattva, or rajas, tamas and sattva together.[11] That which is pure sattva is of the realm of the devas, that which is pure tamas is in the mineral realm, that which is rajas and tamas is in the animal realm and that which is mixed is in the human realm. In this way, everything is a mix of the guṇas with a predominance of certain guṇas.

It is important to understand that the guṇas are relative. Reading books may be a sāttvika activity, but within that, there is consciousness-expanding literature which is sāttvika, romance novels which are rājasika, and illicit jargon that is tāmasika. Sex may be a rājasika activity, but within that, there is loving sex with one's spouse that is sāttvika, pleasure seeking sexual activity that is rājasika, and base practices with random partners that is tāmasika. War is a tāmasika activity, but within that, there is war for defending a just neighbor which is sāttvika, war for monetary gains which is rājasika and senseless war born from misunderstanding which is tāmasika. In this way, within actions there can be variations of all the guṇas. This variation can continue down into tertiary levels as well.

Material things are also divided into these various levels. Jyotiṣa may be a sāttvika brāhman activity, but within that, there is spiritual Jyotiṣa for self-growth which is sāttvika, and business Jyotiṣa which is rājasika, and then the use of astrology for black

[11] Mahābhārata , Book 12, Śānti Parva CCCXV

magic and overcoming enemies which is tāmasika. But what if the astrology is being used to help a good king overcome his evil enemies? In this way, there are many levels.

Meat is considered tāmasika but within that there are certain meats which are sāttvika. Yājñavalkya and Manu Smṛti as well as Patañjali, Caraka and Suśruta all discuss the animals that can be eaten and those that are to be avoided.[12] Fish is considered more sāttvika than red meat. Of the sāttvika fish, the Rohi (a type of carp) is an herbivore considered the most sāttvika, while other types of fish fall into another tertiary group. Of red meat the gentle herbivore deer is considered the most sāttvika. For people eating a diet heavy in red meat, to eat deer instead of cow is a recognizable step towards sattva.

The guṇa will also be relative to the individual station as well. For the weak and emaciated Caraka says to feed them certain meats, or meat soups. In wasting diseases, Caraka recommends eating the meat of carnivores and drinking wine to help digest it. For an emaciated individual or one with a wasting disorder, the meat is becoming a medicine and cannot be considered tāmasika. It is bringing life and health to the individual, and restoring balance (sattva). When Iyengar speaks of ahiṁsa he says, "Blood-thirsty tyrants may be vegetarians, but violence is a state of mind, not of diet. It resides in a man's mind and not in the instrument he holds in his hand. One can use a knife to pare fruit or to stab an enemy. The fault is not in the instrument, but in the user."[13] In this way, a vegetarian[14] that *looks down* on others because of their diet, has lost the sattva of not eating meat.

From the spiritual perspective alcohol is considered tāmasika, but Caraka Saṁhitā has an entire chapter on wine. He says if a person of sāttvika nature drinks wine in moderate doses and in a proper manner, it works like nectar,[15] as it increases assimilation by opening the channels and helps re-establish the nutrient flow to the tissues.[16] Caraka sayswine was worshipped by the kings as nectar and established in sacrifices,[17] and this is still done in certain Tāntrika traditions.

Caraka gives the rules for social drinking (*pānagoṣṭi*): which foods to eat beforehand, which types of wines for different constitutions, and who should avoid wine.[18] Caraka describes three types of drinking parties (*pānagoṣṭikā*). Sāttvika drinking is when the rules of ingestion have been followed; the setting is comfortable and clean with a good mood and good company, and one's sense of cheerfulness and love increases without the senses being disturbed. Rājasika drinking is when the speech becomes slurred, varies every moment along with the emotions which may become rude and the drinking ends in an

[12] Chottopadhyay p.77
[13] Iyengar, B.K.S. p.32
[14] Manu Smṛti (5.53-55) says it make one like a sage (*muni*) while living like as a householder.
[15] Caraka Saṁhitā, Sūtrasthāna XXVII.191-192,
[16] Valiathan, p.305-306 and Chottopadhyay p.75-89
[17] Caraka Saṁhitā, Cikitsāsthāna XXIV.3-10
[18] Caraka Saṁhitā, Cikitsāsthāna XXIV.11-25, discussion on topic in Chottopadhyay p.99-114.

unhappy condition. Tāmasika drinking is when the speech loses its cheerfulness, there is discontent with the food and drink taken, the person is not enjoying themselves anymore and which ends in bewilderment, passion and passing out.

Caraka mentions that some people used alcohol in excess but he did not try to stop it but to help people remain within limits and enjoy (*joṣa*) it. In this way, we see the Vedic philosophy is for proper use being more important than prohibition. Caraka says that food which sustains life, if taken in excess or improperly becomes like poison. Even poison when taken properly acts like medicine.[19] In this way, proper use is sāttvika and improper use is due to deficiency, excess or wrong timing.

Caraka says that the body follows the mind, and the mind follows the body.[20] The use of intoxicants of any kind is avoided by one seeking sattva. Any intoxication which comes from outside is not productive of the highest level of sattva in the spiritual aspirant. But few are able to be pure saints, and one should be settled with their own nature. By accepting oneself where one is at, real growth is possible and spirituality can increase naturally. Some individuals do not have the nature to follow the path of pure sattva and therefore the proper use of non-sāttvika methods should be understood. For example, the average person with tāmasika grahas (especially Rāhu) in the second house from lagna will not be vegetarian. They may try to be in the daśā of a sāttvika planet, but in the daśā of a tāmasika planet they will eat meat (unless a sāttvika planet gives virodha from the 12th house). In such a case, you can advise them to only eat the meats which are sāttvika. In the case of a benefic in the second house one should avoid eating meat or else they are reducing the power of that planet. In this way, an astrologer must understand the guṇas to be able to suggest the best path for an individual.

The guṇas are relative to the state of an individual as well as the focus and method of use. The guṇas have relativity depending on various levels of application and at different moments in time. The astrologer advises an individual towards sattva in a way that will allow them to live to their highest potential according to their nature and to gain the most knowledge in this life.The Bhagavad Gītā (XIV.11) says that when sattva is dominant,the light of knowledge becomes visible in the body.

From sattva is born knowledge (*jñāna*), from rajas greed (*lobha*), and from tamas comes negligence (*pramāda*), delusion (*moha*) and ignorance (*ajñāna*) (XIV.17). The guṇa is the foundational state in which everything else is processed. The guṇas create a cycle in which the mind is as it acts. If the mind is tāmasika, it will do tāmasika actions which will maintain the tamas. To break the cycle, a sāttvika lifestyle helps to raise the level of sattva in the mind, but only according to one's nature.

[19] Caraka Saṁhitā, Cikitsāsthāna XXIV.60
[20] Caraka Saṁhitā, Śārīrasthāna IV.36

We aim to follow sattva but must not be attached to it. Sattva can create attachment to happiness (*sukha*), rajas gives attachment to action (*karma*), and tamas gives attachment to negligence, carelessness, or indifference (*pramāda*). The attachment to sattva is binding. For spiritual growth we must follow sattva but not become a sattva snob, as that attachment is far from spiritual. The guṇas are Prakṛti and not Puruṣa, they are a worldly means and not an end.

The Bhagavad Gītā (XIV.5) says that the imperishable one (*avyayam*), is bound into the body by the guṇas born of prakṛti. In this way, the soul is tied to the body because of the guṇas. They are like strings which tie you down and limit the soul. Sattva may help to bring knowledge and right understanding but it still needs to be transcended. The Bhagavad Gītā says that sattva is pureness (*nirmala-tva*), illuminating (*prakaśaka*), and free of disease (*anāmaya*). It binds the soul through attachment to happiness and knowledge (XIV.6). Rajas is the nature of passion (*rāga*) arising from desire/thirst (*tṛṣṇā*) and attachment and binds by attachment to action (*karma*) (XIV.7). Tamas is born of ignorance (*ajñāna*) and confuses everyone. It binds the soul with indifference (*pramāda*), laziness (*ālasya*), and sleep (*nidrā*) (XIV.8).

One follows sattva to the best of their ability, but doesn't get egotistical about it by either getting snobbish about how sāttvika they are or acting above the guṇas. Humility is very important to true sāttvika living. Humility is to be aware of the control the guṇas have over your own actions and those of others. You are in the guṇa you are in presently because that is the guṇa you are in presently. What you do and what happens in your life is the result of the guṇas on your mind.

The Bhagavad Gītā (XIV.19) says when the observer (*draṣṭā*) perceives nothing other than the guṇas as the doer [the cause behind actions], and knows that which is higher than the guṇas, he approaches the Supreme Being. That one attains the Amṛta (XIV.20).

So what does someone who is above the guṇas look like? The Bhagavad Gītā says that one that is above the guṇas does not desire sattva, rajas or tamas. They do not seek or hate illumination (*prakāśa*) or actions (*pravṛtti*) or delusion (*moha*). This does not mean they don't have some of these elements happening, they are just not seeking after nor avoiding the guṇas themselves (XIV.22). Things are as they are. The person that is beyond the guṇas 'sits as if they sit apart', they are not disturbed by the guṇas. They see the guṇas as setting all things in motion and therefore stand unagitated (XIV.23). They are self-abiding and are the same in happiness and suffering, the same to a lump of earth, precious stone or gold, the same to the friends and non-friends, and being stable even in blame and praise of themselves. They are equal to honor and dishonour and impartial to friends and enemies (XIV.24-25). They are happy to just be themselves and live their life as it is. This is the quality of someone who has transcended the guṇas (*guṇātīta*).

How do you feel when someone compliments your practice and calls you incredible? How do you feel when someone says that you are worthless and that you don't understand what you are doing? Is your reaction the same to both? Do you want to be appreciated? Are you as giving and friendly to non-friends as you are to your friends? Such a person is very rare. A person who can stay centered when both tamas and rajas are thrown at them is firm in the truth of who they are.

Our goal is to watch ourselves, to be aware, and to do our best to not fall into the traps of the mind which will only take away our clarity. The Supreme Place is everpresent, yet it is missed because we aren't present.

When an individual gets a little angry they are able to observe themselves getting angry, but when they get very angry they lose themselves to the emotion. The 'unagitated stance' the Gītā describes is to remain in the seat of the observer (*draṣṭā*).

As long as one is alive, actions will continue to happen and emotions will continue to rise in the mind. By remaining in the seat of the observer, the relationship to those actions and emotions is no longer unconscious. One stays abiding in the self (*svastha*) and keeps their mind focused on the highest goal; and the world continues on, moved by the guṇas. Time continues moving everything; churning the guṇas. Even in the charts of great saints and avatāras, time moves the guṇas to make karmas unfold.

"There is nothing either on earth or in heaven among the gods, which is born of Prakṛti, which can exist free from the three guṇas" (XVIII.40). Everything in creation therefore has a predominance of various guṇas. Parāśara discusses these guṇas in the chapter on *The Results of Sattva, Etc.*[21] He teaches that the world is composed of the three guṇas and through their mixture four states of action arise. Parāśara says,

अथो गुणवशेनाहं कथयामि फलं द्विज ।
सत्त्वग्रहोदये जातो भवेत्सत्त्वाधिकः सुधीः ॥ १ ॥

atho guṇavaśenāhaṁ kathayāmi phalaṁ dvija |
sattvagrahodaye jāto bhavetsattvādhikaḥ sudhīḥ || 1||

Now, I narrate the results of the guṇa which predominates an individual,
When sattva planets are rising, the individual will have
a noble disposition (*sattvādhika*) and a good sense of understanding (*su-dhī*).

रजःखेटोदये विज्ञो रजोगुणसमन्वितः ।
तमःखेटोदये मूर्खो भवेज्जातस्तमोऽधिकः ॥ २ ॥

rajaḥkheṭodaye vijño rajoguṇasamanvitaḥ |
tamaḥkheṭodaye mūrkho bhavejjātastamo'dhikaḥ || 2||

If rajas planets are rising then know that the person is endowed with rajas guṇa.
If tamas planets are rising the individual is dull witted, among other ignorant qualities.

गुणसाम्ययुतो जातो गुणसाम्यखगोदये ।
एवं चतुर्विधा विप्र जायन्तो जन्तवो भुवि ॥ ३ ॥

guṇasāmyayuto jāto guṇasāmyakhagodaye |
evaṁ caturvidhā vipra jāyanto jantavo bhuvi || 3||

When the person is born with planets [of various guṇas] rising, there is a mixture of guṇas.
In this way, there is a fourfold division of all created beings.

उत्तमो मध्यमो नीच उदासीन इति क्रमात् ।
तेषां गुणानहं वक्ष्ये नारदादिप्रभाषितान् ॥ ४ ॥

uttamo madhyamo nīca udāsīna iti kramāt |
teṣāṁ guṇānahaṁ vakṣye nāradādiprabhāṣitān || 4||

[The above mentioned dispositions are called] accordingly:
excellent (*uttama*), middling or average (*madhyama*),
low or base [*adhama*], and neutral (*udāsīna*),
These attributes which I will speak of were explained by Nārada and other sages.

[21] Bṛhat Parāśara Horā Śāstra, Sattva-ādi-guṇa-phala-adhyāya

Parāśara describes these four dipositions:[22]

Uttama	Madhyama	Adhama	Udāsīna
Sattva	Rajas	Tamas	Mixed
calm, contented (*śama*), self-controlled (*dama*), austere (*tapas*), cleanliness (*śaucha*), patient (*kṣānti*), sincerity (*ārjava*), non-covetousness (*alobha*), truthfulness (*satyavāditva*) ǀǀ 5ǀǀ	valour (*śaurya*), sharpness (*teja*), resolution, firmness (*dhṛti*), capability (*dākṣya*), not retreating from a fight, protecting the virtuous, conscious (*ceti*) ǀǀ 6ǀǀ	greedy (*lobha*), untruthful (*asatyavāditva*), cold, lacking compassion (*jāḍya*), lazy (*ālasya*), and good at doing the work of a servant (*sevākarma*) ǀǀ 7ǀǀ	skilled at commerce (*vāṇijya*), agricultural work (*kṛṣikarmaṇi*), keeping livestock (*paśupālana*), and speaks both truth and lies ǀǀ *8*ǀǀ
Brāhmans	**Kṣatriyas**	**Śūdras**	**Vaiśyas**

These four varieties of the guṇas relate to the four castes (*varṇa*). The four caste system was created according to the distribution of the guṇas and their acts.[23] This means one is in a caste according to their predominant guṇa. In medieval and modern Indian society, the caste system was something a person was born into. This *is possible*, as the fruit doesn't fall far from the tree. Social, economic and educational conditions have a tendency to keep individuals in the same guṇa as their parents. Karma will often attract a soul to a womb that has similar karma and guṇas. But this is *not always* the case, and in present day society, the belief in free will and hard work has allowed people to enter any caste of society. Therefore, we do not limit an individual because of their birth into a particular family. But castes *do* exist, according to nature, as a quality of activity that an individual performs.

गतैश्च लक्षणैर्लक्ष्य उत्तमो मध्यमोऽधमः ।
उदासीनश्च विप्रेन्द तं तत्कर्माणि योजयेत् ॥ ९ ॥

gataiśca lakṣaṇairlakṣya uttamo madhyamo'dhamaḥ ǀ
udāsīnaśca viprenda taṁ tatkarmaṇi yojayet ǀǀ *9*ǀǀ

Using the indicated characteristics for uttama, madhyama, adhama, and udāsīna,
The individual should be employed in the proper type of work.

द्वाभ्यामेकोऽधिको यश्च तस्याधिक्यं निगद्यते ।
अन्यथा गुणसाम्यं च विज्ञेयं द्विजसत्तम ॥ १० ॥

dvābhyāmeko'dhiko yaśca tasyādhikyaṁ nigadyate ǀ
anyathā guṇasāmyaṁ ca vijñeyaṁ dvijasattama ǀǀ *10*ǀǀ

If two or more qualities are dominant consider the most predominant,
Otherwise know that it is of mixed guṇa.

[22] Bhagavad Gītā XVIII.42-44 has a similar list of attributes (almost exact for brāhmans and kṣatriyas).
[23] Bhagavad Gītā, IV.13 and XVIII.41

There is also the possibility of mixed indications, which is particularly prominent in the modern world with all its opportunities. Normally, the strongest planet will dominate, but in our time, all planets influencing will have their say in various daśā. It is not uncommon to find a farmer (sudra) making movies (vaisya work), or a banker (vaisya) studying astrology (brāhmana work).

Uttama guṇa means there is a predominance of sattva guṇa and such a person is a brāhman. These qualities lead a person to be a brāhman, and do brāhman work. If those qualities are not there the individual is not a brāhman. Merely being born in a brāhman family doesn't mean you are a brāhman,[24] though in modern India hereditary caste is considered like an ethnicity. This heritage will not be used for determination of profession.

Caste (*varṇa*) is based upon an individual's innate nature (*svabhāva*).[25] There are some modern religious issues with birth in a certain caste, and the belief that this is the indication for caste, but the Gītā, Parāśara and other texts indicate that the qualification for one's work is based upon the innate nature (*svabhāva)*of the individual. As astrologers, we need to see the guṇas of the individual to make proper recommendations for career as well as relationship compatibility.

The sattva guṇa leads one to the Brāhman path, while tamas leads one to the śudra path. Rajas does not have balance. "Nobody is perfect rajas. Rajas can never be perfect. Rajas has an upper rajas and lower rajas. Upper rajas is madhyama, the kśatriya. The lower rajas is udāsīna, the vaiśya. Both kṣatriyas and vaiśyas are rajas. The kṣatriya want power and the vaiśya want money".

There is an important differentiation between the three guṇas as attributes of one's nature and as tendencies for one's career. One should always strive to attain sattva in their actions; to act honestly, with good intention, clarity, and to do all action remembering the true doer. But it is advised by the Bhagavad Gītā (XVIII.45-49)that it is best for one to do the work that comes naturally (*sahajaṁ karma*). By doing one's own innate duty (*svadharma*), one can focus their mind on the Supreme goal and attain this much more easily. In this way, the higher spiritual teaching is that it is not about *what* you do but about *how* you do it that matters. Therefore individuals are advised do the work that they were created to do.

The planets do not make you a certain guṇa. The chart is not "controlling you" and "taking away your free-will". The planets and guṇas *indicate* one's nature. Who is making you have the eye color you are born with? Who is forcing you to be the height you are? These things are just how we are born, they are our nature.

[24] Rath, Sanjay. Opening lecture 0018

[25] Bhagavad Gītā, XVIII.41

There is a saying that the cause of budding rice is in its own seeds. It will grow as it is meant to grow according to its own self-nature (genetic material). Its growth will happen only at a particular season as a result of the instrumental agency of rain (*varṣa*).

At the right time, the nature of an individual will manifest. An individual can decide to be a pacifist or a soldier at a time of war. Either role needs a war to bring out the individual nature which was already present in the individual like the nature of a plant in its seed. In this way, daśā are indicating circumstances happening in our life, and our nature reveals itself at those times. The guṇa of the daśā will bring about different results in different people according to their nature.

Guṇa and Gaze

The Bhagavad Gītā (XIV.18) says that 'those established in sattva go upward, the rājasika stay in the middle, and the tāmasika, established in the lowest, go downwards. 'When someone of sāttvika disposition dies, they will go to higher planes of existence or a better next life. Those who are rājasika continue in the same station, and the tāmasika incarnate in the lower realms or in situations which incur suffering (XIV.14-15).[26] Those who keep a sāttvika disposition will have uplifted spirits, the rājasika will be enmeshed in their day to day ups and downs and the tāmasika will be depressed and lost in their problems. The upward and downward directions are also seen in traditional sayings; when things are positive people say they are "looking up" or feeling "uplifted". When someone is suffering with tamas, people ask "what has you down".

"When we have tama guṇa we look down. When we have sattva guṇa we look up and rajas we look slightly on the side or we look straight. So when a person comes to show you his chart, first see how the person has generally got his neck. If the person is always looking down, 'oh got so many problems' his gaze is down that means tamo-guṇa is dominating over him. If his gaze is up 'yes I have great plans, was thinking of writing another book, yes, will see if can do that' if the head is up he is sattva guṇa. If it is straight it is rajas, slightly up slightly down it is still rajas; Rajo-tamas, rajo-sattva. So we have three main positions, and in the rajas group there are two intermediate positions: straight-slightly up, straight-slightly down. So we have how many positions? Four positions. The top position looking up is called uttama, the best; looking up. Ideally a person doing a guru mantra like *'auṁ gurave namaḥ'*, will start looking up, it will cause your head to go up. Just start it tomorrow. Do Śani mantra and your head will start going down. Why? Because these grahas have guṇas. Based upon the graha who is sitting on your head, [determined by] the mantra you are doing, either you look down or you look up. So

[26] *Sāṅkhya Kārikā* 44 says that 'by dharma one goes upward, by adharma one goes downward, from jñāna one gets freedom (*apavarga*), and through ignorance one gets bound (*bandha*).'

whose mantra should you do ideally? You should do a sattva guṇa mantra. Always try to do a sattva guṇa mantra."[27]

Caste (*varṇa*) is nothing but a predominant guṇa; the predominant guṇa will decide your varṇa. Pandit Sanjay Rath teaches that "none of us are in perfect guṇa all the time. Our mind can be in a guṇa, our body can be in a guṇa, our objective can be in a guṇa."[28]

Guṇa Determination

The lagna shows the guṇa of the intelligence, which is the intrinsic guṇa that shows the overall personality of the individual. Therefore we must study the ascendant (*udaya lagna*) to see the intrinsic nature. Parāśara says to look at the guṇa of the planets rising (*udaya*). Planets in the lagna will have the largest effect on the individual. The sign that the planet is placed in will also be very important (whether the lord is sattva, rajas or tamas), as well as full aspects on the sign/planet. The lagna lord must also be studied, and even more so if there are no planets in the lagna. The guṇa of that planet, the sign it is placed in, and planets it is conjunct will all influence the overall guṇa of the individual. Powerful planets in the tenth will also have a say on the guṇa and the quality of work the individual does.

The author has Gemini lagna with no planets present, but there is a fifth house aspect of Rāhu. The lagna lord is placed in its exaltation with the Sun. Exaltation makes a planet give sāttvika results and the Sun will make the changeable planet Mercury give sāttvika results. In this way, the rajas nature has become sāttvika and the sāttvika indication are more prominent than the aspect of Rāhu which would give a tāmasika nature.

Salvador Dali has a Gemini lagna,with no planets or full aspects, and the lagna lord is retrograde Mercury placed in Taurus with Mars. Mars gives some tamas but the lord, the planets and the sign are rajas, so that guṇa predominates. Bill Gates has Gemini lagna,with no planets or full aspects, and the lord Mercury is exalted and conjunct Mars with the aspect of the Moon. All the indications are basically different indicating mixed guṇa showing a vaiśya (businessman). In this way, the lagna and lagna lord are to be studied with conjunctions, lords, and aspects. Looking at many charts and seeing the variation is key to get a better understanding.

After the guṇa of the individual is understood then one analyzes the daśā and how the present guṇa is affecting the individual. The guṇa of the mahādaśā relates to the actions of the individual. The antaradaśā shows the guṇa of the changing mind during that time. The pratyāntara daśā shows the guṇa of the intelligence relative to the decisions that the person makes. This is a basic fundamental of reading.

[27] Rath, Sanjay. Opening lecture 0018
[28] Rath, Sanjay. Opening lecture 0018

The guṇa of the daśā is based on the guṇa of the ruling planet. Jupiter daśā is generally sattva unless it is severely afflicted with tamas grahas and/or debilitated. Rāhu and Ketu will give tāmasika results but can be influenced by the planets they are conjunct. The guṇa of a daśā can either support a person's innate nature or alter it, for better or worse.

"The Lagna is telling us what your intrinsic nature is. Nothing stops you from changing. That is the beauty of all this knowledge, otherwise why are we learning Jyotiṣa? If we cannot change, we cannot improve. If we cannot know what to do to become better or have a life full of knowledge, then why study Jyotiṣa? Jyotiṣa is meant to increase our guṇas."[29] It is not changing what you are doing with your life but the quality with which you are changing your life. Jyotiṣa is about improving your guṇas, and maximizing your potential and possibility.[30]

The best remedy for a negative daśā is the actions and mantras of sāttvika planets. If you focus on the tamas graha, then you perpetuate it. By focusing on the sattva that overcomes that form of tamas, you manifest the higher frequency. The tamas of Saturn is overcome by the sattva of the Sun. The tamas of Rāhu is overcome by the sattva of Jupiter, while the tamas of Mars is overcome by the sattva of Moon. In this way, the tamas of Saturn is overcome by mantras like the Gāyatrī, or taking a leadership role in a club or in the community, or reading spiritual texts. The attributes and actions of sāttvika planets have the power to remove the negativity of the tāmasika planets.

It is important to note that nīca planets become tāmasika and ucca planets become sāttvika relative to the results they will give. The state of the planet will have a slightly different effect than the guṇa, but will still influence the final result. For example, the integrity of a person is seen from the status of the lagna. If the lagneśa is exalted the individual will not compromise integrity. If the lagneśa is in its own sign, they will not compromise on their personal integrity but they will let the lack of integrity of others pass. In a friendly sign, there will be integrity based upon the workability of situations. In an inimical sign, the integrity will fall when challenged. If the lagneśa is nīca, integrity becomes questionable and the individual should do their best to strengthen the lagneśa. This will still exist within the quality of work indicated by the guṇa of the planets and signs.

These are the general rules. Occasionally certain combinations (*yoga*) will overrule the chart to give their indications. This is seen in the case of a fully functional *mahāpuruṣa yoga*. There is also an advanced technique using the Varṇada Lagna (VL), which can be integrated with the above understanding. It says that the work one will do is seen from the guṇa of the eleventh from Varṇada Lagna. If the eleventh from the VL is a water sign

[29] Rath, Sanjay. Opening lecture 0020
[30] Rath, Sanjay. Opening lecture 0020

it indicates Brāhmana work. Fire signs show kṣatriya work, earth signs show vaiśya work while air signs show śudra work. The guṇa of planets placed there will predominate.

Exercise

1. Look at all the charts you have collected and observe the planets in the lagna and the situation of the lagna lord. [For advanced study, also analyze any planets in the 10th house.] See how the guṇas are showing the individual's nature and the quality (caste) of work they are doing in life, and note your findings.

2. Look at the charts of ten individual's you know well and see how the daśā has shown the various changes in the type of work they do in life. Remember to see the guṇa of the daśā within the context of the overall guṇa of the individual.

सेव्यसेवकयोरेवं कन्यकावरयोरपि ।
गुणैः सदृशयोरेव प्रीतिर्भवति निश्चला ॥ ११ ॥

sevyasevakayorevaṁ kanyakāvarayorapi |
guṇaiḥ sadṛśayoreva prītirbhavati niścalā || 11||

The relationship between a boss and employee or a husband and wife
will remain favorable if the guṇas are similar.

उदासीनोऽधमस्यैवमुदासीनस्य मध्यमः ।
मध्यमस्योत्तमो विप्र प्रभवत्याश्रयो मुदे ॥ १२ ॥

udāsīno'dhamasyaivamudāsīnasya madhyamaḥ |
madhyamasyottamo vipra prabhavatyāśrayo mude || 12||

The relationship of udāsīna and adhama, udāsīna and madhyama,
madhyama and uttama, have happiness (*muda*).

अतोऽवरा वरात् कन्या सेव्यतः सेवकोऽवरः ।
गुणैस्ततः सुखोत्पत्तिरन्यथा हानिरेव हि ॥ १३ ॥

ato'varā varāt kanyā sevyataḥ sevako'varaḥ |
guṇaistataḥ sukhotpattiranyathā hānireva hi || 13||

If the guṇa of the girl is lower than the man, or the employee lower than the boss,
Then this will produce happiness (*sukha*), otherwise there will be failure (*hāni*).

This is a general rule in marriage compatibility. If the guṇas are the same, it brings a steady happiness, which is a relationship that works. If they are not the same, Parāśara gives the guṇas that will work well together, but there is a slight catch to this combination. The *dominant individual* in the relationship should be the higher guṇa. For example, udāsīna and adhama may work well together, but the relationship will not last unless the dominant individual is udāsīna.

In marriage, the male should generally be a higher guṇa than the female in order for there to be happiness in the family. This is from a point of view where the husband makes the majority of decisions. But from any perspective, what wife would want to be honest and have her husband make her lie? In this way, the wife will find more happiness having a husband of higher standards than herself.

In the workplace, problems are more likely to occur when the boss has lower values. It may be one thing for the employee to cut corners with a boss who makes sure the proper job is done, than to have an employee that wishes to give quality work, or to be accurate and have a boss that makes them rush, or enter incorrect data. Therefore, the dominant figure in any union should be of the same or a higher guṇa to have a long-term beneficial result; to live a harmonious life together.

If one arranges an Iyer Brāhman to marry another Iyer Brāhman because they are the same birth caste and does not analyze the chart further, then it is a blind arrangement. Some astrologers and computer programs just use the guṇa associated with the Moon's nakṣatrato see compatibility, but this is not enough. The actual guṇa must be seen. When very sāttvika-minded people are married to rājasika or tāmasika minded spouses then the individual suffers, and this does lead to divorce. The alignment of guṇa allows two people, even if they have different interests, to at least approach life in the same way.And as life changes, they will be able to ride the waves of time in the same manner.

वीर्यं क्षेत्रं प्रसूतेश्च समयः सङ्गतिस्तथा ।
उत्तमादिगुणे हेतुर्बलवानुत्तरोत्तरम् ॥ १४ ॥

vīryaṁ kṣetraṁ prasūteśca samayaḥ saṅgatistathā |
uttamādiguṇe heturbalavānuttarottaram || 14||

Strong planetary placements[31] at birth, as well as the associations one keeps
Will cause the various guṇas (such as uttama, etc.) to be stronger and primary.

Planets affecting the lagna indicate the primary guṇa of the individual (*svabhāva*). This can be modified by strong planetary placements such as a mahāpuruṣa yoga, or a gajakesarī yoga, etc. It can also be modified by ones associations. If one is by nature tamas but spends large amounts of time with sattva people, they will take on sattva attributes and likings. In the same way, a person of sattva nature may do tamas things if constantly hanging out with a bad crowd. Therefore, one should keep the crowd in which the guṇa is appropriate.

Changing one's association is also a remedy for tamas and rajas afflictions. I often recommend this when there is a papa-kartari on the lagna; for one to be careful of whom they associate with. In the spiritual scriptures, good spiritual association is regularly promoted for spiritual growth and to create firmness on the spiritual path. Unfortunately, cults have taken this to the extreme to control people, so sāttvika application is important.

अतः प्रसूतिकालस्य सदृशो जातके गुणः ।
जायते तं परीक्ष्यैव फलं वाच्यं विचक्षणैः ॥ १५ ॥

ataḥ prasūtikālasya sadṛśo jātake guṇaḥ |
jāyate taṁ parīkṣyaiva phalaṁ vācyaṁ vicakṣaṇaiḥ || 15||

The guṇa of the individual is according to the **time** of birth,
Therefore the clear-sighted (*vicakṣaṇa*) speak these results
after careful examination (*parīkṣya*).

[31] Other translators have given this as father-*vīrya*-sperm and mother-*kṣetra*-womb but this does not fit with the next verse (though it may be a double meaning). If one sees how Varāhamihira in Bṛhat Samḥita uses vīryā-ga and according to Monnier Williams Sanskrit Dictionary, then this translation will prove more in line.

कालः सृजति भूतानि पात्यथो संहरत्यपि ।
ईश्वरः सर्वलोकानामव्ययो भगवान् विभु ॥ १६ ॥

kālaḥ sṛjati bhūtāni pātyatho saṁharatyapi |
īśvaraḥ sarvalokānāmavyayo bhagavān vibhu || 16||

Time creates, protects, and destroys all beings, and is
Lord of the whole world, all that goes away, the omnipresent lord.

तच्छक्तिः प्रकृतिः प्रोक्ता मुनिभिस्त्रिगुणात्मिका ।
तथा विभक्तोऽव्यक्तोऽपि व्यक्तो भवति देहिनाम् ॥ १७ ॥

tacchaktiḥ prakṛtiḥ proktā munibhistriguṇātmikā |
tathā vibhakto'vyakto'pi vyakto bhavati dehinām || 17||

The sages have declared that the power of material nature (*prakṛti*) is the three guṇas.
And that this separates the unmanifest (*avyakta*) from the manifest (*vyakta*)
And gives [reality] embodiment.

चतुर्धाऽवयवास्तस्य स्वगुणैश्च चतुर्विधः ।
जायन्ते ह्युत्तमो मध्य उदासीनोऽधमः क्रमात् ॥ १८ ॥

caturdhā'vayavāstasya svaguṇaiśca caturvidhaḥ |
jāyante hyuttamo madhya udāsīno'dhamaḥ kramāt || 18||

His own nature is of four parts and in that manner arises in four ways:
uttama, madhyama, udāsīna and adhama.

Parāśara is relating the time of birth (*janmakāla*) with the greater Time (*mahākāla*). The time of birth determines our individual guṇas just as the greater Time created all things and moves them through the guṇas.

Parāśara follows the philosophy that the All-pervasive takes the form of four beings (*cāturātmya*) arising from the combinations of the qualities.[32] The three vyūhas and Vāsudeva are the four aspects of the divine[33] which represent the four levels of consciousness known as the waking state (*jāgrat*), dreaming state (*svapna*), deep sleep (*suṣupti*), and the transcendental state (*turīya*).[34] Creation replicates itself below as above. In this way, the Brāhman by nature is concerned with the transcendental state, the kṣatriya is concerned with the essence of things, the vaiśya is concerned with your mind and advertising, and the śudra works the material reality.

Creation replicates itself below as above and the ancient way to teach this is to put it into an anthropomorphic analogy.The supreme person (*puruṣa*) is one being who

[32] Ahirbudhnya Saṁhita, V.20, V.41
[33] Varadachari, Īśvarasaṁhitā, Volume I, p.98. "The four vyūha deities are said to constitute an aggregate called Cāturātmya."
[34] Varadachari, Īśvarasaṁhitā, Volume I, p.101.

represents the energies contained in all of us, but which manifest in different ratios in different people.

उत्तमे तूत्तमो जन्तुर्मध्येऽङ्गे च मध्यमः।
उदासीने ह्यदासीनो जायते चाऽधमेऽधमः॥ १९॥
उत्तमाङ्गं शिरस्तस्य मध्यमाङ्गमुरः स्थलम्।
जंट्टाद्वयदासीनमधमं पदमुच्यते॥ २०॥

uttame tūttamo janturmadhye'ṅge ca madhyamaḥ |
udāsīne hyadāsīno jāyate cā'dhame'dhamaḥ|| 19||
uttamāṅgaṁ śirastasya madhyamāṅgamuraḥsthalam |
jaṅghādvayadāsīnamadhamaṁ padamucyate|| 20||

The head is the highest portion from which come the uttama quality people.
The chest [power of the arms] is the middle portion from which come madhyama people.
The two shins are the udāsīna portion from which these type of beings come from,
and the feet is the lowest portion from which come the adhama quality beings.

Parāśara divides up the four castes in this same way as the Ṛgveda divides the parts of the Puruṣa. The head or mouth[35] represents the higher portion of the body from which the higher guṇas exist guiding the being.[36] The arms are the part of the being that is acting and making things happen on a physical level similar to how politics controls the way things are done. The legs are the actual means of getting around as the merchant class creates the wealth to make things work properly. The feet are the lowest part of the body, yet provide a foundation which roots everything in the world and allows society to stand. The guṇas and castes can be understood in this analogy as the Puruṣa refers to the anthropomorphized cosmic being, as an archetypal blueprint of the world and human nature- it is that which is above that is being reflected below. The need of all these parts to be

Puruṣa Sūkta: Ṛgveda 10.90

यत्पुरुषं व्यदधुः कतिधा व्यकल्पयन्।
मुखं किमस्य कौ बाहू का उरू पादा उच्येते॥११॥

yatpuruṣaṁ vyadadhuḥ katidhā vyakalpayan|
mukhaṁ kimasya kau bāhū kā urū pādā ucyete||11||

When they immolated the Puruṣa,
into how many portions did they divide him?
What was his head called, what of his arms,
what of his thighs, what were his feet called?

ब्राह्मणोऽस्य मुखमासीद् बाहू राजन्यः कृतः।
ऊरू तदस्य यद्वैश्यः पद्भ्यां शूद्रो अजायत॥१२॥

brāhmaṇo'sya mukhamāsīd bāhū rājanyaḥ kṛtaḥ|
ūrū tadasya yadvaiśyaḥ padbhyāṁ śūdro ajāyata||12||

His head became the Brāhmaṇa,
his arms became the Rājanya,
his thighs became the Vaiśya,
the Śudra was born from his feet.

[35] Mahābhārata , Book 12, Śānti Parva 342, Viṣṇu Purāṇa I.6
[36] Ahirbudhnya Saṁhita addsdestiny (*niyati*) from the forehead, time from the eyebrows, and guṇa from the ears.

functioning properly in a human is important to the function of the whole person in the same way that all four castes make up a society and are needed to be functioning in a healthy way for a prosperous and just society.

The Ahirbudhnya Saṁhita explains that there are four archtypes of human beings (*manus*) who represent the four qualities of action.These are personified as four couples who are the archetypal dispositions of action (*karmādhikāra*), which exist within the Puruṣa. They are the power and nature of all actions (*kṛtsnakarmādhikāra*).[37] They are said to descend to earth copulating and creating the four types of humans in the land of actions (*karmabhumi*).[38]

The Ahirbudhnya Saṁhita explains that the highest (*kūṭastha*) Puruṣa is an aggregate of souls like a hive of bees [with various positions based upon their nature]. The soul was originally unlimited (*sarvatomukha*) and all-knowing (*sarvajña*) but those souls are pierced by ignorance of various degrees. The souls are dulled by the dust of beginningless predispositions and are moved by Time to perform karma accordingly.

एवं गुणवशादेव कालभेदः प्रजायते ।
जातिभेदस्तु तद्भेदाज्जायतेऽत्र चराचरे ॥ २१ ॥

evaṁ guṇavaśādeva kālabhedaḥ prajāyate |
jātibhedastu tadbhedājjāyate'tra carācare || 21||

In this way, time is classified by qualities that control
all creatures and even the gods (vaśa-ādeva),[39]
distinguished by natural disposition/ properties,
and that division is given to all animate and inanimate things.

एवं भगवता सृष्टं विभुना स्वगुणैः समम् ।
चतुर्विधेन कालेन जगदेतच्चतुर्विधम् ॥ २२ ॥

evaṁ bhagavatā sṛṣṭaṁ vibhunā svaguṇaiḥ samam |
caturvidhena kālena jagadetaccaturvidham || 22||

In this way, the lord created existence similar to his own guṇas,
The fourfold Time as the fourfold Universe.

[37] Ahirbudhnya Saṁhitā, IV.57, VI.32, VI.40, VII.37

[38] Viṣṇu Purāṇa I.6.7-21. Ahirbudhnya Saṁhitā, VI.8-46 These archetypes are developed by Aniruddha into the material world with the creative energy (*bhuti śakti*) who is made of Time and the guṇas.

[39] Bhagavad Gītā XVIII.40 There is no being either on earth or among the gods which can exist free of the three guṇas.

Chapter 5

Five Elements

"I was absent-minded; I did not hear.
I was absent-minded; I did not see.
It is thus evident that a person sees with the mind,
hears with the mind.
Desire, determination, uncertainty,
belief, disbelief, steadiness,
unsteadiness, shame, intellect, fear-
all these are in the mind alone.
Therefore, when touched from behind,
a person knows by mind."
-Bṛhadaranyaka Upaniṣad

Five elements (Pañca-Mahābhūtas)

The entire universe is made of five (*pañca*)great (*mahā*) material elements (*bhūtas*): earth, water, fire, air and ākāśa. They are the essence of not just the physical universe but of reality.

Bhūta has many meanings (as the past participle of bhāva), but basically means to have become, to exist, to actually have happened. Living beings that have become and are existent are also called bhūtas. Mahābhūtas are the great existing principles. They are that through which everything has, is or will come into existence.

The mahābhūtas are also called the *pañca-tattvas*. They are the grouping of five elements out of the 25 tattvas which manifest reality, which all come from the paramatattva- the transcendental essence of reality. The word *tattva* literally means *tat-tva* or that-ness. It is the true essence or the real substance. When referred to as the *pañca-tattva*, it means the five elemental building blocks of reality, the five core principles which manifest reality. The tattvas are the basic building blocks of creation to which everything can be reduced. Even the elements of the periodic table can be reduced down into five groups relating to the five tattvas.

These five tattvas are represented in the five elemental planets. The Sun represents fire and the Moon represents water on a higher level. They are the first dichotomy of reality; male-female, mother-father, mind-soul, hot-cold, etc. This is seen among the rāśi as the Sun and the Moon each have one sign, then each of the five elemental planets own a sign which is odd (masculine/solar) or even (feminine/lunar). So it is clear that there is the division of two (lunar-solar) and then the division of five (elements). The soul/Sun is generated with the causal realm (*suṣupti*), the mind/Moonis generatedwith the subtle realm (*svapna*) and the ahaṅkāra/Rāhu is generated with the material realm (*jāgrat*).[2] Then the material elements are generated as the building blocks for the soul-mind-identity to manifest within.

In the Vedic delineation of creation, there are three aspects of ahaṅkāra from which all things become. From the tamas ahaṅkāra (*bhūtādi*) come the five elements (ākāśa, air, etc) and the tanmātrā (sound, touch, etc). According to Parāśara, from rajas ahaṅkāra (*taijasa*) the 10 indriya are created; the powers of cognition and action. Five of these organs are receptive (hearing, feeling, etc) and are called jñāna-indriyas (cognition senses). Five of these organs are utilitarian (speaking, touching, etc) and are called karma-indriyas (action senses). Each of these correlates to one of the five elements.

[2] This is why the *Kālacakra Tantra* with the three divisionsof the maṇḍala talks about the Sun, Moon, Rāhu together.

Ahaṅkāra (I-sense)			
Bhūtādi (tamas-ahaṅkāra)		Taijasa (rajas-ahaṅkāra)	
Tattva and Tanmātrā		Jñāna-Indriya	Karma-Indriya
Space (*ākāśa*)	Sound(*śabda*)	Ear/hearing (*śrotra*)	Speech/ vocal organ (*vāc*)
Air (*vāyu*)	Touch (*sparśa*)	Skin/feeling (*tvac*)	Hand/ handling organ (*pāṇī*)
Fire (*agni*)	Sight (*rūpa*)	Eyes/seeing (*cakṣus*)	Feet/ locomotive organ (*pāda*)
Water (*jala*)	Taste (*rasa*)	Tongue/tasting (*jihva*)	Urethra/generating organ (*upastha*)
Earth (*pṛthvī*)	Smell (*gandha*)	Nose/smelling (*nāsikā*)	Anus/ evacuation organ (*pāyu*)

The linked relationships (*anvaya*) such as Space-Sound-Speech-Hearing or Air-Touch-Hand-Skin are an important part of Vedic science. There are many variations to Sāṅkhya in different traditions but these correlations remain the same in all of them. They are a standard that needs to be meditated upon and deeply ingrained in the psyche.Their relation reveals the reason why massage (touch) has the ability to pacify vāta (vāyu in the body), the reason ringing a bell (sound) in worship clears the space (ākāśa), or why astrologers use Agni mantras to improve their predictive powers (sight). This is how *khecarī mudrā* (raising the tongue to top of mouth) allows sexual energy to rise into spiritual energy. These correlations can also be seen in the cakras relating to the specific element. The throat-ākāśa relates to sound, the heart-vāyu relates to touch and the healing power of the hands. The navel-agni gives us protection from toxins and relates to our vision and its clarity. These correlations are the logic that is applied in many techniques of Āyurveda, Yoga and Jyotiṣa.

Below we take a closer look at the tattvas and the associated tanmātrās to deepen our understanding and therefore our ability to perceive more clearly. Caraka says that earth is characterized by hardness/solidity (*khara-tva*), water by flowing/liquidity (*drava-tva*), fire by heat (*uṣṇa-tva*), air by mobility (*cala-tva*), and ākāśa by lack of resistance (*apratighāta-tva*).[3] This is the general nature of each element which can be noticed on a physical, mental or spiritual level. That which has solidity, firmness or hardness relates to earth, and that which is running, flowing, dripping, in a fluid manner is water. That which is hot, transforming, or cooking is fire, and that which is moving, fluctuating, unsteady like the wind is air. Ākāśa is free of resistance, free of struggle or obstruction, everywhere making space (*avakāśa*) for everyone to get along. When you see someone dance you can recognize the element which is stronger in the way they move, you can see it in their walk, and in how they hold themselves or how they talk.

The elements make everything work, as everything is composed of them and is functioning through them. In this way, we look at what functions each rules within the body and environment.

---

[3] Caraka Saṁhitā, Śārīrasthānam I.29-30

Element		Definition according to Śrīmad Bhāgavatam	Nature of the Elements: Charaka Saṁhitā, Śārīrasthāna IV.12
Space	ākāśa	Provides accommodation of room (*chidra-dātṛtva*) for all living beings both internally and externally, it is the field for the activities (*dhiśṇyatva*) of the prāṇa, the senses and the ātman. 3.26.34	Sound (*śabda*), hearing (*śrotra*), lightness (*lāghava*), subtlety (*saukṣmya*), and proper discrimination (*viveka*)
Air	vāyu	Moving (*cālana*), mixing (*vyūhana*), guiding expression/ speaking (*netṛtva-dravya-śabda*), proper functioning of all the senses (*sarva-indriyāṇām ātmatva.* 3.36.37	Touch (*sparśa*), sense of touch (*sparśana*), dryness (*raukṣya*), impelling (*preraṇa*), formation and transportation of the dhātus (*dhātu-vyūhana*), and bodily movement (*ceṣṭa-śārīra*)
Fire	agni	Illumination/ explaining/ meaning (*dyotanam*), cooking/ digesting (*pacana*), drinking (*pāna*), eating (*adana*), removing cold (*hima-mardana*), evaporating (*śoṣaṇa*), hunger (*kṣut*), and thirst (*tṛṣ*).3.36.40	Sight (*rūpa*), sense of vision (*darśana*), visibility/ appearance/ elucidation/ lighten (*prakāśa*), digestion (*pakti*), and heat (*uṣṇa*)
Water	jala	Moistening/ lubricating (*kledana*), coagulating (*piṇḍana*), satiating, giving contentment (*tṛpti*), rejuvenating/vivifying (*prāṇana*), refreshing, causing fullness (*āpyāyana*), moistening/ softening (*undana*), removing heat (*tāpa-apanoda*), bringing increase/ abundance (*bhūyastva*). 3.36.43	Taste (*rasa*), sense of taste (*rasaṇa*), coldness (*śaitya*), softness (*mārdava*), unctuousness (*sneha*), and moisture/wetness (*kleda*)
Earth	pṛthvī	Place for all attributes of existence to manifest (*sarva-sattva-guṇa-udbheda*), making forms (*bhāvana*), building (*sthāna*), giving shape/ holding (*dhāraṇa*), delineating space, distinctiveness (*sat-viśeṣaṇa*). 3.36.46	Smell (*gandha*), sense of smell (*ghrāṇa*), heaviness (*gaurava*), solidity/firmness (sthairya), and perceivable form (*mūrtisceti*)

Ākāśa is one of the hardest tattvas to understand, as it is the most subtle. Many ancient Buddhist philosophers have even denied its existence, while some Hindu scholars have associated it with divinity itself. Ākāśa by its own nature is unimpeded (*avyāhatagati*), everywhere (*nitya*), all-pervading (*vibhū*), it has singularity (*pṛthaktva*), it connects things (*saṁyoga*) or takes them apart (*vibhāga*) depending on its presence. Ākāśa makes protons and electrons *attracted* to each other so they form into atoms. Ākāśa is the field in which all the other elements exist, the space in which they work. The earth is the form of the body, ākāśa is the channels. Vāyu (prāṇa) moves through those channels operating life.

We will use a very gross example to demonstrate the need for ākāśa. In the spine, there is a proper amount of space between each vertebra. They are padded and lubricated. If excess water accumulates in the spine, then there is swelling.If excess fire accumulates then there is inflammation. If excess air is in the spine then there is pain, decay, and cracking. If there is not enough space, then the spine compresses nerves or wears away unevenly. The elongation of the spine, which gives proper space for all processes and motions to happen healthily, creates an experienceof spaciousness in both the body and mind. This space is the tangible experience of ākāśa. After practicing yoga-āsana the body should feel lighter and more expansive because of the increased ākāśa in the physical, prāṇika and mental bodies.

If there is enough space in the joint area it will move smoothly. If there is too little space it will move with friction. Friction creates heat. Fire is thus created when ākāśa is removed creating more density. In the same way, the movement of molecules will take form into different tattvas according to the change in ākāśa.

The *Vedānta Pañcadaśī* (II.60-78) teaches that ākāśa derives its existence from Brahman (god). Brahman only has existence (*sat*), while ākāśa has ākāśa (space) and existence. Ākāśa is a property of existence, and also has the ability to communicate sound. Brahman is completely all pervasive, ākāśa less pervasive, and vāyu much less. The Supreme is absolutely everywhere as all things and unlimited. Ākāśa is all-pervasive also, but there are areas that can become deficient or excessive, as it is an element which can be limited. In this way, ākāśa is the most pervasive element, though if it was the same as god, then how could we say that there is not enough, or that it is afflicted. The Supreme is omnipresent beyond manifestation, while ākāśa is the reflection of this quality into the physical manifestation.

The proceeding tattvas each have a portion of the prior tattva.[4] This is often made into a fraction of a tenth (*daśama*) or an eighth (*aṣṭama*), both which are proportions that can denote a "small part" as well as a specific amount. In this way, air is created from a small part of ākāśa. Fire is generated from a small part of air. Ākāśa has only one quality (sound), air has two qualities (sound, as well as movement/sensation). Fire contains the qualities of the previous tattvas in addition to sight, while earth has all the qualities of the elements. The *Bhāgavata Purāṇa* (3.26.49) says the cause (*parasya*) is observed in the characteristics (*dharma*) of its effect (*aparasmin*), therefore the peculiarities (*viśeṣa*) of *all* the elements exist only in the earth element. This means that earth can be smelled, tasted, seen, felt and heard. The earth element contains all other elements, while water contains all elements except earth. Fire contains only ākāśa, air and itself, while air contains only itself and ākāśa, and finally ākāśa has only the characteristics of ākāśa.

---

[4] Caraka Saṁhitā, Śārīrasthānam I.28 and Vedānta Pañcadaśī II.88

In manifestation, the elements intermingle to create the world. Time is mixing these 25 principles[5] and everything is a mix of these elements and what we see is the predominance. It is similar to having a kāraka and sub-kārakas, and tertiary kārakas. For example, food is primarily ruled by the Moon, while fruit issub-ruled by Jupiter, and peaches ruled on a tertiary level by Venus. Smells can be earthy, sweet (watery), spicy (fiery), as well as light and ethereal. At the same time music (sound) can be ethereal (ākāśa), or sexy (water), or exciting (fire) or earthy. Music will invoke dance according to its predominant element. In this way, any sensory object will affect the area it works on according to the nature the elemental predominance.

Tanmātrās

The pañcatattva, through the impulse of time (*kāla-gatyā*), generate the material reality in which we discern and interact through the tanmātrās: sound, touch, sight, taste and smell. Caraka says that the tanmātrās are characteristics of the five elements.[6] Living beings evolve with the ability to sense these tanmātrās, therefore all creatures develop a method to hear, feel, see, taste and smell the five elements. The tanmātrās are the objects of the sense organs.

It is important to understand the main characteristics of the elements and their inter-relationships. This should be understood between the tattvas, tanmātrās and senses. The Śrīmad Bhāgavatam gives the nature of each tanmātrā, listed in the graph below:

Tanmatra		Definition according to Śrīmad Bhāgavatam	
Sound	śabda	3.26.33	That which conveys the meaning of an object (*artha-āśrayatva*) and signifies the presence of a speaker (*śabdasya liṅgatva*).
Touch	sparśa	3.26.36	Sensation of soft and hard, cold and hot, etc [the sensation of motion and speed]
Sight	rūpa	3.26.39	Establishes (*saṁsthātva*) the visible appearance (*vyakti*), shape (*ākṛtitva*), and qualities (*guṇatā*) of an object (*dravya*), and effulgence/energy/power (*tejastvam*) from fire (*tejasa*)
Taste	rasa	3.26.42	Due to interaction with the other elements (*bautika*) the single taste becomes divided into astringent (*kaṣāya*), sweet (*madhura*), bitter (*tikta*), pungent (*kaṭu*), sour (*amla*) [and salty].
Smell	gandha	3.26.45	Due to the properties (*avayava*) of various substances (*dravya*) the single odor becomes pleasing/ fragrant (*saurabhya*), pleasant (*śānta*), mixed (*karambha*), putrid (*pūti*), pungent (*ugra*), sour (*amla*), etc.

[5] Śrīmad Bhāgavatam, 3.26.15 *etāvān eva saṁkhyāto brahmaṇaḥ sa-guṇasya ha sanniveśo mayā prokto yaḥ kālaḥ pañca-viṁśakaḥ*. See also Śrī Kālacakra Tantra I.4 *kālācchūndyeṣu (kālātūlyeśu) vāyu jvalena jaladhara....*

[6] Caraka Saṁhitā, Śārīrasthānam I.27 *mahābhūtani khaṁ vāyuragnirāpaḥ kṣitistathā| śabdaḥ sparśaśca rupaṁ ca raso gandhasca tadguṇaḥ||*Śārīrasthānam I.31 *arthaḥ śabdādayo jñeyā gocarā viṣayā guṇaḥ||* This is also stated in Vedānta Pañcadaśī II.2.

Philosophical Variations

The *Sāṅkhya Kārikā* of Iśvara Kṛṣṇā says that the tanmātrās generate the tattvas (38). The *Sāṅkhya-Pravachana Sūtra* (1.61) says that the gross elements (*sthūla-bhūtāni*) come from the subtle elements (*tanmātras*). Then it says '*stūlāt pañca tanmātrasya*' which literally means 'five tanmātras from the gross' and is often taught as 'knowedge of the five tanmātras are inferred from the material elements' (1.62).

The view of the 4th century *Sāṅkhya Kārikā* and *Sāṅkhya-Pravachana Sūtra* is a linear view with a dual foundation (Puruṣa and Prakṛti). The *Sāṅkhya Kārikā* is non-theistic (as god cannot be proven). Prakṛti separates from Puruṣa and then Mahat is created from which Ahaṅkāra is generated. The 10 indriyas come into existence through sattva moved by rajas and the tanmātrās come into existence from tamas moved by rajas.[7] The tanmātrās then become dense and manifest the five elements.

The foundation of the view that the tanmātrās manifest the five elements into material reality is that the five elements are material reality, and that the subtle reality (*tanmātrā*) must manifest first.The sound in thesubtle body produces physical space. As the thought of something that tastes good makes the mouth salivate, the tanmātrā of taste produces the water element. There is the subtle element (*tanmātrā*) of sound which creates vibration making space and from it the sense of hearing originates. When there is no physical body there is still the sense of hearing (as in a dream one still hears). The sense of hearing manifests the ears on the material level and the power of speech manifests the mouth. In this way the subtle elements create the world by densifying the subtle level.

Parāśara teaches a theistic trinity (Puruṣa, Prakṛti, Kāla) generating causal, subtle, and waking consciousness, and the three guṇas, then the jīva, manas, and ahaṅkāra with all of these elements existing in a seed form of the creation similar to a map of a human in the DNA of a sperm and egg. The pañcatattvas, tanmātrās, senses and sense organs are all created as part of that root matter (*pradhānā*). Then the material world that we perceive takes manifestation out of this root matter (like an incubating cosmic egg) and beings take form.

From the astrological perspective, the pañcatattvas manifest in the physical realm as tangible physical objects, but they are much more than this. The pañcatattvas exist in a subtle state on each level of consciousness. This is how there can be five aspects of mind divided into the five elements, or how each element can manifest different emotions, or how a planet becomes an Ātmakāraka (soul level). Parāśara is using a system of

[7] All schools of Saṅkhya have the pañcatattvas arising from tamas. Parāśara teaches that the indriya arise from the rajas and the deva arise from sattva. Texts like *Lakśmī Tantra* and *Vedānta Pañcadaśī* (I.17-21) have the jñāna-indriya arising from sattva and the karma-indriya arising from rajas. Suśruta Saṁhitā (Śārīrasthānam I.4-7) uses the same division of *Sāṅkhya Kārikā* but with devas as Parāśara.

pañcatattvas that are the essence of reality (tat-tva); "that" which reality is composed of. We do not correlate Jupiter to sound, we correlate him to ākāśa, the tattva, the essential nature. Venus is associated with water, water will make you understand Venus, taste is a secondary manifestation as are the genitalia associated with the water tattva. In this way, we *understand* the core building blocks of reality which all manifest through the five tattvas.

This is a philosophical difference, but it validates how we use our language in astrology. In all systems the basic linked associations (ākāśa-sound-ear-mouth) remain the same. Everyone agrees that ākāśa is linked to sound which is made by the mouth and heard by the ear. In astrology, we need to utilize the basic linked associations to correctly perceive reality.

Indriya

The five sense faculties are made of all five elements but one becomes predominant. The sense faculty perceives its most dominant element because that is its nature.[8] In this way, the eye is created by the fire element and has vision because of fire. The objects (*artha*) the sense faculties perceive are the tanmatras: sounds, touch, sight, taste, and smell.[9]

By understanding the relationship between the five senses and the pañcatattva, a deeper understanding of both can develop. The attribute of akāśa is sound, it is ethereal and cannot be touched, yet we sense it all the way through us. We are moved by it as it densifies to air (movement). We evolved a mouth to speak and communicate. We can make sound with our hands clapping, but it is the connecting and communicating power of ākāśa/sound that comes through our mouth. And the ears hear; they take in knowledge and understanding, allow us to relate to the environment and to learn and progress. This is the root nature of Jupiter. The attribute of air is touch/sensation, which is created from movement. We externally feel something through our skin/sensory neurons when there is motion. Internally we feel something when we bring our mind/prāṇa to that area of focus, still there is a motion or change happening to have a touch sensation.As the mouth generates sound, the hands generate touch. The hands represent action, work (karma), creating, generating, and grasping on both a physical and mental level. The hands lead us to either do good karma or bad karma, and the results of what we do is worn on our hands, as one who murders has 'the blood of those killed upon his hands'. This is the root nature of Saturn.

The five senses relate to the five modes of perceiving and interacting with the five essences of reality. Each sense correlates to one of the five elements. In this way, there are not seven or eight senses, there are just five. The *Vedānta Pañcadaśī* (II.6-9) says that the five senses function through their external apparatus: the ears, skin, eyes, tongue and nose. But we also hear sounds made by our breath and other sounds when our ears are closed and we feel the internal sensation of hot and cold when we consume food and water. There are sights, tastes and smells generated from inside as well, therefore the sense organs give rise to things within the body as well as outside the body. Therefore we must not be limited by the sense of sight, but understand on all levels the concept of sight that fire indicates, which even includes insight.

Some believe that there are 12 or more senses as opposed to the gross five senses. The Vedic perspective is that there are five root senses, but they have a much broader field as one understands the nature of the pañcatattva. For example, the sense of movement is an internal sense of air compared to the external sense of touch. The sense of balance is an internal sense of ākāśa compared to the external sense of sound.

[8] Caraka Saṁhitā, Sūtrasthāna VIII.14, Śārīrasthānam I.24

[9] Caraka Saṁhitā, Sūtrasthāna VIII.11

In this same way the *Vedānta Pañcadaśī* (II.10) says that all actions can be classified into five groups of speech, grasping, movement, elimination, and sexual intercourse. Even actions performed in agriculture, commerce, service and such can be included into one of these five groups. And these actions are performed through the five organs of action: mouth, hands, feet, genitals and anus (II.11). These can be corrolated to the actions of communication (speech), grasping/achieving, transporting/movement, reproduction, and eliminating/cleaning. This is taken more figuratively than literally. Therefore it is understood that all sensory reception and actions can be correlated to the nature of one of the five elements.

The *Sāṅkhya Kārikā* (33) mentions 13 indriyas acounting for the five jñāna and five karma-indriya plus the three internal instruments of perception (soul, mind, ahaṅkāra). The 'sense' of life, thought and I-ness mentioned by Rudolf Steiner refers to an awareness of these internal instruments preceding the mahābhūtas.The *Sāṅkhya Kārikā* (35) says, the three internal instruments are the cause of comprehension. They are like a house, while the senses are like gates. The five jñāna and five karma-indriyaare the action and the cognitive nature of the five elements (relating to the five planets), and the internal instruments (*antaḥkarana*) relate to the Sun, Moon and Rāhu.[10] The *Bhagavad Gītā* (VII.4) lists these as the eight-fold division of material nature (*prakṛti*): earth, water, fire, air, ākāśa, soul, intelligence, and ahaṇkāra.[11] We can see that this is the root eight principles (*tattva*) from which the other Sāṅkhya principles transform (*vikāra*).

The mahābhūtas/tanmātrās relate to the planets. The sense/attributes related to each become strong when that planet is well placed and strong in the rāśi or navāṁśa trines. The indriya also relate to the houses. The five jñāna-indriyas are indicated by the ninth house from the houses ruling their sense organs as they are the dharma of that sense organ. The lagna is seen for complexion and skin, while the ninth house indicates touch. The second house indicates the eyes, while the tenth house indicates vision. The third house represents the ears and the eleventh house represents hearing. The fourth house represents the nose and the twelfth house represents smell. This is important to differentiate the cause for a certain issue, like whether a person is deaf because of a physical malformation which is operable or whether it is the internal process that does not function, (the kāraka planet as well as the house need to be afflicted to indicate a problem). These houses also indicate the many layers the senses represent. For example, the fifth house is tongue/taste, while it also shows what a person likes, what they are attracted to, what they desire (*iṣṭa*). The fifth house shows us what deities a person likes to worship because it represents what energy they desire in their life (what they are hungry for).

---

[10] Vimalaprabhā, commentary on Śrīkālacakra Tantra I.2

[11] Caraka Saṁhitā, Śārīrasthānam I.63-64 gives a similar concept of 8 prakṛtis and how these transform (*vikāra*) into 24. 'Manas' has been translated as 'soul' (mahan/jīva) in this context according to Vedānta Sūtra II.4.12, Sāṅkhya-Pravachanasūtram 1.71, Sāṅkhya Kārikā 35 for the purpose of staying consistent with the present use of terminology.

We can also see excesses or deficiencies based on planetary strength and malefic and benefic placements in these houses . Planets/houses conjunct Rāhu can show misuse of particular senses. Sensory information is a form of nutrition for the mind, it is what comes through the gates of the house and then resides in the house. Proper sounds, sensations, sights, tastes and smells are essential for physical and mental health. The underuse, overuse or wrong use of any sense can lead to mental and physical disorders by imbalancing the elemental nature of an individual.[12] This is even more important for a child to develop a balanced brain and consciousness. In our time, excessive television and plastic objects over stimulate some senses (sight/sound) and under stimulate others (touch, taste, smell). Living beings, and especially developing children, need balanced sense activation for healthy growth and happiness. Disharmony in the body and mind can be balanced by sense therapies; with particular types of music, massage, colored lights, foods and essential oils.

Sensory Perception

The *Vedānta Pañcadaśī* (II.17) says that the objects in which sound, touch, etc are discernable are products of the five elements. With the help of scriptural texts and reasoning it is understood that even the senses and the [cognitive] mind are made of the five elements. Caraka goes into depth explaining the nature of the sensory system according to the five elements and their interaction with the sense organs and the tanmātrās.[13]

The senses are being perceived with the mind who is considered their ruler, while the mind needs the senses in order to function in relation to external objects. In this way, Caraka says that perceiving is not just the senses and their objects, but sense perceptions are produced from the combination of the senses, the sense objects, the mind and the soul.[14] Sensory information needs the internal instruments (*antaḥkaraṇa*) in order to be understood (*saṁgraha*).

If you don't pay attention to something it is possible that it does not become conscious. When you are focused on a particular task, you may not hear someone talking to you. The sense faculties perceive their respective objects only when they are motivated by the mind.[15] In this way, when we learn something, we notice it in a way we would not have in our ignorance. Perception is very subjective.

Caraka says these sense perceptions are 'momentary' and we use them to 'determine' the nature of our reality. They are momentary in that we sense them and then they go

[12] Caraka Saṁhitā, Śārīrasthānam I.118-131, discussed by Caraka immediately following karma-ja disease

[13] Caraka Saṁhitā, Sutrasthana VIII.1-14 and Śārīrasthānam I.17-38 (particularly I.24, 32-34), also Vedānta Pañcadaśī II.12-13

[14] Caraka Saṁhitā, Sūtrasthāna VIII.12-13

[15] Caraka Saṁhitā, Sūtrasthāna VIII.7

away. We use a momentary sensation to feel and evaluate our reality. Our experience is determined by how and what is being perceived through the senses. Yet the mind determines what it focuses on thereby guiding what we experience of a particular environment. In this way, different people are present for the same event but have very different experiences of that event.And as the event (and the sensory experience from it) is momentary we are left only with a mental image (memory) to judge our experience which is distorted more by the guṇas of the memory.

The mind and what it perceives is guided by the guṇas. What you experience and how you judge it is determined by the guṇa of your mind. The guṇas are guiding how the mind is using the senses and the sensory function is based on the elements. Therefore it is the guṇas and the pañcatattvas that are determining an individual's perceived reality. We can see based upon planetary combinations, what guṇas and tattvas are leading the mind and creating a person's perceived reality. We see the guṇa and elements in all areas of their life through the planets.

This affects our entire view of life as well as the little day to day things that we 'chose' to do. For example, there was a time you looked at yourself and thought you looked good with long hair. Another time period you looked at yourself and thought you looked good with short hair. Where did this thought come from that made you feel this or that looked better? When we are unaware of where are perceptions are coming from, we think that we chose to like or dislike something, and thereby chose whether to have short or long hair. We think we chose the fashion, nature and quality of our clothing. Yet, all our choices are being guided by the likes and dislikes, attraction and repulsion that exist from the way the guṇas and elements are creating the perception based on their predominance, strength and weakness.

That which we call reality (the world) is nothing but the perception of sensory stimuli. What you call reality is only the perceptions of your senses registered by the guṇas of your mind. What you see is only based on what you know and what guṇas are controlling the mind. Your choices are the result of this perception. Daśā changes the guṇas and elements and so your perception changes and therefore your actions change.

What is real? What can you be attached to? To fully understand this is to put ourselves in great humility, and to be unattached to our perceptions. Once we understand the mechanism that makes this body-mind work, we actually have the ability to look from a higher vantage point and not be controlled by simple desires. The soul nature has room to work and see itself. The ability to chase after one's choice is actually bondage to desire, and the mind is then clouded by the guṇa and element of that desire. Freedom is the space of seeing it all as it is.

This leads us to focus on That which is actually Real; 'whose form is the blissful perception of absolute unity (*kevala-anubhava-ānanda-svarūpa*); the bliss of That which perceives the wholeness; also called as Sat-chit-ānanda. The Real is aware of all apprehension (*sarva-buddhi-dṛk*).That which was before the guṇas, elements, sense organs and intellect cannot be apprehended by them. That which is all, the essence of all, the nature of reality has no inside or outside, no boundary circumscribing.'[16] The scriptures teach us to understand the nature ofcreated reality (how it is created/perceived) and to meditate on that which is its foundation.Then we realize that the mind, thoughts, and feelings that make the average person suffer are just the results of guṇas and tattvas and we become aware of our real nature.

The System of the Five Elements in the Modern World

In Āyurveda, these linked associations (*anvaya*) are used to understand disease and formulate treatments of both the body and mind. In Yoga and Vedānta, thelinked relationships are understood to realize that we are beyond themby showing us the reality of our perceptions. This understanding allows the mind to properly discriminate and not identify withmaterial creation and therefore naturally supports unattachment.We then can focus our attention on the unchanging.

In the *Yoga Sūtras*, Patañjali says,

स्थूलस्वरूपसूक्ष्मान्वयार्थवत्त्वसंयमाद्भूतजयः ॥ ४४ ॥

sthūlasvarūpasūkṣmānvayārthavattvasaṁyamādbhūtajayaḥ || 3.44||

By profound meditation (*saṁyama*) on the gross and subtle forms of the elements, their linked associations, and their significance one gains mastery over the elements.

ग्रहणस्वरूपास्मितान्वयार्थवत्त्वसंयमाद् इन्द्रियजयः ॥ ४७ ॥

grahaṇasvarūpāsmitānvayārthavattvasaṁyamād indriyajayaḥ || 3.47||

By profound meditation on the form of the sense organs relative to the I-sense, with their linked associations and significance one gains mastery over the senses.

ततो मनोजवित्वं विकरणभावः प्रधानजयश्च ॥ ४८ ॥

tato manojavitvaṁ vikaraṇabhāvaḥ pradhānajayaśca || 3.48||

From that comes swiftness of thought, the ability to modify one's mental state, and mastery over primordial matter (*Pradhāna*).

To the ancient yogīs, the correlation of the elements, tanmātrās, senses, etc. was a roadmap to transcend reality. The theory is not a faith based belief, but is intended to be investigated, and realized. Vedic and Yogic (*vaidika and yaugika*) science is based on this.

[16] Śrīmad Bhāgavatam, Vasudeva's Hymn, 10.3.13-22

Therefore you must deepen your awareness and experience these principles with your own perception. Comprehending them only by reading is not understanding them fully, and will not give complete utilization.

In the industrialized mind, there is an egotistical misconception that modern science is better than anything the ancients had, and that ancient science was patchy guess work. Modern science has improved our understanding of many things, but it has also lost the essence of the human being in its approach. For example, a modern doctor is trained to use machines that test for any issues that may be diseased. An Āyurvedic doctor trains their awareness to be able to recognize disease. The western doctor does not grow in inner knowledge of the self by learning about the machines, while the Āyurvedic doctor is continually refining his awareness to perceive the individual and universe better, which thereby allows him to be more aware of his self and the universe we live in. Western science has many wondrous advancements to add to our practice, but we must be aware not to lose the essence the Vedic paradigm gives us.

The ancients did not base how advanced they were on what material machines they created nor on how they were able to manipulate natural resources. They based their advancement on their state of consciousness. It may be hard for a person living in an industrialized society tofully understandwhat advancement is; to live in a cement house, with hazardous insulation, paint that is off-gassing chemicals, bio-hazardous materials that a chemical company convinced one would 'clean' their house, and constant influx of other materials that destroy the eco-system of the earth....to think that this is more advanced than a healthy, eco-friendly, thatched mud hut is an industrialized view (not advancement). The consciousness of the individual in the hut could be tremendously more aware and more educated, and this is what advanced means in the Vedic paradigm. The unconscious, unsafe, profit-driven manipulation of matter is a false attachment of the industrialized mind. For example, with the creation of the calculator, the mind has become lazier. To contemplate and calculate math in the head creates a healthy balanced logic, which has become weak due to the advanced technology of the calculator.

The Vedic paradigm is intended to increase the capacity of the physical mind, refine our skills, expand awareness, cultivate our higher consciousness, and manifest the higher abilities that are found within the human system. In the *Yoga Sūtras*, Patañjali says,

श्रोत्राकाशयोः संबन्धसंयमाद् दिव्यं श्रोत्रम् ॥ ४१ ॥

śrotrākāśayoḥ sambandhasaṁyamād divyaṁ śrotram || 41||

By profound meditation (*saṁyama*) on the relationship of the ear to the ākāśa one gains the power of supernatural hearing.

बहिरकल्पिता वृत्तिर्महाविदेहा । ततः प्रकाशावरणक्षयः ॥ ४३ ॥

bahirakalpitā vṛttirmahāvidehā| tataḥ prakāśāvaraṇakṣayaḥ|| 43||

By profoundmeditation on the thoughts (*vṛtti*) in the astral body (*mahāvidehā*) when it is outside the physical body all coverings are removed from the Light (*prakāśa*).

Patañjali is not discussing a machine that can be patented to be able to have supernatural hearing. Or a computer system to tap phones with voice activated word recognition programs. He is speaking of refining our own consciousness, at no monetary cost, to be able to perceive what we need to, when we need to. It is something that when acquired will never need to be upgraded. He is talking about something that requires high states of concentration and anadvanced enough consciousness to attain awareness of our energetic body.

Without modern technology, this book might not be in your hands, so there are many benefits to advanced technology. What we have to avoid is to think that because we have a greater ability to manipulate nature, or look at a molecule, that the knowledge of the ancients has become inferior.

The theory of the five elements is not an outdated system created by some ignorant people who did not have the equipment to know better. It is a system of quantifying reality into aspects which the mind can organically perceive and utilize. It is a system which utilizes awareness and thereby expands awareness. Living in this modern age, it is important that we work on *updating* our own concept of what is "advancement".

When you look at a person, can you tell what planets are strong, and what daśā they must be running? When you hear someone speak, can you tell what elements are deficient? Can you feel what cakras are blocked when a person sits in front of you? Can you quiet your mind, and sit in deep peace? Can you stay conscious at night when you fall asleep? These are the areas we need to work to become advanced. Understanding the five elements and their linked associations is a tool to help us progress.

Caraka says that the individual is known as the compilation of the 24 principles of creation. And the individual consciousness is united (*yukta*) with them through rajas and tamas, and freed (*nirvarta*) from them through the cultivation of sattva (*sattva-vṛddhatha*). Actions and their fruit, understanding and delusion, happiness and suffering, life and death are based on this (*atra pratiṣṭhita*); [based on the guṇa one is stationed in]. One who knows these elements (*tattvena*) knows creation and dissolution, traditional medical treatment (*pāramparya cikitsā*) and whatever else that is knowable (*jñātavya*).[17]

[17] Caraka Saṁhitā, Śārīrasthānam I.35-38

Deities Associated with Pañcatattvas

The five elements have a deity relationship used in pūjās. In the Vedic paradigm, the element itself is a divinity. Jala or Āpas is water as a goddess, the element is seen as divinity itself. There is little differentiation between fire as something that is burning and fire as the god Agni. In fact, the word was the same, and differentiation of material element or deity is a matter of context. The Vedic paradigm sees the world as divinity and all aspects of it as faces of that divinity.

Element	Diety
Ākāśa	Viṣṇu
Vāyu	Śiva
Agni	Sūrya
Jala	Śakti
Pṛthvi	Gaṇeśa

In modern religious schools there are varying correlations. There are two common systems used which give good results. The first is a system which divided each of the primary deities in Hinduism into one of the five elements. There are those that worship these five deities everyday to insure that everything in their life is in harmony. This devatā can also be utilized when there is disharmony with that particular element. Viṣṇu is the all-pervasive ākāśa, Śiva is the destructive wind. Sūrya is the fire, the Goddess is water, and Gaṇeśa relates to the earth element.

Element	Form of Śiva
Ākāśa	Īśāna
Vāyu	Tatpuruṣa
Agni	Aghora
Jala	Vāmadeva
Pṛthvi	Sadyojāta

The great god, Śiva, is also considered the lord of the five elements, as the material five elements manifest from the *tamas* ahaṅkāra. The five faces of Śiva relate to the elements in most Tantras and Purāṇas, and there are various visualizations and mantras for each. In Kaśmiri Śaivism, Śiva is considerd as the highest god and in that system the face of Śiva relates to kriyā, jñāna, icchā, ānanda, and cit which are higher level tattvas. But for general purposes the five forms of Śiva relating to his five faces is used to represent the five elements.

Planets and Tattvas

Sage Parāśara discusses the tattvas in the chapter on the Effects of the Five Elements (*pañca-mahābhūta*).[18] His description elucidates the relationship between the elements, the tanmātrās, the planets and the daśās. Sage Parāśara says,

अथ पञ्चमहाभूतच्छायाज्ञानं वदामि ते ।
ज्ञायते येन खेटानां वर्तमानदशा बुधैः ॥ १ ॥

atha pañcamahābhūtacchāyājñānaṁ vadāmi te |
jñāyate yena kheṭānāṁ vartamānadaśā budhaiḥ || 1||

Now I will speak about perceiving the five elements within
From the present condition (*vartamānadaśā*) of the planets, Intelligent one.

शिखिभूखाम्बुवातानामधिपा मङ्गलादयः ।
तत्तद्बलावशाज्ज्ञेयं तत्तद्भूतभवं फलम् ॥ २ ॥

śikhibhūkhāmbuvātānāmadhipā maṅgalādayaḥ |
tattadbalāvaśājjñeyaṁ tattadbhūtabhavaṁ phalam || 2||

Fire, earth, ether, water, air, are ruled by Mars etc.
Those elements exist in all beings,
but will give results according to that which dominates in strength.

Parāśara indicates he will elucidate the relationship between the planets and the elements. The word he uses for planets is *kheṭānāṁ* which means 'that which moves in the sky.' He is poetically saying he will teach the relationship between the five elements within us in relation to that which moves in the sky, or it can be said as 'the relationship between the below and the above'.

Fire is ruled by Mars, earth is ruled by Mercury, ākāśa/ether is ruled by Jupiter, water is ruled by Venus and air is ruled by Saturn. The list is given in the order of the weekdays.This order is important to indicate the elements relating to the planets or the planets relating to the elements. For example, the Pañca-Mahāpuruṣa yogas are given in this order, indicating they are relating directly to the elements; (the techniques taught below alsoneed to be applied to the ṣaṣṭyaṁśa to indicate how much the element supports the unfoldment of the Mahāpuruṣa yoga). The following verses continue to speak about the elements in this same weekday order.

[18] Bṛhat Parāśara Horā Śāstra, Pañca-mahābhūta-phala-adhyāya

सबले मङ्गले वह्निस्वभावो जायते नरः ।
बुधे महीस्वभावः स्यादाकाशप्रकृतिर्गुरौ ॥ ३ ॥

sabale maṅgale vahnisvabhāvo jāyate naraḥ |
budhe mahīsvabhāvaḥ syādākāśaprakṛtirgurau || 3||

If Mars is with strength then fire will be the inherent disposition of the individual.
If Mercury is with strength then earth is the inherent disposition,
If Jupiter is strongest then ākāśa is the constitution.

शुक्रे जलस्वभावश्च मारुतप्रकृतिः शनौ ।
मिश्रैर्मिश्रस्वभावश्च विज्ञेयो द्विजसत्तम ॥ ४ ॥
सूर्ये वह्निस्वभावश्च जलप्रकृतिको विधौ ।

śukre jalasvabhāvaśca mārutaprakṛtiḥ śanau |
miśrairmiśrasvabhāvaśca vijñeyo dvijasattama || 4||
sūrye vahnisvabhāvaśca jalaprakṛtiko vidhau |5a|

Venus will give a watery inherent disposition, Saturn will give an air constitution,
And know that mixed planets will give a mixed natural disposition.
The Sun gives a fiery inherent disposition, and the Moon gives a watery constitution.

Sage Parāśara has given the planet-tattva relationship, and indicates that the planet dominating in strength will give the characteristics of its tattva to the individual. The strongest planet will often be a very strong planet in kendra, in the lagna or conjunct the Moon. A planet in lagna is not enough, it must be the most strongly influencing planet. If an individual has Venus in Aries lagna with Sun and Mars in the tenth house, then the agni tattva will be dominant. In this way, a proper examination of strength should be done, as well as more specific techniques to see which planet is most strongly influencing the individual.

Parāśara has listed the elemental planets and has added that the luminaries are also indicating fire and water respectively. Even though the Sun and Moon are a higher level of manifestation, they still will have their quality which manifests on the physical realm. The energy of the mind is watery, and the energy of the soul is fiery with all the qualities of light.

स्वदशायां ग्रहाश्छायांव्यञ्जयन्ति स्वभूतजाम् ॥ ५ ॥

svadaśāyāṁ grahāśchāyāṁ vyañjayanti svabhūtajām || 5b||

The planets will also display their elemental qualities during their daśā.

There is the inherent nature of an individual, and then there is the nature which arises at that time (*tātkālika*), during a specific daśā. An individual will tend to be leaner during Sun daśā and gain more weight during Moon daśā. Other changes that occurred at the beginning of the daśā will relate to the quality of the element.

Parāśara then describes individuals according to each predominant element.

क्षुधार्तश्चपलः शूरः कृशः प्राज्ञोऽतिभक्षणः ।
तीक्ष्णो गौरतनुर्मानी वह्निप्रकृतिको नरः ॥ ६ ॥

kṣudhārtaścapalaḥ śūraḥ kṛśaḥ prājño'tibhakṣaṇaḥ |
tīkṣṇo gauratanurmānī vahniprakṛtiko naraḥ || 6||

The person of fiery nature is bothered by hunger, has a voracious appetite, is strong (*śūra*), and lean (*kṛśa*).They change their mind often (*capala*), are intelligent, sharp (*tīkṣṇa*), and proud(*mānī*) and have a bright complexion (*gaura-tanu*).

कर्पूरोत्पलगन्धाढ्यो भोगी स्थिरसुखी बली ।
क्षमावान् सिंहनादश्च महीप्रकृतिको नरः ॥ ७ ॥

karpūrotpalagandhāḍhyo bhogī sthirasukhī balī |
kṣamāvān siṁhanādaśca mahīprakṛtiko naraḥ || 7||

The person of earth nature smells like camphor and water-lily, is wealthy (*āḍhya*), and enjoys life (*bhogī*).They have steady happiness, are robust (*balī*), patient (*kṣamāvan*), and sound like a lion (*siṁha-nāda*) [strong will power or firmness (*dṛḍha*) in their voice].

शब्दार्थवित् सुनीतिज्ञो प्रगल्भो ज्ञानसंयुतः ।
विवृतास्योऽतिदीर्घश्च व्योमप्रकृतिसम्भवः ॥ ८ ॥

śabdārthavit sunītijño pragalbho jñānasaṁyutaḥ |
vivṛtāsyo'tidīrghaśca vyomaprakṛtisambhavaḥ || 8||

One with an ākāśa nature knows linguistics (or the meaning of words, or oral tradition), Is an expert in diplomacy/has good guidance (*sunītijña*), is confident (*pragalbha*), knowledgeable, has an easy to read face (*vivṛta-āsya*), and long stature [holds themselves upright].

कान्तिमान् भारवाही च प्रियवाक् पृथिवीपतिः ।
बहुमित्रो मृदुर्विद्वान् जलप्रकृतिसम्भवः ॥ ९ ॥

kāntimān bhāravāhī ca priyavāk pṛthivīpatiḥ |
bahumitro mṛdurvidvān jalaprakṛtisambhavaḥ || 9||

One with a water nature is beautiful or well-adorned (*kāntimān*), can carry large burdens, has kind speech (*priyavāk*), lives like a king, has many friends, and has an understanding of how to be gentle (*mṛdurvidvān*).

वायुतत्त्वाधिको दाता क्रोधी गौरोऽटनप्रियः ।
भूपतिश्च दुराधर्षः कृशाङ्गो जायते जनः ॥ १० ॥

vāyutattvādhiko dātā krodhī gauro'ṭanapriyaḥ |
bhūpatiśca durādharṣaḥ kṛśāṅgo jāyate janaḥ || 10||

Know that abundant vāyu tattva gives wrathfulness (*krodhī*), a light complexion,
fondness for roaming (*aṭana priya*), the individual is lord of the earth,
is difficult to be attacked or insulted, and is thin bodied (*kṛśāṅga*).

Parāśara first gives a verse for each element (in the order of the weekdays) and then he again gives a verse for each element. The qualities indicated are those which cannot be differentiated between the planet and the element itself. The tanmātrās related to the element are also the senses through which that element finds pleasure. In this way, when earth element predominates the individual will desire good smells, and if Mercury is very strong they will even have a naturally good smell about them. When the fire element predominates, the individual will have a desire for shiny bright things, and will also have a luster to their skin or aura. When the ākāśa predominates the individual has a deep interest in sound and language, which therefore gives good knowledge in these related subjects. If the senses are being utilized there will also be some interaction of the associated jñāna and karma-indriyas.

स्वर्णदीप्तिः शुभा दृष्टिः सर्वकार्यार्थसिद्धिता ।
विजयो धनलाभश्च वह्निभायां प्रजायते ॥ ११ ॥

svarṇadīptiḥ śubhā dṛṣṭiḥ sarvakāryārthasiddhitā |
vijayo dhanalābhaśca vahnibhāyāṁ prajāyate || 11||

The individual who shines like the fire element has the luster of gold,
good vision (*śubhā dṛṣṭi*), he achieves success in all work,
wins competitions (*vijaya*), and gains wealth.

इष्टगन्धः शरीरे स्यात् सुस्निग्धनखदन्तता ।
धर्मार्थसुखलाभश्च भूमिच्छाया यदा भवेत् ॥ १२ ॥

iṣṭagandhaḥ śarīre syāt susnigdhanakhadantatā |
dharmārthasukhalābhaśca bhūmicchāyā yadā bhavet || 12||

When the earth is predominant the body has a desirable smell (*iṣṭa-gandha*),
Smooth/thick/glossy fingernails and teeth, and there is gain of dharma, wealth, and happiness.

स्वच्छा गगनजा छाया वाक्पटुत्वप्रदा भवेत् ।
सुशब्दश्रवणोद्भूतं सुखं तत्र प्रजायते ॥ १३ ॥

svacchā gaganajā chāyā vākpaṭutvapradā bhavet |
suśabdaśravaṇodbhūtaṁ sukhaṁ tatra prajāyate || 13||

The clear sky element (*ākāśa*) gives one expertise in speech (eloquence),
And one will get pleasure (*sukhaṁ*) from listening to beautiful sounds (*su-śabda*).

मृदुता स्वस्थता देहे जलच्छाया यदा भवेत्।
तदाऽभीष्टरसस्वादसुखं भवति देहिनः ॥ १४ ॥

mṛdutā svasthatā dehe jalacchāyā yadā bhavet |
tadā'bhīṣṭarasasvādasukhaṁ bhavati dehinaḥ || 14||

When water predominates, the individual has natural softness to the body [roundness, curves, excess weightor even edema], and enjoys desires for tastes (*rasa*) and flavors (*svāda*).

मालिन्यं मूढता दैन्यं रोगश्च पवनोद्भवः।
तदा च शोकसन्तापौ वायुच्छाया यदा भवेत्॥ १५ ॥

mālinyaṁ mūḍhatā dainyaṁ rogaśca pavanodbhavaḥ |
tadā ca śokasantāpau vāyucchāyā yadā bhavet || 15||

When the air predominates there is impurity, ignorance/folly/stupidity (*mūḍhatā*), Miserable/mean (*dainyaṁ*), vāta disorders, sorrow (*śoka*), and afflictions (*santāpa*).

The chart below is a summary of the above for quick reference and cross study.

Agni	Mars	hunger, voracious appetite, strength, lean, fickle, intelligent, sharp, proud, and bright complexion. (6)	luster of gold, good vision, achieves success in all work, wins competitions, and gains wealth. (11)
Pṛthvī	Mercury	smells like camphor and water-lily, wealthy, bhogī, steady happiness, patient , and has firm determination in their speech. (7)	desirable smell, glossy fingernails and teeth, gain of dharma, wealth, and happiness. (12)
Ākāśa	Jupiter	knows linguistics, expert in diplomacy, good guidance, confident, knowledgeable, easy to read face, and upright stature. (8)	eloquence, pleasure from listening to beautiful sounds (*su-śabda*). (13)
Jala	Venus	well-adorned, can carry large burdens, kind speech, lives like a king, many friends, and knowledge of gentleness. (9)	softness to the body, enjoys desires for tastes and flavors, full-bodied. (14)
Vāyu	Saturn	easily angered, light complexion, fond of roaming, lord of the earth, difficult to be attacked or insulted, and thin bodied. (10)	impurity, ignorance, consumption of alcohol/ cowardliness, vāta disorders, sorrow, and afflictions. (15)

These indications can be compared to the results of the Pañca-Mahāpuruṣa yogas to get better depth of understanding the planets and elements. Suśruta Saṁhitā mentions that there are some who view the human constitution according to the five elements (*bautika prakṛti*).[19] He explains the standard three consitutions and adds that the earth consitution

[19] Suśruta Saṁhitā, Śārīrasthāna, IV.76 (IV.64-76)

(*pārthiva*) has a firm (*sthira*) and thick (*vipula*) body and that they are patient (*kṣama*) like the earth herself. The ākāśa constitution (*nābhasa*) is pure (*suchiratha*), long-lived (*cirajīvin*) and has large passages. With five element constitutions a doctor still analyses the three doṣas as causing problems (*doṣa*) within the five constitutions. The vāta-pitta-kapha constitution (*prakṛti*) of an individual is based on the lagna and planets associated with it, as will be discussed in the Āyurveda chapter. The predominant element is based on the chart as a whole, with an emphasis on the lagneśa.

एवं फलं बुधैर्ज्ञेयं सबलेषु कुजादिषु ।
निर्बलेषु तथा तेषु वक्तव्यं व्यत्ययाद् द्विज ॥ १६ ॥

evaṁ phalaṁ budhairjñeyaṁ sabaleṣu kujādiṣu |
nirbaleṣu tathā teṣu vaktavyaṁ vyatyayād dvija || 16||

In this way, these results are to be realized if the planets are with strength,
If they are weak (*nirbala*), then one should speak the opposite (*vyatyaya*).

नीचशत्रुभगैश्चापि विपरीतं फलं वदेत् ।
फलाप्तिरबलैः खेटैः स्वप्नचिन्तासु जायते ॥ १७ ॥

nīcaśatrubhagaiścāpi viparītaṁ phalaṁ vadet |
phalāptirabalaiḥ kheṭaiḥ svapnacintāsu jāyate || 17||

Also, if the planet is in debilitation or an enemy's sign the results will be the opposite,
And if the planet is weak (*abala*) the planet will give results only in imagination.

In the natal, chart if the planet is strong the individual will in general have the beneficial attributes of that element. If the planet is weak or afflicted the individual will lack those qualities. During the daśā of a planet, the qualities of the element become prominent. If the planet is strong, then the results of the element will be very favorable. If the planet is weak, then during the daśā there will be problems with the associated tattva, tanmātrā, and through the related senses. For example, if the Moon (water-taste) is afflicted, in its daśā the individual will have a hard time finding food that is satisfying to them. In the same way, if Moon is in the sixth house, eighth house or its debilitation there will be other issues related to the water element.

If the planet is well-placed but weak, the benefits of the element will be experienced only in the imagination (*svapnacintā*). For example, in Mars daśā, if Mars is very weak then the individual will dream of winning competitions but may not even enter one. This is why it is good to have negative placements be weak and positive placements be strong.

Saturn is the planet of suffering, so his indications are negative if he is strongly affecting the points which relate to the self in the chart. If he is placed in the third, sixth, tenth, or eleventh house then he will give beneficial results by alleviating some of his qualities. Understanding this, one can contemplate the indication for an alcoholic: Saturn associated with the Lagna, Ārūḍha lagna and/or the Moon. Saturn shows the use of alcohol, and therefore the more points of the self that he is influencing the more his qualities will appear in the individual's nature. In this way, the stronger the planet influences the points indicating the self, the more it will influence the individual.

Everyone is a mixture of all elements, though one or more elements may become predominant. The planet lording the active daśā will increase an element's influence on the individual. Variations will change according to daśā, as planets that were not prominent enough will get enough energy to show their results.

तद्दुष्टफलशान्त्यर्थमपि चाज्ञातजन्मनाम् ।
फलपक्त्या दशा ज्ञेया वर्तमाना नभःसदाम् ॥ १८ ॥

taddustaphalaśāntyarthamapi cājñātajanmanām |
phalapaktyā daśā jñeyā vartamānā nabhaḥsadām || 18||

If the birth information is unknown (*ajñāta-janman*),
Then this can be used to determine the remedy (*śānti*) for problems (*duṣṭaphala*),
The planet *(sky-dweller)* of the present daśā should be known by the ripening fruit.

If the birth data is unknown, the remedy can be given according to the elemental indications that are causing a problem. For example, if there is problem in the love-life (water) then Lakṣmī can be worshiped. If there are problems with not having enough energy then a Mars remedy can be utilized. This is meant for situations when the birth data is unknown or one cannot determine the problem from the chart. The cause of the problem should be inferred from the issue. Unfortunately, this is an extremely overused rule and it should NOT be the standard to give remedies. However, one should know this to help people even when one cannot look at the chart.

When there is lack of birth time but one has the information to cast a chart, the running daśā can also be inferred according to the nature of the elements in the individual's life. In a day, there is only so much variation to which daśā would start the life (according to the nakṣatra). But how much of that daśā has passed and where the present individual is can be determined according to the "ripening fruit" which are the consequences of the daśā.

Parāśara began the *Pañca-mahābhūta-adhyāya* by saying he will speak about perceiving the five elements within from the present condition (*vartamāna daśā*) of the planets. He gives examples of elemental qualities which can be perceived in an individual's life. The good astrologer will be able to see events happening and quantify it into a change of a certain element.

Assignment

Collect the charts of ten people who have the qualities of each elementas described above. Analyze these charts to find the nature of how that element becomes strong. Nothing compares to the experience of seeing charts. Yet seeing charts for thirty years without knowing what to look at gives little fruit. With specific intention, collect these charts and categorize them, so they can teach you.

Svara Śāstra (Science of Breath)

When looking at a chart or answering a question *Praśna Mārga* says the predominating element can be determined by [1] examination of the astrologer's breath, [2] from the first letter of the word uttered by the individual, or [3] from the time of the query. First we will discuss the breath, afterwards we discuss the vowels, and I just mention the elements of the kālacakra.[20]

There are three branches of Jyotiṣa: Gaṇita, Horā, and Saṁhitā. *Svara Śāstra* is a Saṁhitā science which focuses on observing the five elements in the breath. Svara has a few meanings: a tone in music, a vowel, the voice, and the air breathed through the nostrils. Here it means the air breathed through the nostrils and the observation of the quality of that breath.

Mahat has three aspects: buddhi, prāṇa and kāla. As we breathe, thought moves, and time turns. Buddhi has the five aspects of the tattvas (seen in psychology), kāla has the five aspects of the tattvas (seen in the pañcāṅga), and prāṇa has the five tattvas (seen in the five-fold division of the vāyus). Furthermore, each of these five-fold divisions of each of these can take on the qualitative nature of the five elements. The water element of the buddhi (mind) can have a hot emotion like anger. The fire element of kāla (vāra) can have an ākāśa day like Thursday. In the same way, the outgoing breath can take on the qualities of each of the elements. Therefore we must understand the elements in the outgoing breath.

Time turns and we breathe. The base unit of time is a prāṇa (a breath of 4 seconds), of which six make a vighaṭikā (24 seconds), and 60 vighaṭikās make a ghaṭīkā. Two and a half ghaṭikās make an hour. Each hour can be divided into the five elements with each element ruling 12 minutes (approximately 180 prāṇa). In the sky, each sign is divided into two halves, solar and lunar and each rises for an hour. In this same way, the nostrils run on the solar side (*Piṅgalā*) for one hour, and on the lunar side (*Īḍā*) for one hour.

On a Sunday, the breath generally starts in the right nostril at sunrise. It will run through each element, lasting approximately (not exactly) 12 minutes. Then it will switch to the left nostril, and run through each element. In this way, the nāḍī is active for about 15 degrees (a horā) and the element is active for 3 degrees (a daśāṁśa). In one day the breath will move through 120 elements (5 X 24 horās).

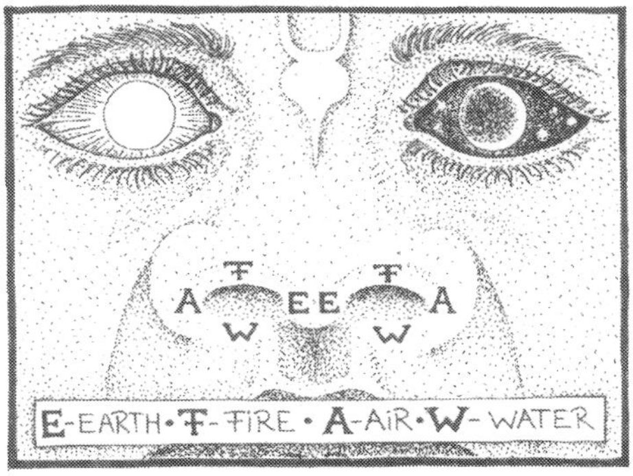

[20] We discuss the vowels according to the standard kulākula cakra, compared with those given by Harihara: a- pṛthvī, i- jala, u- agni, e-vāyu, and o-ākāśa.

With a slow inhale and exhale one can easily be aware of the difference between the flow of breath between the two nostrils. With more subtle awareness, one can be aware of how the air is moving through the active nostril. Earth moves along the middle of the nasal passage, water moves on the lower portion close to the body (like snot running out of the nose). Fire runs along the top side of the nostril opposite the water, and air runs along the outer side of the nostril. Ākāśa runs through the center or can be felt as moving more evenly through the nostril. Those who have studied Āyurvedic pulse diagnosis should be able to easily feel the difference in the movement of the breath, as it is distinct yet subtle, similar to the pulse.

An astrologer should perform *svara sādhana* at some point to gain awareness of the qualities of breath. Svara sādhana involves awakening early, and sitting for meditation one hour before sunrise. One can see the breath move through the elements, and should mediate on the elements as they are active (color, cakra, bīja). At the moment of Sunrise, one can observe the breath becoming balanced between the two nostrils. This is the moment that the breath is changing from the lunar nāḍī (*Īḍā*) to the solar nāḍī (*Piṅgalā*). This happens every hour, but the sunrise and sunset change is longer, deeper, and easier to be aware of. It is also a very important spiritual moment, where the breath naturally flows in the central channel (*suṣumnā*). One then watches the breath for another hour as the breath moves through each element in the other nāḍī.

The nāḍīs are active from sunrise to the next sunrise. The breath will indicate the moment of sunrise, if one is paying attention to the changes of the qualities. Many texts indicate the use of the standardized horās that are an equal length of 60 minutes each, though I have not found this to be the case. This may vary per person, or may vary according to different places. An astrologer should take awareness of the movement of breath in the nostrils (*svara*) to be aware of how they can percieve the lunar and solar currents and the movement of the elements. Various activities, emotions, or sickness will also change the svara and one should be aware of these changes.

The flow of the breath will change according to the day of the week and the tithi of the Moon. In Astrology, a good or bad day, or other results are determined by the ruling vāra, tithi, and nakṣatra at sunrise. These will affect the flow of prāṇa in the nāḍīs. One who is expert with the svara (*svaravid*) can know the time of day from their breath.

The *Pavana Vijaya Svarodaya* says that svara is the brain of astrology. Therefore an astrologer without the knowledge of svara is considered as a body without a head. In general, svara is used by Yogīs. Awareness of the breath allows one to perform actions according to the most auspicious moments.

To begin utilizing the svara, one should be aware of two important movements of the breath. One should only eat when the solar nāḍī is active, otherwise digestion will not be as proper. One should go to sleep only when the lunar nāḍī is active or else sleep will not be as restful. If one can become aware of these simple activities relative to the placement of the svara then slowly one will gain proficiency in this subject. When actions are performed in alignment with the running element they have good results, when opposed to the running element there is difficulties. Being aware of the svara will increase the intuition (*pratibhā*) and therefore the accuracy of astrological interpretations and predictions.

Kālacakra Elements

The Kālacakra divides the day into eight parts (90 minutes long). The odd parts are divided by the elements of earth (30 minutes), water (24 minutes), fire (18 minutes), air (12 minutes) and ākāśa (6 minutes), while the even parts are divided in the reverse by ākāśa, air, fire, water and earth with the same time period for each element. This is used by some astrologers to determine the predominant element when someone asks a question (*praśna*) to be able to give a quick answer. Praśna Mārga says that, according to this system, earth and water indicate auspiciousness. Fire, air and ākāśa do not give good results [7.30]. When the division of earth is indicated, things will remain the same, in water they will soon be accomplished, in fire there will be enmity, in air things that are coming and going are successful, and in ākāśa there is disease and failure [16.32-35].

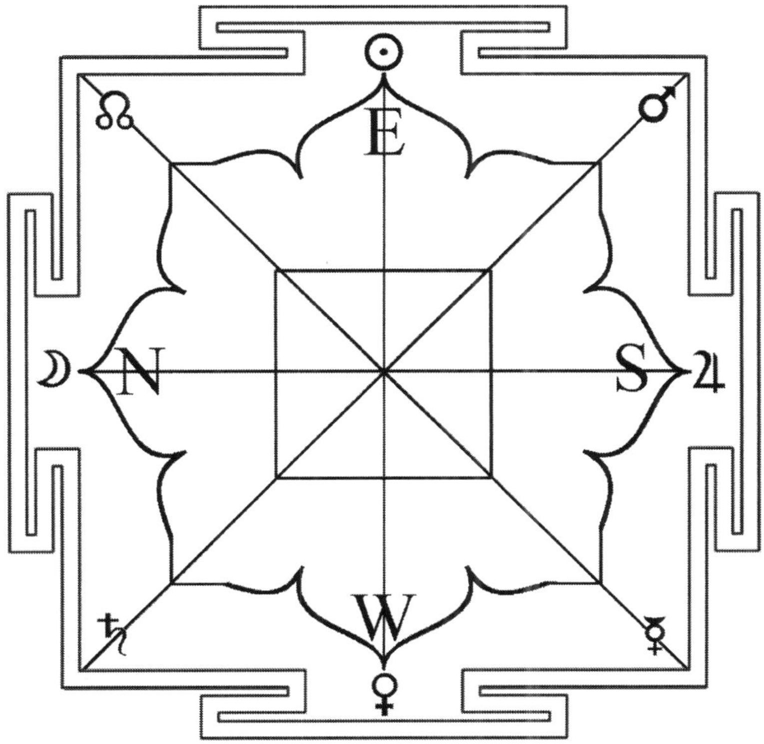

Kulākula Cakra

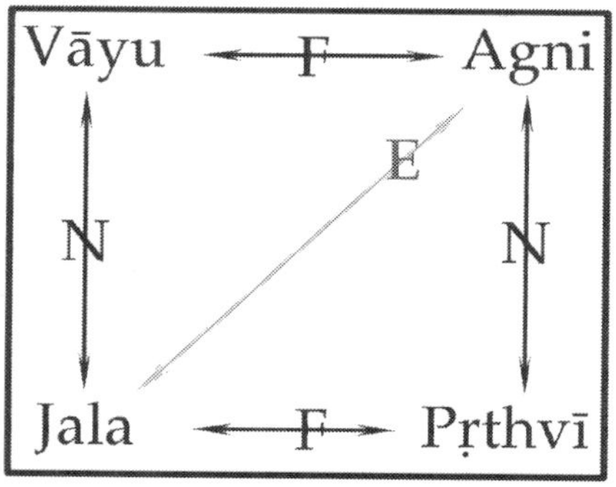

The family (*kula*) and the not-family (*akula*) cakra is a grouping of the Sanskrit letters into the five elements to show how they interact. Each element interacts with other elements in either a friendly, neutral, or inimical way.

Fire and Water are inimical (enemies) as well as Earth and Air. Fire and Air are friendly as well as Water and Earth. In the diagram you can see the relationship: side by side is friendly, above and below is neutral, and diagonal is inimical. Notice the ordering is similar to the insideof the human nostril; Fire on top, Water on the bottom, Earth on the inside, Air on the outside.

Looking at the signs of the zodiac, each sign has an opposite that balances or supports it. Opposite the fire sign is an air sign. Fire needs air to burn, therefore Vāyu and Agni are friendly. Opposite the water sign is an earth sign. Water needs a container to hold it or give it shape, therefore these elements are friendly. The primary gaṇḍāntas are the crossing from fire to water signs, and the minor gaṇḍāntas are the crossing from earth to air signs. The relationship is seen among the rāśi, not among the planets (Sun and Moon or Mercury and Saturn are not inimical). These relationships indicate the nature of how various elements interact in the material manifestation.

The science of mantra (*mantra śāstra*) has multiple cakras to check for various types of suitability. The Kulākula Cakra checks the relationship between the elements of the sounds to see the level of benefit for the individual. The first letter of the individual's name is compared to the first letter of the mantra. For example, a woman named Jill wants to do a Kālī mantra. *Ja* is ruled by Earth and *ka* is ruled by Air, which makes a mantra starting with Kālī's name inimical. She is better to do a mantra of Bhadrakālī as *Bha* is ruled by Water which is friendly to her name sound.

Kulākula Cakra					
Planet	*Air*	*Fire*	*Earth*	*Water*	*Ether*
Sun	a ā	i ī	u ū	ṛ ṝ	lṛ lṝ
	e	ai	o	au	aṁ aḥ
Mars	ka	kha	ga	gha	ṅa
Venus	ca	cha	ja	jha	ña
Mercury	ṭa	ṭha	ḍa	ḍha	ṇa
Jupiter	ta	tha	da	dha	na
Saturn	pa	pha	ba	bha	ma
Moon	ya	ra	la	va	śa
	ṣa	kṣa	ḷa	sa	ha

Since Air and Fire or Water and Earth are friendly they will give quick results. Air and Water or Fire and Earth are neutral and give medium results. Fire and Water or Earth and Air are inimical and can give negative side effects. All mantras that begin with the ākāśa letters benefit everybody.

Mantras that begin with *Auṁ namo bhagavate*... are ruled by ākāśa and benefit everyone. The mantra *Auṁ Somāya namaḥ* is not as beneficial to people whose names begin with Fire sounds. By chanting *Auṁ namaḥ Somāya,* the ākāśa element is predominant and therefore the elemental flaw is removed. The prasiddha mantra *Auṁ namaḥ Śivāya* utilizes this format.

Piṇḍa-Brahmāṇḍa Tattva

The concept of the *Piṇḍa-Brahmāṇḍa,* taught by Śrī Acyutānanda Dāsa, is that the body (*piṇḍa*) is a replica of the Universe (*Brahmāṇḍa*), or microcosm is a reflection of the macrocosm. As the universe is made, so is the human made.The five elements (*pañcatattva*) are the building blocks of the material world. Everything is composed of them, in manifold mixture and varying amounts.

The Puruṣa Sūkta (Ṛgveda 1.90. 13-14) says that from the mind of the original Puruṣa the Moon was born, from his eyes the Sun was born, and the wind (*vāyu*) from his breath. The atmosphere (*antarikṣa*) from his navel, heaven from his head, earth from his feet, and the directions from his ears. The world is being manifest by the various parts of the cosmic being. This is not taken literally as a giant being cut into parts but as the analogy of the reflection of the divine in the universe and the universe in the human being.

The term "as above so below" is not to be taken as an interesting philosophical notion in Jyotiṣa. It is the foundation upon which the entire science rests. The movements in the sky above are not causing an event to take place, they are a reflection of the karma that is being played out. If your hair looks bad in a mirror you will comb your hair, not the mirror. We are not fixing planets, we are fixing our own karma. The outside is inside, the inside is outside. The spiritual practice of realizing the universe and the divine in the human body is called *kāyā sādhana* by Śrī Acyutānanda Dāsa. He says,

Within your body there is infinite space,
The cosmos itself is within your body.
The person who has not penetrated the body,
His wisdom is of no avail.

In Āyurveda this theory is called the *loka-puruṣa samya*. After Caraka describes the elements, he says that 'the individual is the same as the universe (*loka-sammita puruṣa*). All material, mental, and spiritual phenomena in the world (*loka*) is in the individual, and all that is in the individual is in the world. This is how the wise perceive.' Through spiritual practice one cultivates seeing the world in themselves and themselves in the world. This develops universal vision (*parāvara-dṛśa*) and peace rooted in wisdom (*śantir-jñāna-mūla*).[21]

Śrī Acyutānanda says, "The individual (*piṇḍa*) is small and the universe (*brahmāṇḍa*) is huge. But this wonderful experienceof merging the huge in one's small is possible by expanding the limits of one's mind."[22]

[21] Caraka Saṁhitā, Śārīrasthānam IV.13, V.20 (entire chapter V)

[22] Acyutānanda, *Chayāliśa paṭaḷa* XXIX, translated by Tandra Patnaik, p184.

Chapter 6

Birth Circumstances

Even though people may be well known,
they hold in their hearts the emotions of a simple person
for the moments that are the most important of those we know on earth:
birth, marriage and death.
–Jackie Kennedy

Circumstances of Birth

Nothing at the moment of birth is accidental; from the number of people in the room to the weather of the day. The circumstances of birth relate to who we are and reveal the nature of our personality and karma. These factors are also very benefical for chart rectification.

Birth is the moment we come out of the womb and enter an 'individual existence'. This sounds like a simple definition but has actually been a debate among scholars for many millenium. When exactly does 'individual existence' start? Advanced astrologers rectify the birth time to 24 seconds using the nāḍyaṁśa (D-150) and ardha-nāḍyaṁśa (D-300), yet still there are so many variables that there is still disagreement about the exact moment of birth. Many people get fundamental about this topic (fundamentalism is a disease of Ketu) but we will avoid this and focus on understanding the sides of each factor of determination, as well as the actual science of being born. Then we will look into details about the circumstances of birth reflected in the rāśi and navāṁśa and what this means about ourselves.

Life

Life starts before we are actually born. A living baby can be born premature or die within the womb-meaning it is alive. So when exactly does 'life' begin? There are many theories, we will try to understand this question from both a scientific and an astrological perspective. After we understand some of these theories, we will look at when 'individual life' begins.

Creating a new life begins with the sexual act called *mithuna*. The transiting seventh house shows the emotion between lovers during intercourse. If Mars is in the seventh house, then the individuals are fighting and arguing. If Saturn is present, then there is lack of satisfaction and closeness. If benefics are in the seventh house, the sex will be amorous and playful. The karmas of the incarnating soul are attracted to the mental state of the man and woman at the time of copulation (which can be seen in the seventh house of the copulation time). The incarnating soul's mental and physical nature relates to the predominat guṇa and doṣas (*vāta, pitta, kapha*) of the parents at the time of copulation. Sperm is released into the female partner. This is called the *niṣeka,* which literally means sprinkling or infusion and in this context means ejaculation (Moon is kāraka). The released sperm travel into the womb to fertilize the female ovum (egg) which can take anywhere from ten hours to five days. Every text containing the topic of niṣeka begins with calculations for the menstruation cycle, and how it relates to Moon and Mars. Ovulation (ṛtukāla[2]) was understood to be sixteen days from the beginning of menstruation or twelve days from the end of it.

The moment of 'conception' is called the *ādhāna*. Ādhāna literally means depositing or placing as well as kindling or lighting a fire, in this context it means conception (Sun is kāraka). The niṣeka can be controlled by man, but the ādhāna is controlled by a higher power. The semantics of the English term 'conception' is debated and not used in scientific literature as it does not differentiate: the *fertilization* of the ovum (sperm meeting egg) or the merging of the sperm's nucleus with the egg's to make a *zygote* (taking about 30 hours), or the *implantation* of the resulting cell mass (blastocyst) onto the wall of the uterus (1-2 days later).

When fertilization happens it is the beginning of a process, yet this actual process was started by the niṣeka, and the process is still taking place. When the sperm and egg combine into a zygote all the genetic material that will be used to create that individual is then in place, yet the seed has no field to grow in. This cell mass continues to divide as it travels into the uterus. If there is no implantation then there is no pregnancy. In this regard, the Āyurveda texts define the embryo (*garbha*) as: the combination of sperm (*śukra*), ovum (*śoṇita*) and soul (*jīva*) when it has become stationed in the uterus (*garbhāśaya-stha*).[3]

Caraka Saṁhitā says the combined sperm and ovum go to the uterus and then the jīva, conjoined the mind, descends into the womb (*avakrama*) to create the embryo.[4] The mind forms the bridge between the physical matter which will become body and the jīva which is transmigrating. Caraka Saṁhitā states that the gross body is a result of the subtle body (*sūkṣmaśarīra*) and can only manifest when associated with the subtle body guiding the formation of the gross body and mind according to the results of past actions.[5] This may seem clear but if the jīva does not enter until in the womb then how was the genetic material which will make the body according to its karma already processed before descending to the uterus?[6] The jīva had to be present even before the niṣeka if it was attracted by the parent's mental state during mithuna. Therefore when does the jīva enter the physical or is the jīva guiding the entire process in a transcendental state. These are the main issues of debate.

---

2 Ṛtukāla refers to the time of the female ovulation each month as well as the time of life between puberty and menopause when a woman is capable of child-bearing.

3 Caraka Saṁhitā, Śārīrasthānam III.3, Suśruta Saṁhitā, Śārīrasthānam IV.3, and Prasūti Tantra IV.1

4 Caraka Saṁhitā, Śārīrasthānam III.1 *yadā cānayostathāyukte saṁsarge śukraśoṇitasaṁsargamantargarbhāśaya-gataṁ jīvo›vakrāmati sattvasamprayogāt tadā garbho›bhinirvartate* |

5 Caraka Saṁhitā, Śārīrasthānam II.36

6 Rigorous research has not confirmed that there was a proper understanding of the uterus, the fallopian tubes, or the female ovum within the ancient Āyurvedic texts. There is mention of uterine veins, and ducts, etc., but their function has not been described satisfactorily for modern correlation. See *The Origin of the Life of a Human Being* by Rahul Peter Das, p14-29 for more on this topic.

It makes minor differences for our calculations but it makes a huge difference relative to the abortion laws and regulations of a country; are drugs that stop implantation to be called as birth control or abortificiant? Did life begin at fertilization, or implantation? If there is no pregnancy (garbha/ embryo formation) can it be said that life has begun?

Jyotiṣa has various calculations to differentiate the *niṣeka* from *ādhāna*; the niṣeka is obvious as it is the finishing of copulation, the adhana has some adjustment calculations. For each of these times, a chart can be cast and indications about the pregnancy and future child can be seen. Some astrologers do not differentiate the difference between niṣeka and ādhāna. In the case of In-Vitro fertilization, these times can be drastically different. There is a case where a woman at Israel's Hadasa Hospital became pregnant with embryos that had been frozen for twelve years.[7] The niṣeka and adhana were twelve years apart. Bṛhat Jātaka mentions certain combinations for delayed delivery, one of which refers to twelve years.[8] The niṣeka and fertilization were done at one time, then frozen. The conception/ implantation/ ādhāna happened twelve years later.

These conception charts indicate the health of the mother during pregnancy and delivery as well as the formation of the child. For example, if at the moment of conception malefics occupy the twelfth house, and benefics don't aspect the lagna, or Saturn occupies the lagna and is aspected by Mars the pregnant woman will pass away.[9] Most of the combinations that indicate death of the mother, will indicate delivery complications in this age. Relative to the child, when the lagna of the conception chart is occupied or aspected by a benefic planet, the child will be healthy, prosperous, and strive for all types of knowledge.[10] There are also combinations for producing a female, male, hermaphrodite, or twin children. There are simple and complicated calculations for timing delivery.[11] There are also negative combinations such as: if a malefic conjoins the Moon (with no benefic influence) in the last navāṁśas of Cancer, Scorpio, or Pisces then the child will be born deaf.[12] There are various combinations to be avoided. For this reason in ancient times, royal families were very particular about times to concieve children. Many traditional Jyotiṣa texts give detailed information about determining conception time.

The *Horāsāra* states that all rules of the niṣeka chart are also applicable to a praśna of the same topic. This text also gives various techniques to predict about the gender of the child and the time of delivery using praśna.[13]

---

7 Revel, Human Reproduction, p. 238
8 Bṛhat Jātaka 4.22
9 Bṛhat Jātaka 4.6
10 Jātaka Pārijāta III.20
11 See Sathanam, R. *Essentials of Predictive Hindu Astrology*, Chapter 23: On Prenatal Epoch, or refer to Jaimini Upadeśa Sutra 4.3.3-9
12 Bṛhat Jātaka 4.18
13 Horāsāra IV.22-28

Conception Chart Calculation

How many people actually have their conception chart? Very few. The Ṛṣis also had this issue and therefore discovered techniques to work backwards from the natal chart to get the conception time. A few rules have been listed below to determine the conception time from the birth chart. There are other techniques available but these are simple guidelines which give relatively accurate results.

1. Count 273 days backward from the birthdate. [This technique will not work if the individual was born premature.] A sidereal lunar month is 27.3217 days. This multiplied by 10 months is 273 days. (Thirty days in a solar month multiplied by nine results in 270 days).

2. Notice whether the lagneśa is in the visible (*dṛśya*) or invisible (*adṛśya*) half of the zodiac. The invisible side is the middle (15°) of the ascendant to the middle of the seventh house. If the lagneśa is in the invisible side then the the birth took less time while if it is in the visible portion it took more time.

3. Saturn and Gulika are the kārakas for the pāpa-karma, un-wholesome action, which leads to your re-birth. They represent suffering and its results. Calculate the difference in degrees between Saturn and Gulika, then reduce by multples of thirty to have a number under 30. Turn these degrees into days and either subtract or add this to 273 days depending on whether the birth took less time or longer.

4. The Moon at conception should be in kendra to the natal Moon. This is used to rectify the day calculation to the appropriate Moon sign.

5. The lagna of the conception chart is the seventh from the child's Janma Lagna. That which was the seventh house of the conception chart becomes the lagna [or navāṁśa lagna] of the individual. There is a great revelation hidden in this technique. The seventh house of the conception chart shows the mental and emotional qualities between the parents at the moment of creating the individual. This seventh house sign then becomes the rāśi or navāṁśa lagna of the individual's birth chart. In this way, the guṇa (levels of rajas and tamas) and doṣas (levels of the elements) of the parents dominant at the time of conception influences the nature of the child as stated in the Āyurveda texts.

Creating the Perfect Child

How to make the child you want to have. If only there was a good recipe that was sweet and simple. Can you control the birth time? Or at least the circumstances of the birth?

As you will see below, there are all types of combinations showing the nature of the individual soul and how this reflects in the circumstances of birth. One such combination in the child's chart shows whether the father was present at the birth or not, so then is that the father's decision or the child's. A woman's father was in the delivery room for many hours waiting for her arrival. After the night had passed he left to get a morning coffee. When he returned twenty minutes later, his daughter had been born. In her chart, the Moon does not aspect lagna or lagneśa. He missed the birth even though he was right there trying to be present.

In my own daughter's navāṁśa chart, Sun and Ketu were conjunct and in trine to Jupiter. Wow, if Jupiter could be in the navāṁśa lagna and Sun and Ketu in the fifth, then she would be an incredible astrologer. I put the ghee lamp in the northwestern direction to allow the Sun to be in the fifth. There were complications during labor and we had to go to the hospital for final delivery. Now, with that Jupiter in the navāṁśa seventh and in trine to Sun and Ketu she'll marry a good astrologer.

An associate of mine was consulted by a gentleman who wanted a chart to have his child born through cesarean (when the doctor surgically removes the child). He asked for a chart best for politics and wealth. There was no reason for the mother to have a cesarean birth except that the father was trying to control the child's destiny. In these cases, negative combinations show up in the chart which were overlooked by the astrologer, or other such things happen. We must be careful how we try to control destiny- as destiny is *daiva,* which comes from the devas, and it is not our job to play god.

We get what our karma gives us. A child is only the power of ones own fifth house. Caraka says that the child resembles those things which the mother thinks in her mind during conception.[14] Therefore instead of trying to control the destiny by fixing the lamp in the room in a certain way or manipulating the birth we must instead focus on inner cultivation of ourselves. Everything in our life is just a reflection of our own growth and consciousness- therefore we must clean the dirt from ourselves not from the mirror. *Garbhādhāna-saṁskāra* is the purification process done before two prospective parents decide to conceive.

Tradition teaches us that before conceiving we should do various sadhanna and rituals to purify and prepare ourselves. In our Jyotiṣa tradition, the paramguru fasted for forty days and went on pilgrimage to the temple of the family deity (*kuladevatā*) before conceiving.

[14] Caraka Saṁhitā, Śārīrasthānam II.25

In this way one must perform spiritual penance, and pray to the divine for a child. How to get an artist- pray to the goddess Sarasvatī and perform her rituals. In this way, we ask destiny (*daiva*) to bless us and we earn this blessing. The moment of niṣeka is also to be performed with intention and at a beneficial muhūrta. Then you surrender (*prapatti*) and trust in the Supreme. Muhūrta is like archery. You take your time, eye the target, watch your breath and mind, and at the right moment you release the arrow. Once it is released there is nothing you can do but surrender, if the wind blows or you didn't aim properly then the arrow will miss. It is the intention and action at the beginning that determines the outcome. In this way we strive for the proper intention when we create a child.

When people come to the astrologer with the wrong intention, it is almost impossible to find a good muhūrta. While people of good actions with pure intention choose beneficial muhūrtas by chance. So what happens when a pregnancy comes by accident? We often end up with a child who does not know their purpose in life. Their intention for creation was accidental and unconscious and this lack of clarity gets reflected in their life. The fifth house (which is the basic representation of offspring) is our mindfield (*citta*) and desires, therefore what we create. As individuals we need to be conscious of what we are trying to create in this world, where we are headed, and what we are trying to achieve with our life. An individual who prays to Viṣṇu everyday to be of service to the Lord and offers their life to the betterment of the world, or one who prays to Sarasvatī everyday to create things that bring more light into this creation are sure to have their creations blessed and guided by a higher power. Therefore, an accidental birth of such an individual will carry the same intentions. In this way, to create a wonderful child, we purify ourselves; our actions and desires.

The Months of Pregnancy

Each month of the pregnancy is ruled by a planet. If there is any weakness in a planet at the time of conception there may be issues in the month of development ruled by that planet.[15] There is a difference in the rulership of the months between Jaimini and Varāhamihira. We will analyze Varāhamihira's as they relate to the natural significations of the months of pregnancy.

The first month ruled by Venus is called *Kalala*, which is when the sperm and ovum mix and begin multiplying exponentially. Caraka Saṁhitā says that there is no distinct form in this month, yet all organs exist in their latent form.[16] Generally, in Jyotiṣa, calculations of pregnancy are calculated as 273 days based on the sidereal lunar months (39 weeks). Allopathic medicine considers pregnancy (called gestation) to last 40 weeks (280 days) but this is counted from the last menstruation. Conception is possible about two weeks

[15] Bṛhat Jātaka 4. 16
[16] Caraka Saṁhitā, Śārīrasthānam IV.9

after menstruation- which makes actual pregnancy about 38 weeks (266 days). This means when using allopathic gestational weeks to enumerate the time frame of pregnancy the first month is actually only two weeks, as the month is counted from the last menstruation. When an individual says they are 8 weeks pregnant (western gestational weeks), they are approximately 6 weeks from conception. Vedic reference is counted from the conception.

	Month	Lord	Jaimini Lordships
1	Kalala	Venus	Venus & Sun sign
2	Ghana	Mars	2nd house from Sun
3	Aṅkura	Jupiter	Moon & 3rd from Sun
4	Asthi	Sun	Mars & 4th from Sun
5	Charma	Moon	Mercury & Sun's 5h
6	Aṅgaja	Saturn	Jupiter & 6th from Sun
7	Cetanatā	Mercury	Saturn & 7th from Sun
8	Bhavana	Lagnesh	Rahu & 8th from Sun
9	Udvega	Moon	Ketu & 9th from Sun
10	Prasava	Sun	10th house from Sun

The second month ruled by Mars is called *Ghana* which means 'solidified' and relates to the densification of the embryo. The Greek roots of the word embryo relate to 'inner-swelling'. In this month, the size will go from a poppy seed to a kidney bean with developing organ tissues.

The third month ruled by Jupiter is called *Aṅkura* which means to sprout. Caraka Saṁhitā says all sense organs, limbs of the body and internal organs manifest themselves simultaneously in this month according to the modification of the five elements. This month marks the end of the embryonic period (where there is the greatest chance of any malformation to take place) and the beginning of the fetal period. Suśruta Saṁhitā says when the embryo (*garbha*) develops hands, feet, sense organs, etc. it is called a body (*śarīra*); though in western medical terms it is now called a fetus. All material and spiritual phenomena of the universe are present in the fetus and everything in the fetus is present in the universe.[17] All deities can be identified in the body- Vāyu as the life force (*prāṇa*), Ākāśa as the porous parts, Indra as the ahaṅkāra, the Aśvins as complexion, etc.[18] The body grows according to the same components that compose and guide the universe.

As the senses manifest, there is pulsation in the fetal heart tissue and the mind begins to feel. The fetus experiences desires related to its past life. The mother enters *dauhṛdāvasthā*- the state of two hearts. The fetal blood is oxygenated in the mother's lungs. The mother begins to share the desires of the child because of this state of two hearts. The Āyurvedic texts caution that one must give the mother everything she desires (as long as its not harmful) because if not there could be vāta distrubance resulting in developmental issues or loss of the fetus at this time.

The fourth month ruled by the Sun is called *Asthi* which means 'bone' and is when the fetus develops structure. The bone begins to harden, teeth buds develop, the arms and

[17] Caraka Saṁhitā, Śārīrasthānam IV.13

[18] Caraka Saṁhitā, Śārīrasthānam V.5

legs develop to the proportion of the body, and reflexive movement stimulates kicking and stretching.

The fifth month is *Carma* which means 'skin'. The skin grows in excess to be filled with fatty tissue later, the pigmentary and sweat glands become more clear, the vernix caseosa forms on the skin as a protective layer, the nervous sytem develops myelin and sensory development increases. The aspect of mind (*manas*) which processes sensory stimuli is developing. The fetus is aware of sounds outside the womb, sensitive to light, as well as smell and tastes which show up in the amniotic fluid of the mother quickly after ingestion.

The sixth month ruled by Saturn is called *Aṅgaja* which means produced from the body and represents the growth of hair and nails. The fetus is also practicing the use of its digestive system by taking the amniotic fluid into its digestive track and creating meconium. The lungs also take the amniotic fluid in and out while the muscles of the lungs function to prepare the muscles for breathing. Locomotor control in the brain begins to develop at this time (though just reflexive movements), as the nervous sytem and muscles integrate.

The seventh month ruled by Mercury is called *Cetana-tā* which means the state of sentience or consciousness- this is when the fetus is said to become fully aware of inside and outside the womb. The brain (*mastiṣka*) grows very quickly at this time. Modern research shows the thalamocortical connections are formed at this time which allows the true sensations of pleasure and pain. Some traditions say that this is when the soul enters the body as this is when it becomes conscious. Suśruta Saṁhitā's opinion is that the fetus

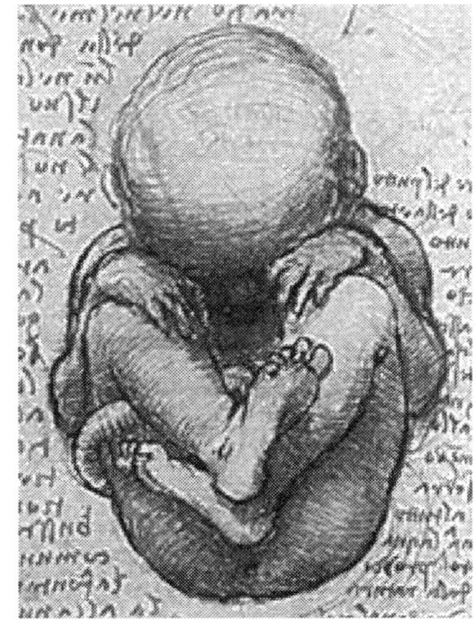

gets *cetanā dhātu* in the fourth month when its heart begins to operate fully as the heart is the seat of consciousness. The Āyurveda texts agree that the soul is needed to enter for the formation of an embryo to be established,[19] therefore it is the working of the intelligence that starts during the seventh month. It is the mundane awareness of the buddhi which is ignited not the higher awareness of the jīvātman.

The eighth month ruled by the lagneśa is called *Bhavana* which means a place, abode or coming into existence. The nutritional demands of the fetus increase and the mother is eating more. The ancient texts mention that this is when the fetus begins to feel desires of hunger and thirst; most likely this view was in response to the mother's enlarged appetite for nutritious foods. Previously, the focus was on functional development while now the focus is growing bigger and the fetus begins putting on body fat at this point to prepare for

[19] Caraka Saṁhitā, Śārīrasthānam III.8

emerging from the womb. There is a symbiotic relationship in the eighth month between the fetus and mother to develop the ojas (*ojassañcaraṇāvasthā*).

The ninth month ruled by the Moon is called *Udvega* which means agitated. The fetus is fully functional and is moving excessively in the womb. Visible feet are seen on the mother's belly as the fetus kicks and stretches. This was interpreted as the fetus showing readiness to leave the womb. Though by the end of this month and beginning of the next the movement slows down as the fetus grows so big it has no room to move.

The tenth month is called *Prasava* which means 'to bring forth' or delivery, it is also called the delivery month (*sūti-māsa*). Suśruta Saṁhitā says delivery is normal in the ninth or tenth month. In modern thought, thirty-seven to forty-two gestational weeks is considered full-term. Before that is pre-term delivery (34-36 weeks) and after 42 weeks is late. Only five to six percent of pregnancies go over forty-three weeks and these are more likely to have complications. A strong Venus will indicate earlier delivery (*apūrṇakāla-ja*). Venus is the kāraka for premature delivery, and when Venus is placed in the first or eighth house it can indicate premature delivery.[20] A very strong Jupiter will indicate later delivery and the baby should be born with more weight.

Jaimini also relates the houses from the Sun of the conception chart to the months of pregnancy.[21] The Moon is the sustainer of the body, but the Sun (*Savitṛ*) is the creator of the body. Therefore the first month relates to the house in which the Sun is placed- relating to the creative force driving the individual's creation. The second month relates to the second house from the Sun- and so forth. The tenth house is the achievement of the creative being and the time to bring forth the creation.

The life process begins with mithuna, niṣeka, ādhāna, and the forty weeks of pregnancy. The grand finale is the actual birth (*janma*) at the appropriate birth time (*janma-kāla*).

---

[20] If Venus is in lagna or eighth it indicates the doṣa is from the father and he should worship the holy fire and purify himself. If Venus is in AL or eighth from AL then it is caused by the mother's doṣa, and she should worship the goddess Durgā. Mṛtyuñjaya Homa should be done for Venus and caution should be taken for the child's first daśā.

[21] Maharshi Jaimini's Upadeśa Sutra 4.3.95-103

Birth and Birth-time

When the female cervix (*śukrapraveśinī peśī*) dialates to about 10 cm active labor begins. During a normal healthy birth the fetal head is facing downwards helping the cervix to flatten and dialate. Birth feet first (breech) is generally avoided due to possible delivery complications, and only about 3-4% of births end up being breech.[22] Women are reccomended to perform certain yoga postures to insure the head emerges first.

While in the womb, the fetus does not breathe or digest, the placenta (*aparā*) does all this for the fetus.[23] Carbon dioxide and waste products from the fetus are sent back through the umbilical cord (*nābhi nāḍī*) and placenta to the mother's circulation to be eliminated. The fetal lungs are collapsed and are not used for breathing since all oxygen and nutrition is supplied through the umbilical cord. The fetal heart is pumping blood through the body but only using two chambers, this 'fetal circulation' changes at birth. With the first few breaths, the collapsed lungs expand into air filled sacs. This change of pressure at birth allows blood to flow into the lungs activating all four chambers of the heart to begin to work.

The first few breaths are the hardest for the newborn as the lungs need to open and fill with air for the first time, and often the first few breaths are short and irregular and may take a few hours to stabalize. The baby should breathe within 30 seconds to one minute after delivery. Often the baby will need some physical stimulation, though labor itself can stimulate the first breath. What is it that makes the baby take its first breath? Some say it is the lack of oxygen coming from the placenta, or sulfactants, or pressure, but this natural function of life happens and must happen as soon as we leave the womb/enter the atmosphere.

At the moment of birth the fetus oxygenates its own blood and takes an independent body. In Jyotiṣa the body is represented by the lagna. Sanjay Rath says, "the moment of separation of the body of the created being from that of the mother is the time of birth as it is at this moment that an independent body (Lagna) has come into being."[24] 'Individual life' is the time we utulize to tie down the exact degree of the ascendant (*lagnasphuṭa*). The allopathic medical system uses the moment the infant's body is completely out of the womb (*bhū patana*) as the birth time. Some systems use the first breath/cry, others the cutting of the umbilical cord. There is no agreement among scholars about this exact moment, therefore rectification is always essential. Let us now understand the arguments for and against the various birth time determination.

[22] Gaskin, p.384
[23] Gaskin, p.298
[24] SJVC, Question on birth time, 23 February 2002

Fire: The sighting of the head (*śiro-darśana*), also called crowning, as the birth time is the first time any part of the infant is outside of the womb. Before crowning, the fetal head is slightly visible but is going in and out slowly stretching the vaginal canal (*garbhamārga*) to be ready for exit. This is called the 'ring of fire' where the nerves of the mother are stretched and compressed- at first burning then becoming numb. When the head has come out to a position in which it does not go backwards again, this is called crowning. Labor may take over 24 hours but once the head has crowned the infant leaves the womb in approximately one to ten minutes after this. It is the first time that any of the infant has left the womb, like the first step of one leg out of the house to begin a journey. The argument against using this as the birth time is that the infant is not fully out of the womb, nor breathing on its own, and therefore not a separate entity. In cases where the birthing infant is not aligned properly it is possible for the doctor to push the head in and realign the child (before it starts breathing). In one situation, the child's head came out and was pushed in twice until the shoulders were in the proper position for delivery.

Air: The first breath as the birth time is generally taken from the first cry. It is hard to hear the first inhale, but the first exhale is loud and clear. Death is officially defined as the "cessation of vital functions including heartbeat, brain activity and breathing". In general, the last breath leaving the body is considered the moment of dying. In this way, the first breath entering the body would be birth. In yoga it is believed that destiny gives us a number of breaths not years, so 'individual life' would be the first breath to the last breath. The first breath inflates the lungs, changes the fetal circulation to normal four chamber circulation, and allows the infant to live separate from the placenta and mother. The argument against using this as the birth time is that an infant can *completely* leave the mother and not start breathing for some time. In water births, the child can be born under water, allowed to open its eyes, use its senses and move about for over a minute before being brought up for its first breath. In some situations the breathing needs to be induced. What if the infant dies without ever having taken a breath- it was born. Othertimes, the infant can cry when not completely out of the mother's *garbhamārga*, and therefore not be separate from the mother yet.

Earth: Bhū Patana literally means descending to the Earth, and is taken as the infant's complete exit of the womb. This is what is used in modern allopathic medicine, as the focus is on the physical body leaving the mother. Where as the first breath takes into account the independent working of the prāṇa. The complete physical exit is easily determined. Satyācārya reccommends this time for its ease of determination.[25] The argument against using this as the birth time is primarily that the other indications are better: crowning- she's already been out, first breath- out doesn't mean taking in oxygen and pumping her own blood, cutting the umbilicus- is the final separation.

[25] Satya-Jātakam, Upodghataḥ 5

Water: Cutting of the umbilical cord (*nābhi nāḍī*) independant from the placenta (*aparā*) has the largest range of variation in time. The placenta delivery is five to fifteen minutes after the infant's delivery (it is called the afterbirth). The placenta is created within the first divisions of the zygote to blastocyst and is the same genetic material as the child. It implants into the uterine wall to regulate nourishment. Once the baby leaves the womb the uterus begins to contract and pushes out the placenta. The umbilical cord pulsates strongly for about five minutes after birth and can continue for about twenty minutes. In allopathic hospitals, the cord is cut directly after birth whether there are fluids flowing or not and before the delivery of the placenta itself. The cutting of the cord is a human action, and not nature itself. In cases where the cord is rapped around the infant's neck it has to be cut immediately- even before the child completely exits the womb. More holistic births will not cut the cord for five to twenty minutes after delivery when the pulsation has stopped. Some individuals wait for the umbilical cord to naturally fall off which takes about four days, this is called a lotus birth. In Chinese medicine, the umbilical cord is burnt (not cut) after it has stopped pulsating. The argument against using this as the birth time is that it does not inhibit 'individual life' from existing if the cord is not cut, nor does it show full delivery if it is cut. Excluding the lotus birth (variation of four days), the average time of cutting the umbilical cord can vary from not out of the womb to twenty minutes. Also, the placenta itself is created from cells in the original blastocyst- not from the mother herself. Therefore cutting the umbilicus is separation from the placenta not the mother.

Head Visible	12:46 AM
Crowning	12:51:08
Bhu Patana	12:51:36
First Cry	12:52:05
Cutting Cord	12:52:42

Different traditions give priority to one of these birth times. There is no consenses. Some advise using the yuga of the prāṇapada lagna to indicate which time should be used; for fire signs (satya yuga) use the śiro-darśana time, for eath signs (kali yuga) use Bhu Patana and so on. One must be aware of the possible variation when rectifying the chart. Below is the example of my daughter's birth times. As it was an allopathic hospital setting we were unable to let the umbilical cord stop pulsating before it was cut as we had wished.

When the infant is born the senses are wide open and receive everything with extreme intensity. It is best to avoid bright lights, intense smells, and loud noises (particularly mechanical noises). Some traditions teach for the mother to not leave the house for forty days and then chose a beneficial muhūrta when they do so. If the mother sings while the child is in the womb and also when it is outside, it creates a nourishing environment that has familiar sensory stimuli, which is emotionally comforting. The singing of the Mother is the best medicine for the infant as it increases the energy of the Moon, and the first year is the Moon naisargika daśā.

Birth and Death: the cycle of life

At the moment of birth, death is inherent, the cycle of life includes death. Birth and death are moments where the individual soul enters the physical world and leaves it. The moment of birth is a result of all previous actions from the past lives. Karmas that were not balanced in the previous life and unfulfilled desires that were unable to fructify, due to the present life karmas, are guided to take place by this life's combinations supporting those karmas to be experienced. For example, if a native has extreme poverty yogas then no matter what positive service they gave, their money situation could only become minimally better. But on the next birth a new stage is set and strong desires left unfulfilled are given fertile soil to bear fruit. In the Bhagavad Gītā, Arjuna asks Kṛṣṇa, what happens to the individual who has faith (*śraddhā*) and strives towards the changeless foundation (*sthitiṁ sthirām*) in the path of yoga, yet does not succeed. He is told that such an individual will be born into a family of wise yogins, which is a great blessing and hard to achieve. In this way, the individual will learn the knowledge of the last life, and be carried on- even against his will- to attain the supreme goal (*parāṁ gatiṁ*).[26]

Some situations are blessings from a previous life, other situations are punishment from past actions. There is a story of a boy who had a crippled leg who came to see Satya Sai Baba with his mother to be healed. They made it to have special time with Sai Baba and watched as he healed many other people that day. When it came to their turn, they were told that it was not the best path for them to be healed. That in a previous life the boy had been a crooked judge and this was his punishment, and that the mother was the secretary of that judge. In this way, circumstances in early childhood are not the karma created in this life but are purely the results we have earned in the past incarnations.

The life process starts with a conception chart guiding our formation, then individual life gets a birth chart with what we are destined to experience. The yearly charts are based on the birth chart and can be calculated for the whole life from the beginning. The chart cast the moment an individual dies, called a *Puṇya Chakra*, will show how soon an individual is reborn and what karma they did in this life that needs more work. The moment of death determines the next life and its incarnation. The karma entering this world is seen in the birth chart, how we worked with this karma is seen in the puṇya chakra. Death to birth is the journey between bodies (puṇya chakra to birth chakra). Birth to death is the journey of embodiment. From the physical perspective it may seem like a long journey but from the soul's perspective a lifetime is a fleeting moment. In soul awareness, one realizes the short time of incarnation and makes the most beneficial use of embodied time. Every individual is born with strengths and weaknesses and as astrologers we are here to guide people to attain their highest potential in all four aims of life. Only that which is not born does not die. This unborn, undying nature is the Amṛta- the immortal- the supreme goal (*parāṁ gatiṁ*).

[26] Bhagavad Gītā, VI.33-45

Casting the Chart: the child is born

The circumstances of birth are used to indicate the correct time and show that *everything* at the moment of birth is important. Parāśara talks about casting the chart when a child is born. In the *Sūtikā-adhyāya*, Parāśara begins,

अथाहं सूततिकाध्यायं वक्ष्यामि श्रृणु सुव्रत ।

athāhaṁ sūtikādhyāyaṁ vakṣyāmi śṛṇu suvrata।

Maitreya, now I speak about the circumstances of birth.

पुरा प्रसङ्गवशतो ब्रह्मणा कथितं यथ ॥१ ॥

purā prasaṅgavaśato brahmaṇā kathitaṁ yathā।।1।।

Long before, there was an occasion that Brahma spoke about this.

यन्त्रैः स्पष्टतरो वेद्यो जन्मकालस्तथा पुनः ।

yantraiḥ spaṣṭataro vedyo janmakālastathā punaḥ।

That exact time of birth should be known with the help of a clock (*yantra*).

साध्याः स्पष्टखगाश्चैवं लग्नं साध्यं यथोदितम् ॥२ ॥

sādhyāḥ spaṣṭakhagāścaivaṁ lagnaṁ sādhyaṁ yathoditam।।2।।

With this time, the correct positions of the planets and ascendant are calculated,

लग्नद्वादशभावेषु ग्रहाः स्थाप्या श्दिवा जनौ ।

lagnadvādaśabhāveṣu grahāḥ sthāpyā divā janau।

The lagna and twelve houses are established, and the grahas placed there in.

Sundials, hourglasses, water clocks, etc. were used in ancient days to keep time. Parāśara says that we must use these instruments to find the accurate time. In the modern day, this is the correctly set watch. With this time, the chart is cast and the whole life is seen. The accuracy of this time will effect the accuracy of your chart interpretation.

In the *Uttara Kālāmṛta*, Kālidāsa says to use the gnomon[27] (*śaṅku*) and other yantras. To determine the *nāḍīs* and *vināḍīs* that have elapsed from sunrise to the moment of birth. He explains how to calculate proper time from the tropical (*sayana*) position of the Sun. Then calculations are made using dṛg gaṇita [with ayanāṁśa] to get the location of planets and houses.[28] The gnomon is basically a sun dial. This is a stick that angles the same

[27] Gnomon comes from the Greek *gnōmōn* which means one who knows or examines. It derives from the same roots as the Sanskrit word jñānin (*jña* becomes *gno* in the west) which means one who knows or is endowed with knowledge. In Sanskrit, it is also a word denoting an astrologer.

[28] Uttara Kālāmṛta, Kāṇḍa I, Chapter 1 verse 4

degree as the location's lattitude, and casts a shadow. The Sun moves fifteen degrees westward every hour and the gnomon's shadow on the sundial moves at the same rate. When set up properly it can be accurate from one to two minutes. There is also a water clock (*ghaṭa*), which is a small pot with a hole in the bottom that allows for water flow and therefore time measurement. These are the types of instruments (*yantra*) referred to in these verses. Examples of larger classical instruments can be seen in the observatories set up by Mahārāja Jai Singh in Delhi and Jaipur.

Kālidāsa says to determine the nāḍīs and vināḍīs that have elapsed from sunrise to the moment of birth. Nāḍīs are also called *ghaṭikās* (24 minutes) and vināḍīs are also called *vighaṭikās* (24 seconds). There are 60 ghaṭikās (or nāḍīs) in a day. Birth time was traditionally calculated by how many ghaṭikās had elapsed from sunrise or sunset. If you end up seeing older Indian clients, you will sometimes still get their birth time in ghaṭikās from sunrise and will need to determine the time of sunrise on that day and calculate the time based upon the number of twenty-four minute periods passed.

There are 300 vighaṭikās in a sign therefore, when a chart is accurate to 24 seconds the ardha-nāḍyaṁśa (D-300) is accurate. This chart gives the janma-vighaṭikā-graha or the planet that lords the D-300 ascendant. This planet shows the gender of the individual.[29] This is more advanced astrology, for the beginner the key is to make sure the rāśi, navāṁśa and daśāṁśa are correct. This will allow an astrologer to discuss the health, skills and career of the child.

Parāśara , after discussing the proper calculation of the horoscope in these verses, gives techniques to show various circumstances at the birth- both for interpretation purposes as well as for indicating the proper chart if there is some discrepancy. If the rāsi or navāṁśa chart were very close to changing these indications could solve the issue. When a child becomes older, we can rectify according to other qualities and indications. But if you are given the chart of a newborn baby, you still must rectify it before reading the chart, especially if the ascendant of the rāśi or navāṁśa is near to change. A forty year old individual asking for a consultation may not know how many people were in the room at their birth but the mother or father of an infant will remember these circumstances. Once the rāśi and navāṁśa are rectified the dvādaśāṁśa (D-12) can be rectified based on the situation of the parents. When the D-12 is rectified the D-10 should be in relatively good standing.

[29] Jaimini Upadeśa Sūtras 4.3.9-12

Circumstances of Birth

In holistic western medicine the circumstances of birth are said to effect the emotional health of the individual for their entire life. Even Sigmund Freud in his "Introductory Lectures to Psychoanalysis" mentions that anxiety of the birth experience may possibly effect later anxieties. In the west, birth trauma has been associated with emotional issues in the individual. The Vedic sages went into much more detail showing how the moment we are born is an imprint of our entire karmic history. Everything in the chart correlates to the environment and situation of birth; the number of people present, their qualities, the place, directions of the doors, the weather, color of the neighbor's house, the temple/church down the road, everything.

The intention of the first rule given by the sage is rarely applicable to the modern world as most births happen in one's own home or the hospital. Traditionally, the wife would stay with the elder women of the family during the delivery and this verse shows which side of the family she is more likely to stay with. I have given this verse even though it seems to have little modern application, to look at the principles in it. Parāśara says,

सूर्यो रात्रौ सूर्यपुत्रो जनकौ परिकीर्तितौ ॥३॥

sūryo rātrau sūryaputro janakau parikīrtitau||3||

If birth occurs in the daytime then the Sun [is to be regarded as the father],
if it is during the night then Saturn is to be regarded as the father.

तथैव सितचन्द्रौ तु विज्ञेयौ मातृसंज्ञितौ ।

tathaiva sitacandrau tu vijñeyau mātṛsañjñitau|

Similarly Venus and the Moon will represent the mother
respectively during day and night time.

तयोर्मध्ये बली यः स्यात्तस्य गेहे जनिर्भवेत् ॥४॥

tayormadhye balī yaḥ syāttasya gehe janirbhavet||4||

The birth of the child has taken place in the house of that
parent whose significating planet is stronger.

The first verse given by Parāśara gives a specific rule for birth kārakas. If the birth is during the day the Sun is the kāraka for father, if at night the kāraka is Saturn. The mother is signified by Venus during a day birth and Moon during a night birth. These kārakas are used for seeing the fortune of the parent after birth and the some general relationship dynamics with the parents, not to be confused with other rules such as in longevity where the father is the stronger between the Sun and Venus. Certain kāraka systems are used for certain situations, and should not be confused. Sun/Saturn and Venus/Moon kārakatattva show the function of the mother and father in the individual's life. It can be used to see the nature of the individual's daśā on the parents and the nature of their interation, the role the parent is playing with the child. The planet *not* indicating the parent will show the male and female relatives respectively.

Pandit Sanjay Rath teaches that if the indicator of the parent is in the 6th or 11th house there can be a financial decline after the child is born. The sixth house can show some type of punishment, or legal issues. The eleventh will show first a rise in position and then a fall. The eighth house can show diseases or distress, while the ninth house will show the steady fortune of the parent.

My daughter was a night birth and her Saturn is in Leo with the Sun conjunct an ucca Mercury, showing a father who could be an astrologer and a writer. A woman born in the day had Venus in the eighth house with Rāhu and had a mother who was a researcher at a laboratory who died early in her life. Often when the parent indicator is in a duḥsthāna there is separation from that parent at some point in time. For example, a day birth individual had ucca Venus in the 12th house and her mother was a famous dancer but she died when the individual was thirteen years of age.

Pandit Sanjay Rath teaches that a day birth will often complain that the mother (Venus) loves the other sibling more. In a night birth the mother is always being motherly and never stops playing the motherly role, whereas when the significator is Venus the mother can eventually become a friend. This can be applied to the significator (Sun or Saturn) of the father as well. Planets in the 12th often show something you are attached to. If the planet which is indicator of parent is in the 12th, it can show the individual is very attached to them.

The stronger planet being a parent indicator is considered a shelter (*śraya*) or anchor for the individual's life direction. If that parent dies or there is some separation then the individual may feel lost till the time of marriage. In this case, the remedy is to worship either Śiva (Saturn) or Pārvatī (Moon) for a night birth and Lakṣmī (Venus) or Nārāyaṇa (Sun) for a day birth. These are simple ways to use these karakas.

The above dictum by Parāśara states that the stronger planet will indicate the side of the family the delivery home will be within. For example, if the planet indicating the mother is stronger, then birth may be in the mother's home, or her parent's home or one of her friend's homes. Birth in a hospital will be decision of the parent who is the stronger indicator (in this case the stronger ṣaḍbala is used). The Sun/Saturn or Moon/Venus need to be strong to indicate the home of the parent or that parent's relative or friends. When the ṣaḍbala of these planets is very close it can often make the situation not either of their choice.

By looking at the planets in this way, it shows that it is not just about placement but that the strength of the planet needs to be evaluated. In many of the following rules, the most powerful grahas and combinations will give results. This means you must be aware of stronger combinations that will cancel out the results of other grahas. Jupiter may be showing an easy delivery by its placement but the aspects of Saturn and the affliction to the Moon may be so bad it will overpower that and cause difficulties. The strength of the planets will show their influence in the delivery circumstances. Parāśara says,

सबलो भौमदृष्टश्च स्वक्षेत्रादिषु संस्थितः ।

sabalo bhaumadṛṣṭaśca svakṣetrādiṣu saṁsthitaḥ।

When the Sun with strength is situated in its own sign aspected by Mars,

सूर्यो यदा तदा ज्ञेयं बहुदीपान्वितं गृहम् ॥६ ॥

sūryo yadā tadā jñeyaṁ bahudīpānvitaṁ gṛham।।6।।

then know that there are many lights in the house.

जलभांशगतश्चचन्द्रश्चतुर्थे भवने भवेत् ।

jalabhāṁśagataścacandraścaturthe bhavane bhavet।

If the Moon is in a watery sign/aṁśa in the fourth house,

युक्तो मन्देन वा दृष्टोऽन्धकारे जायते जनिः ॥७ ॥

yukto mandena vā dṛṣṭo'ndhakāre jāyate janiḥ।।7।।

conjunct or aspected by Saturn then birth will be in darkness.

This rule shows the influence of light and darkness (in all their actual and metaphorical meanings) at the time of birth.When the Sun is strong and supported by Mars (another agni tattva graha) then the fire element is strong in the person and there is much light at the time of their delivery. This also represents knowledge, and educated people, and that the person will live a life striving to attain jñāna. When the Moon is in a water sign/aṁśa and in association with Saturn, then the delivery is without light. Varāhamihira says that if the Moon is in a division of Saturn in the fourth house, or Saturn aspects from a watery sign, or is conjunct [Saturn] then birth is in darkness.[30] Kalyāṇa Varma says that delivery is in darkness if the the Moon is in a Saturn aṁśa, or a water aṁśa or in the fourth conjunct or aspected by Saturn.[31] The Moon is digbala in the fourth house making it strong. Moon in association with Saturn is Kālika yoga and brings the energy of the dark goddess Kālī. Moon and Saturn sambandha can also show depression or tamasic association, as well as financial difficulties in the place of birth. Moon's association with Rāhu will show similarly the path of leaving light for tamas. The strongest energy of the planets will show their significations on the place of delivery when they are strong.

[30] Bṛhat Jātaka V.17
[31] Sārāvalī of Kalyāṇa Varmā IX.27

Location

Birth occurs on the way to the place of delivery when the Moon is in the lagna and benefics are in debilitation. Parāśara says,

नीचराशिगताः सौम्या ग्रहदृष्टिविवर्जिताः ।

nīcarāśigatāḥ saumyā grahadṛṣṭivivirjitāḥ |

If the benefics are situated in their signs of debilitation
and are not aspected by any planet and

चन्द्रो यदि भवेल्लग्ने पथि जन्म विनिर्दिशेत् ॥५॥

candro yadi bhavellagne pathi janma vinirdiśet ||5||

the Moon is placed in the Ascendant,
then the birth is to be told as occuring on the way.

Varāhamihira says that when benefics are debilitated the delivery is under the trees (*taru-śala-ādi*) or in such similar situations, [in less controlled environments or in the wilderness, etc]. And in this situation, if the ascendant and Moon are devoid of aspect then the birth is in a place devoid of people.[32] Kalyāṇa Varmā adds that if the Moon is debilitated in the fourth or lagna then birth is on the ground (not even on a bed). In this way, weak planets create a negative (or less protected) circumstance during birth. When there are many debilitated planets, everyone at that time is not born the same way, these experiences will be based on the postion of the weak planets and how much they are affecting the individual.

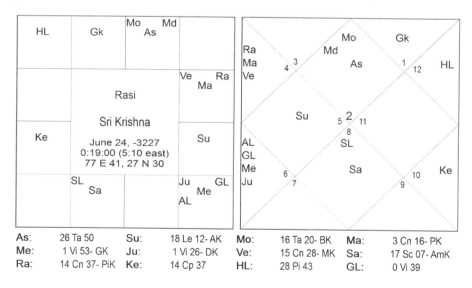

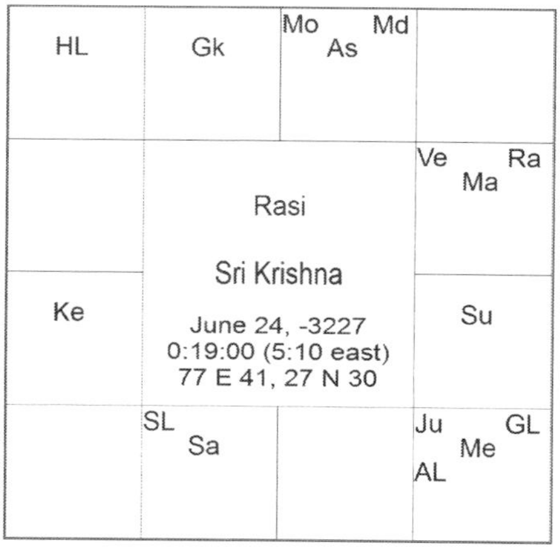

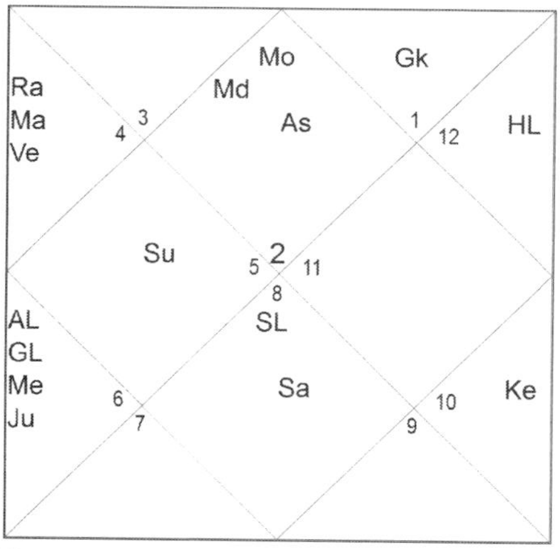

As:	26 Ta 50	Su:	18 Le 12- AK	Mo:	16 Ta 20- BK	Ma:	3 Cn 16- PK
Me:	1 Vi 53- GK	Ju:	1 Vi 26- DK	Ve:	15 Cn 28- MK	Sa:	17 Sc 07- AmK
Ra:	14 Cn 37- PiK	Ke:	14 Cp 37	HL:	28 Pi 43	GL:	0 Vi 39

[32] Bṛhat Jātaka V.16

Kalyāṇa Varmā says the place of delivery will correspond to the rāśi or navāṁśa at birth; a fixed sign/aṁśa indicates delivery in one's own place, as well as a vargottama lagna. A dual sign indicates birth on the way [or changing the place of labor, or going to the place of delivery during labor]. Movable signs indicate going to a place other than your own home for the delivery.[33]

In Śrī Kṛṣṇa's chart, the Moon is stronger (it is exalted in the lagna) and it was raining heavily when he was born. Since the Moon is stronger for a night birth it indicates a maternal place, and he was born in the maternal uncle's dungeon. Saturn is aspecting the Moon indicating he was born in a place of darkness. The lagneśa of his rāśi is in the third conjunct Mars and Rāhu indicating dungeons (bandhana yoga). The lagna is a fixed sign in Śrī Kṛṣṇa's chart but the lagneśa (Venus) is in a parivartana yoga with the ucca Moon. This shows he was carried away from his birth place to a place of the Moon in Taurus (cow herders) and switched (*parivartana*) with his female cousin.

Now there may be some confusion as to whether to look for these results in the rāśi or the navāṁśa. Varāhamihira says to determine the strength between the rāśi and navāṁśa to determine the birthplace. In general practice, unless there is a strong combination in the rāśi overriding the navāṁśa indications, these rules will be found to be very successful when applied to navāṁśa. Therefore all rules utilized hereforth will be applied to the navāṁśa unless otherwise mentioned (but be aware that these rules can be applied to rāśi in certain situations, as well as to relevant divisional charts). To determine the stronger varga, kendra bala becomes very important. A varga with no planets in kendra becomes very weak and gives less results.

If the lagna and Moon are in water signs the delivery will be close to water [also representing a waterbirth]. This will also happen if the lagna is a water sign and it is either aspected by a Moon with fullness or the Moon is in the fourth, seventh or tenth [kendra].[34] Waterbirth can also seen when lagna and fourth are occupied by benefics and the moon is in a water sign.[35]

Sometimes a woman plans for a waterbirth and the labor continues for an extended period- then as soon as she leaves the water and lays in another place the delivery progresses. Other times, the child is not coming forth and the lights are turned dim and the delivery progresses. In this way, certain birth circumstances may be planned by the parents but may not actually come to pass according to the karma of the child.

---

[33] Bṛhat Jātaka V.13, Sārāvalī of Kalyāṇa Varmā IX.3-4, and Jātaka Pārijāta III.66
[34] Bṛhat Jātaka V.8-9, and Jātaka Pārijāta III.62
[35] Sārāvalī of Kalyāṇa Varmā IX.5-7

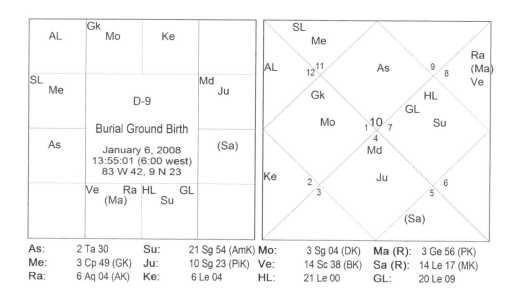

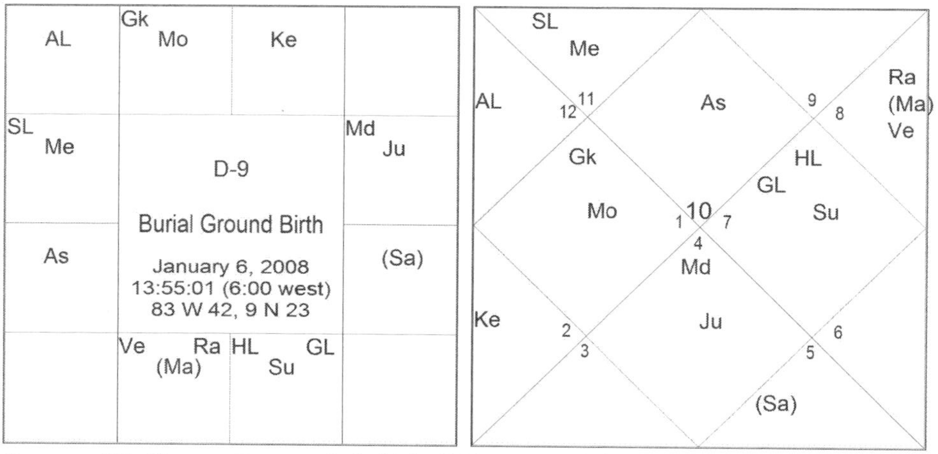

As:	2 Ta 30	Su:	21 Sg 54 (AmK)	Mo:	3 Sg 04 (DK)	Ma (R):	3 Ge 56 (PK)
Me:	3 Cp 49 (GK)	Ju:	10 Sg 23 (PiK)	Ve:	14 Sc 38 (BK)	Sa (R):	14 Le 17 (MK)
Ra:	6 Aq 04 (AK)	Ke:	6 Le 04	HL:	21 Le 00	GL:	20 Le 09

Varāhamihira says that if the lagna has Saturn in a nara rāśi[36] with the aspect of Mars the birth will be in a graveyard (*śmaśāna*).[37] Saturn and Mars sambandha is called Yama-yoga, and Yama is the Lord of death. Saturn Mars in lagna can give birth in/near a graveyard, as well as Capricorn lagna (the natural sign of graveyards) with the aspect of Saturn and Mars. Saturn Ketu can give birth in a place where there are disembodied spirits. In this way, the yogas will give their results.

In the example navāṁśa chart, the child was born on land that was an old tribal burial ground (which was no longer in use). The chart has Capricorn navāṁśa lagna with Saturn and Mars giving rāśi dṛṣṭi. The navāṁśa changes in three minutes to Aquarius (a nara rāśi) with Saturn and Mars giving graha dṛṣṭi, which would show a burial/creamation gound which is still in use. Rāśi dṛṣṭi shows the place, while graha dṛṣṭi shows the desired intention of the people using the place. In the example chart, the lagna has the graha dṛṣṭi of exalted Jupiter showing the present use of the land is by spiritual people for an educational and holistic healing center.

[36] Nara rāśis are one's which have a human (*nara*) image associated with them: Gemini- a couple, Virgo- virgin woman, Libra-shopkeeper with scale, Aquarius-person holding water container, and the first half of Sagittarius.

[37] Bṛhat Jātaka V.12, Sārāvalī of Kalyāṇa Varmā IX.10, and Jātaka Pārijāta III.65

Nāḍī Text Examples

There are some Nāḍī texts where Pārvatī asks the various sages to interpret a chart.[38] Below are some excerpts from these to see the nature of what the Ṛṣī sees.

[2] Parāśara says: This is the horoscope of a male child that lives with name and fame. His birth house is south-facing. The street extends from east to west. [3] There is a temple for Mahāviṣṇu in the eastern side. The south-east side adores a temple for Hanumān while the north-east side has an abode of worship for Śrī Mahākālī. [5] The native is the sixth child of his parents. Oh Pārvatī, I will explain to you about the native's parents, wife, progeny, etc. in detail.

In the above example, Parāśara starts looking at the chart and speaks first about the cicumstances of birth before moving forward into the individual's life. These are just examples to demonstrate that these above techniques were put into use while doing readings. Here is another example below:

[2] The native is a male. The house in which he is born faces the south. There are no other houses in the opposite direction. Situated in the north-east side of the house is a dilapidated temple of Kṛṣṇa. [3] The native's father had a total of eleven coborns out of whom some died. Only three sisters and three brothers have long lives. The father is of dark complexion and has a symetrical body…

Vāstu

Saturn represents both incarnation and death. Death or birth are said to cause impurity (*aśaucha*) for forty days both to the person's present and the location of the happening. Saturn is also the natural kāraka of vāstu which is the *situation of the land and home.* The situation of Saturn indicates the nature of the house of birth.

Varāhamihira says if Saturn is in a water sign [showing human activity] and connected to Mercury then birth is in/near a sports/ amusement area, connected to the Sun shows a temple area. The Moon indicates places with saline soil (*soṣara-bhumi*). When Saturn is in a human sign [showing human activity] and connected to Venus and Moon the birth is in a place enjoyed by people. When Jupiter influences the child is born in a home where religious practices (*agni-hotra*) are performed. The Sun gives royal mansions, cowsheds, or temple premises. Mercury indicates a workshop (of a carpenter, artist, sculptor, etc) and libraries/ centers of knowledge.[39] If Mercury was associated with Saturn in an earth sign, the location would be a garden- a place not particularly meant for the purpose of

[38] These nāḍīs are translated under the title "Wisdom of the Seers" and found in chapter 17 and 26-31 of R. Santhanam's

[39] Bṛhat Jātaka V.11-12, Sārāvalī of Kalyāṇa Varmā IX.8-11, and Jātaka Pārijāta III.64-65

humans. In this way, Saturn shows the nature of the living environment at birth.

The strongest planet will effect the nature of the *house of delivery*, sthāna bala specifically. If Saturn is the strongest, the house will be a remodeled older house. Mars shows a house that has been burnt, the Moon shows a new house, the Sun shows a house made of wood. Mercury shows a house built by many craftsman, Venus shows a new, decorated and pleasing house. Jupiter shows a very strong house. The strongest planet indicating the birth house can then be taken as the lagna and the nature of other houses around it can be seen.[40] The first three signs from that planet represent east, the fourth to six signs from it represent south, etc. In this way, the nature of the house and the entire *neighborhood* can be seen. The lagna (or the sign lording the strongest planet in kendra) will indicate the direction of the delivery room in the house. The delivery bed can also be seen, as well as the type of clothe on it.[41] The direction of the doors in the delivery room can be seen from the direction ruled by the planets in kendra, and if no planets then the direction of the strongest sign in kendra.[42]

[40] Bṛhat Jātaka V.19, Sārāvalī of Kalyāṇa Varmā IX.15, and Jātaka Pārijāta III.72
[41] Bṛhat Jātaka V.20-21, Sārāvalī of Kalyāṇa Varmā IX.13, 18-20, Jātaka Pārijāta III.73-74, and Uttara Kālāmṛta I.I.9
[42] Bṛhat Jātaka V.18, Sārāvalī of Kalyāṇa Varmā IX.16, and Jātaka Pārijāta III.71, and Uttara Kālāmṛta I.I.10

Nurses in the Room

The number of nurses in the room when the child is born is a technique utilized in the rāśi chart. This will often show the number of people in the room helping, whether they are nurses or not. Parāśara says,

लग्नचन्द्रान्तरालस्थग्रहैः स्युरुपसूतिकाः ।

lagnacandrāntarālasthagrahaiḥ syurupasūtikāḥ।

The planets placed inbetween the lagna and Moon show the people helping the mother.

दृश्यादृश्यविभागाभ्यां बहिरन्तश्च ताः स्मृताः ॥१२ ॥

dṛśyādṛśyavibhāgābhyāṁ bahirantaśca tāḥ smṛtāḥ।।12।।

Whether they were inside the room or outside the room
is known from the visible and invisible divisions of the houses.

स्वक्षादौ द्विगुणा ज्ञेया वक्रोच्चे त्रिगुणा मताः ।

svarkṣādau dviguṇā jñeyā vakrocce triguṇā matāḥ।

Regard planets in their own sign as double and retrograde or exalted as triple.

यत्रोभयस्य सम्प्राप्तिस्त्रैगुण्यं तत्र वै सकृत् ॥१३ ॥

yatrobhayasya samprāptistraiguṇyaṁ tatra vai sakṛt।।13।।

If there is both [own sign and exaltation] then it will gain triple.

पापैस्तु विधवा ज्ञेयाः शोभनैः सधवाः स्मृताः ।

pāpaistu vidhavā jñeyāḥ śobhanaiḥ sadhavāḥ smṛtāḥ।

Malefics indicate widows and benefics indicate married women.

The focus of this verse is the number of women in the room at birth. The tradition in ancient times is that a pregnant woman would go to one of the parent's homes and the sisters, cousins and elder women would help her through the delivery. The number of people in the delivery room could be seen by counting the number of planets from the lagna to the Moon. Planets in the invisible (*adṛśya*) side of the chart, from the middle of the lagna till the middle of the seventh house, are inside the birthing room. Planets in the visible (*dṛśya*) side of the chart are outside the delivery room- visible and seen by others.

When counting the planets to determine the number of people, a planet in its own sign is counted as two people, while an exalted planet is counted as three people. This is a standard rule for counting items. For example, the number of properties a person owns would be seen by planets in the fourth house of chaturthāṁśa and counted as two properties for own sign and three for exaltation. For certain techniques a debilitated planet can count as negative one (-1). Parāśara adds that if the planet is in its own sign and exalted it counts as only three. The only graha that does this is Mercury who is exalted in his own sign.

The nature of the people in the room is indicated by the qualities of the planets. Malefics will indicate women who are older and may have lost their husband. Benefics indicate younger married women. Their strength will also be apparent in the people who they represent, according to their state at the time of delivery. In general, all the people present can be identified according to the planets in the child's birth chart.

In the example rāśi chart below, (1) Ketu represents a female acupuncturist who was present as a friend to give support. (2) Saturn represents the doula, who is an attendant specifically for the needs of the mother during labor (the word actually comes from the Greek for slave). As this is a servant role it relates to Saturn who rules servants. (3) The Sun represents a female Āyurvedic practitioner who was present. (4) Mars is well placed when it is in a three planet conjunction and gets the good results of the other planets. It represents the primary nurse assisting the delivering mother. Mercury is exalted which will often indicate male, it is also conjunct with Mars and Sun which would also make it male. Therefore, Mercury is representing three men, and there were three men at the delivery; (5) the delivery doctor, (6) the father and (7) the father's friend. It indicates a good doctor because it is the fourth lord strong in its own house.

Venus is debilitated and afflicted by Mars (most subha graha and least subha graha interact). The birth was planned to be at the Mother's home but due to complications the

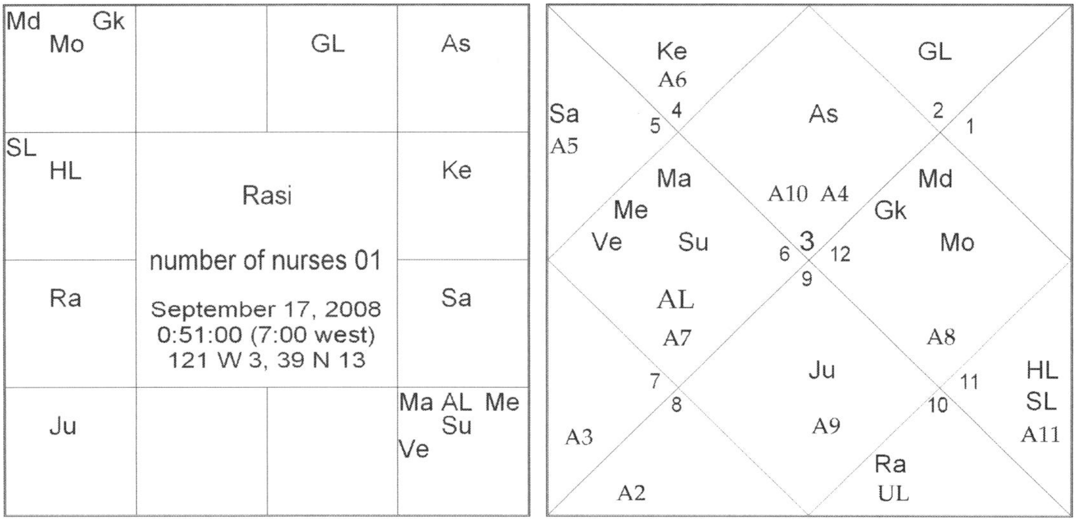

As:	18 Ge 23	Su:	0 Vi 49 (DK)	Mo:	25 Pi 55 (BK)	Ma:	24 Vi 46 (MK)
Me:	26 Vi 31 (AmK)	Ju:	18 Sg 41 (PK)	Ve:	27 Vi 43 (AK)	Sa:	19 Le 36 (PiK)
Ra:	22 Cp 35 (GK)	Ke:	22 Cn 35	HL:	29 Aq 58	GL:	29 Ta 48

(8) midwife panicked and the birth ended up in the hospital (moving during labor is seen from both rāśi and navāṁśa lagna being dual signs). Venus represents the midwife and her panic is due to the debilitation, which is removed by Mercury (the doctor) being that Mercury gives nīca banga to Venus, as well as the interaction of Venus and Mars (the primary nurse). The affliction of Venus by Mars is also seen in that the midwife was in the process of a divorce (a process ruled by Mars).

Jupiter is eighteen degrees, so it is just outside the delivery room, but in this hospital the actual room was divided into two parts, an entry area and a delivery area. Jupiter in its own sign represents two individuals. There were two respitory nurses that came into the entry room just before the birth in case there was any issues with the baby starting or stopping its breathing. Rāhu represents the secretary working outside the room in the Newborn and Infant Care Unit. In this way, all the planets represent people at or near the delivery, according to the strength and weakness of the planets. In the same way, each person indicates the strength and weakness of those planets.

Now to sum up some of the above mentioned principles. The chara, sthira, dvisvabhāva nature of the sign relates to whether the location of delivery is at home, on the way/ transition, at a set place, or away. The nature (rāśi and sambandha) of Saturn relates to the vāstu of the place of delivery. The strongest planet shows the nature of the house of delivery, and planets from that show the neighborhood. The strongest planet in kendra shows the doors to the delivery room. The number of planets from Lagna to Moon show the number of attendants at the time of delivery.

The information on location may seem too detailed for just seeing the birth place alone. Rectifying the chart is important, but why so many verses on these details? These are all general principles. They are being enunciated by the sages relative to place of birth, but they can be used in many other situations. For example, in Praśna, if someone came with a question about a stolen item, you could precede to tell them not just about the thief and whether they would get the item back or not, but with this level of detail you have the ability to describe the location the stolen item is being kept with great accuracy. Like this, these are general principles and if we learn them in this situation they can be applied again and again. The sages give a few techniques here and a few over there, and it is up to the intelligent to put them all together. The sages don't give a huge list of planetary qualities, this list is relatively short as the nature of the planets becomes obvious as you read various dictums such as these on location. As you understand that Saturn and Mars in a human sign give death related situations you could also see this in the tenth house as a career for a person. In this way, these are general principles that are being enunciated and we must understand them at this deeper level.

At the same time, the moment of birth is a hologram of our chart. A praśna answers the question that arises at that moment, because the stars above relate to the question in that moment's circumstance, as well as the answer. A muhūrta shows the nature of that which is being created, as well as the circumstances and intentions at the moment it is created. The circumstances of birth are reflective of the characteristics of the individual, which are percieved by the placement and status of planets in the birth chart. In this way, the chart above reflects the circumstances (or the particular energy) on the earth at that given moment. That which is "born" during that moment has the nature of that energy within it.

Even the weather can be percieved in the navāṁśa lagna. Nikola Tesla was one of the worlds greatest mechanical and electrical engineers, and the PBS special about him was called "Master of Lightning". He was born during an electrical storm and has Mars and Ketu in his navāṁśa lagna representing an electrical storm. Another individual with exalted Saturn in navāṁśa lagna was born during a blizzard (large snow storm) and Saturn represents cold. What is manifesting relates to the entire environment, the stars and what they are manifesting on earth, and the event which happens at that moment.

The Dīpa

Dīpa means the lamp or light. Traditionally it was a ghee lamp placed in the wall of the room. The light represents being, knowing, knowledge, or the tripod of life: the Sun, Moon and Lagna. Parāśara says,

यस्मिन् भागे भवेत्सूर्यस्तत्र दीपं वदेत् सुधीः ।

yasmin bhāge bhavetsūryastatra dīpaṁ vadet sudhīḥ|

The dīpa is indicated from the region/sign in which the Sun is placed.

लग्नाद्वर्त्तिस्तथा चन्द्रात्तौलं वाच्यं मनीषिभिः ॥८॥

lagnādvarttistathā candrāttaulaṁ vācyaṁ manīṣibhiḥ||8||

The ascendant indicates the wick, the Moon indicates the oil.

चरेऽर्के चंचलो दीपः स्थिरर्क्षो तु स्थिरो भवेत् ।

care'rke cañcalo dīpaḥ sthirarkṣo tu sthiro bhavet|

If the Sun is in a moveable sign the lamp will flicker,
If the Sun in a fixed sign it will be steady

द्विभे स्थितिर्द्वयोर्ज्ञेया सूर्यर्क्षवशतो बुधैः ॥९॥

dvibhe sthitirdvayorjñeyā sūryarkṣavaśato budhaiḥ||9||

The Sun in a dual sign is known to be both flickering and steady.

How these dīpa techniques relate to todays modern lamps is debatable. For example, the nurses kept dimming the lights during my daughter's delivery and I kept turning them up (lots of light shows a strong Sun). Her Sun's aṁśa is in a moveable sign which shows flickering (my debatable modern interpretation). The techniques are mentioned here for the understanding of the technique itself. The kāraka Sun represents light, its placement in the chart represents where the light is. In vāstu, this will help determine the best place to put a lamp in one's office or the best place to put the temple/alter in the home (Sun is kāraka for temples). Venus shows the best place to put the bedroom in the house or the bed in the bedroom. In this way, the the nature of the kāraka can be understood in deeper terms.

Parāśara mentions that the dīpa is placed in the direction related to the house/sign in which the Sun is placed. The word used can mean house or sign, in our tradition we use the house placement of the Sun. Lagna/Aries represents the eastern direction of the room, the fourth house/Cancer represents the North, the seventh house/Libra the south, etc. The nature of the flame is steady or flickering based on the motion associated with the sign in which the Sun is placed.

The classics say that if the wick of the lamp is newly lit, the ascendant is in its early degrees while being at the end of itself the ascendant is towards the end of the sign. But this creates a difficulty in that many lamps were made to burn all night long, and the wick lasts all night. The amount of oil in the lamp is seen by the Moon's degrees. Some commentators have said it is based on the fullness of the Moon but Bhattotpala (a respected ninth century commentator of Varāhamahira) has discredited this with the fact that not all children born on the new-moon are born in the dark. In general philosophy, the dīpa container itself represents one's home, the oil in it represents the body, and the wick represents the intelligence (*dhī*). When making a dīpa for pūjā one chants mantras to the Iṣṭa-devatā while making the wick- so the divine can guide the mind. In this way, the ghee lamp indicates the strength of the lagna; body, dhi-śakti, health and longevity. This is an application of reading kārakas. For example, my daughter was born with a very strong Moon and there was plenty of food for the people to eat at her delivery. The general kāraka for food is the Moon, and the extra food showed that the Moon was strong. In this way, the significations of the planets at birth should be perceived and understood.

Pain to Mother

Birth is not always a painful experience and other times it is a terrible experience which scars the mother. Pain relates to Saturn and other malefics. Birth is painful when the Moon is associated with malefics (especially Saturn) or in kendra to them (especially the fourth house). Varāhamihira says that if there are malefics conjoined, fourth or seventh

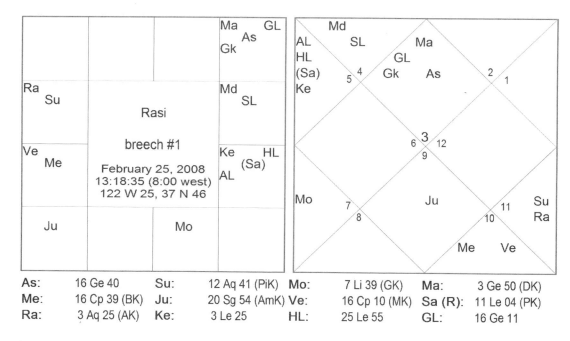

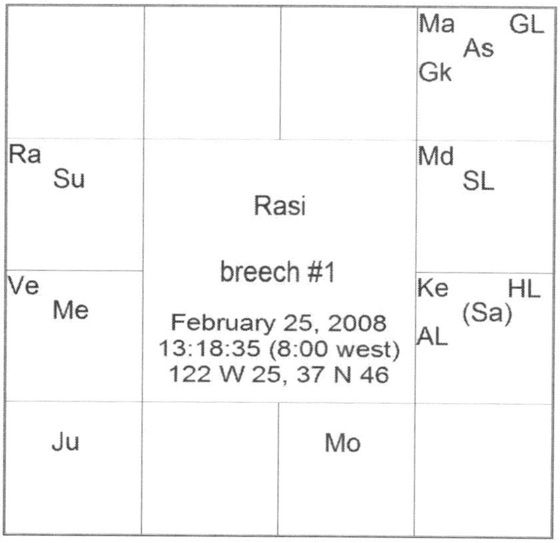

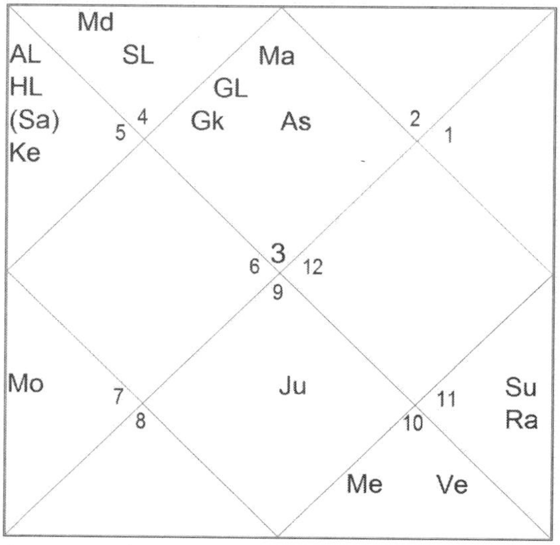

As:	16 Ge 40	Su:	12 Aq 41 (PiK)	Mo:	7 Li 39 (GK)	Ma:	3 Ge 50 (DK)
Me:	16 Cp 39 (BK)	Ju:	20 Sg 54 (AmK)	Ve:	16 Cp 10 (MK)	Sa (R):	11 Le 04 (PK)
Ra:	3 Aq 25 (AK)	Ke:	3 Le 25	HL:	25 Le 55	GL:	16 Ge 11

from the Moon then the delivery is very painful (*kleśa*).[43] Kalyāṇa Varmā says if there[44] are beneficial aspects then the delivery was comfortable, while malefics make it difficult (*kaṣṭa*).[45] He says that benefics in the tenth and fourth house cause birth to be in a good condition (*sampatti*) and in a spacious place (*vipulā*).[46] The fourth house is the most important house from the Moon to see for pain caused to the mother during delivery. The seventh is the fourth from the fourth, and the tenth is aspecting the fourth. In this way, the condition of the fourth from the Moon of the rāśi, navāṁśa and dvādaśāṁśa should be seen. Benefics show an easy birth in a comfortable place. Malefics show complications and painful experience to the mother.

In the *Horāsāra*, it says in a praśna to first see the stronger between lagna and Moon. Then see the fourth house from there. If the lord of the fourth is strong and has beneficial combinations then the child will be happy in the womb[47]. In this way, if the query is about the birth it will also show a comfortable delivery, as all the above presented rules can be applied to praśna with proper discrimination.

If the birth is breech or there were problems with getting the fetus to turn before the delivery the classics mention[48] that the acendant should be a pṛṣṭhodaya rāśi (sign rising from behind: Aries, Taurus, Gemini, Sagittarius, and Capricorn). This cannot

---

[43] Bṛhat Jātaka V.17, and Jātaka Pārijāta III.70
[44] The reference does not mention lagna or Moon but the preceding verse is referring to the lagna rāśi.
[45] Sārāvalī of Kalyāṇa Varmā IX.2
[46] Sārāvalī of Kalyāṇa Varmā IX.31
[47] Horāsāra IV.26-28
[48] Bṛhat Parāśara Horā Śāstra, *Sūtikā-adhyāyaḥ* 10, Bṛhat Jātaka V.17

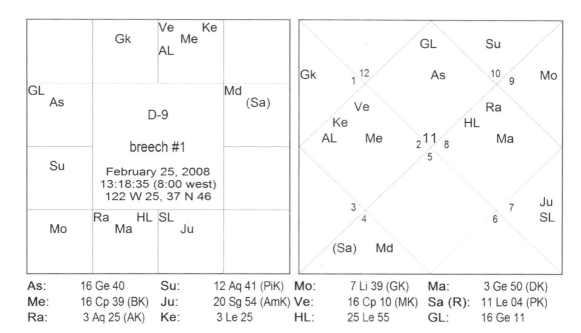

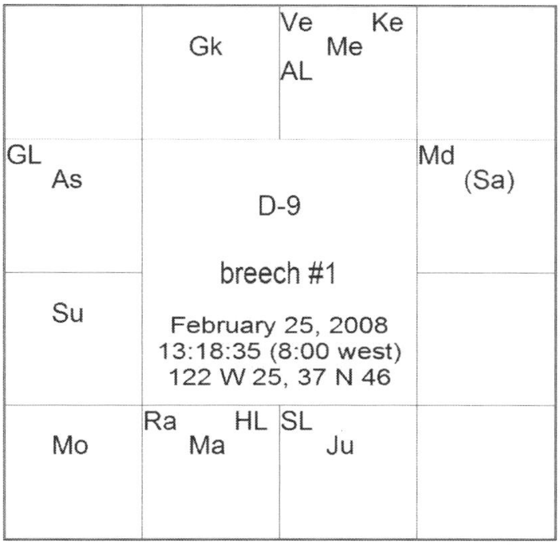

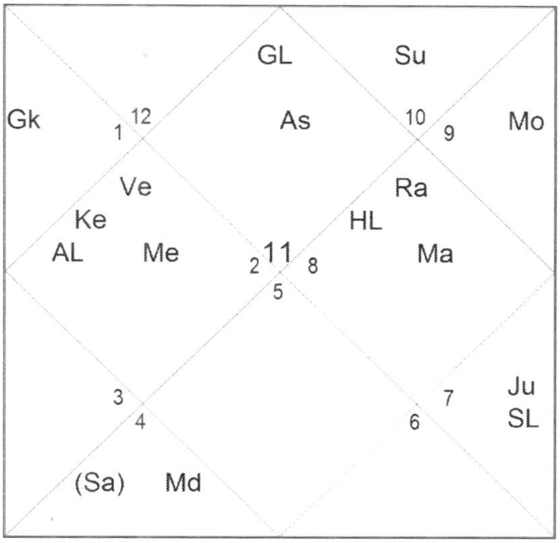

As:	16 Ge 40	Su:	12 Aq 41 (PiK)	Mo:	7 Li 39 (GK)	Ma:	3 Ge 50 (DK)
Me:	16 Cp 39 (BK)	Ju:	20 Sg 54 (AmK)	Ve:	16 Cp 10 (MK)	Sa (R):	11 Le 04 (PK)
Ra:	3 Aq 25 (AK)	Ke:	3 Le 25	HL:	25 Le 55	GL:	16 Ge 11

be predicted as only three to four percent of births are breech and five out of twelve signs (41%) are pṛṣṭhodaya. In general, the head is ruled by the Sun and the head birthing first shows the strength of the Sun as the leading planet. When the Sun is not the boss of the chart Rāhu takes over; it is similar to when the mafia become stronger then the king/ government. When Rāhu becomes stronger than the Sun to be the boss of the chart this can be indicated by a breech birth. Aquarius navāṁśa lagna or stronly placed Rāhu may also give a breech birth but the primary factor is the strength of Rāhu over the Sun. In the example chart, the rāśi chart of a footling breech birth had Gemini lagna with Sun conjunct Rāhu in Aquarius, Saturn was placed opposite giving an exchange of Sun and Saturn. Rāhu was the Ātmakāraka, and the navāṁśa lagna was Aquarius with Rāhu and Mars in the navāṁśa tenth house. This illustrates how Rāhu takes over the chart in the case of a breech birth.

Rāhu also shows the use of forceps during birth as Rāhu rules metals, metal tools, and things that are not normal. Rāhu influencing navāṁśa lagna can indicate birth with forceps. Mars indicates caesarian birth, as he rules cutting and invasive operations by surgeons. In the previous example, the breech birth had to be delivered by caesarian, and Mars has fourth house graha dṛṣṭi on the navāṁśa lagna. Ketu will often cause reversals, such as the heart being on the opposite side than normal. Scorpio will tend to cause some type of deformity, especially if it is with Mars or Ketu. For example, in the chart of Adolf Hitler, the navāṁśa was Scorpio with Venus, Ketu and Mars and he only had one testicle. In this way, malefics will cause some type of disruption to the birth process and the child.

Absence of Father

Importance is placed on the presence of the father during delivery. If the Moon has sambandha with the lagna or lagneśa then the father is present. These techniques are utilized in the rāśi chart. The Moon represents the blood lineage. When studying lineage in a chart, one analyzes the fourth and ninth from the Moon. The trines (particularly ninth) to the Moon shows the continuance of lineage. The kendra (particularly fourth) to the Moon shows the support to the lineage. When the Moon does not associate with lagna or lagneśa there is a going away from the lineage in life. It also shows that at some point the father will not be there when needed or will let the native down during an important time. Parāśara says,

लग्ने मन्दो मदे भौमश्चन्द्रो लग्नं च पश्यति ।
बुधशुक्रान्तरे चन्द्रः परोक्षे स्याञ्जनिः पितुः ॥२६ ॥

lagne mando made bhaumaścandro lagnaṁ ca paśyati|
budhaśukrāntare candraḥ parokṣe syāñjaniḥ pituḥ||26||

Saturn in the lagna and Mars in the seventh and Moon not aspecting the Lagna,
When the Moon is placed between Mercury and Venus, indicates the father is not present at the delivery.

अष्टमे नवमे वापि चरमे यदि भास्करः ।
परोक्षे जन्म जातस्य पितुः स्यान्नात्र संशयः ॥२७ ॥

aṣṭame navame vāpi carame yadi bhāskaraḥ|
parokṣe janma jātasya pituḥ syānnātra saṁśayaḥ||27||

When the Sun is in a moveable sign, in the eighth or ninth house,
Then the father will be absent from the delivery.

कर्मभावं विना दृश्ये चरभे यदि भास्करः ।
लग्नं चन्द्रे न पश्येश्चेद् दूरसंस्थः शिशोः पिता ॥२८ ॥

karmabhāvaṁ vinā dṛśye carabhe yadi bhāskaraḥ|
lagnaṁ candre na paśyeśced dūrasaṁsthaḥ śiśoḥ pitā||28||

When the Sun is in a moveable sign, except the tenth house,
And the Moon does not aspect the ascendant,
it is understood that the infant's father resides far away.

These are combinations that might not stand out at first but will be seen only with further research when studying the chart. The first combination says if Saturn is in Lagna and Mars is in the seventh house and the Moon is between Mercury and Venus not aspecting the lagna then the father is absent at the birth. In the example chart, Saturn aspects the lagna with his third house graha dṛṣṭi, and Mars aspects the seventh house with his seventh house dṛṣṭi. Moon is in between Mercury and Venus and does not aspect

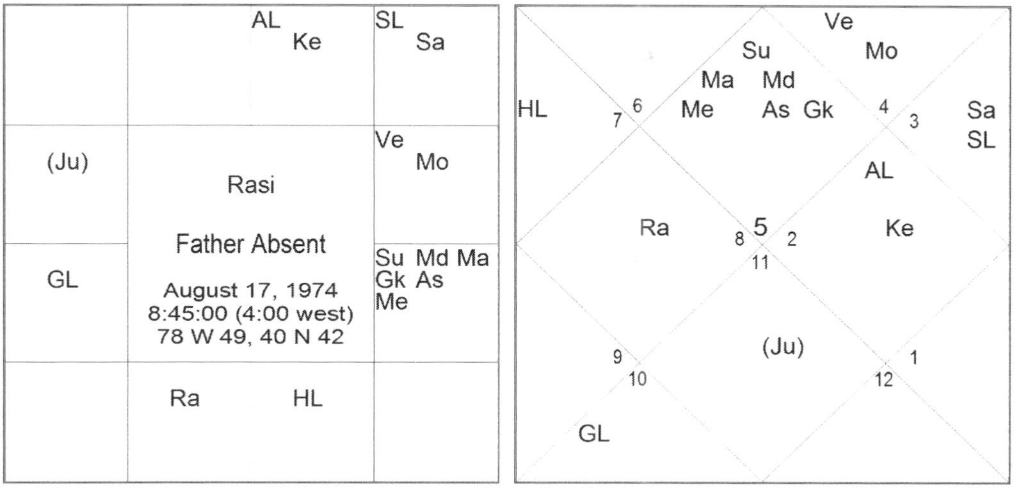

As:	26 Le 56	Su:	0 Le 44 (DK)	Mo:	26 Cn 59 (AK)	Ma:	19 Le 41 (MK)
Me:	0 Le 51 (GK)	Ju (R):	21 Aq 49 (AmK)	Ve:	9 Cn 36 (PiK)	Sa:	20 Ge 45 (BK)
Ra:	22 Sc 19 (PK)	Ke:	22 Ta 19	HL:	7 Li 13	GL:	17 Cp 04

the lagna from the twelfth house. The individual's father was with the mother during the entire night of the labor. As the Sun rose, he went to get a coffee at the local store since the labor was taking so long. When he returned the child was born. He had intended to be present for the birth but because of the child's chart was not able to be. The mother eventually left the father, and the child grew up primarily with the mother, so the father was in the child's life very little. Because of his fear of flying he was unable to attend the child's marriage. In this way, the father was not present for the birth and was not able to be present for many important events in the child's life. Parāśara says,

रात्रौ जन्म यदा यस्य भौमयुक्तः शनैश्चरः।
चरस्थः परदेशे तु तातस्य निधनं वदेत्॥२९॥

rātrau janma yadā yasya bhaumayuktaḥ śanaiścaraḥ||
carasthaḥ paradeśe tu tātasya nidhanaṁ vadet||29||

A night birth in which Saturn and Mars are conjunct,
And placed in a moveable sign, indicates the father will have
destruction in a foreign country.

In this dictum, the child is born at night so that Saturn becomes dominant to give results for the father. Saturn and Mars together is Yama-yoga which indicates circumstances of death. The moveable sign indicates the father's location in a distant place and the yoga indicates death. This could be a combination in which the child loses the father while he is fighting a war in a foreign land.

Varāhamihira states that if malefics planets are in malefic signs in the fifth, seventh, or ninth from the Sun, the child is born while the father is in bondage (jail). The sign occupied by the Sun will indicate the locality of the bondage. This means if the sign of the Sun is fixed the father is in jail nearby while if the Sun is in a moveable sign the father is in jail in a distant place. There are also combinations for the mother giving birth in jail[49] and the death of the mother after birth.[50] But these verses delineating the situation of the father at birth show that his circumstances are as important as the mother's.

अष्टमे वा व्यये पापा् लग्नेशो बलसंयुतः ।
सुखेऽथ नवमे वापि रोगयुक्तस्तदा पिता ॥३० ॥

aṣṭame vā vyaye pāpā lagneśo balasaṁyutaḥ|
sukhe'tha navame vāpi rogayuktastadā pitā||30||

If malefics are in the eighth or twelfth and
the lagneśa is strongly placed in the fourth or ninth,
Then the father will get an illness [after the birth of the child].

लग्नस्थं सबलं सूर्यं शनिभौमौ प्रपश्यतः ।
जन्मकाले तदा तस्य रोगयुक्तः पिता भवेत् ॥३१ ॥

lagnasthaṁ sabalaṁ sūryaṁ śanibhaumau prapaśyataḥ|
janmakāle tadā tasya rogayuktaḥ pitā bhavet||31||

If the Sun is in strength in the ascendant and Saturn and Mars aspect,
Then the father will have illness during the birth time.

चतुर्थे दशमे वापि शनिभौमार्कखेचराः ।
शुभसम्बन्धहीनश्चेत्तदा पितृसुखं नहि ॥३२ ॥

caturthe daśame vāpi śanibhaumārkakhecarāḥ|
śubhasambandhahīnaścettadā pitṛsukhaṁ nahi||32||

If the fourth and tenth are malefic with the planets Saturn, Mars and Sun,
With no benefic association, the native is devoid of happiness from the father.

We can learn a lot about ourselves by looking at our children's birth charts. In the chart from the example of the number of nurses in the room during delivery, we can see the first dictum listed by Parāśara here. There is a malefic in the eighth house and the lagneśa is placed with strength in the fourth house. The father also has combinations for sickness in his chart. This sickness could be timed using the father's chart or the child's chart, as the indication exists in both and should have an alignment with timing.

[49] Bṛhat Jātaka V.10
[50] Sārāvalī of Kalyāṇa Varmā IX.34-36

Adoption Combinations

The magic of Jyotiṣa is that everything is interconnected, and exactly the way its supposed to be. The child will be born exactly when they are supposed to be born. If a child is to be given away in adoption or was concieved in an illegitimate relationship, then this is representative in the birth chart.

An adopted child is called a datta-putra (given-son). An individual will tend to adopt a child when Mars and Saturn are in the ninth house of the saptāṁśa. Sometimes this combination may block children from being born, but as soon as the couple adopts a child they are able to move to the next house of the saptāṁśa indicating the next child which can be born naturally through the couple. In this case, adopting a child can sometimes be a remedy, if there are no other indications blocking children. This should be applied very gracefully as it would not be appropriate for a couple to adopt a child just to get their own, as an adopted child is to be cared for as the couple's own child. The dharma śāstra gives the adopted child the same right to inheritance as the natural born child. An adopted child is also called *kṛtrima* which means not natural, made by artifical means, simulated, assumed, or adopted. It may not be a natural child but is treated as if it were one.

Adoption is said to happen to a child if the Moon or Sun is in the ninth or fifth from Saturn and Mars.[51] Sārāvalī adds that Mars and Saturn conjunct in the same aṁśa or Mars in the seventh aspected by Saturn can also indicate adoption. I have not seen this rule to work very well in modern situations, as their has been great variability in the combinations of different charts of adopted individuals. In the charts I have seen, one of the luminaries is conjunct or trine Mars or Saturn and has rāśi aspect of either Mars or Saturn or is in their sign so that it has connection to both of them; in both rāśi and navāṁśa.

The classics also mention whether the child is well cared for after adoption or not according to its birth chart. If Jupiter aspects the planet causing the adoption, the child will live long and prosper in its new family. If the Moon is afflicted and has Mars seventh from it, then the child will suffer. If a benefic aspects the Moon, it can save the child, through an individual or relative represented by that benefic planet.

There are also combinations to see if the child was born from an illegitimate relationship.[52] This type of information is very sensitive and even ancient authors caution about its use. If you tell a person that their father was not actually their biological father this can be very disturbing. If you tell a husband that the child does not belong to him, then you are creating some very severe reactions that will result in your own negative karma. In these type of situations one must differentiate between what they tell an individual and the information they see which is used to give proper advise without speaking directly about the situation. Good discernment is very important for an astrologer.

[51] Bṛhat Jātaka V.14-15, Sārāvalī of Kalyāṇa Varmā IX.37-40, and Jātaka Pārijāta III.52-53, 67, 68

[52] Jaimini Upadeśa Sutra 1.4.44-48, Bṛhat Jātaka V.6, Sārāvalī of Kalyāṇa Varmā IX.32-33, and Jātaka Pārijāta III.48-49

Birth Marks and Body Markings

Just as the place of birth and its circumstances are seen in the stars of the moment. The stars also stamp their marks on the body with markings as well as the shape and proportion of every feature. Parāśara mentions the placement of planets and their corresponding marks on the physical body. He says,

कालाङ्गे यत्र भौमार्कौ तत्र ज्ञेयं तिलादिकम् ॥१४ ॥

kālāṅge yatra bhaumārkau tatra jñeyaṁ tilādikam||14||

Where the Sun and Mars are in the kālapuruṣa there will be a mole.

शनिराहू स्थितौ यत्र तत्र श्यामलमादिशेत् ।

śanirāhū sthitau yatra tatra śyāmalamādiśet|

In the place of Saturn and Rahu will be a dark colored spot.

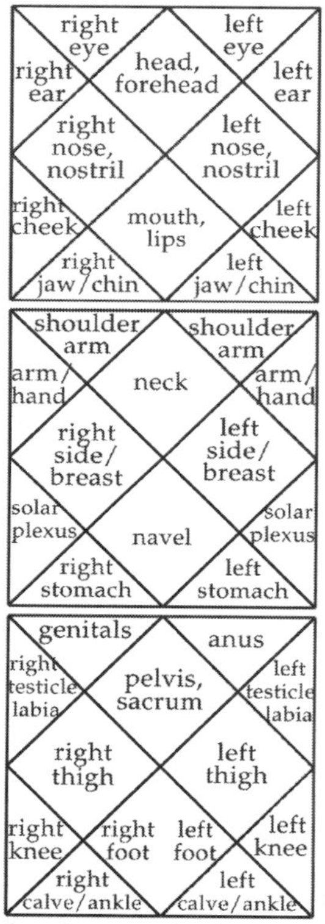

The marking will have the color or other significations of the planet indicating it.[53] Mars can give red spots, red moles, or scars. Parāśara gives more verses, some of which need a large amount of work decoding. Varāhamihira uses a simple way to see the marking on the body according to the dreṣkāṇa, or three divisions of the sign. The first dreṣkāṇa (first ten degree of the sign) represents the upper third of the body, above the neck. The second ten degrees represents the middle third of the body, while the last ten degrees represents the lower portion of the body below the navel. While the first third represents the upper head, the lagna represents the forehead, the second house the right eye, the third the right ear, the fourth the right nose, the fifth the right cheek, the sixth the jaw area, and the seventh the mouth. Notice that each sense (eyes, ears, nose) are dual and have two houses, while the mouth is central/single and is found in a single house. The specifics of the head are mapped into each house of the first dreṣkāṇa. The markings on the body are seen accordingly as planets are placed in these divisions.

There is a method by which the dreṣkāṇa of the lagna degree of the head.[54] Therefore if the lagna is 14 degrees, it falls in the second dreṣkāṇa which then represents the head. The third dreṣkāṇa then represents the torso, and the first dreṣkāṇa represents the lower portion of the body. If the lagna degree was in the third dreṣkāṇa, then the third will represent the head portion, the first represents the

[53] Bṛhat Parāśara Horā Śāstra, *Sūtikā-adhyāyaḥ* 16-17

[54] Bṛhat Jātaka V.24, based on the interpretation of *uditairdrekkaṇabhāgaiḥ*

torso, and the second represents the lower body. The author has had beneficial results with this method. Birth marks may also show on the body according to the planets in nakṣatras.

Parāśara mentions that these markings may not show up till a later time, which means that they may not be present at birth.[55] Varāhamihira states that benefics give birth-marks. Malefics will give sores or wounds caused by the nature of the malefic planet. Saturn indicates wounds from stones or vāta disorders, Mars from fire, weapons or poison. When Mercury becomes malefic it will give wounds due to earth related accidents, the Sun indicates quadrupeds or wood, while the Moo n indicates horned or aquatic animals.[56] Though the aspect of a benefic indicates it will be a marking only. These markings can be predicted and can also indicate to the astrologer the nature of the planet, or be used for rectification. When these malefic planets are in fixed or own sign/aṁśa then the signs will accompany birth. Otherwise they will come by accidents later in life.[57]

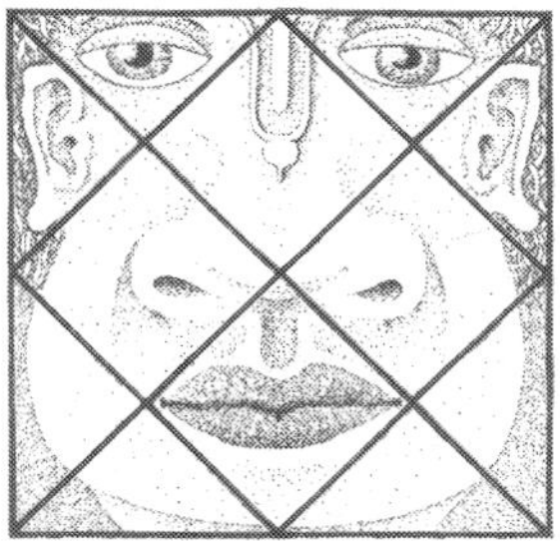

The imagery and placement of tattoos is based upon the same rules as body markings. Tattos of malefic images indicate the nature of the planet in its placement. A bad wound or disturbing image in a particular area should be analyzed as it is an indication to the astrologer about the disturbing nature of the graha and its need of remedy.

The state of the stars can be read in the circumstances of birth, they can be read on the body of the thing created at that moment. In this way, we also become aware of the importance of mūhurta- choosing a good time to begin important events. Projects will be 'marked' by the situation of the stars according to their position when the project begins. In this same way, the nimitta (omens) at the time an event transpires indicate the nature of the stars being favorable or not favorable. For example, having understood this, what would be the difference between signing a contract for a job in an old dilapitated house versus signing that contract in a grand mansion. Successful powerful people perform such events in grand places which also indicates the beneficial disposition and strength of the planets. Even a contract itself will be marked by the planetary positions. If there are significations for war during the signing of a peace treaty, the treaty will lead only to a greater war. A contract will have issues within it according to the planetary situation when it is contracted. In this same way, the body is marked by the planetary positions at birth.

[55] Bṛhat Parāśara Horā Śāstra, *Sūtikā-adhyāyaḥ* 17-18
[56] Bṛhat Jātaka V.25, Jātaka Pārijāta III.78 and Horā Makaranda V.31-33
[57] Bṛhat Jātaka V.25, Jātaka Pārijāta III.78, and Horā Makaranda V.31-33

Naming

In the beginning of creation, there was no sound (*aśabda*) and no vibration (*nispanda*). With vibration (*spanda*) came sound (*śabda*), they are the same. The first sound was 'auṁ' which was called as god or god-sound (*śabdabrahman*). From this came the causal body of sound (*pasyanti*), where the name, the object and its meaning are all the same. At this level, there is no difference between and object and its name-sound-vibration, the sound is the object. From this evolved the subtle body of sound (*madhyama*), where the name and the object are closely related. As in a dream, you think of an object and it appears, or think of a place and you are there, the apprehension of an object and the object itself are co-related. The externally manifest sound (*vaikharī*) exists in the physical world and is heard by the ears. The mind as the subject has apprehension (*pratyaya*) of objects (*artha*), and names those objects by words (*śabda*).[58] In the physical realm the sound, object and apprehension are all separate. We percieve an object and name it, and then when more than one person knows that name, they can share the same apprehension when they say that name. In this way, you can name an object and that name not correspond to what the object actually is. You can also percieve the vibration (*spanda*) or sound (*śabda*) of an object and give it a name which correlates to what it actually is. The power of sound must be considered on this level when naming a child.

Humans are very complex vibrations, having both postive and negative qualities. The study of a birth chart can reveal the sounds a person vibrates to or certain vibrations and sounds that bring out the best qualities in a person and support the individual to be successful in life according to who they are. There are many techniques to chose a name for a new born child based upon the natal chart. In initiations, names can be chosen for this reason, or they may be chosen to help the individual overcome certain inner obstacles. Someone who is noisy may get the name Śānti (peace). These spiritual names have a broader range of purposes, but can still be made more benefical to the overall being by some astrological guidance.

There are many considerations to take into account when choosing a name but we will focus on three. The sound the name begins with (*nāma-akṣara*), the number of syllables in the name and the general meaning of the name.

Speech comes from a very deep place inside a human and touches a very deep place inside those who hear one's words. Speech is a very powerful force. Every time someone hears their name it is affecting them on a very deep mental and spiritual level. The first sound of a question in praśna reveals the answer to an individual's problems. The first sound of the name of a deity can be meditated upon in tantra to understand the essence of that form. Mantras are even chosen as beneficial or not in tantra according to the first sound of an individual's name. In this way, there is a large emphasis on the first sound

[58] Woodroffe, Sir John, Garland of Letters, p.23

of the name. The first 'sound' is very important- not just the letter but the actual audible sound. The word 'Cat' in English begins with the letter 'C' but has the 'Ka' sound in Sanskrit. In this way, it is the sound that matters not the written letters.

The first sound will generally be related to the nakṣatra pada the child's Moon is placed within. These sounds are found in the hoḍa chakra.[59] This can also be chosen according to the pada of the lagna degree or a very beneficial planet if that planet needs to be activated better to help an individual attain their highest purpose. Some use the sounds of the strongest planet according to Ṣaḍbala. In some traditions, this first sound is based on the sounds associated with the rāśi, but given the same type of determination. Some systems use the same sounds for the rāśi as exist in the padas connected with them, while other systems have various other rāśi chakra correlations. Sometimes the names of Viṣṇu associated to the twelve signs of the zodiac are used in this way as well. It is important to examine the chart and determine any negative combinations. One should avoid the sounds connected to the planet which is causing negative situations. For example, if there is a cursed Venus maraṇa-kāraka-sthāna in the sixth house, then you want to avoid the sounds of Venus (cha, chha, ja, jha).

The first vowel sound can be chosen according to the avasthā of the planets and pañcha-svāra daśā, as we saw in the Sudarśana Cakra section. The katapayādi chakra can be used to see which sign the overall name is influencing, but this is again an advanced technique.

The number of syllables may not seem that important until you hear a two-year old try to learn how to speak. They focus very intently on each syllable, and often start with only two syllable words. In mantra śāstra the number of syllables becomes very important to give the pertinent results in a person's chart. In this way, the number of syllables in a name is chosen according to the motion of the sign ruling the lagna. Chara rāśi use one syllable, sthira rāśi use two syllables, and Dual rāśi use three syllables, (though some traditions prefer to use two, four or six syllable names only).

The meaning of a name will help a person achieve their fullest potential. There are various techniques for understanding this. Spiritual gurus use their higher capacities to understand an individual and their vibrations. Parents of a new-born are in an altered state where they are more sensitive to actually feel the correct name of a child. If your astrological analysis is correct it should generally align with the parents ideas if they are spiritually in-tune individual's. If there is a certain combination that is highly beneficial it can be used to give a name representative of what it indicates. Sometimes the name is given according to an association with the family deity (*kula-devatā*). Other situations, the nakṣatra pada of Jupiter is taken and is used to understand the nature of the individual's wisdom or to enhance it. Nārada Ṛṣi gives a list of the nakṣatra pada results in the Nārada

[59] Science of Light, Volume 1, Chapter 11: Nakṣatras

Purāṇa, which can be used to choose the topic of the name. These can be used to see what the name is best to represent, such as a royal name or eloquent name, or spiritual name, etc. Other texts used by the astrologer can also be applied, such as Sārāvalī has a list of the results in each nakṣatra pada, as well as the results of the Moon in various navāṁśas. The better qualities of these positions can be used to help choose a name that promotes the individual's better qualities to shine. Choosing a name which contains this type of idea or energy will prove very beneficial to the individual throughout their life.

Naming in the Native American cultures was often related to omens at birth. When the child was born if two deers were seen running across a clearing, the child could be named two deers running, or soaring eagle, or bearpaw, etc. according to omens that were seen during the circumstances of birth or when deciding the name. Names were fluid as well and could change as natural initiations took place. In this same way, in the eastern traditions after an initiation into a tradition one would often receive a spiritual name reflecting a new birth. Birth and name relate to each other, just as birth and the external circumstances relate to each other. After understanding how nothing at the moment of birth is by chance and that it all represents the energy within the child's chart, omens play an important role in chosing a name.

Sometimes the name will come by an omen or a dream, or there may be a tradition that the family follows. These family traditions are important to insure the happiness of the ancestors. For example, in one tradition every other generation is a Śaiva and then Vaiṣṇava name. In the Jewish tradition, the name of a passed on relative is used, even if it is the first sound of that relative's name only. The astrological rules listed above can be applied in all these contexts, even if the individual wants a Christian biblical name, the meaning of these names can be understood and the sounds they begin with and number of syllables can be analyzed according to the basic premises of Jyotiṣa.

A nickname can be given as well, using either the same techniques or utilizing the techniques that were not able to be applied for the primary name. The nickname should be a simple, sweet name that is easy to say and pleasing to the parents.

When a child is born it is auspicious to have their chart done by a proper astrologer. There is a misconception that an infant's chart should not be read, but this is very untrue. The chart should be well understood for the nāma saṁskāra, so that a proper name can be given to the child. The chart should be checked to see if there are any bālāriṣṭā (infant death) combinations, so they can be immediately remedied. Then the chart should be seen for pañchāṅga doṣas which will need remedies by the parents. These will protect both the child and the health and wealth of family members. Other events or qualities can be seen in the chart, but these three are the most important to see as soon as the child is born.

The first ritual done after birth, when the child has had the fluids removed from it, is for the father to look at the child's face and into the child's eyes. At this moment all ancestral debt (*pitṛ-ṛṇa*) is removed from the father. There are two ways to remove pitṛ-ṛṇa, either to have children to carry on the ancestral lineage or become a renunciate and burn ones negative past karma as well as ones ancestral karma. A short prayer to Viṣṇu and sprinkling oneself with water is advised for the father after this.

The jātakarma is the first rituals done at a proper muhūrta to the child. These rituals have many variations depending on the tradition. It consists of either writing Auṁ on the child's tongue or touching it three times with ghee saying certain prayers to put the proper speech on the child's tongue from the beginning. Some also whisper mantras into the child's ear to remind it of its true divine nature.

The ritual done for naming the child is called the nāma kāraṇa saṁskāra, or simply nāma saṁskāra, or nāmakāraṇam, which means the naming ceremony, or name giving. If worship (*pūja*) was done in order to conceive the child then a pūja should be done as a thank you to the same deity after the birth and naming.

Other rituals for the child should be learned along with muhūrta, as the timing of them is important. They include the first wearing of ornamentation, the first time the infant is swung in a cradle, the first time leaving the house, first time eating solid food, ear piercing (*karṇa vedha*), first haircut (*muṇḍana*), learning the alphabet, starting education, and initiation into one's religious heritage (*upanayana saṁskāra*).

This has been an overview of the information needed to understand the circumstances of birth.

Chapter 7

Special Ascendants

Jaiminīya Brāhmaṇa says the morning Agnihotra
is to be performed before the cattle are released to the pastures (1.5).
Since Prajāpati created beings after the day-break,
therefore it is offered in the morning.
By offering Agnihotra in the day and evening
one puts food in the mouth of the day and night (I.6)

Special Ascendants: Viśeṣa Lagna

Parāśara teaches about special (*viśeṣa*) ascendants in the *viśeṣa-lagna-adhyāya*, and mentions them a few other places as well. The viśeṣa lagnas are related purely to time (*kāla*). In general, the mathematical calculations of the chart relate to time and space, as we will discuss. But the viśeṣa lagnas relate only to kāla and do not depend on space at all.

Speed is created by the movement of time over a distance in space. Without space there is no variation of speed and the viśeṣa lagnas progress (*krama*) regularly (*kālāvadhi*) from sunrise till birth (*iṣṭa kāla*). This regular movement in time irrelavant of space/speed is used to calculate the primary viśeṣa lagnas. In this way, they represent a higher force of Time, a rhythm, which we are able to read in the birth chart. As a higher force beyond spacial manifestation/limitation they are seen as the workings of the devatās.

Studying the calculations of a technique is essential to understand its use. Therefore, first we will learn to calculate and then understand the first three viśeṣa lagnas who represent the trinity of Brahmā, Viṣṇu and Śiva. Where were you when Brahmā was creating you? Where were you when Viṣṇu was giving out wealth? Where were you when Śiva was giving power (*rājya*)? How you are receiving/perceiving the blessings of these devatās is seen according to the placement of the viśeṣa lagnas.

Parāśara says,

अथाहं सम्प्रवक्ष्यामि तवाग्रे द्विजसत्तम ।
भावहोराघटीसंज्ञलग्नानीति पृथक् पृथक् ॥ १ ॥

athāhaṁ sampravakṣyāmi tavāgre dvijasattama |
bhāvahorāghaṭīsañjñalagnānīti pṛthak pṛthak || 1||

Best of brahmins, now I completely explain
The knowledge of bhāva, horā and ghaṭī lagna one by one.

सूर्योदयं समारभ्य घटिकानां तु पंचकम् ।
प्रयाति जन्मपर्यन्तं भावलग्नं तदेव हि ॥ २ ॥

sūryodayaṁ samārabhya ghaṭikānāṁ tu pañcakam |
prayāti janmaparyantaṁ bhāvalagnaṁ tadeva hi || 2||

Counting from sunrise (*sūryodaya*) every five ghaṭikās [120 minutes]
The bhāva lagna advances all the way through a sign.

The bhāva lagna advances uniformly through one sign in 2 hours. Five ghāṭikas (24 minutes X 5) is equal to 120 minutes (or 2 hours) which is the natural time-length of a sign. Depending on the latitude and the time of the year, a sign takes a varying period to rise. It averages to two hours a sign yet is rarely exactly that. The bhāva lagna does not take into account the space or location of the individual but rises uniformly for everyone. Therefore the bhāva lagna will show the deviation of space on time in an individual's reality. In this way, the bhāva lagna has very similar connotations to the bhāva cakra, yet it shows your perception of your role in this world.

इष्टं घट्यादिकं भक्त्वा पंचभिर्भादिजं फलम्।
योज्यमौदयिके सूर्ये भावलग्नं स्फुटं च तत्॥ ३॥

iṣṭaṁ ghaṭyādikaṁ bhaktvā pañcabhirbhādijaṁ phalam |
yojyamaudayike sūrye bhāvalagnaṁ sphuṭaṁ ca tat || 3||

The time passed from birth (*iṣṭa kāla*) in ghaṭī, vighaṭikā, etc. is divided by five
And the result is added to the Sun at sunrise for the bhāva lagna degree.

Parāśara says to take the birth time in ghaṭikās, divide it by five and add it to the Longitude of the Sun at sunrise. The degree of the Sun at sunrise is the degree of the sunrise itself in the birth chart, and in this way the special lagnas begin from the moment of sunrise. As modern time is recorded in hours and minutes we will calculate the bhāva lagna accordingly. Calculate the amount of time passed from sunrise to the time of birth (*iṣṭa kāla*). Divide that by two and add that to the Sun's longitude at sunrise.

	October 9th, 1976	December 12, 1976
Sunrise	7:04 AM	7:12 AM (Dec 11th)
Birth time	22:06	2:06 AM
Iṣṭa Kāla	15 hours 02 minutes	18 hours 54 minutes
Divide by 2	7 hours 32 minutes	9 hours 27 minutes
Convert to signs/degrees	7 signs and 15 degrees 30 min	9 signs 13 degrees 30 min
Sun degree at sunrise	22° 45′ Virgo	26° 11′ Scorpio (Dec 11th)
Bhāva Lagna	8° 15′ Taurus	09° 41′ Virgo

2 hours is equal to 1 sign, so to make the math easy, when the time is divided in half 1 hour is equal to 1 sign. Then each hour is equal to one sign added to the Sun's sign. These are added in a non-inclusive count. 4 minutes is equal to 1 degree, so divided in half, 2 minutes is equal to 1 degree. Divide the minutes in half again and they are equal to degrees to add to the Sun's longitude. There are other ways to do the math, this is just a simple method which does not require a calculator.

तथा सार्धद्विघटिकामितादर्कोदयाद् द्विज।
प्रयाति लग्नं तन्नाम होरालग्नं प्रचक्षते॥ ४॥

tathā sārdhadvighaṭikāmitādarkodayād dvija |
prayāti lagnaṁ tannāma horālagnaṁ pracakṣate || 4||

Thus, it is said that the lagna that advances 2½ ghaṭikā [60 minutes]
measured from sunrise (*arkodaya*) is called the horā lagna.

इष्टघट्यादिकं द्विघ्नं पञ्चाप्तं भादिकं च यत्।
योज्यमौदयिके भानौ होरालग्नं स्फुटं हि तत्॥ ५॥

iṣṭaghaṭyādikaṁ dvighnaṁ pañcāptaṁ bhādikaṁ ca yat |
yojyamaudayike bhānau horālagnaṁ sphuṭaṁ hi tat || 5||

The *iṣṭa kāla* in ghaṭī, vighaṭikā, etc. is multiplied by two and divided by five,
And the result is added to the Sun at sunrise for the horā lagna degree.

The horā lagna moves at one sign every hour. It is twice as fast as the bhāva lagna or 2X the speed of the bhāva lagna. This 2X the speed is connected with the second house of wealth and sustenance and explains why this lagna is used in financial astrology as well as longevity calculations. The mathematical calculation can be done similar to the bhāva lagna, without divided the first result by 2. Alternatively, the difference calculated for the bhāva lagna can be multiplied by two and then added to the Sun at sunrise.

कथयामि घटीलग्नं सृनु त्वं द्विजसत्तम।
सूर्योदयत् समारभ्य जन्मकालावधि क्रमात्॥ ६॥

kathayāmi ghaṭīlagnaṁ sṛnu tvaṁ dvijasattama |
sūryodayat samārabhya janmak ālāvadhi kramāt || 6||

एकैकघटिकामानात् लग्नं यद्याति भादिकम्।
तदेव घटिकालग्नं कथितं नारदादिभिः॥ ७॥

ekaikaghaṭikāmānāt lagnaṁ yadyāti bhādikam |
tadeva ghaṭikālagnaṁ kathitaṁ nāradādibhiḥ || 7||

Listen to my explanation of the ghaṭī lagna.
Counting from sunrise, the lagna progresses (*krama*) regularly (*kālāvadhi*)
Through a sign in one ghaṭī [24 minutes].
That is called the ghaṭikā lagna by Narada and other sages.

राशयस्तु घटीतुल्याः पलार्धप्रमितांशकाः।
योज्यमौदयिके भनौ घटीलग्नं स्फुटं हि तत्॥ ८॥

rāśayastu ghaṭītulyāḥ palārdhapramitāṁśakāḥ |
yojyamaudayike bhanau ghaṭīlagnaṁ sphuṭaṁ hi tat || 8||

The ghaṭīs are equal to the number of rāśis,
The vighaṭikās are divided in half to yeild the degrees/minutes,
And the result is added to the Sun at sunrise for the ghaṭī lagna degree.

Each sign is 24 minutes (1 ghaṭīkā), therefore the ghaṭī lagna progresses one sign every 24 minutes, as its name implies. In this calculation using ghaṭīs there is no conversion needed, similar to using hours with the horā lagna. Each ghaṭī past sunrise is one sign. When doing the calculations with hours the iṣṭa kāla is multiplied by 2.5 and then added to the longitude of the Sun at sunrise accordingly.

क्रमादेषां च लग्नानां भावकोष्ठं पृथक् लिखेत्।
ये ग्रहा यत्र भे तत्र ते स्थाप्या राशिलग्नवत्॥ ९॥

kramādeṣāṁ ca lagnānāṁ bhāvakoṣṭhaṁ pṛthak likhet |
ye grahā yatra bhe tatra te sthāpyā rāśilagnavat || 9||

Draw a separate house chart for each lagna and
Place the grahas where they are according to the rāśi lagna.

Parāśara advises us to make three separate charts to be analyzed. In this way, he is indicating that the houses from special lagna can be analyzed as a lagna itself. Normally, a separate chart is not prepared, but the viśeṣa lagna is anaylazed within the primary chart itself. For a beginner though, it is good to first look at these lagnas individually.

Practice Exercise

1. For your chart and one other, calculate the three viśeṣa lagnas indicated by Parāśara in these verses.

2. The viśeṣa lagnas are all moving in a circular fashion like the hands of a clock. Make a chart which includes all three viśeṣa lagnas in their respective places and draw a circle/spiral from the Sun to the location using a different color for each lagna. Notice the spiral and distance of each lagna.

3. Draw three charts, one for each of these lagnas (unless they happen to fall in the udaya lagna).

Bhāva Lagna

The bhāva lagna (BL) is signified by the Sun and relates to your concepts about yourself. It can show the difference between what you are and what your brain/ego believes yourself to be. The bhāva lagna is the roles you play, while the lagna is your actual role.

The bhāva lagna relates to the devatā Brahmā, and shows what he wanted to create. When the BL aligns with the lagna then it shows an alignment with your genetics. When they misalign then there is a misunderstanding of your own genetic strengths and limitations as well as your roles in life. We have different roles at different times, lover, friend, guru, father, and those roles can change over time. The bhāva lagna shows how in tune you are with yourself.

To fully understand both the bhāva lagna and the general principles of viśeṣa lagnas we should study the Equal-House Chart (*bhāva cakra*) and the Deviated-House Chart (*bhāva-calita cakra*). This deviation from viśeṣa lagnas to house calculations will actually help elucidate the working of the bhāva lagna as well as the principles of how space distorts reality.

Bhāva Cakra and Bhāva-Calita Cakra

There are three standard types of calculations to produce the placement of signs and planets in houses. These three charts all work simultaneously on different levels. The *Rāśi Cakra* (sign chart) is the standard chart where each house has exactly one sign in it. The *Bhāva Cakra* (equal house chart) is the horoscope where the signs and houses do not line up exactly but deviate based upon the lagna. The *Bhāva-Calita Cakra* (*Śrīpati*) takes into account the lagna and the tenth house to create a chart where the signs are different lengths and the houses and signs do not line up.

The **rāśi cakra** is the standard chart used so far in this text. Wherever the lagna degree is the entire sign becomes the lagna and each sign fits perfectly into each house. The rāśi cakra takes the middle of the head as the center of the ascendant no matter where the ascendant degree (*lagna sphuṭa*) is located. The rāśi divisions are natural and each house is the size of one 30 degree rāśi. This chart is important for using house lordships, and aspects that affect an entire house. The whole sign system was used by most of the ancient world including the Greeks and early medieval astrologers. As the houses and signs are in their natural order they relate to the divine order (*ṛta*) of the universe, therefore showing all things as they are.

In the **bhāva cakra**, the lagna degree becomes the middle of the sign and the signs and houses will not line up. For example, if the lagna degree is at 3 degrees of Gemini, the middle of the lagna becomes 3 degrees Gemini. The last 12 degrees of Taurus will be in the beginning of the lagna and the last 13 degrees of Gemini will be in the second house. The cusp (*bhāva madhya*) of each house is the same degree as the rising (*udaya*) lagna. Bhāva here means astrological house, and it is translated as the equal house chart. The bhāva cakra takes into account the lagna sphuṭa, and divides the houses and signs accordingly which can shift some planets from where they are located in the rāśi cakra. The focus on the lagna spuṭa brings the focus on the individual's reality and not the natural order, and from the Vedic perspective shows how the person perceives and interacts with reality. It shows what is in the person's head, more than what actually is.

The diagrams below show the difference in calculation between the rāśi and bhāva cakras. The triangles are the houses and the circle is the signs. Notice the alignment of the houses, signs and midpoints in the rāśi cakra and the difference between the houses and signs in the bhāva cakra. Though Jupiter stays in Aries it changes houses in the bhāva cakra.

Rāśi Cakra

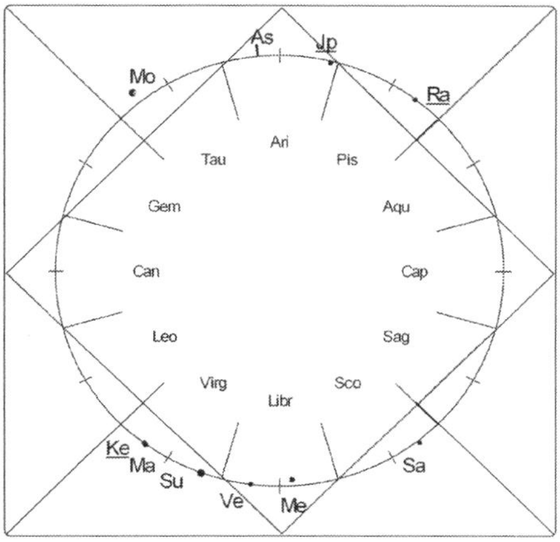

Bhāva Cakra

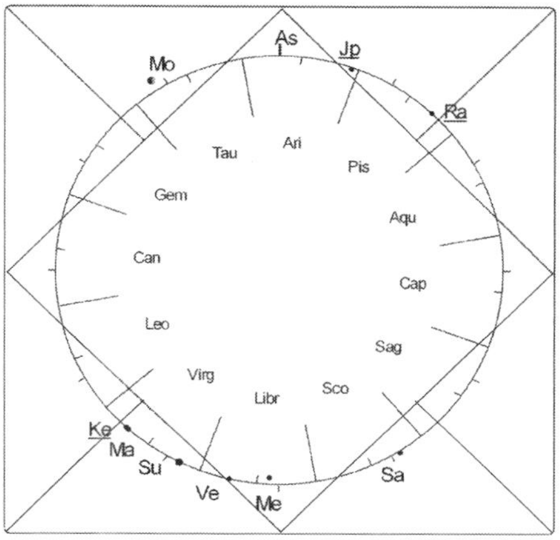

Sometimes in life we refuse to see things the way they are, but instead choose to live inside our idea of what it could be. For example, a woman who has a terrible relationship with an abusive man and who denies that it is as bad as it is. Sometimes we create situations that are based on our dream reality and then they do not have the same longevity or happiness as if we just accepted the natural situation. When planets have shifted houses in the bhāva chart, you can see the way a person thinks about an area and the difference from how it really is. Though what happens eventually is what we project.

The lord of the bhāva is the sign falling on the cusp (*bhāva madhya*) of the house. The cusp is the middle (*madhya*) of the house in Vedic astrology, while in western systems it is the beginning of the house. The mind does not keep the same borders as nature and the shifting planets show a distortion in thinking which can confuse the mind. They are interpreted according to the significations of the planet as well as the significations of the houses which the planet is shifting from and to. For example, when the Sun shifts, the person may run away from success, or when Venus shifts the person may run away from relationships. If a sixth house Venus shifts to the seventh, the person will pursue situations in love and relationship that lead them into suffering and inimical situations. If a 7th house Sun is shifting to the eighth house, the person is believing that certain solar attributes of people that they are attracted to and who are attracted to them are a problem. If a 10th house Mercury is shifting into the 11th house then the individual is mixing up their work associates and clients with their friends.

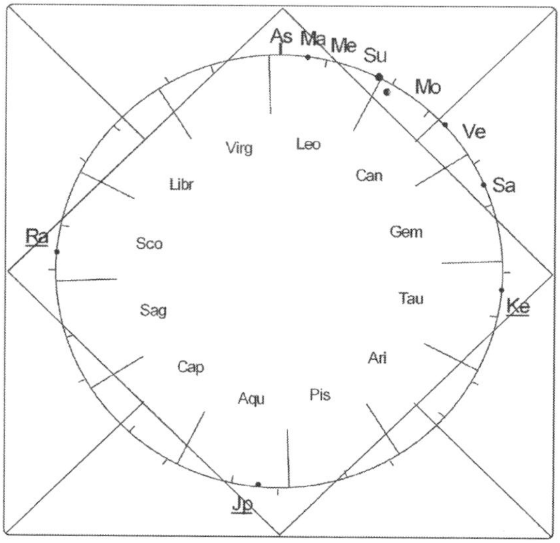

For example, an individual has the Sun in the rising sign indicating a strong willed person who shines among other people. The Sun moves to the twelfth house in the bhāva cakra, so she will think that she hides herself and that nobody sees or respects her. The Sun has moved to its marāna kāraka position and she feels like she is suffering a lack of recognition much more than it actually is. If there is a planet in either the house that the Sun is naturally in or the house that it has moved to which does not change between the two charts, that planet has the ability to show the person reality. For example, if that planet was Mars who is in the first house in both charts, then the individual can have brothers or male friends help remind them of the actuality of their situation, which in this case is being a person who is seen and respected by people.

This fixed/firm (*stheya*) planet helps to anchor the shifting planet into reality. An arbitrator or one who settles disputes between people is called *stheya*, and in this way the planet helps settle the different perceptions between the planet and reality. If there were two planets in the seventh house, Venus and Sun, and Venus moved to the sixth house in the bhāva cakra, while the Sun became stheya, then the father or elder male figures would provide the best relationship clarity for the illusions that the person has about the spouse being an enemy. The recognition of this unaligned thinking can naturally occur between the natural ages of those planets (from age 21 to age 28), but may require the help of the individuals seeing the reality (stheya) throughout life if the shifted planet is weak.

The energy of the planets and signs exists on an archetypal plane, seen as the world of the gods. Just as light shifts its angle when it passes through water, the light of this archetypal reality shifts as it enters the material plane. This distortion is the deviation between the reality of what is and what is going on in our heads or how we are using our heads.

In the **bhāva-calita cakra**[2] the sign length variation is taken into account bringing focus on the exact lagna and tenth house degrees. Calita means moved from one's usual course or deviated, and relates to the deviation of the signs taken into account by the speed of their rising which makes some signs larger than others. In the northern hemisphere the

[2] Bṛhat Parāśara Horā Śāstra, Viśeṣa-lagna-adhyāya, v.18-23

sign Virgo takes the longest to rise and Pisces the fasted to rise, on the southern hemisphere this is reversed. The farther away from the equator an individual is born the more the signs will vary from their natural length.

The example below is the same chart as given in the rāśi and bhāva cakra example. Notice how the signs in the bhāva-calita cakra have either condensed or lengthened in comparison to the bhāva cakra. It does not change the chart too much in Pennsylvania as it would for the same rising sign in Alaska.

Bhāva-Calita Cakra (Pennsylvania)

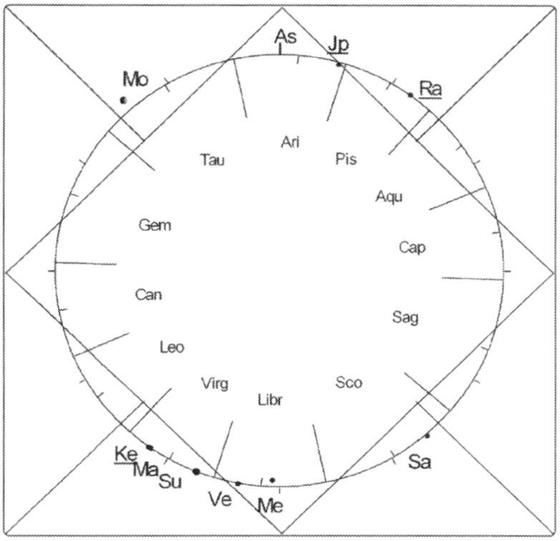

Bhāva-Calita Cakra (in Alaska)

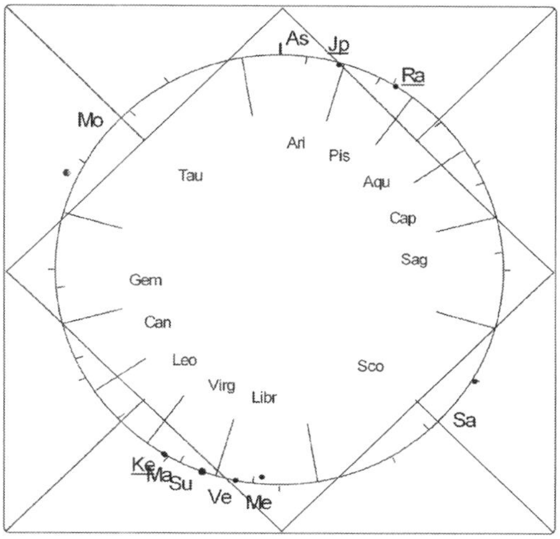

The bhāva-calita cakra puts the exact lagna sphuṭa in the middle of the lagna and the exact svarga sphuṭa (midheaven) in the middle of the tenth house. The signs are proportioned accordingly. As it takes into account both the lagna and the tenth house it shows the deviation in our minds that is caused by our own mind and the influence of society. The rāśi cakra gives importance to the natural order of the universe. The bhāva cakra gives importance to the lagna (the individual), and the bhāva-calita cakra gives equal importance to the lagna and tenth representing the individual and society. In the rāśi cakra we use both rāśi and graha aspects, in the bhāva cakra we use only the graha aspects and in the bhāva-calita cakra we are not using aspects at all (or only those calculated by degree).

The rāśi and bhāva cakras can have the midheaven fall anywhere from the 8th to the 11th house depending on the latitude of birth. The closer to the equator the closer the midheaven will be to the tenth house and the more balanced the houses will be. The farther away from the equator the more deviated the houses become. Western astrologers use a system that takes into account the lagna and midheaven as a preference, but some argue its impracticality for people born closer to the north or south poles. We utilize all three variations of calculations for their specific purposes

The variation in space/speed creates a distortion in the way the stars and planets are mapped into our reality. The rāśi cakra avoids the distortion created by space/speed and therefore indicates the natural order of the universe. But even though the rāśi are mapped out equally, the actual lagna sphuṭa is determined according to the variation of space and time by taking into account elliptical motion of what is actually rising at the moment of birth. The viśeṣa lagnas use a uniform circular motion and speed which allows them to progress regularly (*krama kālāvadhi*) from sunrise throughout the day. Parāśara states that the janma lagna is to be calculated according to the birth place (*svasvadeśa*) while the viśeṣa lagnas are calculated the same everywhere (*sarvatra samakriyā*) [v.24]. Each sign is given an equal motion without taking into account the deviation of space/speed that we can see happening in the bhāva-calita cakra. The Bhāva lagna is the progression of time from Sunrise till your birth in an equal and uniform motion. It shows how much distortion there was between the movement of uneven elliptical time and even cyclical time.

In the above chart, because of the variation of latitude, Scorpio was rising for about 5 hours, and Sagitarius and Capricorn for about two hours to both rise; a little longer than an hour for Sagittarius and a little shorter than an hour for Capricorn. The Bhāva lagna moves through each of these signs in two hours without taking this variation into account. If sunrise was in Scorpio and the person was born six hours later the rising (*udaya*) lagna is in Sagittarius. But the Bhāva lagna moving equally through the signs will have moved three signs and be placed in Capricorn.

Understanding these calculations allows one to understand the parameters in which you are reading the universe and therefore allows you to interpret it properly. Whenever you are trying to understand the difference between various similar techniques always come back to the procedures of calculation. In general, we can see that the method (or differences of methods) in calculation indicate the import of a technique and its applications. Understanding the meaning of the archetypal regularity of the rāśi cakra helps one understand the regularity of the viśeṣa lagnas which are not perceptions or appearances, but are indicating the hands of Time.

Bhāva Lagna Interpretation

The bhāva cakra shows the misconceptions in your thinking process and your interaction with the world; what is the world offering you and how are you receiving it. The Bhāva lagna (BL) shows your personal misconceptions about yourself; how in tune with yourself you are and whether you understand your own physical genetics as well as your roles in the world. The Bhāva Lagna also relates to how aligned your decision making is with your intelligence.

It is significant to notice whether the Bhāva lagna (BL) is before or after the lagna, to see whether you are ahead or behind where you need to be. It is interesting to note that if the BL is behind the lagna it can often look similar to one's tropical natal chart. If the BL is ahead of the lagna it shows a more forceful masculine nature, while if it is behind the lagna it shows a more gentle feminine nature in the roles you take. If the BL is behind the lagna is creates a more passive individual who has their roles and thinking forced on them by the world, while if it is too far ahead they are forcing their roles and thinking on others. The odd and even nature, the cara or sthira nature and the actual nature (Aries forceful, Taurus stubborn) of the sign in which the BL is placed will also alter its role.

The amount of distortion is important to see how an individual is seeing their roles in the world and making decisions. A huge amount of difference between the lagna and BL, which happens at the higher latitudes, indicates more psychological problems. If you are born a Sagittarius lagna and are acting like a Capricorn, there will be greater issue than if the change is only a navāṁśa or a nakṣatra shift. In the case of an Aries lagna that has the bhāva lagna in Pisces, the individual will tend have the intensity of Aries but in their decision making and the roles they take in their life will be more passive like Pisces. There are also the complications of when planets become involved. If the BL is in Virgo with Rāhu and the lagna is Leo with Jupiter and Mercury, then not only are the signs different but the guṇa of the planets add to the distortion in one's roles.

The lagna shows what your role is and the Bhāva lagna shows what you are thinking/ acting your role is. In the varga charts, the BL shows the distortions which exists to your role in that area of life. For example, if in the daśāṁśa (D10), the Bhāva lagna is in the eleventh house, then the tenth house (which is the kāraka bhāva) is in the twelfth house from it indicating you think your roles at work are causing you a loss instead of a gain. In general, your view of an area of life has a distortion if the kāraka bhāva of the pertinent varga chart falls in a duḥsthāna from the Bhāva lagna.

Pandit Sanjay Rath says, "We are all somewhat distorted, now we at least know we are and can do something about it." The Bhāva lagna shows our personal misconceptions about ourselves and the bhāva cakra shows our misperceptions in our interaction with the world. The bhāva cakra should be seen to help remove psychological blockages created by our own misperceptions, though the Bhāva lagna is rarely used in giving a reading as some of its deeper implications are often uncomfortable and lack validity for daily life. Just as Brahmā is rarely worshiped among the trinity, this viśeṣa lagna is the least used among them.

Horā Lagna

The horā lagna is twice the speed of the bhāva lagna which indicates the circular uniform motion of the second house. The second house is wealth and sustenance which relates to Viṣṇu. The second house sustains the material body and is therefore related to health. It sustains us in the material world and therefore relates to wealth. The second house is not income. Income is money being earned, that is coming into one's life that is why it is called a gain. The second house is what you have; you could say what you have in your bank account instead of your pay check. On a larger scale it is all the accumulated possessions and financial savings that give an individual value. Some individual's have huge incomes but no wealth; while others are born with wealth and do not even need to think about income. The horā lagna relates to wealth. The artha trikoṇa (2, 6, and 10) is the trine where one pursues their material well-being as a basic necessity of a human being and society.

The horā lagna represents Viṣṇu and his sustenance. It relates to wealth, the second house, and the second divisional chart (*horā cakra*). The horā lagna shows what we value and therefore what we have that is valuable. It shows where we were when Viṣṇu was giving out wealth. The primary significator of the horā lagna is the Moon (for sustenance and health) and secondary significator is Jupiter (wealth) as he is the significator of the second house.

Viśeṣa Lagna	Time in a Sign	Movement per Day	Speed	House Kāraka	Planet Kāraka
Bhāva Lagna	120 minutes	360 degrees	1X	1	Sun, (*lagna*)
Horā Lagna	60 minutes	720 degrees	2X	2	Moon, Jupiter
Ghaṭī Lagna	24 minutes	1,800 degrees	5X	5	Sun, Jupiter
Prāṇapada	6 minutes	7,200 degrees	20X	3	Mars, Sun, (*Agni*)

Pandit Sanjay Rath teaches that the HL "represents the 'concept of wealth' for the individual. The house and sign occupied by the horā lagna shows the concept of wealth that motivates the mind."[3] The horā lagna can be called the intellect of the second house and we value it. If the HL is in the fourth, the individual values home, mother, happiness and other fourth house indications. The sign lord and the planets conjunct the horā lagna will modify your values.

[3] Sanjay Rath. *Horā Lagna*, p.5

Jupiter will indicate knowledge, and this knowledge will be in the area indicated by the house. If the HL is in a sign of Jupiter or is conjunct or opposite Jupiter then knowledge is valued by the individual. If Venus is the sign lord, then looks are often more important than knowledge or quality (or quality will be based on looks). If the HL is in the seventh house in a sign of Jupiter then the individual will value the spouse's knowledge and understanding. If Venus is in the 7th with the HL, the individual will value their wife's beauty, clothing and jewelry. The Sun associated with the HL will show the person may value the father, government, or Vedānta. Agni grahas need to associate with the HL for one to value Jyotiṣa. The sign can be taken more specifically, such as Britney Spears has HL in Gemini in the tenth house, therefore she values her work performances and her professional communications.

As the HL lord shows the nature of what you value, you will find that many of your friends will have the same sign lord or planet conjunct the HL, or at least association with planets that have similar values. We value people who share our values or *who provide* what we value to us.

When the HL lord has sāttvika associations the individual values quality over quantity. When there are rājasika associations quantity is more valuable. If the HL was in the fifth house in a Venus sign with Mercury then quantity of students is more valued. If the HL was in the fifth house with Jupiter and the Sun then a few good quality students is more valuable. When Rāhu is conjunct the HL it can show negative ideas, or confusion about what wealth is, how to manage it, or how it is best used.

The strength and house placement of the lord of the HL will give indications about the nature of one's values. The HL becomes strong if its lord is ucca, sva or conjunct an ucca graha or benefic, or if there is an uccha or sva graha conjunct the HL. The horā lagna lord is always better for wealth and values if it is strong and well- placed. Therefore it is good to strengthen the lord in a positive way according to its house placement. If the HL lagna is in the seventh house, it is made strong by getting married. If it is in the ninth house it is made strong by getting a guru in one's life.

Horā Lagna in Houses

It is always important to look at the axis the horā lagna is placed in as well as the specific house. In the 1-7 axis relationship becomes very important. In the first house exercise, health, good name become important. The HL placed in the first or seventh is a natural dhāna yoga (combination for wealth) because wealth is always on the mind. The individual believes they have a right to wealth and to control wealth and its distribution in the world. They may become known because of their wealth. If the HL is conjunct other planets the person may become known for their values relative to those significations.

The Dali Lama has HL in Gemini lagna with Sun, Mercury and Ketu. Śrī Aurobindo has HL in lagna with ucca Jupiter and Mars (*Guru-maṅgala yoga*) showing his values are for the greater good of the world. Sadam Hussein had HL in lagna with a nīca Jupiter.

HL in the seventh house shows the individual values relationships, marriage, networking, business as well as other significations of the seventh house. These individuals give great value to their relationships and marriage breaking is a severe loss to them. When you lose what the HL values it creates a lot of suffering, as if the meaning of life has been lost. In this way, if the HL is in the seventh house, the situation of divorce is very traumatic to the person, if the HL is in the ninth the death of the Guru is very traumatic. In a consultation, we know to place extra emphasis on the axis where the HL is placed.

In the 2-8 axis the family and community becomes important. They are concerned with issues relevant to the family or close community. The second house shows value given to wealth, finances, and the people that connect you to that (like Mother or social services if the Moon is there, or common people/coal/oil if Saturn is there).

Gandhi had HL in the second house and his concern was for his larger community well being over his own; Saturn was there showing concern for the common people. Speech (one's word) is also a value to individuals with second house HL as Gandhi found great value in truth. In Gandhi's chart the HL being conjunct Saturn shows he renounced the pursuit of wealth later in his life. In this way, malefics will alter results. Martin Luther King had HL in the second house with Jupiter in Aries showing the intensity of the truth in his words which was his greatest asset.

The eighth house shows insurance, debts, inheritance or other people's money. In the eighth house the horā lagna has a sense of destiny to fulfill. Adolf Hitler has HL in Taurus in the 8th house with its lord Venus in a planetary war with Mars in Aries (he also has Rāhu in the ninth and Jupiter was MKS). Padre Pio has HL in Taurus in the eighth with Sun, Mars and Mercury and the HL lord has gone to the ninth house, (in his case Jupiter was in Lagna). Hitler valued destruction and war, while Padre Pio was a saint who valued deep spirituality and healing. In this way, the planets conjunct the horā lagna and the placement of its lord will influence the values indicated by the house placement of the HL.

In the 3-9 axis the guru and guru-upadeśa are highly valued. The ninth is knowledge and the third is seeking knowledge. The HL in the third or ninth house values knowledge and higher learning if associated with benefics or lorded by benefics. The third house relates to seeking knowledge, listening, entertainment, sports depending on the lord and the planets associated. If the HL is in the sign of Mercury or Jupiter it makes a very studious individual. The third house is the ear and the individual values listening to teachings or music; the third is communication resources.

Albert Einstein had a third house HL in Leo. The lord of the HL is in an intelligence combination (*dhīmanta yoga*) showing a high level of intelligence. If malefics associate then the higher learning is used for negative purposes and can make a criminal. Einstein has Jupiter in the ninth house opposite the HL.

The ninth house indicates that one values the guide, guru, dharma or religion. This becomes the value that life revolves around. The ninth is also connected to the world at large and an expanded view and understanding of the world. Akbar the Great had a ninth house HL conjunct an exalted Moon and he had an open minded world view that allowed all religions and arts to flourish under his rule. If HL is conjunct pāpa grahas in the ninth house it can indicate that the individual values darker forms of religion or materialism.

The 4-10 axis shows that one values mother, home, residence, nationality, happiness, work, or the office. When the HL is placed in the fourth house, the individual will value their home and will often live in rich or good quality homes or places. If the lord is not well placed, this can indicate a person who puts all their resources into living in a very nice place. If the HL lord is well placed or strong it can show an individual who has many property resources. Al Gore has the HL in the fourth house which shows he values not just his home but his environment. He has worked with environmental awareness since finishing his vice-presidency. The tenth house gives a career focus. The person values their career life and puts a lot of weight behind their position in their job. Britney Spears has HL in the 10th house (this can be compared to Madonna who has the HL in the second house).

The 5-11 axis shows that one values learning, children, students, and associates. There is a lot of value given to speculation, planning for the future, and innovation. The visionary William Blake has HL in the fifth house with Jupiter, Mercury and the Sun. Harish Johari has fifth house HL in Sagittarius. Emperor Aurangzeb had a fifth house HL but the lord was conjunct a nīca Sun in the ninth house. He had a value of the knowledge of one religion only, and broke temples to build mosques so the future would have only his religion.

The eleventh house relates to friends, associates, and income. It can show the individual values their work associates or those that are friends they can look up to (like an elder brother). It will also show they value their monetary gains highly. Yasser Arafat had an Aries HL in the eleventh house with Moon and Rāhu and the lord is placed in the fourth house with exalted Mercury. This gave a mixed indication, Mercury is showing wealth, but Rāhu is showing a confusion or misuse of wealth. It is said that after his death it was discovered that he had his millions of aid money in Swiss banks. Fidel Castro has HL in the 11th house with Mars in Aries. This would be beneficial except that Saturn is in the fifth house creating a negative yoga (*unmada*) that blocks healthy future planning.

The 6-12 axis shows one values service, employees, pets, debates, or fighting disease. The sixth house will not only show that they value their employees but will show in which way they value them. If the HL is in the sixth with Saturn and Ketu the individual wants mindless employees who do just as they are told. If the lord of the HL is weak then they mistreat their employees. If HL is with benefics in the sixth the individual will want their employees to think for themselves and benefit from their work. They value hard work as well as others working for them. Edgar Cayce has Sagittarius HL in the sixth house with Jupiter and Mars showing his value of service to others. The twelfth house shows sleep, bedroom pleasures, travel, alone time, as well as the spiritual master or guide. In this way, the houses containing the HL should be seen and studied.

Second House from Horā Lagna

The second from the HL is important in timing when you'll get what you value and how long you'll have it. There are many yogas that indicate wealth at different times of life, but in general on can say that if the HL is strong one can be born into wealth, while if the second from the HL is strong one will gain the wealth. The second house from HL is key for timing.

Bill Gates has Sagittarius HL in the seventh house and the second lord from it is exalted in the fifth house. Andrew Carnegie has Virgo HL in the twelfth house and its lord has gone to the second from it with an exalted Saturn. Nelson Rockefeller has an Aquarius HL in the sixth house with the second lord from it, Jupiter, exalted in the eleventh house.

Princess Dianna has Aries HL in the eighth house with the UL. This shows the wealth comes with marriage even though it is in the eighth house representing the breakage of marriage. Second from the HL is Venus in its own sign showing a rise in wealth.

Dhana Yogada

The horā lagna shows what you value. It also shows the resources that are valuable to your success. Planets conjunct or having rāśi dṛṣṭi on the horā lagna become a *dhana-karta;* they have the power to bring wealth and resources. If they don't associate with the lagna then the individual will not enjoy the wealth, but the associated house and lords will enjoy the wealth. Many astrologers take into account association with the seventh house as the individual will be able to enjoy the increase of wealth through the spouse.

For the individual's utilization of the indicated resources, the HL needs to somehow associate with the lagna. The planet connecting the lagna and the HL connects you to your resources (men, money, materials) and therefore your fortune. This planet is called a *dhana-yogada;* it is a planet that will bring prosperity in its daśā.

In the chart of Donald Trump the HL is in the fourth house indicating that he made his wealth through real estate development. The lord of the HL is placed in the lagna thereby Mars connects the HL to the lagna and becomes a dhana-yogada. Mars is the planet signifying property.

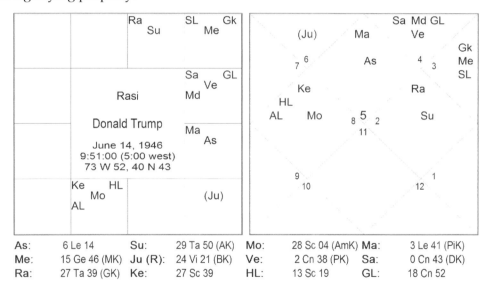

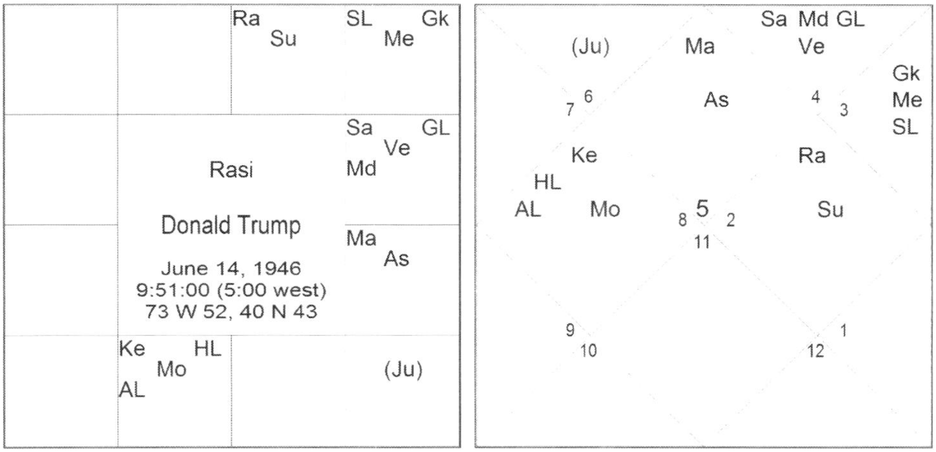

As:	6 Le 14	Su:	29 Ta 50 (AK)	Mo:	28 Sc 04 (AmK)	Ma:	3 Le 41 (PiK)
Me:	15 Ge 46 (MK)	Ju (R):	24 Vi 21 (BK)	Ve:	2 Cn 38 (PK)	Sa:	0 Cn 43 (DK)
Ra:	27 Ta 39 (GK)	Ke:	27 Sc 39	HL:	13 Sc 19	GL:	18 Cn 52

The HL becomes important because we put energy and time into the things we value. When horā lagna becomes involved in other combinations, it gives them value thereby helps to bring success to those indications. The HL becomes very important when studying finances in a chart and in the practice of financial/business astrology. HL shows what you will get compared to what you want. It shows what will come in abundance.

It is important to note that the HL is important for health (being connected to the second house). This is why it is used in longevity calculations (*āyurdāya*) such as the rule of three pairs, which will be discussed in the chapter on Āyurjyotiṣa.

The *varṇada lagna* (VL) is calculated from the composite of horā lagna and lagna. This lagna shows the type of work (*karma*) that is done to achieve one's wealth in life, and how accomplished one becomes in their respective area. The varṇada lagna (and then 11th from it, and then 11th from that, etc.) can be used to see various job situations. Parāśara teaches an entire daśā for the varṇada lagna to shows situations in the career and health.

Ghaṭīkā Lagna

The ghaṭīkā lagna (GL) is calculated by five times the movement of the lagna which indicates the circular uniform motion of the fifth house. It relates to the fifth house significations, the pañcāṁśa and its kāraka is the Sun. The rājya of the fifth house (natural Leo) and the Sun relate to the power of Śiva. The ghaṭīkā lagna is primarily used to see political power but can also be used to see jñāna as it is the power of Śiva from the fifth house. The placement of the GL will show where and what you derive your power from.

The GL becomes important in political astrology (*rāja jyotiṣa*). In political astrology the fifth house relates to the king's power and those who support him. The more support and control, the more power. The fifth house from GL (and the kāraka lagna) is important for timing when an individual rises to power. It is used heavily when determining which candidate may win an election and if they can remain in power.

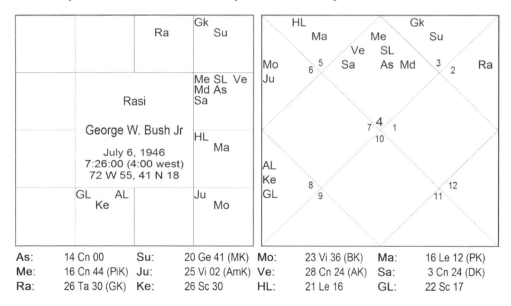

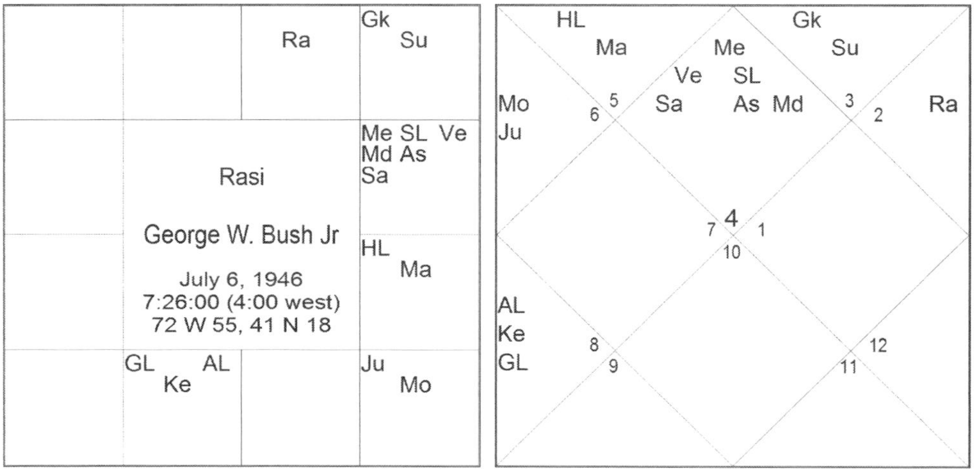

As:	14 Cn 00	Su:	20 Ge 41 (MK)	Mo:	23 Vi 36 (BK)	Ma:	16 Le 12 (PK)
Me:	16 Cn 44 (PiK)	Ju:	25 Vi 02 (AmK)	Ve:	28 Cn 24 (AK)	Sa:	3 Cn 24 (DK)
Ra:	26 Ta 30 (GK)	Ke:	26 Sc 30	HL:	21 Le 16	GL:	22 Sc 17

Just as the HL associating with combinations strengthens them by giving them value, the GL will strengthen by giving power, leadership and control. The GL shows where your power comes from. George Bush Jr. has the GL in the fifth house with Ketu indicating he gets his power from the secret service (Ketu) who are his subordinates (fifth house). The fifth from GL shows what you do beforehand to get rāja yoga and when the power will come. George Bush Jr. has the ninth house fifth from his GL indicating that getting power is related to his father. One could also conclude it has to do with the religious (ninth house) right that helped him get elected.

In Barak Obama's chart the GL is in the fourth and the fifth from it has Rāhu and Mars. Mars and Rāhu are military combinations and in Leo it shows politics. This shows there was some military support for Obama according to the actions he would take as president. Being the fourth from Moon and the eighth from lagna could also indicate the large amount of people losing their homes played a role in his coming to power. In general malefics fifth from GL indicate someone who runs after power but then suffers once they get it.

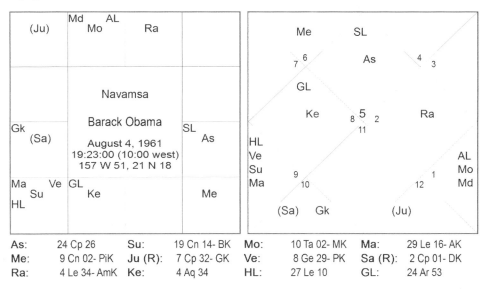

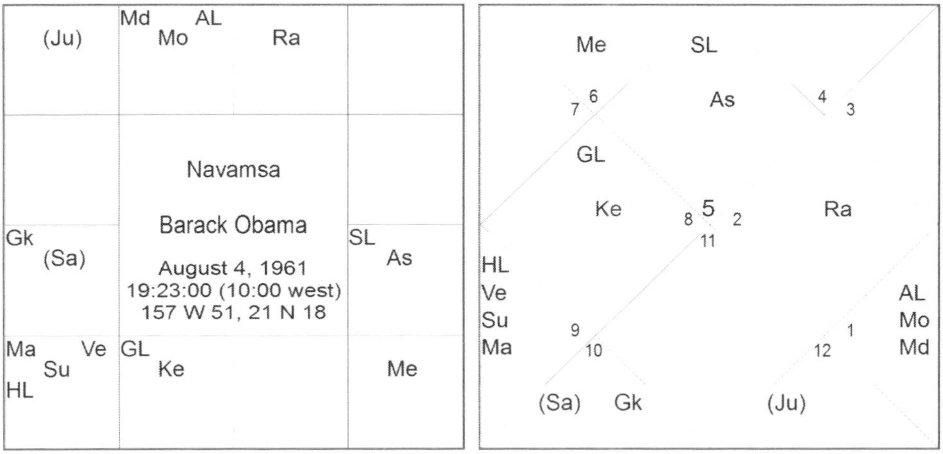

As:	24 Cp 26	Su:	19 Cn 14- BK	Mo:	10 Ta 02- MK	Ma:	29 Le 16- AK
Me:	9 Cn 02- PiK	Ju (R):	7 Cp 32- GK	Ve:	8 Ge 29- PK	Sa (R):	2 Cp 01- DK
Ra:	4 Le 34- AmK	Ke:	4 Aq 34	HL:	27 Le 10	GL:	24 Ar 53

In many places Parāśara uses the word *vilagna*. The '*vi*' prefix has many meanings which include intensifying, negating, or distinguishing. In this way it is interpreted to mean 'from the lagna or other lagnas for their distinctive aspects seen from them'. Therefore there are various yogas that can be seen according to the lagna or the viśeṣa lagnas, where you would only see the combination relative to money for horā lagna or relative to position for ghaṭikā lagna, or image for arūḍha lagna. Therefore when doing either financial astrology (HL) or political astrology (GL) all houses (and yogas) can be seen from the viśeṣa lagna.

Rājya Yogada

Planets connected to the GL are called *rājya-karta* and planets connected to both the GL and the udaya lagna are called *rājya-yogada*. In the chart of George Bush Jr., Mercury, Saturn, Venus and Ketu are all rājya-yogadas. Cancer and Scorpio have rāśi dṛṣṭi on each other and thereby the planets in those signs are linking the lagna and the ghaṭīkā lagna supporting him to rise to power. Yogadas can be seen in the rāśi, the navāṁśa and the Jagannatha dreṣkāṇa.

Mahāyogada

If the yogada planet (for HL or GL) is also the lord of the Moon sign (*subhapati*), then it becomes a kevala yogada and becomes more powerful to give its results. If a planet connects the horā lagna, the ghaṭīkā lagna and the udaya lagna then it becomes a mahāyogada and can bring power and prosperity in its daśā. In Obama's chart, Rāhu and Mars are mahāyogadas as they are conjunct the HL and have rāśi dṛṣṭi on both lagna and GL.

In the chart of Bill Gates, there are three mahāyogadas: Moon, Mars and Mercury. The lagna is a dual sign and the HL and GL are in dual signs, which shows that any planet in a dual sign is aspecting both the lagna and the viśeṣa lagna. Therefore Mercury, Mars and Moon are aspecting the lagna, the HL and the GL.

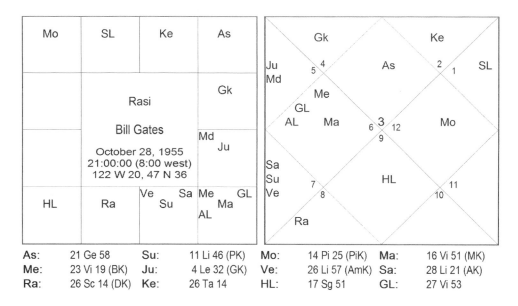

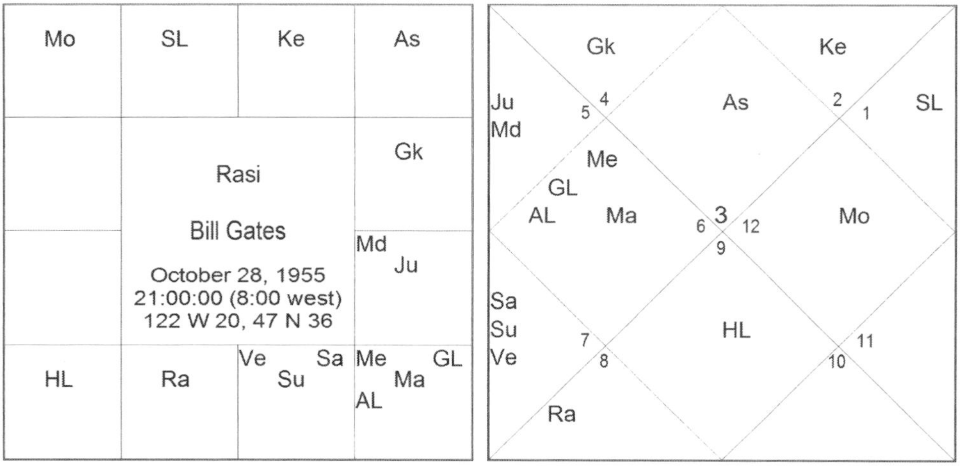

As:	21 Ge 58	Su:	11 Li 46 (PK)	Mo:	14 Pi 25 (PiK)	Ma:	16 Vi 51 (MK)
Me:	23 Vi 19 (BK)	Ju:	4 Le 32 (GK)	Ve:	26 Li 57 (AmK)	Sa:	28 Li 21 (AK)
Ra:	26 Sc 14 (DK)	Ke:	26 Ta 14	HL:	17 Sg 51	GL:	27 Vi 53

Other yogas in the chart associated with the yogadas will alter the results they give. The yogadas will generally support other combinations to give their fruit. The ghaṭīkā lagna also relates to knowledge (*jñāna*) and the mahāyogada give a high level of knowledge which allows the individual to achieve their goals. A mahāyogada also has the ability to give a high level of spiritual attainment when associated with spiritual combinations. This can be seen in the chart of Maharshi Mahesh Yogi who has four mahāyogadas: Moon, Mars, Mercury, and Saturn.

The bhāva lagna, horā lagna and ghaṭīkā lagna are the first three viśeṣa lagnas. They are all moving in a cyclical fashion like the hands of a clock. The BL is like the hour hand, the HL like the minute hand and the GL like the seconds hand. In ancient times there was a whole school of Jyotiṣa based just on these types of calculations. They put emphasis on the calculations from sunrise time (*sūryodaya*) to the birth time (*iṣṭa kāla*).

There are many other viśeṣa lagnas for other indications that use varying calculations. We will briefly mention the varṇada lagna so you are aware of it, but will not go into depth. We will discuss the Śrī lagna to understand its calculation and see how it relates to timing. Then we will look at the prāṇapada lagna which is an extremely sensitive point but which yields a rich amount of knowledge when understood.

Varṇada Lagna

The varṇada lagna (VL) is taught next by Parāśara. He teaches both the calculation of the VL and the varṇada daśā which he says by knowing one can speak about the longevity of the individual.[4] This means that the varṇada daśā is primarily an āyurdaśā used in Āyurjyotiṣa though it can also be used to see the health of your professional life.

The varṇada lagna relates to our work and the type of career we have. Varṇa means caste, and the varṇada is the giver of the caste; it shows the quality of the work one will do. There are many intricacies of the varṇada lagna, particularly relative to longevity, which we will not discuss. Here we will just introduce the concept for familiarity with this viśeṣa lagna. Parāśara teaches,

ओजलग्नप्रसूतानां मेषादेर्गणयेत् क्रमात् ।
समलग्नप्रसूतानाम् मीनादेरपसव्यतः ॥ ११ ॥

ojalagnaprasūtānāṁ meṣādergaṇayet kramāt |
samalagnaprasūtānām mīnāderapasavyataḥ || 11||

If the natal lagna is odd (*oja*), then count direct (*kramāt*) from Aries to Lagna.
If the natal lagna is even (*sama*), then anti-zodiacal (*apasavya*) to mīna.

Oja	Krama	Sama	Utkrama
1 Aries	+1	2 Taurus	-11
3 Gemini	+3	4 Cancer	-9
5 Leo	+5	6 Virgo	-7
7 Libra	+7	8 Scorpio	-5
9 Sagittarius	+9	10 Capricorn	-3
11 Aquarius	+11	12 Pisces	-1

If the natal lagna is odd, such as Gemini then one counts direct from Aries to Gemini which is +3. If the natal lagna was Leo, then from Aries to Leo is +5. If the natal lagna is Taurus, then count from Pisces to Taurus in an anti-zodiacal direction to get -11. If the lagna is Cancer then reverse count from Pisces to Cancer to get -9. All the houses from lagna can be understood simply in the chart below. Though it is important to understand the calculation and not just rely on the chart which is only to aid understanding. Notice that the number arrived at can only be odd. This number will be added or subtracted from the number arrived at in the next calculation.

मेषमीनादितो जन्मलग्नान्तं गणयेत् सुधीः ।
तथैव होरालग्नान्तं गणयित्वा ततः परम् ॥ १२ ॥

meṣamīnādito janmalagnāntaṁ gaṇayet sudhīḥ |
tathaiva horālagnāntaṁ gaṇayitvā tataḥ param || 12||

Just as the janma lagna is counted to Aries and Pisces by the wise (*sudhī*),
Another count is done from the horā lagna.

[4] *yasya vijñānamātreṇa vadedāyurbhavaṁ phalam || 10||*

Just as the count was done from the natal lagna, the same count is done from the horā lagna. If the HL is odd the count is direct to Aries and if the HL is even it is reverse count to Pisces. In this way, one can use the same chart as above and just use the HL instead of the udaya lagna. These two numbers derived from the lagna and HL are then used to find the varṇada lagna.

ओजत्वेन समत्वेन सजातीये उभे यदि ।
तर्हि संख्ये योजयीत वैजात्ये तु वियोजयेत् ॥ १३ ॥
मेषमीनादितः पश्चाद्यो राशिः स तु वर्णदः ।

ojatvena samatvena sajātīye ubhe yadi |
tarhi saṅkhye yojayīta vaijātye tu viyojayet || 13||
meṣamīnāditaḥ paścādyo rāśiḥ sa tu varṇadaḥ |14a|

If both are from the odd signs, or both from even signs then add the numbers,
If they are hetrogenous (*vaijātya*), then subtract [to get the difference between them].
The varṇada rāśi is then seen [counting from] Aries or Pisces.

The numbers are either added together or subtracted to get the final number, which will make the result an even number by nature of the math. If the lagna is odd then it is counted directly from Aries and if the lagna is even it is counted in reverse from Pisces. There are techniques to calculate the VL with longitude but there is no need.[5] The entire rāśi is seen as the varṇada lagna and the daśā counted from it is a rāśi daśā with years counted by sign.

Bill Gates has Gemini lagna (odd sign) which gives us the count +3. The HL is placed in the seventh house in Sagittarius (odd sign) which gives the count +9. These are added together to give the count as +12. When twelve is added to Aries, the resulting sign is Pisces, therefore Bill Gates has VL in the tenth house.

President Obama is Capricorn lagna which gives the count of -3. His horā lagna is placed in Leo which gives a count of +5. Because one is an even sign and the other an odd the difference is calculated: five minus three is two. Since the lagna is even then two is counted anti-zodiacal from Pisces to get the varṇada lagna in Aquarius.

Parāśara continues to calculate varṇada daśā and explains not only how to see ones own health but to look at the seventh from VL to see the spouse's health, and the fourth from VL to see the mother's health, the fifth from VL to see the childrens's health, etc. These combinations are also useful to see how one relates to these individuals in the workplace, and the health of the work relationship. As the varṇada lagna is calculated from the lagna and the horā lagna it has the nature of the physical body and its sustenance both on a health and monetary level.

[5] Some interpret lagna-anta and horā-lagna-anta as meaning with degrees (with the end point), while others interpret it as to take the complete sign.

Interpretation of Varṇada Lagna

The varṇada lagna shows what you relate to as work. The house it is placed in and the house lords it relates to will show the type of work one may be associated with. In the ninth house or associating with the ninth lord will show work with universities. In the tenth or associating with the tenth lord will show work with a company. In the seventh or associated with the seventh house will show work with sales. In this way, the first very general level of the VL can be understood.

The stronger of the VL or its seventh is then seen. Then lord of the eleventh from that sign of the varṇada lagna is said to show the caste of the individual. This and the previous rule are hard to apply because caste is not inherited in our society and such rules may not apply in our modern day. Though, it is still good to understand the calculations.

The general rule is that the tattva of the sign lord (11th from the VL or its seventh) determines the caste of the person's work [4.1.32]. The water signs indicate brahman (intellectual/religious) type of work: Cancer shows doctors, Scorpio shows researchers, and Pisces shows priests. The fire signs indicate kṣatriya type of work: Aries shows the armed forces, Leo shows politics, and Sagittarius shows bureaucracy. The vāyu signs indicate vaiśya type of work: Libra shows stores, Aquarius shows factories and production, while Gemini shows the traders and middle-men. The earth signs indicate śūdra type of work: Capricorn shows hard manual labor, Taurus shows laborers and farmers, and Virgo shows secretaries or people who serve businessmen. Planets in these places can alter the results according to their caste and livelihood.

The varṇada lagna in kendras and trikoṇa will often show socially accepted work, depending on its conjunctions. If it is conjunct Rāhu in a trine it may show less socially accepted activities while if it is with Jupiter in a negative house it can show accepted work.

The varṇada lagna gives financial benefits in the second house [4.1.34]. If placed in the twelfth house it is said to give demonical attitudes (*āsura*) which allows the individual to gain by the loss of others, like a gambler or a thief [4.1.33]. Benefics or strong planets associating with the VL show happiness with one's work, while malefics show unhappiness.

The second house from VL becomes important for financial success. In businesses this will also show wealth and resource management. Benefics there are good, malefics are not. Association of the VL and the second lord from VL is a type of dhana yoga.

Bill Gates has the VL in Pisces with the Moon (1 planet), and exalted Mercury and Mars (2 planets) are in the seventh house from it making the seventh house stronger. The eleventh from the VL seventh house is Cancer; a brahman sign showing intellectual work. An exalted planet seventh from VL and the Moon conjunct the VL shows he enjoys his work and it prospers. The second lord from the VL is in the seventh house having rāśi dṛṣṭi on VL creating a dhana yoga and good wealth management in his company.

We studied the importance of the HL and the GL relating to the second and fifth house of wealth and power. In the same way, the second and fifth from the VL become important. The fifth from the varṇada lagna will show power and position in one's work. Association between the lord of the fifth house from VL and the varṇada lagna is a type of rāja yoga. Bill Gates has the fifth lord from his VL, the Moon, conjunct the varṇada lagna itself. The viśeṣa lagnas bring out the blessings in his chart.

George Bush Jr. has the VL in the sixth house. The VL is aspected by Sun, Moon and MKS Jupiter, showing he enjoys his work though there is some suffering that comes from it. The stronger of the VL and its seventh is the seventh as the Sun is placed there. The eleventh from the VL seventh is Aries (with its lord in Leo) showing kṣatriya work like the military and politics. The second lord Saturn does not have aspect on the VL lord or VL lord Jupiter (who is MKS) showing poor financial/resource management at work. The fifth from the VL lord is Mars which has no aspect on the VL or its lord showing the individual does not have full power/control at work. He does have the third lord from VL and sixth lord from VL conjunct in lagna showing he does have intelligence for his work.

Sage Jaimini mentions some more detailed combinations to see from VL. In general, the varṇada lagna can be read as a complete lagna in itself and the yogas seen from it can be seen as what brings one success or downfall in their line of work.

Tithyaṁśa

Parāśara teaches that the signs are divided into 30 degrees, with 15 degrees on each side of the cusp (*bhāva madhya*) of the house. He described this as the *tithyāṁśa,* where the word tithi represents the number fifteen. The 15 degrees before the bhāva madhya are called pravṛtti, which means they are increasing like the light of the Moon in śukla pakṣa. The fifteen degrees after the bhāva madhya are pūrti, which means completed and coming to an end like the Moon in kṛṣṇa pakṣa. In this way, the bhāva madhya is taken as the Full Moon and the sandhis are the Dark Moon.

Planets have more strength to give results in the brighter degrees, from lagna and from the other viśeṣa lagnas. Planets that are within five degrees either direction of the viśeṣa lagna have more light of that viśeṣa lagna. For example, if the horā lagna was in 10 degrees of Gemini, then planets that fall within 5 to 15 degrees in any sign have more light from the HL and will have more ability to bring prosperity in their time periods. Planets that are close in degree to the GL have more power to bring rise to the individual during their time periods.

There is a beautiful teaching revealed here that is key to understand. Just as the 30 degrees of the sign can be made into tithi, the twelve degrees of the tithi can be divided into twelve signs for various calculations. A sign can also be divided into 27 nakṣatra or the nakṣatra can also be divided into twelve signs.

Śrī Lagna

Śrī is another name for the goddess of prosperity, Lakṣmī. The Śrī lagna is calculated based upon the degrees of the Moon and the lagna. HL relates to the Viṣṇu and the SL relates to his consort, the goddess Lakṣmī. The placement of the SL is where Śrī sits in an individual's chart.

Parāśara does not teach this special lagna in the viśeṣa lagna chapter, but uses the SL in the *Daśā-adhyāya* as the starting point for *lagnādi rāśi daśā*; a daśā used to time prosperity. Parāśara teaches the *Sudaśā vrata* in the Viṣṇu Purāṇa to obtain the blessings of Lakṣmī. Traditionally, this daśā is called *sudaśā* (good-daśā) because it shows when and where Lakṣmī will shine on us and allow prosperity into our lives.

Sudaśā shows Lakṣmī moving through the houses of the chart indicating when prosperity will flow and when it will dry up. It shows the blockages to prosperity during different periods of our life, as well as when monetary combinations will fructify. Some astrologers also use it to time marriage.

In the Daśā-adhyāya, Parāśara teaches,

ऋक्षे लग्नादिराशीनां दशा राशिदशा स्मृता ।
भयातं रविभिर्निघ्नं भभोगविहृतं फलम् ॥ १८८ ॥
राश्याद्यं लग्नराश्यादौ योज्यं द्वादशशेषितम् ।

ṛkṣe lagnādirāśīnāṁ daśā rāśidaśā smṛtā |
bhayātaṁ ravibhirnighnaṁ bhabhogavihṛtaṁ phalam || 188||
rāśyādyaṁ lagnarāśyādau yojyaṁ dvādaśaśeṣitam |189a|

The rāśi daśā known from the nakṣatra (*ṛkṣa*) is called the lagnādi rāśi daśā.
Bha-yatā is multiplied by twelve and the result is divided by the bha-bhoga.
The rāśi indicated is added to the lagna rāśi to start the twelve.

The method taught by Pandit Sanjay Rath is to divide the nakṣatra into twelve portions related to the twelve signs.[6] As each rāśi has 30 tithis, and each tithi has 12 signs, each nakṣatra can be divided into 12 signs.[7] See the amount the Moon has progressed in the nakṣatra (*bha-bhoga*), which is basically seeing in what nakṣatra rāśi that Moon is placed.

---

6 Rath, Jaimini Upadesa Sūtra, p.215. *tārārkāṁśe mandādyo daśeśaḥ||2.4.27||*
7 A nakṣatra is 800 minutes of arc (48,000 seconds) which is 4000 seconds of arc for each rāśi.

Then add that many signs and the degrees to the lagna. This point is called the Śrī lagna (SL) by traditional astrologers.

The Śrī lagna is as many signs from the lagna as it has passed in the nakṣatra. To get the exact degrees one can divide the elapsed degrees in the nakṣatra (*bha-bhoga*) by the length of a nakṣatra. That fraction multiplied by 360 degrees gives the degrees progressed which are added to the longitude of the lagna.

1. The progressed degrees in the nakṣatra/length of nakṣatra = fraction of bhabhoga
2. Fraction of bhabhoga X 360 = degrees of zodiac progressed
3. Degrees of zodiac progressed + longitude of lagna = Śrī lagna

Bill Gates' Moon is 14°25'12" Pisces. Uttarabhādra nakṣatra is 3°20' to 16°40' Pisces. Therefore the Moon has crossed 11° 05' 12" of Uttarabhādra nakṣatra.

11-05-12/13-20 is 665.2 minutes over 800 minutes (665.2/800) =0.8315
0.8315 X 360 = 299.34 degrees
(9 X 30 = 270), 299.34 – 270 = 29.34 (29' 20" 24") =
9 signs and 29 degrees 20 minutes 24 seconds
Bill Gates lagna is 21°58'23" Gemini or (3) 21-58-23
+ (9) 29-20-24
(13) 21-18-47 which is
(1) 21-18-47

Bill Gates has his Śrī lagna in Aries 21° 18' 47". This is placed in the eleventh house of his chart and lorded by Mars who is conjunct an exalted planet in the fourth house. Aries will be where the sudaśā starts in his chart. As this is a chapter on viśeṣa lagnas I will not go into the calculation of sudaśa here, but the calculation of the daśā is given in the proceeding verses of Bṛhat Parāśara Horā Śastra.

In these verses Parāśara mentions the calculation of this lagna and the daśā calculated from it, he does not go into any other details. Sage Jaimini gives rules for interpreting the Śrī lagna and the results of the sudaśā. In this way, Jaimini always expands the teachings of Parāśara and never contradicts or shows a different system of astrology.

Interpretation of Śrī Lagna

Horā lagna shows what we value, and what we have of value. Śrī lagna shows what level of comfort our prosperity is giving to us in life. Ṛṣi Jaimini teaches that if the lord of the SL is uccha or nīca then the native is endowed with wealth (*Śrīmanta*). Pandit Sanjay Rath teaches that the results given by Jaimini apply to the lord of SL, planets conjunct the SL and the individual results of the daśā sign of the sudaśā.[8]

If the lord of Śrī lagna is in own sign or a friendly sign it corresponds to the native's wealth accordingly [2.4.29]. This indicates that own sign will show upper class and friendly sign shows middle class status. If the lord of SL is in an inimical sign it indicates the native is unfortunate (*durgata*) [2.4.30]. The status of the lord of SL indicates the financial status of the individual, or their level of comfort in life. The status of the SL is primary and the status of the various daśā will influence this. Planet status, and benefics and malefics will show ups and downs in the various sudaśā [2.4.35-36]. The daśā of the sign lord conjoining or aspecting the lagna is also very prosperous. In Bill Gates' chart the SL lord Mars has rāśi dṛṣṭi on the lagna as well as being a mahāyogada.

When a malefic is conjunct the Śrī lagna it can show blockages to one's prosperity or blockages to comfort in life. The indications can be analyzed and the donation to those significations will help allow prosperity to flow better in one's life. When one does not give Lakṣmī what she wishes then they will lack her blessing. Pandit Rath says, "People will always ask what can the goddess of prosperity give to me, but they will rarely ask what they can do for her."

To allow Lakṣmī (prosperity and abundance) to come into our life, we must give her what she asks for. The house, sign, planet and their lordship conjoined the SL will indicate what we need to give to Śrī. For example, if the SL is in the ninth house with Venus, the individual can give or sponsor art at their temple when they want to increase prosperity.

When one properly understands the indications they will find either that the person is already giving the indications on their own accord (especially if there is association of the lagna or ninth lord), or that they have excess of that which is indicated to give away.

The Śrī lagna is an aspect of Lakṣmī and the lord of the SL (*Śrīpati*) is an aspect of Viṣṇu. Pandit Sanjay Rath teaches that when either one of these aspect (rāśi dṛṣṭi) the fourth house, it shows that the heart lotus is open and that the heart is very giving. If neither aspect then the heart may be less open (unless other benefics aspect) or the lord of the fourth is well placed and strong. When the heart is open a person is more giving (unless the twelfth house is afflicted by malefics). The giving of the twelfth house relates to material giving, while the giving of the fourth house relates to giving from the heart.

[8] Rath, Sanjay. Jaimini Upadeśa Sūtras, p.217. *tasmitrucce nīce vā śrīmantaḥ || 2.4.28 ||*

A benefic Jupiter in the twelfth house can show a person who is very giving to beneficial causes- but the fourth house and Śrī lagna will show whether this is just a material giving or a deep giving from the heart.

Horā lagna shows what we value, and what we have of value. Śrī lagna shows what level of comfort our prosperity is giving to us in life.

Viśeṣa Lagna	Calculation	Devatā
Bhāva Lagna	1X speed	Brahmā
Horā Lagna	2X speed	Viṣṇu
Ghaṭī Lagna	5X speed	Śiva
Varṇada Lagna	Lagna + HL	*[Indra]*
Śrī Lagna	Lagna + nakṣatra bhoga	Lakṣmī
Prāṇapada Lagna	20X speed	Garuḍa

Prāṇapada Lagna

Thousand-rayed, existing in a hundred forms, the Sun rises as the breath of beings.[9] From the Sun we calculate another special ascendant. The prāṇapada lagna (PP) shows where the prāṇa resides in a birth chart. It is a very sensitive point that is hard to calculate correctly, but which yields great insights when understood. The prāṇapada shows how prāṇa is moving in a person's reality; within themselves and among others in their life. Prāṇa is the life force and the real essence of our breath. The prāṇapada relates to the third house where breathing is initiated as it causes the lungs to expand and contract. The prāṇapada lagna regulates the speed of breath, the movement of the mind, and the strength of the life force.

When we care about something in our life we give it prāṇa, and when something cares about us, it is giving its prāṇa to us. That which we don't give prāṇa to has a weak connection with us, and that which we put prāṇa into plays an important part in our life. Sometimes we chose to put our prāṇa into ventures or people that cause us great joy, while other times we chose things that cause great suffering. In this way, the prāṇa guides us and our mind to focus on certain areas in our life.

[9] Maitrī Upaniṣad VI.8

Calculation

Each minute of time equals five degrees of prāṇapada movement. Therefore the prāṇapada moves through a sign in six minutes. Any inaccuracy of birth time severely influences the final result. There are four main opinions on how to calculate sunrise which can alter the time by over six minutes. The tradition teaches to use the time of sunrise as the appearance of the first ray of Sun on the horizon. It is techniques like these where such accuracy becomes important in Vedic Astrology. Not everyone agrees to use this definition of sunrise and most software programs give you the option to choose your definition.

The calculation of the prāṇapada lagna is mentioned in BPHS after the calculation of the aprakāśa grahas and upagrahas in the *Graha-guṇa-svarūpa-adhyāya*. Parāśara says,

भांशपादसमैः प्राणैश्चराद्यर्कत्रिकोणभात् ।
उदयादिष्टकालान्तं यद्भं प्राणपदं हि तत् ॥ ७१ ॥

bhāṁśapādasamaiḥ prāṇaiścarādyarkatrikoṇabhāt |
udayādiṣṭakālāntaṁ yadbhaṁ prāṇapadaṁ hi tat || 71||

The prāṇa moves in a uniform bhāṁśa-pada [in one ghaṭīkā],
in the moveable signs of the Sun's trine (*arka-trikoṇa*).
[calculated from] sunrise to iṣṭa kāla; that sign is the prāṇapada.

Prāṇapada moves through a sign in six minutes (15 vighaṭīkās or 360 seconds). Prāṇapada will move four signs (1/3 the zodiac[10]) in 1 ghaṭīkā (24 minutes). It moves through the first series of nakṣatras (*bhāṁśapāda*) in 1 ghaṭīkā; one gaṇḍanta to the next gaṇḍanta or 120°. As the prāṇapada takes six minutes to go through a sign, one minute of time is equal to 5° of arc.

The time from Sunrise till the birth time (iṣṭa kāla) is used to calculate prāṇapada. There is a small variation compared to the first three viśeṣa lagnas. While the time difference was added to the Sun wherever it is placed, the movement of the prāṇapada starts from the moveable sign in the Sun's trine (*arka-trikoṇa*). Prāṇa comes from the Sun, but only in its moveable sign where movement/breath is happening.

[10] *tri tri bhāgāḥ carasthirarobhayaparyāt||JUS 4.3.22||*

स्वेष्टकालं पलीकृत्य तिथ्याप्तं भादिकं च यत्।
चरागद्विभसंस्थेऽर्के भनौ युङ्ग नवमे सुते॥ ७२॥
स्फुटं प्राणपदाख्यं तल्लग्नं ज्ञेयं द्विजोत्तम।

sveṣṭakālaṁ palīkṛtya tithyāptaṁ bhādikaṁ ca yat |
carāgadvibhasaṁsthe'rke bhanau yuṅ navame sute || 72||
sphuṭaṁ prāṇapadākhyaṁ tallagnaṁ jñeyaṁ dvijottama |73a|

The iṣṭa kāla is turned into vighaṭīkā (*pala*), and divide by 15 (*tithi*).
The rāśi, degrees, etc. are added to the position of the Sun in moveable (*cara*) sign,
The ninth (*navama*) there from if Sun is in a fixed (*aga*) sign, fifth in a dual (*dvi*) sign.
This point (*sphuṭa*) is called the prāṇapada lagna by the wise.

As the prāṇapada moves 15 vighaṭikās a sign, Parāśara teaches to turn the birth time totally into vighaṭikās and then divide by fifteen to see how many signs it has progressed through. Since our preference of time unit is hours and minutes, we use the prāṇa speed as one sign in six minutes. Therefore, we can convert the iṣṭa kāla into minutes and divide it by six for the same result.

The distance arrived at is added the Sun if it is in a moveable sign. Otherwise the moveable sign in trine to the Sun is taken with the Sun's degree. Pandit Sanjay Rath calls this *koṇārka*, the same longitude in the cara trikoṇa from the Sun, where the Sun god breathes life prāṇa into you. Therefore if the Sun is in Aries, the degrees are added to the longitude of the Sun in Aries. If the Sun is in Leo, the degrees are added to the longitude of the Sun from Aries. If the Sun is in Sagittarius, then the degrees are added to the longitude of the Sun from Aries; always the moveable sign in trine.

Bill Gates was born at 9:00 PM and sunrise was at 6:47AM. The iṣṭa kāla is 14 hours and 13 minutes or 853 minutes. This is multiplied by 5° of arc, and reduced by multiples of 360: 853 minutes X 5° = 4265 – 3960 = 305° (10 signs and 5°). The rising Sun on the day Bill Gates was born was at Libra (7) 11° 10′

+ (10) 05° 00′

(5) 16° 10′ [17-12 signs =5]

Bill Gates has his prāṇapada lagna in Leo 16° 10′. Seconds of birth and Sunrise should be taken into account for accuracy, especially with the importance of the prāṇapada in navāṁśa. George Bush Jr. was born at 7:26AM and sunrise was at 5:25AM. The iṣṭa kāla is 2 hours and 1 minute, or 121 minutes. This is multiplied by 5° of arc, and reduced by multiples of 360: 121 minutes X 5° = 605 -360 = 245° (8 signs and 5°). The rising Sun when George Bush Jr. was born was in Gemini, so we take the moveable trine to that which is Libra with the same degrees: (7) 20° 36′

+(8) 05° 00′

(3) 25° 36′ [15-12 signs =3]

House placement

Parāśara first mentions good and bad houses for the prāṇapada in the *Graha-guṇa-svarūpa-adhyāya*. Then in the *Aprakāśa-graha-phala-adhyāya* (v.74-85) he gives specific results for each house placement. We will look at the simple results he lists and then look at the rational so that we can give a deeper and more personalized interpretation. In the *Graha-guṇa-svarūpa-adhyāya*, Parāśara says,

लग्नाद् द्विकोणे तुर्ये च राज्ये प्राणपदं तदा ॥ ७३ ॥
शुभं जन्म विजानीयात्तथैवैकादशेऽपि च ।
अन्यस्थाने स्थितं चेत् स्यात् तदा जन्माशुभं वदेत् ॥ ७४ ॥

lagnād dvikoṇe turye ca rājye prāṇapadaṁ tadā || 73b||
śubhaṁ janma vijānīyāttathaivaikādaśe'pi ca |
anyasthāne sthitaṁ cet syāt tadā janmāśubhaṁ vadet || 74||

If the prāṇapada is 2, 5, 9, 4, 10 or 11 from the natal lagna,
It indicates a good birth (*śubha janma*).
Placed in other houses there will be a not-good birth (*aśubha janma*).

Parāśara teaches that the prāṇapada lagna is well-placed in the fifth and ninth, fourth and tenth, and second and eleventh houses. Pandit Sanjay Rath teaches that the placement in the fifth or ninth will indicate the individual is attracted to a Vaiṣṇava form of god in this life. Viṣṇu forms are those associated with devotion (water) and being saved. The placement of the prāṇapada in the fourth or tenth houses indicates the individual is a Śākta, therefore is attracted to the mother goddess in this life. The prāṇapada placed in the second or eleventh houses indicates an individual who is attracted to a Śaiva form of god in this life. Śaiva forms are those which punish and need penance (fire) for one to get over their karmas. These houses will be modified by the house lords they are conjunct. For example, if the prāṇapada is in the second house but conjunct the lord of the ninth house, it will indicate Viṣṇu. Obama has the prāṇapada in the eighth house but it is conjunct the fourth and second lords.

These houses give good results while houses 6, 7, and 8 as well as 12, 1, and 3 are not auspicious in their results (as seen below). Parāśara mentions the prāṇapada in each house from lagna, which deepens the previous statement. Prāṇapada placed in:

Lagna: weak (*kṣaṇo*), sickly (*rogi*), mute (*mūka*), disordered mind (*unmatta*), a defective or missing limb (*jaḍāṅgastu hīnāṅgo*), unhappy (*duḥkhita*), under weight (*kṛśa*).

2nd house: lots of grains (*bahudhānya*), lots of wealth (*bahudhana*), many servants (*bahubhṛtya*), many offspring (*bahupraja*), and fortunate (*subhaga*). [Devoted to the spouse (7th house).]

3rd house: cruel (*hiṁsra*), arrogant/haughty (*garva*), harsh/ harshness of speech (*niṣṭhura*), ūti, a thief (*malimluca*), lacks respect for teachers (*gurubhaktivivarjita*).

4th house: happy (*sukhī*), pleasing, agreeable (*kānta*), loved by friends (*suhṛdramāsu vallabha*), wholly devoted to teachers (*gurau parāyaṇa*), cold (*śīta*), intent on truth (*satya-tatpara*).

5th house: enjoys happiness (*sukhibhāj*), commences good acts (*sukriya-upeta*), full of compassion (*dayānvita*), possessed of all that one desires (*sarvakāma-samanvita*). [Devoted to one's boss and work (tenth house).]

6th house: under the dominion of relatives and enemies (*bandhu-śatru-vaśas*), sharp/harsh/ vehement (*tīkṣṇa*), weak digestion (*mandāgni*), unmerciful (*nirdaya*), low/base (*khala*), sickly (*rogī*), protects one's acquisitions (*vittapa*), short life (*alpa-āyus*).

7th house: jealous[11] (*īrṣyālu*), continually desirous/lustful (*satata kāmī*), intense (*tīvra*), fierce form (*raudra-vapus*), difficult to overcome (*durārādhya*), deficient in learning or having bad opinions (*kubuddhimān*).

8th house: distressed with disease (*roga-san-tāpita-aṅga*), distressed (*pīḍita*), and death-like suffering due to the king, relatives or children (*pārthiva duḥkha*). [Devoted to oneself.]

9th house: will have children (*putravān*), possessed of wealth (*dhanasampanna*), fortunate (*subhaga*), pleasant to look at (*priyadarśana*), servants are never bad (*bhṛtya sada-aduṣṭa*), clear-sighted (*vicakṣaṇa*). [Devoted to family (second house).]

10th house: heroic/vigourous (*vīryavān*), intelligent (*matimān*), talented/skilful (*dakṣa*), carries out the king's business/ government work (*nṛpa-kāryeṣa*), learned (*kovida*), wholly devoted to worshipping the gods (*deva-arcana-parāyaṇa*).

11th house: famous (*vikhyāta*), endowed with good qualities (*guṇavān*), intelligent (*prājña*), having enjoyments (*bhogīdha nasamanvita*), fair complexioned (*gaurāṅga*), devoted to mother (*mātṛvatsala*).

12th house: wicked/vile/mean (*kṣudra*), evil-natured (*duṣṭa*), defective limbs (*hīnāṅga*), aversion to brahmins and relatives (*vidveṣī dvija-bandhu*), eye disease (*netrarogī*) or one-eyed (*kāṇa*).

One must remember not to look at the prāṇapada in isolation. Parāśara adds at the end of the chapter that before properly declaring these results one should consider the light-giving planets which move through the sky by their positions, lordship, aspects and strength and weakness determination.[12] In this way, one should always see these types of

[11] According to Suśruta it also denotes those who get aroused by watching the copulation of others, which could indicate those who look at pornography.

[12] *ityaprakāśakheṭānāṁ phalānyuktāni bhūsura | tathā yāni prakāśānāṁ sūryādīnāṁ khacāriṇām || 86||*
tāni sthitivaśātteṣāṁ sphuṭadṛṣṭivaśāt tathā | balā'balavivekena vaktavyāni śarīriṇām || 87||

results among other factors in the chart. We will try to understand some of the significations of the prāṇapada lagna to be able to understand why Parāśara has made these statements.

Jaimini teaches that the third from prāṇapada lagna indicates with which parent we will have a closer connection (*niyojita*). If there are benefics third from PP then the individual is attached to the father [4.1.48]. Donald Trump has PP in the lagna and third from it is Libra with no planets placed there indicating attachment to his father. Obama has the same signification in his chart (Libra third from PP), which we will look at more deeply below.

If there are malefics in the third from PP then the individual is attached to the mother [4.1.49]. George Bush Jr. has Mars in Leo third from his PP showing he is attached to his mother. If both benefics and malefics are in the third from PP, then the individual is attached to co-borns [4.1.50]. Bill Gates has Saturn, the Sun and Venus third his prāṇapada showing more attachment to siblings, nephews or close friends.

If benefics are in the third and aspected by malefics or malefics in the third aspected by benefics then there are mishaps (*virūpa*) [4.1.51]. For example in Obama's chart the third from the PP is Libra with no planets showing attachment to the father, but it is aspected by Ketu, Moon, Rāhu, and Mars. The malefics indicate that in their daśā there is some mishap that changes this situation. In George Bush's chart there is no planet aspecting the third from PP so there is no break in his love and attachment to his mother.

The sixth house is seen similar to the third, except the sixth will show who you serve based upon the significations of the house. Parāśara teaches that we are completely devoted (*parāyaṇa*) to the individuals signified by this house. Parāśara says when the prāṇapada lagna is in the fourth house the individual is devoted to teachers (6th from PP is the 9th house). Parāśara says that PP in the sixth house makes one devoted to protecting their acquisitions (6th from PP is the 11th house). PP in the tenth house indicates one who is wholly devoted to worshipping the gods, or devoted to the third house of guru upadeśa and pūjā. Parāśara says, the prāṇapada lagna in the eleventh house indicates devotion to the mother. In this way, we can understand the sixth house from the prāṇapada lagna, and know that prāṇapada in the second house will make one devoted to their spouse.

The significations of the eighth house from prāṇapada will indicate those who serve you, as we see when the PP is in the fourth house the individual is loved by friends (11th house). When the PP is in the tenth, one carries out the king's business and has many subordinates (5th house) serving him to execute the commands.

Jaimini teaches that that happiness and sorrow are seen from the fifth house from prāṇapada lagna [4.1.52]. Benefic planets in the fifth house from PP show love and affection blessing your life. Malefics there take away what you care about, break your attachment, and that loss causes great sorrow. Even if the malefic is exalted it will cause losses that make one suffer (and the Moon or ātmakāraka aspecting ensure the loss). The planets in that house can indicate those who bring happiness or suffering into your life. In this way, planets in the ninth from prāṇapada can shows those who you bring happiness and suffering to. From prāṇapada lagna to its seventh house is the out breath where you are giving prāṇas, and from the seventh back to prāṇapada is in breath where you are receiving prāṇas. The fifth is what you give your prāṇa to, that will make you happy or make you suffer, while the ninth house is those that give you prāṇa whom you will make happy or sorrowful. In the chart of Bill Gates and Obama, the fifth house from prāṇapada lagna is lorded by a benefic showing they put their energies into beneficial things that bring them happiness.

Pandit Sanjay Rath teaches that the fourth house from prāṇapada shows our mental strengths; where our prāṇas are strong. And the tenth house shows where we have some mental weaknesses. In the chart of Obama, the fourth from prāṇapada lagna is the eleventh house indicating great strength in making gains for the country. The tenth house from the prāṇapada lagna is the fifth house of speculation showing some weakness in planning the future, and with the Moon there it shows a lack of truly understanding the public (though he will still win re-election to a second term because of other indications). In the chart of Bill Gates, he is devoted to the eighth house of his researchers and developers. He is served by the tenth house of commercial companies. The fourth from PP is the sixth house, showing his knowledge of overcoming the competition (through whatever means with Rāhu there). His mental weakness is in understanding the foreign markets of the twelfth house from lagna.

The twelfth house from prāṇapada lagna is a house getting destroyed; the prāṇas are disturbed. Planets placed in that house will get depression, die early or may even kill themselves. Moon there-placed can show a Mother who is depressed, may die early or may even commit suicide. Venus would show the spouse or sister in such a condition. In Obama's chart, the Sun is placed twelfth from his prāṇapada showing the disturbance in his relationship with his father. His parents split when he was two, and his father only visited him once from Kenya when he was 10 years old before dying in an automobile accident in Obama's twenty-first year (Sun maturity).

The positions from the prāṇapada should be integrated with the lagna, AL, AK and other key points and lagnas. Sage Jaimini also speaks about the sign placement of the prāṇapada: in Aries the PP gives strength (*bala*) [4.1.41]. Poor longevity is indicated by prāṇapada in Cancer [4.1.42]. To summarize these, the prāṇapada is good in the signs of Mars and the Sun as its nature is fiery. The prāṇapada relates to the fire element and its kāraka is the Sun represented by the king of birds, Garuḍa. It is second best in the balance of the Jupiter signs, and then has strength in the slowness of the Saturn signs. It is weakest in the Moon's signs and next weakest in Venus signs as it does not like the jala tattva. This is the same for the planets conjunct and aspecting the prāṇapada. The nodes are inimical to the prāṇapada as sarpas are eaten by Garuḍa.

Navāṁśa Prāṇapada Lagna

The prāṇapada is a very sensitive point that was calculated in ancient times without computers. There were various ways to confirm the accuracy of the prāṇapada placement. When one understands how to read the prāṇapada as a lagna it will help to confirm the calculated position or move the time a few minutes/seconds so that the prāṇapada is in the correct sign.

The other special lagnas are based on the movement of the lagna and added to the Sun's longitude at sunrise. The prāṇapada is taken from the koṇārka, the moveable trine to the Sun which takes into account other subtle factors of creation. In the navāṁśa, the relationship of prāṇapada to the Moon adds to this subtlety of the prāṇa and its role in keeping the mind and body functioning.

In the navāṁśa, the prāṇapada must be in trines or seventh from the Moon to insure that the being is alive and breathing. This can be used for rectification after the chart is corrected to at least the ṣaṣṭyaṁśa as it is an extremely sensitive point in the navāṁśa, changing signs every 40 seconds. A breathing being cannot be born without the prāṇapada related to the Moon. The Moon is the need for prāṇa; it triggers the breath to keep us alive. The prāṇapada is the supplier of prāṇa (coming from the Sun).

The prāṇapada lagna regulates the prāṇa by being the supplier. The prāṇapada navāṁśa therefore indicates the quality of a person's breathing or issues related to it. The natural speed of the planet ruling the sign placement relates to the speed of the breath. Saturn ruled signs show slow breathing , Leo shows steady breathing, Cancer shows fast and irregular breathing.

The navāṁśa prāṇapada rectification enables a very subtle fine tuning that will help when using the viṁśottarī daśā down to the sixth level. That level of daśā is used to predict the time of things like being late to work, tripping in the sidewalk, getting on a plane, and very fine tuned predictions.

Conclusion

This chapter hase given a general idea about the viśeṣa lagnas. Understanding the conceptual framework for their calculations their practical usage becomes easier to understand. The usage of these viśeṣa lagnas will bring a new level of deeper refined vision to the astrological chart.

Chapter 8

Nārāyaṇa Daśā

The indications (*lakṣaṇa*) of a seed
are the cause of the type of tree (*dravya*)
that follows (*kāraṇa-anugata*).
The character (*lakṣaṇa*) of what we are made of (*dravya*)
is the cause of what we become (*kāraṇa-anugata*).
-Viṣṇu Purāṇa (II.7.33)

Nārāyaṇa Daśā

There are many wheels turning inside a watch. Time has many cogs and many levels of possibilities to activate. There is the natural time that is the foundation of everything. There are graha daśās that show the interactive level of reality and then there are the group of *rāśi daśā* that indicate the *situations* that are becoming active in our life. There are hundreds of daśā, but it is advised to start with a foundation of three: naisargika daśā, a graha daśā and a rāśi daśā. Understanding these three types of daśā will give a strong foundation to understand all the other various daśā that have very specific application.

We have studied naisargika daśā and some of its variations. These show the natural state or phase of life a person is in and help us have a proper vantage point to make other predictions. We have learned viṁśottarī daśā as the first daśā. This and other udu daśā are based on the nakṣatra and therefore relate to the Moon. They show the 'experience' in life which can be irrespective of the events surrounding the individual. Rāśi daśā are calculated from the Sun signs which are related to the resources the Sun provides.

The first phalita rāśi daśā (rāśi daśā for predicting life results) that I recommend a student to start with is Nārāyaṇa daśā. Different traditions will have different emphasis on different daśā. Nārāyaṇa daśā is the phalita rāśi daśā given importance in this tradition. It is also known as *Rāśi-pada-krama daśā* in south India.

Rāśi dasās show the circumstances and direction of life. For example, a new job can give you a new office, new associations, and new income. Moving to a new home or office will change the circumstances that will be presented to you in your life. Rāśi daśās are very effective in timing circumstancial situations.

A seed is inactive until it is given the right circumstances to grow. A seed needs soil, water and Sun to sprout forth (*praroha*), just as our karmas need the right situation, resources and energy to manifest their results. In this way, a combination for being a great leader needs a circumstance of a company or organization to be fruitful within. Or the combination for being a great entertainer needs the circumstance of the theatre and an acting company.

There is an inherent nature of that which is born, that unfolds according to its environment. The seed of a tree will become a tree, the seed of a flower will become a flower. A sunflower seed won't become a rose bush. A great leader is born to be a great leader and a great actor is born to be a great actor. It is not about predetermination by something other than you. It is about you becoming fully you. It is about following your heart and being yourself fully. We are each born unique with the callings of our heart. Our own soul brings these 'callings' with us into this body. These callings are seeds inside of us, and as a particular type of tree will follow from a particular type of seed, so our nature follows from our callings. The Viṣṇu Purāṇa (II.7.33) says that the indications (*lakṣaṇa*) of a seed are the cause of the type of tree (*dravya*) that follows (*kāraṇa-anugata*). The character (*lakṣaṇa*) of what we are made of (*dravya*) is the cause of what we become (*kāraṇa-anugata*).

The Viṣṇu Purāṇa (II.7.33-36) says that in the proper space and time the root, stem and branches spring from a seed and then grow and produce other seeds. In the same way the root matter produces Mahat, the other tattvas, and the elements (*bhūtāni*) which creates the beings in this world (*bhūtasargaṇa*).

सन्निधानाद् यथाकाशकालाद्याः कारणं तरोः ।
तथैव परिणामेन विश्वस्य भगवान् हरि ॥३६

sannidhānād yathākāśakālādyāḥ kāraṇaṁ taroḥ|
tathaiva pariṇāmena viśvasya bhagavān hari||36

Just as space (*ākāśa*) and time (*kāla*) cause (*karaṇa*) the tree,
So in a like manner, all developments (*pariṇām*) are caused by the lord (*Bhagavān Hari*).

व्रीहिबिजे यथा मूलं नालं पत्रांकुरौ तथा ।
काण्डं कोषस्तथा पुष्पं क्षीरं तद्वच्च तण्डुलाः ॥

vrīhibije yathā mūlaṁ nālaṁ patrāṅkurau tathā|
kāṇḍaṁ koṣastathā puṣpaṁ kṣīraṁ tadvacca taṇḍulāḥ||37||

As a seed of rice has the root, stalk, leaf, shoots,
branches, bud, flower, sap, grain,

तुषाः कणाश्च सन्तो वै यान्त्याविर्भावमात्मनः ।
प्ररोहहेतुसामग्रीमासाद्य मुनिसत्तम ॥

tuṣāḥ kaṇāśca santo vai yāntyāvirbhāvamātmanaḥ|
prarohahetusāmagrīmāsādya munisattama||38||

husks, and seed finally become manifest because of its nature,
The reason (*hetu*) for the sprouting forth (*praroha*) is completely attained.

तथा कर्मस्वनेकेषु देवाद्याः समविस्थिताः ।
विष्णुशक्तिं समासाद्य प्ररोहमुपयान्ति वै ॥

tathā karmasvanekeṣu devādyāḥ samavisthitāḥ|
viṣṇuśaktiṁ samāsādya prarohamupayānti vai||39||

In this way, the actions (*karma*) of men and gods are situated similarly, and
By the power of Viṣṇu their results come growing forth.

स च विष्णुः परं ब्रह्म यतः सर्वमिदं जगत्।
जगच्च यो यत्र चेदं यस्मिंश्च लयमेष्यति ॥

sa ca viṣṇuḥ paraṁ brahma yataḥ sarvamidaṁ jagat |
jagacca yo yatra cedaṁ yasmiṁśca layameṣyati ||40||

This Viṣṇu is the supreme spirit (*paraṁ brahma*) from which the entire universe proceeds, Who is the universe itself and to whom it dissolves back into.

The Nārāyaṇa daśā indicates the space and time for things to manifest. It indicates the circumstances of the present situation in which a seed may grow. Seeds are tendencies (*saṁskāra*) within us from past actions in this life or past lives. These seeds will sprout at the right space and time.

Rāśi daśās move from sign to sign and have signs as antardaśā. The planets represent people in a chart; that which has the power to grasp, to grab, and to make happen by its will. Rāśi are the situations these graha act within; what they have, what quality they have, how much of it they have. Nārāyaṇa daśā is the "when" in that equation.

The grahas are controlled by a quality of time and the rāśi are controlled by another quality of time. The experience of reality is the experience of time. Time takes its flavour from the graha and rāśi, their qualities both naturally and according to that individual's chart.

Calculation of Nārāyaṇa Daśā

The calculation is technical, and understanding the rules is crucial to understanding other rāśi daśā. Some daśās may start from different signs, or have a different progression, or utilize different direct and anti-zoadiacal rules, but the general calcuations will be variations of the standard. The determination strength rules will also be important for other daśās and predictions.

[1] The first rule of Nārāyaṇa daśā is that it starts from the stronger of the lagna or its seventh house.[2] This is called the axis of truth (*satya-pīṭha*). The lagna is like Brahmā (the rising Sun) and the seventh house is like Śiva (the setting Sun). The seventh house is the seed desires that bring us into this life. It is the thoughts that were present in your parent's mind when you were created. The stronger of the lagna or seventh shows whether your head or your root desires are guiding you more.

The partner is a reflection of you, as a manifestation of your basic seed desires. Sometimes the reflection is more powerful to cause results. You are creating your partner, who is creating you. In this way, the seventh house can be seen as the stronger of what is

[2] Bṛhat Parāśara Horā Śāstra, Antardaśā-adhyāya v.6, Jaimini Upadeśā Sūtras 2.4.7

creating you. Whichever one is guiding is perfect for this life and Nārāyaṇa begins from there.

Strength Rules

The rules for determining the stronger sign in either the lagna or seventh are based on the Cara daśā rules in Bṛhat Parāśara Horā Śastra and modified according to the upadeśa of Jaimini.[3] The order presented here is according to these texts as taught by Pandit Sanjay Rath and my understanding of these teachings.

The first rule is based on planets; the sign with more planets has more weight to insure that it will give results.[4] If this rule determines the stronger then the calculation is complete. If both signs have no planets or both have the same number of planets then one utilizes the next rule. The sign aspected by Jupiter, Mercury or its own lord is stronger. If the aspects are the same, then the next rule is to look at the status (ucca, mūlatrikoṇa, sva, etc) of the planets in the sign.[5] If that gave a result then one does not proceed, but if there is still equality then the next rule is utilized.

Standard strength rules state that cara signs are stronger, then the sthira, then the dual signs.[6] This rule is not utilized for finding the stronger of the lagna or seventh because they are the same type of sign. Therefore the next rule, if they are still equal strength, is that the lord in a different oddity is stronger. That means if it is an even sign, it is stronger if its lord is in an odd sign, and an odd sign is stronger if its lord is in an even sign. If they are the same, then the sign giving higher number of daśā years is the stronger.[7]

a. The sign with a planet is stronger

b. The sign with more planets is stronger
[*Jaimini says a sign aspected by Jupiter, Mercury, or own lord is stronger*]
[*Jaimini says if equal number, then examine status: ucca, mūlatrikoṇa, sva, etc.*]

c. If equal number [*or status*] then the strength of sign determines:
Cara signs are strongest, then sthira, then dual
[*Jaimini says if still the same, then use the one with higher degrees*]
[*Jaimini says if still the same, use the lord in a different oddity than its own sign*]

d. If the same, then the one giving a longer daśā is stronger
[*Jaimini says if still the same, the sign whose lord is ātmakāraka is stronger*]
[*If still the same, use the lord who has higher degrees according to cārakāraka*]

3 The source text of these rules is examined with the mūla daśā calculations on pages 383 to 387.
4 Bṛhat Parāśara Horā Śāstra, Daśā-adhyāya v.161
5 BPHS, Daśā-adhyāya v.162
6 BPHS, Daśā-adhyāya v.163a
7 BPHS, Daśā-adhyāya v.163b

Progression of the Daśā

[2] Once the stronger of the lagna and seventh has been decided, then the direction of the daśā is determined. This is done by looking at the ninth from the starting sign and seeing whether it is an odd or even footed sign.[8] The footedness of signs deals with dharma, as the Vāmana avatāra takes three steps to uphold dharma. The Vāmana Gāyatrī found in the Ṛgveda and many other Vaidika texts says,

त्रीणि पदा वि चक्रमे विष्णुर्गोपा अदाभ्यः ।
अतो धर्माणि धारयन् ॥१ ।२३ ।१८ ॥

trīṇi padā vi cakrame viṣṇurgopā adābhyaḥ |
ato dharmāṇi dhārayan || *Ṛgveda 1.23.18*

Viṣṇu the protector, invincible,
took three steps and upheld dharma.

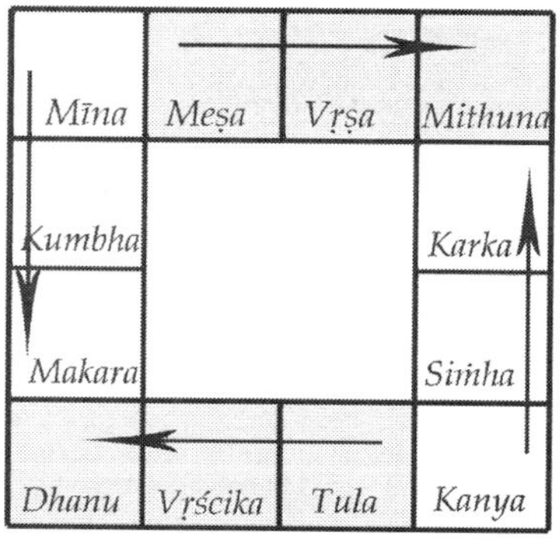

Starting from Aries (as well as kṛtikkā) every three signs is considered as odd footed (*viṣama-pada*) or even footed (*sama-pada*). The first three rāśi of the zodiac are odd footed (Aries, Taurus, Gemini), the next three are even footed (Virgo, Leo, Cancer). Then the next three are again odd footed (Libra, Scorpio, Sagitarrius) and the last three are even footed (Pisces, Aquarius, Capricorn). If the ninth house is odd footed then the direction of the daśā is zodiacal (Aries, Taurus, Gemini, Cancer, Leo, etc). If the ninth house is even footed then the order of the daśā is anti-zodiacal.

[3] The next determination will be the order of the daśā based upon the nature of the initiating sign (*ārambha rāśī*).[9] There are three progressions based upon the three natures of signs.

a. Cara signs are regular: for zodiacal it is Aries, Taurus, Gemini, Cancer, etc
for anti-zodiacal it is Cancer, Gemini, Taurus, Aries, etc

b. Sthira signs are every sixth: zodiacal is Aries, Virgo, Aquarius, Cancer, etc
for anti-zodiacal it is Cancer, Sagittarius, Taurus, Libra, etc

c. Dvisva signs are trines, then 10th: zodiacal is Aries, Leo, Sagittarius, Capricorn, etc
for anti-zodiacal it is Cancer, Pisces, Scorpio, Libra, Gemini, etc

[8] BPHS, Daśā-adhyāya v.157 and 167: verse 157 mentions the daśā direction of odd and even footed signs and verse 167 clarifies to calculate this *pada krama* from the ninth house; also Jaimini Upadeśa Sūtra 2.3.29.

[9] BPHS, Antardaśā-adhyāya v.7-9, also presented in Jaimini Upadeśa Sūtra 2.4.8-10: this is a distinction between some interpretations of cara daśā and Padakrama daśā/Nārāyaṇa daśā.

Length of the Daśā

[4] The next step is to find the length of the daśā for each sign. Count from the daśā rāśi to its lord.[10] If the daśā sign is odd footed, then count zodiacal. If the daśā rāśi is even footed, then count anti-zodiacal to the lord of the sign.[11] Subtract one year from it to make it a non-inclusive count. For example, in Aries daśā, if Mars is in Gemini it gives 2 years. In Leo daśā, if the Sun is in Gemini then it gives 2 years. Subtract one for nīca sthāna and add one for ucca sthāna.[12] So in Leo daśā, if the Sun is in Aries it gives 5 years, and if the Sun was in Libra it would give 9 years. If Jupiter is in Capricorn, Sagittarius daśā will be 0 years, and if Jupiter is in Capricorn, Pisces daśā will be one year. If a planet is in its own sign it gives 12 years.

There is a standard exception to this order regarding Saturn (Brahmā) and Ketu (Gaṇeśa). If Saturn is placed in the sign, then the order will always be direct. If Ketu is placed in the sign, then the order will always be anti-zodiacal. If they are conjunct in a sign, then the direction of the stronger or higher degree will be utilized.

Aquarius and Scorpio both have two lords. The stronger lord needs to be determined to calculate the length of the daśā (and sometimes for the strength of the sign).[13] If the lords are placed in the same sign, then the daśā will be the same and there is no need to calculate which is stronger. Only the stronger lord is utilized for adding and subtracting a year for ucca and nīca planets.

a. If one is in its own sign and the other is elsewhere, use the planet not in its own sign.
b. If both lords are elsewhere, the stronger of the two signs gives the daśā period.
c. If the signs are of equal strength, use the lord contributing the larger daśā (counting zodiacal or anti-zodiacal based upon the sign even or odd footedness: direct from Scorpio and reverse from Aquarius).

After the daśā of all twelve signs, the remainder from twelve of each daśā gives the next legnths of daśā. For example, if the first daśā of Aries is 4 years, then the second Aries daśā will be 8 years. If the first daśā of a sign was 12 years then its second daśā will be 0 years. This makes the Nārāyaṇa daśā 144 years in length.

---

[10] Bṛhat Parāśara Horā Śāstra, Daśā-adhyāya v.155
[11] BPHS, Daśā-adhyāya v.156
[12] BPHS, Daśā-adhyāya v.165
[13] BPHS, Daśā-adhyāya v.157-160

Antardaśā Calculations

The final calculation is the antardaśās. First find the stronger of the first or seventh from the daśā rāśī. And then use the placement of the lord of that sign to start the antardaśā. If it is an odd sign go zodiacal and if it is an even sign go anti-zodiacal.[14]

As there are 12 months in the year, when a daśā is divided evenly it is given 1 month for every year.[15] So if the rāśi daśā is 4 years then each sign is given four months in the antardaśā. Each antardaśā is of equal length. So if the antardaśā started from Libra, then the next antardaśā would be Scorpio, then Sagittarius, Capricorn, etc in regular order.

1. Find the stronger of the seventh or the daśā rāśi
2. Start from the sign placement of the lord of the stronger sign
3. Odd and even starting sign determine direct or anti-zodiacal direction
    a. Saturn or Ketu in the initiating sign (ārambha rāśī) alter the direction.
    b. Saturn or Ketu in the daśā sign alter the direction.
    c. If Saturn is in one and Ketu in the other, then use the stronger sign.
4. The months are related to the number of years of the daśā

Calculation Example

[1] The first step is to determine the stronger of the lagna or seventh. In the example chart, there are no planets in the first or seventh house. Neither the lagna nor the seventh

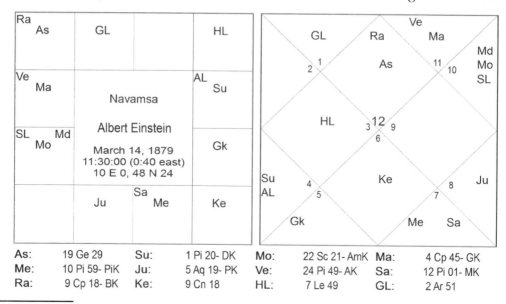

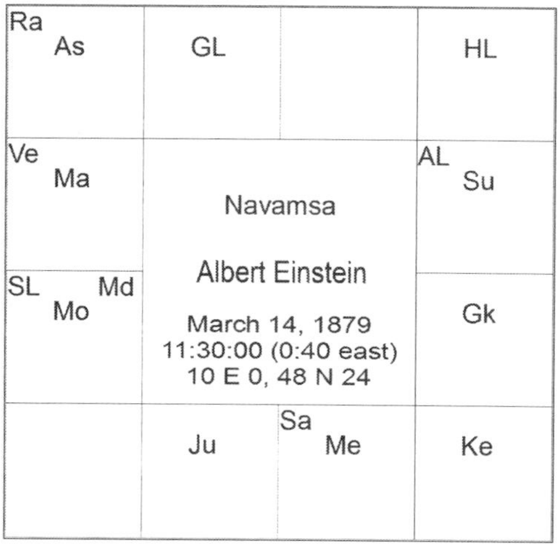

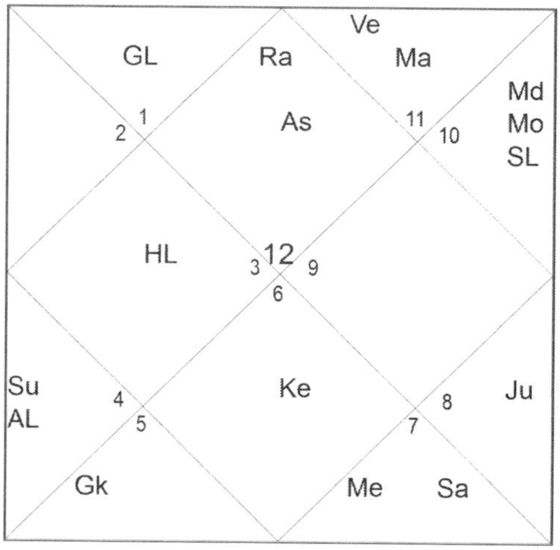

As:	19 Ge 29	Su:	1 Pi 20- DK	Mo:	22 Sc 21- AmK	Ma:	4 Cp 45- GK
Me:	10 Pi 59- PiK	Ju:	5 Aq 19- PK	Ve:	24 Pi 49- AK	Sa:	12 Pi 01- MK
Ra:	9 Cp 18- BK	Ke:	9 Cn 18	HL:	7 Le 49	GL:	2 Ar 51

14 Bṛhat Parāśara Horā Śāstra, Antardaśā-adhyāya v.6 also JUS 2.4.13
15 BPHS, Antardaśā-adhyāya v.5 and serial order noted in Carādi-daśā-phala-adhyāya v.90

are aspected by Jupiter but both the lagna and the seventh have rāśi aspect of Mercury. For the lagna it is the own lord aspecting and for the seventh it is not. This makes the lagna the stronger of the two houses.

[2] The ninth house is Aquarius which is even footed making the order of the houses go anti-zodiacal.

[3] The initiating sign is dual and so the order goes in trines: Gemini, Aquarius, Libra, then Virgo, Taurus, Aquarius, then Sagittarius, Leo, Aries, and Pisces, Scorpio, Cancer.

Mahādaśā			**Leo Antardaśā**	
Gemini	1879-03-14		Pisces	1932-03-14
Aquarius	1887-03-14		Aquarius	1932-08-16
Libra	1898-03-14		Capricorn	1933-01-13
Virgo	1904-03-14		Sagittarius	1933-06-14
Taurus	1909-03-14		Scorpio	1933-11-16
Aquarius	1920-03-14		Libra	1934-04-13
Sagittarius	1930-03-14		Virgo	1934-09-16
Leo	1932-03-14		Leo	1935-02-12
Aries	1937-03-14		Cancer	1935-07-16
Pisces	1947-03-14		Gemini	1935-12-16
Scorpio	1948-03-14		Taurus	1936-05-14
Cancer	1951-03-14		Aries	1936-10-16
Gemini	1958-03-14			
Aquarius	1962-03-14			

[4] Then the length of the daśā is calculated, by counting from the sign to the lord. Gemini is odd footed, so we count zodiacally to Mercury (10) and subtract 1 to make it non-inclusive. Then subtract one because Mercury is in nīca sthāna, which gives the number of years as 8 (1879 + 8 = 1987).

The next daśā is Aquarius which has two lords. Rāhu is with one planet and Saturn is with three other planets, so Saturn is stronger. Aquarius is even footed, so count from Aquarius to Saturn in an anti-zodiacal direction (12) and subtract one to make the count non-inclusive), which gives the number eleven (1887 + 11 = 1898).

The next daśā moves zodiacal because Libra is odd footed. Venus is six signs away from Libra, minus one, which gives five years. Venus is exalted so we add one year (1898 + 6 = 1904). Then, Virgo is even footed, so we count in reverse to Mercury (7), and minus one (6). Mercury is nīca so we subtract another year to get five years (1904 + 5 = 1909). Next, Taurus is odd footed so we count direct to Venus (11) minus one (10) and then add one year for the exaltation to get eleven years (1909 + 11 = 1920). When done in the software, the actual hours are calculated and will add a day after some time. In general, when the mahādaśā is changing it will take place on the birth date, for this example it is March 14th.

[5] Then the antardaśā are calculated. For Leo antardaśā, we start from the stronger of the first or seventh from Leo (the daśā rāśī). In this case, it is Aquarius because it has one planet present, and the lord of Aquarius (Saturn is stronger) is placed in Pisces. Therefore the first daśā is that of Pisces, an even sign, so the direction of the daśā is anti-zodiacal. The antaradaśā moves in a normal order, so the antaradaśā of Leo start with Pisces and go reverse to Aquarius, Capricorn, Sagittarius, etc. [If Saturn was in Aquarius, it would have made the order direct, but this is not the case].

[6] The length of the antardaśā are related to the length of the mahādaśā. Leo mahādaśā is five years long. This makes each antardaśā five months long. Leo Pisces starts 1932 (3) March, 14th with the addition of five months becomes 1932 (8) August, 14th. The computer adds in the variations of the days of the month, but for quick calculation one can just use the same day of the month for each daśā.

Practice Exercises

1. Calculate the Nārāyaṇa daśā for your chart and two others. Calculate the active antardaśā.

Interpretation

Nārāyaṇa daśā has a universal application similar to viṁśottarī daśā among the nakṣatra daśās. Parāśara teaches how to see the results of various types of rāśi daśā in the *Carādi daśā phala adhyāya*. Each of the rāśi daśā also have various special techniques and particulars to utilize and bring out their full potential. Here we look at the basics which underlie them all. Parāśāra says,

चरस्थिरादिसंज्ञा या दशाः प्रोक्ताः पुरा द्विज ।
शुभाऽशुभफलं तासां कथयामि तवाऽग्रतः ॥ १ ॥

carasthirādisañjñā yā daśāḥ proktāḥ purā dvija |
śubhā'śubhaphalaṁ tāsāṁ kathayāmi tavā'grataḥ || 1||

Twice born, I have already taught the calculation of the cara, sthira, etc daśās,
Now I tell about the most important good and bad results.

लग्नादिद्वादशान्तानां भावानां फलकीर्तने ।
तत्तद्राशीशवीर्येण यथायोग्यं प्रयोजयेत् ॥ २ ॥

lagnādidvādaśāntānāṁ bhāvānāṁ phalakīrtane |
tattadrāśīśavīryeṇa yathāyogyaṁ prayojayet || 2||

Speaking of the results of the twelve houses from the various lagnas
caused by the strength of the rāśi lord according to its capability (*yogya*).

बलयुक्ते च राशीशे पूर्णं तस्य तदा फलम् ।
फलं मध्यबले मध्यं बलहीने विपर्ययः ॥ ३ ॥

balayukte ca rāśīśe pūrṇaṁ tasya tadā phalam |
phalaṁ madhybale madhyaṁ balahīne viparyayaḥ || 3||

If the lord of the rāśi is with strength it will give full results,
Medium if with medium strength, and with out strength the reverse.[16]

There are two primary factors to judge the results of the daśā. First the strength and capability of the planets in the rāśi daśā are analyzed. The capability (*yogya*) refers to the natural significations of the planet, the malefic and benefic nature, and the quality of the house lordships.

The natural order of benefic and malefic are utilized: Jupiter, Venus, Mercury, Moon, Sun, Mars, Saturn then Rāhu. The malefic and benefic nature of the signs is based upon their lordships. The malefic/benefic sign and planet relationship will bring about the growth or decrease of the significations of that house. A benefic in the sign will indicate association with people or situations that relate to the significations of that planet. In this

[16] JUS 2.4.14 *svāmibalaphalāni pragvat||*

way, the rāśi daśā containing the Sun could give government punishment if not well placed. With Mars it would give arguments and even lead to court related issues.

The rāśi daśā of Venus or a strong and beneficial seventh lord will increase the likelihood of marriage. Parāśara says the daśā rāśi which has the lords of the fifth, eleventh, tenth, fourth, ninth, or lagneśa will give good results if they are benefics or in own sign.[17] The strength and capacity of the planet will indicate the overall results.

The second primary factor to judge the results of the daśā is the planetary placements *from* the rāśi daśā. Paraśāra says,

यो यो दशाप्रदो राशिस्तस्य रन्ध्रत्रिकोणके ।
पापखेटयुते विप्र तद्दशा दुःखदायिका ॥ ४ ॥

yo yo daśāprado rāśistasya randhratrikoṇake |
pāpakheṭayute vipra taddaśā duḥkhadāyikā || 4||

If the eighth house or trines (fifth and ninth) from the daśā rāśi has
malefic planets that daśā will give suffering (*duḥkha*).

तृतीयषष्ठगे पापे ज्यादिः परिकीर्तितः ।
शुभखेटयुते तत्र जायते च पराजयः ॥ ५ ॥

tṛtīyaṣaṣṭhage pāpe jyādiḥ parikīrtitaḥ |
śubhakheṭayute tatra jāyate ca parājayaḥ || 5||

It is said that malefics in the third and sixth overpower others (victory),
And if benefic planets are there then the native is overcome (defeat).

लाभस्थे च शुभे पापे लाभो भवति निश्चितः ।
यदा दशाप्रदो राशिः शुभखेटयुतो द्विज ॥ ६ ॥

lābhasthe ca śubhe pāpe lābho bhavati niścitaḥ |
yadā daśāprado rāśiḥ śubhakheṭayuto dvija || 6||

Benefics or malefics in the eleventh house will definitely give gains,
As well as a daśā with a benefic planet in the rāśi.

Planets in the daśā rāśi give the primary results to the daśā. If there is a benefic there then everything is interpreted in a better light. Then the houses from that are read as if the daśā rāśi is the lagna. If there is a benefic in the fourth house from the daśā rāśi, there will be good results in the home. Paraśāra says, if there are malefics in the fourth from the daśā rāśi there will be loss of property, home (moving) and pets/livestock (or other products of the land). If that planet is Mars the loss will be due to fire from carelessness. Saturn will give pain in the heart (*hṛdaya-śūla*). Sun will give problems with the government

[17] Bṛhat Parāśara Horā Śāstra, Carādi-daśā-phala-adhyāya, v.66

(*rāja-prakopa*). Rāhu will give all types of losses (*sarva-haraṇa*), and fear of poison/cancer (*viṣa*), and theft (*cora*).[18]

Planets in the ninth will affect dharma and who is guiding you. Planets in the tenth house will affect career, and in the eleventh will affect the success of ventures. Planets in the seventh affect relationship (they can bring one, make one better/worse, or break a marriage). Planets in the fifth can show children or career advancement or growth of students. Planets in the sixth and eighth will give problems according to the significations of planets placed there.[19]

The trines are the support of a house and when there are malefics there, it indicates some issues. The fifth house is mantra; it is what you are constantly repeating to yourself. Malefic there are bad mantras, even things like, "I am not good enough", or "I can't do this". Benefics in the fifth give good results and good mantras. Parāśara says that Rāhu or Ketu in trines to a sign will cause suffering with children, loss of objects, wandering in a foreign land, distress (*kleśa*) or fear at every step.

Generally, malefics give negative results and benefics (or the lord of the sign) will give positive results of the house. Though any planet in the eleventh will give gains, and malefics in the third show accomplishment, while malefics in the sixth can show victory (over the conflict that arises). If the malefics in the third and sixth are weak, then they don't give their results and if they are strong in the third and sixth they give good results. Benefics can make a person spiritual in the third and sixth if they are strong; it is good for spiritual life but not for material life.

Planets that become kendra to daśā rāśi play a greater role during that particular period, and more so during its antardaśā. The Sun in kendra to the daśā rāśi gives new beginnings and the Moon in Kendra gives social support. The udaya lagna in kendra will show a change in character and the ārūḍha lagna in kendra will show a change of image.

The seventh house from the daśā rāśi will show the direction (*gati*) during the daśā. It is what the mind desires and wants. If there is a planet in the seventh from the daśā rāśi its indications will be prominent during that time period. In this way, we are generally reading the houses as an axis of first and seventh.

---

[18] Bṛhat Parāśara Horā Śāstra, Carādi-daśā-phala-adhyāya, v.62-63, see also v.68-71

[19] BPHS, Carādi-daśā-phala-adhyāya, v.60-61, 65-67

Daśā Results

शुभक्षेत्रे हि तद्राशेः शुभं ज्ञेयं दशाफलम् ।
पापयुक्ते शुभक्षेत्रे पूर्वं शुभमसत्परे ॥ ७ ॥

śubhakṣetre hi tadrāśeḥ śubhaṁ jñeyaṁ daśāphalam |
pāpayukte śubhakṣetre pūrvaṁ śubhamasatpare || 7||

A benefic sign is known to give good daśā results,
A malefic in a benefic sign is good at first and bad (*asat*) later on.

पापर्क्षे शुभसंयुक्ते पूर्वं सौख्यं ततोऽशुभम् ।
पापक्षेत्रे पापयुक्ते सा दशा सर्वदुखदा ॥ ८ ॥

pāparkṣe śubhasaṁyukte pūrvaṁ saukhyaṁ tato'śubham |
pāpakṣetre pāpayukte sā daśā sarvadukhadā || 8||

A benefic in a malefic sign will be happy at first and then not good,
A malefic in a malefic sign will always give suffering in the daśā.

शुभक्षेत्रदशा राशौ युक्ते पापशुभैर्द्विज ॥ ९ ॥
पूर्वं कष्टं सुखं पश्चान्निर्विशङ्कं प्रजायते ।
शुभक्षेत्रे शुभं वाच्यं पापर्क्षे त्वशुभं फलम् ॥ १० ॥

śubhakṣetradaśā rāśau yukte pāpaśubhairdvija || 9||
pūrvaṁ kaṣṭaṁ sukhaṁ paścānnirviśaṅkaṁ prajāyate |
śubhakṣetre śubhaṁ vācyaṁ pāparkṣe tvaśubhaṁ phalam || 10||

A benefic sign with both a malefic and a benefic,
without hesitation, will bring forth difficulty at first then happiness afterward.
Benefic signs give good results and malefic (*pāpa*) signs bring misfortune (*aśubha*).

If all indications are beneficial then beneficial circumstances will be present the entire daśā, or the opposite if it is a clearly malefic daśā. A malefic in a benefic house will first give the nature of the house and then the malefic will destroy those significations as the daśā progresses. A benefic in a malefic sign will present good situations that do not retain their beneficial nature.

The natural trend of the rāśi daśā is to give its good results in the beginning. The period of the daśā can be divided into three parts. Beneficial *signs* give their results in the beginning third of the daśā and malefic *signs* give their results towards the end third of the daśā. The middle part of the rāśi daśā will tend to give the results of the rāśi lord. Benefic *planets* will give their results in the beginning of the daśā and malefic *planets* will tend to give their results in the last part of the daśā. Simply put: the good will come in the beginning and the malefic results will be in the end of the rāśi daśā.

Pisces is an exception in that it gives the results of the sign in the middle of the daśā. If there are both benefic and malefic planets in the daśā rāśi, advise the individual to utilize the significations of those benefics in their life. These planets will uplift the individual and help them overcome any problems they may encounter. These are general trends and the antardaśā have the ability to modify the unfolding of these results.

द्वितीये पञ्चमे सौम्ये राजप्रीतिर्जयो ध्रुवम् ।
पापे तत्र गते ज्ञेयमशुभं तद्दशाफलम् ॥ ११ ॥

dvitīye pañcame saumye rājaprītirjayo dhruvam |
pāpe tatra gate jñeyamaśubhaṁ taddaśāphalam || 11||

Benefics in the second and the fifth definitely make one loved by the king and victorious. Malefics gone there are known to give unfavourable daśā results.

चतुर्थे तु शुभं सौख्यमारोग्यं त्वष्टमे शुभे ।
धर्मवृद्धिर्गुरुजनात्सौख्यं च नवमे शुभे ॥ १२ ॥
विपरीते विपर्यासो मिश्रे मिश्रं प्रकीर्तितम् ।

caturthe tu śubhaṁ saukhyamārogyaṁ tvaṣṭame śubhe |
dharmavṛddhirgurujanātsaukhyaṁ ca navame śubhe || 12||
viparīte viparyāso miśre miśraṁ prakīrtitam | 13a |

Benefics in the fourth or eighth house give happiness and health (*arogya*). Benefics in the ninth indicate increase of dharma, and happiness from gurus and people. The opposite will give opposite results and mixed planets will give mixed results.

The fourth and eighth relate to the protection of Mars. Together they show the longevity, health and strength of the immune system (*ojas*). The eighth house is also problems and debts. Benefics in the eighth from daśā rāśi indicate the paying off of debts, while malefics there will increase debts and give all types of things to worry about.

Pāka and Bhoga

पाके भोगे च पापाढ्ये देहपीडा मनोव्यथा ॥ १३ ॥

pāke bhoge ca pāpāḍhye dehapīḍā manovyathā || 13b||

If the pāka and bhoga are malefic there is body pains and mental agitation.

The general effects of the daśā rāśi are judged from the planets in the sign and the nature of the sign lord, and then we can see more particulars. The placement of the lord of the sign is called the *pāka*. It indicates the amount of effort and the use of intelligence within that period of time.

Count as many houses from the daśā rāśi as the pāka has gone, and that will give the *bhoga*; it's the ārūḍha of the daśā rāśi calculated from the pāka.[20] The bhoga rāśi indicates the results from the effort indicated by the pāka. Pāka means to cook and bhoga means to enjoy the fruits, or eat the food. This shows the quality and amount of effort that is put in and the level of results that one achieves during a particular daśā.

The nature and quality of the results are based on the planet's significations, malefic/ benefic nature, lordship and status. The pāka gives better results if it is well placed like a kendra or trine from the lagna. The placement from lagna indicates the nature of the results (2nd-money, 7th-relationship, 10th-work, etc.). Beneficial pāka in the second will make an individual take action to make more money, while a beneficial bhoga in the second results in the accumulation of wealth. Jupiter will give more wealth than Mercury, and an exalted Jupiter will give even more wealth than if just in a friendly sign. If no planet is there see the strength and nature of the sign. A malefic pāka in the second will indicate actions that cause the loss of money, and a malefic bhoga in the second will indicate that financial fruits are lost.

Basically, the lord of a sign has gone to a particular house and therefore gives certain results according to where the lord has gone.[21] If the second house lord has gone to the eighth or twelfth there is loss of money. If the second lord has gone to the fifth or ninth there is good investment and luck with finances. Therefore during the rāśi daśā of the second house the significations will be activated according to the placement of the lord as this is the nature of the house. The bhoga is the ārūḍha of the house, which is the manifestation of that house, and therefore the fruit of the rāśi daśā.

The daśā rāśi and its lord are like the lagna and malefics there will afflict the health and physical nature. Malefics with the ārūḍha of the rāśi daśā will afflict more the mental level during the daśā. In this way, Parāśāra indicates that when the malefics are in both the pāka and the bhoga there is bodily pain (*dehapīḍā*) and mental distress (*manovyathā*).

[20] Bṛhat Parāśara Horā Śāstra , Antaradaśā-adhyāya v.9-12
[21] BPHS, Carādi-daśā-phala-adhyāya, v.51

And therefore, we can also understand that benefics in the pāka give health and benefical actions, while benefics in the bhoga bring happiness accordingly. Paraśāra says,

सप्तमे पाकभोगाभ्यां पापे दारार्तिरीरिता ।
चतुर्थे स्थानहानिः स्यात्पञ्चमे पुत्रपीडनम् ॥ १४ ॥
दशमे कीर्तिहानिः स्यान्नवमे पितृपीडनम् ।

saptame pākabhogābhyāṁ pāpe dārārtirīritā |
caturthe sthānahāniḥ syātpañcame putrapīḍanam || 14||
daśame kīrtihāniḥ syānnavame pitṛpīḍanam |

Pāka and bhoga in the seventh with malefics will bring sickness to the spouse,
or loss of home in the fourth, and pain to the children in the fifth house,
loss of reputation in the tenth, and pain to father in the ninth house.

पाकाद्रुद्रागते पापे पीडा सर्वाप्यबाधिका ॥ १५ ॥
उक्तस्थानगते सौम्ये ततः सौख्यं विनिर्दिशेत् ।
केन्द्रस्थानगते सौम्ये लाभः शत्रुजपप्रदः ॥ १६ ॥

pākādrudrāgate pāpe pīḍā sarvāpyabādhikā || 15||
uktasthānagate saumye tataḥ saukhyaṁ vinirdiśet |
kendrasthānagate saumye lābhaḥ śatrujapapradaḥ || 16||

Pāka gone to the eleventh with malefics gives pain and all types of obstacles,
Benefics in the said houses give happiness.
Benefics in kendra give gains and pacify the enemy.

Transits

जन्मकालग्रहस्थित्या सगोचगग्रहैरपि ।
विचारितैः प्रवक्तव्यं तत्तद्राशिदसाफलम् ॥ १७ ॥

janmakālagrahasthityā sagocagagrahairapi |
vicāritaiḥ pravaktavyaṁ tattadrāśidasāphalam || 17||

The position of planets at the time of birth, as well as the transiting planets are considered before declaring the rāśi daśā results.

The natal planets are factored in with the nature of transits. This is seen two ways: at the time of consultation and at the time the daśā begins. Transits to the daśā rāśi will give more results than average, and those transits can activate indications of the sign. All transits of the chart can be understood according to the houses from the daśā rāśi. For example, Jupiter transiting the daśā rāśi or its second will bring wealth. Rāhu transiting the daśā rāśi hurts the reputation, while in the second from daśā rāśi will create financial losses. The slow moving planets like Jupiter, Rāhu and Saturn are the most important to notice. The Sun will activate already present indications and the other planets will show results of shorter duration. Some use the finer divisions (like the prāṇāntardaśā) of Nārāyaṇa daśā to time when the transit will give its results for things such as exact day of a car accident or meeting of the spouse.

There is a technique called *daśā praveśa*, which means the chart at the moment of entering the daśā. This can be done for all dāśā, but ones like viṁśottarī have too much room for error. The cara daśās are much more likely to be accurate and give good results. In the daśā praveśa, the strength of the lagna, Moon and the rāśi daśānath are all important. The house position of Rāhu at the moment the daśā starts will suffer the entire daśā.

यश्च राशिः शुभाकान्तो यस्य पश्चाच्छुभग्रहाः ।
तद्दशा शुभदा प्रोक्ता विपरीते विपर्ययः ॥ १८ ॥

yaśca rāśiḥ śubhākānto yasya paścācchubhagrahāḥ |
taddaśā śubhadā proktā viparīte viparyayaḥ || 18||

If there is a benefic in the daśā rāśi and a benefic planet after it (*paśca*), then that daśā will give good results. The opposite is said if it is reversed.

त्रिकोणरन्ध्ररिष्फस्थैः शुभपापैः शुभाऽशुभम् ।
तद्दशायां च वक्तव्यं फलं दैवविदा सदा ॥ १९ ॥

trikoṇarandhrariṣphasthaiḥ śubhapāpaiḥ śubhā'śubham |
taddaśāyāṁ ca vaktavyaṁ phalaṁ daivavidā sadā || 19||

Benefics in trines, eighth or twelfth give good results and malefics there give unfortunate results in that daśā and this is always spoken by the astrologer (*daiva-vid*).

उच्चस्वर्क्षग्रहे तस्मिञ्छुभं सौख्यं धनागमः ।
तच्छून्यं चेदसौख्यं स्यात्तद्दशा न फलप्रदा ॥ २२ ॥

uccasvarkṣagrhe tasmiñchubhaṁ saukhyaṁ dhanāgamaḥ |
tacchūnyaṁ cedasaukhyaṁ syāttaddaśā na phalapradā || 22||

A Benefic planet in exaltation or own sign will give happiness and wealth,
while if [the daśā rāśi] is empty, then that daśā will be unhappy and without results.

If nothing is in the rāśi during its daśā there is less excitement. The results will then primarily be analysed on the nature of the sign lord, the pāka and bhoga and the placement of the antardaśā from the rāśi daśā.

Bādhaka

Parāśara gives the calculations for bādhaka-sthāna[22] and indicates that in the rāśi daśā of the *bādhaka-sthāna* or the *bādhakeśa* there will be obscuration, great trouble, (*mahāśoka*), blockage (*bandhana*), and misfortune. Then Parāśara mentions that Rāhu in duḥsthāna or in the bādhakasthāna [from the daśā rāśi] will cause suffering. This indicates to utilize a temporal bhadaka-sthāna, which some say also indicates that there can be a bādhaka-sthāna from each house.

बाधकव्ययषडरन्ध्रे राहुयुक्ते महद्भयम् ।
प्रस्थाने बन्धनप्राप्ती राजपीडा रिपोर्भयम् ॥ २३ ॥

bādhakavyayaṣaḍrandhre rāhuyukte mahadbhayam |
prasthāne bandhanaprāptī rājapīḍā riporbhayam || 23||

If Rāhu occupies the bādhaka-sthāna, twelfth, sixth, or eighth house [from the rāśi daśā],
there will be great danger, or blockage during a journey,
or suffering caused by the government, or fear of enemies during the [rāśi] daśā.

The bādhaka graha will force its results on an individual. Bandhana being caused by argalā or other yogas will also force their results, and be more likely to happen during an antardaśā associated with the bādhaka.

Cursed planets will create situations which result in suffering. Since curses are primarily seen from benefic planets, the circumstances look good at first and then are revealed to be negative, or turn into negative situations. A cursed benefic will give its results though the various rāśi daśā according to the nature of its placement from the rāśi daśā sign.

[22] Carādi-phala-adhyāya, v. 20,21,23; Discussed in its own chapter.

Antardaśā

The antardaśā are interpreted similar to the mahādaśā; see the strength and nature of the antardaśā rāśi and then see the houses *from the antardaśā rāśi*. The only difference is to see the antardaśā signs relative to the daśā sign, not the lagna. For example, Parāśāra says the antardaśā of signs in the duḥsthāna (6, 8, 12) from the daśā rāśi (or signs containing nīca or krūra grahas) will bring about quarrels (*kalaha*), disease (*roga*), danger of death, etc (*mṛtyu-bhayādika*).[23] If the daśā rāśi has a malefic or krūra planet it will be more likely to give results during the antardaśā of a malefic or duḥsthāna.

A benefic antardaśā of an auspicious mahādaśā will give really good results,[24] while a malefic antardaśā of a malefic mahādaśā will activate the negative results. In a malefic antardaśā of a benefic mahādaśā, the time period will start good and then the malefic will give its results.[25] The full results of the mahādaśā will be in the antardaśā of the rāśi/planet that is strongly tied to the daśā rāśi/planet by conjunction or other yoga (*ātmasambandhin*) or by the rāśi/planet that has the same innate nature (*nijasadharmin*) that is being indicated by the mahādaśā. Parāśara says,

रव्यारराहुशनयो भुक्तिराशौ स्थिता यदि ।
तद्राशिभिक्तौ पतनं राजकोपान् महद्भयम् ॥ २४ ॥

ravyārarāhuśanayo bhuktirāśau sthitā yadi |
tadrāśibhiktau patanaṁ rājakopān mahadbhayam || 24||

When Sun, Mars, Rāhu, or Saturn is stationed in the antardaśā rāśi
In those rāśi daśās there will be ruin, anger of the king and emergencies.

भुक्तिराशित्रिकोणे तु नीचखेटः स्थितो यदि ।
तद्राशौ वा युते नीचे पापे मृत्युभयं वदेत् ॥ २५ ॥

bhuktirāśitrikoṇe tu nīcakheṭaḥ sthito yadi |
tadrāśau vā yute nīce pāpe mṛtyubhayaṁ vadet || 25||

The antardaśā of a debilitated planet placed in trine
or conjunct a debilitated or malefic planet will give fear of death.

भुक्तिराशौ स्वतुङ्गस्थे त्रिकोणे वापि खेचरे ।
यदा भुक्तिदशा प्राप्ता तदा सौख्यं लभेन्नरः ॥ २६ ॥

bhuktirāśau svatuṅgasthe trikoṇe vāpi khecare |
yadā bhuktidaśā prāptā tadā saukhyaṁ labhennaraḥ || 26||

A planet in own sign or exaltation in trine from the antardaśā rāśi,
will acquire happiness and gains in that antardaśā,

---

23 Bṛhat Parāśara Horā Śāstra, Carādi-phala-adhyāya, v. 20,21,23; Discussed in its own chapter.
24 BPHS, Carādi-phala-adhyāya, v.12-13
25 BPHS, Carādi-daśā-phala-adhyāya, v.37

नगरग्रामनाथत्वं पुत्रलाभं धनागमम्।
कल्याणं भूरिभाग्यं च सेनपत्यं महोन्नतम्॥ २७॥

nagaragrāmanāthatvaṁ putralābhaṁ dhanāgamam |
kalyāṇaṁ bhūribhāgyaṁ ca senapatyaṁ mahonnatam || 27||

become head of a town or community, gain children, have financial gains, nobility, abundant luck, or become an army commander of high rank.

पाकेश्वरो जीवदृष्टः शुभराशिस्थितो यदि।
तद्दशायां धनप्राप्तिर्मङ्गलं पुत्रसम्भवम्॥ २८॥

pākeśvaro jīvadṛṣṭaḥ śubharāśisthito yadi |
taddaśāyāṁ dhanaprāptirmaṅgalaṁ putrasambhavam || 28||

If the lord of the rāśi daśā is in a benefic sign with the aspect of Jupiter, that daśā has financial gains, auspiciousness, and birth of a child.

The above is the primary techniques to begin to utilize for interpretation, and there are also many ways to fine tune results. Yogas will modify everything.[26] For example, a Mahapuruṣa planet will surely give good results in its rāśi daśā. A viparīta yoga would at first seem to give bad results but will prove beneficial. Also pay attention to the yogas of the lord of the rāśi daśā. In this way, the significations of the yoga will give results, not just the nature of the planets.

Other factors to consider are the effects of avasthās[27] like combustion, planetary war or maraṇa-kāraka-sthāṇa. You can see suffering of the karāka in its rāśi daśā, and you can also see when certain planets enter MKS position for a particular daśā. Also consider special significations like mārakas[28] or deha and jīva.The results of argalā are seen from the daśā rāśi, and can be timed from the rāśi antardaśā.[29] The Pachakādi Sambandha of planets in the daśā rāśi will give their effects to respective houses, planets and ārūḍhas. The aṣṭakavarga of the signs will influence their results.[30] See the sarvāṣṭakavarga of the daśā rāśi for its strength, the individual bindhus a planet is contributing to see the significations in that daśā, and also the aṣṭakavarga of the lord of the daśā rāśi. Generally speaking, a Cara daśā is activating the latent significations in the chart that are already present. Narāyāṇa daśā can be used to help time the fructification of these circumstances and events.

Many examples can be found in *Narāyāṇa Daśā* by Sanjay Rath, and we will only take a brief look at the chart of Albert Einstein. He was a big promoter of pacifism in his Sagittarius mahādaśa, with Jupiter as the rāśi daśā lord being placed in the ninth house. In

[26] Bṛhat Parāśara Horā Śāstra, Carādi-daśā-phala-adhyāya, v.38
[27] BPHS, Carādi-daśā-phala-adhyāya, v.86 (84-87)
[28] BPHS, Carādi-daśā-phala-adhyāya, v.73-77
[29] BPHS, Carādi-daśā-phala-adhyāya, v.43-45
[30] BPHS, Carādi-daśā-phala-adhyāya, v.53-55

his Leo daśā, Hitler became Chancellor. In Leo Sagittarius, running the antardaśā of the bādhaka house and a multitude of planets in the fourth from the antardaśā rāśi, Einstein immigrated to the United States. The bhoga of that daśā is in the eleventh house which contains the Ghaṭī lagna, and the ārūḍha of the ninth house, and at that time he took up a teaching position in Princeton, NJ.

Einstein entered Aries daśa in 1937, with Mars in the tenth house from daśā rāśi but eighth house from the lagna. Einstein did great research but would later wish he did not and called his connection to the atomic bomb the greatest mistake of his life. Mars conjunct Rāhu is a combination for fighting or war. In the antardaśā of Capricorn containing Rāhu and Mars (which support the action of Aries), Einstein wrote a letter to President Roosevelt recommending nuclear research in fear that Germany might build an atomic bomb first. In Aries Leo, Einstein worked for the research and development division of the U.S. Navy.

After the war, Einstein's Pisces daśā began, ruled by Jupiter, and his focus became disarmament for peace. This small use of Narāyāṇa daśā shows how circumstances change and bring about different situations in one's life.

Exercises

2. This is the first quarter of the Carādi-daśā-phala-adhyāya. Read both the Cara daśā chapter (*Carādi-daśā-phāla-adhyāya*) and the Computation of Antardaśā chapter (*Antardaśā-adhyāya*) of Bṛhat Parāśara Horā Śāstra and be familiar with the contents of these chapters.

Varga Nārāyaṇa

One of the best reasons to become proficient in Nārāyaṇa daśā is that it can be used in all varga charts. This will give accurate results for timing properties in the D-4 or work related situations in the D-10. When someone is interested in details about business expansion, change in position, vacations, slow times, or times to start a new business, the D-10 Nārāyaṇa daśā is a wonderful tool. When someone is interested to know about a vehicle, its problems and accidents, see the D-16 Nārāyaṇa daśā. In this way, when you are timing things based on the indications seen in specific houses of the divisional charts the rāśi daśā of that varga chart will give good results. The key is to understand the specific indications of the houses of that division.

There are two variations on calculation. [1] The first variation is to start from the numerically related house lord of the rāśi in that varga, and [2] the second variation is to start the varga daśā from the varga kāraka bhāva. For example, [1] the daśā for the D-9 Nārāyaṇa daśā starts from the rāśi ninth lord placement in the navāṁśa. Or [2] the D-9 Nārāyaṇa daśā starts from the stronger of the ninth house and the third house (first or seventh from the kāraka bhāva). Sanjay Rath advises the first rule.

If you are looking at divisional chart D-*n*, take the nth house (take out multiples of 12 if more than 12). For the D-4 Nārāyaṇa daśā, use the lord of the rāśi fourth house in the D-4 chart to start the daśā. For the D-16 Nārāyaṇa daśā, also use the lord of the rāśi fourth house in the D-16 chart to start the daśā. Take that planet's rāśi as the lagna and see if the first or seventh from that is stronger. All other rules for calculation remain the same. In the case of Einstein, the lord of the tenth house is Jupiter. Jupiter is in Pisces in the fourth house of the daśāṁśa (D-10). Jupiter is conjunct Saturn and there is no planet in the tenth house of the daśāṁśa. Therefore the D-10 Nārāyaṇa daśā begins from Pisces. The Varga Nārāyaṇa daśā can be broken down into antar daśā, pratyantar daśā, sūkṣmāntar daśā, and prāṇa daśā levels and transits can be seen within these levels for very fine tuned prediction.

The house activated gives results according to its significations from the divisional lagna, as well as planetary placements in the rāśi daśā and the strength of the rāśi daśa lord determines the results. The varga Nārāyaṇa daśā will work in the particular area of life under consideration according to the confines of the Nārāyaṇa daśā in the rāśi chart, just as any event in a varga would behave. For example, the Bhaṁśa (D-27) can show the ups and downs of financial status with the D-27 Nārāyaṇa daśā based on the status of the D-27 rāśi daśā and its lord. This financial status will be up and down based upon the confines of the natal chart indications.

The example is of the author's daśāṁśa, since dates and events are known clearly. The author's rāśi tenth lord is Jupiter, which is placed in the tenth house of the daśāṁśa in Pisces. There is no planet in the seventh from it, which makes it the strongest to start the daśā. The first daśā is Pisces for twelve years, as the lord is in the sign itself. The daśā moves zodiacal because the ninth house (Scorpio) is odd footed (*viṣama-pada*), and in trinal motion becase the starting rāśi is dual. This makes the next daśā Cancer (even footed sign) for eleven years. Next is a year long daśā of Scorpio (odd footed sign), since Mars is the stronger lord because it's conjunct a planet. The next daśa is the tenth from that in zodiacal order which is Sagittarius for three years. This is followed by eight years of Aries and eight years of Leo.

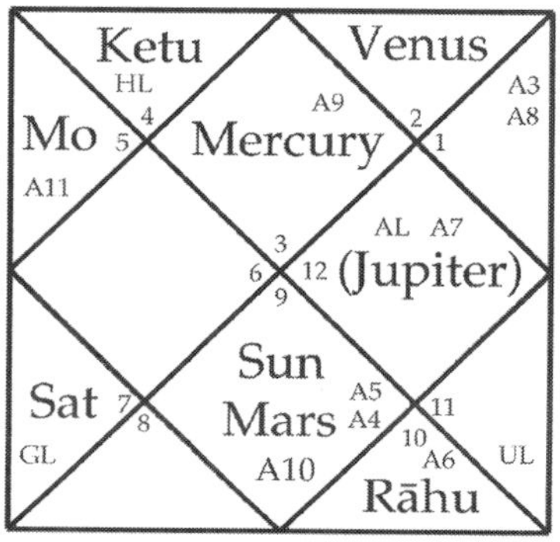

In Aries Virgo, the author bought a home in California which was a place to live, work and teach. In Aries Libra Libra the author took a large business loan (exalted eighth lord) and bought his own development company. Libra as the fifth house indicates change in position, and the author went from working for someone to being the boss of a company. Two malefics in the third house from the daśā rāśi gave a viparita argalā to fuel the endeavour which took a lot of energy. In Scorpio antardaśā (lord in a friendly sign, second from daśā rāśi and in the house of business from lagna), there was hard work and gains; Mars and Sun give a dhana argalā, and Rāhu gives another viparita argalā. Jupiter in the fifth from the daśā rāśi shows there was a large amount of learning at this time. Mercury in the eighth from the daśā rāśi shows the lack of writing that was done at that time.

In Sagittarius antardaśā (lord in own sign and tenth from lagna as well as ninth from daśā rāśi), the business profitted and doubled in size. Jupiter is giving sukha argalā to the daśā rāśi, and the main office was moved to a much nicer location. With Rāhu giving a pāpa argalā, corners were cut and codes were violated to make larger profits. In Capricorn daśā, there were legal disputes (A6 with Rāhu) that severly hurt the business and were complicated by the failing housing economy. Rāhu in Capricorn is tenth from the daśā rāśi so the malefic planet directly hit the business. Aquarius antardaśā continued the legal issues and brought more losses as the lord of the antardaśā, Rāhu, has gone to the twelfth from itself, which is also the eighth from lagna. In Aquarius daśā, the savings of the business were utilized to keep it running indicated by the negative activation of the ārūḍha of the twelfth house of expenses (not marriage in the daśāṁśa). In Pisces antardaśā, with Jupiter in its own sign, the author became a full time astrologer and astrology teacher with no other side businesses. In Aries Aries, which is the eighth from the fourth house, the development business was sold in a break-even deal.

Then Leo daśā began and the Sun as the lord of Leo is in the seventh house with Mars (two planets). There is one planet in the seventh from it, which means that the sign of the Sun is stronger to start the antardaśās. The first daśa of Leo is Sagittarius, with Sun and Mars. At this time the author hired a professional artist to "re-brand" the teaching material and advertisements. A new website was made to make the author's Vedic astrology teachings more accessible to a larger international audience. In this way, when individuals ask about their position in a company or the situation of their business, the D-10 Nārāyaṇa daśā will make it clear why certain events happened in the past and what to predict for the future.

Conclusion

Knowing how and when to use various types of daśā is key to being able to answer any question that an individual may have. Practice makes perfect, and utilizing this daśā everytime you look at a chart will allow you to get how it works.

The rāśi shows us the situations that are presented to us. They are that which happens *to* us, as opposed to a graha daśā which indicates what we perceive and therefore how we react. The rāśi show us what is there, what is to become.

So much of our work is helping people accept who they are. Helping them discover themselves or giving them the support they need to believe in what is already present in them. For example, a woman came asking me about how to be successful at her Yoga teaching. Her chart indicated that she was creative like an actress. She confirmed that she had a Masters in Theatre, but she believed she couldn't make money at it. Her chart indicated fame through acting and when that would happen. So we discussed ways to integrate the self-development of yoga into acting and children's theatre projects that she had set aside because of financial fears. We are who we are, we just have to let ourselves flower. Remove the weeds and create the right circumstances.

A great leader is born to be a great leader and a great actor is born to be a great actor. It is not about predetermination by something other than you. It is about you becoming fully you. It is about following your heart and being yourself fully. We are each born unique with the callings of our heart. Our own soul brings these 'callings' with us into this body.

Chapter 9

Āyurjyotiṣa

"Days and nights are ceaselessly running,
bearing away in their current
the periods of life of all human beings.
Like currents of rivers,
these flow ceaselessly without ever turning back.
The ceaseless succession of the waxing and waning pakṣas
is wasting all mortal creatures
without stopping for even a moment in this work.
Rising and setting day after day, the Sun,
who is himself undecaying,
is continually cooking the joys and sorrows of all men.
The nights are ceaselessly going away,
taking with them the good and bad incidents that befall man."
-Mahābhārata, Śānti Parva CCCXXXII

Āyurjyotiṣa

Āyurjyotiṣa is divided into two branches: kārmik disease (*daiva-cikitsā*) and longevity (*āyurdāya*). The first branch is in the realm of the doctor (*vaidya*) with a strong understanding of the principles of Āyurveda. The second branch belongs to the *kārtāntika*, the astrologer who can calculate the time of death.

I. Daiva-Cikitsā

There are three primary divisions of disease according to their origination: inherent (*ādhyātmika*), external (*ādhibhautika*), and kārmik (*ādhidaivika*). Ādhyātmika relates to that which is an intrinsic disorder of the body or mind. The imbalance of physical doṣas according to the individual constitution relate to this category. Ādhibhautika relates to disorders proceeding from extrinsic causes such as being cut by an inanimate object, hurt in a car accident or war, or attacked by an animal. Ādhidaivika relates to disease which arises due to kārmik debts or spiritual issues.

Daiva means the fate one has earned according to one's karma, and the astrologer is one who can read this previous life karma (*Daivajña*[60]). Cikitsā is medical treatment. To treat a disorder of the body or mind with Vedic astrological remedies is called daiva-cikitsā.

All aspects of Āyurveda can be seen in the astrological chart: the constitution, the imbalances, and the timing of imbalances. These general factors can be treated without looking at a chart, and are the job of the Āyurvedic doctor (*vaidya*) to analyze and treat with herbs, diet and related therapies. There are three areas that astrological analysis becomes necessary: [1] removal of blockages, [2] timing, and [3] kārmik disease.

Occasionally, the Vaidya will prescribe certain lifestyle remedies which the patient is not able to enact due to being stuck in old patterns (kārmik tendencies). Through astrology, these blockages can be removed so that physical therapies can be followed and sustained. The goal is to remove the basic causes of disease (tamas and rajas) which are the result of a lack of sattva.

There are periods of life where disease is more likely; daśās of negatively placed planets, or daśās of malefic planets that are afflicting beneficial factors in life. Remedial measures can be done before disease appears to help prevent it. When a disease has already arisen, astrology can help time when the suffering will come to an end, or when a cure will become possible.

[60] See appendix "Names for Astrologer"

Then there is the area of disease that does not make physical sense, or does not respond to physical or mental treatment. This is because there are kārmik reasons for the disease which need to be corrected before any remedy will be effective. Small children getting cancers or genetically inherited disease are a few types that fit into the category of kārmik disease. These types of disease are the realm of the astrologer.

Basic Causes of Disease

Jyotiṣa focuses on harmonizing what Ācyutānanda calls the *Piṇḍa-Brahmāṇḍa*, which is the individual reflecting the universe. Āyurveda focuses on *Loka-Puruṣa-Sāmya*,[61] which is creating equilibrium (*sāmya*) between the individual (*puruṣa*) and the environment (*loka*).[62] The primary cause of intrinsic disease is lack of harmony between the individual and the environment.

There are three agents which cause this root imbalance: chronobiological influences (*kāla*), intelligence (*buddhi*), and the objects of the senses (*indriyārtha*). These three causative agents relate to the three sāttvika planets: Jupiter, the Sun and the Moon. Disease is therefore caused by the disturbance of the sattva (sustaining) force of the body which imbalances how the individual relates to their environment.

Normal function and interaction of these three agents is important for a healthy balanced life. The harmony of sattva can be disturbed in three ways. Through the nature of rajas (Mercury and Venus) there is excess utilization (*atiyoga*). Through the tamas of Saturn there is lack of utilization (*ayoga*), and through the tamas of Rāhu there is improper utilization (*mithyāyoga*). When the three causative agents malfunction in any of these ways they are called kāla pariṇāma, prajñāparādha, and asātmyendriyārtha.[63] All other causes of intrinsic disease are secondary to these three primary causes.

Kāla Pariṇāma

Kāla Pariṇāma literally means time-transformations, or time-development. It can refer to the changing of the seasons as well as chronobiological changes (aging) in the body. The gross level of kāla pariṇāma relates to the ability of the individual to live appropriately according to the change of the seasons and environment. It relates to the appropriate actions to be performed at the appropriate times of day. It means changing the diet and lifestyle regimes according to the temperature, humidity, and other weather factors to harmonize the imbalances they cause in the individual's body.

[61] Caraka Saṁhitā, Śārīrasthāna, IV.13 and V.2-5 *Loka-Puruṣa-Sāmya* is said to be "how the wise perceive."
[62] In many ways, these terms can be used interchangeably, so the distinction is very minimal.
[63] Caraka Saṁhitā, Śārīrasthānam II.40, 43, 44

Kāla Pariṇāma refers to the integration of lifestyle and therapies that fit the chronological aging of the individual. This chronological aging relates to the naisargika daśā which is similar for all individuals. An infant in its first year has a certain diet, which varies from that of a growing child. The young and active can eat lots of high fat foods (or just about anything) and there are no issues but, as one gets older the metabolism slows down and the diet has to change accordingly. The elderly need a diet that is easy to digest and which supports their slowly decaying condition.

Caraka Saṁhitā says that "Man is caused by Time, and Time determines his diseases. The entire world depends on Time, and Time is the causation of everything (*sarvatra kāraṇam*)."[64] At a subtle level of kāla pariṇam, all the various daśās have their effects on the individual's physical, mental and spiritual health. Certain daśās need astrological remedial measures to insure the health of the individual stays in balance. The daśās of negatively placed planets such as benefics in duḥsthānas or malefics in kendra or trine, or daśās of malefic planets or malefic lords that are afflicting beneficial factors in life, or daśās where the mahādaśā and antardaśā lord are in a six-eight relationship can cause health problems. Negative transits can also cause suffering, cancer, operations, etc. that can be greatly helped with astrological remedial measures.

The Sun is important for the first house significations of health and the body. The body is affected by age, which is ruled by Saturn. In this way, Saturn is the child of the Sun; the Sun is the great time-maker while Saturn is the power of time to age and decay. Saturn is the planet ruling aging and death while the Sun rules life and vitality. They are two opposed forces, one keeping you alive and the other taking you closer to death.

The Sun brings forth the light and ability to perceive the correct way to live according to time. It is the Sun that allows a Jyotiṣī to look into the astrological chart and perceive aspects of a person's life. In the same way, it is the Sun that allows a person to look into their life and see what they need to do to live appropriately for their space and time. The strengthening of the Sun strengthens this ability and the overall health associated with the lagna. The sattva of the Sun helps one to attune to the cycles of time and to live life in harmony with them. One should analyze the condition of the Sun, aspects of malefics and the sixth and eighth lord, the Sun's dispositor, and the condition of the lagna bhāva to give appropriate remedies if needed.

[64] Caraka Saṁhitā, Sūtrasthāna XXV.25, this can be compared to the Kāla Sūkta of the Atharvaveda.

Prajñāparādha

Prajñāparādha is the mistake of the intellect. *Prajñā* is wisdom and understanding. *Aparādha* means a mistake, a wrong, an offense, or a transgression. Prajñāparādha is the inability to listen to the body's natural wisdom or the minds better understanding.

Prajñāparādha is when the person does not follow their own better understanding of their need for healing. Sometimes this will be having knowledge of the correct actions and not following them. For example, when a person knows that large amounts of alcohol are negative to their health but they continue to consume the substance. This includes an individual who continues to smoke tobacco, even though they have friends or family who have died from lung cancer.

In this way, living an unwholesome or dishonest life can lead to disease. Caraka says that righteous acts and living bring happiness and unrighteous acts bring misery to the body and mind which are the seats of disease.[65] Any action creating negative (rajas or tamas) emotions will eventually cause disease. Stress (rajas) is a major cause of disease by its depletion of the immune system (*ojas*), and is in many ways a condition of mental perspective.

Prajñāparādha will also indicate a person not listening to the body's own innate wisdom such as when a person believes that a certain substance is good for them even though their body does not respond well to it. They may continue to use the substance that is not good for their health and actually make themselves sick because they did not listen or were not aware of the body's understanding. For example, a western study said that a glass of alcohol reduces the chance of heart disease. Western studies do not differentiate between constitutions. For a kapha individual, a single class of alcohol with food will improve digestion and therefore improve health. For a pitta individual, it may cause ulcers, skin conditions and other problems related to too much heat. The pitta individual may get symptoms like hyper acidity from the alcohol, but due to Prajñāparādha will ignore these signs of the body and continue to use alcohol believing it is good for them. This example could also be seen with milk; for a vāta constitution it is medicine, while a kapha constitution may develop illness from milk which directly starts with congestion after drinking milk. Prajñāparādha is also seen in a situation such as when the body is stiff or sore from not enough movement, and the individual just takes a pill to cover it up instead of giving the body some healthy movement. Or not getting enough sleep and taking coffee to give the body enough energy to go to work in the morning. The body will always let us know what keeps it healthy, but does the mind listen to the body or follow its own desires. When tamas is very strong the individual is not aware of what the body feels, when rajas is very strong the individual listens to their mind even if the body disagrees.

[65] Caraka Saṁhitā, Śārīrasthānam II.41

This application of intelligence (*dhī śakti*) relates to the planet Jupiter who is the kāraka for the pāka lagna (the position of the lagneśa). How an individual applies their intelligence is seen relative to the pāka lagna. An afflicted or negatively placed lagneśa will show the situation of prajñāparādha. Negative placement, or affliction to lagneśa, as well as bad daśās or negative transits can all lead to living an unhealthy lifestyle and ignoring the innate wisdom.

There is a deeper level to the decisions made by an individual. The soul (*ātmakāraka*) is very important to how we live. If the AK is negatively placed in the navāṁśa it can cause wrong decisions which lead to ill health and even issues that are primarily due to wrong decisions made in our previous lives.

Asātmyendriyārtha

Asātmya means unwholesome or disagreeable. *Indriyārtha* is the object of the senses, as the smell of a rose is to the nose (smell, taste, sight, touch and sound). *Asātmyendriyārtha* is unwholesome contact of the sensory objects which includes excessive use of the senses, lack of use of the senses and wrong use of the senses.

Most sensory addictions are the result of mental issues. The Mind is that which reads the senses, it is fed through the senses. This includes excessive sugar or chocolate intake based on eating addictions. This includes excessive touch addictions which include hyper sexuality. Asātmyendriyārtha includes bad movies with "unhealthy" images for the mind. This would also include situations of war trauma or gang violence related emotional issues.

Just as certain smells have the ability to bring balance to the elements and emotions (as used in aromatherapy), certain smells can create disease. In the modern work place there are machines off-gasing chemicals (such as a photocopier), or cleaning agents that give people migraines, or polishing agents, or glues, that can give stomach aches, headaches, or build up enough toxicity in the body to create liver problems and cancer.

Of the senses, the nose, tongue, and skin function in proximity to its stimuli, while the mind, eyes, and ears function with remoteness.[66] In this way, their utilization will also vary from gross to subtle. Sensory over stimulation can lead to all sorts of vāta related disorders, and can drain the body's natural immunity. Wrong use of the senses imbalance the elements that relate to that particular sense and lead to the associated mental problems. The wrong or unwholesome use of the senses is caused by a lack of sattva and increases that lack of sattva, creating a cycle which leads to ill health.

---

[66] Suśruta Saṁhitā, Śārīrasthānam I.3

The Moon should be analyzed along with the fourth house and the Ārūḍha. The sattva of the Moon needs to be strengthened, and remedies should be of a very sāttvika nature. The yogic practice of pratyāhāra is also beneficial for the overuse of the senses and rejuvenation of the mind and body. When the Moon is weak or afflicted it is very common to have sensory addictions to deal with the associated mental issues. These issues should be understood and dealt with through counselling.

The root cause of intrinsic disease is lack of harmony between the individual and the environment. These are the three agents that will align the individual or misalign the individual with the environment: time (Sun), right use of intelligence (Jupiter) and proper use of the senses (Moon). Understanding the three basic causes of disease will allow a medical astrologer to pinpoint the cause of disease and give a general remedy to help balance the tamas or rajas at the root. This will allow an individual to integrate the therapy and lifestyle changes recommended by the Vaidya. If an individual is sick because of an addiction to the wrong use of the senses, they may be told to stop, but without strengthening the Moon it will be very difficult. With the addition of mantras or other sāttvika remedies, the Vaidya is able to remove the root cause of the disorder. Then treatment is applied to the manifestation of the disease and it is treated from both ends.

Buddhi	Use of Intelligence	Lagneśa	Hare
Kāla	Proper Time	Sun	Rāma
Indriyārtha	Use of the Senses	Moon	Kṛṣṇa

In the Śrī Acyutānanda Paramparā, the mantra *Hare Rāma Kṛṣṇa* and its variations are used to strengthen the three pillars of life: Jupiter, the Sun and Moon. By strengthening the three sāttvika planets, the whole life becomes more balanced. In ancient Vedic ritual these three were worshipped as Indra, Agni and Soma (known as the adhidevatās of Jupiter, Sun and Moon).

Caraka Saṁhitā says, "A man who's thoughts, speech and actions are done with good intention (*sukhānubandha*), who is established in sattva (*sattvaṁ vidheyaṁ*), has clarity of judgement (*viśadā buddhi*), knowledge (*jñāna*), is devoted to penance (*tapas-tatpara*), and meditation does not come down with disease".[67]

[67] Caraka Saṁhitā, Śārīrasthānam II.47

Components of Āyurveda

It is not possible to teach Āyurveda here, but a few simple concepts should be understood by every Jyotiṣī. Caraka says that the understanding of the nature of the body provides the knowledge regarding the factors which are responsible for its wellbeing[68]. Here we will become familiar with a few Āyurvedic principles like the source texts and branches of Āyurveda, the three doṣas and their twenty attributes, Agni, Āma and Ojas, pathology and timing disease. Then a look at the various subtle levels of our being and disease. This is just a brief introduction to basic Āyurvedic principles so that one can begin to think about health from a Vedic perspective and not a western mechanical perspective.

Āyurveda

There are three primary Āyurvedic texts called the 'Great Trio' (*bṛhattrayi*), which are are studied by Āyurvedic physicians. They are called *Caraka-saṁhitā* by Agniveśa (and redacted by Caraka), *Suśruta-saṁhitā* of Suśruta, and the *Aṣṭāṅga-Hṛdaya* by Vāgbhaṭa. Each contain 120 chapters relating to the years of a full span of longevity.

There are eight traditional branches of Āyurveda. The first is *Kāyacikitsā* which is treatment of the body (called internal medicine). The second is *Śālākya* which is treatment of head and neck diseases. *Śalyāprahartṛka* is the extraction of foreign bodies through surgery. Āyurveda has utilized surgery for hundreds of years and fully supports surgery when it is needed. The astrologer should be able to give a beneficial time for surgery to be successful. The fourth branch is *Viṣagara-vairodhika-praśamana* which is the treatment of conditions caused by poisons (antidotes) or which utilize poisons as medicine. *Bhūta-vidyā* is literally the 'science of *has-beens*', which relates to psychology and the mental problems caused by unhealthy past-thought (subconscious issues) and troubles from spirits (past away beings) and their possession. This topic is discussed in the chapter of bhādhaka. The sixth branch is *Kaumāra-bhṛtya* which is the care of the pregnancy, birth and treatment of children. *Rasāyana* is the science of rejuvenation and removing the weaknesses or troubles of old age (geriatrics) and support of the immune system. The eighth branch is called *Vājikaraṇa* which is focused in the maintenance of sexual health; vitality in men and fertility in women. Internal medicine (*Kāyacikitsā*) is the standard form of Āyurveda learned and discussed by general practitioners and astrologers.

[68] Caraka Saṁhitā, Śārīrasthānam VI.3

Tri-Doṣa

From a Vedic perspective, the body is not made of chemicals; it is made of the five elements which are analyzed as the three doṣas in the body's functioning. The biological components are called doṣas (problems or faults) because they become vitiated and vitiate each other. When the elements function in the body they can be classified into three doṣas, vāta, pitta and kapha, according to their functioning and the problems they cause. The Vedas say we are made by mother Earth and father Sky; the pṛthvī tattva is the vessel which contains all the other elements, and ākāśa is that space in which they interact. Vāta is composed primarily of air, pitta is composed primarily of fire with a small amount of water, and kapha is water. Small details vary about the tri-doṣas between Caraka, Suśruta, and Vāgbhaṭa, but the general theory is the same.[69]

The three doṣas can be understood as conceptual constructs to explain human physiology. Vāta controls the transportation of substances in the body, all its motions and sustains all organs of the body (through prāṇa, udāna, samāna, apāna and vyāna). Pitta is concerned with the processes of conversion, consumption, and other chemical processes happening in the living body. Kapha maintains the body-fluid, controls growth and durability of the body.

Some have tried to relate the doṣas to physiological substances (like pitta and bile) but the authorities disagree as the doṣas are biological factors that have been grouped by function into three categories and are not restricted to gross substances. The bio-chemicals of the body are the agents of the doṣas and act according to them.[70] Pitta governs conversion

Doṣa	**Vāta**	**Pitta**	**Kapha**
Tattva	Vāyu	Agni *and Jala*	Jala
Seated in the body	Seated in the large intestines	Seated in the small intestines	Seated in the stomach
Associated organs	urinary bladder, kidney, brain & nervous system	liver, gall bladder, spleen, heart, uterus	lungs, pancreas, testes, breasts
Periods of Increase	Increases in old age, last period of the day and night, final stage of digestion	Increases in mid-life, midday and midnight and while food is under digestion	Increases in childhood, morning and early hours of the night,
Normal function	In a normal state gives enthusiasm, inspiration, expiration, movements, normal metabolism, proper elimination of toxins.	In a normal state gives good vision, good digestion, normal temperature, normal appetite and thirst, bodily softness and luster, happiness and intelligence.	In a normal state gives unctuousness, cohesion, steadiness, heaviness, virility, strength, forbearance and patience.
Attributes	Dry, cold, light, subtle, mobile, clear, rough	Unctuous, hot, sharp, flowing, acidic (*amla*), fluid (*sara*), pungent (*katu*)	Heavy, cold, soft, unctuous, sweet (*madhu*), static, cloudy

[69] Valiathan, M.S. *The Legacy of Caraka*, p.liv
[70] Rao, Dr. Namburi, *Pañcabhūta Theory*, p.21

and consumption and therefore relates to the digestion in the stomach (and all associated chemicals and hormones), as well as the digestion of light on the skin (and the associated chemicals which change the skin color). Pitta also relates to the eye and the digestion of images by the mind. In this way, pitta is not associated with a gross substance but a function of the fire element within the body.

Constitution: Prakṛti

The planets relate to the doṣas of the body.[71] Sun and Mars and Ketu are pitta, and the Sun is said to be drier than Mars. Jupiter is kapha, and Saturn and Rāhu are vāta. Venus is kapha-vāta and will give a body with thin aspects and voluptuous part as the ideal model. The Moon will be either more vāta while new or more kapha while full. Mercury is tri-doṣik (composed of all three doṣas) and therefore gives disease where all three doṣas are out of balance (*sannipata*), which makes it harder to cure. There is a difference between the problem (*doṣa*) and the constitution (*prakṛti*). The constitution is the most likely doṣa to be aggravated by lifestyle. But the planet causing disease will indicate the doṣa of the disease an individual will suffer.[72]

Sun	Pitta
Moon	Vāta-Kapha
Mars	Pitta
Mercury	VPK
Jupiter	Kapha
Venus	Kapha-Vāta
Saturn	Vāta
Rāhu	Vāta

There is often a misunderstanding between ākāśa and vāta.[73] Caraka says that while earth gives the form of an individual, ākāśa is all the hollows/channels (*suṣirāṇi*) of the body, and vāyu is the prāṇa moving through those channels.[74] Ākāśa is evenly permeated through all the doṣas, tissues, and organs. It holds them all together, and allows them to work harmoniously together. Jupiter is ākāśa in nature but he is kapha in doṣa, as the ākāśa is attractive and it holds; it is not a more spread out form of vāyu. Ākāśa holds things together, it has great memory (ākāśik records) and large body mass.

Vāta is vāyu and these two words are used interchangeably by Caraka. In the chapter on vāta, he praises the Wind god (*Vāyu*) as the lord responsible for our actions and thoughts, creating happiness or suffering, he is death (*Mṛtyu*), the lord of death (*Yama*), the lord of creatures (*Prajāpati*), the creatrix (*Aditi*) and the creator (*Viśvakarma*).[75] These significations of Vāyu relate to Saturn. Caraka teaches that one must understand Vāyu at a deeper level in order to forewarn their patients of its disastrous effects when it causes disease.

[71] Bṛhat Parāśara Horā Śāstra, Graha-guṇa-svarūpa-adhyāya v.23-29, Yavanajātaka 1.113, Bṛhajjātaka 2.8-11, Sārāvalī 4.21-27, Phala Dīpikā 2.8-14, and Praśna Mārga XI.3

[72] Praśna Mārga, XII.29

[73] Aṣṭāṅga Saṅgraha (Sūtrasthāna 20.1-3), which is a later text, states that Vāta is composed of ākāśa and vāyu. This is not taught by Caraka.

[74] Caraka Saṁhitā, Śārīrasthānam V.5

[75] Caraka Saṁhitā, Sūtrasthāna XII

The five elements exist in all substances but one will predominate to give its results. The three doṣas exist in all living things but one will often become predominant. The innate amounts of predominance of the doṣas in a human at birth is called the prakṛti (constitution). There is no prakṛti better than another, just the ability to live in balance with one's individual constitution.

An Āyurvedic doctor understands the prakṛti from examination of the individual. The astrologer will determine the prakṛti according to the planets influencing the lagna, and confirm through questions if the consultation is not in person.[76] Rāśi aspects are very important for determining the prakṛti, and a strong planet will influence more than weak planets. Powerful yogas influencing the lagna will also influence the constitution of the individual, but they must be strong yogas, not just good yogas. In this way, negative yogas (such as a new Moon) will also influence the constitution.

Vikṛti is the modifications (imbalances) that happen to the root constitution. This will change according to transits and daśā. In general, a vāta prakṛti will more easily get vāta imbalances but it is possible for them to get pitta or kapha imbalances (*vikṛti*) as well. A kapha constitution is more prone to kapha imbalances but can also get vāta problems. For example, the transits of Saturn through the lagna will be more difficult on health for a vāta constitution, while for a kapha constitution there will not be the same level of vāta imbalance.

Vāta causes the most diseases, pitta next and kapha causes the least amount of disease. This is indicated by the greatest malefics being vāta constitution, the secondary malefics being pitta and most benefics containing some kapha. An Āyurvedic doctor is trained to tell the difference between prakṛti and vikṛti. The attributes of the doṣas in the body should be well understood for a holistic treatment.[77]

[76] For long term treatment of serious disorders one should consult a physician in person.

[77] See Sārāvalī 38.16-21 where he first explains guṇas, then elements, then doṣas. One must also be familiar with the Āyurvedic literature.

The Qualities of the Doṣas in an Individual Constitution		
Vāta	**Pitta**	**Kapha**
Tall or short frame, thin, prominent joints and veins	Medium build, developed muscles	Large, wide frame, stocky, heavy, easily puts on weight
Skin is cold, dry, cracked	Skin is warm, moist, has color, freckles, acne, skin irritations	Skin is white or pale, thick, moist, soft
Head is thin, forehead small, features tend to be small and thin	Moderate head, sharp angular features	Large head, wide forehead, rounded soft features,
Thin eyebrows, small unsteady eyes	Eyes tend to have some color, easily inflamed, piercing, sensitive to light	Bushy eyebrows, thick eyelashes, wide attractive round eyes
Small, crooked teeth	gums bleed easily	Large, thick, white teeth
Joints small and cracking	Loose and flexible joints	Large, well built joints
Variable appetite, variable thirst	Excessive, unbearable appetite and thirst	Slow but steady appetite, scanty thirst
Scanty urine, difficult to discharge, colorless, frothy	Profuse urine, yellow, easily gets infections	Moderate urination
Feces is dry, hard, tends toward constipation	Feces is loose, yellowish, tends towards diarrhea, excess pitta creates a burning sensation	Moderate, solid, excess kapha creates mucus in the stool
Minimal sweat, no smell	Profuse sweating, strong odor	Moderate sweating, pleasant smell
Quick, fast, hyperactive, has a hard time sitting still	Motivated, goal setting, concerned with purpose	Slow but steady, can be lazy
Talkative, fast speech	Argumentative, convincing	Good tone, not talkative
Learns quickly, forgets quickly, indecisive, into trivia, wide but general knowledge, restless	Intelligent, critical, sharp and clear memory, deep knowledge in area of interest, aggressive	Slow thinking, slow learning but once known doesn't forget, calm and content
Fearful, anxious, nervous, insecure, unpredictable, ungrounded, spiteful	Angry, irritable, frustrated, jealous, aggressive, fearless	Greedy, attached, sentimental,
Dreams are fearful, flying, jumping, running, restless, nightmares, movement	Dreams are colorful, fiery, violent, bloody, passionate, and have conflict, competition, etc.	Dreams are watery, with shells or lilies, sentimental, emotional, and the sleep is heavy
Poor immune system strength	Medium immunity, prone to infections	Strong immunity
Tend to : Nervous systems diseases, pain, arthritis, degenerative diseases, hysteria, anxiety, insomnia, trembling	Tend to: Infections, inflammatory diseases, skin problems, hyperacidity, heartburn, rage, tantrums	Tend to: Respiratory diseases, congestion, edema, diabetes, sorrow, lethargy

The Twenty Attributes

In Āyurveda, there are twenty attributes that are used to understand the nature of substances.[78] Vāta, pitta and kapha are understood according to the twenty attributes. Caraka does not define the doṣas according to the five elements; he defines them according to these twenty attributes. He then states that the opposite attribute brings harmony to the doṣa.[79] These attributes will apply to metals, gemstones and mantras as well as food and herbs.

Āyurvedic treatment is based upon balancing with the opposite quality; if there is too much heat then give cold, too much dry then give wet. Too much dull then give sharp. The human being is in constant interaction with the environment around them. As the individual (*ahaṅkāra*) may see itself as a different entity than its environment, the human body and mind is affected by its food, environment, and life cycles making it not separate from the environment. The exchange between the individual and the environment follows the law of homologous or similars (*sāmānya*) and heterologous or opposites (*viṣesa*). Like increases like, and opposites create balance. Basic treatment consists of restoring the balance of pañca-mahābhūtas in the body and mind, and the harmony in the relationship between the individual and the loka.

Cold (śīta)	Hot (*uṣṇa*)
Unctuos (*snigdha*)	Dry (*rūkṣa*)
Heavy (*guru*)	Light (*laghu*)
Gross (*sthūla*)	Subtle (*sūkṣma*)
Dense (sāndra)	Flowing (*drava*)
Static (*sthira*)	Mobile (*cala*)
Dull (*manda*)	Sharp (*tīkṣṇa*)
Soft (*mṛdu*)	Hard (*kaṭhina*)
Smooth (*ślakṣṇa*)	Rough (*khara*)
Coudy (*picchila*)	Clear (*viśada*)

Vāta	Dry, cold, light, subtle, mobile, clear, rough
Pitta	Unctuous, hot, sharp, flowing, acidic (*amla*), fluid (*sara*), pungent (*katu*)
Kapha	Heavy, cold, soft, unctuous, sweet (*madhu*), static, cloudy

Āyurveda has no practice that is good for everyone. It is about individualizing and teaching the individual to get in tune with what is good for their constitution. A person who is primarily pitta with some secondary vāta will need to eat differently than an individual who is kapha. It takes an expansion of awareness for an individual to be aware of the factors around them which increase or decrease the doṣas. An Āyurvedic doctor does not just prescribe medicine, but teaches an individual about how to be in balance with their environment, food and time so they make the correct choices in life for their long term health.

[78] Caraka Saṁhitā, Sūtrasthāna XXVI.10-11, Śārīrasthānam VI.10
[79] Caraka Saṁhitā, Sūtrasthāna I.59-63 (see chart)

Agni

Disease relates to Virgo (natural 6th house) because it is generally associated with the intestines and the entire digestive system. In Āyurveda, disease is based on the digestive system and Agni (the digestive fire). Agni is the key to health. In Jyotiṣa, Mars is called the general who regulates the health of the body and protects it from disease. If the Agni is strong then no toxins can enter the body, there is no toxic build up in the body, the mind and senses are clear and the individual possesses the energy to change the lifestyle in a positive direction. Internal disease starts from the digestive system.

Toxins are called Āma and are primarily caused by improper digestion, undigested toxins, or improperly developed rasa[80] caused by diminished Agni prone to produce pathological syndromes. Āma is associated with Rāhu and Saturn, and toxic build up caused by Rāhu and Saturn leads to disease. Āma is not a doṣa, it is foreign to the body. It is improperly developed rasa, therefore its formation is based on the strength of the Agni in the body. A simple way to remove Āma is through drinking hot water, the water strengthens rasa (lymph and blood) while the heat strengthens the digestive Agni (Mars). By sipping hot water one strengthens the Agni. In severe cases, Āyurvedic purifications are performned to remove the toxins from the body before other medications are given.

Ojas is the immunity, the glow to the aura, and the prime energy reserve of the body. Ojas and Āma are opposites, when there are toxins the Ojas is less, when the Agni is strengthened and the toxins removed the Ojas increases. By increasing the Agni and Ojas the body's natural immunity is strengthened.

As digestion is very important, there is large emphasis placed on the types and quality of food one eats. Wholesome food causes the growth of healthy bodies and unwholesome food for the growth of disease. The quality of food an individual eats is based upon the second house and planets placed there. The guṇa of a daśā will also highly influence the quality of food an individual eats.

Wholesome food is that which maintains the equilibrium of the doṣas and helps eliminate their disturbance.[81] There is also a mental component. Caraka Saṁhitā says that even wholesome food creates toxins in the body when eaten while feeling anger, confusion, envy, grief, anxiety, sorrow, etc.[82] Detailed knowledge of *how* to eat is given by Caraka,[83] such as that food should be eaten in a pleasant place and not in a hurry.

80 The product arrived at from the digested food transported by the blood to nourish the body.
81 Caraka Saṁhitā, Sūtraasthāna XXV.30-34
82 Caraka Saṁhitā, Vimānasthāna 2.9
83 Caraka Saṁhitā, Vimānasthāna 1. 24-25

Āyurveda teaches that the body has its own natural resistance or immunity (*vyādhikṣamatva*) which needs to be supported. This relates to the two gurus of the sky, Venus and Jupiter who support the health and immunity (*ojas*) of the body and mind. Jupiter and Venus well placed and unafflicted in the rāśi give the body strong natural immunity. The strength and support of these two planets is important for the body to remain healthy or overcome disease and are therefore the primary astrological remedies for disease. In this way, it is not just about fighting disease, but about making the body healthy enough to have its own resistance to fight disease.

Natural disease resistance based on past life karma will be seen in the fourth house of the navāṁśa. Benefics in the navāṁśa fourth house give a strong natural resistance while malefics will indicate the person gets sick easily and often. The fourth from Moon can be seen similarly as it brings the cure to disorder and any malefics there will be a blockage to getting proper treatment.

Āyurveda teaches that the body is inherently endowed with its own power to heal itself (*svabhāvoparamavāda*). This can be seen in a river that is polluted; nature will clean up the river itself washing away all the debris if people would just stop polluting it. In this way Āyurvedic medicine aims to assist nature and the body's natural ability to heal itself when disease causing factors are removed. When an immune system is fighting itself allopathic medicine has tried to fight the immune system to stop it, but Āyurveda would look more for the reason the immune system is fighting and work to support the body in what it is doing to protect itself. By strengthening the Agni and increasing Ojas the body will begin to heal itself.

It is important to understand Āyurvedic philosophy when looking at health in the astrological chart. The weaknesses and strengths, transits and daśās are reflecting the moving of the elements in the body and the resulting disease caused through the elements. To use a western bio-mechanical perspective is to miss the beauty that the sciences of Jyotiṣa and Āyurveda offer. At the same time, Āyurveda is big enough to integrate western medicine into itself. Āyurvedic medicine does not have to be an herb, for centuries physicians have used all types of chemicals in medicine. In order to apply a chemical medicine in an Āyurvedic way would be to take into account its elemental attributes and to use it to support the body's natural ability to heal, not just stop the manifest problem.

Dhātus

The body is made of seven dhātus which relate to the seven physical planets.[84] The correlations all have various symbolisms. For example, the Sun is the dharma which supports the world, like the bones giving structure and support to the body. Caraka mentions that there are 360 bones at birth (the degrees of the zodiac). There are 54 bones in both hands (the navāṁśas in an ayana). There are 30 bones in an arm or leg which relate to the maximum longevity (30 X 4= 120). There are 27 bones in the spine and 28 bones in the skull relating to the two systems of nakṣatras.[85] In this way the bones relate to the divisions of time just like the Sun. Mars is an Army general and controls everything like the nervous system controls the body. Those who have strong "nerve" have a strong Mars. In this way, the physical *and* psychological characteristics of the dhātus relate to the planets, and any issues will show up on both the physical and psychological levels.

When the planet lording the dhātu becomes weak, afflicted or cursed then there are problems in that associated tissue.[86] The doṣas will locate themselves within a dhātu and create ill health. In this way, the astrologer must understand the doṣa causing the problem, the place in the body, and the dhātu that has become the site of disease. For a simplified example, Mars in Libra afflicting Mercury can cause excess pitta in the rasa dhātu which causes skin irritation (rashes) in the genital area. Caraka says that even if a physician doesn't know the name of a disease, it can still be treated by understanding the symptoms/doṣas, site of manifestation and pathology.

	Dhātu	**Tissue**	**Upadhātus**	**Mala (waste)**
Mercury	Rasa	Lymph (rules taste)	Top layer of skin, lactation, mentruation	Kapha
Moon	Rakta	Blood	Blood vessels & tendons	Pitta (bile)
Saturn	Māmsa	Muscle	Skin, ligaments, subcutaneous fat	Earwax, sebaceous secretions
Jupiter	Meda	Fat, adipose tissue	Flat muscles, sinews, tendons, the omentum,	Sweat
Sun	Asthi	Bone (& cartilage)	Teeth	Nails & hair
Mars	Majjā	Nerve, marrow	sclerotic fluid in eyes, tears	Tears & eye secretions
Venus	Śukra	Reproductive	Ojas	Smegma

[84] Bṛhat Parāśara Horā Śāstra, Graha-guṇa-svarūpa-adhyāya v.31, Yavanajātaka 1.123-136, Varāhamihira's Bṛhat Jātaka 2.11, JātakaPārijāta 2.28, Phala Dīpikā 2.8-14, and Praśna Mārga, XI.3

[85] Modern medicine lists 350 bones at birth, and only 26 bones in the spine (though the sacrum is 5 bones which are fused with age and the coccyx is 4 or 5 bones which also become fused).

[86] Praśna Mārga (XI.6-7) says if the eighth house is not occupied by any planet then disease is due to the dhātu and doṣa indicated by the eighth lord or the lord of the 22nd drekkāṇa.

The upadhātus and malas can help give additional information for diagnosis. For example, if there is a problem with the bones the nails will become brittle. The Sun is also associated with balding, and here, hair is seen as an upadhātu related the Sun.

With a further study of Āyurveda, one can properly diagnose imbalances and recommend physical remedies such as treatments, purifications, and herbal medicines. But even if one is not going to be a physician, the study of Āyurveda will deepen one's ability to see health properly in the birth chart, and will allow one to live a more harmonious life.

Nidāna: Āyurvedic Pathology

Disease relates to the natural 6th house because it is associated with the digestive system. In Āyurveda, disease is based on the digestive system as the three doṣas are seated in specific places in the the digestive tract. Kapha is seated in the stomach, pitta is seated in the small intestines, and vāta is seated in the large intestine.

1	Doṣa-sañcaya	accumulation
2	Prakopa	aggravation
3	Prasara	dissemination
4	Sthāna-saṁśraya	localization
5	Vyakti	manifestation
6	Bheda	explosion

Pathogenesis has six consecutive stages: accumulation (*doṣa-sañcaya*), aggravation (*prakopa*), dissemination (*prasara*), localization (*sthāna-saṁśraya*), manifestation (*vyakti*), and explosion (*bheda*). Pathogenesis starts with excess doṣa accumulating in the site of manifestation (in the digestive system). When it becomes too much it becomes aggravated and leaves its seat (dissemination). The excess doṣa travels though the channels (*srotas*) and localizes itself in a particular weak tissue or organ. The weakest part of the body is often the placement of the 6th or 8th lord or a place damaged by a malefic. And the weak tissue is indicated by the weak or afflicted planets.

In this fourth stage the first syptoms become noticed (*pūrvarūpa*), as when a person knows a cold is coming on but has not gotten it yet. Then the stage of manifestation in which an actual disease/disorder is named. The final stage is when the disease deepens as a cold can become pneumonia by going deeper into the lungs and becomes more severe and harder to cure. The final level of disease is bheda, which means blossoming, bursting forth, bursting asunder, breaking, injury, disturbance change, and alteration. This is the level where the disease blossoms into its full effects, for example, where arthritis would cripple a person so they cannot walk. It disturbs the normal activity and alters the normal functions of the healthy body.

Saturn and Mars aspecting a planet curse it and aspecting a house damage the significations of that house. Saturn and Mars together are called Yama yoga (the combination of the lord of Death). Their joint aspect hurts the health significations of a house. The portion of the body suffering from this is seen from the Moon.

A more advanced principle, is that Saturn is detrimental to the Sun and Mars is very detrimental to the Moon. And accordingly, Saturn afflicts health in trines to it and Mars afflicts the kendras to it. The houses that are both in kendra to Mars and in koṇa to Saturn will also have health challenges. The severity weakness is seen according to the types of combinations, strengths of the planets, kārakas and houses, as well as the daśā.

Understanding the weak planets and houses, afflicted planets and houses and then the planets involved in created the disorders is the key to understanding the root pathology. When the root is understood, then the disease can be treated on the physical, mental and spiritual level. Medicines can be given, the mental patterns can be addressed, and the kārmik remedies (mantras, pūjās, and donation) can be recommended. Mantras can bring harmony and raise frequencies, gemstones can strengthen dhātus or organ systems, and donation can balance karma.

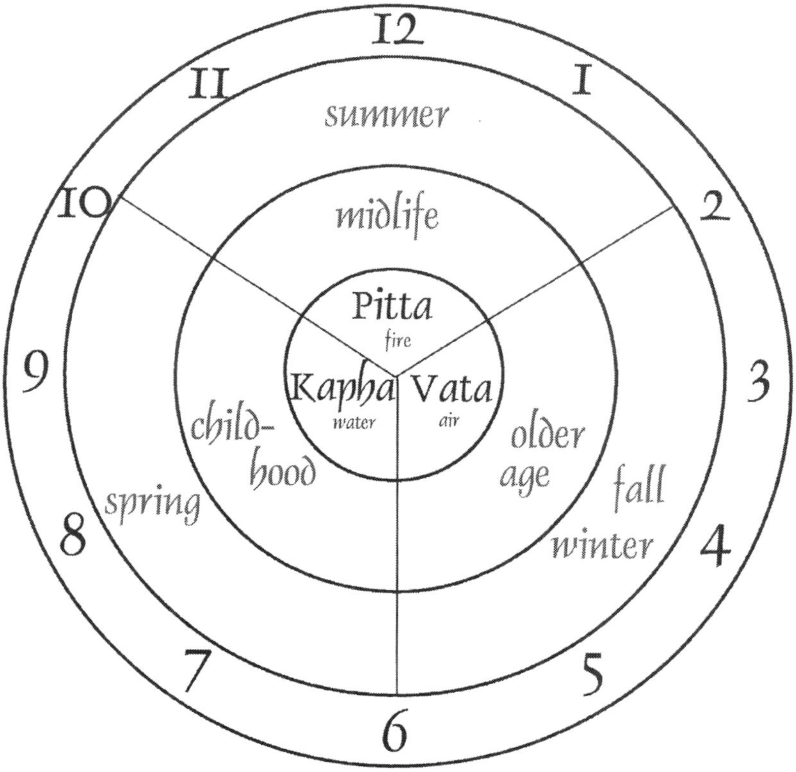

Timing Disease

The *Mahābhārata* says that even physicians who are well-skilled and well-versed in their scriptures and well-equipped with excellent medicines, are themselves afflicted by disease like animals assailed by hunters. As larger animals attack smaller ones, ailments are seen to afflict even invincible kings with fierce energy.[87] Malefic planets are in every chart, it is just a matter of where and when they will afflict us.

In the Rāśi, planets in favourable houses give good health, and planets in bad houses give ill health. This means that benefics do best in kendra or trines, and malefics do best in 3, 6, 8 and 12 to give good health (and therefore longevity). It is even said that malefics in any house other than the third or eleventh will eventually cause a disease.[88] When planets are in negative places and inimical to the lagna, they will bring disease.

Praśna Mārga (XIV.49) states that when Saturn or the 8th lord from a house transits the house, and at the same time the active daśā is of the 6th, 8th, or 12th lord, then the house will come to grief or diseases of the body associated with the house will come to pass. Planets placed in or aspecting the eighth house will also indicate disease during their time period. The disease will relate to the planet in the eighth or having an aspect on it.[89] In this way, transits and daśā are utilized together in order to predict disease and its cause. One should study many examples, to understand the applications of these techniques.

Ṣaṣṭāṁśa (Kaulakas)

The Ṣaṣṭāṁśa is taught by Jaimini (3.3.59-129) and is used to fine tune disease after it is seen in the rāśi.[90] The drekkāṇa divides the body into third portions (10°) to indicate specific areas of the body. Those thirds are divided in half (5°) which makes six kaulakas in a sign.

The kaulakas are calculated direct in odd signs and in reverse for even signs. So if the Sun is in 9° Aries it is in the second kaulaka, while if it is in 9° Taurus it is in the fifth kaulaka.[91] Āyurveda divides the origin of disease into proximate/near (*sannikṛṣṭa*) and distal/from afar (*viprakṛṣṭa*), and into extrinsic/outside (*bāhya*) and intrinsic/from within (*ābhyantara*). The odd kaulakas indicate disease of internal origin, while the even kaulakas indicate disease of external origin. For example, if the Sun was damaging the

---

[87] Mahābhārata, Śanti Parva CCCXXXII

[88] Praśna Mārga, XII.77. The combinations for long and short life given by Parāśara can be studied with these concepts in mind.

[89] Phala Dīpikā14.1-9

[90] A complete study is given by G.K. Goel in his article "Kaulaka (Shastamsa)" in the text *Varga Chakra* edited by Sanjay Rath. This is only a very general outline to begin the study of this divisional chart.

[91] Rāhu and Ketu are calculated in reverse (3.3.66), so Rāhu in 9° degrees Aries is in the fifth kaulaka.

region of the head and it was in an odd kaulaka the indication is a brain problem, while if the Sun was in an even kaulaka it could be a hair problem.

The ṣaṣṭāṁśa can also be studied independently to understand pathology. One can use viṁśottarī daśā to see malefics (or disease causing planets). These planets in the trines to the sixth house of the ṣaṣṭāṁśa indicate disease that is arising from problems with the digestion. Malefics in trine to the eleventh indicate disease from unknown causes (such as bādhaka). Malefics in trines to the ninth indicate diseases that are understood and diagnosed, while trines to the twelfth indicate that the disease is undiagnosed or has supernatural pathology.

The ṣaṣṭāṁśa has its own daśās called the paryāya daśās. In this daśā, the sixth and the eleventh house (6th from the 6th) indicate problems. The second house indicates death, and malefics in the second or eighth can give disease or early death. Though the ātmakāraka must also be under affliction to give disease or death. There is also a method to see the health and death of all relatives using the kaulakas, the carakārakas and this daśā.

Āyurvedic Remedy

Āyurvedic cure is based on śodhana, the purification of the of the excess doṣa through processes like pañcakarma. The excess doṣa is removed from the seat where the disorder began. Then śamana, the pacification of the disturbed doṣa by herbs, lifestyle, etc. Treatment is done at the root level of the disease, as well as treatment of the actual disorder. This wholistic approach is the foundation of Āyurvedic treatment. It insures the initial stage of accumulation is removed with the disorder so that the disease will not return and other disease will not arise. When disease is caused by lack of energy or strength of the body then rejuvenation (*rasāyana*) therapy is done to enliven the body._

There are many discernable causes for disease such as doṣas, the environment, spirits, or planetary movements. But in the end there is only one actual cause, and that is a person's past actions.[92] Once the kārmik cause of the disease/disorder has been understood, one applies the standard rules of astrology in order to correct the issue. If Venus is weak and creating low Ojas, the standard Venus remedies are applied. If Rāhu is causing a cancer, the standard purification remedies for Rāhu will apply. After the kārmik remedies have been given, the physical therapies need to be applied by the Vaidya. The two work together, not separately.

[92] Praśna Mārga, XIII.30-32

When the disease is arising from the physical activities of the body it is important for the astrologer to recommend an individual to an Āyurvedic doctor unless one is also trained in Āyurveda. When a Vaidya sees that the disease has kārmik issues that need to be resolved then they should recommend daiva-cikitsā.

It is best to visit the doctor on the day of the fourth lord, and if that is not possible then the day of the lagneśa (or the horā of the fourth lord). The Āyurveda Saukhyaṁ advises that one should not start treatment on a bad nakṣatra, vāra or tithi because such actions can have harmful effects. While if treatment is initiated when these factors are auspicious, then the objective of treatment is accomplished (5.36). The various astrological texts on muhūrta discuss choosing a proper time for treatment.

The *Āgniveśya Gṛhyāsūtra* advises to worship the nakṣatra lord every year for long life and health. Pūjā to the devata of the janma nakṣatra lord is beneficial for health and to get proper treatment.

Recovery from disease depends on the force of the astrological combination causing disease, the daśā, as well as timing according to the rules of praśna for recovery. In order to predict recovery, one must clearly understand what caused the disorder and how it was activated by the daśā. In this way, when the negative period ends, recovery will begin naturally. The transit of Jupiter (protector of life), and the daśā of the fourth lord (house of cure) are also beneficial in predicting recovery. Negative karma should be purified or pacified to aid any medical treatment to work efficiently.

The Purāṇas teach various systems, based on the nakṣatras, to know how long a cure will take. For example, a patient that comes to the doctor on Puṣya nakṣatra will be cured easily, whereas a person that comes in Śatabiṣa will be very hard to cure. There are also other combinations, for example, the *Āyurveda Saukhyaṁ* (5.22) says when Venus is in Ārdrā or Āśleṣa then the disease is very difficult to cure and such a physician is really rare.

Science of Taste: Rasa

Taste is a flavor we experience on our tongue as well as in our experiences. It is a flavor we crave or dislike on both a physical and mental level.[93] Caraka says that the Moon is the presiding deity of water,[94] and it is water which manifests taste (*rasa*). Taste is directly linked with emotional experience and can be utilized to deal with the emotional aspects of the planets.

The five elements are the efficient cause of the six tastes, and therefore taste will indicate the predominant elemental (*pāñca-bautika*) composition of food and herbs. Though every material is composed of all five elements there is a predominance of one of them and substances are classified accordingly. Because of the interaction of the five elements there is nothing which is not therapeutic when used in the appropriate conditions and situations.[95] In this way, taste alone can be used as a medicine for both physical and psychological issues.

Each taste is composed of two elements, and takes on their qualities. Sweet is composed of earth and water. Sour is composed of earth and fire. Salty is composed of water and fire, pungent composed of fire and air. Bitter is composed of air and ākāśa and astringent composed of earth and air.

Taste	Element	Planet
Sweet	earth and water	Jupiter
Sour	earth and fire	Venus
Salty	water and fire	Moon
Pungent	fire and air	Sun
Bitter	air and ākāśa	Mars
Astringent	earth and air	Saturn
Mixed	Mixed	Mercury

Sweet is cold and heavy and therefore it increases kapha and decreases vāta and pitta. Sweet is connected to Jupiter. It brings agreeableness and happiness to the mind, as well as sweet feelings. Excess sweet creates attachment, greed and possessiveness. Sour is hot and light and therefore increases pitta, slightly increase kapha, and slightly decreases vāta. Sour increases alertness, appreciation and discrimination. It relates to Venus and because of this it is recommended to have yogurt (sour) in the morning for those with immune diseases or cancer to increase the Ojas. In the west people take vitamin C (sour taste) when they need to get over a cold (which is a sign of weak immunity). Excess sour can lead to being overly critical and judgmental, as one often feels towards an ex-partner after a relationship breaks.

Salty is hot and heavy so therefore increases pitta and kapha and decreases vāta. Not enough salt in the diet creates dullness and depression. Salty relates to the Moon and a proper amount of salt gives interest and enthusiasm to the mind. Excess salt can give

[93] Taste is described in Caraka Saṁhitā, Sūtrasthāna XXVI.14-79

[94] Caraka Saṁhitā, Sūtrasthāna XXVI.39. This gives the flavor to experience: moments to savor, sweet times, hot bodies, sour feelings, or bitter endings.

[95] Caraka Saṁhitā, Sūtrasthāna XXVI.10-11

kapha disorders and support the minds addictions and attachments. Pungent is hot and light and therefore increases pitta and vāta while decreasing kapha. Pungent taste is ruled by the Sun and gives enthusiasm, determination, and vitality. It removes obstructions and brings clarity of perception. Excess pungent can make the mind irritable, competitive, aggressive, and angry. Those with anger issues are advised to avoid pungent and eat more sweet.

Bitter is cold and light and therefore increases vāta while decreasing pitta and kapha. Though bitter is not an enjoyable taste in itself, it promotes the flavor of other tastes. Bitter kills germs and bacteria, is anti-inflammatory, and cleanses the liver. Bitter relates to Mars and it is said to make the mind celibate; to withdrawal your mind from temptations, and make one more self-aware. The bitterness of Mars relates to the resentment, which is often incomplete or unexpressed anger and frustration. Excess bitter can make one cynical, lonely, and isolated. Astringent is cold and heavy and is known to increase vāta and decrease pitta and kapha. The astringent taste can create dryness in the mouth and throat and makes speech difficult. It is ruled by Saturn who has difficulty speaking in front of people. The proper amount of astringent in the diet allows the mind to be grounded and organized. Excess astringent can create insomnia, fear, anxiety and make the mind scattered and disorganized.

Understanding some basic attributes of the tastes we can see that the planetary correlations are based upon the functions of the tastes. The science of taste is very deep and an important science to understand if one is using food and herbs to treat patients.

The planet's taste can directly strengthen all the psychological attributes of the planet. Taste occurs in the trines as that is where fire is located (*agni koṇa*). To pacify a malefic planet, it is taken to the nearest trine with the vāra cakra in direct order (minus Rāhu and Ketu which don't have tastes). For example, when Saturn is in the eleventh house it gives a certain level of disorganization. Saturn gives the Moon's taste (salty) in the lagna [Saturday- 11th, Sunday- 12th, and Monday- lagna]. If Saturn is in the fourth house, there is a coldness in the heart which can use the pungent taste to remove the negative emotions of Saturn [Saturday-4th, Sunday-5th house]. If Mercury is in the fourth house, then sweet taste will be present in the fifth house trine, and sweet taste will allow Mercury to be brilliant.

Planets can be emotionally pacified by their taste in a trine. For example, you can help someone suffering from depression by taking Saturn into its nearest trine. The most important planet to take to the trine is the Moon as it is the lord of taste (*rasa*). Of benefics, the Moon is the lowest, as it can easily change which side it is on. If the Moon is in the twelfth house it is easily angered and so gives the taste of bitter on the lagna which will help to pacify it. This taste in trine indicates what the planet in that house needs; what rasa that planet is indicating. These tastes are working primarily on the psychological level.

Inherited Disease: Ādibala-Pravṛtta

There is no difference between genetics and karma. The past life karma is written in one's genetics. If the body shape and features are seen in the chart, then how is it separate from genes? The karma carried by the soul decides which attributes one's body takes from the available genetic material available to them. In this way individual karma and family karma are mixed. We can share the negative karma of our ancestors and suffer disease according to the paternal and maternal misdeeds done before our birth.[96]

Caraka and Suśruta have both identified disease inherited from the parents and divided them into two divisions (paternal and maternal). In this way, whether a disease has been inherited or not is seen in the khavedāṁśa (D45) and the akṣavedāṁśa (D45). A similar combination which is causing the disease in the rāśi will be present in these vargas to indicate the disease was inherited. If it is in the D45 then it is from the paternal side, and if in the D40 it is from the maternal side.

For example, leukoderma is a condition related to weak Mercury and Saturn afflicting the Sun. In a gentleman's chart, Mercury and Sun were together aspected by Saturn and a nīca Mars. In the D45 he had the Sun aspected by both Saturn and Mars showing the disease was inherited from the paternal side of the family.

Soul Level Disease: Svāṁśa

Happiness and suffering cannot occur without the soul (*jīvātman*), as the soul is the observer of actions and their results. The soul is the root cause of the living being as well as disease.[97] The soul in the living body is said to reside in the cave of the heart. The jīvātman is our true guidance in this world, but it is contained within the body and the mind. The body and soul are forced go where the mind wants them to. Those on the spiritual path quiet their minds and listen to the guidance of the soul. When an individual chooses to ignore the voice of the soul to follow society's or the mind's desire, then the jīvātman will disrupt the body in frustration and develop disease.

With Jyotiṣa it is possible to see what type of disease is caused by the unhappiness of the jīvātman. It is very important to take note of this, as a vaidya's goal is to get to the root of the disease. If a disease is caused by the soul's unhappiness, balancing the doṣas will take extra effort and will be temporary. When we see a person suffering at the soul level it is our duty to help them look at the deeper desires in their heart and help them give importance to their heart-song.

You can use these aspects of disease in different ways. If you normally cast a chart for your patients then just take note of the disease tendency of the jīvātman. Or if you have a

[96] Atharvaveda X.30.4 mentions the suffering of disease from the mother and father's sins.
[97] Caraka Saṁhitā, Sūtrasthāna XXV.8-9

hard to treat case that seemed simple but just won't be cured, then it may be wise to check the disease indicated by the jīvātman.

Well placed the kārakāṁśa protects the health of the body. If the kārakāṁśa is placed in the navāṁśa sixth or eighth house, the person will suffer chronic disease throughout their life.[98] This is often used for rectification of chronically ill individuals, particularly if a few minutes difference has the kārakāṁśa in the eighth house.

The sign containing the kārakāṁśa or the sign lording the navāṁśa lagna will show the diseases manifested by the soul. For example, if the navāṁśa lagna is Gemini there will be skin problems if the individual's soul is discontent. These skin conditions have a deeper need to be met and external therapies will not completely solve the situation.

In the chart below, are listed the problems (or blessings) arising from the signs containing the navāṁśa lagna or the kārakāṁśa.[99] These do not all relate to physical disorders, as they are a blend of attributes to elucidate the nature of the navāṁśa sign. I have also added significations of the signs from Praśna Mārga to deepen the possibilities.

	Parāśara	Praśna Mārga VIII.16-19
Aries	Problems from rats and cats	Diseases in the head, eyes, high fever, itches and wounds
Taurus	Quadrupeds, etc	Diseases in the sexual organs, aversion to eat and drink, swelling and water caused diseases
Gemini	Skin conditions	Nose, skin, breathing troubles
Cancer	kapha disorders	Stomach and eye problems, spiritual affliction, diseases from extreme heat
Leo	Proplems from canines or tigers	Diseases in the breast, tongue, face, lack of taste for anything, and watery complaints
Virgo	Skin conditions, inflammation, etc	Nose, skin, breathing troubles
Libra	Business, trading in clothing, etc	Diseases in the sexual organs, aversion to eat and drink, swelling and water caused diseases
Scorpio	Snakes and lack of mother's milk	Diseases in the head, eyes, high fever, itches and wounds
Sagittarius	Fall from heights	Mental troubles (*buddhi-bhrama*) and ear complaints
Capricorn	Problems or gains from aquatic animals	Mental confusion (*buddhi-bhrama*), debility, indigestion, inability to walk
Aquarius	Construction of water reservoirs	Suffer itches and wounds
Pisces	Spirituality	Mental troubles and ear complaints

98 This is mitigated if the navāṁśa lagna and the 6th or 8th placement have the same lordship.

99 Bṛhat Parāśara Horā Śāstra, Kārakāṁśa-adhyāya, v.2-8

A deeper understanding of the three bodies, five kośas and disease is needed to be better able to diagnose and treat disorders at their root. For a physician, determining whether a disorder is based in the body, mind or soul takes experience to master. But when understood allows one to create a healing program that places greatest emphasis on the source of the disorder allowing there to be primary treatments and supporting treatments. For example, if the navāṁśa lagna is Gemini and there are skin conditions. The soul searching changes in life can be the primary remedy while herbal medicine for the skin is a supporting treatment. If the navāṁśa lagna is Libra and the individual is a stressed business executive who has skin conditions that are linked to stress, then mental therapies are primary and herbal medicine supportive. If it is someone with the sixth lord in lagna or Moon in the sixth house, who has a food allergy, then diet will be the primary treatment for the skin condition and mantra will be a supportive treatment. In this way, the cause will help direct the method of treatment, and the emphasis on the various aspects of treatment.

The Three Bodies (Tri-Śarīra)

The physical body (*sthūla śarīra*) is that which is most easily seen. Made of flesh and bones, this body is composed of the food taken into it according to digestion and assimilation. The quality of food, vitamins and herbs as well as proper exercise determines the functioning of the physical body. This body can be cut, bruised or broken and is the primary focus of allopathic medicine.

The mental body, or subtle body (*sūkṣma śarīra*), is the thinking-emotional body, which is the focus of psychology. This body can get mental or emotional disorders which can be self-contained or which can deteriorate the physical body. One becomes aware of this subtle body while in a dream or trance. There is perception of sound and form but this form is only a mental creation within the dream world, and even though it is a dream, the dream body still experiences emotion and mental cognition.

The causal body (*kāraṇa śarīra*) is the individual essence of a person which reincarnates from life to life. *Kāraṇa* means the cause, the reason, the motive, or origin of anything. The causal body is the cause of our thoughts in the mental body and the actions of the physical body. The causal body contains the tendencies and nature of an individual.

A	U	M
Physical Body (*Sthūla Śarīra*)	**Mental Body** (*Sūkṣma Śarīra*)	**Causal Body** (*Kāraṇa Śarīra*)
Material world	Dream world	Deep Sleep
Vaikharī Vāc	Madhyamā Vāc	Paśyantī Vāc
Awake Consciousness (*jāgrat*), normal consciousness	Dream Consciousness (*svapna*), subconscious	Kārmik Tendencies (*Saṁskāras*)/seed desires, supraconsciousness (suṣupti)
Body to **act** upon thoughts	Mind, thoughts, emotions	The objective of thoughts/desires
Annamaya kośa	(Prāṇamaya kośa), Manomaya kośa	(Vijñānamaya kośa), Ānandamaya kośa
Jagrat + Sattva = Ahaṅkāra	Svapna + Rajas = Manas	Suṣupti + Tamas = Jīvātman
Body	Mind	Soul

The Five Fields: Pañca-Kośas

In yogic philosophy there is another system of five kośas. *Kośa* is the casing or enclosure of a state of manifest consciousness, it can also been understood as the field of manifestation. The *anna-maya kośa* is the food casing which creates the physical body. The *prāṇa-maya kośa* is the energetic field of prāṇic energy which works between the physical and mental body. The *mano-maya kośa* is the mind field which holds the cognitive energies to create the mental body. Prāṇa motivates the body and controls all its functions, while the mind controls the movement of prāṇa (consciously or subconsciously). The prāṇa goes and moves within the body according to the mental condition and the focus and awareness. One controls the movement of prāṇa by controlling the mind and place of awareness.

The *vijñāna-maya kośa* is the field of knowing which works between the mental body and the causal body. The *ānanda-maya kośa* (bliss field) is the aspect of you which gives you individuality from the supreme. At this level of your being there is awareness of all lives, it is your individual essence (*ātmā*) which can be called the soul. This soul is the cause of your individual nature and composes the causal body. The causal body has tendencies (*saṁskāras*) which generates the knowing-body and decisions which then govern the mental processes. If one's causal body has the tendency to be an atheist, then when they hear about the soul or god they 'know' that it is too religious and have emotions in the mental body of dislike. In this way, the tendencies of the ānanda-maya kośa manifest through the vijñāna-maya kośa to give the mind the nature of its thoughts.

To really understand the nature of the interaction between the tri-śarīra and the pañca-kośa one should study the five platonic solids and their interaction. Three solids are independent and two are created by interlinking the other three. Their evolution also relates to the manifestation of the ākāśa to the pṛthvī and the soul to the material body.

Āyurveda focuses on the treatment of the levels of the tri-śarīra, while Yoga focuses on the intricacies of the pañca-kośa.

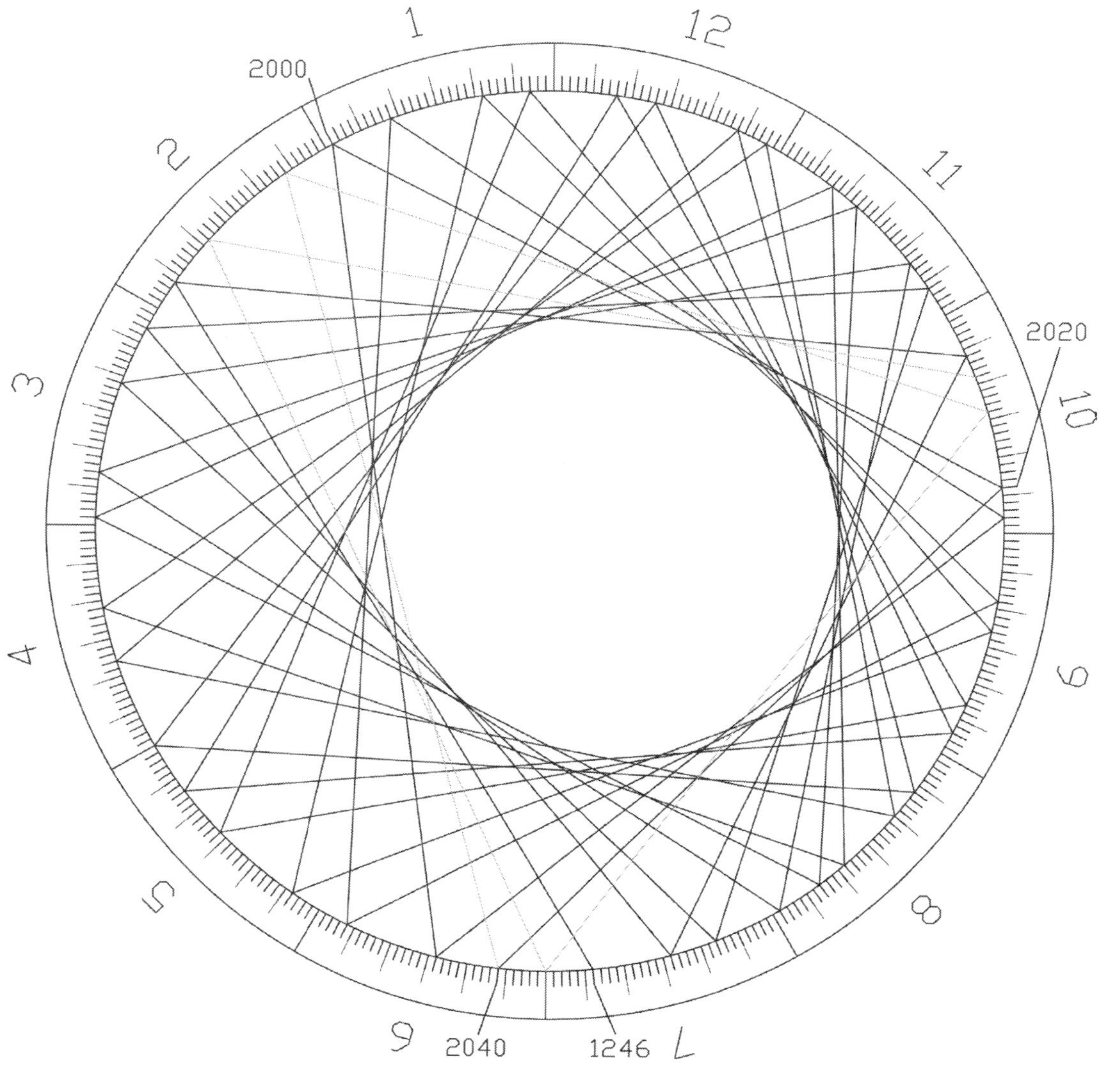

Treatment

The diagnosis of disease is done according to the distinctions (*viveka*) of the three bodies and therapeutic approach is of three types based on the focus of treatment applied. A cut on the foot, a broken arm, or a bad stomach from eating spoiled food are physical body disharmonies which are to be treated directly on the material plane. Physical problems are easy to see and diagnose according to physical symptoms of the body. The cause is often clear and easily understood, such as clogged arteries from a high fat diet. Simple disorders rooted on the physical plane such as a cold or sun burn will take simple herbal remedies like ginger for the cold and aloe vera for the sunburn. Physical measures are applied to the physical body such as taking high blood pressure medicine for the heart or guggulu for arthritis. These physical level medicines are called *yuktivyapāśraya*. *Yukti* means to join, *vyapa* means to diminish, and *aśraya* means to take shelter, so this is treatment that takes the shelter of joining together herbs and medicines that will diminish the imbalances. Major physical disease is seen in the rāśi chart with the lords of the 6th and 8th house, the A6, and weak planets. This is the realm of standard rational medicine.

Disorders rooted in the mental body will generally manifest within the body system.[100] Blood conditions, odd pains, organ blockages or failures. Emotions lock themselves in their respective places within the body and then cause disharmony there. For example, worry relates to the stomach. An individual with stomach ulcers, indigestion, irritable bowel syndrome must be questioned by the physician as to whether there is a physical cause or if there are some issues with worry in their life. If they have an incredibly acidic diet then it may only be physically related, but if there is excess worry in their life no physical medicine will properly cure the affliction. Anger is stored in the liver and gall bladder and issues with gall stones, toxic blood or related conditions can indicate that the individual needs to address issues of anger. Cancers often relate to the holding of negative patterns or beliefs in the areas of life relating to the afflicted body parts. These diseases rooted in the mental body have two approaches to treatment; physical remedies are given for immediate relief and psychological remedies are used to truly heal and prevent recurrence.

The treatment for mental disease (*mānasa roga*) is not relative to vāta, pitta and kapha but to the mental doṣas of rajas and tamas. When the disorders relate to the mind such as bipolar disorder, depression, phobias, etc. the psychiatric treatment is called *Sattvāvajaya*. *Sattva* means balance, and *vajaya* means to impel or inkindle, thereby meaning the increasing of balance (*sattva*) in the mind. This can be seen in the chart based on the Moon and the fourth and fifth house.

---

[100] Caraka Saṁhitā, Sūtrasthāna XXV.20-22

All disorders have some existence in the causal body as everything experienced relates to the causal karma.[101] But disorders directly rooted in the causal body are ones that are often abnormal or hard to cure. Uterine cancer in a 19 year old girl is generally not related to toxins from the environment, and is most likely too early for trauma to manifest on the physical body from the mental. Rare or genetic diseases, as well as chronic and debilitating diseases generally relate to the causal body. Causal body disorders also include those that are the result of not following one's inner callings. These diseases stagnate, linger and have little benefit from physical medicine. The karma behind the disorder needs to be dealt with in order to allow any healing to happen. People with disease rooted at this level may go to many doctors without finding a cure. This is the realm where an astrologer becomes necessary for the healing process.

The third type of therapy for disease rooted in the causal body is called *daivyapāśraya* or *daiva-cikitsā*, which both refer to kārmik medicine prescribed by the astrologer (*Daivajña*). In the Artharvaveda, this is the main method of treatment. Herbs were used but with mantras and the intention to propitiate energies. Amulets were used to heal and protect. When the Āyurvedic saṁhitās were being written as well as the present time, yuktivyapāśraya is primarily used with daivyapāśraya being resorted to when the normal methods fail. Most people try modern methods to heal first and only when everything on the physical plane fails do they go to faith healers, astrologers or pūjarīs for kārmik medicine. Allopathic medicine blindly tries to treat on the physical level first where Āyurveda looks for the root of the problem and treats at the appropriate level/s from the beginning.

We are a holographic image of all three bodies, but there are different *distinctions* on different levels. The diagnosis of the primary origin of disease is crucial for best treatment, though all levels affected are treated with the appropriate medicine. By addressing all aspects of the disorder, harmony is quickly achieved, or in severe cases, harmony becomes available.

[101] Caraka Saṁhitā, Sūtrasthāna XXV.19. An astrologer should be able to look through this chapter of Caraka Saṁhitā and understand the combination for each of the causative factors of disease.

Internal Medicine and Longevity

Internal medicine and the use of daiva-cikitsā is one aspect of Āyurjyotiṣa. The second branch relates to the calculation of life an individual has been born with. As everything has its roots in the causal body, the longevity has an important role on the health and when certain issues will arise in an individual's life.

Caraka Saṁhitā discusses the conceptual aspects of calculating longevity.[102] If longevity is predetermined (*daiva*), then what use is human effort (*puruṣakāra*)? Caraka discusses that karma has three levels of intensity, and human effort also has three levels of intensity. According to the strength of one's past karma the lifespan will be determined and according to one's present action (relative to the past karma) the life span will be either shortened or lengthened. Caraka Saṁhitā says that both daiva and puruṣakāra play their roles in determination of the lifespan, therefore one should not have a one-sided view that one is more responsible than the other.

From the astrological viewpoint, if the combination causing a disease has the ability to have a cure then, the right medicine or doctor will manifest. A cure will come through the signification indicating a remedy to the combination causing affliction. The greatest doctor who can cure an individual's ailment may live a minute away, but does the individual have the karma to meet that doctor to be cured? In this way, the factors giving a cure must be strengthened to allow the individual to find a method of healing. The factors extending life need to be strengthened to extend longevity. Both healing and longevity will depend on the strength of combinations causing disease and lifespan, and the strength of the actions done by the individual. If there is fixed (*dṛḍha*) karma indicating short life, then simple action (like just changing the diet) cannot change the situation. If there is changeable (*adṛḍha*) karma for long life, and the individual lives a very unhealthy life, then they can easily die early. The *Mahābhārata* says if the fruits of man's acts were not dependent on other circumstances, then one would obtain whatever object one would desire.

The *Mahābhārata* says, "The period of life, of every man, is like a steed.... Its nature is exceedingly subtle; minutes (*kṣaṇas*), seconds (*nimeṣas*) and milliseconds (*truṭis*) are the hair on its body. The twilights are its shoulder joints. The śukla and kṛṣṇa pakṣa are its two eyes of equal power. Months are the other limbs on that steed which is running incessantly. If your eyes are not blind, and you behold the invisible course of that steed incessantly moving forward, then you will set your heart on righteousness, after hearing what your preceptors have to say about the next world. "[103]

[102] Caraka Saṁhitā, Vimānasthāna, III.28-38
[103] Mahābhārata, Śānti Parva CCCXXII

II. Āyurdāya: Longevity Calculations

Parāśara speaks about longevity calculations in the chapter on Āyurdāya. Dāya has two meanings: [1] giving, presenting or a donation and [2] a portion, share or inheritance. *Āyurdāya* is the portion of life that one has been given, and it is also the name of the branch of predicting the length of life. Parāśara devotes one chapter to these calculations, Jaimini devotes about a third of his Upadeśa to these calculations.

An ancient name for astrologer is *Kārtāntika*[104] which means one who can calculate the time of death. Antaka is a name of Yama, since it means 'causing an end', or death. The one who can calculate (*kārta*) the time when Yama will come is called Kārtāntika. Sometimes people are surprised that longevity can be seen in the astrological chart, but as everything has its time, why not the human body? It is attachment to the body that causes any disbelief. The chart is the Kālapuruṣa who reveals the time of all things. The soul moves from one body to another temporary body when the māraka daśā comes. Do the longevity calculations work? They work, according to the ability of the astrologer who uses them.

When a doctor treats an individual with severe illness, they are first to consider the longevity of the individual.[105] In the modern world, doctors will charge exuberant fees for therapies on people who have no chance to live. This is considered inappropriate in Āyurveda, and disrespectful to Life. If death is near, one should not waste time or money on therapies to try to live longer, but must begin spiritual practices to begin the transition into the next world. This determination is the job of an astrologer competent in longevity calculations.

Maitreya asks,

धनाधनाख्ययोगौ च कथितौ भवता मुने ।
नराणामायुषो ज्ञानं कथयस्व महामते ॥ १ ॥

dhanādhānakhyayogau ca kathitau bhavatā mune |
narāṇāmāyuṣo jñānaṁ kathayasva mahāmate || 1||

Oh Sage, you have spoken about the combinations for wealth and poverty,
Oh great-minded one, could you speak about determining the longevity of human beings.

---

[104] Kārtāntika is listed as a synonym for astrologer in the fifth century Amarakoṣa (see Appendix).

[105] *Āyurveda Saukhyaṁ* of Toḍarānanda, "The physician should first examine the span of life of the patient, and only thereafter, initiate his treatment. If the span of life is over then where is the need of treatment (5.2)?" In this text the author advises many techniques of praśna to determine the success or failure of treatment (5.3-55) before he gives physical analysis. The author uses the Kālacakra to determine the span of life (5.30)

Parāśara replies,

साधु पृष्टं त्वया विप्र जनानां च हितेच्छया ।
कथयाम्यायुषो ज्ञानं दुर्ज्ञेयं यत् सुरैरपि ॥ २ ॥

sādhu pṛṣṭaṁ tvayā vipra janānāṁ ca hitecchayā |
kathayāmyāyuṣo jñānaṁ durjñeyaṁ yat surairapi || 2||

The beneficent inquiry by you is for the goodwill of all human beings.
I shall narrate that knowledge that is difficult even for the gods to understand.

आयुर्ज्ञानविभेदास्तु बहुभिर्बहुधोदिताः ।
तेषां सारांशमादाय प्रवदामि तवाऽग्रतः ॥ ३ ॥

āyurjñānavibhedāstu bahubhirbahudhoditāḥ |
teṣāṁ sārāṁśamādāya pravadāmi tavā'grataḥ || 3||

Many people have spoken of many different ways to calculate the longevity,
This is a brief summary (*sārāṁśa*) that I speak before you.

Parāśara mentions that there are many different views and techniques for longevity calculation. Many of these are available in different texts; there are many, but others are sure to have been lost. Parāśara has taken (*ādāya*) from all these systems a small summary (*sārāṁśa*) or just some key points to be considered.

Longevity calculations are the subject of an entire book,[106] as there are so many techniques for various circumstances. This is a study that should be given multiple years and ample application to master. But we all have to start somewhere. The beginner first approaches the science of longevity calculation with the *Method of Three Pairs*. This allows the individual to start understanding the basic compartments of lifespan (*āyus*), with increases, and decreases in the compartments. After this, other techniques of Parāśara and others can be studied, which we will mention only briefly.

There are three branches of Āyurdāya: [1] mathematical (*nitya*), [2] incidental (*anitya*) and [3] that which is caused by Yogas. For the most accurate predictions all of these need to be utilized to come to a conclusion, unless certain indications insure that one will work over the other. Parāśara teaches all three branches in his brief summary. Mathematical methods generally calculate the lifespan indicated by each planet and add them for an exact final longevity. Parāśara narrates three different *mathematical* longevity calculations: aṁśāyu, piṇḍāyu, and nisargāyu, which are chosen according to the strength of the lagna, Sun and Moon respectively.[107]

[106] Mukunda Daivajña's *Āyurnirṇaya* is one like this, but presently only available in Hindi translation.
[107] These are all Parāśara mentions here but there are also other calculations such as those mentioned in the of Āyurdāya-adhyāya of Jātaka Pārijāta (5.33): Piṇḍaja (Sun), Nisargaja (Moon), Bhinna-Aṣṭakavargaja (Mars), Rāśmija (Mercury), Kālacakraja (Jupiter), Nakṣatraja (Venus), Sāmudāya-Aṣṭakavargaja (Saturn) and Aṁśaja (Lagna).

In observational methods (*anitya*), elements in the chart are used to get a general age range and then daśā and transits are utilized for fine tuning. Parāśara teaches the *Method of Three Pairs.* The branch of Yogas is about understanding how certain combinations will alter the lifespan insuring an individual lives a full span of life or not.

Lifespans

Different individuals are born with different lifespan. Parāśara mentions seven categories of lifespan, each of which has various compartments. Maitreya asks,

कतिधा सा कदाऽनायुरमितायुः कदा भवेत् ॥ ५१ ॥

katidhā sā kadā'nāyuramitāyuḥ kadā bhavet || 51b||

How many kinds [of āyus are there], what is the time span of shortened life,
and what is the time span of immeasurable life?

Parāśara replies,

बालारिष्टं योगारिष्टमल्पं मध्यञ्च दीर्घकम् ।
दिव्यं चैवाऽमितं चैवं सप्तधायुः प्रकीर्तितम् ॥ ५२ ॥

bālāriṣṭaṁ yogāriṣṭamalpaṁ madhyañca dīrghakam |
divyaṁ caivā'mitaṁ caivaṁ saptadhāyuḥ prakīrtitam || 52||

It is stated that [1] bālāriṣta, [2] yogāriṣṭa. [3] short, [4] middle, [5] long,
[6] supernatural and [7] immeasurable (*amita*) are the seven-fold [lifespan].

बालारिष्टे समा अष्टौ योगारिष्टे च विंशतिः ।
द्वात्रिंशद् वत्सरा अल्पे चतुष्षष्टिस्तु मध्यमे ॥ ५३ ॥

bālāriṣṭe samā aṣṭau yogāriṣṭe ca viṁśatiḥ |
dvātriṁśad vatsarā alpe catuṣṣaṣṭistu madhyame || 53||

[The lifespan of] bālāriṣṭa is till eight years, yogāriṣṭa till twenty,
short life is till thirty-two years, middle life till sixty-four,

विंशाधिकशतं दीर्घे दिव्ये वर्षसहस्रकम् ।
तदूर्ध्वममितं पुण्यैरमितैराप्यते जनैः ॥ ५४ ॥

viṁśādhikaśataṁ dīrghe divye varṣasahasrakam |
tadūrdhvamamitaṁ puṇyairamitairāpyate janaiḥ || 54||

120 for long life, a thousand years for supernatural (*divya*) lifespan, and
anything above that is immeasurable (*amita*) lifespan,
which is acquired by those who have immeasurable virtue (*puṇya*).

There are seven types of longevity. The first two are *bālāriṣṭa* and *yogāriṣṭa*. Bālāriṣṭa is when a child dies before 8 years of age (some calculate till age 12). *Sadyoriṣṭa* is an aspect of bālāriṣṭa which is when an infant dies soon after birth (or within the first year), this includes Sudden Infant Death Syndrome (SIDS). Bālāriṣṭa calculations are important to do for new born children, to insure if any issues are present, remedial measures can be performed before the problem arises. Yogāriṣṭa is death before the age of twenty, or while the person is still in the student section of life. Bālāriṣṭa and yogāriṣṭa combinations will be the topic of another chapter. Parāśara teaches these in the Riṣṭa-Ariṣṭa Adhyāya, where in the first verse he indicates one should make sure that the individual lives to enjoy the results of your predictions. In the second verse he mentions that one should not predict 'death' for an individual until the janmāriṣṭa period is complete (after 24 years of age). One can call these times where death is indicated as "dangerous periods for health" and recommend remedial measures, but should avoid giving predictions which can cause trauma. It is taught that if one predicts death of an individual under 24, they may loss the power of prediction (*gāyatrī doṣa*).

Short (*alpa*), middle (*madhya*) and long (*dīrgha*) are the three compartments of longevity that will be the focus of our present study. Supernatural (*divya*) lifespan is attained by special yogis and sages. Above a thousand years, cannot be measured in the birth chart, therefore it is called immeasurable (*amita*). Parāśara indicates a few combinations in the chart where divya or amita āyus can be obtained by an individual.[108] It is important to note that the combination is not called immortal (*amṛta*) lifespan as all beings are destroyed at the end of a kalpa.[109] One may seek to extend the life to an immeasurable span, but death will eventually come to the body, as it is nature that all created things are eventually destroyed, including the universe itself. The immortality sought by the Vedic sages is conscious merger with the eternal unmanifest (*śāśvataṁ avyayaṁ padam*).

Method of Three Pairs

The method of three pairs is the first longevity technique taught to a student.[110] It is not the final answer to longevity, as it needs fine tuning. In general usage, it is meant to give the astrologer an idea of the time to begin examining more closely, called the apparent lifespan (*sphuṭam-āyus*). If you had to analyze the entire life it would take a very long time, which would be important for certain predictions. But for general predictions, the method of three pairs takes a minute once learned and helps focus into a certain area of life. The rules that go along with the three pairs for increase and decrease of compartments are a good introduction to lifespan alteration. Parāśara says we should know that,

[108] BPHS, Āyurdāya-adhyāya v.55-58, see also Sārāvalī 40.22, Horā-Sāra VI.51-59, Sarvārth Cintāmaṇi 12.54-83.
[109] Viṣṇu Purāṇa. II.8.90
[110] See also the Jaimini Upadeśa Sūtras 2.1.0 -2.1.18

कैश्चिल्लग्नाष्टमेशाभ्यां मन्देन्दुभ्यां तथैव च ॥ ३३ ॥
लग्नहोराविलग्नाभ्यां स्फुटमायुः प्रकीर्तितम् ।

kaiścillagnāṣṭameśābhyāṁ mandendubhyāṁ tathaiva ca || 33||
lagnahorāvilagnābhyāṁ sphuṭamāyuḥ prakīrtitam |34a|

It has been stated by some that the positions of the lagna lord, eighth lord, Saturn, Moon, Lagna, and Horā Lagna show the apparent (*sphuṭa*) longevity (*āyus*).

आदौ लग्नाष्टमेशाभ्यां योगमेकं विचिन्तयेत् ॥ ३४ ॥
द्वितीयं मन्दचन्द्राभ्यां योगं पश्येद् द्विजोत्तम ।
लग्नहोराविलग्नाभ्यां तृतीयं परिचिन्तयेत् ॥ ३५ ॥

ādau lagnāṣṭameśābhyāṁ yogamekaṁ vicintayet || 34b||
dvitīyaṁ mandacandrābhyāṁ yogaṁ paśyed dvijottama |
lagnahorāvilagnābhyāṁ tṛtīyaṁ paricintayet || 35||

The lagna lord and the eighth lord together are considered the first group,
Saturn and the Moon together are seen as the second group,
Lagna and Horā Lagna are considered the third.

1	Lagneśa	Aṣṭameśa
2	Saturn	Moon
3	Lagna	Horā Lagna

These are six factors put into three groups of two. The lagna lord (*lagneśa*) and the eighth lord (*aṣṭameśa*) are key factors governing the actions/functioning of the body and its longevity. The Moon is kāraka for life and prāṇa while the Saturn is the kāraka for suffering and death. The lagna is the body itself and the Horā Lagna is a point related to the sustenance of the body both financially and through prāṇa.

Lagna	**Vṛddha 8th**
Aries	Scorpio
Taurus	Gemini
Gemini	Capricorn
Cancer	Sagittarius
Leo	Cancer
Virgo	Aquarius
Libra	Taurus
Scorpio	Sagittarius
Sagittarius	Cancer
Capricorn	Gemini
Aquarius	Capricorn
Pisces	Leo

There is more than one way to calculate the eighth lord (*aṣṭameśa*). For this rule we use the "advancing" calculation called *vṛddha kārakas*. In this system the eighth house (*mṛtyu bhāva*) from Aries is Scorpio, then the eighth from Taurus becomes Gemini (which is the eighth from Scorpio). For these longevity calculations, one should utilize the vṛddha eighth lord to get the best results.

In this way, these six points have been determined to show the longevity of the individual. Parāśara uses the term *Sphuṭam-āyus*, where spuṭa can mean clear, evident, or apparent. Sphuṭa also means the degree of a planet; the clearly apparent placement. Therefore, this calculation gives the apparent lifespan (*sphuṭamāyus*).

चरराशौ स्थितौ द्वौ चित् तदा दीर्घमुदाहृतम् ।
एकः स्थिरेऽपरो द्वन्द्वे दीर्घमायुस्तथापि हि ॥ ३६ ॥

cararāśau sthitau dvau cit tadā dīrghamudāhṛtam |
ekaḥ sthire'paro dvandve dīrghamāyustathāpi hi || 36||

If both [of the pair] are in moveable signs then long life is declared,
If one is fixed and the other dual then also there is long life.

एकश्चरे स्थिरेऽन्यश्चेत् तदामध्यमुदाहृतम् ।
द्वौ वा द्वन्द्वे स्थितौ विप्र मध्यमायुस्तथापि च ॥ ३७ ॥

ekaścare sthire'nyaścet tadāmadhyamudāhṛtam |
dvau vā dvandve sthitau vipra madhyamāyustathāpi ca || 37||

If one [of the pair] is in a moveable sign and the other in fixed
then middle life is declared,
If both are situated in a dual rāśi then also there is middle life.

एकश्चरेऽपरो द्वन्द्वे द्वौ वा स्थिरगतौ तदा ।
जातकस्य तदाऽल्पायुर्ज्ञेयमेवं द्विजोत्तम ॥ ३८ ॥

ekaścare'paro dvandve dvau vā sthiragatau tadā |
jātakasya tadā'lpāyurjñeyamevaṁ dvijottama || 38||

If one is in a moveable sign and the other in dual sign or if both are in fixed sign
then know that the individual will have short life.

Parāśara has stated the combinations for short, middle and long life. To understand the basis of this will make it very easy to remember. Sthira is tamas, not moving, so it gives short life. Cara is rajas and is moving very much giving long life, while dual signs are in the middle giving middle life. If both pairs are in a cara rāśi then the life is long, as both in a sign will be the length of that sign. If they are in different signs then the third sign (not present) becomes the longevity. So if one is in sthira and the other is dual, the longevity of cara is indicated.

Long life: Cara	**Middle life: Dual**	**Short life: Sthira**
Cara + Cara	Dual + Dual	Sthira + Sthira
Sthira + Dual	Sthira + Cara	Cara + Dual

First one analyzes the lagneśa and the aṣṭameśa. If the lagneśa is in Aries (cara) and the aṣṭameśa is in Leo (sthira), then the longevity indicated is middle life. Then the second pair is analyzed. If Saturn is in a Virgo (dual) and Moon is in Pisces (dual) then again middle life is indicated. If two of the three pairs agree then that is taken as the apparent longevity.

योगत्रयेण योगाभ्यां सिद्धं यद् ग्राह्यमेव तत्।
योगत्रयविसंवादे लग्नहोराविलग्नतः॥ ३९॥
लग्ने वा सप्तमे चन्द्रे ग्राह्यं मन्देन्दुतस्तदा।

yogatrayeṇa yogābhyāṁ siddhaṁ yad grāhyameva tat |
yogatrayavisaṁvāde lagnahorāvilagnataḥ || 39||
lagne vā saptame candre grāhyaṁ mandendutastadā |40a|

If the three groups achieve agreement then accept that,
If the three groups disagree then one should use the Lagna and Horā Lagna.
If the Moon is in the lagna or the seventh house then accept Saturn and the Moon.

If they agree (two out of three) use that length for longevity. If they disagree use the longevity indicated by the Lagna and HL unless Moon is in lagna or seventh which indicates to use the longevity calculated from Saturn and Moon.

When using 120 years as the maximum longevity (*viṁśottarī*) the compartments are divided into 40 years. With balariṣṭa the first twenty, short life is 20 to 40. Middle life is 41 to 80, and long life is 81 to 120. When using 108 years as maximum longevity (*aṣṭottarī*) then the compartments are divided into 36 years. Short life is 20 to 36, middle life is 37 to 72 and long life is 73 to 108. And a third shorter lifespan takes maximum longevity to be 96 (*ṣaṇṇavati-sthira daśā*), with compartments of 32 years each. The method of three pairs will indicate one of these various longevity compartments.

Praśna Marga (IX.11-12) mentions that when the lagneśa and aṣṭameśa are nīca then short life is indicated, while their exaltation gives long life. The association of benefics and malefics with the factors (of the three pairs) and their strength will also alter the longevity (IX.18-24).

ह्रासो वृद्धिश्च कक्ष्याया विचिन्त्या सर्वदा बुधैः॥ ४०॥

hrāso vṛddhiśca kakṣyāyā vicintyā sarvadā budhaiḥ || 40b||

The wise always consider [factors which] decrease (*hrāsa*)
and increase (*vṛddhi*) of the compartment (*kakṣyā*).

The compartment (short, medium, or long) is determined first. Then the rules for adjustment are utilized which either increase the longevity or decrease the longevity indicated. *Kakṣyā hrāsa* is the decrease of longevity and *kakṣyā vṛddhi* is the increase of the longevity compartment.

दीर्घे योगत्रयेणैवं नखचन्द्रसमाब्दकाः ।
योगद्वयेन वस्वाशा योगैकेन रसांककाः ॥ ४१ ॥

dīrghe yogatrayeṇaivaṁ nakhacandrasamābdakāḥ |
yogadvayena vasvāśā yogaikena rasāṅkakāḥ || 41||

If all three combinations indicate long life it is equal to 120 years (*nakha-20, candra-1*),
If two groups 108 (*vasu-8, āśā-10*), and if only one combination then 96 (*rasa-6, aṅka-9*).

मध्ये योगत्रयेणैवं खाष्टतुल्याब्दकाः स्मृताः ।
द्व्यगा योगद्वयेनाऽत्र योगैकेनाब्धिषण्मिताः ॥ ४२ ॥

madhye yogatrayeṇaivaṁ khāṣṭatulyābdakāḥ smṛtāḥ |
dvyagā yogadvayenā'tra yogaikenābdhiṣaṇmitāḥ || 42||

If all three groups are middle then it is known to be equal to eighty (*kha-0, aṣṭa-8*) years,
If two groups then 72 (*dvi-2, aga-7*), and if one group it measures sixty-four (*abdhi-4, ṣaṭ-6*).

अल्पे योगत्रयेणाऽत्र द्वात्रिंशन्मितवत्सराः ।
योगद्वयेन षट्त्रिंशत् योगैकेन च खाब्धयः ॥ ४३ ॥

alpe yogatrayeṇā'tra dvātriṁśanmitavatsarāḥ |
yogadvayena ṣaṭtriṁśat yogaikena ca khābdhayaḥ || 43||

If all three indicate short life then the years are measured to thirty-two,
Two groups indicate thirty-six, and one group indicates forty (*kha-0, abdhi-4*).

एवं दीर्घसमाल्पेषु खाब्धयो रसवह्नयः ।
खण्डा दन्तमितास्तेभ्यः स्फुटमायुः प्रसाधयेत् ॥ ४४ ॥

evaṁ dīrghasamālpeṣu khābdhayo rasavahnayaḥ |
khaṇḍā dantamitāstebhyaḥ sphuṭamāyuḥ prasādhayet || 44||

In this way, long, middle, short is measured to 40, 36 (*rasa-6, vahni-3*), and
32 (*danta*), when reduced by a section (*khaṇḍa*) of apparent longevity.

	Short	Middle	Long
Short	20- 32	33- 64	65- 96
Middle	20- 36	37-72	73- 108
Long	20- 40	41-80	81- 120

Below is a graph indicating the basic longevity compartment (*kakṣyā*) that a person falls into. Short, middle and long are again divided into their respective short, middle and long. The life compartments are a cakra, a cycle that does not begin or end. If short life is made longer it becomes middle life. If short life is made shorter it becomes long life. If long life is made longer, it becomes short life.

In the chart of Mahatma Gandhi, the lagna lord is Venus placed in a moveable sign (long) and the vṛddha eighth lord is Taurus. But the eighth lord and the lagna cannot be the same, so the eighth from the eighth (Sagittarius) is used, which has Jupiter placed in a moveable sign (long). These two indications together indicate long life. Then the second

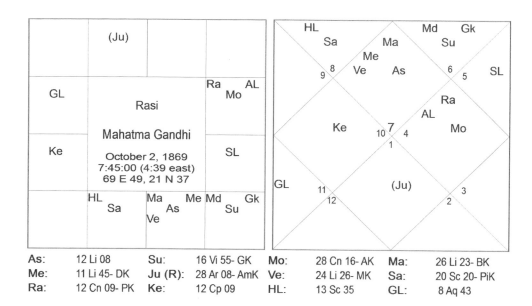

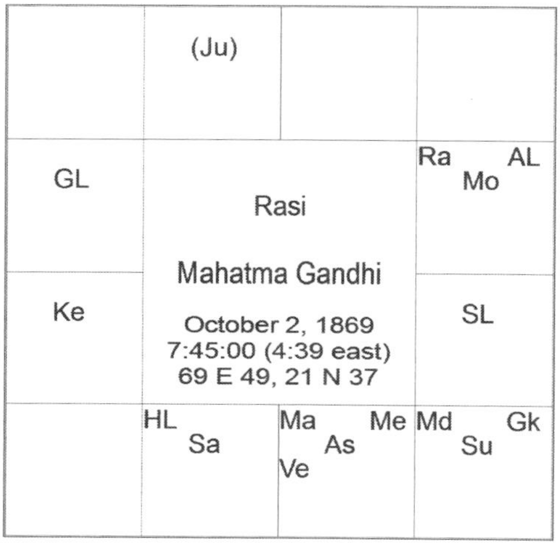

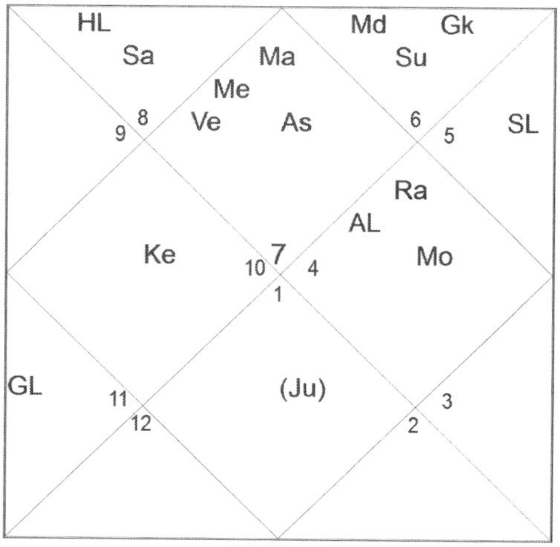

As:	12 Li 08	Su:	16 Vi 55- GK	Mo:	28 Cn 16- AK	Ma:	26 Li 23- BK
Me:	11 Li 45- DK	Ju (R):	28 Ar 08- AmK	Ve:	24 Li 26- MK	Sa:	20 Sc 20- PiK
Ra:	12 Cn 09- PK	Ke:	12 Cp 09	HL:	13 Sc 35	GL:	8 Aq 43

pair: The lagna is moveable (long) and the HL is fixed (short) which indicates middle life. The third pair: Saturn is placed in a fixed sign (short) and Moon is placed in a moveable sign (long) which indicate middle life. When two groups give middle then the life span is indicated to be between 41 to 80 years of life. Mahatma Gandhi died at the age of 79.

योगहेतौ शनौ कक्ष्याह्रासोऽन्यैर्वृद्धिरुच्यते ।
न स्वर्क्षतुङ्गगे नो वा पापमात्रयुतेक्षिते ॥ ४७ ॥

yogahetau śanau kakṣyāhrāso'nyairvṛddhirucyate |
na svarkṣatuṅgage no vā pāpamātrayutekṣite || 47||

A yoga caused by Saturn gives compartment decrease (*kakṣya hrāsa*)
others say it gives compartment increase (*kakṣyā vriddhi*),
Not if in own sign or exaltation, or not if only aspected or conjunct a malefic.

लग्नसप्तमगे जीवे शुभमात्रयुतेक्षिते ।
कथितस्यायुषो विप्र कक्ष्यावृद्धिः प्रजायते ॥ ४८ ॥

lagnasaptamage jīve śubhamātrayutekṣite |
kathitasyāyuṣo vipra kakṣyāvṛddhiḥ prajāyate || 48||

If Jupiter is in lagna or seventh house, and only aspected or conjunct a benefic,
It should be told that the lifespan is increased (*kakṣyā vṛddhi*).

अनायुश्चेद् भवेदल्पमल्पान्मध्यं प्रजायते ।
मध्यमाज्जायते दीर्घं दीर्घायुश्चेत् ततोऽधिकम् ॥ ४९ ॥

anāyuśced bhavedalpamalpānmadhyaṁ prajāyate |
madhyamājjāyate dīrghaṁ dīrghāyuścet tato'dhikam || 49||

Very short life will become short, short should become the middle life,
Middle life will become long, and if long life it will become very long life.

योगहेतौ गुरावेवं कक्ष्यावृद्धेश्च लक्षणम् ।
एतस्माद् वैपरीत्येन कक्ष्याह्रासः शनौ भवेत् ॥ ५० ॥

yogahetau gurāvevaṁ kakṣyāvṛddheśca lakṣaṇam |
etasmād vaiparītyena kakṣyāhrāsaḥ śanau bhavet || 50||

Yoga caused by Jupiter is characterized by kakṣyā vṛiddhi,
It will be the reverse when Saturn will cause kakṣyā hrāsa.

Jupiter in lagna (or seventh) will increase the lifespan and Saturn will reduce it, this is a standard rule with most longevity calculations. Saturn will only decrease the longevity in the lagna if he is not in own sign or exaltation. In this way, benefic combinations and houses increase longevity. Negative combinations, malefics, and the houses which Saturn is kāraka will decrease longevity.

The standard rules can be applied to other living beings for calculation of their longevity, but the life compartment ratios need to be fit to the animal's recognized lifespan.[111] The method of three pairs is good for a younger person. If someone comes and they are in their late seventies, you would not use this technique. They have already entered later life, so why look for what part of life they will pass. More specific rules with daśā and transits are required.

[111] Bṛhat Parāśara Horā Śāstra, Āyurdāya-adhyāya, v.23

Āyurdāya Yogas

सुयोगैर्वर्ध्यते ह्यायुः कुयोगैर्हीयते तथा ।
अतो योगानहं वक्ष्ये पूर्णमध्याल्पकारकान् ॥ ५९ ॥

suyogairvardhyate hyāyuḥ kuyogairhīyate tathā |
ato yogānahaṁ vakṣye pūrṇamadhyālpakārakān || 59||

Beneficial yogas increase the lifespan and negative yogas decrease it.
Therefore, I speak about the yogas bringing about full, medium and short lifespan.

The graph below is a summary of the longevity yogas given by Parāśara.[112] These yogas will alter the longevity even if other indications are in the chart. When Saturn is creating a reduction, it shows bad lifestyle, lack of preventative care, and wrong foods and other wrong use of the intellect. When Jupiter is giving an increase of the lifespan, it indicates good guidance, right livelihood, and good luck getting the proper medicines or therapies. Benefic situations with the lagna show good use of one's intelligence (making the right decisions for oneself). The first yoga for long life has three planets all having lots

Pūrṇāyus (96, 108, 120)	**Dīrghāyus**	**Alpāyus** (32, 36, 40)
lagneśa in kendra with benefics and beneficially placed with the aspect of Jupiter. (60)	Three planets in 8th house, in own, exaltation, or friendly divisions (*varga*), while lagneśa is strong. (63)	Mars and 3rd lord, or Saturn and 8th lord are combust or aspected/ conjunct malefics.(74)
Lagneśa in a kendra conjunct with Jupiter and Venus or aspected by them. (61)	Saturn and 8th lord conjunct with an exalted or own sign planet. (64)	Lagneśa in 6th, 8th , or 12th house, conjunct with malefics or devoid of benefic aspect/conjunction, then no children and short life. (75)
Three planets exalted, consisting of or conjunct (*saṁyuta*) with the lagneśa and aṣṭameśa, and 8th house devoid of a malefics. (62)	Malefics are in 3rd, 6th and 11th house, while benefics are in kendras or koṇas. (65)	Malefics in kendra, devoid of benefic aspects, and weak lagneśa.(76)
If 6th, 7th and 8th house are occupied by benefics, while malefics are in 3rd house. (66)	Malefic is in 8th house, while 10th lord is exalted. (68)	Malefics in 12th and 2nd house and devoid of beneficial aspect/ conjunction. (77)
Aṣṭameśa friendly to the Sun, while malefics in 6th and 12th house, and lagneśa in kendra.(67)	Lagna a dual rāśī, while lagneśa in kendra, koṇa or exaltation.(69)	lagneśa and aṣṭameśa in duḥsthāna, without strength, are knows as short life, and if mixed influences it will be middle life. (78)
	Lagna is a dual rāśi, lagneśa is strong, and two malefics in kendra.(70)	

[112] See also Horā-Sāra VI. 2-50, Sarvārth Cintāmaṇi 11.74-22, 12.1-52, and Jātaka Tattva (*Aśṭama Viveka*) for more yogas on longevity. Discussion in various texts is found in Pingree's commentary on Yavanajātaka (p.340).

of livelihod in them,[113] showing a lot of support in one's life and surroundings, and the lagna is strong indicating the proper use of all this energy. In this way, these combinations can be understood.

Longevity is determined by past karma, and past karma is indicated according to the various yogas in a chart. Yogas are that which connect the individual with the results of their karma.[114] The extremely short life seen in bālāriṣṭa and yogāriṣṭa as well as extremely long life such as amitāyus are only seen from yogas (and not daśās).

The various yogas for longevity will alter lifespan. When calculating the lifespan of an important chart, one should also see the charts of the individual's spouse and children. There is a saying that a man cannot die if his wife is running a good daśā (how could she have such a bad event happen in a good daśā?). Longevity of a close relative can be seen in a person's chart. In many ways, the death of the father or mother is a very important event in the person's life. Therefore one could use a man's chart and cross reference it to his wife and children's indications for the highest level of accuracy in predicting longevity.

Parāśara stated that this was just a small summary, and there are many other techniques. The key to using all these techniques is about learning when the various methods apply, and all the special exceptions. Most of the techniques are relatively simple, it is more about learning when to properly apply them that is difficult. In this way, understanding the nature of death becomes important, as the reason for death will also indicate which system of timing is best.

Nature of Death

Parāśara speaks about the nature of death according to the situation of the third house from lagna (*lagnāt tṛtīyabhāve*), but does not specify which lagna. If you use these techniques from lagna, they will not work. Jaimini mentions the same combinations but specifies to use them from Ārūḍha lagna, and by doing so you will get very accurate results very easily. If the eighth from AL is stronger than the third from AL (or more malefic) then it will indicate the circumstances of death.

The place of death will be according to the sign of the third from AL (or eighth if stronger). Parāśara gives the standard distances of far from home (*paradeśa*) with a cara rāśi, at home (*svagehe*) with a sthira rāśi and on the way (*pathi*) with a dual rāśi.[115] A very clear example is Mahatma Gandhi who was assassinated while walking through a garden. Third from his AL is Virgo with the Sun. Virgo is a dual sign which shows he is on the way, Virgo also relates to gardens. The Sun indicates firearms, and his assassination

[113] In mathematical calculations, own signs/ navāṁśa/drekkāṇa as well as vargottama doubles the planets portion of longevity, while exaltation and retrogression triples.

[114] Praśna Marga IX. 45-48

[115] Bṛhat Parāśara Horā Śāstra, Māraka-bheda-adhyāya, v.34

for political reasons. Houses lorded by benefics (or benefics placed there) indicate a nice place of death (*subhadeśa*), while malefics indicate the opposite (*kīkaṭadeśa*). The planets placed in that house will also influence the nature of the place of death.

The cause of death will be seen according to the planets placed in or having rāśi dṛṣṭi on the third from AL (the navāṁśa of planets placed in the third will also be informative). Malefics indicate a painful death (*duṣṭa maraṇa*), while benefics indicate a painless/easy death. Saturn will indicate a slow death due to chronic disease, while Rāhu will be a quick death, like a cancer that kills the person a few months after diagnosis. If Saturn is present the individual has time to come to terms with death, while with Rāhu there it happens before the person comes to terms with dying. A near death experience (*apa-mrityu*) will often resemble the final cause of death. For example, an individual with Moon third from AL had two surfing accidents before eventually drowning. Below is a graph of the causes of death as given by Parāśara for the third and eighth house. I have added other common

	Third House	Eighth House	Additional Indications
Sun	Caused by the king/politics (*rājahetu*) [25]	Fire	Firearms, burns, punishment, bone diseases, spinal disorders, etc.
Moon	Pulmonary disease (*yakṣmā*) [26]	water	Kapha disorders, tuberculosis, lung related problems, etc (Moon in Saturn sign gives death by hanging).
Mars	Ulcers/ wounds (*vraṇa*), weapons/ knives (*śastra*), or burned by fire (*agnidāha*) [26]	weapons	Sharp objects, surgery, wounds, abscesses, boils, cancer, burns, pitta related disorders,
Budha	Fever (*jvara*) [30]	fever	Blood or skin disorders
Jupiter	Swelling, tumour, edema (*śopha*) [30]	diseases	Vomiting, inability to keep food down, or no desire to eat for days before, etc.
Venus	Urinary disease, diabetes, (*meharoga*) [31]	Hunger, digestive functioning (*kṣudhā*) [35]	Kidney diseases, diabetes related disorders, immune system failure, etc.
Saturn	Poison (*viṣa*), pain (*ārti*), jalādvā, fire, misfortune/ calamity (*pīḍana*) [27], (with Moon shows) falling (*prapatanāt*) into a deep hole (*gartāduccāt*) or jail, bondage, hanging (*bandhana*) [28a]	Thirst (*pipāsā*) [36]	Vāta disorders, indigestion, beating/ bludgeoning, pierced (*bhedana*), slow degenerative diseases with lots of suffering, etc.
Rāhu			Death comes quickly and is a shock, can indicate poisoning (snakebites) or toxicity, radiation, brain tumors from cell phones, bad death, etc.
Ketu			Mistakes that lead to death, parasites, viral diseases, insect transmitted diseases, small pox, etc.
Māndi	(with Moon shows) parasites (*kṛmi*) and leprosy (*kuṣṭha*) [28]		(with Moon shows) choking, or poisoning, (with Saturn shows) snakebite or bondage

causes, but one should be able to infer all possibilities of death by understanding these combinations and the nature of the planets.

Certain yogas for death will indicate other methods of dying.[116] The stronger of the yoga and the combination in the third house from AL will then determine death. If no planets are in the third house the sign and aspects indicate the nature of death. If there was a specific yoga indicating a certain type of death, then it will definitely take place if there are no planets in the third or eighth from AL because it is automatically stronger. For example, if the third from AL is Pisces with no planet it indicates a peaceful death, but a Rucaka Mahāpuruṣa Yoga indicates death through a Mars related means (fire or enemies), and will override the peaceful death. If Jupiter was in Pisces in the third from AL, then the stronger of Jupiter or Mars will indicate the nature of death.

If Saturn is in the eighth from lagna, and the Moon is weak and aspected by Mars the individual will die from an operation. If the Moon is conjunct Mars, Saturn, Rāhu, and Mandi in a duḥsthāna, and aspected by Lagneśa, the person will die a violent death. The Moon in lagna, weak Sun in eighth, Jupiter in twelfth and a malefic in the fourth indicates death from being attacked by thieves in the night. And for death by impalement, the lucky soul needs the Moon with a malefic in the first, fifth or ninth, while Saturn is in the tenth and Sun or Mars are in the fourth. These are types of combinations that will alter indications of the third house from Ārūḍha lagna.

After determining the nature of death in the chart, a praśna can be cast to confirm the nature of death. In the praśna, death is due to the planets aspecting the eighth, placed in the eighth and in their absence the eighth lord itself.[117] The significations of the planets are the same as mentioned above, as well as the rules used for the third house from AL.

Parāśara gives combinations about the fate of the corpse (*śava*), such as whether it will be burned, put in water, dried up in the ground, etc., according to the 22nd dṛkkāṇa which maps onto the eighth house.[118] Certain combinations for the nature of the body at death will also indicate how the body will die. For example, if the person dies in a fire and their body is burnt, or they drown and the body is not recovered from the water.

Sometimes death comes all of a sudden and one is unaware, like a heart attack. Some people fall into a coma before they die, and therefore die in unconsciousness (though peacefully). For the spiritual aspirant, full consciousness at the time of death is very important.

---

[116] See Bṛhat Jātaka XXV, and Jātaka Pārijāta (Va.2-11) for more detailed information.
[117] Praśna Marga, XI.20
[118] Bṛhat Parāśara Horā Śāstra, Māraka-bheda-adhyāya, v.38-39, and see also Jātaka Pārijāta (v.13).

तृतीये गुरुशुक्राभ्यां युक्ते ज्ञानेन वै मृतिः ।
अज्ञानेनाऽन्यखेटैश्च मृतिर्ज्ञेया द्विजोत्तम ॥ ३३ ॥

tṛtīye guruśukrābhyāṁ yukte jñānena vai mṛtiḥ |
ajñānenā'nyakheṭaiśca mṛtirjñeyā dvijottama || 33||

Jupiter and Venus being connected to the third gives knowledge of death,
Know that other planets give unconsciousness or lack of knowledge of death.

The third house is the nature of how one acquires things in their life. If malefics are there, it indicates a certain degree of aggressiveness (which is beneficial for someone like a soldier). If benefics are placed there it indicates a gentle disposition. In this way, a spiritual aspirant, even if they have malefics in the third from AL can overcome them by how they carry themselves in everyday life. Benefics in the third and sixth from AL is called *Sādhu Yoga*; it makes a person unattached to getting things, therefore very peaceful and non-aggressive. This unattached action (as if Jupiter is in the third from AL) will allow one to retain consciousness at the time of death.

Jaimini repeats this teaching (*guru-śukrābhyāṁ jñāna-pūrvakam*) indicating that the combination gives prior knowledge of death [2.2.28]. The association of Jupiter and Venus with the third house will give a person the ability to know about their death beforehand. Malefics do the opposite, so when an astrologer sees malefics in this place, the chance of predicting the native's time of their death is quite small, as they are not meant to know. Venus and Jupiter are the natural gurus who will reveal higher knowing to the individual.

The third house shows the nature of the death, but this is not used to time death. The longevity calculations show when death will come. And the nature of death is an indicating factor for choosing the various methods. When using the three pairs one needs to use daśā and transits to fine tune the time of death. It is also said that when there are no yogas indicating the age of death, then one must be guided by daśā to determine the period of death.[119]

A daśā which is for karma phala (the results of actions) is not applicable to determine āyus, as the time of death is not a fruit to be gained. There is an entire class of daśā called āyurdaśās which are used to calculate health and longevity. Śūla daśā, Niryāṇa Śūla daśā, Brahmā daśā, Sthira daśā, Maṇḍūka daśā, navāṁśa daśā, varṇada daśā and the paryāya daśās are some of the common āyurdaśās taught in the classics. Each has their particular application for health and longevity. One of the more popular āyurdaśās is the śūla daśā.

[119] Praśna Marga, X.3

Śūla Daśā

Śūla daśā is an important daśā for anyone doing Āyurveda or looking at the longevity (*āyus*) in a chart. The Śūla (or triśūla) is the weapon held by Śiva. This daśā shows when the destroyer will take your life with his śūla, or when there will be periods of severe health problems. This is a rāśi daśā which shows the situation of the body and its weakness toward disease. Parāśara says, "the course of suffering (*yāmāriṣṭa*) will happen in the daśā period of the stronger (*prabala*) Śūla rāśi."[120] This daśā becomes very important when dealing with chronic diseases or an elderly individual who may die from the disorder or disease they are suffering. Suffering is the key word; śūla daśā works best when the individual dies while suffering (like a painful cancer).

This is an introduction to the calculation and basics of śūla daśā, so one can become familiar with its presence and use. Further study should be done to understand the daśā variations needed to make accurate predictions. If you do astrology for 40 years and don't look at this daśā when there is illness or death, then your astrology is a fruit tree in unfertile soil. Even if you are not masters with all the variations, by beginning to utilize this daśā, it is nutrients in the soil which will yield good fruit in the future.

Calculation of Śūla Daśā

In the *Daśā-adhyāya*, Parāśara teaches the calculation for Niryāṇa Śūla daśā,

निर्याणस्य विचारार्थं कैश्चिच्छूलदशा स्मृता ।
लग्नसप्तमतो मृत्युभयो यो बलवान् भवेत् ॥ १८१ ॥

niryāṇasya vicārārthaṁ kaiścichūladaśā smṛtā |
lagnasaptamato mṛtyubhayo yo balavān bhavet || 181||

It is taught by some sages that śūla daśā is for determining the departure from life (*niryāṇa*),
The stronger of the lagna or seventh will give the fear of death (will start the śūla daśā).

तदादिर्विषमे विप्र क्रमादुत्क्रमतः समे ।
दशाब्दाः स्थिरवत् तऽ बलिमारकभे मृतिः ॥ १८२ ॥

tadādirviṣame vipra kramādutkramataḥ same |
daśābdāḥ sthiravat tatra balimārakabhe mṛtiḥ || 182||

From that starting [sign], if it is odd (*viṣama*) the order will be direct,
and if it is even (*sama*) then the order will be anti-zodiacal (*utkrama*),
The daśā years are the same as sthira daśā [which is 9 years for each daśā],
Death (*mṛti*) happens in the stronger māraka rāśi.

[120] BPHS, Viśeṣalagnādhyāya, v.23. Parāśara first mentions Śūla daśā in the special lagna chapter when he explains that the daśā calculated from the Varṇada lagna can cause death similar to the rules of Śūla daśā.

Śūla daśā starts from the stronger of the first or seventh house for the individual. When this daśā is being used for relatives, it will start from the first or seventh from the kāraka bhāva. For example, for the death of mother, the śūla daśā will start from the stronger of the fourth or tenth house. The rules to determine the stronger of the first and seventh are the same as Cara daśā (as taught in the Nārāyaṇa daśā chapter).[121]

For our calculation of Śūla daśā, the order always goes direct. The length of the daśā is the same as sthira daśā which is nine years for each sign. The first nine years relates to the Rāhu-Ketu return, and the next nine years relate to the nodal return, accordingly for each nine/eighteen years. The first four signs are equal to thirty-six years, the second four relate to middle life, and the last four daśā relate to long life (9 X 12 = 108). Antardaśās start from the sign itself[122] and proceed in regular zodiacal order. Each antardaśā is nine months.

The most malefic planet will kill an individual- this will be discussed in the chapter on mārakas. The stronger or more dangerous (*prabala*) relates to the fourth rule of strength which means that which is more malefic. Śūla rāśi will indicate when the suffering or killing nature of a planet becomes activated. It will also show the length of suffering, or the time period that needs to be crossed in order to recover.

Death will occur in the śūla daśā of severely malefic combinations and trines to the *Rudra* (and *Prāṇi Rudra* planets). This same sign (calculated in the rāśi) can also be seen in the aṣṭāṁśā (D-8). Jupiter is Śiva (as the guru) and his conjunction or aspect represents his protection. If Jupiter or the ātmakāraka is aspecting the sign, it is unlikely that death will occur in that śūla daśā. In this way, there are some fine-tuning rules which help clarify when the śūla will kill. This daśā gives a time period of nine months, the month should be clarified with transits to the mṛtyupada. The day is clarified with nakṣatra cakras or the degree of planets aspecting the fifth house added to the saṅkrānti of the month of death. The time of death is calculated according to the movement of the yoginis and the mṛtyu sphuṭa, or based upon the Ārūḍha lagna.

When the māraka relates to a negative Śūla daśā the same remedies given for mārakas can be utilized. There is also a stotra of the 108 names of Śiva in the Śiva Puṛana[123] where the demon Andhaka is lodged on the tip of Śiva's trident, and he chants the 108 names of Śiva in order to please the deity and is allowed to live.

[121] Bṛhat Parāśara Horā Śāstra, Daśā-adhyāya v.161-164

[122] Some utilize the stronger of the first and seventh from the daśā rāśi to start the antardaśā, and some teach to start from the sign containing the lord of the daśā sign.

[123] Śiva-Mahāpurāṇam, Rudra Saṁhitā, Yuddha Kaṇḍa, chapter 49

Calculation of Brahmā, Rudra and Maheśvara

Parāśara says, "the consideration of loss of life-force (*vāyu-maraṇa*) is made from the Śūla daśā of the Rudra planet (*rudraśūla*) or its trines."[124] Brahmā, Rudra and Maheśvara calculations are utilized in many āyurdaśās like Śūla, Brahmā, Sthira daśā, etc. One should be able to calculate these planets for use in Āyurdaśās, even if most computer software does this for you.

Brahmā Planet

The sthira daśā starts from the *Brahmā graha*. Maitreya asks Parāśara to elucidate how to find the Brahmā graha.[125] The Brahmā graha will be one among the six planets from Sun to Venus (Saturn cannot become Brahmā graha as he is the kāraka). The stronger of the 6th, 8th, or 12th lord (taken in regular order- not vṛddha kārakas) becomes the Brahmā. The following steps are what we use to identify the Brahmā graha:

1. This is taken from the stronger of the first or seventh (same as the śūla daśā).
2. Strength here is based on predominance of odd and visible signs.
3. If planet is not odd and visible, then importance is given to odd sign first, then visible sign. If more than one qualifies, take the stronger.
4. If no planet qualifies then the duḥstha houses from the weaker of the first and seventh are taken to calculate Brahmā.
5. Since Saturn and nodes do not become Brahmā, when calculations show Saturn as the strongest then replace with Mars, Rāhu is replaced with Mercury, and Ketu is replaced with Jupiter.
6. There is an exception: If the lord of the eighth from AK is placed in the eighth from lagna then it automatically becomes the Brahmā planet overriding all other rules.

Rudra

Rudra holds the prāṇa within the body. The stronger of the second and eighth lord becomes the Rudra graha. Malefic association can make one lord stronger than the other, which means that the most malefic becomes Rudra. The śūla daśā of trines from the Rudra can cause accidents or death. The natural lords of the second and eighth are Venus and Mars, and when conjunct or aspected by the Moon they can become Rudras to cause accidents in śūla daśā.

[124] Bṛhat Parāśara Horā Śāstra, Viśeṣa-lagna-adhyāya, v.20
[125] BPHS, Daśā-adhyāya, v.170-173

Maheśvara Planet

The eighth house from each sign is considered it's Rudra as it destroys that house. The lord of the eighth house from the Ātmakāraka, has the ability to destroy the individual soul, and is therefore called as *Maheśvara*. In the Gītā, it is said, that "among the Rudras, I am Maheśvara" indicating the higher position of Maheśvara among the Rudras.

1. If the 8th from the AK is exalted or in own sign then it cannot be Maheśvara (as it is too benefic to take life). Therefore the eighth/twelfth lord (whichever is stronger) from the eighth house is taken as the Maheśvara graha.
2. If Rāhu or Ketu are first or eighth from the AK then the Maheśvara is calculated in reverse; the sixth lord from AK becomes Maheśvara.
3. If Rāhu or Ketu becomes Maheśvara then Rāhu is replaced by Mercury and Ketu is replaced by Jupiter.
4. The Brahmā graha cannot be Maheśvara. Therefore the eighth/twelfth lord from the eighth house is taken as the Maheśvara graha.

Mahādaśās		Gemini Antardaśās
Li: 1869-10-02		Ge: 1941-10-03
Sc: 1878-10-02		Cn: 1942-07-02
Sg: 1887-10-02		Le: 1943-03-31
Cp: 1896-10-02		Vi: 1944-01-01
Aq: 1905-10-03		Li: 1944-10-03
Pi: 1914-10-03		Sc: 1945-07-02
Ar: 1923-10-04		Sg: 1946-03-31
Ta: 1932-10-03		Cp: 1947-01-01
Ge: 1941-10-03		Aq: 1947-10-04
Cn: 1950-10-04		
Le: 1959-10-04		
Vi: 1968-10-03		

The śūla daśā (or Brahmā daśā) of the Maheśvara or its most malefic trine can cause death. These three planets (Brahmā, Rudra, and Maheśvara) are not becoming malefics. They will not hurt an individual in their vimśottarī daśā. They are specific to āyurdaśās, and the timing of longevity.

In the above chart of Gandhi, the stronger of the second and eighth lord is Venus (as it is in its own sign). And Venus is conjunct Mars, so it becomes the Rudra planet. The Mars lord the eighth house from the ātmakāraka and therefore become the Maheśvara planet. As the Rudra and Maheśvara are conjunct, death is likely in their trines. The sign Libra (which contains them) is aspected by Jupiter (who is the ātmakāraka) so it is unlikely to kill. The seventh house has Jupiter so again is unlikely to kill. Between Gemini and Aquarius, the sign lorded by Saṭurn and Rāhu is more likely to cause death, it is also the eighth from AL, and has rāśi dṛṣṭi from Mars and Rāhu.

Śūla daśā starts in Libra as it has more planets making it stronger than the seventh house.[126] Proceeding in zodiacal direction, his death occurred in the Mahādāśa of Gemini which started in October 1941. Starting the antardaśās

[126] If you are using software, always insure that you have chosen the correct options for calculation.

of nine months each in zodiacal order from Gemini itself, the antardaśā of Aquarius was running at the time of death. Both the Mahādaśā and antardaśā were trine to Rudra and Maheśvara.

Conclusion

This chapter has covered a wide range of topics, which has left little room for an in depth study in this book. The intention has been to open the awareness to the various techniques and procedures one needs to understand to see health and longevity (*āyus*) in astrology. This chapter has therefore set the context to learn more about Vedic medical astrology. With a proper teacher, other research material, and practice, one can master these techniques to give accurate results.

Chapter 10

Bādhakādi

Even physicians, that are well-skilled and
well-versed in their scriptures and
well-equipped with excellent medicines,
are themselves afflicted by disease
like animals assailed by hunters.

-*Bhagavata Purāṇa* CCCXXXII

Māraka and Bādhaka

Planets have their natural significations as well as temporal significations taken on by ownership of certain houses. For example, Jupiter may be a naturally beneficial planet but takes on the role of debt-giver when he becomes the eighth lord. There are other significations that a planet can take upon itself; for example, when a planet becomes the bhādakeśa it will give some results similar to Rāhu. When a planet becomes māraka it will give some results similar to Saturn during its daśā. In this way, we must study these special significations of planets to give proper predictions as well as specific remedial measures.

Māra means killing, death, or pestilence. The *'ka'* suffix[2] is similar to the "-er" in English, so if māra means kill then *māraka* means kill*er*, murder*er*, a deadly disease or plague. Māraka relates to the death-giving nature of Saturn. Ghāta means to hurt, bruise, or devastate. *Ghātaka* means the pain-inflictor, destroyer, or that which ruins, and relates to harmful aspect of Mars. Bādhā means obstacle, hindrance, annoyance, affliction, harassment, torment, or trouble. *Bādhaka* is the oppressor, harasser, blocker, or that which is opposing. It represents the confounding blockages related to Rāhu.

Māraka

Parāśara speaks about māraka planets in a chapter called the *Māraka-bheda-adhyāya,*[3] which means the chapter on being pierced by the killer planets. Bheda means piercing, tearing, destroying, or disturbance, and represents the ability of these planets to indicate disturbance in the individual's life. Maitreya asks Parāśara,

बहुधाऽऽयुर्भवा योगाः कथिता भवताऽधुना ।
नृणां मारकभेदाश्च कथ्यन्तां कृपया मुने ॥ १ ॥

bahudhā''yurbhavā yogāḥ kathitā bhavatā'dhunā |
nṛṇāṁ mārakabhedāśca kathyantāṁ kṛpayā mune || 1||

Oh Sage, you have spoken much about longevity (*āyus*),
Could you please tell about being pierced by the mārakas.

2 अक (ण्)
3 Bṛhat Parāśara Horā Śāstra, Māraka-bheda-adhyāya

Parāśara replies,

तृतीयमष्टमस्थानमायुःस्थानां द्वयं द्विज ।
मारकं तद्व्ययस्थानं द्वितीयं सप्तमं तथा ॥ २ ॥

tṛtīyamaṣṭamasthānamāyuḥsthānāṁ dvayaṁ dvija |
mārakaṁ tadvyayasthānaṁ dvitīyaṁ saptamaṁ tathā || 2||

The third and eight houses are the two places of longevity (*āyuḥ-sthāna*),
The twelfth houses from them are mārakas, which are the second and the seventh houses.

The eighth house is known as the house of longevity, it shows how much life (*āyus*) is within a person. The third is the eighth from the eighth and therefore also becomes a house of longevity. The second and seventh houses are twelfth from the houses of longevity; they indicate loss of that longevity. The seventh house is the natural house of exaltation for Saturn and the second house is the natural house of āyus exaltation for Rāhu. The lords of these houses are called mārakas. When one is pierced by these house lords, it is like a pointed object putting a hole in a container of water; the life-force leaks out. This can lead to sickness or death.

तत्रापि सप्तमस्थानाद् द्वितीयं बलवत्तरम् ।
तयोरीशौ तत्र गताः पापिनस्तेन संयुताः ॥ ३ ॥
ये खेटाः पापिनस्ते च सर्वे मारकसंज्ञकाः ।

tatrāpi saptamasthānād dvitīyaṁ balavattaram |
tayorīśau tatra gatāḥ pāpinastena saṁyutāḥ || 3||
ye kheṭāḥ pāpinaste ca sarve mārakasañjñakāḥ |

Among these two, the second house is the more powerful māraka.
Those lords, malefics gone there, and malefics conjunct them,
All have the opportunity to be māraka planets.

The second and seventh houses are called *mārakasthāna*. The second house is more powerful in its māraka effects. Malefic planets placed in a mārakasthāna become mārakas as they have the ability to indicate loss of longevity. The lords of these houses are called *mārakeśa*. Malefic planets conjunct a mārakeśa also become mārakas, which means in their daśā they could cause health problems, or in the proper time could be the daśā for leaving the body.

Determination of Māraka Status
Lords of the second and seventh house
Malefics in the second and seventh house
Malefics conjunct the second and seventh lords

The planet which becomes lord of a māraka house becomes more malefic. Therefore, when discussing the situation of health and wealth we will add the designation of māraka when referring to the planet. For example, one can say "the individual suffered a recurrence of malaria during the daśā of māraka Venus". Benefics can be māraka but unless heavily afflicted are not likely to kill. In calculating longevity, the more malefic planet becomes the indicated māraka.

तेषां दशाविपाकेषु सम्भवे निधनं नृणाम् ॥ ४ ॥
अल्पमध्यमपूर्णायुः प्रमाणमिह योगजम् ।
विज्ञाय प्रथमं पुंसां मारकं परिचिन्तयेत् ॥ ५ ॥

teṣāṁ daśāvipākeṣu sambhave nidhanaṁ nṛṇām || 4||
alpamadhyamapūrṇāyuḥ pramāṇamiha yogajam |
vijñāya prathamaṁ puṁsāṁ mārakaṁ paricintayet || 5||

At the ripe period (in the daśā which gives the results),
Destruction/suffering (*nidhana*) will come to the individual.
Death will be according to short, medium, or long life combinations
The wise consider the first māraka of the individual.

Calculations for short (*alpa*), medium (*madhya*) and long (*pūrṇa*) life should be done before looking at any other longevity calculation. The māraka planets will only show small suffering unless it is the life compartment indicated for the individual to die. Timing death has many technicalities and is the topic of an entire book, but one must understand that these are time periods of weakness to the life force. The life force is like water in a container that has been pierced by the māraka.

Whether the hole makes the entire water leak out depends on how malefic the planet was that caused the hole. The more malefic the māraka is, the worse the danger of losing life-force. For example, when one māraka is positioned in another māraka house and afflicted by malefics its ability to kill becomes very strong. One must understand what planets have the power to kill, the intensity of this power, and the amount of life-force (*āyus*) in the individual.

The amount of water in a container is important; a small hole can make a container with a small amount of water run dry quickly, while a big hole can take a long time to make a well-filled container run dry. In general, a healthy young person will have minor suffering from a māraka, while an older sick individual will have great suffering from a māraka daśā. Longevity must be calculated and understood to determine a māraka's ability to kill. In general it will just perturb health unless there are other afflictions and indications for early death.

All houses have a māraka to their significations. For example, the fourth and eleventh houses are māraka to the tenth house of career. In the daśā of those planets māraka to the tenth, career will suffer and can even be lost. In this way, māraka planets can be used to see the ending of any area of life. In dire cases when an individual needs to end a situation, the lords of these houses are activated using tamasik energies or deities.

Other Mārakas

Any planet that has the power to kill is also called a māraka. Parāśara says that loss or death can also happen when a benefic is associated with the twelfth lord, or in the daśā of the eighth lord. He says the daśā of a planet which is completely malefic can also cause destruction (*nidhana*) in its daśā. One must use discernment to see what is significantly acting like a māraka.[4]

Māraka means that which will make you suffer or cause *nidhana* (death, destruction, or loss). It is creating māra; causing the dying process or the lessening of the life-force to take place. This means that in the daśā of a planet that becomes māraka there is suffering, disease and possibility of death.

Saturn is the natural (*naisargika*) māraka, but when he is also in a temporal position of being a māraka he will exceed the suffering of all other planets. Parāśara says,

मारकग्रहसम्बन्धान्निहन्ता पापकृच्छनिः ।
अतिक्रम्येतरान् सर्वान् भवत्यत्र न संशयः ॥ ९ ॥

mārakagrahasambandhānnihantā pāpakṛcchaniḥ |
atikramyetarān sarvān bhavatyatra na saṁśayaḥ || 9||

If Saturn is ill-disposed and associated with a māraka planet,
there is no doubt he will be the worst māraka among all planets.

Parāśara gives a special rule from the Moon. Instead of seeing the second and seventh, he indicates to see the second and twelfth.

आद्यान्तपौ च विज्ञेयौ चन्द्राक्रान्तगृहाद् द्विज ।
मारकौ पापखेटौ तौ शुभौ चेद्रोगदौ स्मृतौ ॥ १८ ॥

ādyāntapau ca vijñeyau candrākrāntagṛhād dvija |
mārakau pāpakheṭau tau śubhau cedrogadau smṛtau || 18||

The second and twelfth from the Moon are also considered mārakas if they are malefic.
If they are benefic they just bring disease (*roga*).

4 Bṛhat Parāśara Horā Śāstra, Māraka-bheda-adhyāya, v.6-7

The dusthāna lords can also become mārakas, especially when associated with a māraka. This is because they are taking on the role of the kāraka of their bhāva who is the *naisargika māraka*.

षष्ठाधिपदशायां च नृणां निधनसम्भवः ।
षष्ठाष्टरिष्फनाथानामपहारे मृतिर्भवेत् ॥ १९ ॥

ṣaṣṭhādhipadaśāyāṁ ca nṛṇāṁ nidhanasambhavaḥ |
ṣaṣṭhāṣṭariṣphanāthānāmapahāre mṛtirbhavet || 19||

Destruction (*nidhana*) may happen to an individual in the sixth lord's daśā,
Death (*mṛta*) may come in the antardaśā of the sixth, eighth, or twelfth lords.

Many planets can get association with māraka status but the results will depend upon the strength of the planet, its natural disposition, the quality of health in the individual, and the length of life indicated in the individual's chart. Parāśara says,

मारका बहवः खेटा यदि वीर्यसमन्विताः ।
तत्तद्दशान्तरे विप्र रोगकष्टादिसंभवः ॥ २० ॥

mārakā bahavaḥ kheṭā yadi vīryasamanvitāḥ |
tattaddaśāntare vipra rogakaṣṭādisambhavaḥ || 20||

If many planets are māraka, and be endowed with strength,
In those respective daśā and antardaśā there will appear disease, suffering, etc.

उक्ता ये मारकास्तेषु प्रबलो मुख्यमारकः ।
तदवस्थानुसारेण मृतिं वा कष्टमादिशेत् ॥ २१ ॥

uktā ye mārakāsteṣu prabalo mukhyamārakaḥ |
tadavasthānusāreṇa mṛtiṁ vā kaṣṭamādiśet || 21||

Mārakas when endowed with strength primarily hurt the life-force (*māra*),
But according to their avasthā and disposition they indicate death (*mṛta*) or suffering (*kaṣṭa*).

Rāhu and Ketu can also become māraka in the lagna, seventh, eighth and twelfth houses, and have the power to kill during their daśā. Rāhu in the sixth, eighth or twelfth house will give suffering (*kaṣṭa*) during his daśā unless conjunct or aspected by a benefic.[5] Malefic aspects or association will make a māraka stronger to make an individual suffer while benefic aspect of association will make the māraka give less suffering.

[5] Bṛhat Parāśara Horā Śāstra, Māraka-bheda-adhyāya, v. 22-24

Prosperity

The mārakeśa is not just negative for health but also has negative effects on finances. In the Poverty Combination Chapter (*Daridra-yoga-adhyāya*) there are combinations for poverty that are increased by the association of the mārakeśa.

If the ascendant lord is in the twelfth, and the lord of the twelfth is in the ascendant conjunct or aspected by a mārakeśa the person will be without property or have money problems (*nirdhana*). The same will be true if the lagneśa goes to the sixth house and the sixth lord goes to the lagna and is conjunct or aspected by a mārakeśa.[6] In general, a malefic planet placed in the lagna (except for the 9th or 10th lords) and associated with a mārakeśa will hurt finances.[7] The mārakeśa has the significations of Saturn. The lagna shows one's disposition, and the malefic associated with the mārakeśa hurts ones disposition and ability to make clear and healthy decisions leading to financial issues during the daśā of the malefic or the mārakeśa. If Jupiter has association with the lagna or the mārakeśa, then utilize him for remedial measures. Otherwise use the Sun to strengthen the lagna. Jupiter represents the protection of prāṇa and the Sun represents vitality, both improve the condition of the lagna.

The fifth and ninth lords are the most important planets for prosperity. If these planets are placed in the sixth or twelfth house and aspected by a mārakeśa they will bring money problems. The fifth lord represents your planning, while the ninth lord represents your advice and advisors. Being placed in a dusthāna, whose kāraka is Saturn, and aspected by a planet giving the significations of Saturn these areas will suffer financial misfortunes. If the fifth lord is involved in this situation, then advise the person to seek good council. If the ninth lord is in this position, advise the person to trust their judgement and be weary of advice.

There are other combinations given by Parāśara involving the mārakeśa in the poverty combination chapter. The basic idea is to understand that the second and seventh lords are not beneficial for finances when associated with planets deciding finances; fifth and ninth lords and the lagna/lagneśa. They are acting like Saturn, and will become more negative with malefic aspect and less troublesome with benefic aspect. The second house is associated with finances, and the second lord is sometimes seen as beneficial for money. The second lord should be studied very closely as it can hurt as much as it can help depending on its position, association and combinations.

6 Bṛhat Parāśara Horā Śāstra, Daridra-yoga-adhyāya, v. 2-3
7 BPHS, Daridra-yoga-adhyāya, v. 8

Daśā

Parāśara gives teachings on mārakas in multiple places. At the end of the chapter on māraka-bheda, Parāśara says,

अन्यान् मारकभेदांश्च राशिग्रहकृतान् द्विज ।
दशाध्यायप्रसंगेषु कथयिष्यामि सुव्रत ॥ ४६ ॥

anyān mārakabhedāṁśca rāśigrahakṛtān dvija |
daśādhyāyaprasaṅgeṣu kathayiṣyāmi suvrata || 46||

Other planets and signs and their aspect of giving māraka effects,
Will be told in the chapter discussing timing (*Daśā-adhyāya*).

In the teaching of ayurdaśās, there are many different ways to calculate māraka planets and signs which will indicate death depending on daśā suitability. When a calculation is done to determine what indications will kill you or take you close to death, those indications become mārakas in the chart for that daśā or technique. For example, in śūla daśā the planet becoming Rudra or Maheśvara is a māraka for the śūla daśā. And for determining when the prāṇa leaves (*niryāṇa*) the body, Parāśara says that the individual will die during the śūla daśā of the strongest māraka sign (*balimārakabhe mṛtiḥ*).[8]

The viṁśottarī daśā of a māraka planet as explained in the māraka-bheda chapter is considered negative as it can bring either health complications or monetary issues. Parāśara, in the *Viśeṣa-nakṣatra-daśa-phala-adhyāya* states that the lord of the 2nd and 7th houses will give fear of death during their daśā. And a planet combining with the lords of the 2nd or 7th houses or posited therein will also give unfavourable results during their daśā. Parāśara predicts clear results of the daśā of planets that have māraka status.[9] He primarily focuses on the antardaśā māraka graha.[10] For example, in Rāhu-Sun daśā there will be serious disease if the Sun becomes māraka. In Sun-Mars there are physical and mental diseases. In Venus-Rāhu when Rāhu becomes māraka there is laziness in the body. Ketu-Mars can give high fever, fear of poison, distress to the wife and mental agony, while Venus-Mars gives financial hardships. Mars-Rāhu will give loss of wealth and emergencies (*mahad-bhaya*). In Mercury-Mercury there is death to a relative while in Mercury-Ketu there is loss of a co-born when the antardaśā lords become māraka. These predictions have been surprisingly accurate, as are the rest of the daśā results listed by Parāśara.

[8] Bṛhat Parāśara Horā Śāstra, Daśā-adhyāya v.181-182

[9] BPHS, Viśeṣa-nakṣatra-daśā-phala-adhyāya, see also Carādi-daśā-phala-adhyāya v.43-50

[10] Māraka results are mentioned just for antardaśās except for mentioning māraka status and remedies of Rāhu and Venus in the Daśā-phala-adhyāya

Remedies for Mārakas

The propitiation of Śiva (*Śaṁkara prasāda*) and the use of the Mṛtyuñjaya mantra is the general remedy for a māraka. Āyurvedic remedies or yoga-therapy (*yoga-chikitsā*) should also be prescribed for all the disorders which arise from the mārakas. These disorders are rooted in the body's imbalances and triggered by one's karmic indications. Mantra and other propitiations insure the disorders are corrected immediately and avoid un-needed expensive or invasive procedures.

Mṛtyuñjaya Mantra

The Mṛtyuñjaya mantra was given by Śiva to Venus after great austerities. In its full form, it gave Venus the power to bring the dead back to life (*Mṛtasañjīvanī*).[11] We can understand this as bringing the ojas back into the vāta-depleted dying body. In this way, the mantra will increase ojas, supporting the body's own immunity and allowing the body to heal itself. Its power is so great that it will even attract the proper doctors and medicines into an individual's life.

This mantra is normally advised to be done one mālā in the morning and one mālā in the evening for forty days, or until the disorder goes away. This equals 80 mālās, or approximately 8,000 repetitions of the mantra. If a person is too sick to be able to chant the mantra, a tape can be played with the mantra near them, and another person can do the mantras and offer them to the sick individual. Mṛtyuñjaya homa (offering sesame seeds with 800 repetitions[12] of Mṛtyuñjaya) and associated rituals are also beneficial if they can be done. The Ṛgveda[13] Mṛtyuñjaya mantra is:

त्र्यम्बकं यजामहे सुगन्धिं पुष्टिवर्धनम्
उर्वारुकमिव बन्धनान् मृत्योर्मुक्षीय मामृतात्

tryambakaṁ yajāmahe sugandhiṁ puṣṭivardhanam
urvārukamiva bandhanān mṛtyormukṣīya māmṛtāt

[11] Śiva-Mahāpurāṇam, Rudra Saṁhitā, Yuddha Kaṇḍa, chapter 50
[12] 1/10th the amount done in japa is offered in homa for best results.
[13] Ṛgveda, Maṇḍala 7, Śūkta 59, v.12

Mahā-mṛtyuñjaya Mantra

The same mantra from the Ṛgveda has special bījas added to it in the Tāntrik traditions.[14] Parāśara recommends the Mahā-mṛtyuñjaya for Ketu-Jupiter daśā when Jupiter is a māraka. It will also give more complete results for those who have the ability to do a larger mantra.

ॐ हौं ॐ जुं सः भूर्भुवः स्वः
त्र्यम्बकं यजामहे सुगन्धिं पुष्टिवर्धनम्
उर्वारुकमिव बन्धनान् मृत्योर्मुक्षीय मामृतात्
भूर्भुवः स्वरौं जुं सः हौं ॐ

aum̐ haum̐ aum̐ jūm̐ saḥ bhūrbhuvaḥ svaḥ
tryambakam̐ yajāmahe sugandhim̐ puṣṭivardhanam
urvārukamiva bandhanān mṛtyormukṣīya māmṛtāt
bhūrbhuvaḥ svaraum̐ jūm̐ saḥ haum̐ aum̐

Mṛtyuñjaya Bīja

For those that do not have the ability to say a Vedic mantra, the bīja mantra can be used instead.[15]

ॐ जुं सः
aum̐ jūm̐ saḥ

Mṛtyuñjaya homa can also be done by priests for a sick and suffering individual. A homa is beneficial in cases of chronic or life-threatening diseases like high fevers. It can also be used for protection from calamities, black magic, and mental suffering.

One can also do Mṛtyuñjaya homa or Mṛtyuñjaya mantra as a general practice to prevent disease or to protect from danger. The best day for this is on the individual's janma nakṣatra. It is also beneficial on the 3rd, 5th, and 7th stars from the janma nakṣatra. Some also advocate performing this mantra on days when the Moon is in gaṇḍāta nakṣatras, for protection of the mind.

In addition to Mṛtyuñjaya mantra each planet has some specific remedial measures to be performed. These remedies are for the planet being a māraka, associated with a māraka or in a house for which Saturn is a kāraka (6th, 8th, and 12th). This is a general summary below for ease of memory:

[14] Mantra Mahodadhi, Taraṅga 16
[15] Mantra Mahodadhi, Taraṅga 15.108-109

Planet	Māraka Remedies
Sun	Worship of the Sun (*sūrya-prīti*)
Moon	Worship of a devī-rūpa and donation of a white cow or female buffalo
Mars	Chanting Śrī-Rudram and donation of a bull or ox
Mercury	Viṣṇu-sahasranāma, donation of silver image [of Viṣṇu] and/or a goat
Jupiter	Śiva-sahasranāma, donation of gold image [of Śiva] and/or a cow
Venus	Devī worship and donation of white cow or female buffalo
Saturn	Homa with sesame seeds and donation of black cow or buffalo
Rahu	Durgā mantras and donation of a black cow or female buffalo
Ketu	Durgā mantras and donation of a goat

One should study the daśā section for the exact remedy recommended by Parāśara. For example, for Jupiter-Sun daśā it is specifies to chant the *Āditya Hṛdaya*. Ketu-Moon daśā recommends a śānti-pūjā for the Moon be done. While for Mars antardaśās a bull is given in donation (*vṛṣa-dāna*), for Mars-Mars daśā one should donate an ox for pulling a cart (*anadvāha*). For Ketu-Mars daśā, Ketu takes predominance and one should donate a goat (*chāga-dāna*). For Mars-Mercury daśā it specifies the donation of horses (*aśva-dāna*).

We can see how a planet becoming māraka is behaving like Saturn, and how the remedies also relate to this. When a planet becomes ghātaka it acts like Mars. In this way, planets take on various roles and energies based upon how they are situated in the chart.

Bādhakasthāna and Bādhakeśa

The Bādhaka acts like Rāhu and therefore represents unseen (*adṛṣṭa*) obstructions. In the case of mārakas, one has a disease or disorder that is causing the problem which can be seen by others and diagnosed. The bādhaka is a shadow like Rāhu; there are problems but the reason is not understood. Blockages keep coming up that are unforeseen and their cause or reason is unknown. They not only delay or block situations but they also confuse those who suffer them.

In the chapter on the results of rāśi daśās,[16] Parāśara mentions bādhaka signs,

मेषकर्कतुलानक्रराशीनां च यथाक्रमम् ।
बाधा स्थानानि सम्प्रोक्ता कुम्भगोसिंहवृश्चिकाः ॥ २० ॥

meṣakarkatulānakrarāśīnāṁ ca yathākramam ǀ
bādhā sthānāni samproktā kumbhagosiṁhavṛścikāḥ ǀǀ 20ǀǀ

Aquarius, Taurus, Leo, and Scorpio, in that order,
Are called as bādhasthāna to Aries, Cancer, Libra and Capricorn.

पाकेशाक्रान्तराशौ वा बाधास्थाने शुभेतरे ।
स्थिते सति महाशोको बन्धनव्यसनामयाः ॥ २१ ॥

pākeśākrāntarāśau vā bādhāsthāne śubhetare ǀ
sthite sati mahāśoko bandhanavyasanāmayāḥ ǀǀ 21ǀǀ

The lord of those signs or the bādhasthāna is unfortunate/evil (*śubhetara*),
Thus situated there will be obscuration, great trouble (*mahāśoka*), blockage (*bandhana*) and misfortune.

Parāśara says that the eleventh sign from a chara rāśis is the *bhādhaka-sthāna*. In this same way, the ninth sign from a sthira rāśi is the bhādhakasthāna and the seventh sign from a dvisvabhāva rāśi[17]. There is a mnemonic to easily remember this which includes reasoning related to Rāhu. There are different types of movement related to different planets. Rāhu relates to maṇḍūka-gati, which means leaping like a

Sign	#	Bādhakasthāna	Bādhakeśa
Aries	11th	Aquarius	Saturn/Rāhu
Taurus	9th	Cap	Saturn
Gemini	7th	Sag	Jupiter
Cancer	11th	Taurus	Venus
Leo	9th	Aries	Mars
Virgo	7th	Pisces	Jupiter
Libra	11th	Leo	Sun
Scorpio	9th	Cancer	Moon
Sagittarius	7th	Gemini	Mercury
Capricorn	11th	Scorpio	Mars/Ketu
Aquarius	9th	Libra	Venus
Pisces	7th	Virgo	Mercury

[16] Bṛhat Parāśara Horā Śāstra, Carādi-daśā-phala-adhyāya
[17] Praśna Mārga XV.111-113 shows other opinions on the topic, also see XV.35 and XV.163 for usage.

frog, or skipping several parts. In relation to movement in the zodiac it relates to one sign jumping over another sign. And since it is Rāhu the jump moves backwards. In this way, from the lagna there is a jump over the twelfth house to the eleventh house, then a jump over the tenth house to the ninth and another jump over the eighth to the seventh house. Rāhu moves like a frog, sitting inactive, observing and then suddenly taking a large move. The first move is to the eleventh house, which relative to Aries is ruled by Aquarius- the natural house of Rāhu. In this way, the eleventh house/Aquarius is the natural bādhakasthāna. The chart to the side lists the bādhaka for each sign but one should just remember: eleventh from moveable signs, ninth from fixed signs, and seventh from dual signs is the bādhakasthāna. The lord of this house then becomes the bādhakeśa. When two planets are indicated to be bādhakeśa use the fourth rule of strength which utilizes the one which is more malefic in the chart.

Some astrologers debate whether to use the bādhaka in areas other than health and longevity but when one understands that the planet is carrying the effects of Rāhu then it will give Rāhu-like results in any area of life. The statement by Parāśara is in no way limiting itself to any one area, but just states there will be major issues related to the bhādhakasthāna. Planets placed in this house, or the placement of its lord will show the area of these results in an individual's life.

The bādhaka for cara rāśis is the house of hearing. They have a tendency to listen very subjectively, and hear what is convenient with a limited focal point. The bādhaka for sthira rāśis is the ninth house, which relates to touch. So touching or feeling on all levels can get closed down and leave the individual feeling stuck. It makes it harder for them to relate to other people or their lack of sensitivity can lead to being betrayed by their feelings. The bādhaka for dvisvabhāva rāśis is the seventh house of dṛṣṭi or sight. They have a hard time seeing what others want and have trouble shifting perspective to see other people's viewpoint. They often live in their own opinions and get shocked when things turn out differently. There are many other ways to look at the houses causing bādhaka and the implications. For example, the movable rajas signs perceive the eleventh house of earnings/money as a limitation. The fixed tamas signs perceive religion, dharma, or government as a limitation. The dual sattva signs perceive marriage and relationship as a limitation. But this can also be seen from signs. Aquarius has Libra as its bādhaka rāśi and will consider marriage as a place to get stuck. Pisces has Virgo as its bādhaka rāśi and will consider details and orderliness as a place to get stuck.

The bādhaka is not a malefic, the ninth lord is not becoming a malefic; it is becoming bādhaka. Just as the second and seventh are not becoming 'malefics' but they are becoming mārakas. This means that it will not cause a curse or create problems on its own. But by being bādhaka- if it is one of the planets causing a disease (meaning it is in a malefic combination) it will make the disease one that is hard to treat, and hard to get rid of. In this way it will not cause a problem like a 'malefic' but will give 'bādhaka' results. Harihara goes into great detail on this fact, and we see Parāśara mention this as well when he says,

बाधकव्ययषड्रन्ध्रे राहुयुक्ते महद्भयम् ।
प्रस्थाने बन्धनप्राप्ती राजपीडा रिपोर्भयम् ॥ २३ ॥

bādhakavyayaṣaḍrandhre rāhuyukte mahadbhayam |
prasthāne bandhanaprāptī rājapīḍā riporbhayam || 23||

If Rāhu occupies the bādhaka, twelfth, sixth, or eighth house [from the daśā rāśi],
there will be great danger, or bandhana[18] during a journey,
or suffering caused by the government, or fear of enemies during the [rāśi] daśā.

In this situation Rāhu is associated with the bādhakasthāna (or the 6th, 8th or 12th) in order to create the suffering during the rāśi daśā. This gives two important teachings. The first is that a malefic like Rāhu is needed to activate the suffering of the bādhaka. The second is that every sign has a bādhaka, which is used particularly in rāśi daśās. In general, we only utilize the bādhaka from lagna because it is the body/intellect that experiences blockages. The bādhaka from the fourth house would relate to your mother's obstacles, in this way, the bādhaka can be seen from any house but must be seen according to its significations.

The bādhakeśa will at times give very good results if it is a beneficial planet and well-placed. But if the planet is afflicted or the bādhaka aspect is activated then remedial measures need to be done. Bādhaka is not based on planetary friendships or enemies or anything of this nature. A bādhaka planet will not become an enemy to the lagna, because of it being bādhaka. It just has a dual purpose in the chart and will represent some unseen karma related to the planet itself. This can also be utilized in praśna to understand unseen blockages and their remedies.

The bādhaka is best seen with rāśi daśās as it is unseen (*adṛṣṭa*) and therefore hard for the mind (*nakṣatra daśā*) to see. If the bādhaka is unafflicted it should only give negative results in its rāśi daśā. Though it can still give effects according to a nakṣatra daśā, you can notice this particularly in āyurjyotiṣa when looking at hard to cure diseases. It is also applicable in situations where people are focused on visas- relating to foreign travel and the blockages that happen in these situations. The bādhaka can also show that the native will be travelling abroad, as it relates to Rāhu.

If bādhakeśa is in lagna or lagneśa is in bādhakasthāna then the individual is the cause of their own obstacles. Otherwise one should see the house and planet significations to understand the reasons for the blockage.

[18] Bandhana means to be bound, and be as little as being delayed and stuck in an airport or as severe as going to jail depending on significations.

The primary remedy for bādhaka is the worship of Gaṇeśa, also known as Vighneśvara- the lord of obstacles. The bādhakeśa acts like Rāhu blocking the doorway of a circumstance and seventh from Rāhu is Ketu who represents the key. The method to remove the naisargika bādhaka (Rāhu) is to worship the form of Gaṇeśa associated with its opposite house: Ketu. This mantra should be a standard of all astrologers since Rāhu and Ketu play such a 'key' role in Jyotiṣa. In the same way, we can take the form of Gaṇeśa associated with the sign opposite the bādhakeśa to overcome the blockages being caused.

गजानन *gajānana*	वक्रतुण्ड *vakratuṇḍa*	एकदन्त *ekadanta*	कृष्णपिङ्गाक्ष *kṛṣṇa-piṅgākṣa*
गजपति *gajapati*			गजवक्र *gajavakra*
विनायक *vināyaka*			लम्बोदर *lambodara*
भालचन्द्र *bhāla-candra*	धूम्रवर्ण *dhūmra-varṇa*	विघ्नराज *vighnarāja*	विकट *vikaṭa*

The Mantra is created by placing the damana bīja (*huṁ*) after the name of Gaṇeśa.[19] Damana means to subdue, tame, or overpower. Huṁ is the damana bīja and gets one back in control of one's situation; it clears away the negativity and blockages. In darker tantra this is used to remove an issue or individual outside of yourself (such as *uccāṭana*). But in Jyotiṣa we realize that everything reflected in the chart is our own karma and therefore something that is manifesting within ourselves. Huṁ is therefore eradicating the negativity of our own minds, restraining the mind from doing wrong things and guiding it to a better direction. One can suffer externally to learn a lesson or one can practice mantra to purify the internal ignorance. Allowing the proper understanding to exist within one's own self allows the situation to pass without much affliction. To practice a mantra is tapas. It takes discipline to sit everyday for a certain period of time and recite the mantra. It is this tapas that burns away the ignorance, purifies the karmas, and allows the individual to have peace. Practicing the right mantra allows us to purify that specific issue directly and therefore hopefully allow for quick results.

Sign opposite Bādhakeśa	
Aries	vakratuṇḍāya huṁ
Taurus	ekadantāya huṁ
Gemini	kṛṣṇapiṅgākṣāya huṁ
Cancer	gajavaktrāya huṁ
Leo	lambodarāya huṁ
Virgo	vikaṭāya huṁ
Libra	vighnarājāya huṁ
Scorpio	dhūmravarṇāya huṁ
Sagittarius	bhālacandrāya huṁ
Capricorn	vināyakāya huṁ
Aquarius	gajapataye huṁ
Pisces	gajānanāya huṁ

For a standard Gaṇeśa mantra one can use their Ketu position. For example, if Rāhu is in Libra, then Ketu is in Aries and one would use the name of Vakratuṇḍa (the curved-tusked one). If the bādhakeśa is in Taurus, then the opposite sign of Scorpio would show the key and one would use the name Dhūmravarṇa (the smoke-colored one) to remove

[19] The nyāsa, puraścaraṇa, etc. of this mantra can be seen in Taraṅga II of *Mantra Mahodadhi* and one can accordingly perform the same (with proper variation) to each of the names of Gaṇeśa.

the bādhaka. In general, all bādhaka remedies need some aspect of spirituality (Ketu), which requires worship of things that are unseen.

The natural cancellation of the bādhaka happens when the bādhakeśa goes to the twelfth house.[20] All the suffering of the kāraka will be removed. In this situation one is advised to worship the bādhaka graha directly and that planet will remove all obstacles in one's path; it will give *ariṣṭa-bhaṅga* or cancellation of suffering. An exceptional example of this is seen in the chart of Mahātmā Gandhi who had a Libra lagna with the Sun as bādhakeśa. The Sun was placed in the twelfth house and he constantly chanted the name of Rāma (the Viṣṇu incarnation related to the Sun). Whatever obstacles stood in his way fell with the power of his mantra with this combination. Not even the government could stand up to him when he faced it.

As previously seen in the cara daśā chapter, Parāśara mentions that there are issues when Rāhu is in bādhakasthāna of a rāśi. There are many more situations where the bādhaka is indicating some type of negative karma. Harihara of *Praśna Mārga* goes into details on these other combinations. The basic premise of his teaching is that the problems are caused by an unseen (*adṛṣṭa*) source, and these unseen entities or energies are angry (*kopa*). The various combinations taught hereafter reveal that unseen source, that which is the cause of the anger/irritation (*kopasya kāraṇaṁ*). This thereby allows one to perform the appropriate remedy to calm/soothe/extinguish the anger (*kopa-śamana*). The various types of bādhaka are all circumstances signified by Rāhu. They are called devatā-bādhaka (anger of the gods), sarpa-bādhaka (anger of the serpants), pitṛ-bādhaka (anger of the ancestors), preta-bādhaka (haunting by spirits), dṛṣṭi-bādhaka (blocked perception), and abhicāra (black magic). All these circumstances deal with an adṛṣṭa source, and the remedy will also involve adṛṣṭa elements. In general, donation or seva, etc will not be enough to remove the bādhaka as they are external practices.

Anger of the Deity: Devatā-bādhaka

The deity we worship will either bless us or curse us in the next life depending on our care of that deity. Someone with an extremely strong Sun could have been a great Rāma devotee in the past life, or at least a very dharmic person. The spiritual work we do in this life will follow us and gives blessings for lives to come, just as our mistakes will haunt us as curses. [The deities we worship or good works we do will also show in the charts of our children, which mean our children have the blessing of that deity, or they themselves worshipped that deity in a previous life.] A planet with beneficial association placed in the lagna shows the blessings of the particular indicated deity. Though if the ninth lord is in the bādhakasthāna the deity the native used to worship has been neglected and will cause suffering. The practices of that neglected deity should be reinvigorated.

[20] Parāśara indicates this cancellation of bādhaka in Ariṣṭa-bhaṅga-adhyāya v.6, Harihara in XV.14

Harihara says when the bādhakeśa occupies an unfavourable house the devatā associated with the planet will cause affliction (*pīḍā*).[21] This can be an unfavourable house or a malefic combination. The cause of the deity's anger (*devatā-kopa*) can be seen according to the planetary placements in the various houses.

Just as the twelfth house from the kārakāṁśa indicates the Iṣṭa devatā in this life the twelfth house from the bādhakeśa shows the maintenance of the deity from the past life. If the bādhaka is negatively placed and a malefic is placed in the twelfth house (or aspecting) it shows the deity from the past life is angry because of improper care of its image (*vapuṣi vikalata*). Mars indicates the deity was not well protected or may have had broken accessories. If the associated planet is Saturn then the deity was worn out or impure (proper ritual purity was not followed). If Rāhu or Gulika are so placed then image is polluted from contact with serpents (this could mean poisonous people interacted with the image or could relate to dark practices such as snakes being offered to the deity). This will bring the anger of the deity according to the placement of the bādhakeśa - but will be caused by the twelfth house indication.

If the bādhakeśa is in the lagna and conjunct a malefic then the image the person worships may be in a negative condition (according to the malefic conjoining). In a praśna, this will indicate the present situation, in the natal chart it will happen when the bādhaka becomes active. If the image is in a temple then it should be repaired or replaced with one's donation. If it is an image on one's personal altar then it should be properly taken care of. The gifting of an image to a temple is very beneficial, or to an individual who needs such an image.

If the bādhaka situation is in the fourth house then the temple building is in a negative situation similar to the malefics it associates with. Mars would show it is in need of repair or replacement, Saturn would show it is in need of cleaning or purification, and Rāhu would show the need of cleanliness both of the place and the practices done there. If the bādhaka is placed in the second or eleventh then the wealth (or other items) being offered to the deity/temple are being misappropriated. This can be a misappropriation of the offered wealth from the past life or failure to offer the proper amount of one's income in this life to higher purposes (and often a combination of the two). It can also indicate one has made a commitment to make certain offerings but has not kept their promise.

A simple teaching hidden here is that one should keep one's alter and deity images clean and in good condition. It is much better to have a small and simple altar that is well cared for, then a large altar with multiple deities that is not cared for. It is much better to go to a small temple that is sincere than a large temple that is corrupt. If one goes to temple, one should participate in the upkeep of the temple, and the care of

[21] Praśna Mārga XV.8-9

the deity (offering new jewellery, clothing, sandalwood, etc.). The temple or personal altar is an external reflection of one's own inner devotion, beliefs and perceptions.

Any sambandha of the fourth house and the bādhaka will indicate a situation with the kula devatā. If the bādhakeśa is in the fourth house (or its lord's other sign), or the fourth lord in the bādhakasthāna (or its lord's other sign) it will show association to the deity worshiped by the family. This will also be the case if the Sun or Moon occupies the bādhakasthāna. In these situations, one must understand the family's traditional religious practices (or deity's rites) and ensure that they are performed by the family. Sometimes the rites are very clear, other time they may be harder to see. For example, if a person has bādhakeśa Mars in the fourth, and their grandmother always had the entire family go together to Mass on certain occasions. And this ritual stopped after her passing, and soon after there were family problems, one should consider continuing the grandmother's ritual. The family deity ensures the health and prosperity of the entire family.

Bhāveśa	**Offering made to Deity**		
Mars/Sun	*pradīpa*	ghee lamp, candle, illumination	om raṁ raṁ raṁ agnyātmakam dīpaṁ samarpayāmi
Venus/Moon	*pāyasa*	milk, rice, rice-pudding, ghee	om vaṁ vaṁ vam amṛtātmakaṁ naivedyaṁ samarpayāmi
Mercury	*candana*	sandalwood paste or fragrant oils	om laṁ laṁ laṁ pṛthivyātmakaṁ gandhaṁ samarpayāmi
Jupiter	*mālā*	garland, wreath, flowers	om haṁ haṁ ham ākāśātmakaṁ puṣpaṁ samarpayāmi
Saturn	*bhūṣaṇa*	Decorating, jewellery, clothing (*vasana*)	om yaṁ yaṁ yaṁ vāyavyātmakaṁ dhūpaṁ samarpayāmi

When the bādhaka is afflicted and causing a problem one must first properly determine the devatā indicated by the planet which is bādhakeśa. It is not a planet (*graha*) but a devatā whenever bādhaka remedial measures are applied. The bādhaka destroys the tattva of the bhāveśa and therefore this must be corrected by offering the tattva to the deity. The tattva will correct the misunderstanding that is causing a blockage. For example, when the bādhaka is in a fire sign there is a lack of clarity which is removed by offering fire to the devatā. Bādhaka remedies are best done regularly during the time indicated by the bādhakeśa in the Kālacakra.

House of Bādhakeśa		
1	*pratibimbadāna*	donation of image of deity
2	*japa*	mantra repetition
3	*pūjā*	Worship
4	*dhāma*	renovation of temple
5	*saṁtarpaṇa*	Feeding, offering refreshment
6	*pratikāra*	medical treatment, mediation
7	*nṛtya*	dance
8	*bali*	gift, tribute, propitiatory offering
9	*devopāsanā*	worship, dharma-devatā
10	*danti-skanda pūja*	worship of Gaṇeśa
11	*tarpaṇa*	ritual water offerings
12	*gīta-vādya*	singing and music (*no bādhaka*)

The house from lagna indicates the action which should be undertaken to calm the deity. For example, if a Scorpio lagna individual has bādhakeśa Moon in Pisces in the fifth house, Moon is strong so it takes the form of Durgā, and the fifth house shows standing. Pisces indicates the ākāśa tattva of Jupiter which means one should offer flowers or a mālā of flowers to a standing form of Durgā on Thursdays between 12-1:30. One should also go to a Durgā temple and help make food, or serve people during events, or donate money specifically for feeding. These remedies need to be fit to the culture, maturity, and spirituality of the individual. For a Christian individual this can be a standing form of Mother Mary. A Muslim could use the name of Allah with lunar qualities like 'Takwin'- which means everything depends on Him. For materialists and atheists bādhaka remedies are not easy to do as Rāhu has become very strong in the chart and has more power over the individual's mind which will not allow them to perform the remedial measures. This relates to the fact of Rāhu becoming maraṇa-kāraka-sthāna in the ninth house. Spiritual individual's (those with strong Ketu) will enjoy the ability to have spiritually constructive ways to direct their energy.

When a planet is placed in the bādhakasthāna and is causing issues because of a certain daśā then it also must be remedied. Harihara says if the planet is Sun or is placed in the Sun's sign..., if the planet is Moon or placed in the Moon's sign... and gives the remedy. In general one should use the remedy of the planet placed in the bādhakasthāna (but the astrologer should be aware of the options).

Planet Placed in Bādhakasthāna		
Sun	*devārādhana*	Worship of the devatā, pacification of possible diseases
Moon	*saṅkhabhiṣeka*	Donation of rice, conch shell libations, free distribution of 'rice-milk'
Mars	*dīpa, havana*	Offering a lamp, fire ceremony/worship with fire offering
Mercury	*nṛtya-karaṇa*	Arranging festivities and dancing for the devatā
Jupiter	*dvija-bhojana*	Feeding Brahmins (spiritual people) and homa
Venus	*Roga-śamanāyānna pradeya bahu*	Consoling and taking good care of the sick, feeding the sick, hospice
Saturn	*nīcānāmannadāna*	Donation of food to fallen and nameless people (the poor)

The individual should see some aspect of results within a month depending on the level of affliction. The more malefics involved, the worse the houses and the weaker the planets the longer the time it will take to give results. The afflictions of the twelfth house from bādhaka also will show the magnitude of past life devatā bādhaka and the time for remediation. When the bādhaka becomes retrograde it gains strength (*ceṣṭa bala*) and becomes very difficult to overcome.

Anger of the Serpents: Sarpa-bādhaka

Rāhu represents serpents and all the good and bad associations with them. There are three main combinations which give sarpa-bādhaka: [1] Rāhu placed in bādhakasthāna, [2] Jupiter in sambandha with bādhakeśa in a duṣṭhāna, and [3] when Rāhu is placed in a kendra or a duṣṭhāna and associated with the bādhakeśa or sthāna. The first two combinations are divine serpents while the third is nature serpents.

I. Divine Serpents (superior & inferior)	II. Nature Serpents
Rāhu placed in bādhakasthāna	Rāhu is placed in a kendra or a duṣṭhāna and associated with the bādhakeśa or sthāna
Jupiter in sambandha with bādhakeśa in a duṣṭhāna	

Rāhu placed in bādhakasthāna gives sarpa-bādhaka. If Rāhu has association with the Sun then the bādhaka is from superior serpents (*sarpanamuttamam*). If Rāhu has association with the Moon then it is from inferior serpents (*sarpaṇa-hīna*). Superior serpents cause various problems to the individual but often have a higher purpose. For example, they may derange the mind or actions but allow the person to understand abstract mathematics, physics, nuclear technologies, or esoteric knowledge. Inferior serpents cause problems but have no purpose except to disturb the individual. It is a dark snake (parasitic entity) in the subtle body that creates negative thoughts and emotions which are in the individual but not coming from the individual. When either the superior or inferior serpent becomes unhappy there is sickness, inability to have children and other mishaps.

If Jupiter becomes the bādhakeśa or is conjunct the bādhakeśa and is placed in a duṣṭhāna (6/8/12) and is in kendra to Rāhu then there is sarpa-bādhaka. When in kendra to Rāhu it will give problems from superior serpents. When it is in kendra to Gulika it will show the anger of inferior serpents. Jupiter represents life and his association with Rāhu or bādhakeśa shows suffering from the disrespect of life or taking of life in the past life.

The deities represented by the benefics aspecting Rāhu should be worshipped to protect and help the individual. The Daṣṭoddhāraṇa Pañcamī Pūjā[22] can also be used to help remove sarpa bādhaka of divine serpents. A large pūjā is done for the divine serpents after bathing with ghee. They are worshiped on the fifth tithi (*pañcamī*) in the month according to the tattva of the sign they occupy.

Tattva	Rāhu position	Vedic Month	Solar Month
Jala	Water signs	Śravaṇa	Sun in Cancer
Agni	Fire signs	Bhādra	Sun in Leo
Pṛthvī	Earth signs	Āśvina	Sun in Virgo
Vāyu	Air signs	Kārttika	Sun in Libra

There are many interpretations of bādhaka among astrologers and much confusion around the topic (it is signified by Rāhu). My interpretation of sarpa-bādhaka caused by nature serpents varies slightly with others, as I believe it needs a more modern understanding. Traces of tree and serpent worship have been found in all cultures across the globe.[23] The snake, its connotations and powers has been propitiated or worshipped throughout time. This is a basic aspect of the collective human consciousness. Taking the collective understanding of the snake in various cultures and metaphoric interpretation of sarpas and nāgas we can gain a deeper understanding of sarpa-bādhaka. The fourth house remedial measures, as well as the causes for sarpa-bādhaka given by Harihara, show the link between the sacred groves and the nāgas.

When Rāhu is in the fourth and associated with the bādhakeśa then the installation of a *citra kūṭa* stone is indicated. A citra kūṭa is an image of a nāga or the nāga king which is placed by a large tree or in a sacred grove (*sarpa kavu*[24]) where the sarpas/nāgas are said to live. These groves were often in the south-western direction. Traditionally large trees were always given space and worshiped. They were a habitat for animals, birds and insects (and ethereal beings)- an entire ecosystem alone. The sacred groves were parts of large properties or temples that were left undisturbed. Often they were the sources of perennial water sources. They relate in some way to modern day nature reserves, or watersheds. Some of the ensuing

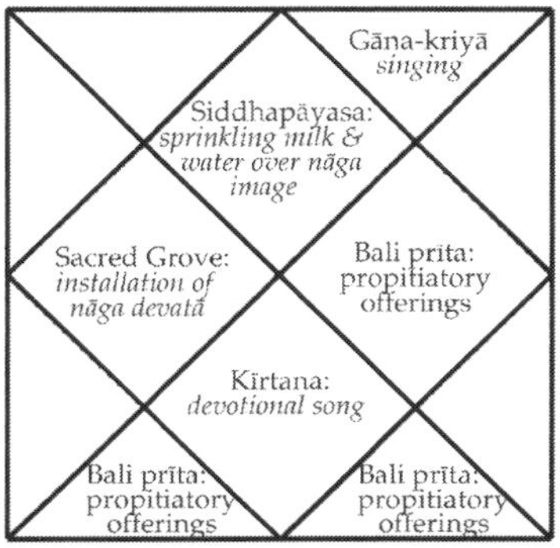

[22] Garuḍa Purāṇa 1.129.27

[23] See *Tree and Serpent Worship* by James Fergusson for a detailed study of this over time and cultures.

[24] Sarpa-kavu is the term used in south Indian, which comes from the Sanskrit sarpa-kuñja

remedies will also relate to environmental remediation. Rāhu in his Viṣṇu form is the one who saves the earth. In the negative, Rāhu becomes disturbed when one either destroys the environment or has destroyed natural habitat in a past life. The nāgas and sarpas can be seen as nature energies, and as the protectors of the nature spirits in the natural environments. Nature is a powerful force with many faces that needs to be respected. Propitiation of the nāgas is often seen as snake worship (ophiolatry), but it can be seen more as the propitiation of nature, its forces, and its protectors.

When Rāhu is placed in the lagna and associated with bādhaka then the remedial measures are to offer milk and water to the image of the nāga. This image is found by an old tree or in a sacred grove in India. In the west some type of nature shrine which gives respects to the nature element can be used instead. Rāhu placed in the seventh or twelfth and connected to bādhaka indicates the offering of song and music. This was normally done at the nāga image or in the sacred grove. The propitiatory rites to be offered when Rāhu is in the sixth, eighth or tenth are also best done in these places.

When Rāhu is in a cara rāśi the cause for the serpents anger is the destruction of serpent eggs. The traditional remedy is the donation of small golden eggs to the deity. The number of golden eggs relates to the bādhaka house; eleven eggs for moveable lagnas, nine eggs for fixed lagnas, and seven eggs for dual lagnas. In a modern interpretation, the cara rāśi represents the destruction of ecosystem breeding grounds, and one should donate to an organization which works to improve this part of the environment. The number of golden eggs would indicate the proper amount to give in donation. One can follow the traditional remedy, a modern interpretation or do both.

Moveable	Destruction of serpent's eggs
Dual	Killing young serpents
Fixed	Cutting trees near serpents abode

When Rāhu is in a dual sign it indicates the killing of the young serpents. The traditional remedy is to offer small golden snakes in the number according to the lagna. The modern interpretation of this is that the karma relates to destruction of ecosystem where the young animals, serpents, birds, etc. mature and live. The modern remedy would be the support of conservation programs. Rāhu in a cara rāśi would support a project to raise the young in captivity to be released into nature, while in a dual rāśi they would support protection and remediation programs. Rāhu in a fixed sign indicates the serpents are angry due to the cutting of trees (inanimate nature destroyed), and the tradition remedy is the replanting of trees. In the traditional sacred groves, whenever a tree was removed another tree was planted right away. In the modern world there are many reforestation projects and other projects where one can donate to or plant trees themselves if space allows.

Harihara gives further indications for the destruction of the environment (*nāgālaya*) which will later cause problems for the individual. If Mars is in kendra to Rāhu the reason for trouble is the destruction of the serpents abodes. This includes the levelling of forests, burning or cutting trees without replanting fresh trees, taking the earth, or levelling the anthills. If Saturn or Gulika are in kendra to Rāhu the abode of serpents has become unclean with trash and human waste. Low minded people hang out in the area, elephants trample the earth, or people freely plough and use the land for agriculture. The remedial indications are to keep the sacred groves well guarded, clean, plant fresh trees and do regular purification rites to the area.[25] In modern day interpretation, one should properly keep their sacred grove if it exists. Otherwise, one should donate to parks and help ensure their upkeep.

Anger of the Ancestors: Pitṛ-bādhaka

The Ancestors refer to the blood lineage one has been born into, and all things associated with this. In the modern world people often like to forget where they came from. But in the traditional world the blood in your veins and the actions and positions of your ancestral family are extremely important.

When the Sun or Moon are in the bādhakasthāna and in the sign or navāṁśa of Mars then the native suffers *pitṛ śāpa*- an ancestral curse. This means if the Sun or Moon are in either Aries or Scorpio in the rāśi or the navāṁśa and this same planet is placed in the bādhakasthāna then there is suffering due to the ancestors anger. For example, if the lagna is Capricorn and the Moon is placed in the eleventh house in Scorpio then there is pitṛ-bādhaka from the maternal side. If it is Aries lagna and the Sun is in bādhakasthāna Aquarius in the rāśi and Scorpio in the navāṁśa, then this is also pitṛ-bādhaka but because it is the Sun it would show that the condition comes from the paternal side of the family.

If the bādhakeśa is afflicted by malefics and happens to be placed in Cancer or Leo it can show pitṛ-bādhaka. If Saturn is associated then it shows some practice or ritual has been forgotten, Mars shows something has been broken or there is some anger from something not performed. Rāhu will show the wrong actions/rites are being performed, or improper performance. Saturn indicates a total lack of care. If the parents are alive one should serve them properly, if they have passed then one should perform the proper annual rituals. This will differ from a normal curse (*śāpa*) in that who is cursing the individual is bādhaka because it is indirect, unseen, yet causing blockages in the individual's life and family.

[25] Praśna Mārga XV.36-38

Additionally, Harihara mentions that if a malefic is in the bādhakasthāna conjoined Jupiter or it is a sign ruled by Jupiter then the curse is of spiritual people (Brāhmaṇa-bādhaka) which could include the Guru, or it could also represent devatā-bādhaka. In these cases, the general curse (*śāpa*) rules apply but when in association with the bādhaka they must have a more refined remedy to ensure there are results.

Anger of Spirits: Preta-bādhaka

Some people tend to have issues with ghosts (*piśāca*) or spirits (*preta*)[26] while other people have never had an encounter. Of those that encounter spirits some have beneficial relations while others are troubled. Gulika associated with the bādhakasthāna indicates trouble from ghosts or those who have died but not moved onwards (*piśāca*).

If Gulika[27] is in the sign or aṁśa of Mars or is conjunct or aspected by Mars then the ghost had an unnatural death such as burns, weapons or infectious disease. If Saturn has the same connection then the ghost will have died in suffering or poverty in a lonely or foreign place. If Rāhu has a connection to Gulika then the person died of snake-bite, poison, or cancer. Sudden or unexpected death may block a person from leaving this plane as well as the lack of proper services performed after one's death.

The nature of the ghost's death can be seen from the sign of Gulika. For example, if Gulika is in a water sign they may have drowned. The lords of the bhāvas that are associated with Gulika may indicate the relation to the ghost. For example, if Gulika is conjunct the third lord, it may be the ghost of a brother, if it is the ninth lord it may be the father, a boss, or a guru. If Gulika is in any way connected to the fourth house or lord, then the ghost is from within the family. In this way, the nature of the ghost is to be ascertained. If Gulika is in a fixed sign it shows the individual died recently, and a moveable sign shows they died long ago.

It is said that if the condition is the result of a preta or piśāca then the remedial measures will show immediate results. On should perform proper rituals (*śrāddha*) for the past individual. In severe cases one should enlist the help of a professional who deals with disembodied spirits and can remove them (*piśāca-cātana*). The person being haunted should do ugra mantras of the bādhaka devatā to help remove the spirit.

The conjunction of Mars and Ketu is also called piśāca-bādhaka, it shows problems from angered spirits or a person who denies an angry part of themselves which takes on its own identity in their psyche. It can bring extreme anger where the person loses their mind and is overcome with the anger of the spirit or their repressed anger. Such piśāca-bādhaka combinations can seem like another entity lives in the person, or that the individual has

[26] These terms are often used interchangeably with other terms for disembodied beings.
[27] Praśna Mārga says Gulika but tradition says Ketu can also be used in the same way in these calculations.

another personality within them. If the combination of Mars and Ketu is afflicted by other malefics and on the Lagna or Moon it will give very intense results. This combination placed in the seventh or with the Upapada (UL) will give these qualities to the wife. If this combination is in the third it will give this nature to the sibling, in the fourth the mother could have this anger issue or there could be spirits haunting the home, other houses can be seen accordingly. It is believed by some that this combination is cancelled in the signs of Jupiter; in Sagittarius by Rāma and in Pisces by Kṛṣṇa. Ketu and Mars in kendra to each other when associated with lagna can also cause piśāca-bādhaka. Proper Viṣṇu mantras calm the mind and help control the anger. Fasting on Ekādaśī is beneficial for getting over the karma associated with the anger. The oil of khus (*Vetiveria zizanioides*) is beneficial for cooling the mind, and keeping it under control.

The conjunction of Saturn and Ketu will cause preta-bādhaka, which shows trouble from ghosts. This will give results during the proper daśā. When either Mars-Ketu or Saturn-Ketu are associated with the bādhakeśa there is definite aḍṛṣṭa activity from the combination. The same rules previously applied to Gulika can be used for Ketu to see the nature of the spirit. For preta-bādhaka, an ugra form of Gaṇeśa is the best remedy, unless it is placed in the lagna. When placed in lagna, one must determine whether it is in the visible or invisible side of the lagna sphuṭa. In the invisible side of lagna it becomes a pitṛ-doṣa from the maternal side and from the visible side of lagna it becomes a pitṛ-doṣa from the paternal side.

There are also spirits which bother small children which are called *bala-piśāca*. Mercury represents young girls, and Saturn young boys. Bala-piśāca is indicated when Mercury or Saturn are in the bādhakasthāna or the bādhakasthāna is Gemini or Capricorn. In these cases, disorders that cannot be diagnosed by normal methods should be understood to have unseen causes. Proper protective mantras, yantras and amulets should be used.

Cursed Speech: Jihvā Doṣa

When the second lord is in association with the bādhakeśa the person suffers from *jihvā doṣa* (literally the tongue problem). This is when the problems arise from the wrong use of words, or saying the wrong thing. When an event fails because it was spoken about it is said that it was jinxed. This means that there was suffering from having spoken about something; this is jihvā doṣa. Since the second lord is a māraka it can also cause disease. Remedial measures are to worship the devatā associated with the bādhakeśa and watch ones tongue; if you don't have something good to say then don't say anything.

Blocked Perception: Dṛṣṭi-bādhaka

Dṛṣṭi-bādhaka is often translated as the "evil eye" according to early translators, but I have chosen to translate it as blocked perception or bādhaka to one's perceiving-consciousness as it is also called *dṛṣṭibhava-bādhaka*. This is a form of bādhaka which is related to psychological disorders. In ancient times these disorders or compulsions were all seen as spirits that possessed the individual.

This particular topic is much more a focus of abnormal psychology. The combinations relate to spirit possessions which cause disorders that are today called obsessive compulsive or anti-social type of disorders or schizophrenia. For example, an individual possessed by apasmāra-piśāca falls unconscious with shooting eyeballs, spits large quantities of phlegm, bites his teeth, and recovers consciousness after some time.[28] This is called an epileptic seizure in modern terminology.

This topic will not be discussed in detail here but a small summary of available material will be given for those who may come across a situation in which they need to do further research for particular situations. More research needs to be done to correlate modern diagnostic terminology with these ancient dṛṣṭi-bādhaka combinations to give a proper use of the astrological information.

Harihara discusses the indications of general dṛṣṭi-bādhaka (troubling of spirits/compulsions), the state of individuals attacked by them, and the places where they are activated. He speaks about the various types of spirits (compulsions/disorders), and their differentiation. He lists the types of spirits related to each planet when it is placed in the bādhakasthāna.

The general indications of dṛṣṭi-bādhaka relate to association of bādhaka with lagna or lagneśa and the lagna and the Moon being afflicted by malefics. All the spirits are categorized into three groups according to the purpose of affliction. They are called rati (rantu) kāma, hantu kāma, and bali kāma based upon their desire (*kāma*) to distress the individual. Below is a table listing the traditional understanding of the spirit, and a *modern* psychological interpretation[29] of the disorder category. This is followed by the combinations creating each of these situations.

[28] Praśna Mārga XV.90-92

[29] This list is not a definitive list and needs much more extensive research. The disorders are listed here according to some of the actions indicated by various spirits to give an idea of what could be a modern interpretation.

Rati kāma	Hantu kāma	Bali kāma
Spirits that want to enjoy through the person	Spirits that want to destroy or kill the person	Spirits that want to be fed, to get offerings
Unfulfilled desires or needs turning into compulsions, sex and drug addiction	*Either murderous or suicidal tendencies, anxiety, paranoia, schizophrenia*	*Compulsions and addictions, bipolar disorder, eating disorders, trichotillomania, obsessive rituals*
(can be pacified)	(doesn't leave until victim dies)	(leave after getting their dues)
Bādhaka & lagneśa friendly	Bādhaka & lagneśa inimical	Bādhaka & lagneśa neutral
Bādhaka joined lagna or the lagneśa	Bādhaka joined sixth or eighth house or lord	Bādhaka conjoined other house lords

A spirit can be seen as a formation of psychic energy. A psychological disorder is a possession by a formation of psychic energy, regardless of how exactly this formation formed or where it came from. From the modern allopathic perspective, these psychic energies are formed within the individual. From the Vedic perspective, these psychic energies may be from within the individual (present or past) or come from an outside source.

Dṛṣṭi-bādhaka can be seen as spirits that may be forcing the individual to perform a certain action, as Madame Blavatsky used to smoke large amounts to supposedly appease the spirits she worked with, or some Aghoris will drink large amounts of alcohol to keep the spirits they work with appeased. Dṛṣṭi-bādhaka can also be seen as a psychological issue that is not well understood, even by today's science.

The Spiritist movement, primarily based in Brazil, works with these psychological disorders from the perspective of spirits that can be interacted with. Their mental hospitals employ both western and Spiritist therapies. These mental hospitals show improvement among 60% of schizophrenics and 70% of those with bipolar disorder.

Vedic remedial measures focus on strengthening the well placed benefics having association with the negative combination. The proper devatā are to be worshiped and gemstones or yantras worn.

Black Magic: Abhicāra

Abhicāra literally means magic and spells, but has a general connotation of magic done for negative purposes. Modern people often think there is very little black magic in the modern world, but there are cases. Sometimes people travel in rural areas, and find themselves having strange problems. Sometimes lovers break up and do things to take revenge. Sometimes politicians employ specialists to ruin their opposition. Sometimes people dabble in what they think is small, simple magic and get stuck in much bigger, complex problems. The primary purposes for black magic are to make individuals give away all their money (evil minded store owners will do this to make you spend too much). People may wish to make an individual leave their abode and go away. Old lovers may try to either hurt their ex-partner or control them to get them back, or make things difficult for them. And sometimes people will try to kill others through magic, as there is no court that will convict one of first degree murder with a spell.

Confusion when in a store or around a certain person which goes away when not in the presence of that person or store is an indication of abhicāra. Falling sick during important times and having it accompanied by a pet dying or other strange occurrences indicates abhicāra. In this way, a good astrologer learns to be aware of certain events which indicate that there are more than average happenings taking place. A praśna will verify that abhicāra is actually the case, but the indications should also be present in the individual's chart.

Parāśara mentions abhicāra in the *Bhāveśa-phala-adhyāya* [42] in regards to the sixth lord in the fourth house. The sixth lord relates to abhicāra and it acts like Mars/Saturn (kārakas of the sixth house). When this goes to the house of emotion (the heart) then the person uses the power of Mars- abhicāra. If that planet is a malefic it is used for negative purposes, and if it is a benefic planet then it is used for good purposes. In the same way, when we see a combination for abhicāra, we can determine the intentions of the magic. Though no matter what the intention may be, manipulation of someone else is manipulation. The sixth house/lord and Mars are the signifiers of abhicāra.

The association of the bādhaka with the sixth house is an indication of health problems being caused by abhicāra. This is indicating that someone external is doing some act which is causing sickness in the individual. Harihara states that there are two variations of disease: one caused by the imbalance of the three doṣas, and one caused by abhicāra which aggravates the doṣas. If the sixth house and bādhaka are associated and the lord of the lagna or eighth house is stronger then it is caused by the imbalance of the tridoṣa. If the sixth lord or bādhakeśa is stronger then it is caused by abhicāra.

When Mars is in lagna (or aspecting) and the sixth lord is placed in the lagna, seventh or twelfth there can be abhicāra. Mars is a planet related to occult studies.[30] One should notice that in the ruchaka mahāpuruṣa combination Mars is said to be skilled in mantras and spells (*mantra-abhicāra-kuśalī*). The presence of Mars in the lagna will be stronger abhicāra than his aspect (unless he is conjunct the sixth lord). The graha aspect of Mars will show a person's anger while the rāśi aspect will show a hurt or breaking situation. Mars placed in the bādhakasthāna and aspected by the sixth lord is another combination for abhicāra.

The motive for the abhicāra is seen from the dispositor of the sixth lord and its house. A Venusian sign would show it may be because of love, a Mercurial sign would show it would relate to money, etc. If the sixth lord was in the seventh it would relate to love, if it was in the second or eleventh house it would relate to money. If the sixth lord was placed in the eleventh house in a Venusian sign then it could indicate money from a relationship, or a love relationship that was just for money. In this way, the house and sign of the sixth lord is studied to see the motive of the abhicāra. The type of abhicāra is seen from the sixth lord; if it is benefic then it is big magic (*mahā-abhicāra*), if it is a malefic then it is lower magic (*kṣudra-abhicāra*). The caste or occupation of the person doing the abhicāra is seen from the nature of the sixth lord. The accomplice or person they employ to perform the abhicāra is seen from the bādhakeśa. There is debate on whether the bādhakeśa being strong is a good or bad thing. In this situation, a strong bādhakeśa shows a very good accomplish to help your enemy achieve their aims. Details about who the person is that is doing the abhicāra can be seen from the bhaveśa conjunct/aspecting the sixth house. If the tenth lord is in the sixth house then a work related individual is creating the abhicāra. Much more details can be seen with techniques given in Praśna Mārga relative to the articles and spells used and other such specifics.

Ketu in the lagna, fourth or tenth with Mars in lagna (or aspecting) can cause abhicāra. Ketu and Mars in kendra to each other when associated with lagna can also cause piśāca-bādhaka. In this situation it may be a piśāca-bādhaka which has been created through abhicāra. Remedies should be done for the piśāca-bādhaka as well as for the abhicāra if both are indicated.

For removal of abhicāra one should perform Mṛtyuñjaya japa, and/or Gaṇeśa homa and the worship of an ugra devatā which has beneficial aspects on the combinations. Kālī mantras or Jagannātha worship are also very beneficial for protection and removal of abhicāra. There are various pūjās related to the planet becoming the sixth lord which should be done by a professional if need be. The professional should be of a sattva, rajas, or tamas nature depending on the rāśi and navāṁśa of the bādhakeśa.

[30] In the Viṣṇu Purāṇa (II.6.14), Parāśara says that those who do rituals to harms others (*duriṣṭa-kṛt*) go to the hell of insects (*kṛmīśa*), which indicates that black magic relates to the Mars aspect of Scorpio.

Conclusion:

Planets can act like more than their simple naisargika significations. Māraka and bādhaka are significations that will change the results of planets during certain times. These types of combinations should be studied and understood for proper prediction and to be able to give the most appropriate remedies.

Chapter 11

Curses

Forgiveness is a virtue of the weak,
and an ornament of the strong.
Forgiveness subdues (all) in this world;
what is there that forgiveness cannot achieve?
What can a wicked person do unto him
who carries the sabre of forgiveness in his hand?
Fire falling on the grassless ground is extinguished of itself.
An unforgiving individual defiles himself with many enormities.

eko dharmaḥ paraṁ śreyaḥ
Righteousness alone is the supreme good;
kṣamaikā śāntir uttamā
Forgiveness alone is the highest peace;
vidyaikā paramā dṛṣṭir
Knowledge alone is supreme vision;
ahiṁsaikā sukhāvahā
and peacefulness (*ahiṁsa*) alone is happiness.

- Mahābhārata, Udyoga Parvan XXXIII

Curses

Ṛṣi Parāśara speaks of curses in the chapter on illuminating (*dyotana*) curses (*śāpa*) from a previous birth (*pūrva-janma*). This indicates we are looking at some suffering that was caused by actions in a previous life. It shows a weak area that we were born with and where we have work to do in this life.

Śāpa is translated to mean "curse." It comes from the root *śap*[2] which in the Ṛgveda it is used to mean swearing an oath, or to execrate (to make something holy or curse it). It has the connotation of swearing, which could be for a positive thing or a negative. The Mahābhārata uses the word śāpita as when one is made to take an oath (sworn). In the Atharveda, the term is used to mean 'to curse', such as a scolding or malediction. Therefore śāpa is defined as a curse, malediction, abuse, or an oath. When in the accusative it means to pronounce or utter a curse on someone.

The word curse is a very loaded word in English that sometimes has strange connotations. In English, the word *curse* is defined as a profane oath; a wish that misfortune, evil, doom, etc., befall a person or group. As well as a formula or recitation intended to cause misfortune on another. The word 'curse' was first used around the 10th century in Old English and has an unknown origin. Similar to that is the word *swear*[3] which means to take an oath (such as being sworn into office). It is also used as making a profane oath or using profane language. In this way, the word śāpa and swear are both getting a similar use of making an oath, and the tendency of humans to make negative language and statements when upset. Foul language is also called cursing and many people take such foul language lightly.

We create our reality through speech. Thought is word, and word manifests. When someone is angry and they shout profanities there is negative energy directed at an object or person and this is called cursing. The words or actions do not have to be done externally, as the negative emotion is thought internally and still has its impact. This could be something simple such as cursing someone to have a bad day or bad experience. Though, we aren't looking in the chart for when someone used foul language at you in the previous life. In the ancient texts, śāpa refers to when someone does something that angers another, and they curse them to 'be separated from their wife' or such things. For this very curse, Rāma had to live without his beloved. In average human charts, we have what seems like a much more simple experience. Someone may cheat you and you just say, "damn him, damn that %#$&!. It is not the actual words that are cursing but the emotion being invoked which is channelled through our speech (out loud or in our

---

[2] Dhātupāṭha (xxiii , 31 ; xxvi , 59) *ākrośe*: assailing with harsh language , scolding , reviling , abuse

[3] Which comes from the PIE root swer which means to say or reply.

thoughts). Those emotions affect you and the other person; in this life and the next. A simple one time action will not create a curse from the previous birth, but intense or repeated actions will be carried to the next life.

Every second, with every thought and action, you are having an impact on others. You are impacting your life and the life of those around you. There is no action, word, or thought that is not influencing the direction your reality is manifesting. The more intense the action and its impact the more intense the karma associated with it.

If the Moon is cursed, then in a previous birth, the individual caused a motherly figure to suffer. Therefore in this life, they have a cursed Moon and they have issues with their mother and emotional struggling. If Venus is cursed, then in the previous life the individual acted negatively towards the wife, or sister or women in general. Therefore in this life there are struggles with women or relationships.

When negative things happen to us, or other people hurt us, we blame them as the cause of the hurt. This justifies holding negative emotions within ourselves. When we *blame* this external source, we lose our power, and get lost in the illusion of the world (*māyā*). If we *blame* karma, as an external force, then we again point a finger at something else causing the negative situation. Karma is the results of *our* own actions, no one elses. In the horoscope, curses are caused by the negative planets (*papa grahas*) and represent negative thoughts and emotions we have within ourselves. The seeds of karma exist inside of us and generate our view of the world. We cause our reality at every moment with how we act, what we say and how we think. It takes a high level of awareness and self-acceptance to see these thoughts and emotions and to shift our perspective.

The most efficient way to overcome a curse is to find the root thoughts and beliefs that manifested the negative experience and bring them back into alignment with our higher nature. In most cases, we start by recommending specific mantra and donation or service work and just mention the out of alignment views that need to be looked at. Mantra, donation and service help to loosen up the rut of karma and allow a shift in attitude/ viewpoint to be lived into.

Curses in the Chart

The basic definition of a curse is when a planet or sign is conjunct or aspected by two or more malefics. The house/planets that are hemmed within malefics (*pāpakartari*) can also be called cursed, as if the planets it is within (*krūrāntara*) are conjunct it. A planet that is combust (*astaṅgata*) means it has been 'brought to an end' is also considered cursed. Mars indicates anger, Saturn indicates sorrow and grief, and Rāhu represents shock and anxiety.

A complete curse needs the conjunction or aspect of one malefic agni graha and one vāyu graha. The vāyu graha causes suffering and the agni graha ignites it. Therefore a true curse is the aspect or conjunction of Mars and Saturn or Mars and Rāhu. When the affliction is being caused by Saturn and Rāhu or Mars and Ketu, it is actually an affliction (*ṛṣṭa*), which is discussed in regards to bādhaka. Some individuals consider the Sun a malefic and also use its aspect or conjunction to indicate a curse. Taking it as an agni graha it does have the ability to ignite a curse, but in my experience the Sun should be a functional malefic in order to do this.

A cursed planet (*śāpata graha*) will show that there is suffering with the significations of that planet (issues with a particular archetype). This suffering causes negative views towards those significations which therefore continue to attract a negative experience for the individual regarding that area of life. For example, if Jupiter becomes cursed, the individual will have negative experiences with teachers, which leads to not trusting gurus. The individual may not have the ability to commit to a living guru, and validate that as a good thing. The person who will not call an individual person guru has a cursed Jupiter. This attitude will cause suffering in marriage, especially for women. For men it indicates issues with commitment, while for women it is also the kāraka of the husband. An individual with a cursed Jupiter may have blockages to accepting religious beliefs or maybe accepting a living teacher's advice and not consider that a problem, but when there are problems with a long term committed relationship that they are trying to create in their life, then it is considered an issue.

Malefics cause sorrow, grief, fear, anxiety, anger, resentment, coldness, hatred, and distance. If only malefics aspect a poorly placed planet then there are hard emotions associated with the significations. Venus is love, and when it is cursed the individual will look for love in the wrong places. Wrong thinking attracts wrong relationship and/or attracts unavailable partners. If Saturn aspects Venus, there is a lack in what one feels they deserve, and if Mars is aspecting Venus there are anger and control issues in relationship. Sometimes these feelings and there source experience in this life may be apparent and other times they may be subconscious because they were created when the mind was still young.

When Venus is cursed, there will be an initial negative experience with relationship which is seen to create a negative template in the mind. This makes the mind run off of a programming which generates similar negative experiences in the future. A cursed Venus will give resentment/distrust/etc. towards the opposite sex and will attract situations that will fulfil that energy into one's life. Some systems of psychology look to find that initial experience in this life and release or reprogram from that point. This gives very beneficial results but doesn't look at the reason for the initial negative experience. A curse of Venus comes from some mistreatment of women or one's partner in a previous life. The negative actions in that life can be rectified in this life by beneficial actions to the indications of the suffering of Venus. By both treating the kārmik seed (propitiating the curse of Venus) and doing this inner work, results are guaranteed to last for the long term.

Wrong desires make us want things that aren't beneficial for us. Malefic conjunctions or aspects give us these wrong desires associated with the afflicted kāraka. The mind dwells again and again on that which it desires and makes excuses and reasons to validate those desires, no matter how absurd or counterproductive those desires are. Most of these desires are below the conscious thought process but form the foundation of where and how our thoughts are arising.

There are no external causes to anything- everything is in our life because we have brought it because of something inside us. In this way, the mind can be a dangerous thing and its understanding and control is the key to peace. If malefics are with the Moon this will add to negative thoughts, and if the lagna is weak this will make the situation that a curse will bring harder to get over.

Garden's need to be weeded, not once in a lifetime, not once in a year, but they need very regular weeding. Negative thought processes, self-defeating internal dialogues need to be caught and removed before they manifest suffering in the environment. Depending on the strength of the affliction, remedies can be performed to open the movement for the kārmik tendencies to be cleared.

People act as if there is a world out there that they don't have an influence on. Everything you think, and how you think, how you see the world, generates the world that you live into. Everything is inside, everything outside is just a reflection. There are layers (or levels) of the maṇḍala of your life. The planetary energies work first inside your psyche, then in your body, then in your family relationships and then in your worldly interactions. For example if the Sun is afflicted there are self-confidence issues, bone or spinal problems, tension with the father and conflict with authority. One level of that maṇḍala will show itself more than another, but all are related. Some people blame their father for their confidence issues, but there is no reason to blame anything, that is just the karma. To understand the root cause as karma is not meant to disempower, it is meant to stop blaming other things and create growth in the present. Anything that a person blames is just an excuse which only leads to being stuck in the karma. Being responsible for one's karma allows forward action which creates forward motion in life. Swami Vivekananda says,

"We only get what we deserve. It is a lie when we say, the world is bad and we are good. It can never be so. It is a terrible lie we tell ourselves.

"This is the first lesson to learn: be determined not to curse anything outside, not to lay the blame upon anyone outside, but be a man, stand up, lay the blame on yourself. You will find, that is always true. Get hold of yourself."

"Is it not a shame that at one moment we talk so much of our manhood, of our being gods- that we know everything, we can do everything, we are blameless, spotless, the most unselfish people in the world; and at the next moment a little stone hurts us, a little anger from a little Jack wounds us- any fool in the street makes "these gods" miserable! Should this be so if we are such gods? Is it true that the world is to blame? ....The very fact that you complain and want to lay the blame upon the external world shows that you feel the external world- the very fact that you feel shows that you are not what you claim to be. You only make your offence greater by heaping misery upon misery, by imagining that the external world is hurting you, and crying out, "Oh, this devil's world! This man hurts me; that man hurts me! " and so forth. It is adding lies to misery.

We are to take care of ourselves- that much we can do- and give up [blaming] others for a time. Let us perfect the means; the end will take care of itself. For the world can be good and pure, only if our lives are good and pure. It is an effect, and we are the means. Therefore, let us purify ourselves. Let us make ourselves perfect."

Working on another person doesn't work; we have to work on ourselves. This is an understanding that you must come from. Yet, as an astrologer, we do not tell people that they are the cause of all their suffering and it is their entire fault. That would be disempowering. That is the wrong use of our astrological vision. We have to see the combinations in the chart and listen to where the individual is stuck. Then we can empower them to get over limiting beliefs and recommend remedies to support that process.

Everything is inside, everything outside is just a reflection. Something between you and others is really between you and you. We are communicating with our own reflections. The first level of the planetary maṇḍala outside of the body is one's family members and close friends. If an individual with a cursed Moon has not gotten over their mother issues, then that energy will follow them into their home life, stability, their social network and their ability to get along with others in the community. For a practical remedy, one can work with the immediate family who are a direct mirror of one's karma. The specific individual the planet is indicating can be understood by the people represented by the planet as well as the houses the cursed planet is placed in and house lordships. Facing the issues one has with close family is one way to overcome the blockages and afflictions that an afflicted planet puts in our life. If an individual cannot connect with their immediate family members, there is a blockage with the representative planetary significator or house.

It doesn't matter what the father did, or the mother didn't do, or why the wife did that, or how bad that guru did something to someone. What matters is what actions are being taken from the present moment forwards. We need to accept what has happened, because it is what is. Denial of 'what is' is unconsciousness. Acceptance is coming to terms with your karma and allowing the attention to be in the present. When giving a reading, a client may be in denial that there is an issue with that person in their life, or you may not be noticing the correct person because of house lords, houses, etc that are involved- so it takes time to learn which area is being afflicted, and it takes a good listening to be able to hear the difference between denial and your wrong interpretation. The key is to find the family or close community member that the curse is showing itself with. Remove the blame and the limiting beliefs. You don't need to tell them what to do, just help bring to awareness what is occurring and how that impacts other areas of their life. This awareness shifts things naturally. It's the things we don't see that impact us the most. The Jyotiṣi brings jyoti; that which is of light brings light, and therefore removes the shadow.

To do this for others, we must do it for ourselves first. You have to see where you can get over you own curses, and then you can really help others with theirs. Most astrologers have lots of flaws in their chart, if they didn't they would have a hard time understanding other people's suffering.

Forgiveness

Planet	Guru Form
Sun	Dakṣinamūrti
Moon	Mahāvidyā
Mars	Hanuman
Mecury	Vyāsa, Dattatreya
Jupiter	Bṛhaspati, Śiva
Venus	Bhṛgu Ṛṣi
Saturn	Ṛṣi, ancestors
Rāhu	Patañjali
Ketu	Vedamūrti

Svami Vivekananda shares that 'what our attention is focused on will become our reality'. Blame keeps our attention on the past. Attention on the past only generates the same experience in the future. It is one's own responsibility to clean up resentments.

Acceptance allows us to be in the present, to let go and forgive. This can happen naturally with the aspect or transit of Jupiter over the cursed planet, or a Jupiter/ guru mantra for the lord of the sign the cursed planet is placed in. Resentment held by the ahaṅkāra stops one from forgiving. Gandhi said, 'The weak can never forgive. Forgiveness is the attribute of the strong.' It takes the strength of Jupiter to not take a situation personally (*aham*), to see the nature of karma, and to forgive.

Actions will continue based on the past unless you let go and forgive. If one resents someone, or holds pain or anger towards them, or other ill emotions, it means they have something that is needed to be forgiven. In a practical remedy, one can work on forgiving the issues they hold against the graha (as it manifests in one's life; sun-father). True forgiveness sets us free of the past, it allows the heart to be open and give love freely, and it allows one to stop repeating the past negative patterns and gain the benefits of that kāraka in their life.

The Sun warms everyone and the wind cools everyone equally. There is no reason to hold resentments towards anyone in our lives and those whom we have blockages with show which planets have blocked energy. As an astrologer, one should make sure they are working on this with any cursed planet in their own chart. Anywhere there is blockage there will be bias, and therefore unclarity that will lead to mistakes. For the greatest clarity we need to clear out our own baggage. One can ask, "What can be given up that lets the blocked situations with people in your life move forward and not be held in the past?"

If Mars and Rāhu are conjunct or aspecting Venus, the individual may feel their wife, or lovepartner, or sister has abused them, lied and cheated them and is too dangerous to trust. If it was in a sign of Mercury, then this all happened around money, finances or communication. If it is in a Venus sign, it all happened around sexuality, love and relating. Whatever the situation is, that fear, anger, and resentment blocks the heart and doesn't allow a healthy relationship to be present for any of the significations of Venus. Forgiveness is clearing our negative emotions attached to an individual. This doesn't mean one needs to stay in an abusive relationship, or keep being cheated, but it means to live each moment in a state of peace and clarity with all aspects of you.[4] Forgiveness is allowing the power of Jupiter (joy) to transcend the results of the malefic conjunctions and aspects.

There are a few words that relate to forgiveness in Sanskrit that fall into two groups. We'll look at them to broaden our understanding. The first words relating to forgiveness are about bearing with what was done, it is about accepting. *Marṣaṇa* means to endure, to have patience, to pardon or forgive. *Samanujña* means to fully permit or to approve of, to pardon, forgive, or make allowance for faults. *Kṣam* also means to bear, to be patient, to pardon and forgive. Kṣam also is a word for the Earth who is patient and bears all things equally upon her. These words refer to the understanding and compassion in forgiveness.

The second group of words for forgiveness relate to letting go, and setting free. *Vitīrṇa* is a word for forgiveness that means to have penetrated beyond, or passed beyond or gone over. It is about moving forward above what was in the past, as the past being what

[4] Mahābhārata, Vana Parvan, XXVIII Draupadī encouraged Yudhiṣṭhira to battle, but he first forgave King Dhṛtārāṣṭra and the Kurus, so his mind was clear and decision to go to battle correct.

has stuck you. *Vimuc* is a word for forgiveness that means to unleash, unharness, release, set free, or liberate. It relates to the bond that not forgiving puts on one's own self. One can forgive someone and be friends again or forgive and not continue to associate, but to not forgive is a weight that is carried by the person with the grudge, not the one who the grudge is against. *Niryat* is another word which means to *give back, to restore*, to forgive, or to set free. This comes close to the English word *for-give* which literally means to *give* as be*fore*.

In the Mahābhārata, Yudhiṣṭhira sings a verse by the sage Kaśyapa:

"Forgiveness is virtue; forgiveness is sacrifice,
forgiveness is the Vedas, forgiveness is the sacred transmission.
He that knows this is capable of forgiving everything.
Forgiveness is God; forgiveness is truth;
forgiveness is stored ascetic merit; forgiveness protects the ascetic merit of the future;
forgiveness is asceticism; forgiveness is holiness;
and by forgiveness is it that the universe is held together.
Persons that are forgiving attain to the regions obtainable by those that have
performed sacrifices, or are conversant with the Vedas, or having high ascetic merit...
Forgiveness is the might of the mighty; forgiveness is quiet of mind.
Can one like us abandon forgiveness, which is such,
and in which are established God, truth, wisdom and all the worlds?
The man of wisdom should ever forgive,
for when he is capable of forgiving everything, he attains to God.
The world belongs to those that are forgiving; the other world is also theirs.
The forgiving acquires honours here and a state of blessedness hereafter.
Those men that ever conquer their wrath by forgiveness, obtain the higher regions.
Therefore has it been said that forgiveness is the highest virtue."

Your mother and father are the source of your life and relate to the soul and the mind. Your mother and father and immediate family make your initial experience of reality on which everything else is based. This is the first and most important place to forgive unconditionally and restore good relationship into one's life and balance the karma associated with those related planets. Our relationship with our family has a ripple effect on our entire life. In this same way, how you are to people has a ripple effect on the entire world.

Mantras, donation and service help shift energy, and forgiveness (unattachement to your issues) is really letting go of the person (graha affliction) inside of you. It lets go of the poison (malefics) you hold which poisons your experience of reality. We pay our debts to the past and burn that karma to allow a new future. Astrology does not need to be pessimistic; it can bring clarity into what needs to be cleared.

Understanding Curse Combinations

Parāśara discusses the affliction of each graha. Rahu causes the curse of serpents (*sarpa śāpa*). Sun indicates the curse of forefathers (*pitṛ śāpa*). Moon indicates the curse of mother (*mātṛ śāpa*). Mars causes the curse of brother (*bhrātṛ śāpa*). Mercury indicates the curse of maternal uncle (*mātula śāpa*). Jupiter indicates the curse of a priest/spiritual person (*brahmana śāpa*), while Venus indicates the curse of wife (*patni śāpa*). Saturn causes the curse of spirits (*preta śāpa*). Parāśara doesn't mention Ketu which is often called the curse of a saint (*sādhu śāpa*) and is used by some traditions.

The chapter in Bṛhat Parāśara Horā Śāstra on curses from a previous birth (*Pūrva-janma-śāpa-dyotana-adhyāya*) focuses on curses that cause loss of children (*suta-kṣaya*). Though, these same principles are applicable in other areas. The chapter begins with Maitreya asking,

महर्षे भवता प्रोक्तं फलं स्त्रीणां नृणां पृथक् ।
अधुना श्रोतुमिच्छामि त्वत्तो वेदविदांवर ॥ १ ॥

maharṣe bhavatā proktaṁ phalaṁ strīṇāṁ nṛṇāṁ pṛthak |
adhunā śrotumicchāmi tvatto vedavidāṁvara || *1* ||

Honorable sage, in many ways you have spoken about results for women and men,
At this time, oh knower of the Vedas, I want to hear more from you.

अपुत्रस्य गतिर्नास्ति शास्त्रेषु श्रूयते मुने ।
अपुत्रः केन पापेन भवतीति वद प्रभो ॥ २ ॥

aputrasya gatirnāsti śāstreṣu śrūyate mune |
aputraḥ kena pāpena bhavatīti vada prabho || 2 ||

Oh sage (*muni*), the ścriptures say that one who is childless doesn't pass onwards,
Oh master (*prabhu*), kindly explain, what sin (*pāpa*) does one do to be childless?

The fact that a person doesn't pass onwards (*gatirnāsti*) refers to not leaving this plane after death. The soul stays and haunts others because of their desire for children which they did not have. In this way, the *lack of fulfillment* of children binds the soul to this life by the suffering. "Not passing onwards" also refers to a lack of direction (*gatirnāsti*) indicating the direction we gain from the fifth house. Without or beyond children this also includes one's students (on all levels of life) and spiritual practices. It also indicates that there is lack of proper direction of any house that is afflicted or cursed, and the nature of the houses of a cursed planet are also lost.

जन्मलग्नाच्च तज्ज्ञानं कथं दैवविदां भवेत् ।
अपुत्रस्य सुतप्राप्तेरुपायं कृपयोच्यताम् ॥ ३ ॥

janmalagnācca tajjñānaṁ kathaṁ daivavidāṁ bhavet |
aputrasya sutaprāpterupāyaṁ kṛpayocyatām || 3||

In what manner will the astrologer (*daiva-vid*) have the knowledge from lagna
that makes one childless, please speak about the remedy (*upāya*) to attain a child.

Here the astrologer is called the destiny-knower (*daiva-vid*). And Maitreya wants to know how these curses can be seen from the lagna. This request indicates that curses are read from the lagna, they are not read from AL or other special lagnas in the rāśi. The present effect will be seen from the rāśi and D60 lagna (and the past life situation is seen from the AL of the D60). From the AL, we will see more deeply how and where that afflicted planet is disturbing the life, but the story and choice of remedy for that will be based on the rāśi lagna position. Parāśara replies to Maitreya's request.

साधु पृष्टं त्वया विप्र कथ्यते हि तथा मया ।
यथोमया हि पृष्टेन शिवेन कथितं पुरा ॥ ४ ॥

sādhu pṛṣṭaṁ tvayā vipra kathyate hi tathā mayā |
yathomayā hi pṛṣṭena śivena kathitaṁ purā || 4||

Good question, learned one, I will tell you that
Which Śiva told previously when asked by Uma.
The wife of Śiva, known as Uma (or Parvatī), asked Śiva,

केन योगेन पापेन ज्ञायतेऽपत्यनाशनम् ।
तेषां च रक्षणोपायं कृपया नाथ मे वद ॥ ५ ॥

kena yogena pāpena jñāyate'patyanāśanam |
teṣāṁ ca rakṣaṇopāyaṁ kṛpayā nātha me vada || 5||

What negative combinations are known to destroy children,
Please tell me the protective remedies (*rakṣa-upāya*).

Śiva replies to her,

साधु पृष्टं त्वया देवि कथयामि तवाऽधुना ।
सन्तानहानियोगांश्च तद्रक्षोपायसंयुतान् ॥ ६ ॥

sādhu pṛṣṭaṁ tvayā devi kathayāmi tavā'dhunā |
santānahāniyogāṁśca tadrakṣopāyasaṁyutān || 6||

Good Question, Goddess, I will narrate this now,
The combinations for deprivation of offspring and the related protective remedies.

While replying to mother Uma, Śiva states he will give the remedies for the deprivation (*hāni*) of progeny/family/lineage (*saṁtāna*). This is a less common term to call children, which leads us to understand a hidden meaning, or the first remedy given. One of the most common remedies for childlessness is the *Saṁtāna Gopāla* mantra; worshipping baby Kṛṣṇa.[5]

देवकी सुत गोविन्द वासुदेव जगत्पते ।
देही मे तनयं कृष्ण त्वामहं शरणं गतः ॥

devakī suta govinda vāsudeva jagatpate |
dehī me tanayaṁ kṛṣṇa tvāmahaṁ śaraṇaṁ gataḥ ||[6]

Son of Devakī, Govinda, son of Vasudeva, Lord of the Universe,
Give me a child, Kṛṣṇa, I have surrendered to you.

Then Śiva proceeds to teach two basic combinations indicating the root issues causing a curse denying children. This is followed by differentiating various types of curses. We will look at the first two verses and understand the basic principles.

गुरुलग्नेश दारेशपुत्रस्थानाधिपेषु च ।
सर्वेषु बलहीनेषु वक्तव्या त्वनपत्यता ॥ ७ ॥

gurulagneśa dāreśaputrasthānādhipeṣu ca |
sarveṣu balahīneṣu vaktavyā tvanapatyatā || 7||

If Jupiter, lagneśa, seventh lord (*dāreśa*) and the fifth house (*putra sthāna*)
Are all without strength, then it is said, there is childlessness.

रव्याारराहुशनयः सबलाः पुत्रभावगाः ।
तदाऽनपत्यता चेत् स्युरबलाः पुत्रकारकाः ॥ ८ ॥

ravyārarāhuśanayaḥ sabalāḥ putrabhāvagāḥ |
tadā'napatyatā cet syurabalāḥ putrakārakāḥ || 8||

If the Sun, Mars, Rāhu and Saturn are strongly placed in the fifth house,
And the significator for children (*putra-kāraka*) is weak then there is childlessness.

In the first combination, we see the kāraka planet and the kāraka bhāva for children are both weak. Then the lagna and its seventh are weak indicating the individual and their spouse do not have the strength to overcome the obstacles they are presented with. This means that a strong lagna or seventh can overcome general situations of lack of resources or other issues causing lack of (or loss of) children. This gives us more than one option

[5] *Saṁtāna gopāla* mantra is for getting children, *Bāla Gopāla* mantra is for insuring the child's health, and *Gopāla* mantra is for one's own health.
[6] For women, change '*śaraṇaṁ gataḥ*' to '*śaraṇaṁ gatā*' for proper grammar.

to give a remedy. If the fifth lord was afflicted in the 8th house, then one can strengthen Jupiter and the lagneśa. If Jupiter was afflicted in a bad placement, then one can strengthen the fifth house and the lagneśa. In all these ways, we have multiple options for a planet which can bring children. If all these factors are beyond repair, then it becomes a fixed karma which indicates a curse denying children.

The second verse discuses multiple malefics being placed in the fifth house. In general, if malefics are causing a curse, if they are weak then it shows less power for them to hurt significations, and if they are strong then they have more power to hurt the significations they are harming. Malefics situated in or aspecting a house will harm it (unless it is their own house). If the significator is also weak then the significations of that house will suffer severely. If the significator can be made strong and some benefic aspects strengthened on the house then there is hope for a remedy. If there is no ability to strengthen these factors then it has become fixed karma caused by negative actions in the past life relating to that area of life.

This fits the standard teaching that has been presented so far and clarifies it. Then Parāśara mentions specific curses next.[7] These verses can be looked at as individual combinations and we can also utilize these verses to understand the principles behind them. They are not combinations that the average individual will likely be able to remember, but by studying them one is able to put together the general idea of where a curse is being caused and how to seek the repayment of the debt so that the curse may be propitiated properly. The first combinations given are the curse of the serpants (*sarpa-śāpa*). Śiva tells Uma,

पुत्रस्थानगते राहौ कुजेन च निरीक्षिते ।
कुजक्षेत्रगते वाऽपि सर्पशापात् सुतक्षयः ॥ ९ ॥

putrasthānagate rāhau kujena ca nirīkṣite |
kujakṣetragate vā'pi sarpaśāpāt sutakṣayaḥ || 9||

Rāhu in the house of children aspected by Mars, or is in the sign of Mars,
Indicates destruction of children due to the curse of sarpas.

पुत्रशे राहुसंयुक्ते पुत्रस्थे भानुनन्दने ।
चन्द्रेण संयुते दृष्टे सर्पशापात् सुतक्षयः ॥ १० ॥

putraśe rāhusaṁyukte putrasthe bhānunandane |
candreṇa saṁyute dṛṣṭe sarpaśāpāt sutakṣayaḥ || 10||

The fifth lord conjunct Rāhu, and the child of the Sun (Saturn) in the fifth house
Conjunct or aspected by the Moon, indicates destruction of children from curse of sarpas.

7 This is also disussed in *Crux of Vedic Astrology* by Sanjay Rath, p.172-174

कारके राहुसंयुक्ते पुत्रेशे बलवर्जिते ।
लग्नेशे कुजसंयुक्ते सर्पशापात् सुतक्षयः ॥ ११ ॥

kārake rāhusaṁyukte putreśe balavarjite |
lagneśe kujasaṁyukte sarpaśāpāt sutakṣayaḥ || 11||

When the kāraka is conjunct Rāhu, and the fifth lord is without strength,
And the lagneśa is conjunct Mars, it is destruction of children from curse of sarpas.

कारके भौमसंयुक्ते लग्ने च राहुसंयुते ।
पुत्रस्थानाधिपे दुःस्थे सर्पशापात् सुतक्षयः ॥ १२ ॥

kārake bhaumasaṁyukte lagne ca rāhusaṁyute |
putrasthānādhipe duḥsthe sarpaśāpāt sutakṣayaḥ || 12||

When the kāraka [Jupiter] is connected to Mars, Rāhu is conjoined the lagna,
The fifth lord is in a duḥsthāna [6, 8, 12], then the curse of sarpas destroys the children.

भौमांशे भौमसंयुक्ते पुत्रेशे सोमनन्दने ।
राहुमान्दियुते लग्ने सर्पशापात् सुतक्षयः ॥ १३ ॥

bhaumāṁśe bhaumasaṁyukte putreśe somanandane |
rāhumāndiyute lagne sarpaśāpāt sutakṣayaḥ || 13||

If the fifth lord is the child of Soma (Mercury), in a division or associated with Mars,
And Rāhu and Māndi are in Lagna, then the curse of sarpas destroys the children.

पुत्रभावे कुजक्षेत्रे पुत्रेशे राहुसंयुते ।
सौम्यदृष्टे युते वाऽपि सर्पशापात् सुतक्षयः ॥ १४ ॥

putrabhāve kujakṣetre putreśe rāhusaṁyute |
saumyadṛṣṭe yute vā'pi sarpaśāpāt sutakṣayaḥ || 14||

If the fifth house is lorded by Mars, the fifth lord is conjoined Rāhu, or
Conjunct or aspected by Mercury, then the curse of sarpas destroys the children.

पुत्रस्था भानुमन्दाराः स्वभानुः शशिजोऽङ्गिराः ।
निर्बलौ पुत्रलग्नेशौ सर्पशापात् सुतक्षयः ॥ १५ ॥

putrasthā bhānumandārāḥ svabhānuḥ śaśijo'ṅgirāḥ |
nirbalau putralagneśau sarpaśāpāt sutakṣayaḥ || 15||

The Sun, Saturn, Mars, Rāhu, Mercury, and Jupiter in the fifth house, and
The lagneśa and fifth lord are weak, then the curse of sarpas destroys the children.

ग्नेशे राहुसंयुक्ते पुत्रेशे भोमसंयुते ।
कारके राहुयुक्ते वा सर्पशापात् सुतक्षयः ॥ १६ ॥

lagneśe rāhusaṁyukte putreśe bhomasaṁyute |
kārake rāhuyukte vā sarpaśāpāt sutakṣayaḥ || 16||

Lagneśa conjunct Rāhu, and the fifth lord conjunct Mars or
The kāraka [Jupiter] conjunct Rāhu indicates the curse of sarpas destroys the children.

We can see the standard rules at work here, but the cause of the sarpa curse is being revealed. The first verse [9] has Rāhu in the kāraka bhāva (with malefic aspects), while the second verse [10] has Rāhu conjoined the kāraka bhāva lord. Here a malefic in the kāraka bhava is hurting the house, and the aspect of the Moon is insuring the results. In the third verse [11], the kāraka is conjunct Rāhu (while the lagna is afflicted and the lord of the kāraka bhāva is weak). In the fourth and fifth verse [12/13], Rāhu is afflicting the lagna, while the kāraka and bhāva lord are afflicted. The next verses will fit under one of these mentioned categories: Rāhu afflicting either the kāraka bhāva, or kāraka bhāva lord, or the kāraka graha or the lagna itself.

There are huge amounts of Jyotiṣa principles hidden within the above combinations, which is more than can be explained here. What is presented here are the very basic principles, but as you study this chapter more in depth, you will see that some of the combinations are very similar and you have to take into account some other factors. For example, verse 75 related to the curse of a priest (*brahma-śāpa*) says if Jupiter is nīca, Rāhu is in the lagna or the fifth, and the fifth lord is in a duḥsthāna [6, 8, 12], then curse of a Brahman destroys the children. This is similar to verse 12 above, except that Jupiter is nīca, indicating it is the cause of the suffering.

Keeping the above understanding in mind, we can look at the next few verses regarding the curse of the forefathers (*pitṛ śāpa*). Śiva said to Uma,

पुत्रस्थानं गते भानौ नीचे मन्दांशकस्थिते ।
पार्श्वयोः क्रूरसम्बन्धे पितृशापात् सुतक्षयः ॥ २० ॥

putrasthānaṁ gate bhānau nīce mandāṁśakasthite |
pārśvayoḥ krūrasambandhe pitṛśāpāt sutakṣayaḥ || 20||

If the Sun is debilitated in the house of children, and placed in the aṁśa of Saturn, and associated or hemmed in by malefics, then the curse of forefathers destroys the children.

पुत्रस्थानाधिपे भानौ त्रिकोणे पापसंयुते ।
क्रूरान्तरे पापदृष्टे पितृशापात् सुतक्षयः ॥ २१ ॥

putrasthānādhipe bhānau trikoṇe pāpasaṁyute |
krūrāntare pāpadṛṣṭe pitṛśāpāt sutakṣayaḥ || 21||

If the fifth lord is the Sun placed in a trine, conjunct a malefic, [or] hemmed within malefics, [or] apected by malefics, then the curse of forefathers destroys the children.

भानुराशिस्थिते जीवे पुत्रेशे भानुसंयुते ।
पुत्रे लग्ने च पापाढ्ये पितृशापात् सुतक्षयः ॥ २२ ॥

bhānurāśisthite jīve putreśe bhānusaṁyute |
putre lagne ca pāpāḍhye pitṛśāpāt sutakṣayaḥ || 22||

If Jupiter [the kāraka] is in the sign of the Sun [Leo], and the fifth lord is conjunct the Sun, And the lagna and fith house have malefics, then curse of forefathers destroys the children.

लग्नेशे दुर्बले पुत्रे पुत्रेशे भानुसंयुते ।
पुत्रे लग्ने पापयुते पितृशापात् सुतक्षयः ॥ २३ ॥

lagneśe durbale putre putreśe bhānusaṁyute |
putre lagne pāpayute pitṛśāpāt sutakṣayaḥ || 23||

If the lagneśa is without strength in the fifth house, and fifth lord is conjunct the Sun, And malefics are in the lagna and fifth house, then curse of forefathers destroys the children.

पितृस्थानाधिपे पुत्रे पुत्रेशे वापि कर्मगे ।
पुत्रे लग्ने च पापाढ्ये पितृशापात् सुतक्षयः ॥ २४ ॥

pitṛsthānādhipe putre putreśe vāpi karmage |
putre lagne ca pāpāḍhye pitṛśāpāt sutakṣayaḥ || 24||

If the tenth lord is in the fifth house or the fifth lord is in the tenth house, And the lagna and fifth house have malefics, then curse of forefathers destroys the children.

पितृस्थानाधिपे भौमः पुत्रेशेन समन्वितः ।
लग्ने पुत्रे पितृस्थाने पापे सन्ततिनाशनम् ॥ २५ ॥

pitṛsthānādhipe bhaumaḥ putreśena samanvitaḥ |
lagne putre pitṛsthāne pāpe santatināśanam || 25||

If the tenth lord is Mars and associated with the lord of the fifth, and the lagna, fifth house, and tenth house have malefics, then the forefather's curse destroys the children.

In all the above and proceeding combinations malefics are mentioned, which means Mars, Saturn and Rāhu. So understanding that Rāhu is involved in almost all these situations you must differentiatiate when the suffering is coming from the serpants or forefathers (and all the other planetary curses involved). We see this when we study the chart in depth, we will see a theme that starts repeating. There is a story that goes with every situation which reveals itself.

Two principles are introduced here. The large involvement of a single planet and the use of the houses and houselords involved. The first few verses show that the Sun is heavily tied to the area of life relating to children in the specific chart and that its severe affliction leads to the pitṛ śāpa. The later verses start using the house of the biological father (10th) to indicate the pitṛ śāpa, (the ninth house is used for brahmana śāpa).

In this way, we see what is most affecting the individual; in trines, associated with the lagna, etc. to see the source of the suffering. What are the most negative indications? Which planets are unhappy (*nīca*). Which houses and house lords are involved? The large involvement of a specific factor will indicate the roots of an issue. Sometimes students complain when a simple rule they learned is cancelled out by a stronger situation happening, but this is life. Someone may be a good math teacher and want to teach high school students but end up a computer technition because they were able to find a better paying job doing that work. So the math teacher is cancelled, the stronger combination(s) win. Therefore the simple rules are key for laying a foundation to look at, but one needs to read the chart as a whole and put all the pieces together. The story of the chart needs to be understood.

Who, What, Where

Where the curse is situated in the chart indicates not just who was cursed but which area of your life that affliction is returning to cause suffering. Houses and planetary placements from that planet show the story of how that curse takes form in your life. For example, if Moon is cursed in the tenth house, there could have been a motherly woman whose career was destroyed, and this shows suffering from motherly women in the workplace in this life. If Jupiter is cursed in the eighth house in this life, it could show the person stole from their teacher in the past and in this life the individual will have a hard time finding a teacher. A fifth house Venus may be a daughter, an eleventh house Mercury may be a friend. The planet modified by its placement is taken into account, and it is this individual 'who' is cursing.

If the lagneśa is involved in the curse, then the suffering is very personal and can even hurt the physical health. If the lagneśa is twelfth from a curse it shows that your intelligence ignores the bad situation. If the lagneśa is second from the curse, it shows the cursed individual ignores your intelligence. If the 8th lord is connected to the curse it will show great suffering and can even give chronic disease or disorders. In this same way, if the tenth lord is involved it can show career and financial issues and bad reputation with regards to work. The lords involved will show results in this way according to the daśā activating the combinations. If the ātmakāraka is involved in the curse, then the suffering affects the individual deeply and can even change their direction in life. The curse of the ātmakāraka can be devastating to the individual's dreams, but with proper guidance can lead to great humility (as the individual is forced to get over their ahaṅkāra).

If there is more than one curse, there will always be a predominant one, even if two are active. In this way, analysis is made to determine which is predominant and causing the greater suffering. More malefics conjunct (and next aspecting) is more intense suffering. Duḥsthānas indicate more intense karma to be overcome. Benefics in duḥsthānas (6,8, 12 and 3), whose bhāva kāraka is a malefic, will cause more suffering, and the stronger they are in these houses the stronger the suffering. Benefics will give less suffering if strongly placed in a kendra or trikoṇa, and more suffering if strongly placed in dusthana. Exaltation or retrogression in duḥsthānas will indicate stronger negative results accordingly. This will be similar for malefics in kendra and trikoṇa, the stronger they are the more suffering.

The life circumstance will also be a factor for which curse is more severe. For example, a renunciate with a cursed Venus and cursed Jupiter will suffer the curse of Jupiter more. The curse of Venus is supporting their renunciation, while the curse of Jupiter is blocking their proper guidance on the spiritual realm. In this way, proper analysis will indicate the problem area and allow the proper remedy to be given.

The vimśottarī daśā of the cursed planet will show suffering, especially if it is not well placed or weak. If the cursed planets are conjunct, then the curse (and therefore the remedy) may relate to an indication represented by that conjunction. If the cursed planets are opposite each other in the chart, then the curse may go back and forth between the two planets, and the remedy to one can afflict the other and vice versa. In this case, a more comprehensive remedy can be given with the focus on the more important planet (unless a remedy similar to the conjunction can be given).

If the curse is placed in the kendra or trines, then the curse was caused by an action the individual may not have been aware of in the past life. This unintentional suffering creates a situation where the individual will suffer and the curse will make the person a better individual because of the suffering. If the curse is located in duḥsthāna houses, it indicates the curse was done out of intentional action. In this case, it is unlikely the curse will ever be fully overcome. The best thing to do for this situation is ensure the remedy is done as a lifelong practice to manage the situation.

Curses will be activated both by daśā and by specific actions. For example, if the Sun is cursed in the 10th house, then when you become head of a company the results of that Sun will be activated. Actions related to the curse will aggravate it. For example, if a cursed Jupiter is in the sixth house, then arguing with the guru will aggravate the curse of Jupiter and make it much worse. If the curse is in the fourth house it will relate to the home life, while in the tenth the work life. If the curse is in the ninth house it can show the curse is activated on pilgrimage, or the twelfth house will show the curse is activated while traveling abroad. In a general way, curses in fixed signs will affect you more at home or close to home, while curses in moveable signs will be more activated in foreign places or away from home. In this way, all aspects of placement are taken into account to understand the nature of the affliction and how and when it is becoming worse or can be lessened.

"A curse has the purpose of depriving one of ones attachments. Whether this be one's spouse, job, status, home, friends, siblings, parents, etc. should be determined through the curse yogas. However, the curse will not work if the object of attachment has not manifested yet, i.e. a person cannot suffer the deprivation of spouse if they are not married. Hence curses can initially work towards the manifestation of various attachments only to deprive one of them later on. This all depends on the Yoga in the chart."[8]

If an individual has a cursed Venus, the suffering will be more likely when the individual starts a relationship so remedy can be done at that time, or before that time, or the individual can be more careful in selecting a spouse (who, when, where) and insuring compatibility. This would be the same for Mercury and education, and Jupiter and finding a teacher, etc. In this way, understanding where the curse is activated will help the astrologer give advice accordingly.

The significations of the cursed planet will suffer. Learning, education, the rasa dhātu, and the skin will suffer with a cursed Mercury. Decision making, guidance, finances, and such will suffer with a cursed Jupiter. To understand how this is impacting an individual's material life, see the natural zodiac houses ruled by that planet. For example, if Venus is cursed it will impact finances (2nd house/Taurus) and relationship (7th house/Libra). The planets give the significations to the natural houses of the zodiac, and we can understand their impact deeper by looking at them in this way. When the lagna lord is cursed there is bad decision making and a lack of direction with life; even if the individual has many resources, they will not know how to use them to be effective. The curse of lagna can also hurt the reputation.

The houses owned by the cursed planet will suffer as their lord is under affliction. When looking at the lordship of the planets involved in the curse, see the house signs that contain malefics, the A6 and the A8 to indicate the main cause of suffering. When looking at a malefic planet (who lords two signs) take the sign which contains planets over one that is empty. For example, in a Cancer rising chart with cursed Venus, the fourth and eleventh lord are hurt. If the eleventh is empty but the fourth has the Moon, then the curse will more likely afflict the mother over the colleagues of the eleventh house. The specific difficulties will be seen from the fourth lord as well as the dvadaśāṁśa chart.

[8] Rath, Sanjay. *Moola Dasa: Lagna Kendradi Graha Dasa*. Sri Jagannath Center, Handout, 2001.

To understand the deeper story of the curse, examine the cursed planet (śāpita graha) in the khavedāṁśa (D-40), akṣavedāṁśa (D45), and ṣaṣṭyāṁśa (D60). This will indicate that the curse is related to either the maternal or paternal family's karma, or simply one's own action in a past life. The śāpita graha is examined to see which chart shows the same malefic situation or planetary condition. For example, if Jupiter was conjunct Rāhu, Saturn and Mars in the rāśi, and in the D-40 it is only conjunct Saturn and aspected by nothing else, in the D-60 it is aspected by Rāhu and nothing else, but in the D-45 it is conjunct Rāhu and Ketu and aspected by Saturn, then involvement of paternal karma is indicated. Curses can stay in a family for up to seven generations unless they are pacified. If the cursed Jupiter is placed in the fifth house of the D-45 and cursed again, this could indicate a break in a commitment (Jupiter) and a child outside of the marriage (fifth house with Rāhu) on the paternal family side. These actions and their impact related to that situation are indicating the present life suffering. Often souls return to individuals in the same family to enjoy blessings or curses created within that family. The past can be seen in this way through these charts.

The Curse of Lord Rāma

Bhagavan Śrī Rāma is the first chart to study in the traditional teaching of curses. Some people think that divine beings or Saints are not affecting by curses or karma. If even a divine incarnation like Śrī Rāma can have a curse, then who is above karma? Anything that has incarnated, has been born with a birth chart and exists within the realm of Time. Great Time is moving all things, and the saints and avatars teach us to sail on this ocean by following the divine flow.

In the Rāmāyana of Vālmīki,[9] the birth of Rāma is described in Canto XIX: The Birth of Princes.

The seasons six in rapid flight
Had circled since that glorious rite.
Eleven months had passed away:
Twas Chaitra's ninth returning day.
The moon within that mansion shone
Which Aditi looks kindly on.

Rāma was born eleven month's since the Pūjā to help produce an auspicious son. It was was the ninth waxing tithi of the month of Chaitra. And the Moon was placed in Punarvasu, the nakṣatra of Aditi.

[9] Translated by Ralph T.H. Griffith

Raised to their apex in the sky
Five brilliant planets beamed on high.
Shone with the moon, in Cancer's sign.
Bṛhaspati with light divine.

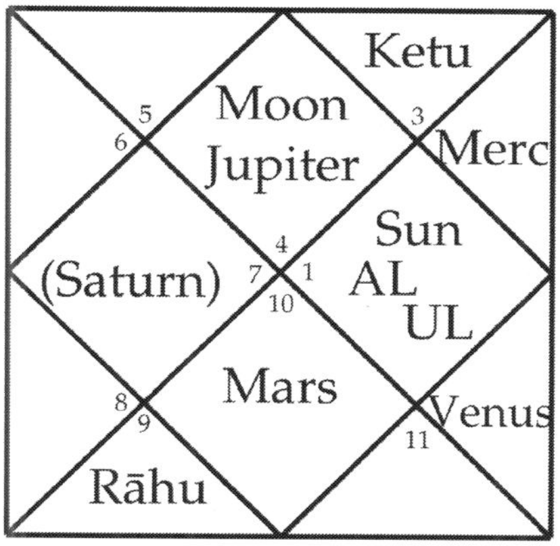

The Moon was with Jupiter in Cancer and there were five exalted planets. This is Jupiter in Cancer, Sun in Aries, Mars in Capricorn, Saturn in Libra, and Venus in Pisces. In this way, the chart of Śrī Rāma has been given.

Śrī Rāma has Moon and Jupiter in lagna indicating great fame and exalted Sun in the tenth house showing his kingship. Jupiter and Moon are aspected by Saturn and Mars. The Sun (with UL) is aspected by Saturn, Mars and Rāhu indicating the curse of the Sun is greater and being placed in the tenth house is indicating a pitṛ curse on career and spouse. As the time for Rāma to take his kingship came, his 'step' mother requested a wish of his father. The stepmother is represented by the 6th house which has Rāhu in it, and Rāhu is the lord of the A6. The sixth house is also lorded by a cursed planet. At the stepmother's request, the father (Sun) sent Rāma to live in the jungle for 14 years. The curse of Sun was activated at the time of his ascension to power. The second house of wealth, lorded by the Sun, became null and void during his time of renunciation in the jungle, and his father passed away in grief while he was away.

Venus is exalted in the ninth house, indicating an incredible wife, but the curse is conjunct his UL and so he was separated from his wife for most of his married life. The lord of Venus is also under a curse, and when the lord of a planet is cursed, the full blessings of that planet lack the ability to be fully enjoyed, unless the curse is lifted. The lagna lord, Moon, is involved in the curse and makes the suffering very personal.

Practice Exercise:

1. Completely read the chapter in Bṛhat Parāśara Horā Śāstra on curses from a previous birth (*Pūrva-janma-śāpa-dyotana-adhyāya*).
2. All the combinations in this chapter apply to the fifth house. Rewrite verses 20-25 in regards to the curse of ancestors denying the partnership of the seventh house.
3. Here we have listed principles, but it is in real charts that we see how it really works. Study three charts of individuals having serious problems, practice the application of these principles and indicate the nature of the issue through planetary and house influences.

Free from a Curse (Śāpa-mukti)

Pandit Sanjay Rath says, "What is good in this world, I do not have to worry, what is suffering is my responsibility… I must see people's suffering. If I cannot see the suffering, I cannot solve the problem." [10] We learn how to see the suffering and then we learn how to help overcome it.

Some curses can be overcome (*viṣapa*), some curses can be nullified (*śapathajambhana*), some curses can be averted (*śapathayāvana*) before they happen. And some curses are jail (*śāpayantrita*) that can be made more bearable. All this depends on the placement of the curse and the severity of the karma.

A mantra or stotra to uplift the afflicted planet is the first thing to give, if the individual is capable of doing a mantra. If needed, a pūjā to pacify and uplift the śāpitā graha can also be done to speed up the process. In the case of Śrī Rāma, he worshiped the Rameśvara Śiva liṅga (associated with the exaltation of the Sun) before re-uniting to get his wife and returning home.

After mantra, pūjā or prayer, the proper actions directed at balancing the karma is to be performed by the individual. Donation and service can be performed by any individual with any religious (or non-religious) views, and thereby get beneficial results. For this reason, it is important to be able to tell an individual which significations will be the most beneficial to donate to in order to rectify their karma.

First we will look at the traditional teachings of Parāśara on how to remove the suffering of a curse (*doṣa-parihāra*). Then we will look at the dynamics of these remedies in order to give them an authoritative modern context for effective remedial measures. After explaining each curse, Parāśara gives us a list of traditional remedies. For curse of the nāgas, Parāśara says,

ग्रहयोगवशेनैवं नृणां ज्ञात्वाऽनपत्यता ।
तद्दोषपरिहारार्थं नागपूजां समारभेत् ॥ १७ ॥

grahayogavaśenaivaṁ nṛṇāṁ jñātvā'napatyatā |
taddoṣaparihārārthaṁ nāgapūjāṁ samārabhet || 17||

Individuals subjected to these combinations considered to cause childlessness,
Undertake (*samārabh*) nāga pūjā for the sake of removing (*parihāra*) this problem.

[10] Curses and their Remedy, Delhi, 2000 36:49

स्वगृह्योक्तविधानेन प्रतिष्ठां कारयेत् सुधीः ।
नागमूर्तिं सुवर्णेन कृत्वा पूजां समाचरेत् ॥ १८ ॥

svagṛhyoktavidhānena pratiṣṭhāṁ kārayet sudhīḥ |
nāgamūrti suvarṇena kṛtvā pūjāṁ samācaret || 18||

In one's home, establish a golden nāga statue according to the rules,
And perform pūjā as done by the wise.

गोभूतिलहिरण्यादि दद्याद् वित्तानुसारतः ।
एवं कृते तु नागेन्द्रप्रसादात् वर्धते कुलम् ॥ १९ ॥

gobhūtilahiraṇyādi dadyād vittānusārataḥ |
evaṁ kṛte tu nāgendraprasādāt vardhate kulam || 19||

Then by donating a cow, land, sesame seed, gold, etc. according to one's level of wealth, surely one attains the tranquility/kindness of the Nāga King and the family increases.

Parāśara speaks of remedies, indicating their importance. Often if a person couldn't have kids, they don't need you to tell them, they already know and are coming to the astrologer for a remedy. People that have a cursed Venus don't need you to tell them they have relationship problems; most of the time they will tell you. People see an astrologer to learn how to overcome their kārmik hurdles. In this way, Parāśara teaches us the remedy after having shown us the problem, just as medical texts talk of the cure after teaching the disease.

First Parāśara indicates a deity to be propitiated. Then he speaks about donation. Parāśara indicates to donate according to *vitta-anusāra-ta. Vitta* (from *vid*) means what is known or understood and *anusāra* means what is natural, prevalent, established by authority or custom. With *-ta* on the end, this term can mean "the nature of what is in conformity with present usage". *Vitta* also means wealth (what has been gained) and therefore also means "donation according to one's level of wealth." Therefore Parāśara recommends that we give according to the nature of our level of wealth and our cultural customs. In the present modern culture, donation happens through organizations or temples that help out particular groups of people. These organizations often have a structure already in place for donation at different levels of wealth.

In the ancient times, there were not large scale organizations, but at the same time, people lived in a small village where all these archetypal problems were apparent in your neighbors or neighboring village. Donating a cow to the local teacher, feeding crows, or a few dogs, or helping a single poor family was practical.[11] In modern times, our lives are busier, and the impacts of our actions have a more far reaching impact. In a powerful chart, the indication could have been caused by a large scale company or organization

[11] See Jātakā-Bharaṇam of Pandit Dhundiraj where there is an entire chapter (*Dāna-adhyāya*) on donation.

the person was running or part of in their last life. In this way, donating to a quality organization which has a large impact in the world gives very beneficial results.

For curse of the Ancestors (Sun), Parāśara recommends a pilgrimage to Gayā, which is in northern India. For curse of brother (Mars), he recommends pilgrimage for planting fig trees near the river Kaveri, which is in South India. These are possible for Hindus in India, but these are not efficient remedies for those in other countries around the world. Remedies need to be *practical* and *possible* for individuals to perform in order for them to get results.

Therefore we now study the nature of the remedial worship and offering and understand its correlate to the individual, in their culture and time period. In order to do this properly, we first must understand the various remedies to get free from a curse (*sāpa-mukta)* as given by Parāśara.

Remedial Measures from *Pūrva-Janma-Śāpa-Dyotana-Adhyāya*	
Curse of Pitṛ	Śrāddha at Gayā, feeding 100 or 1,000 Brāhmaṇas as one can afford [31]. Performing the marriage of a girl [not one's own] (*kanya-dāna*), donation of a cow, and one will definitely be freed of the curse of the ancestors [32]. The family will grow and their will be children and grandchildren. [33]
Curse of Mātṛ	Bathing in the sea by the bridge between India and Sri Lanka (*setu*), and having one lakh (100,000) of Gāyatrī mantra recited. [Donation of] things made of silver, milk, drinks, and donation or actions associated with the planet [48]. Feeding Brāhmaṇas, and going around (*pradakṣiṇa*) the the pipal tree (*aśvattha*) 1008 times with devotion [49]. Indeed the Great Goddess (*mahādevi*) will give freedom from the curse and there will be gain of good children and the family will prosper (*kula-vṛddhi*) [50].
Curse of Bhrātṛ	To get release from the curse of brother, perform Cāndrāyaṇa fast after listening to the Harivaṁśa Purāṇa (the geneology of Viṣṇu), while offering oneself to Viṣṇu (*viṣṇu-sannidhau*) [62]. Plant holy fig trees (*aśvattha*) along the Kaveri river, give ten milk-giving cows through the wife and donate land with fruit trees [63]. One will get his fair portion though a lawful wife, without doubt. One will certainly have children and the family will prosper [64].
Curse of Uncle	To remove this doṣa, establish/preserve a pleasing image of Viṣṇu. Dig a reservoir (*vāpī*), well (*kūpa*), pond (*taḍāga*), etc. for a family member [69]. The children will increase and the accomplishments will grow, this is how the wise pacify these impious combinations [70].
Curse of Priest	To pacify this doṣa, the individual performs Cāndrāyaṇa fast offering prayers three times. Donating a milk-giving cow with a financial gift (*dakṣiṇa*) [79]. Donating five gems (*pañcaratnāni*) along with gold, and afterward feeding Brāhmaṇas according to one's means [80]. Then surely there will be gain of good children, no doubt. There will be freedom from the curse (*mukta-śāpa*), purification of the soul (*viśuddha-ātmā*), and good brains (*sukha-medhas*) [81].
Curse Of Wife	To overcome this curse, help a sincere young girl get married (*kanya-dāna*). If an unmarried girl is not available, a statue of Viṣṇu with Lakṣmī [93] made of gold can be donated along with ten milk-giving cows. Donate a bed, ornaments, clothing, to a [newlywed] husband and wife [94]. Definitely (*dhruvaṁ*) there will be a child and luck (*bhāgya*) will grow [95a].
Curse of Preta	This doṣa is pacified by performing śrāddha at Gayā. Rudra abhiṣeka and donation of an image of Brahmā [106], [donation of] a milk-giving cow, a silver vessel/bowl (*pātra*), and a blue sapphire (*nīlamaṇi*). And afterward, feed Brāhmaṇas and give them monetary donation (*dakṣiṇa*) [107]. This will give humans freedom from the curse, birth of a child and growth of the family [108].
	If the doṣa for obtaining a child is caused by Mercury or Venus then Śambhu pūjā, for Jupiter and Moon utilize mantra, yantra and medicines [109]. If caused by Rāhu, give a marriage offering (*kanya-dāna*), from the Sun worship Viṣṇu (*hari-kīrtana*), donation of a cow for doṣa caused by Ketu, and Rudra jāpa for that caused by Mars and Saturn [110]. All doṣa disappear and one gains a good child (*śubha-santāna*) by listening to the telling of the harivaṁśa (mythology/geneology of Viṣṇu) in the prescribed way, with devotion [111].

Mechanics of Donation

Donation works directly on us, even if it seems indirect. The results of modern quantum science allows us to infer how this works. In classical physics, the *principle of locality* states that an object is influenced directly only by its immediate surroundings. It is a belief that "that which we conceive as existing ("real") should somehow be localized in time and space."[12] This supports the logical material analysis that two separate entities *should not* influence each other without some kind of interaction or communication between them.

Non-locality is the direct influence of one object on another distant object. This is related to *quantum entanglement* theory of quantum physics which says that distant events may under some circumstances have instantaneous correlations with local ones. Research has been done using *photon polarization* with a large spatial separation between the particles and observed events which should require time to elapse when it did not. Therefore, non-locality, though not understood, is a process where distant objects immediately create an effect on others with no lapse of time, no matter the distance they are separated.

The universe is made of consciousness. Its very fabric is consciousness and affected by thought. Sub-atomic particles act according to who you are being. Every thought interacts and manifests the nature of your reality. Every second, with every thought and action you are having an impact on yourself, others and the environment. You are impacting your life and the life of those around you.

You can donate to a children's hospital, woman's shelter, or wildlife organization and get an immediate result in your individual life. Even if these things seem distant or unrelated, they can immediately and directly change the planetary frequencies in your life. You can balance your karmic debt, without needing to be near or connected to those individuals which are being benefited.

The astrologer can see the area of life that is afflicted, see the actions which created that misalignment and determine what positive actions can balance that karma. In this way, proper donation is an action (*karma*) that balances debts. This unlocks doorways, opens new possibilities, and allows thoughts and actions to shift in a way that allows for new possibilities to open in one's life. Why waste time living a few decades as a rock when you can make the world a better place and live the life that you want? Proper donation or service with proper mantra is even more powerful. When there is a disease being caused by a curse, the trained astrologer may also recommend a medicine to fix the root issue and symptoms, in addition to donation or service. Or the kārmik remedy will bring the right doctor and medicine.

[12] Albert Einstein, Letter to Max Born (March 1948)

Donation does not require a particular religious background to practice and is supported by all major religions. The Judeo-Christian concept of donation talks about the benefits of donation and how to perform it. In the book of Tobit [4.6-12] it says,

> *7: To all them that live justly, give charity from your substance; do not let your eye begrudge the gift when you make it. Do not turn your face away from anyone who is poor, and the face of God will not be turned away from you.*
> *8: If you have many possessions, make your gift from them in proportion; if few, do not be afraid to give according to the little you have.*
> *9: So you will be laying up a good treasure for yourself against the day of necessity.*
> *10: For charity delivers from death and keeps you from going into the darkness.*
> *11: Charity, for all who practice it, is an excellent offering in the presence of the Most High.*

The Christian Gospel teaches to sell what you have and give in charity [Luke 12:13], as this is what is considered true wealth in heaven (for the day of necessity). And one is told to give donation privately and not in front of others with the intention to look good or it will not work [Mathew 6:1-4].

Charity can atone for ones sins and redeem one from death [Proverbs 11:4]. As water puts out a blazing fire, donation will atone for sins [Ecclesiastics 3:30]. Jesus teaches to give from what is in you and it will leave you clean [Luke 11:41]. He speaks about giving as that which cleans the inside, similar to washing the outside. In this way, donation cleanses the negative tendencies which are inside, and that is the result of balancing karma.

Mantras from the Vedik path are the same as prayers from the Judeo-Christian path. The remedy for a curse lies in mantra or stotra, ritual if possible and donation. This becomes prayer, fasting and charity/donation in the Judeo-Christian realm. The book of Tobit [12:8-10] teaches,

> *8 Prayer with fasting and charity is better than to lay up treasures of gold,*
> *9 For charity saves from death, purges away sins, and gives a full life.*
> *10 But they that commit sin and injustice are enemies to their own soul.*

Technicalities of Donation

Donation is done according to the basic significations of a planet. You caused some suffering, now you have to directly help those who are suffering in a proportionate way to remedy the situation. It is the emotion/impact that is experienced by those individual's that is balancing the karma and removing the curse (*śāpoddhāra*).

When the planetary frequencies are properly understood, all things can be categorized within them. If a person is having reproductive issues, there is an imbalance with the frequencies of Venus. On the level of the mental body this can often relate to sexual abuse (Venus-Rāhu) earlier in life, or a negative relationship experience, that has caused stagnant energy in the reproductive area. The fact that the abuse can be seen in an individual's chart, indicates that there is a deeper *causal* reason behind the suffering. Each chart will indicate the specific reason relative to past karma. Often the curse of Venus relates to some type of abuse of the feminine energy by the individual in their previous life. The karmic balancing can be done by donating money or time to women's help organizations. The giving of beneficial energy to the frequency of Venus helps clear the kārmik blockages associated with the sister, or the reproductive system or the love relationship or however the curse is manifesting according to house and sign. The best thing about donation is that there are no negative side effects of the remedy. If the astrologer gives the wrong remedy, nothing will shift and there is at least some good karma performed.

Jupiter relates to having children. Often people who have not been able to have children will adopt and then later be able to conceive their own child (after having adopted one). The fact that they adopted a child and are taking care of a child that needed extra help has balanced their Jupiter frequency enough that they have moved through the blockage and been able to have a child themselves. In this way, when parents are having issues conceiving or carrying a pregnancy they can donate to children in need. Often it is beneficial to adopt a child financially through various non-profit organizations.

Many of these kārmik remedies can be performed on an obvious level according to intuition regarding the cause of the disorder. If a child is having learning difficulties donate money or time to children with more severe mental handicaps. If there are money issues in your life, donate your money or time to helping the poor and homeless.

On a deeper level, we understand the frequency of the planetary energy. Mercury relates to the skin as well as learning, so an individual with a bad skin condition can donate to their local school programs. Mars relates to inflammations, and people with a recurring inflammatory condition can donate to veterans or a legal defence fund for a good cause. As Jupiter indicates children and husband, a woman wanting to find a husband can also financially adopt a child to help improve her karma to find a quality husband. Every action we perform has many ripples affecting other people's lives, which is reflected in our own kārmik consequences.

Below are examples of simple remedies that one can ask a patient or client to perform to help remove the kārmik blockages.

Sun	Helping own father or men who have small children, service to a government project, paying other's medical expenses, donation/service to local temple or church, donations for bird protection organizations (or large felines)
Moon	Helping own mother or women in care of children, helping community events, donation to battered mothers or single mothers, helping those with depression or other mental disturbances, donation to water life protection organizations
Mars	Helping the brother, donations to veterans or those wounded in war, or the police or public safety, donations to burn victims, or fire victims, helping those going through a divorce, or any type of abuse, helping those needing a legal defence, donation to public land, parks, reforestation
Mercury	Helping cousins, aunts, uncles, or students, donations to schools, donations of books and other learning material, paying for a poor child to attend a better school, or an individual to attain new skills, donations to canine protection related organizations
Jupiter	Helping husband, guru, priests, actually or financially adopting a child, donations to teachers or spiritual organizations, donation to humanitarian work foundations, fruit trees, donation to help elephants or whales
Venus	Donations to battered wives or other groups that support the upliftment of downtrodden women, organizations that help women get out of the sex industry, helping individuals get married, supporting artistic or performance foundations, donation to equine protection services
Saturn	Helping one's employees, the working class, unions, donating to the elderly, sick/diseased, maimed, handicap, children with foot and leg birth defects, poor and homeless, or reptile protection
Rāhu	Donations to environmental protection or rehabilitation projects, donation to drug education and rehabilitation programs, or helping those with compulsive disorders, or organizations fighting fraud, cheating, and pollution
Ketu	Donation to monks, nuns, āśrams and spiritual healers, donation and service to yoga organizations, prevention and curing of viral diseases, breaking conspiracies, fish or amphibian protection organizations

The more specific the remedy is, the faster it will give results (according to the nature of the individual's karma). If Venus is aspected by Rāhu and Mars, then in a past life the individual may have been abusive to the spouse. If this combination is in Cancer, then the individual may have been psychologically abusive, if it is in Leo then is may have been manipulative and controlling, if it is in Virgo then there is a lack of integrity with low class partners. In this way, the past karma is to be understood and the remedy will therefore be aimed to uplift the fallen significations. If Venus is in Cancer aspected by Rāhu and Mars, then donation can be to a counselling organization for abused women. In Leo, donation could be towards an organization aimed at empowering abused women to have confidence, or learn leadership. If Venus is debilitated, donation can be to helping women who have gone down the wrong path in life, or helping restore a life of integrity back into their womanhood. In this way, the well trained astrologer will understand the past karma and find the exact nature of the situation to donate to.

If a child is having learning disabilities, then there is some blockage regarding the frequencies of Mercury. If Mercury is conjunct Saturn the donation will be to children who are born with some retardation, while if Mercury is conjunct Mars the donation will be to children who are from troubled families and need special attention. If Mercury is with Rāhu and aspected by Saturn, then the donation will be to children who are born with incurable or genetic disorders such as autism, Down syndrome or such conditions. If Mercury is with Rāhu in Aries it will be a genetic disorder that destroys the logic of the child and makes them unable to learn working skills. If Mercury is with Saturn in Gemini it will be children with speech disorders. In this way the donation of time or money will go to the exact frequency which will more quickly allow the individual to work through the karma they need to process.

It is the impact that is experienced by those individual's that is balancing the karma and removing the curse (*śāpoddhāra*). If an individual is donating to an organization that is not actually applying the money to what it is supposed to, then the remedy will not work as it is supposed to. It is the impact the donation has that matter, not just the act of giving the money. When I first asked my guru about that, his response about the donation not getting to serve its purpose was because of the density of the individual's karma; even though they try to remove the negative, it is not happening. In this way, it is important to be aware of what organization you are donating to and to insure that they are actually helping serve the significations that are afflicted.

Sometimes when I talk about what to donate to, people tell me they are already donating to some other good cause. If you need to donate to abused women because of a Venus curse, then donating to hungry children in a foreign land will not help your present problem. If the individual had Saturn aspecting Mercury, it would be beneficial, but otherwise it will show up as a beneficial Mercury in the next life. By choosing what is best to donate to based upon the curses or afflictions in the chart, we are directly impacting the results of karma being experienced in this life. I often take time to explain the karma to the individual; how it is impacting their present life and the karma that could be causing it. Then we look at the possibilities for donating to an organization that can directly impact that kind of signification.

As soon as the person makes the commitment and starts researching what type of organization to donate to, there condition starts to shift. In cases, where the remedy cannot be started until a month or two later, the individual can make a sankalpa (intention/promise) to start donating by a specific time, so the karma can begin to shift. Pandit Sanjay

Rath teaches that when there are additional doṣas like Sankranti or Tithi doṣa, then the remedy (mantra and donation) for the curse will cure those aspects afflicted by pañchāṅga doṣa.

Depending on how the planet is connected to the lagna and Moon, it may not be active at the time of looking at the chart, there may only be subtle traces of the afflicted significations. The curse will become active during the daśā that activates it, and donation remedies are beneficial to do beforehand to lessen the negative experience associated with that planet. Besides the situations which activate the curse there is also the daśā that will activate the curse. This will be seen in either the vimśottarī daśā (or specific udu daśā) *of the cursed planet* when the situation itself is becoming active, or in the mūla daśā *of the planets causing the curse.*

The end of the curse or period of its effect is called the *śāpānta*. When Rāma (the Sun) touched the rock which was Ahalya, it was her śāpānta, she was set free from her infidelity curse. The remedy for the curse (or chance to improve the situation) is seen in the viṁśottarī daśā of the dispositor of the curse, or with the transit of Jupiter, or when beneficial significations giving remedy are in first, eighth and tenth from the Narāyaṇa daśā rāśi, or during the mūla daśā of the remedy planet (bhāva kāraka or dispositor or benefic aspecting) indicating improvement or a chance to resolve the problem. Each of these will work according to the indications of the respective daśā/transit.

These methods of healing karma are meant to benefit the material world. Yoga teaches a deeper philosophy of how to be unattached to your karma, and this is one of the deepest teachings in texts such as the *Bhagavad Gītā*. Every action creates karma; good or bad. Karma binds you to your material existence. Since karma cannot be escaped it is not the action but the perception of action which the yogī changes. This is another topic, but what is to be understood is that what is being taught here is not donation or seva for the purpose of attaining mokṣa (karma yoga). The intention of this type of donation is to remove kārmik blockages which will allow life to be successful and make the world a better place.

These remedies balance kārmik debt and remove blockages in the causal body. As the causal body is very subtle, the results may also be subtle. For example, a man was suffering with immune system problems for many years, and he was told to donate to a women's organization. He signed up for regular donations to be automatically taken from his account. A month after beginning this, he found a doctor that put him on a food regimen that cured his disorder. For years he went to many doctors that could not help him, it was after he began working on his kārmik debts that he was able to find the right doctor. The remedy works with everything on the material plane in which the physical body interacts, not separate from it.

We can have insight into how the remedy may enter into the life and can also guide people along these lines (after a remedy has been done to start clearing the karma). If the lord of the house is beneficial and is helping lift the curse, then the remedial actions will be given to the native by someone directly. For example, if the curse is in the fourth house and lorded by Jupiter, and Jupiter is in the tenth house then the boss may give the individual the direction needed to overcome the curse. If Jupiter was in the ninth house, then the guru will give the direction to overcome the curse. In this way, the significations indicated by the lord will indicate who is giving the information to overcome the suffering. If the person was suffering from an immune disorder, this would be the person that mentions a doctor that could help them. Ārūḍhas with a cursed planet will indicate who is suffering; ārūḍhas with the remedy planet will indicate those who will be helpful to alleviate the suffering. If the Upapada Lagna is with the cursed combination, that marriage will be a curse in itself and will bring suffering, while if the UL is with the remedy planet then the spouse will bring relief accordingly.

The bhāva kāraka of the house of the cursed planet will be approached according to the tattva of the bhāva kāraka, for example, if the bhāva kāraka is Saturn then the deity controlling the vāyu tattva (Śiva) is propitiated to bring the remedy. In this way, Śiva would be beneficial if the Sun was the lord of the sign (Leo) and Śiva will be beneficial if the kāraka is Saturn (vāyu). In one case the deity is used as a planetary overlord (invoking an individual to help), and in the other case as the controller of the kāraka's tattva (invoking a beneficial situation). If the curse is in the second house, Jupiter is the kāraka, and ākāśa is the tattva. Viṣṇu is the controller of ākāśa and he can be propitiated by pūjā to Viṣṇu or by feeding people (a second house remedy related to the sustainer). A cursed Mercury conjunct Saturn in the second house can show donation to an organization feeding children. If the curse is in a fixed sign, it is best in an organization that works locally, if it is in a movable sign, it is best supporting an organization that works in distant lands.

If it is the kāraka of the house that helps with the remedy, then the remedy comes without the individual's knowledge. This could indicate a situation where the vāstu is causing illness and the disease causes financial problems which make a person move their home/office and then the remedy comes into the life because the cause has been removed.

Kārmik intensity of the curse is based on the house, house lord, and bhāva kāraka. If the planet is cursed and the lord and kāraka are also afflicted then it indicates a very fixed suffering, and the proper practice of the Mahāvidyā of the planet can be given to help the situation. The Mahāvidya changes who the person is *being*, and thereby changes the perception of the situation and its results.

Talking about curses is a delicate matter. Even the word 'curse' creates fear and despondency in people. Use the word 'curse' if the individual is mature enough or avoid it if the Moon or lagna is weak. Speak about the area where karma is afflicted and the possible reasons, and explain the remedy the indidivual can perform. This knowledge is meant to open up an area of life that has been blocked. It is giving a person joy where it has not been. If you leave the client feeling challenged and discouraged you have not served them. Empower your clients with this knowledge and show them new possibilities.

Life has consequence; it's not about good or bad. Some individuals get upset at others or even god for their suffering. "How could a kind god have made such suffering?" The law of karma is the law of consequence. You can love someone and allow them to get their consequence. When a child touches something they are not allowed to, the parent gives them the consequence, it does not mean they do not love the child. Blessings and curses are just consequences to our actions; from past lives (birth chart) and right now (praśna).

The situations we get in life our not out to disempower us, it is just life, it is just the results of something we did without consciousness. Adding consciousness and approaching life with intention empowers us. We are perfect as we are, there is just karma that has been picked up that is ready to be cleared. Your true nature is perfect as it is, there is nothing to change, just baggage to let go of.

The Transient Nature of Time

As an astrologer, we leave an individual in a greater state than when they came to us. We empower them to overcome their situation, or help them to find peace with it. Occasionally, there is a suffering that cannot be alleviated, such as a loved one dying, or a job being lost that will not return, or a reputation that has been spoiled. In these cases, it is our duty to remind those suffering of the transient nature of Time.

The Mahābhārata starts by teaching the temporary nature of existence to a suffering king with a special ode to Time.[13] The blind king, Dhṛtāraṣṭra, was distressed about the situation of his children and the coming battle, many of them were sure to die. He grieves to his advisor, Sanjaya, and says he doesn't wish to live anymore.

Sanjaya reminds him that there have been hundreds and thousands of great kings and heroes in the history books (*purāṇa*) and they have all died as well as their sons. These great humans were generous, truthful, pure and even though they had perfected all the good qualities (*sarva-ṛddhi-guṇa*), they have gone to their end (*nidhanaṁ gataḥ*).

Sanjaya tells the king, that his children are evil-natured (*durātman*), burning with hostility (*manyu pratap*), greedy (*lubdha*), constantly in bad conduct (*durvṛtta*), and underserving respect. He says, 'You have heard the teachings (*śrutavan*), and are endowed with brains, intelligence and understanding. By following the teachings (*śruta-anuga*), one's intelligence is not confused. You know about the nature of punishment (*nigraha*) and favour (*anugraha*), the anxiety for your children's safety is unbecoming.'

भवितव्यं तथा तच्च नातः शोचितुमर्हसि ।
दैवं प्रज्ञाविशेषेण को निवर्तितुमर्हति ॥ १८६ ॥

bhavitavyaṁ tathā tacca nātaḥ śocitumarhasi |
daivaṁ prajñāviśeṣeṇa ko nivartitumarhati || 186||

One should not lament for that which will inevitably happen;
Even with excellent understanding, who can avert (*nivartita*) fate (*daiva*)?

विधातृविहितं मार्गं न कश्चिदतिवर्तते ।
कालमूलमिदं सर्वं भावाभावौ सुखासुखे ॥ १८७ ॥

vidhātṛvihitaṁ mārgaṁ na kaścidativartate |
kālamūlamidaṁ sarvaṁ bhāvābhāvau sukhāsukhe || 187||

No one can leave the path of what has been determined by creation,[14]
All that exists or doesn't exist, happy and painful, are rooted in Time.

[13] Mahābhārata (Adhi Parvan) I.I.186-190

[14] Vidhātṛ literally means the distributor/arranger/maker and means either the creator or destiny/fate, as the creation is by itself fated from the moment it is created. The nature of the created is the nature of its destiny. Vidhātṛ-vihita is that which has been apportioned by the creator, which is the destiny.

कालः पचति भूतानि कालः संहरति प्रजाः ।
निर्दहन्तं प्रजाः कालं कालः शमयते पुनः ॥ १८८ ॥

kālaḥ pacati bhūtāni kālaḥ saṁharati prajāḥ |
nirdahantaṁ prajāḥ kālaṁ kālaḥ śamayate punaḥ || 188||

Time matures beings, and Time destroys that which is born,
Time sets beings on fire, and Time bring tranquillity again.

कालो विकुरुते भावान्सर्वाँल्लोके शुभाशुभान् ।
कालः सङ्क्षिपते सर्वाः प्रजा विसृजते पुनः ॥ १८९ ॥
कालः सर्वेषु भूतेषु चरत्यविधृतः समः ॥ १८९ ॥

kālo vikurute bhāvānsarvāṁlloke śubhāśubhān |
kālaḥ saṅkṣipate sarvāḥ prajā visṛjate punaḥ || 189||
kālaḥ sarveṣu bhūteṣu caratyavidhṛtaḥ samaḥ || 189||

Time transforms all states on all planes for good or bad,
Time brings forth all beings and withdraws them again.
Time changes what all beings have preserved.

अतीतानागता भावा ये च वर्तन्ति सांप्रतम् ।
तान्कालनिर्मितान्बुद्ध्वा न सञ्ज्ञां हातुमर्हसि ॥ १९० ॥

atītānāgatā bhāvā ye ca vartanti sāmpratam |
tānkālanirmitānbuddhvā na sañjñāṁ hātumarhasi || 190||

Your condition will pass away and the present rolls forward,
Recognizing that Time created our understanding, it is not proper to give up.

After this talk the king's mind was restored to peace. The lesson here is that understanding that a problem has arisen because of the nature of Time and all these issues will go away for the same reason. All things will pass in Time, all suffering will eventually be in the past.

Timing Results of Curses

An afflicted planet will give negative indications in its daśā according to the area of life of its significations and according to the nature of the daśā. For example, in an āyur-daśā, the afflicted planet is more likely to cause health issues and disease during its daśā than a beneficially disposed planet. The afflicted planet literally becomes *stronger* (to kill you) in its daśā.

In naisargika daśā of an afflicted planet, the time period and the activities natural to that time are more difficult, and will take extra work to accomplish. For example, relationship during and afflicted Venus daśā will be filled with all kinds of suffering in the realm of love, relationship and trying to find the right partner. In this way, during a viṁśottarī daśā of an afflicted planet, situations will arise relative to the nature of the cursed planet. The indications will be based on the indications which that planet desires in the chart and trouble with them being fulfilled. If the māhadaśa and antardaśā lords are both under affliction, there will be much greater suffering in the daśā, and even more so if they are in a six-eight relationship.

Daśās interact with each other and create a stronger situation. For example, the struggles of the Venus naisargika daśā time period will be more prominently activated when a negative Venus viṁśottarī daśā occurs, or if a daśā of the seventh lord is active. The negative indications of an āyur daśā will become more prominent when they align with the health related issues in the viṁśottarī daśā. When negative daśās align to give negative results then there are large issues, when they do not align, then the issues have much less weight. Rāśi daśā and transits will also support or protect a negative daśā.

There is a daśā which is specific to look at curses called *lagna kendrādi graha daśā*, or better known as *mūla daśā*. *Mūla* means root, the foundation or origin. The whole universe has its *mūla* in Time, and is moved by Time. Mūla daśā indicates the root of our karma that Time is bringing to fruition through the three stages of life as seen through the kendras, paṇaphara, and āpoklima houses.

Mūla daśā can be used to time curses and blessings, in both the rāśi and the ṣaṣṭyāṁśa. It is used slightly different than viṁśottarī daśā in that we don't look at the afflicted planet, we look at the daśā of the planets causing the affliction. For example, if Mars and Rāhu afflict Venus, then Rāhu-Mars mūla daśā or Mars-Rāhu mūla daśā will show a situation where the curse will be active in the life of the individual.

"The source of the whole universe is *rooted* in Time,
and in that way, it will go back to Time."[15]

[15] Mahābhārata XVI.9.33 *kālamūlamidaṁ sarvaṁ jagadbījaṁ dhanañjaya* | *kāla eva samādatte punareva yadṛc-chayā* ||

Mūla Daśā

Parāśara teaches the variations of *kendrādi daśā* in the *Daśā-adhyāya* of Bṛhat Parāśara Horā Śāstra. Then a particular variation called *lagna kendrādi graha daśā* is taught in the *Daśā-phalam-adhyāya* (39) of Yavanajātaka, the *Daśā-antardaśā-adhyaya* from Bṛhat Jātaka, the *Daśā-phala-nirupana* from Horā Sāra and the *Mūla-daśā-phala-adhyāya* from Sārāvalī where it is given the name "mūla daśā."[16]

Parāśara indicates four variations of the kendrādi daśās; two according to the place of beginning the daśā and two according to rāśi or graha giving daśā results. Kendrādi-rāśi daśā starts from the stronger of the lagna or seventh and gives results according to rāśi. Kāraka-kendrādi-rāśi daśā starts with the ātmakāraka and gives results according to rāśi. Kendrādi-graha daśā starts with the stronger of the lagna or seventh and gives results according to graha, while the kāraka-kendrādi-graha daśā starts from the ātmakāraka and gives results according to the grahas.[17] Mūla daśā is kendrādi-graha daśā starting from the lagna, therefore called *lagna kendrādi graha daśā.* In the *Daśā-adhyāya,* Parāśāra gives the calculations for kendrādi daśā,

लग्नसप्तमयोर्मध्ये यो राशिर्बलवान् भवेत् ।
ततः केन्द्रादिसंस्थानां राशीनाञ्च बलक्रमात् ॥ १७५ ॥

lagnasaptamayormadhye yo rāśirbalavān bhavet |
tataḥ kendrādisaṁsthānāṁ rāśīnāñca balakramāt || 175||

Between the lagna or seventh, the stronger rāśi will begin, and that kendra-ādi will be established according to the direction of that sign and progresses according to strength.

कारकादपि राशीनां खेटानां चैवमेव हि ।
दशाब्दाश्चरवज्ज्ञेयाः खेटानां च स्वभावधि ॥ १७६ ॥

kārakādapi rāśīnāṁ kheṭānāṁ caivameva hi |
daśābdāścaravajjñeyāḥ kheṭānāṁ ca svabhāvadhi || 176||

In this manner, the signs and planets from the ātmakāraka can also be considered. The years of the daśā are calculated similar to cara daśā; and from planet to own sign.

---

16 In these texts, mūla daśā is mentioned just before naisargika daśā and the naisargika antardaśā are calculated in a kendrādi format. Yavanajātaka varies, where naisargika daśā is first (39.1-5) and then the mūla daśā (39.6-7), which represents a philosophical difference. Yavanajātaka, Bṛhat Jātaka, Sārāvalī, and Horā Sāra are only using mūla daśā and naisargika daśā. It is not till Phaladīpikā of Mantreṣvara that we see the use of Vimśottarī daśā in *this lineage* of texts.

17 Kāraka kendrādi shows the fructification of spiritual experiences; that which is happening to the soul, and its growth. It shows interaction with special devatas (Iṣṭa, Dharma, etc) and other carakārakas. See Larsen's *Kāraka Kendrādi Graha Dasa: The Progress of the Soul*, 2004.

द्विराश्यधिपक्षेटस्य गण्येदुभयावधि ।
उभयोरधिका संख्या कारकस्य दशा समाः ॥ १७७ ॥

dvirāśyadhipakṣeṭasya gaṇyedubhayāvadhi |
ubhayoradhikā saṅkhyā kārakasya daśā samāḥ || 177||

For signs having two lords,[18] calculate (*gaṇya*) both (*ubhaya*) time periods (*avadhi*),
And use the one whose sum gives more daśā years.[19]

To sum up the above, the stronger of the lagna or 7th starts the daśā and that sign (odd/even) determines the direction the daśā progresses (kendra, paṇaphara, āpoklima or kendra, āpoklima, paṇaphara). And within those three groups, the order of signs will be according to the strength of those signs. This daśā can also be calculated from the ātmakāraka (from a planet). The years of the daśā are calculated the same as cara daśā (given a few verses before by Parāśara). This is done by counting from the sign to the lord of the sign for a rāśi daśā, and calculated from the planet to its mūlatrikoṇa sign for a graha daśā. For signs having two lords, the lord giving more (*adhika*) daśā years (*daśā samā*) is used. This and other rules have been delineated in the cara daśā section, but this verse lends importance to the daśā length given by the lord of the sign for kendrādi daśā.

The kendra refer to the 1st, 4th, 7th and 10th. The paṇaphara are the 2nd, 5th, 8th, and 11th. The āpoklima are the 3rd, 6th, 9th, and 12th. The word kendra comes from *kentron*, which is the greek word for the angular houses. Kentron comes from *kenteo* (to prick), and kentron means that which pricks, like a thorn or a bee sting and also referes to a point. This is similar to the Sanskrit, where they were also called the *kaṇṭaka*, the pointed places, indicating their impact. They are also known as the catuṣṭaya, the square, indicating the four 'points' from each other which creates a square.[20] Paṇaphara comes from the greek word *epanaphora* which generally relates to successive repetition, but in astrology refers to the houses that successively follow the kendra,[21] this is why they are often called succedent (subsequent) houses in English. Āpoklima is the house that precedes the kendra: *apo* is a prefix meaning away, off, back, down[22] and *klima* means a downward slope or inclination, so it is the slope away from the kendra, or 'downhill' from there. Sagittarius represents falls from high places, as the tenth house is the height of it all and the downhill (*āpoklima*) is pretty steep from there.

---

18 *vṛścikādhipatī dvau ca ketubhaumau smṛtau dvija | śanirāhu ca kumbhasya svāminau parikīrtito || 157||*
Scorpio has two lords known as Ketu and Mars. Saturn and Rāhu are declared the lords of Aquarius.

19 *dvināthakṣetrayoratra kriyate nirṇayo'dhunā |dvāvevādhipatī vipra yuktau svarkṣe sthitau yadi || 158||*
When there are two lords, determine which one is working. If both lords are conjunct in their own sign, *varṣa dvādaśakaṁ tatra na cedekādi cintayet |ekaḥ svakṣetrayo'nyastu paratra yadi saṁsthitaḥ || 159||*
Then one is considered to give twelve years. If one planet is in its own sign and the other is in a different sign, *tadā'nyatra sthitaṁ nāthaṁ parigṛhya daśāṁ nayet |dvāvapyanyarkṣagau tau cet tamormadhye ca yo balī || 160||*
The one stationed in another lord's house is accepted for the daśā. If both lords have gone to other signs, the counting is according to the stronger [Bṛhat Parāśara Horā Śāstra, Dāśā-adhyāya].

20 Bṛhajjātaka of Varāhamihira I.17

21 Neugebauer and Van Hoesen, *Greek Horoscopes*, p.7

22 It is the exact same as the Sanskrit prefix *apa-*.

The kendrādi daśā starts with the primary kendra and those four houses give their experience in the first part of life. After which, the next group of four signs (paṇaphara) will give their results in the middle of life. The āpoklima are "over the hill", representing the last part of life. In this way, the various texts say that one can understand the condition in the three parts of life.[23] The strength or otherwise of these trinity of signs (kendra, paṇaphara, āpoklima) will decide the effects of the three stages of life.

"The kendrādi daśās, being based on the kendras, work towards the fructification of events in one's life. This arises from the *paraspara kāraka* concept. As the kendras are the pivotal parts of one's life, they have the power to impact ones personality, and planets therein have a profound impact on one's life. Hence the kendrādi daśās are specifically meant to see when the various rāśi/planets will give their kārmik results. This is what makes the kendrādi daśās different from other daśā."[24] The kendrādi daśā are indicating events that impact your personality; events which make you who you are.

How the specifics of the kendrādi daśā are calculated (where it is starting from) then adds to the subtley of what you are looking to perceive. Every daśā has the possibility to perceive an aspect of our life, we just have to understand the dynamics of how it works to interpret it properly. Mūla daśā is a particular kendrādi variation that begins from the strongest lagna (udaya, Sun or Moon) and reads the kendra from that. In this way, it is analysing the root lagna kendra that makes you who you are. Mūla daśā can also be utilized in the D-40 (Moon), D-45 (Sun) and D-60 (lagna).

If a planet is cursed, this daśā can be used to predict that entire area of life. For example, if Venus is cursed or under other affliction, you can time when partners come and go with the mūla daśā very effectively. Mūla daśā can also be used in timing positive and negative yogas in the ṣaṣṭyāṁśa (D60) which shows the deep past life roots of curses and blessings. When this one can rectify the ṣaṣṭyāṁśa and read mūla daśā from here, one's interpretations and predictions will match what people get from psychics and nāḍī readers (and its always fun to compare).

---

23 Yavanajātaka 1.94-98, Horā Sāra of Pṛthvyaśas 8.2

24 Rath, Sanjay. *Moola Dasa: Lagna Kendradi Graha Dasa*. Sri Jagannath Center, Handout, 2001.

Calculation of Mūla Daśā

The mūla daśā begins from the strongest of the Sun, Moon or lagna.[25] Kalyāṇa Varmā calls this the views of Satyāchārya (*satya-bhāṣita*). The stronger of the udaya lagna, Sun and Moon is determined as the root of the manifesting karma. Most software gives and an option to choose just one of these, or to select to only use lagna or Sun or Moon if one prefers. This is important as certain combinations will bring a variance to the standard rules of strength.

After the focal point (lagna) is determined, the first daśā is decided by the strongest planet in that kendra, and then followed by other planets in that kendra in order of strength. When all planets have given their results, then the next set of four signs will give their daśā. According to Parāśara, if the starting sign is odd then paṇaphara give the next four signs and if the starting sign is even then it will be the reverse and the āpoklima give the next daśā. Saturn in the starting point always makes the daśā go direct and Ketu in the starting point makes the daśā always go reverse, as a standard rule.

1. The mūla daśā starts from the stronger of the Sun, Moon or Lagna
2. The strongest planets in that kendra give their daśā first
3. The next group of four is based on odd/even sign of the starting rāśi (Saturn makes it always direct and Ketu always reverse)

The strength is determined according to the standard rules which are elucidated by Parāśara in the teaching on cara daśā.

तत एव दशा ग्राह्या क्रमाद् वोत्क्रमतो द्विजः ।
बलस्याऽत्र विचारे स्याद्ग्रहात् सग्रहो बली ॥ १६१ ॥

tata eva daśā grāhyā kramād votkramato dvijaḥ |
balasyā'tra vicāre syādagrahāt sagraho balī || 161||

Therefore, in this manner, the daśā moves forward or reverse, from the strongest:
The planet accompanying planets is judged as stronger.

द्वावेव सग्रहौ तौ चेत् बली तत्राधिकग्रहः ।
ग्रहयोगसमानत्वे ज्ञेयं राशिबलाद् बलम् ॥ १६२ ॥

dvāveva sagrahau tau cet balī tatrādhikagrahaḥ |
grahayogasamānatve jñeyaṁ rāśibalād balam || 162||

If both are with a planet then the one with more planets is stronger
If both are with equal [number of] planets the strength is based on the sign

[25] Yavanajātaka 39.6-7, Bṛhajjātaka of Varāhamihira VIII.1-2, Horā Sāra of Pṛthvyaśas 8.1, Sārāvalī of Kalyāṇa Varmā 41.1-3, Horā Makarand 10.1

ज्ञेयाश्चरस्थिरद्वन्द्वाः क्रमतो बलशालिनः ।
राशिसत्त्वसमानत्वे बहुवर्षो बली भवेद् ॥ १६३ ॥

jñeyāścarasthiradvandvāḥ kramato balaśālinaḥ |
rāśisattvasamānatve bahuvarṣo balī bhaved || 163||

Know that cara, sthira and dvandva, in that order, possess more strength.
If the nature of the signs are the same, [then the one that gives] more years will be stronger.

एकः स्वोच्चगतश्चाऽन्यः परत्र यदि संस्थितः ।
गृह्णीयादुच्चखेटस्थं राशिमन्यं विहाय वै ॥ १६४ ॥

ekaḥ svoccagataścā›nyaḥ paratra yadi saṁsthitaḥ |
gṛhṇīyāduccakheṭasthaṁ rāśimanyaṁ vihāya vai || 164||

If one is in its exaltation or own sign, and the other is stationed in another place,
The rāśi of the exalted one is considered and the other disregarded.

उच्चखेटस्य सद्भावे वर्षमेकं च निक्षिपेत् ।
तथैव नीचखेटस्य वर्षमेकं विशोधयेत् ॥ १६५ ॥
एवं सर्वं समालोच्य जातकस्य फलं वदेत् ॥ १६६ ॥

uccakheṭasya sadbhāve varṣamekaṁ ca nikṣipet |
tathaiva nīcakheṭasya varṣamekaṁ viśodhayet || 165||
evaṁ sarvaṁ samālocya jātakasya phalaṁ vadet || 166||

One year is added for a planet in the house of its exaltation,
And one year subtracted for a planet in its sign of debilitation.
In this way, the birthchart results can all be considered similarly.

With these rules, the strength of the signs and planets is determined and the sequence of planets in the daśā is determined.

a. The planet [or sign] with a planet is stronger

b. The planet [or sign] with more planets is stronger
[Jaimini adds a sign aspected by Jupiter, Mercury or own lord is stronger]
[Jaimini adds if equal number, then examine status: ucca, mūlatrikoṇa, sva, etc.]

c. If equal number [*or status*] then the strength of sign determines:
Cara signs are strongest, then sthira, then dual
[Jaimini adds if still the same, then use the one with higher degrees]

[Jaimini adds if still the same, use the lord in a different oddity than its own sign]

d. If the same, then the one giving a longer daśā is stronger

These rules will give the stronger sign, then the planets (if more than one) within that sign need to be seen for which is strongest among them to give the daśā sequence. Then the daśā length can be calculated to give the 120 year cycle.

e. A planet in exaltation, mūlatrikoṇa, or own sign is stronger in that order

f. The planet with higher degrees is stronger (according to carakāraka)

g. If the same, the one with higher minutes/seconds is stronger

4. Count from the graha to its mūlatrikoṇa (and deduct 1/non-inclusive count)
   a. add 1 for an exalted planet, subtract 1 for a nīca planet
   c. if planet is in own sign it gets the maximum 12 years (even if exalted)
   d. use Aquarius for Rāhu and Scorpio for Ketu
5. Deduct the result from the viṁśottarī daśā period years of the graha
   a. if the result is larger, then deduct the viṁśottarī years from it.
   b. if the result is zero then use the full viṁśottarī daśā length
6. Calculate all nine planets for the first cycle
7. Subtract the years of the daśā from the viṁśottarī daśā length for the second cycle
8. The antardaśā are the same order and begin from the mahādaśā lord
9. The mahādaśā is divided into 9 equal parts to find the length of the antardaśā

Example of Śrī Rāma

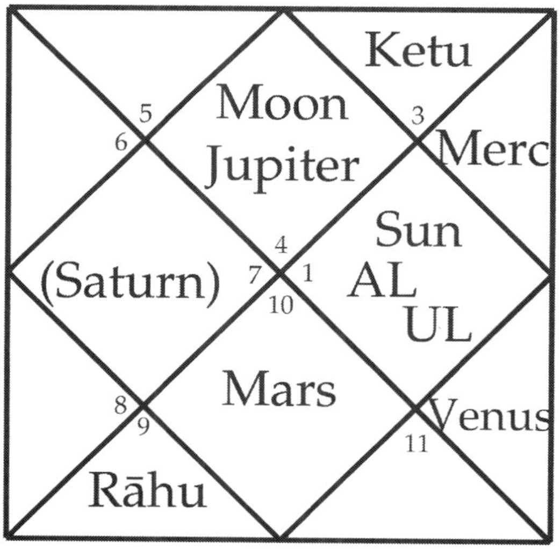

The first chart to calculate mūla daśā and study, according to tradition, is the chart of Lord Rāma. Śrī Rāma had suffered the curse of Nārada and incarnated with the curse to lose his wife and need the help of a monkey to get her back.

The stronger of the Sun, Moon and lagna is calculated first. The Sun is alone, and the Moon is in Lagna with another planet, making the Moon/lagna strongest. The daśā will begin from the moveable signs with the Moon/lagna (having two planets), and then to the kendras in order of strength.

Jupiter is exalted and will give the first daśā, then Moon. Both Libra and Capricorn have the rāśi aspect of Mercury giving them strength, and both those signs contain exalted planets. Mars is stronger because Saturn is retrograde (giving ucca-baṅga). So the daśā following the Moon is Mars and then Saturn. Then Sun is the last planet in the kendra.

Cancer is even, so the next set of signs will be the āpoklima, which are dual signs in this case. Venus gives the next daśā as it is exalted. Then Gemini and Sagittarius have equal number of planets and neither is aspected by Mercury or Jupiter so the status of the lord decides which will be next. As Jupiter, the lord of Sagittarius is exalted; Rāhu gives the next daśā, followed by Ketu.

The last set of four are the paṇaphara houses from the Moon/lagna, which are the fixed signs. This gives the daśā of Mercury. In this way, the rules of strength are used to give the order of the daśā.

According to Sanjay Rath, the length of the daśā is calculated by counting from the planet to its mūlatrikoṇa sign. Jupiter is in Cancer and it is six signs to Sagittarius with an inclusive count, minus one equals five (as a non-inclusive count). One year is added for its exaltation, making six years. The final calculation is to subtract the signs gained from the viṁśottarī daśā of Jupiter which is sixteen years long. This gives the length of Jupiter mūla daśā as ten years.

Daśā Planet	Signs Gained	Additions/ Subtractions	Viṁśottarī Difference	=Years of Daśā	Age
Jupiter	5	+1=6	16	10	0-10
Moon	10	-	10	0=10	10-20
Mars	3	+1=4	7	3	20-23
Saturn	4	+1=5	19	14	23-37
Sun	4	+1=5	6	1	37-38
Venus	2	+1=3	20	17	38-55
Rāhu	2	-1=1	18	17	55-72
Ketu	5	-1=4	7	3	72-75
Mercury	4	-	17	13	75-88
Jupiter			16-10=	6	88-94
Mars			7-3=	4	94-98
Saturn			19-14=	5	98-103

After the first level of the daśā is calculated, the second level takes the remainder of the viṁśottarī years. The first cycle of Jupiter was ten years, which leaves six years remaining. The Moon used its complete years in the first cycle, so the next daśā is that of Mars with four years remaining to be experienced. After all calculations, the final age of 120 years is attained. The antardaśā are composed of each planet proportionately divided up within the mahādaśā.

Pandit Sanjay Rath teaches that after determining the curses, see which are worse and analyse the curse causing planet associated with the eighth house (*nīja doṣa*) for predicting the activation of a curse. When in doubt, use the higher varga charts to determine which curse is more potent.

In the chart of Śrī Rāma, the Moon and Jupiter are aspected by Saturn and Mars, but the strongest curse is the Sun with AL and UL aspected by Saturn, Mars and Rāhu. Saturn is the eighth lord and therefore the most likely to ignite the curse.

Śrī Rāma was born in the daśā of Jupiter, and then educated by Ṛṣi Vasiṣṭha in the daśā of Moon. At this time he was married to Sīta (it is a planet conjunct Jupiter). In the daśā of Mars, he studied warfare from the Ṛṣi Viśvāmitra. Mars aspecting the tenth is good for the tenth house as it is its own sign, meaning it is good for career, in this case his military (Mars/kṣatriya) career. But it is not good for the planet and ārūḍhas aspected by it and other malefics.

In the advent of Saturn mūla daśā, the father of Śrī Rāma decided Rāma is now fit to be king and he can retire to the jungle and focus on his spiritual life. But on hearing this, The 'step' mother (6th house) requested a wish of Śrī Rāma's father. The house represented by her has Rāhu in it, and Rāhu is the lord of the A6. Rāhu is aspected by Saturn giving it a cold selfish desire, and it is lorded by a cursed planet. At her request, the father (Sun) sent Rāma to live in the jungle for 14 years (the daśā of Saturn).

The *original cause* (curse of Nārada) is seen from the houses lorded by Saturn, which in this case are the seventh and eighth house: he separated Nārada from who he wanted to be in a spousal relationship with. As the curse of Sun was activated during Saturn daśā, its house (Leo in the second) became weak and did not fructify: he was away from family and wealth.

When the Sun mūla daśā came, Rāma had reached victory over the demons of the world. His time in the jungle was complete and he was ready to take his throne as an exalted King. Even though the Sun is cursed, it gives its blessing, it is the daśā of the planets causing the curse that are activated in mūla daśā.

The Sun daśā is only one year long and then he enters the mūla daśā of Venus for seventeen years. The lord of Venus is also under a curse, and when the lord of a planet is cursed, the full blessings of that planet lack the ability to be fully enjoyed, unless the curse is lifted. The first portion is Venus Venus and the second antardaśā would then be Venus Rāhu, where false accusations were made against Sīta for her purity, and so the story goes on.

Example of Cursed Divorce

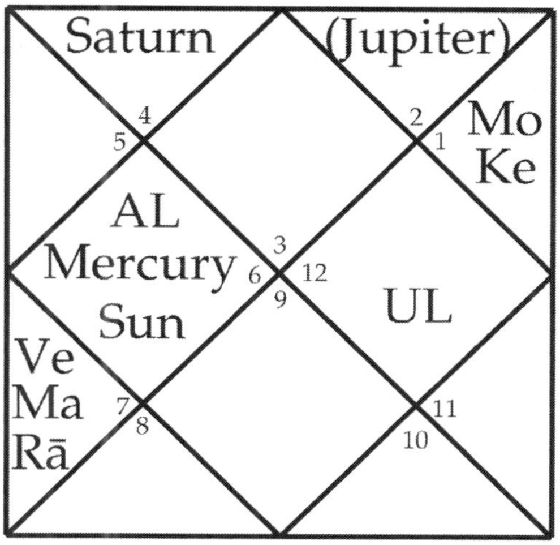

In this chart, the stronger between the lagna, Sun and moon is the Sun, who is conjunct another planet who is in Mahāpuruṣa yoga. So the first four signs will be the dual signs. The strongest between the Sun and Mercury is exalted Mercury, which gives the first daśā, then the Sun gives the next daśā. Since Virgo is even the next four signs will be the āpoklima from Sūrya lagna, which are the fixed signs. The only planet in fixed signs is Jupiter which gives the next daśā.

Then the next set of daśā are given from the paṇaphara to Sūrya lagna, which are the moveable signs. Libra has more planets and will furnish the next set of daśā. Venus in its own sign (*svakṣetra*) is the strongest to give the next daśā, then Rāhu gives the next daśā as its degrees are higher according to the cārakāraka method. Mars finishes the daśā given by Libra. Aries has two planets and Cancer has one, so Aries will furnish the next set of daśā. Ketu is higher degrees and then the Moon. Saturn is the final planet to give the mūla daśā.

Daśā Planet	Signs Gained	Additions/ Subtractions	Viṁśottarī Difference	=Years of Daśā	Age
Mercury	12	+1=13 (12 max)	17	5	0-5
Sun	11	-	6	5	5-11
Jupiter	7	-	16	9	11-20
Venus	12	-	20	8	20-28
Rāhu	4	-	18	14	28-42
Mars	6	-	7	1	42-43
Ketu	7	-	7	0=7	43-50
Moon	3	-	10	7	50-57
Saturn	7	-	19	12	57-69
Mercury			17-5=	12	69-81
Sun			6-5=	1	81-82
Jupiter			16-9=	5	82-87

Venus and the Moon are cursed. Venus is with Mars and Rāhu, and the Moon is with Ketu and aspected by Saturn, Rāhu and Mars. Saturn is the eighth lord, indicating the real activation of suffering. The curse of Moon is the greater affliction with three malefics which includes the aspect of the eighth lord. Venus afflicted will show suffering with relationship and Moon will show suffering with mother and family.

In the case of an afflicted Venus, it is best for the individual to wait till after Venus naisargika dasā to get married, and then perform proper remedies first. The individual did not wait till Jupiter naisargika daśā, as Rāhu mūla daśā began and the curse needed to fructify.

The individual met his first wife in Rāhu-Rāhu mūla daśa. The cursed period brought the wife as a person cannot suffer the breakage of family if there is not one yet. The spouse had an Amāvāsya Moon (ruled by Rāhu) in Āśleṣa gaṇḍānta with the lagna lord Saṅkranti and Mercury combust. This type of spouse is indicated by the nature of Rāhu.

The Moon is aspected by both ninth lords which are both causing the curse. In this way, the Guru is involved in the curse and advised the individual to marry. This is the individual's karma and is of no fault of the Guru, it is in the individual's own chart. The marriage happened during Rāhu-Moon mūla daśā.

During the viṁśottarī daśā of Moon-Venus (the cursed planets) and the Rāhu-Saturn mūla daśā (the planets causing the curse) the wife left the individual and a custody battle over the daughter (Venus in the fifth) ensued. The eleventh lord of friends and colleagues is also aspecting and causing the curse indicating these people aggravated the situation instead of helping. As Moon is the lord of the second house, the finances suffered severely.

The wife, guru and friends are not to blame and if the cursed individual were to be in that perspective they would be stuck in a world in which they don't have power; "other" people do things to them. By being responsible that one's own past life actions created the present life situations, one is acknowledging the root cause within themselves. And when one is responsible for their life, they can forgive, perform remedies, and create the next step of their life.

Saturn indicates the reason for the curse. The houses owned by Saturn in a praśna would indicate the reasons for a curse that has been caused in this life. In this natal chart, Saturn owns the eighth and ninth house which shows that some breaking of dharma or commitment from the past life is incurring the present suffering. The eighth house also rules breakage of marriage.

The suffering lessens when Rāhu-Mercury mūla daśā starts. As the Moon is cursed in an axis with Venus, the remedial measure that would take both into account is the worship of the goddess Annapūrṇa (Venus-Moon). Moon is conjunct Ketu indicating mental disturbances, so donation can be given to mothers who have suffered mental afflictions and abuse.

Levels of the Mūla Daśā

The Mahādaśā lord indicates marriage by its lordship of the ninth and its conjunction with Venus. The antardaśā shows the people who come to give the results. The wife came in Rāhu antardaśā and the marriage happened in Moon antardaśā. At that time the wife herself was in Sun viṁśottarī daśā, and left when she entered her cursed Moon viṁśottarī daśā. The cursed individual had entered Saturn antardaśā, indicating a time of financial hardship and suffering to the Moon, all of which relate to the cursed indications.

Pandit Sanjay Rath elucidates the three levels of mahādaśā, antardaśā and pratyantardaśā to bring events into one's life:

"The **mahādaśā** shows the overall event which is manifesting, i.e. whether it is time for marriage, professional success, children, etc. This again will indicate whether its time for a blessing or curse to manifest. The mahādaśā indicates the overall experience that is about to arrive. The blessing or curse (whichever Yoga is indicated) lasts throughout the mahādaśā with some ups and downs indicated."

"The **antardaśā** indicates those people who have come to give us the results of blessings and curses. As curses arise from another's malign-intent, the one who has come to manifest that ill-intent will be indicated by the antardaśā. This is also applicable to the arrival of blessings."

"The **pratyantardaśā** being more sensitive indicates the time of the actual manifestation of the event and the circumstances that prevail. Curses are however long lasting and the pratyantardaśā merely shows the times of ups and downs within the designated time period, i.e. when the native will meet the one who will carry out the blessings or curses."

Exercises

4. Look up the kendrādi daśā in two or more other texts and read the rules for interpretation and the results of each planet's daśā; in Yavanajātaka, Bṛhat Jātaka, Sārāvalī, or Horā Sāra.

5. Calculate the mūla daśā for your own chart and the three others that were studied for serious suffering in the previous exercise.

6. Look for when the curses and blessings are activated according to mūla daśā in these charts. Analyze how the naisargika, viṁśottarī and mūla daśā are interacting.

7. If possible, in one of the three study charts, see the antardaśā planet when the cursed individual met the person involved in the curse and see the connection of that planet to their chart.

Conclusion

There are a lot of techniques and calculations mentioned in this chapter. The understanding of curses will allow you to better serve those who are suffering. In traditional society, the astrologer was consulted to either pick a good time for a joyous occasion or to help get rid of a problem. Through the centuries astrologers have been criticized for taking advantage of people who are suffering.

To be an astrologer of integrity is to help individuals see their interconnectedness with all aspects of their life, and support them achieving the four aims of life to reach their full potential. We enter a reading with an intention just by the nature of who we are being in the world. If we intend to empower our clients and help them find success and peace in their life, we will be able to express situations in the highest manner. The tradition teaches, first to see god in the client's heart. See the good in them and see them in their full potential. Your intention will manifest that experience.

Life is constantly transforming, nothing is staying the same. Assisting people deal with those changes skilfully is our work. Life is not about right or wrong or should or shouldn't but its about what works and what doesn't work. If the mind is sad, the experience of life is hard and sad, if the mind is happy; the experience of life is light and joyous. Our world is based on our experience of the world. All sensory information of the five elements comes through the mind for interpretation.

When life is good, people complain that astrologers believe in fate and that they as individuals have free will. When life is tough, people act as if there is a world out there that they don't have an influence on. The developed astrologer understands the way things are and where there is possibility of influence. For example, a person who is a big frame kapha constitution will not be a thin model, but they can impact their body weight and their health by how they eat and live. In this way, we are born in a certain way with strengths and weaknesses and karma that requires being experienced. Some things can't change, some things can change, and some will change by our perception of them alone.

Everything you think, and how you think, how you see the world, creates that world that you live into. As an astrologer we have the physical, psychological and spiritual tools to shift and empower the view of life and its manifestation.

Chapter 12

Remedial Measures

Saturn Mantras

Saturn causes suffering in different ways through various charts. The remedies presented here will cover the general nature of Saturn and show the way in which this planet creates troubles. These remedies are traditional mantras found throughout the Vedas, Purāṇas, and Tantras.

Saturn is the kāraka of suffering as he represents our misdeeds in this and previous lives. It is his job to ensure everyone suffers their bad karma. The mantras presented here have the power to purify one's bad karma by washing it clean (Viṣṇu/Kṛṣṇa) or burning it away (Śiva). Viṣṇu is the forgiver of one's sins while Śiva is the remover/destroyer of our sins. The Viṣṇu and Kṛṣṇa mantras purify by forgiving, as the bad karma is washed clean. The Śiva, Bhairava, Rudra, Sūrya, and Hanuman mantras purify by burning one's bad karma away. The nīla-śakti associated with Saturn is related to purifying Saturn and teaching him to act properly as a mother disciplines her child.

Purifying Saturn

There are many ways to approach a planet, and how it is approached will be determined according to the intention one has. This section will reveal mantras for purifying Saturn. Saturn is naturally slow, blocked, dirty and contracted. The Ṛṣi Parāśara says that Saturn can be worshiped as Viṣṇu. By worshipping Saturn as Viṣṇu, one purifies Saturn, removing the dirt and tamas guṇa. Viṣṇu is all-pervasive, everywhere. This expansive vibration removes the constricting energy of Saturn which leads to blockages and heavy build-ups. It creates the proper 'space' for Saturn to work beneficially in, and ensures that Saturn can give pure, healthy results. The mantra to purify Saturn is: Auṁ viṣṇave namaḥ

When Saturn is conjunct or aspecting the lagna, *hūṁ* is inserted into the mantra making it:

|| Auṁ hūṁ viṣṇave namaḥ ||

(Auṁ, praise the all-pervasiveness, dispel negativity)

This mantra purifies the negativity of Saturn on the lagna and brings the focus and foundational strength of Saturn. When Saturn aspects the D-9 lagna, it brings older partners into the person's life; reciting this mantra ensures they are good older people that will help one flourish. By purifying the dirt of Saturn one becomes cleaner themselves (*lagna śuddhi*) or when Saturn is posited in the D-9 lagna or aspecting it one gets a 'cleaner' spouse.

When the AL is conjunct or aspected by Saturn the dirt appears on the image of a person--acknowledgement is slow to come and they get recognition only later in life. To purify this Saturn, insert *śrīṁ* bīja into the mantra. This cool and cleansing mantra will purify the ragged, poor energy of Saturn and remove this from the image one projects to the world.

|| Auṁ śrīṁ viṣṇave namaḥ ||

(Auṁ, praise the all-pervasiveness, cleanse impurity)

Klīṁ is kāma bīja—the desire fulfilling sound, added when Saturn is damaging the seventh house or A7. *Hrīṁ* is added when Saturn is conjunct or aspecting the tenth house or causing problems to the A10. Saturn in the tenth can cause falls from high positions in career. Saturn with the A10 will make a person work very hard and no matter how hard they work they will be asked to work harder. When Saturn is with the A10 the perception is that the person is not working hard enough. So by chanting to Viṣṇu with *hrīṁ* bīja this Saturn becomes cleansed of its hardness and cleansed of the activities that will make a person fall from a high position.

|| Auṁ hrīṁ viṣṇave namaḥ ||

(Auṁ, praise the all-pervasiveness, righteous power)

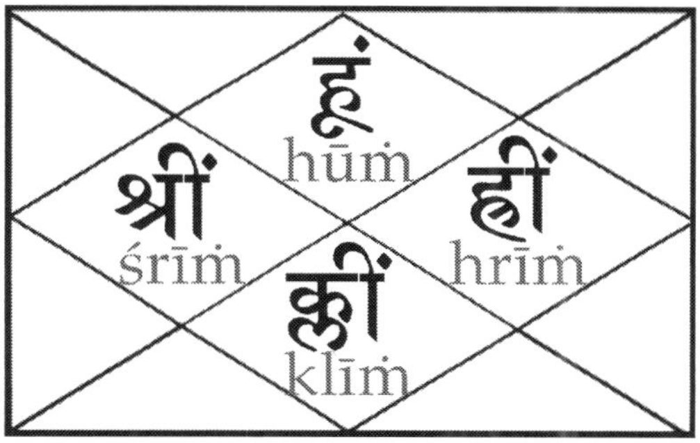

Trines to these kendra positions will use the same mantra. For example, Saturn in the eleventh is trine to the seventh, therefore *klīṁ* bīja is used:

|| Auṁ klīṁ viṣṇave namaḥ ||

(Auṁ, praise the all-pervasiveness,
focus my desire on the positive)

Exception:

In the case of Saturn in the 8th house, the eight syllable mantra is the best mantra for pacification of Saturn.

|| Auṁ namo nārāyaṇāya ||

(Auṁ, praises to that which is the all goal of all humans)

Saturn Afflicting Health

When natal Saturn afflicts the lagna there are health problems related to vāta doṣa throughout the native's life. They will often deal with large amounts of negativity determined by Saturn either placed in the lagna, aspecting it by his third house *hammer* or his 10th house *kick*. Saturn's association with the lagna will also bring more of the tamas guṇa into the person's life, making them lazy, or sullen, or other tamas attributes. The remedy for this is worship of the Sun, though one should also include Āyurvedic remedies such as aśvagandhā.

|| Auṁ ghṛṇiḥ sūryāya namaḥ ||

(Auṁ, praises to the Sun, shine brilliantly)

When Saturn is afflicting the lagna and it is the finances that are suffering instead of health, then there is a variation of the above mantra called the disease and poverty destroying Ravi mantra (*rogadāridrayanāśanam ravermantram*).[2]

|| Auṁ hrīṁ ghṛṇiḥ sūrya ādityaḥ śrīṁ ||

One can use a shorter mantra of the Sun or the famous Savitur Gāyatrī mantra which is extremely efficient instead of the above two mantras. By strengthening the sattva guṇa Sun, kāraka of life and vitality as well as the bhāva kāraka of the lagna, one removes the depletion of Saturn. The Sun burns off the tamas of Saturn, and the body is warmed and strengthened.

|| Tat savitur vareṇayaṁ
bhargo devasya dhimahi
dhiyo yo naḥ pracodayāt ||

'That' which is self evident is the highest awakener,
We mediate upon the self-effulgent source which is the illuminator of all,
Please guide all our intelligence and intuition.

2 Mahīdhara's Mantra Mahodadhiḥ, Taraṅga 15, v.1-3

Saturn Transiting Lagna

Saturn transiting the lagna will cause health problems, as the lord of vāta doṣa is in the body. Saturn is vāta (air) and depletes the body, making it age faster. Natives will often suffer dental problems or other cases of decay. It may also cause financial difficulties. The remedy for this is the worship of Śiva in the form of Bhairava. This form of Śiva protects the lagna and purifies toxins and negativities so they do not accumulate. Bhairava brings strength to the body, and creates a wakeful energetic mental state.

There are a variety of Bhairava forms, Kālabhairava relates specifially to Saturn. The *Śrī Kālabhairavāṣṭakam* is the best for this purpose (unless one has been initiated into a more specific mantra of Kālabhairava. Below is the first verse, one should locate the entire mantra and learn to sing this, as it will be a very beneficial remedy to share with ailing individuals.

Deva-rāja-sevyamāna-pāvanāṅghri-paṅkajaṁ
Vyāla-yajña-sūtram-indu-śekharaṁ kṛpākaram ।
Nāradādi-yogi-vṛnda-vanditaṁ digambaraṁ
Kāśikā-purādhi-nātha-kāla-bhairavaṁ bhaje ।। 1।।

I revere Kālabhairava, who is served by the king of gods,
His feet are as pure as the lotus, snakes as a sacred thread,
He wears the Moon as an ornament and is giving grace,
The yogis like Nārada sing the praises of this sky-clad one,
He is the Lord of the city of Kāśī.

Saturn transiting the 8th lord or its trines can also cause problems with health and finances. Saturn is only the activator of the problems (as kāraka of the 8th lord). The problems will relate to the destruction of the house containing the 8th lord. The remedial measures should be performed according to the nature of the eighth lord and its placement.

Saturn transiting the lagna will create health problems in the area of the body that is weak according to other indications in the chart, it is hurting the vitality and activating the problems. Similarly the 8th lord will destroy the area of life which has a weak kāraka of the house its destroying. If the 8th lord is in the fourth and Venus is weak, then it will hurt vehicles, if Mars is weak it will hurt properties. In this way we specify the problems being activated by the transit.

If the daśā is negative these transits can create much suffering, but a positive daśā will naturally counteract many problems.

Maraṇa-Kāraka-Sthāna Saturn

Saturn is maraṇa kāraka sthāna in the first house, this is where he feels like dying, and thereby his indications in the chart feel like dying. Wherever Saturn is placed he is in the first house of that signified bhāva or ārūḍha, therefore making that area of life feel like it is dying, or suffocating, or trapped. For example, Saturn with the UL will make the marriage feel like it's dying and the spouse will feel suffocated (this also happens if the lord of the UL bhāva is MKS). The worship of the Libra Jyotirliṅgam is used as a remedy to bring life into Saturn. This is often done along with Śiva Liṅgam abhiśeka. A ruby is also recommended (if the Sun is in a beneficial place and beneficial house lord) to strengthen the kāraka of the first house.

|| Auṁ namaḥ śivāya kāleśvarāya hauṁ jūṁ saḥ ||

Auṁ, praises to Śiva, the lord of time,
God and Goddess plant the seed of rejuvenation.

Strengthening Saturn

If Saturn is indicating that he will give good results in a chart and he is weakly placed, then one can do a graha mantra of Saturn to increase his results:

||Auṁ śanaiścarāya namaḥ || (3/8)

Auṁ, praises to the slow moving Saturn

This mantra is good to make Saturn give results similar to Śaśa Mahāpuruṣa yoga, as if Saturn was strong in the first house. The mantra can have *śaṁ* added after Auṁ to make it 4/9, which invokes the traditional learning associated with Saturn. It can also be made 7/12 by adding *praṁ priṁ prouṁ saḥ* after Auṁ which invokes the knowledge of Saturnian sciences such as disease, death and the dying process.

Pacification: Saturn Gāyatrī

The Saturn Gāyatrī (from Ṛg Veda, Maṇḍala 10, Sūkta 9) is recommended by Paraśara (Graha Śānti Chapter) to be recited 23,000 times. This can be done by chanting 6 mālās a day for 40 days and will pacify Saturn.

[Auṁ] śaṁ no devīrabhiṣṭaye
āpo bhavantu pītaye|
śaṁ yorabhi sravantu naḥ|

May the goddess favor us with Peace
and bless us with divine waters to drink
and let health and strength flow to us

Saturn Conjunct the Moon

When Saturn is conjunct the Moon it is called Kālikā yoga as Saturn takes the form of the Devī (goddess). When Saturn is conjunct the Moon, or associated with the fourth house, or in debilitation, the form of Kālī is advised to uplift the effects of Saturn. When Saturn is debilitated it means it is lacking understanding, therefore the Mahāvidyā (great knowledge) of Kālī is needed to educate him, and bring more auspicious results. The Kālī mantra should be calculated to correspond to the placement of Saturn or one can use the sacred Kālī mantra mentioned below.

||krīṁ krīṁ krīṁ hūṁ hūṁ hrīṁ hrīṁ
dakṣiṇa kālike krīṁ krīṁ krīṁ hūṁ hūṁ hrīṁ hrīṁ svāhā||

Auṁ
Auṁ Auṁ
Auṁ Auṁ Auṁ
Auṁ Auṁ Auṁ Auṁ Auṁ
Krīṁ krīṁ krīṁ hūṁ hūṁ hrīṁ hrīṁ
dakṣiṇa kālike krīṁ krīṁ krīṁ hūṁ hūṁ hrīṁ hrīṁ svāhā
In the cycle of creation, preservation, and dissolution,
There is the word (guru) and its meaning (knowledge),
Lead me to create good things and maintain them,
Oh Mother who protects one from Death,
Lead me to create good things and maintain them,
Through the word (guru) and its meaning (knowledge),
Transcending the cycle of creation, preservation, and dissolution,
I offer this prayer to you, So be it.[3]
Auṁ Auṁ Auṁ Auṁ
Auṁ Auṁ Auṁ
Auṁ Auṁ
Auṁ

For those who need a shorter mantra, they can use a simple nāma mantra without Auṁ (3/7). Adding Auṁ directs this mantra for spirituality (4/8).

||krīṁ kālikāyai namaḥ||

For those who will not do a mantra related to a deity, we can just advise *krīṁ* bīja mediation. Dhyāna with this mantra in the evenings for ten to thirty minutes will have a similar effect as the Kālī mantras . It is often advised in many traditions to meditate on this bīja for forty days before beginning one of the larger mantras. This bījas has the power to clean out the internal negativity or karma that manifests into Saturn's negative experiences and in this way, I let people know that krīṁ is like 'clean' for Saturn.

||krīṁ||

[3] Interpretation based on bījārtha of Mahīdhara's Mantra Mahodadhiḥ translation Ram Kumar Rai

Preta Yoga

When Saturn is conjunct Ketu it is called Preta Bādhaka, obstruction by un-embodied spirits still occupying the earth plane. This combination will show problems from unseen spirits either throughout one's life or when activated depending on placement and daśās. For this to be remedied one must ensure that the spirit is properly exorcised or appeased. Sun worship and propitiation of the ancestors may also be beneficial. If the case relates to a spirit lost and trying to find its way then the Śakti Gaṇeśa mantra is best. This Saturn Ketu combination opens up another entire area of Jyotiṣa, called adṛṣṭa, that which can't be seen. One should study the chapter on bādhaka for more details.

Śakti Gaṇeśa Mantra:

|| Auṁ hrīṁ gaṁ hrīṁ mahāgaṇeśāya namaḥ svāhā ||

Auṁ, praises to the goddess empowered Gaṇeśa, the great lord of divisions.

Sāḍhe-Sātī

Sāḍhe-Sātī is the period (7½ years) when Saturn transits over the Moon and over the positions of second and twelfth house argalā. Saturn transiting the houses with low aṣṭakavarga will be a time of the most intense suffering. During this time the Rudra Camakam is chanted to protect one's mind, finances and all things beneficial in life. The Moon gives sustenance and comforts, while Saturn transiting the Moon destroys this supportive ability. There are also more specific remedies relative to the house Saturn is transiting. These more specific remedies may be utilized along with the Rudra Camakam or instead of, depending on the situation of the native.

Saturn Transiting the 12th house:

When Saturn transits the twelfth house from the Moon there may be problems related to domestic life-- this may be issues with childen or the spouse and other problems involving home or property. The remedy for this is the worship of Mother Kālī (either according to the house placement or with the Dakṣina-Kālī mantra).

Saturn Transiting the Janma Rāśi:

When Saturn transits the Janma Rāśi (natal Moon sign) there may be loss of reputation, bad association, failure of endeavors, and other reasons to suffer. For relief from this Hanuman is worshiped. Worship should be performed primarily on Saturdays (worship of Hanuman on Tuesday is for empowering Mars). Given here are two mantras; the first is for removing bad energy and monetary problems, the second is for health and energy level concerns. If more powerful mantras are needed to remove addictions, violence or black magic, one should use the tantric five-headed Hanuman mantras.

|| Auṁ haṁ rudrāya hanumate namaḥ ||

Auṁ, praise to Hanuman the destoyer, bring good space

|| Namo bhagavate āñjaneyāya mahābalāya svāhā ||

I offer praises to the son of añjanī who has great strength

Saturn Transiting the 2nd house:

The transit of Saturn through the second house can cause financial hardship and problems with the government. To resolve this, Viṣṇū is worshiped as Kṛṣṇa. One should either follow the mantra of one's tradition (as initiated) or use,

|| Śri kṛṣṇaḥ śaraṇaṁ mama ||

I take the protection of the Great Sustainer

The transit of navāṁśa Moon should also be taken into account. For example, if Saturn is transiting the sign of Aries in the sky, an individual with navāṁśa Moon in either Pisces, Aries and Taurus will have a navāṁśa Sāḍhe-Sātī.

Some North Indian astrologers recommend worshipping Saturn for Sāḍhe-Sātī problems. In our tradition we do not worship Saturn in this way. Saturn is our pāpa. This can be roughly translated as sin, or bad actions, the opposite of the purva punya (good past karma) seen in the fifth and ninth houses. Saturn is kāraka for the 6th, 8th, and 12th houses. The sixth house is our ṣaḍripu, the sins we do against ourselves (lying, cheating, being jealous, smoking, drinking, etc). The eighth house is the house of nija doṣas (our inherent bad qualities). As the ninth is your luck earned in the last life, the 8th is your bad karma earned in your last life, it's the actions which you have done negative against others. Now understanding this, Saturn is the kāraka for these things, the sins against yourself and the sins against other people, are ruled by Saturn, this is called *pāpa* in Sanskrit.

As the Sun is your sense of self, the Moon is your mind, Mars is your strength, Saturn is your pāpa, He is your sin, your suffering. He is all the bad things you are doing to yourself and others. He doesn't make you suffer. You make yourself suffer. The planets are just indicating your actions, they show the karma YOU have done. They are not external beings who care about making you happy or making you suffer. When Saturn goes over our Moon or Lagna then the results of our own bad karma will come to pass. Any suffering caused by this is due to our own actions past and present.

In this way we worship the Sun to 'protect" us from Saturn. Worship of the Sun 'burns' up our bad karma, our pāpa karma. How does the Sun do this? By worshipping the Sun we live a righteous way performing good actions. By worshipping the Sun we take the path of truth and light. We look at ourselves and take the appropriate actions to correct the frequencies that have been out of integrity in ourselves. By worshipping the

Sun we strengthen the energy of life and vitality (which is opposite to the lord of death and decay). Saturn is darkness and rules ignorance and forgetfulness. By worshipping the light we ask our own ātmā to shine bright like the Sun, for our intelligence (*dhī śakti*) to be bright like the Sun.

There is a modern trend to worship Saturn. Saturn temples are being built all over India in the last few decades. In the past, if one was to worship a planet they did this within the navagraha temples which contained all nine planets. If one studies the Nāḍī texts, the ancient Ṛṣi rarely recommended the worship of Saturn. Why worship your bad karma? Instead worship the Sun, or Śiva who is the Sun in all signs. In this way, the Śiva Liṅga is worshiped with water to purify the pāpa that we have created. The worship of Śiva as Rudra (his ancient form) is utilized to burn up our negative karmas. The worship of Rudra while pouring water over the Śiva Liṅga is called Rudrābhiṣeka.

Rudra Chamakam

The Rudra Camakam is a section of the Śrī Rudram which comes from the Kṛṣṇa Yajurveda. The Camakam is composed of 11 verses (*anuvākas*) that relate to the eleven Rudrāṁśas of a sign. The verse associated with the particular Rudrāṁśa of one's natal Saturn, indicated by Saturn's degree, gives the best results. For the general public, priests and astrologers often prescribe the third anuvāka (verse) as it gives the parākrama (energy/courage) to protect one from the suffering of Saturn.

	Saturn
1	2° 43′ 38″
2	5° 27′ 16″
3	8° 10′ 55″
4	10° 54′ 33″
5	13° 38′ 10″
6	16° 21′ 49″
7	19° 05′ 27″
8	21° 49′ 05″
9	24° 32′ 44″
10	27° 16′ 22″
11	30° 00′ 00″

The Rudra Camakam is chanted after one has taken a shower, having cleansed themselves in preparation for worship. The individual should sit facing the eastern direction. When chanting a single verse (*anuvāka*) one should repeat it eleven times. Below is the third anuvāka,

śaṁ ca me mayaśca me priyaṁ ca me'nukāmaśca me
kāmaśca me saumanasaśca me bhadraṁ ca me śreyaśca me
vasyaśca me yaśaśca me bhagaśca me draviṇaṁ ca me
yantā ca me dhartā ca me kṣemaśca me dhṛtiśca me
viśvaṁ ca me mahaśca me saṁvicca me jñātraṁ ca me
sūśca me prasūśca me sīraṁ ca me layaśca ma ṛtaṁ ca me
'mṛtaṁ ca me'yakśmaṁ ca me'nāmayacca me jīvātuśca me
dīrghāyutvaṁ ca me'namitraṁ ca me'bhayaṁ ca me sugaṁ ca me
śayanaṁ ca me sūṣā ca me sudinaṁ ca me || 3||
Auṁ namo bhagavate rudrāya
Auṁ śāntiḥ śāntiḥ śāntiḥ

Peace is within me, pleasure is within me, love is within me, agreeable desires are within me, sensuality is within me, kindness is within me, prosperity is within me, excellence is within me, self-empowerment is within me, fame is within me, good luck is within me, the most valuable possessions are within me, guidance is within me, support is within me, security is within me, perseverance is within me, wholeness is within me, greatness is within me, reward is within me, intelligence is within me, motivation is within me, productiveness is within me, the capacity to work is within me, relaxation is within me, respectfulness is within me, nectar is within me, healing is within me, health is within me, the life giving medicine is within me, long life is within me, freedom from enemies is within me, freedom from fear is within me, the proper direction is within me, the resting place is within me, the vigor of a new day is within me, good days are in me.
Auṁ, praises to Rudra
Auṁ Peace, Peace, Peace

If this verse is to long for the skill of the individual, then a simple Rudra mantra can be given:

|| auṁ namo bhagavate Rudrāya ||

Conclusion

Among the various remedies there are many which may overlap. The two most important considerations are: the specific problem the native is facing and the individual's chart indications.

The special properties of the mantra and the devatā must be considered relative to the specific problem at hand. For example, Viṣṇu is a sustaining deity while Rudra is a destructive deity. If the significations offer either one as a remedy, then one must more deeply consider the issue. If the native suffers from their life falling apart because of financial lack then a Viṣṇu mantra would be a better choice than Rudra. If the problem is that the person is suffering harsh advances from an enemy or dealing with issues of litigation then Rudra may be the better choice. In this way the specifics of a situation will help determine the best remedy.

The remedy that best fits the overall chart by agreeing with the most significations will give the quickest and easiest results. For example, if the Iṣṭa devata is Viṣṇu and Mercury is the most actively influencing planet in the chart, then the Viṣṇu mantras will override the other mantras in effectiveness. If the Sun is the Iṣṭa, then Śiva or Sūrya mantras will give the best results. Which houses are involved and planetary conjunctions can override other factors and again change the situation for the most effective remedy.

Rāhu Remedial Measures

Rāhu is the always somewhat misunderstood or unclear. His nature is of the shadow; he is not straight (not direct). You can try to understand him, but cannot fully as he is the demented mind, and only the mentally deranged can fully know him. He is the eclipse point, and has the ability to destroy the luminaries, destroy the light, and destroy all sattva. Tamas leads to impurity. When Rāhu is associated with a devatā-bādhaka, then the deity is polluted and impure rituals have been done to it. If Rāhu is strong then the person is very materialistic and does no spiritual purifications. Rāhu clouds the aura, like someone who is addicted to drugs. It creates a cloud in the aura, a sticky energy that would repel a spiritual sādhaka. Rāhu needs to be purified, cleansed, and removed from the system (particularly the aura).

To get into the right mindset (*bhāva*) to work with Rāhu, let's read a bit of a poem by Rabindra Nath Tagore.[2] Rāhu speaks to the Moon thus:

"I am your companion from the beginning of time, for I am your own shadow. In your laughter, in your tears, you shall sense my dark self, hovering near you, now in front, now behind. At the dead of night, when you are lonely and dejected, you'll be startled to find how near I am seated by you, gazing into your face.

Wherever you turn, I am there, my shadow sweeps over the sky and covers the earth, my piteous cry and my cruel laughter echo everywhere, for I am hunger never appeased, thirst never quenched. I am always there, a dagger in your breast, a poison in your mind, a disease in your body.

I shall chase you like a terror in the day, like a nightmare in the night. Like a living skeleton in a famine I shall stretch my hand before you and pester you to give and give and give. Like a thorn I shall prick you day and night, like a curse I shall haunt you, like fate I shall follow you – as night follows day, as fear follows hope."

Rāhu is a point on the ecliptic, the intersection of the Earth's and the Moon's revolutions. It is the Moon's motion that creates the intersectionpoint; therefore, it is called the node of the Moon. This is one of the reasons the nodes affect the mind so much; it is their nature. The mind is not balanced, and this disequilibrium is seen in the motion of the Moon moving above the ecliptic, then crossing a node and moving below the ecliptic. It is oscillating, changing, moving between extremes. Only those who meditate or have some strong spiritual practice can bring the mind into balance. The root energy of mind is feminine, it is goddess, and this Śrī Śakti is called Durgā, who has the power to take the mind out of attraction and repulsion and therefore balance the mind.

---

[2] Rabindra Nath Tagore, "Rahur Prem", *Chhabi o Gan* (Images and Songs), translation by Dutta and Robinson, p.88.

Durga means difficult to access, unattainable, and can refer to a fortress that is well protected, or a place that is very hard to reach. *Durgati* means distress, or someone who has gone on the wrong (*dur*) path (*gati*). *Durgā* is the goddess who gives *durgaghna* (the removal of difficulties, or removal of bad ways). Her prasiddha mantra has 7 words and 17 syllables.

||Auṁ Hrīṁ Śrīṁ Klīṁ Durgati-nāśinyai Mahāmāyāyai svāhā||

Auṁ triple formed Goddess, who is the Great Illusion, destroy my bad direction, so be it.

This mantra is very beneficial during Rāhu daśā and especially Rāhu antardaśās. Durgā is the general remedy for Rāhu. If Rāhu is conjunct the Moon, then Durgā becomes the primary remedy.

The *Navākṣarī Stotra* gives the famous *Navārṇa* mantra, which is 5 words and 9 syllables, placing the Devī in the lagna. This is the best mantra when Rāhu, or Moon afflicted by Rāhu, has a relationship to the dharma trines. When Auṁ is added to the front of the mantra, it becomes the Rāma Tāraṇa mantra, which is what Rāma used before going to battle against Rāvaṇa (a Rāhu-like demon). This mantra has 6 words and 10 syllables, associating it with the artha trines. The mantra is:

||Aiṁ Hrīṁ Klīṁ Cāmuṇḍāyai Vicce||

Oh Triple Goddess, Remover of the dual fluctuations of the mind, cut away ignorance.

When Rāhu is in a Mars sign, or aspected by Mars or Saturn, it takes a more cruel form (*ugra*), or we can say more intense energy is needed to give remedy. In this regard one should call Durgā as *Cāmuṇḍā* or *Caṇḍī*, and accordingly use those mantras. This is the prasiddha mantra of Caṇḍī:

||Auṁ Namaścaṇḍikāyai||

Auṁ praises to the fierce Goddess [who can remove the negative].

The tradition teaches another distinction between the *Navārṇa* and *Caṇḍī* mantras. The Caṇḍī mantra is associated with *Caṇḍa* and the Navārṇa mantra with *Muṇḍa*. Caṇḍa and Muṇḍa are the two demons that the fierce form of Durgādestroys. Caṇḍa means angry, wrathful, cruel or violent, and represents pain and confusion in the heart. Muṇḍa means low, blunt (lack of sharpness), pointless (also hornless or shaved), and it represents pain and confusion in the head. If the lagna or lagneśa is afflicted by Rāhu, then the Navārṇa mantra is indicated. The navārṇa mantra gives lagna correction; it removes the traps and confusions of the brain. The Caṇḍī mantra relates to the fourth house and the removal of the traps, pains and confusions in the heart.

Rāhu and Moon

When Rāhu is conjunct the Moon, then the *Durgā Saptaśatī*[3] becomes very beneficial for the individual. This is a much longer text (700 verses) and will either require someone who is already Hindu, has much dedication, or is in severe mental turmoil (to motivate them to read this on a regular basis). The standard practice is to read the Saptaśatī at around eighto'clock in the evening. A shorter version for those interested but not able to do all 700 verses is the *Durgā-sapta-ślokī,* which is seven key verses to the goddess:

aum̐ asya śrī-durgā-sapta-ślokī-stotra-mahāmantrasya
nārāyaṇa ṛṣiḥ I anuṣṭupādīni chandāṁsi I
śrī-mahākālī mahālakṣmī mahāsarasvatyo devatāḥ I
śrī jagadambā prītyarthe pāṭhe viniyogaḥ I I

jñānināmapi cetāṁsi devī bhagavatī hi sā I
balādākṛṣya mohāya mahāmāyā prayacchati I I 1 I I

durge smṛtā harasi bhītimaśeṣajantoḥ
svasthaiḥ smṛtā matimatīva śubhāṁ dadāsi I
dāridryaduḥkhabhayahāriṇi kā tvadanyā
sarvopakārakaraṇāya sadārdra cittā I I 2 I I

sarva maṅgala māṅgalye śive sarvārtha sādhike I
śaraṇye tryambake gauri nārāyaṇi namo'stu te I I 3 I I

śaraṇāgatadīnārtaparitrāṇaparāyaṇe I
sarvasyārtihare devi nārāyaṇi namo'stu te I I 4 I I

sarvasvarūpe sarveśe sarvaśakti samanvite I
bhayebhyastrāhi no devī durge devī namo'stu te I I 5 I I

rogānaśeṣānapahaṁsi tuṣṭā ruṣṭā tu kāmān sakalānabhīṣṭān I
tvāmāśritānāṁ na vipannarāṇāṁ tvāmāśritā hyāśrayatāṁ prayānti I I 6 I I

sarvābādhāpraśamanaṁ trailokyasyākhileśvari I
evameva tvayā kāryamasmadvairi vināśanam I I 7 I I

---

[3] It is also called the *Devī Māhātmyam* or *Caṇḍī Pāṭha* and is found in the *Mārkeṇḍaya Purāṇa*. There are specific verses for specific conditions that can be advised by those who practice Caṇḍī Pāṭha.

If someone is having severe mental problems related to Rāhu and is not coherent enough to do any type of mantra, then the *Durgā Saptaśatī* can also be played in their environment to benefit them. In very severe cases, the performance of pūjā, homa, etc and the reading of the *Durgā Saptaśatī* for a continuous three, five, or seven days (called *Caṇḍī mahāprayoga*) can be advised. If this *Caṇḍī mahāprayoga* is performed in a place very distant from the individual, they should light an oil lamp (*dīpa*) when the ritual starts. This unbroken light (*akhaṇḍa-dīpa*) should be kept lit for the entire time the ritual is performed. There are some astrologers who do these types of pūjās for individuals; there are also astrologers who sell gemstones to their clients. As an astrologer, one should be aware of one's intentions when benefiting monetarily from remedies. It is best to associate with some pūjārīs you trust and can recommend to people when they are in need of these types of rituals.

When Rāhu is causing problems to the mind, the best herb to remove his effects is calamus (*vācā*).This can be taken as a medicine, or an amulet can be made with the root. When it is taken internally, it should be mixed with the proper proportion of Brāhmī and Jaṭāmāṁsi according to the particular mental disorder and the individual constitution. College students can also use this to increase their concentration, as it removes the wavering of the mind caused by Rāhu. Babas who smoke cannabis use this to remove the cloudy (obscuring) effects on the mind. When a person suffers from an overly Rāhu lifestyle (sensory overstimulation), these herbs and mantras are also beneficial.

Yogis use these herbsas an external method to aid meditation. As an internal practice, they utilize *pratyāhāra,*which is the yogic technique of withdrawing the senses. Rāhu is always focusing outside on the material world, the senses, and on the delusions it places on the world. As much as Rāhu looks at the world, it can't actually see it, because Rāhu is so stuck in its own mental reality and delusional projections. Pratyāhāra is the technique for learning to detach the senses from their outward direction and to teach the mind to look inward, which brings clarity. This allows one to drop some of the stories that Rāhu carries around with it, because one is able to observe oneself and the working of one's own mind. It gives a balance of how much energy is going outward from the senses and rejuvenates the mind.

When Rāhu is afflicting an individual's Moon, it will be noticeable in the area around the person's eyes, the eyebrows, and in the lower forehead. Those with visual sensitivity should observe a few bipolar or depressed people who have Rāhu afflicting the Moon, and they will be able to recognize this easily thereafter. When Rāhu is very strong in a chart, you will also notice it in this region of the face, but instead of compressing the energy, Rāhu just creates a 'darker' frequency.

Ucca and Nīca Rāhu

When Rāhu is exalted or is in a position to benefit or support something, it should be worshipped as the Varāha Avatāra. For example, if it is in the second house and the individual is having money problems, and Jupiter does not aspect, then one should worship Rāhu as Varāha to allow him to act exalted like Viṣṇu and bring prosperity. This also relates to the second from ārūḍha lagna and upapada. Whenever Rāhu is needed to play a supporting role, he can be invoked as the boar with Lakṣmī as the Earth.

||Auṁ bhūr namo bhagavate Varāhāya||

When Rāhu is nīca, or needs to be settled, then it is worshipped as Chhinnamastā. If it is nīca, it is naturally a Mahāvidyā form. Otherwise it is used to calm matters down, such as enemy issues that have developed when an activated Rāhu is in the 12th from lagna or AL. Chhinnamastā is not a saumya devī and should not be used unless specifically needed. It should also only be given by one who is qualified to give Mahāvidyā mantras and understands the precautions. The *Chhinnamastā Aṣṭottaraśata Nāma Stotra* (Her 108 names) is a safe way to invoke the blessing of Chhinnamastā.

Chhinnamastā is visualized as seated in the center of the Sun's disc and holds in her left hand her own severed head with gaping mouth. Three streams of blood come from her neck (iḍā, piṅgalā, and suṣumnā), and she drinks the central stream, while her friends, Dākinī and Varṇinī, drink the other two. She is seated on Rati and Kāmadeva (showing she overcomes material and sexual desires). Mantra Māhodadhi, taraṅga 6, gives a variety of mantras.

||Auṁ Śrīṁ Hrīṁ Hrīṁ Vajravairocinye Hrīṁ Hrīṁ phaṭ svāhā||

||Aiṁ Śrīṁ Hrīṁ Krīṁ Vajravairocinye Hrīṁ Hūṁ phaṭ svāhā||

The first mantra is from Mantra Māhodadhiḥ; the second mantra is that used in the Oriya tradition. Mantra Māhodadhiḥ ends with *hrīṁ hrīṁ phaṭ*, while some other traditions use *hūṁ hūṁ phaṭ*. The Oriya tradition teaches to always use the *hūṁ* bīja before *phaṭ*. One should utilize the mantra of their tradition according to the rules of that tradition.

Rāhu in Lagna

When Rāhu is placed in the lagna it can often cloud the mind, or the direction of the mind. It blocks the dhī śakti from processing information correctly. It can also increase the ahaṅkāra in an unhealthy way, creating excess attachments and issues with those attachments. As Rāhu creates a scandal wherever he goes, in the lagna he can create dishonesty, and other dacoit activities to become prominent in a person's life. The dhī may work for the wrong reasons, such as when Rāhu is placed in Gemini lagna, where it relates to the business of Mercury and will be the best counterfeit money maker. As always, these significations are less malefic if conjunct or aspected by benefics and more negative if associated with malefics.

The standard remedy is to use Jupiter to increase the sattva. One can use Jupiter graha mantras if Jupiter is wellplaced; otherwise, one can use a guru form according to the sign of Jupiter. The standard is to use either Dattātreya or Dakṣiṇāmūrti mantras (particularly Medhā-Dakṣiṇāmūrti mantras). Sadāśiva (an ākāśa form of Śiva) mantras can also be used to clear the lagna.

||Auṁ namo bhagavate Sadāśivāya||

Rāhu Transiting Lagna

Some fear the transit of Saturn, but Rāhu is just as disastrous in his retrogression through the zodiac. When Rāhu transits lagna he will often cause vāta diseases similar to Saturn, accept his are harder to diagnose and treat. The transit of Rāhu through the lagna or over the Sun can also bring an onset of cancer; therefore, those in remission need to be more aware during these times. All the kārakas can be seen in this way, for example, Uturine cancer is more likely when Rāhu transits Venus.

The transit of Rāhu over the AL and its second house can cause negative reputation. If this time coincides with a negative daśā or periods like sāḍhe-sātī, the individual can even be falsely accused of things that could ruin their reputation. When the nodes create an eclipse, the luminaries are being obscured or covered (*chādana*). The word chādana also means to deceive, or conceal, or to tolerate offences if useful for one's aims (similar to a "cover-up" of an illicit activity).

This is how Rāhu can disrupt the lagna, pāka lagna, AL or other personal points in the chart. One is advised to wear a devī kavaca (which has been activated by a sādhaka or priest). This is a protective talisman or yantra of the goddess Durgā. One can also chant the Devī Kavaca found in the Durgā Saptaśatī, which is like armour against negative energies.

Maraṇa-Kāraka-Sthāna Rāhu

Rāhu is MKS in the ninth house. This will often indicate an individual who has great doubt, and can be very disrespectful towards their elders or gurus, or can even be an atheist (*nāstika*). They will not take advice from others. This will be lessened by Rāhu being Ātmakāraka, or other such spiritual significations.

This is a combination that might not come up until the individual enters the daśā of Rāhu. It can be a headache for a teacher when seen in their student's chart, and in this case a remedy is mandatory.The individual should wear a yellow sapphire to strengthen the kāraka of the ninth house, or if Rāhu is a beneficial house lord the individual can wear *gomūtragomeda*. Gomeda is a type of garnet associated with Rāhu which is the color of cow's urine (*gomūtra*). The remedial mantra is to the Śiva Liṅga which exalts Rāhu.

|| Auṁ namaḥ Śivāya Nāgeśvarāya sauṁ sauṁ saḥ ||

Auṁ praises to Śiva, the lord of snakes,
[God and Goddess] plant the seed of rejuvenation.

The negative judgement associated with Rāhu in the ninth house can sometimes become prominent during the daśā, or at other times when Rāhu becomes very strong. This is particularly true if Rāhu is ninth from the Moon, lagneśa, Ātmakāraka, Karakāṁśa, or other important point. This mantra is also beneficial when the attributes of Rāhu in the ninth house are present, such as being disrespectful or unable to take advice.

Strengthening Rāhu

In some cases one may need to strengthen Rāhu directly through a graha mantra. One can do a nāma mantra or the Rāhu Gāyatrī. A normal graha mantra can be taken from the 108 names of Rāhu. If one is going to use a graha mantra, one should at least ensure that the number of syllables is beneficial for the chart, match the meaning of the name to the issue being worked upon, and ensure that the sounds of the name are beneficial for the individual in the mantra chakras.

||Auṁ Rāhave namaḥ ||

Praises to Rāhu.

||Auṁ Svarbhanave namaḥ ||

Praises to the Light of Heaven.

For example, if Rāhu is well placed in the 11th house of gains, and the individual is suffering a spiritual disconnect and is lost because of Rāhu, you can give them the form of Rāhu as Svarbhānu, which was before he had his head severed from his body. It is the unity of the extreme and Rāhu in a very high light. In this way the name should correspond to the issue at hand. After this is chosen, the first sound of the devatā's name should be compared to the first letter of the individual's name to ensure compatibility.

Pacification: Rāhu Gāyatrī

Sometimes Rāhu is in a place that is dangerous to touch and he is causing problems. In these situations, pacification is a good method to remove the problems Rāhu is causing. The Rāhu Gāyatrī (from Ṛgveda, Maṇḍala 4, Sūkta 31, verse 1) is recommended by

Parasara (Graha-Śānti chapter) to be recited 18,000 times with homa. This can also be done by chanting five mālās a day for 40 days and will pacify Rāhu.

कया नश्चित्र आ भुवदूती सदावृधः सखा । कया शचिष्ठया वृता ॥

kayā naścitra ā bhuvadūtī sadāvṛdhaḥ sakhā| kayā śaciṣṭhayā vṛtā||

Oh messenger of the sky, ever prospering friend,
In what manner, and by which method can we achieve clarity.

Solar Eclipse

Rāhu with the Sun is called Dakṣiṇāmūrti Yoga, where the Sun takes on the form of Śiva as a teacher. The negativity of this yoga is that it can create ego issues related to loss of self, misunderstanding of self-role, identity and control issues. It can often be seen on an astral level as energetic blockages in the solar plexus. On the beneficial level, it is the spiritual energy of a solar eclipse where the individual self is removed and there is a clear non-dual reality experienced. When this is connected to the lagna, the individual will struggle with ego delusions, having a too large or too small ego, and projecting this delusiononto others. Often they will make their ego bigger by the delusion of calling it very small, while constantly talking about what a small ego they have. Everyone has an ahaṅkāra; it is an absolutely necessary organ of existence, and we just need healthy ones that are balanced. On a spiritual level, we work to identify the Self with the divine instead of the ego- though the ego will still be present- or else there would be no one to brush your teeth and wipe you after the toilet. Everyone has an "I", which appreciates being loved and cared for. The ahaṅkāra lets you know that those are your teeth, you need to care for them. But who is this "you" truly? That is the question to follow to an answer that is beyond words, and this is the teaching of Dakṣiṇāmūrti Śiva.

Dakṣiṇāmūrti is worshipped during a solar eclipse caused by Rāhu. This mantra is given in the tradition to cross over the effects of Rāhu:

||Auṁ Dakṣiṇāmūrti-ra-tar-om||

One verse of the Śrī Dakṣiṇāmūrtī Stotra, by Ādi Śaṅkara, says that the brilliance of the Sun exists even when taken by Rāhu, just as True Reality exists even when unrecognized in Māyā. He makes the comparison between Māyā racking the mind with illusion to Rāhu eclipsing (*chhādaka*) the Sun on a New Moon conjunction.

Rāhu-grasta-divākarendu-sadṛśo māyā-samā cchādanāt
sanmātraḥ karaṇopasaṁharaṇato yo'bhūt suṣuptaḥ pumān |
prāgasvāpsamiti prabodhasamaye yaḥ pratyabhijñāyate
tasmai śrīgurumūrtaye nama idaṁ śrīdakṣiṇāmūrtaye || 6||

The swallowing of the Sun and Moon by Rāhu is similar
to the obscuration of the Single Reality caused by Māyā,
As when a man's senses are withdrawn in sleep and
After awakening from a dream he remembers who he is,
To the guru Śrī Dakṣiṇāmūrti (who reveals the true nature) I bow.

Dakṣiṇāmūrti is visualized as sitting under a banyan tree, his hand in jñāna mūdrā, in the company of great sages. The banyan tree represents the body and he sits within. He is always abiding (*vartamāna*) at any age, in any state, always throbbing (*sphurantaṁ*) as one's own self ready to be seen. As one will understand from reading the Sanskrit stotra, he is the form of Śiva who is an expert (*dakṣam*) in cutting (*cheda*) the bondages of material nature, and this is why he is called Dakṣiṇā[4]-mūrtī (the form of the expert).

The Dakṣiṇāmūrti Upaniṣad has other mantras and dhyānas. These are particularly beneficial when Rāhu has corrupted the mind. As an astrologer, these are extremely beneficial to do during a solar eclipse to strengthen the memory and intellect. *Medhā* is mental power, literally brain-power, and these mantras invoke Dakṣiṇāmūrti for increasing this attribute. Here are a variety of mantras which mean about the same thing, but vary in number of syllables.

||Auṁ namo bhagavate dakṣiṇāmūrtaye mahyam medhām prajñāṁ pratyaccha svāhā ||9-24

Praises to the power of Dakṣiṇāmūrti, please grant me brain-power and understanding, so be it.

||Auṁ namo bhagavate dakṣiṇāmūrtaye mahyam medhām pratyaccha svāhā ||8-20

Auṁ Praises to the power of Dakṣiṇāmūrti, please grant me brain-power, so be it.

||Auṁ hruṁ namo dakṣiṇāmūrtaye mahyam jñānaṁ dehi svāhā||8-18

Auṁ hrūṁ, Praises to the power of Dakṣiṇāmūrti, please give me knowledge, so be it.

||Auṁ namo bhagavate dakṣiṇāmūrtaye||4-13

AuṁPraises to the power of Dakṣiṇāmūrti.

Agni- Stambhana

When Mars is with Rāhu, it blocks the fire and is called *agni-stambhana* (fire-stopping). This can give problems physically or mentally. It has a tendency to limit the amount of energy a person allows themselves to put forward into the area indicated by the combination. It can also stop individuals from having the follow-through to finish projects.

This combination is also called Vijayā yoga, relating to Vijayā Durgā because of its

4 In the Ṛgveda dakṣinā refers to a cow that can calve and give good milk, and it also has the meaning of an expert, who, having perfected their art, is able to give properly and abundantly.

fierce form, or the fierce form needed to overcome it. This yoga will often show arguing and fighting with the house or planets it is conjunct. Vijayā Durgā is the form of Durgā who has completed battle and is victorious. The mantra for this form of Durgā is called the Rāma Daśākṣari mantra (or Rāma Tāraṇa). It has 6 words and 10 syllables to ensure the enemy is crushed and you return to the tenth house throne.

||Auṁ Aiṁ Hrīṁ Klīṁ Cāmuṇḍāyai Vicce||

Guru-Cāṇḍāla Yoga

Jupiter is the planet of highest sattva and he becomes polluted when conjunct Rāhu. The tamas of Rāhu is so strong even Jupiter can become confused. When this happens, the worship of the Sun is the best remedy. In general, the Sun will help out Jupiter when he is troubled and Jupiter will help out the Sun when he is in trouble; they watch out for each other. It is the relationship between the king and the priest (Indra and Agni), whose positions depend upon each other's support. Therefore, when Jupiter is suffering due to the conjunction of the *cāṇḍāla* (the dog eater), the worship of the Sun will help Jupiter maintain his sattva, and therefore his beneficial actions.

Jupiter and Rāhu conjunction is also called *Jīva-hatyā Yoga* when it is placed in a position where it can create the taking of life (murder). Rāhu removes the compassion of Jupiter, as one fails to see the Supreme Being inside of all living beings. When this combinations falls into certain placements in the navāṁśa it can indicate the individual will be murdered. When it is in rāśi or navāṁśa lagna it will create a great soldier, as the individual has the power to take another person's life. Once I was sitting with my guru, and he looked at the chart of a man with Jīva-hatyā Yoga in lagna and said with a straight face, "This is the chart of someone who has killed many men." The gentleman replied, "I don't know how many, but I sure killed a lot of them."He had been a fighter pilot during the Vietnam War.This is the nature of Jīva-hatyā Yoga, and one should be aware of it in vargas and praśna charts.

If Jupiter or Venus are afflicted, and the Sun is weak, then Rāhu can cause cancer. If there is cancer caused by Rāhu or some other poisoning, then Garuḍa is worshipped to remove the poison. Garuḍa is a bird and represents the energy of the Sun, which can see Rāhu and destroy the shadow, as an eagle or hawk can see a snake from a great distance and then fly away with it for a meal. The mantra reverses *auṁ kṣipa* to *kṣipa auṁ*. Some mantras for Rāhu use the rule of reversal or duplication to overcome the serpent.

||Kṣipa Auṁ Svāhā||

Praises to the great bird [Garuḍa].

Sarpa Ruling the Directions[5]

Planet	Nāga
Sun	Śeṣa (Ananta)
Moon	Phaṇi (Vāsuki)
Mars	Takṣaka
Mercury	Karkoṭaka
Jupiter	Padma
Venus	Mahāpadma
Saturn	Śaṅkhapāla
Rāhu	Kulika
Ketu	All nāgas

Rāhu is a snake (*sarpa*) in all regards. When he is causing a problems, like a curse, and is conjunct another planet, he can be given various names according to the great serpents which rule the directions. These names relate to either Rāhu or Ketu associating with a planet. In this way, if it is said that there is a problem caused by Takṣaka nāga, then it is most likely a conjunction of Rāhu and Mars. The names of the nāgas are indicated by the planet associating with the node. Parāśara also lists 12 names in Viṣṇu Purāṇa related to Rāhu in each sign of the zodiac.

Rāhu aspected by Mars and Saturn shows an angry snake which will destroy the houses that it aspects. This is a sarpa curse and it is even possible that the people indicated by those houses may die early in life to indications signified by Rāhu. In this case, not only does the proper nāga need to be pacified, but the proper remedies to lift the curse need to be performed.

Karkoṭaka Yoga: Rāhu and Mercury

When Rāhu is conjunct Mercury, he is called Karkoṭaka Nāga. It is called Nārada Śapa (the curse of Nārada) because Nārada cursed Karkoṭaka Nāga for making fun of Vaiṣṇavas (Mercury). Whenever Rāhu is conjunct a planet, it indicates that the individual made fun of, teased, caused shame to, or defamed that individual or signification in their last life.

Mercury is very changeable and moulds to his environment very easily. He therefore takes on the attributes of the planet he conjoins. When the thoughtful nature of Mercury conjoins Rāhu, it is twisted and the intellect can be used for lying and cheating, or coming up with ways to scheme or scam. Mercury shows the nature of one's speech, and being conjunct such a tamas graha lowers the quality and nature of one's speech, as well as dements the nature of one's humor.

The remedy requires the strengthening of Mercury to revive its better qualities. *Budhāṣṭamī vrata* is used to purify Mercury (*Budha*) and remove the effects of Rāhu. According to the Bhaviṣya Purāṇa, this requires fasting on aṣṭami tithi and, according to the Varāha Purāṇa, it requires fasting on Wednesdays. Both agree that when an aṣṭamī tithi falls on a Wednesday, one should fast and do pūjā to Budha graha. The importance of this vāra-tithi yoga can be seen according to the Kālacakra. When Rāhu afflicts Mercury, I advise fasting on aṣṭami tithi.

[5] Garuḍa Purāṇa

Mahāpadma Yoga: Rāhu and Venus

As the snake charmer with his dancing cobra is frightening, he is at the same time exciting and alluring. So Rāhu, even though we know he is negative, puts out an attractive energy to seduce us. When Rāhu is with Venus, he creates a woman who is sensually attractive and has a dark allure. In a female chart, this is the woman herself; in a male chart, this is the women to whom he is attracted. If Venus is in a tamasic sign (rāśi and especially navāṁśa), this will lead to base sexual desires; if the Moon supports, it may also lead to actions. When Venus is weak or afflicted in this combination, it can lead to situations of sexual harassment. If the combination falls on the UL, the spouse could experience situations of sexual harassment.

On an astral level it can be seen as excess energy in the genital area and even leaking energy from this area: sticky sexual energy. Many western movies include some Rāhu-Venus elements to satiate the already sensorily over-stimulated masses.

Venus needs to be purified, and the best way to do this is the Mahāvidyā of Venus. Kamalātmikā (or Kamalā) has the power to purify the instincts of Venus when they have been polluted due to conjunction with Rāhu. Kamalā can remove unfaithfulness and other improper sensual appetitesthat lead to eventual unhappiness or unfulfilment in one's love life.

||Auṁ Aiṁ Hrīṁ Śrīṁ Klīṁ Hsauḥ Jagat Prasutyai namaḥ||

Preta Bādhaka

The combination of Rāhu and Saturn gives Preta Bādhaka.The overlord of Rāhu is Yama and the overlord of Ketu is Citragutpa (the keeper of your deeds to be evaluated at death). These two are the king and the minister of the underworld, which is also called the city of dead spirits (*preta-puri*). Preta Bādhaka was also seen regarding Saturn and Ketu conjunction. But there is a difference in that Ketu has agni, and therefore makes the combination a curse.

Saturn and Rāhu have no agni, they are just vāyu, and therefore it is not a curse, but "something far more evil," as my Guruji says. It has an indication for *bhūtas* (ghosts or disincarnate beings). The word for ghosts literally means "has-been" (past tense of bhava) and indicates the past. This shows problems from the mental past, the past life, or those who have passed on to the other side (and often a mix of these). When this combination of Rāhu and Saturn is aspected by Mars, it will indicate death and a haunting from this lifetime.

When associated with the mind, this combination can increase the internal vāta and its related emotions of fear, anxiety, and insomnia. Saturn relates to fear and Rāhu relates to anxiety. Fear is an emotional response to a consciously recognized threat or danger. Fear has an external origin, while anxiety has an intrapsychic origin, meaning it comes from inside. Anxiety is apprehension, stress, or uneasiness that comes from an unknown or unrecognized source, an anticipation in the mind of something dangerous. The two together can cause various emotional disturbances along these lines.

These two planets together relate to a goddess called *Śītalī*. Her name literally means the "cold one," which can relate to not having the warmth of passion. On a positive note it relates to going above passions, but it often shows a disconnection to one's feelings, insensitivity, apathy, and emotional coldness.When these planets are in the lagna, it will create a very slender frame, possibly even looking emaciated.If this is in lagna or relates to the Moon, the person can be very unemotional or cold. Śītalī is also the goddess connected to small-pox (*śītalā*), and offerings are given to her to protect one's children.

The auspicious (*bhadra*) form of Kālī is used for this combination, called Bhadra-Kālī. The mantras of Kālī use *krīṁ* bīja, but Bhadrakālī uses *klīṁ* bīja.

||Auṁ klīṁ Bhadra-Kālike namaḥ||

Kālasarpa Yoga

When all the planets are between Rāhu and Ketu they are swallowed in the belly of the snake. When they are between Rāhu and Ketu (i.e., when the planets are moving toward Rāhu), it is called *Kālasarpa Yoga*, and when they are between Ketu and Rāhu, with the planets moving toward Ketu, it is called *Kālāmṛta Yoga*. Both will alter the results of the chart, though the Kālasarpa is the more feared as it has a much more deluded progression related to Rāhu. Kālāmṛta Yoga at least takes on into the depths of spirituality as it rearranges your life.

There are many who debate the validity of Kālasarpa Yoga, but this is not because of its effects, it is because of the way some priests have utilized this yoga. They tell people with Kālasarpa that their life is terrible and will only get worse if they do not perform the extremely expensive pūjā which only they can perfom. They scare people into wasting huge amounts of money on these pūjās and in the end only give a bad name to astrology. In some regards, these pūjās are more the result of the Kālasarpa than a remedy for it, but that is the game of Rāhu.

Kālasarpa will delay many indicated results in the chart until later in life (after 42 years of age, which is Rāhu's maturity). In general, many remedies for Rāhu may be only partial until after Rāhu matures. This is also true for Saturn in that many remedies may not be as effective until after the person reaches Saturn maturity (35-36 years of age). The availability and timing when a remedy will be possible relates to many indications in the chart, such as beneficial aspects, house lordships and the placement of dispositors of issues one is trying to remedy.

In a Kālasarpa Yoga, the axis in which Rāhu and Ketu reside will also shape the results of the yoga, show how it effects the individual, and indicate which results will not be overcome until later in life. Do huge pūjās work? Pūjā is always good, always, but it shouldn't rob one's bank account. If it costs more than a cow, one should be suspicious. As astrologers, we have more specific ways to *break* the Kālasarpa.

If a benefic is conjunct the nodes, it has the power to break the grasp of the serpent and to guide it. This is most powerful if the planets are Jupiter or Venus, as they are natural gurus and can guide the nodes. If Jupiter or Venus is in the lagna axis, they can be used to break the serpent's grasp. The lagneśa also has the ability to break the nodal grasp. The indicated planet should be activated and given the proper mantras or *works* to break the Kālasarpa. If Venus (Mahāpadma) is breaking the Kālasarpa, then marriage will break the Kālasarpa (although some remedies may be needed in order to get married).

Conclusion

There are additional remedial measures associated with Rāhu throughout the bādhaka chapter. It is very important to understand the bādhaka when determining the remedy, as the nature of the bādhaka alters various needs and prescriptions.

Understanding the nature of the planets and associated deities is an interdependent learning process. One needs to learn about the planetary combinations, the deities associated with them, the results of these combinations, and how they affect one's life. One needs to give a proper diagnosis to give the proper remedy. The greatest eye medicine in the world will not fix a sore throat; the medicine must match the frequency which has become disturbed.

Astrology is a science and can indicate many of the problems an individual may face in life. The remedies for these issues are often found within the science of Tantra (or other spiritual/religious systems and practices). In this way, if one only learns astrology, one will only be able to diagnose. The study of allied sciences will help one to be able to cure. As astrology is the study of an archetypal reality that can manifest in any culture at any time, these remedies, when properly understood, can relate to native cultural practices of similar archetypal energies.

Ketu Remedial Measures

The planets need to be understood to give them remedy, but to understand Ketu is to think backwards. While Rāhu desires things, desires more, Ketu is not interested and would rather do without. Ketu can give very negative results for certain indications but in other situations, Ketu can give beneficial results. Ketu is a benefic for marriage and spirituality, and can therefore be strengthened just by getting married and having children (lineage), or by becoming more spiritual.

Ketu rules over numbers and mathematics. Ketu rules mistakes, the eclipse of the mind that makes you forget something or not pay close enough attention. In a long mathematical equation (especially with no computers) a mistake can ruin everything. For example, when casting a birth chart, if you make a mistake on the time zone, the entire chart is wrong, all the vargas are wrong, all the daśā are wrong. If you were calculating that all by hand over a period of two days, then a small mistake could be disastrous. Those writing code for a computer program, know that everytime one adds an element, three other processes get a bug. Ketu also rules insects, their bites and all the diseases they can give you (real ones and computer bugs as well).

The primary deity associated with Ketu is Gaṇeśa, whose mantras have already been discussed in the bādhaka chapter. One of the reasons to begin important tasks with Gaṇeśa mantra is to insure there will be no mistakes in your task. Those who work in the IT field must have a beneficial Ketu, and therefore Gaṇeśa becomes very important. Ketu manifests as small machines like watches, and machines with small moving parts like a calculator or a computer. The computer is a manifestation of Gaṇeśa, who always has a mouse by his side.

In modern Hinduism, Gaṇeśa is a Śaivite deity, and Śiva is associated with the Sun. As Rāhu and his upāya become closely associated with the Moon (devī), Ketu's upāya needs the energy of the Sun, and specifically the elephant headed aspect. Elephants are ruled by Ketu, as are all cargo transport vehicles. Gaṇeśa was created by his mother (the Moon) therefore he is a node of the Moon, created by the Moon. But it is his father (the Sun) that makes him loose his head, or who goes and gives him a new head in which he can find himself complete and functional. Ketu relates to psychotic states of mind and schizophrenia. If issues associated with bādhaka are ruled out in schizophrenic states then the luminaries and the lagna need to be strengthened.

Ketu makes a person have a lazy eye, and he can make your brain feel like you are going cross-eyed. Ketu boggles the brain. He rulesover numerical mysteries. Ketu associates numbers and letters which is the foundation of Kaṭapayādi varga and other letter-number meaning systems. The Jaimini Upadeśa Sūtra is written entirely in a number encoded system, where the meaning of the verses cannot be understood without the mathematics of the words. Reading such a text is beneficial for simple Ketu problems, like difficulties with visas, border patrols (customs), foreign residence, etc.

Ketu is a thief (*coraka*), and relates to lost and stolen things (*corita*). As an eclipse, the object has been lost from your sight. For those who have Ketu in a position which makes them lose things often, worship of the Sun should be done. In a situation where you have misplaced something, just take a moment and meditate on the Sun to remove the darkness of the eclipse, and then continue looking. In the case of problems from theft, this remedy needs to be looked at more deeply with planets in the 12th from lagna and AL as well as praśna for the particular situation.

Dhūmāvatī

When Ketu is causing external/material problems such as manifesting as thieves, or psychotic neighbors trying to burn your house down, then the Mahāvidyā of Ketu is used to alleviate the problems. Dhūmāvatīis an old woman, a widow, and one should be aware of the health of one's father and grandfather if utilizing this Mahāvidyā.

Dhūmāvatī also gives intuition (like a wise grandmother she knows). Those who work with solving computer problems for a living will do well to gain the siddhi of Dhūmāvatī who has a magic power over small machines. I always used to ask my guru in different ways what kind of Goddess could rule over computers, and he always replied Dhūmāvatī. I had a hard time believing that a crone goddess could have anything to do with technology. But I was in an āśrama high in the Himālayas, and my older computer decided to totally die, which meant not only no writing, but no casting quick and accurate horoscopes.So I surrendered and did a one day Dhūmāvatī sādhanā. That night, she came in a dream and touched my laptop. The next morning I reluctantly opened it, and it started and ran perfectly. So I put a picture of Dhūmāvatī as the desktop background, and the computer ran great until the day I removed the background, it died. So she has the power to work with microchips, and all the things that move in computer language.

||Auṁ dhūṁ dhūṁ dhūmāvatī ṭa ṭa||

She came quickly to me because I have Moon conjunct Ketu, the mother manifests naturally as the crone goddess. And my mother and both grandmothers are all widows. The planet conjunct the Moon will come very easily to the individual in a Mother form.

Ketu Gāyatrī

The Ketu Gāyatrī (from *Ṛgveda, Maṇḍala 1, Sūkta 6, verse 3*) is recommended by Paraśara (Graha-Śānti chapter) to be recited 17,000 times. This can be done by chanting 4 mālās a day for 40 days and will pacify Ketu.

केतुं कृण्वन्नकेतवे पेशो मर्या अपेशसे समुषद्भिरजायथाः ॥३॥

ketuṁ kṛṇvannaketave peśo maryā apeśase samuṣadbhirajāyathāḥ||3||

Awareness is born like the dawn in man,
Giving brightness to the flame, and form to the formless.

Ketu Śānti: Spiritual Remedies

Ketu gets peace by spirituality, you cannot give something to Ketu to pacify him; you must take something away. The other planets also like to take things away, in the mode of charity (*dāna*), like donating books to a school for a Mercury upāya. But Ketu is not as interested in material things. While all the planets are walking forward attaining the various aspects of this world, Ketu is the renunciate who is walking backwards towards the source from which all things come.

It is said that when Ketu is twelfth from the kārakāṁśa the individual will get mokṣa. When the mokṣa-kāraka becomes the planet that helps you on the spiritual path, then mokṣa can be very close. This indicates that one can be guided to true spirituality, as long as the rāśi chart supports the practice of this spirituality.

Ketu śānti is about renunciation or surrender (*śaraṇāgati*). There are six types of surrender taught in the ancient scriptures. We shall explore them, look at the nirukta of each of the six names, and see how they relate to the nine planets. All six types of surrender relate to Ketu, and Rāhu is the blockage (*virodha*) to surrender, the opposite of surrender; he is attachment. Rāhu shows where our attachments are strongest and Ketu shows where we can surrender the deepest.

Six Aspects of Surrender (Ṣaḍvidhā Śaraṇāgati)

Ketu wants to let go, to forget the world and walk off into the jungle like a sādhu. Ketu is the kāraka for sādhus and renunciation. Though renunciation does not mean that we have to give up everything and be a monk, this is not the teaching of the Bhagavad Gītā, if one is not familiar with this they should study these teachings deeply, as they are the core of Vedic philosophy. One must give up *attachment* to everything, which is true renunciation. And it is this renunciation or surrender that makes Ketu beneficial.

The Pāñcarātra and other Bhāgavata texts say that surrender (*prapatti*) is the most important factor in attaining spiritual realization. The Pāñcarātra teaches a four-fold approach to the eternal abode (*śāśvataṁ sthānaṁ*): jñāna yoga, karma yoga, bhakti yoga and prapatti. This is the foundation of the Vaiṣṇavism taught by Śrī Acyutānanda.[2] Ketu relates to prapatti: *patti* comes from the root *pad* (foot) and means going or walking, and *pra* is a prefix meaning very much or great, so prapatti literally means the great-walk or the highest way to go. Prapatti is defined as *śaraṇāgati*, which means going in the path of *śaraṇa* (refuge, shelter). Both words correlate to the English word surrender, and have been defined as "total and confident surrender of oneself and all that belongs to oneself".

Upāya-Jñāna		Attitudes of Mind
Sun/Moon	Ātma-nikṣepa	Surrender of the self
Mars	Goptṛ	God as the protector
Mercury	Kārpaṇya	Absolute humility
Jupiter	Ānukūlya	Kindness to all
Venus	Mahāviśvāsa	Great faith/trust
Saturn	Prātikūlya	Avoid Antagonism

Namas (*namaḥ*) literally means to bow, which show ones humility before something greater than us out of respect and adoration. To give a complete *namas* is to bow and surrender to the divine. True bowing is to bow before that which is the highest aspect of creation, which is everywhere in everything. Said alone, *Namaste* is just a salutation. But when consciously used, *Namaste* can be a reminder to bow to the divine which is in everything, which is in me and which is in you. The traditional texts teach that the six aspects of surrender are correlated to ***namana*** (bowing, or giving namas) which contains six letters: n-a-m-a-n-a. The 'six aspects of surrender' are called Upāya-jñāna which basically refers to mental attitudes. These are the means of understanding that allow one to completely surrender. Each upāya relate to Ketu (as they are a mode of surrender), their blockages (*virodha orapāya*) relate to Rāhu. In general the lord of Rāhu (or planets conjunct Rāhu) will be the biggest apāya in one's spiritual life. For spiritual benefit in worldly life one should insure to follow the surrender related to the lagneśa, as this is surrendering yourself (lagna). The planets conjunct Ketu (or dispositor if no planets) will be the best surrender to practice for expediting results in the spiritual world. You can't pay a pujārīs to do a ritual to give you any of these, or to remove any of these virodhas. These attitudes are self cultivated, and show the spiritual evolution of the individual.

2 Odiya Vaiṣṇavism (teachings of the Pañcasakha) and many other Vaiṣṇava lineages give importance on the fourfold path. Certain sectarian views only place emphasis on bhakti.

The Sun and Moon

Ātma-nikṣepa is the complete surrender of oneself to the divine. Nikṣepa means to throw down, to cast away, to abandon, or to trust. Ātma-nikṣepa literally means to throw oneself down before a higher power, to cast away the thought that you are the cause, to abandon that you are the doer, to completely trust a higher Spirit other than yourself.

Ātma-nikṣepa relates to the Sun and Moon as they are the soul and mind which manifest the ahaṅkāra (I-sense), or what one considers as 'oneself'. In theAcyutānanda tradition it is called *ātma-samarpaṇa*. Samarpaṇa means to present, to consign, to completely hand over, or the act of placing. In this way, it means to completely hand over the thought that you are the doer or that you control your life, to offer you ātmā to the divine, to hand over yourself and say "thy will be done", it is all your will, I surrender myself to That.

The Gītā says that he who sees himself as the sole doer (*kartāram*) does not really see, because he sees with immature understanding (*akṛta-buddhitva*). That person has not understood the nature of thoughts and actions and where they arise from. With ātma-samarpaṇa one gives up the sense of being the doer (surrenders any sense of I) and therefore gives up the ownership of the fruit of action (*karma-phala-tyāga*). If one has studied the Bhagavad Gītā well, they will understand that this teaching is repeated again and again. One must give up the sense of being the doer, the ownership of actions and the fruit which comes from them.

The blockage (*virodha*) to ātma-samarpaṇa is *phalepsā* (desired-result) which is the ahaṅkāra's desire to enjoy mundane benefits, to own the fruit of actions. "I" am so wonderful, "I" have done so much good work, "I" have earned this, "my" big house, "my" thinking, I, my, me, mine. If one gets a raise at work, the "I" says 'I did such a good job that "I" received a raise'. While the surrendered ātmā says, 'the work has been blessed and Bhagavan is bringing more money'. The attitude is slightly different and the ownership is removed. Some people believe they are the ones controlling their life. The Gītā says to avoid speaking of this knowledge to those who are not ready, or do not want to hear it, and who do not do mantras or pūjā (XVIII.67). This is the teaching of Ketu, the mokṣa-kāraka, when one is not seeking mokṣa why try to feed them food they do not want to eat. These spiritual teachings are for those who are ready.

The Gītā teaches that when we take refuge in our sense of "I" then we will be led by our own material nature which is bound by karma. Whatever action your karma deems to happen will come about, even if you say it won't, because by some delusion (*moha*) you will do something that makes it so (XVIII.59-60). Therefore even if you think you have some will to do as you wish, you are just being led around by your karmic tendencies, a slave to your own past actions. The Gītā says the Lord of all beings abides in the realm of the heart causing all beings to move (XVIII.61). And we should seek refuge (*śaraṇam*) in him alone, with our whole being (*sarvabhāvena*). And from that tranquility, one attains supreme peace (*parāṁ śāntiṁ*) and the eternal abode (XVIII.62). By offering oneself, one becomes prasāda, as food offered to the deity, purified.

In classical Vaiṣṇavism surrender is not something that pertains only to bhakti, as some traditions translate the Gītā. It pertains also to karma yoga, jñāna yoga and even reading someone's astrological chart. Every action, at all times becomes becomes prasāda by offering up the sense of doership to a higher power. And it is this surrender of the "I" that gives one peace.

Mars

Mars is the general, the soldier, the policeman; his job is protecting. The spiritual attitude related to Mars is called **Goptṛ**, which means one who preserves or protects.[3] Life has many events that we have no control over, such as a drunk driver swerving and hitting your car while you are driving. To think that you can protect yourself is limiting and blocks the support of the divine in your life. By surrendering yourself to the protection of a higher power, you invite the higher presence to give you protection, to be your protector (*goptṛ*).

Mars relates to the fire element, which relates to strength in the physical body, and intelligence in the mind. The divine is all powerful, and can protect us from what we cannot control. The divine can also protect our decisions and guide us properly. One of the biggest issues of Mars is carelessness, which can lead to all types of accidents. Goptṛ is when we deliberately chose to make God our primary protector since the all pervasive is the most competent to protect all beings. By surrendering the thought that you can protect yourself, or that you have control over the circumstances that can come into your life, you are *mindfully acknowledging* a higher protection and making room for that in your consciousness. When one goes on a journey and is blessed "May God protect you" or "Jah protect", this acknowledgement puts one into a prayerful attitude.

The blockage (*virodha*) to this is the feeling of indifference (*udāsīna*) caused by negligence/disregard (*upekṣā*). The taxi driver got in the car yesterday and was fine, the day before was just fine, everyday this last three years was fine, so he is indifferent when he gets into the car, he does not think to pray for divine protection before driving off. People get stuck in bad situations, disease, or accidents before they start praying for protection.

[3] The order of the six varies in different saṁhitās and some have argued this shows a different order of importance. Svāmī Deśikan (nyāsa viṁśati śloka 12) has taught that ātma-nikṣepa is the main ingredient and the other five are its aspects. The order is given here according to the order of the planets in the vāra cakra.

There are many stories about divine protection, like Job in the lion's den. In Hawaii, there was a volcano eruption which destroyed an entire village, yet split and missed the house of one shaman. In the Sumatra Earthquake Tsunami, there was an entire city destroyed except for one mosque that was left standing. Or there are the people that called in sick on the day the twin towers fell. These are stories of divine protection from great catastrophes, but in everyday life, there are many moments where divine protection is blessing us. Goptṛ is acknowledging that divine protection, and surrendering ourselves to take a protection that is higher than us.

Mercury

Mercury is a high achiever who likes to accomplish many things. Mercury is the student who is learning and proud of his knowledge. **Kārpaṇya** is absolute humility, it literally means to admit that you are weak and poor, and less than. It is the honest awareness of one's own natural ignorance and impurity from the karma of countless births. Often people ride on the arrogance of parentage, education, or wealth and think that they have the ability to get and know everything by themselves. Kārpaṇya is admitting that one is still filled with faults and ignorance.

Acyutānanda called this the *Śūdra-bhāva* or the mental condition of being a servant. Acyutānanda would often call himself a śūdra (one born in the servant caste). He believed that by thinking one was superior to others because of some birth in a Brahmin or other higher caste or rich family, one became blind to the truth that we are all one. Acyutānanda taught that we should all have the mindset of servants, to humbly serve, to not think that we are better than others, that we have some knowledge or initiation that makes us better.

The path of humility and service removes the attachment to the selfish desire for power and control. If a role of power is given, the mind needs to remain in the śūdra bhāva, to stay in the mood of service. The position is not given for one to have more power and prestige, but given to allow one to be of more service. As astrologers in the tradition of Acyutānanda, we are not special because we know many mantras, or have special techniques to see more than others, we are just servants. Everyone is playing their role according to their karma. The role is not important, the performance and the mindset in which it is performed is the important aspect. We are servants and our job is to help people get over their worldly suffering and find alignment with a higher purpose in their life.

Mercury is the Earth element, and it is the Earth Mother (*Bhūmī*) who is the most humble of all. She carries everyone, you walk all over Her and still she cares for you. We can learn from everyone, at every moment when we humble ourselves. The Earth abundantly provides all things through divine blessings. What can truly be successful without the blessing of the divine? We must humble ourselves and know that it is a higher power that is guiding all things, and who makes all things successful.

The blockage to kārpaṇya is *sva-svātantryāvabodha*, the imagination that one is free, self-independent, and able to do whatever one likes by his own free choice. Parāśara says that Mercury by nature is independent (*svatantra*), he likes to do things on his own, be creative, have his own philosophy. This can be beneficial in some areas, just like it is beneficial for Mars to do his job and protect people. But on the inner spiritual plane, one must realize that life is unfolding faster than one can control. That most of life is out of one's control, that we are just responding to the various situations that are manifesting around us. One must realize that there are those who know better than us, and who can guide us, who we must humble ourselves before and depend upon. One must understand when to follow one's own will and when to submit their will.

The śūdra-bhāva gives one the lowliness to admit one's ignorance, and to let all the blockages of self-importance and pride dissipate. How can the student learn anything if they think they already know it all. The Zen saying is that you need to empty the cup in order to be filled. The Gītā teaches that through humble submission (*praṇipāta*), enquiry (*paripraśna*), and service (*sevā*) the wise (*jñāninas*) who perceive the essence of reality (*tattvadarśanas*) will give the teachings (*upadeśa*) (IV.34). *Praṇipāta*like kārpaṇya is humble submission; it is bowing all the way to ground, or falling at one's feet. Mercury is the student, but will not get the higher knowledge until he humbly submits to the Guru. When the student thinks they know it all already, they lose the chance to get the next level of teachings. In the same way we are all students of the universe, and need to humbly submit to the all pervasive One.

Jupiter

Jupiter is the guru, the spiritual teacher, wise, and filled with abundance of all good things. **Ānukūlya-niścaya** is the resolution to be kind to all beings, to not stop that goodwill or limit it to only certain people. *Ānukūlya* means to have kindness, friendliness, or good-will. *Niścaya*is conviction or firm determination; it is used interchangeably with *saṅkalpa* which means definite intention, conviction or a vow. In this way, the surrender associated with Jupiter, is the surrender of any animosity which creates the genuine opening of the heart to see the divine in all living beings. It is similar to a vow of compassion.

People who look at the physical reality and are unaware of a deeper level only see the physical body. They get trapped into treating those who do not look a certain way to be less, and can even shun or mistreat people they consider different. In the most superficial level, this relates to judging people according to how they dress. The soul takes different births and the social economic class, the features, the religion, all change from life to life. Attachment to any of the body's coverings is a blockage in the mind. Sometimes people hold their knowledge as something that makes them better than others. Sometimes one can becomes attached to their concept of purity and look down on those who are not as pure as them.

Jupiter represents the jīva that is in all living beings. And Jupiter is the ākāśa that is in everything, everywhere, meaning the separate soul inside is really just a reflection of the all pervasive that is everywhere. The Gītā teaches that one who is perfected in yoga sees all beings in the self and the self in all beings (VI.29). That yogin, at all times, sees all beings as the same (*samadarśana*). The ākāśa is the element of harmony, unity and when it is strong we realize we are all one family (*vāsudeva kuṭumbakam*). At the highest level we realize we are all One being with many hands, many eyes, all a part of god. The *Ahirbudhnya Saṁhitā* says that it is the conviction to be kind to all, because all beings are actually the body of god. Ahiṁsa (non-violence) develops naturally from this awareness. Jupiter is the planet of peace and non-violence in body, speech and mind.

Jupiter represents knowledge and the teaching of knowledge (which falls into three categories). The Gītā teaches that knowledge which sees One eternal being (*ekam bhāvam avyayam*) in all beings, the undivided in the divided, is sāttvika knowledge (XVIII.22). The knowledge which separates different beings of various kinds is rājasika. And knowledge which is attached to small actions as if it were all without understanding or without a higher purpose is tāmasika. All these forms of knowledge are needed at some point. A manual to run a device is tamasic knowledge, understanding which customers will buy which products is rājasika knowledge; each is needed at certain times. But the knowledge which one uses to run their life needs to be sāttvika in order to expand one's spirituality. When the sattva of Jupiter is strong within an individual their knowledge will tend towards sattva naturally. When we practice sāttvika knowledge then Jupiter becomes strengthened.

The blockage of the ānukūlya-resolution is *nirākṛti* which is contemptuous or negative attitude to others. *Ākṛis* to bring near, to invite; it is the same root as *ākarṣaṇa* (*ākṛṣ*) which means to bring near, drawing towards one's self, to attract. *Nirākṛ* is to separate, divide, or to reject, refuse, or drive away. Nirākṛti is separating oneself, seeing divisions in the mind, and refusing certain aspects considered different. This could be called non-acceptance of others, or discrimination. The actions that arise from discrimination against one's race, gender, or other material state are negative and cause darkness in the heart.

The Gītā says when one receives the teachings of the wise who perceive the essence of reality (*tattvadarśanas*) then one will see absolutely all beings in the self (*ātmā*) and therefore in the divine (IV.35). In this way, the clear perception of the wise see the supreme being (*adhibhūta*) in everything. With this quality of perception, how can there be discrimination, or murder?

The Gītā says he who sees god everywhere, and sees all things in god, is not lost from god, nor is god lost from him (VI.30). The yogin who is established in oneness (*āsthita-ekatvam*), honors the divine situated in all beings, and therefore dwells in the supreme being whatever action is performed (VI.31).

Venus

Venus is love, compassion, and devotion. Love is something that requires trust, when trust is lost in a relationship then it no longer grows. In the same way, devotion requires a trust in a higher power. Viśvāsa is trust, faith, or confidence in something. The water element is emotion which feels faith and trust. Venus relates to **Mahāviśvāsa** which is a great trust that all is taken care of by a higher power. Lakṣmī Tantra says god's power is easily reached and grace is constantly at hand, always, at all times through this trust.

Everything we have is a blessing. You can lose your eyesight tomorrow, your nervous system could get a degenerative disease and put you in a wheel chair, your closest loved ones can die one day in an accident; disaster and disease are everywhere. Life is delicate, and a properly functioning body is a high blessing that is unrealized until it is lost.

There is a parable of a rich man who believed people only prayed because they wanted things, and because he had money to buy whatever he wanted, he thought he didn't have any need to pray. After suffering a chronic degenerative disorder which crippled him, unable to get a cure, he prayed, asking "why god, why". After a time of great reflection as he was losing his life, his prays were simply thankfulness for having been giving the joy of experiencing life and finding the divine within it.

The Gītā says that by devotion (*bhakti*) to god, one comes to know the immensity and the reality (*tattvatas*) of the Supreme Being. There upon, one enters That, having known the reality of the Supreme (XVIII.55). Mahāviśvāsa is trusting that everything is being moved by a higher power and therefore everything happens as it is supposed to. Such deep felt understanding may not be a cure to every disease, but it gives a fulfilling internal peace. Trusting the divine and appreciating all that is given, opens the heart, to allow the divine into it.

The blockage to mahāviśvāsa is disregard (*upekṣaka*) that one develops by the notion that the results of action (*karma-phala*) are bestowed according to one's self and not granted by the Supreme (*adhidaiva*). Mahāviśvāsa is the understanding that god is the true benefactor of all beings. To think that you are the cause of the good things in your life is a lack of appreciation for the source of where things truly come from. The Gītā teaches the difference between the divine (with light) and the āsurī (without light) paths (XVI). Those who are asura believe that the universe was created without a god and life is just the result of copulation. They are attached to insatiable desires, which lead to the destruction of the natural environment and suffering of other people. They are filled with arrogance, hypocrisy, lust, and have accepted false notions because of delusion (*moha*). Because of this they act without purity, without the radiance of light (*aśuci*).They are filled with anxiety, and seek by unjust means to hoard wealth for the enjoyment of their desires. They believe they have obtained their wealthor their power, as something that is "mine", "earned by me", "me, and me alone". When they give charity, they believe it is their own greatness that is giving. This eventually leads to egotism, pride, desire, envy, indignance, and anger; these types of people come to hate the divine in their own and other's bodies (XVI.17). They cannot be truly happy with themselves, nor do they find deep inner peace that comes with faith and trust.

The Gītā says that there are three types of faith (sattva, rajas, tamas) born of innate nature. Man is made of faith (*śraddhā-maya*), therefore man is whatever faith he has (XVII.3). Faith in the divine is the quality of sattva, therefore those who have faith in a higher power increase sattva within themselves. To have devotion requires loving with no thought of return, to love the divine (*daivam*) just to the love the divine. This giving of the heart without attachment brings deep contentment.

Worship, austerity, or charity done with faith is called sat (true, real), while done without faith is called asat (untrue, without virtue, not in alignment with reality). This type of faith is viśvāsa, to believe in a higher power when religious things are done. Mahāviśvāsa is to have faith in every action, to have trust that all is happening and existing in our life due to the Supreme benefactor. The Gītā teaches that by performing all actions with reliance (*vyapāśraya*) on the Supreme, by grace, one attains the eternal unchanging abode (*śāśvataṁ avyayam padam*)(XVIII.56).

Saturn

Saturn isthe planet of suffering, who relates to the vāyu tattva. The air element creates separation, difference, and a desire to oppose certain proper norms. Saturn is the farmer who doesn't have to wear nice clothing, or the servant who doesn't have all the proper etiquette of the educated.

The other planets are benefics or at least sura grahas, while Saturn is malefic and asura. The spiritual remedy in regard to the other planets is about bringing out their highest attributes, while with Saturn it is about avoiding his attributes. When all of the other elemental planets are placed in the ninth house, they give beneficial results to the spirituality. When Saturn (or Rāhu) is placed in the ninth house it makes one disrespectful to elders and gurus. It makes one disrespect (Saturn) or doubt (Rāhu) the traditions and teachings that have been passed down through the elders and gurus.

When Saturn is associated with Ketu he becomes Yama; the person who fights the rules becomes in charge of keeping them. **Prātikūlya-vivarjana** literally means giving up antagonism. It is about giving up all the antagonism that Saturn has towards the gurus, elders and the teachings of the tradition.It is about giving up antagonism towards god or anything that takes us closer to god.

Saturn disregards śāstra because he is dirty; he rules sin (*pāpa*). To progress in the spiritual path, one needs to use discipline to control one's self and take a more austere path. Therefore one is surrendering the negative personal desires according to the teachings of the elders. Those who are attached to their negative desires hold antagonism to the elders. Sometimes people may even follow the injunctions of scripture but just have hostility because they do not have the surrender, they want to feel like they are in charge. They do not want to be a servant to anyone else, or to bow themselves to another's knowledge.

The scriptures, like the Bhagavad Gītā, talk about what food is sāttvika and what foods should be avoided. These types of non-denominational teachings are given to allow us to live life in harmony. Various living traditions will teach a way of life, which might not agree with everything one desires to do. A spiritual practitioner should examine whether they are not following these practices because of personal desire. There are many old rules that have become socially outdated, and one should be aware of this within their tradition. But disregard for scripture out of laziness or indulgence in personal desire is a blockage. There is also a difference in being devoted to a path, and avoiding certain cultural rules that may not be valid, but being totally devoted to the path, as compared to someone who is adverse to scriptures. There are also individuals who have negativity towards gurus; this can be from a cursed Jupiter or a tamasic ninth house. This negativity is a blockage to them, and to their spiritual unfoldment. Even if they don't take a physical guru, there is no need to hold antagonism towards gurus or elders.

In the Gītā, tāmasika worship is described as devoid of faith, scripture disregarded, food not offered, mantras deficient, and without fee to the priest (XVII.13). All these are qualities of Saturn, the lack of faith, the disrespect for scripture, the improper use of mantra, and being cheap with those who devote themselves to religion or spirituality.

Prātikūlya-vivarjana also relates to giving up antagonism towards others' spirituality. Teachers like Paramhamsa Ramakrishna spent their life proving that all spiritual paths are valid. The nature of antagonism on any level becomes a blockage to seeing god everywhere in everything. Unfortunately, many religious teachers have not removed this from themselves yet are antagonistic either out of blindly following something they were told or out of a base need to protect their own religious beliefs. When one is firm in their belief there is no need to put down other faiths.

The blockage to prātikūlya-vivarjana is *aśāstra-upasevā* which is indulging in actions which are prohibited in the scriptures. The injunctions of śāstra are meant to protect us from creating negative karma (*pāpa*). How can we purify ourselves and get closer to the Supreme if we are constantly polluting ourselves? How can we know the right path if we do not respect the gurus and scripture which contain the things to be done and the things to be avoided?

The Gītā says that one who follows his own desires (*kāmakāratas*) and ignores the knowledge of scriptures does not attain perfection (*siddhi*), nor happiness (*sukha*), nor the highest goal (*paraṁ gatim*). Therefore one should use the teachings of scripture to determine what is to be done and what is not to be done (XVI.23-24).

Conclusion

Ketu is not just the mokṣa kāraka, but also gives intuition. By following the path of surrender (*śaraṇāgati*), we open ourselves up to a higher guidance, a higher knowing, and higher perception. It is this higher perception that allows us to truly help those who come to us for advice. This is also in itself a path to the divine. The *Ahirbudhnya Saṁhitā* gives the analogy of the path of surrender to a passenger who wants to cross a river in a boat. It is the passenger's responsibility to sit in the boat, and then it is the boatman's job to row the boat. The practitioner needs to get in the boat of surrender and then God will take them across the river of illusion to the shore of truth. The practitioner's job is to fully surrender, deeper than just a thought of surrender, but to have that surrender come from the entire body-mind-soul.

Appendix

The Word for Astrologer

The Amarakośa (5th century) lists eight names that were commonly used to refer to an astrologer at that time: sāṁvatsara, jyotiṣika, daivajña, gaṇaka, mauhūrtika, mauhūrta, jñāni, and kārtāntika. The Amarkośa is a collection of synonyms that were commonly used in literature during that time period. The number of names indicates that there were a good number of astrologers and literature about them. The names also reveal the various ways that society perceived astrologers and their function.

Sāṁvatsara is one who knows the saṁvatsara (a Vedic year and later a jovian year). It is a name given to the astrologer since they are the calculators of the calendar; the ones who know the movement of the Sun and Moon, and can calculate when the months and years begin. We take this for granted and just look at a calendar that someone else has prepared, but in ancient times the keeping of a calendar was a process that required an understanding of observational astronomy and advanced mathematics.

Jyotiṣika is the one who practices Jyotiṣa. *Jyoti* means light, but in Sanskrit there are many words for light. For example, *prabhā* means light as that which is shining forth and illuminating. *Dīpti* means light, but generally refers to that made from the fire or from a lamp. *Prakāśa* means light, but is a very strong word that indicates that is bright (not soft like the morning light- prabhā). There are many more words for the various types of light. Jyoti is the light as the source of life (it has a heavenly-soul connotation). The plural of Jyoti refers to the light of the stars and the planets which are lights in the sky. Jyoti with *śa* suffix becomes cerebral *ṣa* because of the vowel *i* in jyoti, thereby becoming Jyotiṣa which means "that which pertains to the light, or that which pertains to the stars and planets".

It is common to use the term Jyotiṣī for an astrologer. Also there is the term Jyotirvid, one who knows (*vid*) about the planets and stars. The *Yukti-kalpa-taru* says that a Jyotiṣika is one who knows the body parts, is an expert speaker at the meetings, comes from a tradition (*kulakrama*), is pure (*śuddha*) and should be appointed by the king. This clearly indicates that there were lineages of astrology in ancient India, and that it was standard for astrologers to interact in politics.

Gaṇaka literally means a counter or one who reckons. It is a name for an arithmetician, as well as someone who calculates horoscopes. A gaṇaka has been defines as one who counts the subha and asubha graha phalam, or the one who calculates the good and bad results of the planets. Gaṇaka also has the meaning of a particular caste which is from a brahmin father and a vaiśya mother, who were a caste of astrologers (those who made their livelihood through the nakṣatra). They are often grouped with the vaidya caste, which was a caste of doctors. Some texts criticize these two castes as impure because the vaidya physically touches people and all their various parts and exudations, while the astrologer is consulted by all castes of people, thereby coming into contact with those considered impure by certain Brahmin belief systems. It is because of this that even Manu Smṛti says that vaidyas and gaṇakas are inauspicious.

Mauhūrtika literally means one who makes muhūrta, or one who knows the moments/ spaces of time and indicates them. Mauhūrta is one who choses Muhūrta. The Mahābhārata defines a Mauhūrtika as one who is *daivachintaka;* who thinks about or is familiar with fate/destiny (*daiva*). The Bhagavata Purāṇa (6.6.9), says the Mauhūrtikas were a group of gods born from Muhūrtā and Yamarāja. In this way, the 30 muhūrtas of the day were seen as children born from Muhūrtā the daughter of Dakṣa. Their job was to deliver to living beings the results born at the proper time (*svakāla*). An astrologer was supposed to know all 30 muhūrtas, their gods, and the positive and negative results related to each.

Vipraśnakā is also a name for astrologers. It is defined as one who can see the answer, one who gives decisions, or an expert. Sometimes it is even translated as a fortune-teller.

Jñāni literally means the one who knows, but it is a word that directly means an astrologer or a fortune-teller, since they are the ones who know what has been, what is, and what will come to be. The practice of astrology (or seeing the past, present and future) is called jñānatva which literally means knowing-ness. An astrologer is also called a trikālajñā, or one who knows the three times. It also has the connotation of one who is omniscient, where it is also used as trikāladarśin (one who sees past, present and future). There are various tantric sādhanās that are performed to gain trikālajñā siddhi.

Kārtāntika is the one who knows the time of your death. Antaka is a name of Yama, since it means 'causing an end', or death. The one who can calculate the time of your death, who knows when Yama will come is called kārtāntika. This shows that calculating the longevity of an individual was an ancient practice done by astrologers, and one which was standard. This is why texts like the Jaimini Upadeśa Sūtras put so much emphasis on longevity calculations; an astrologer was expected to be able to calculate the longevity, so one could plan life accordingly.

Daivajña is one who knows the destiny (*daiva*). Daiva can have many connotations and is beautiful to understand deeply. The most literal translation of daiva is 'belonging to the gods (*devas*)', or 'coming from the gods (*devas*)'. That which comes from the devas is divine will, or destiny. All the various gods and goddesses exist among the planets and stars. Nīca Jupiter is Tārā, Jupiter-Venus is Lakṣmī-Nārāyaṇa, Saturn-Venus is the nature spirits (*yakṣas*). All archetypes that manifest as gods are found among the primal archetypes of reality which are the planets (interacting with the stars). That which is coming from the planets and stars is the map of our life, which is translated into the western concept of 'destiny'. We know that the will of the planets is the creation (or reflection) of our own actions (*karma*), which the word destiny does not *culturally* denote.

The word destiny comes from the Latin *destinare*, which means to determine, appoint, and make firm. It means to completely (de-) become stationed (stinare), as a destination- the firm place where you are going. The birth chart is the map of where we are going.

The position of the planets, which unfolds reality, is that which is coming from the devas (our planetary positions). In the Vedic paradigm, god is not someone or something that is out there different then ourselves. God is in us, we are made of god-goddess which is in everything everywhere as the very fabric of reality. Daiva is the will of the gods, the indications of the planets that a person will receive in life. In this way, the daivajña knows the results of your birth chart, what has been destined (determined) to happen. The daivajña knows the desires of the gods, knows which gods each planet is manifesting as. The daivajña knows what those devas want and how to appease them. This is a very high name for an astrologer and that is why Jyotiṣa is the shining eye (*nirmala-cakṣu*) of the Vedas.

Daiva-lekhaka is another name for an astrologer. Lekhana means to write, and a lekhaka is a writer (scribe). In this way, Daivalekhaka is one who writes the horoscopes, and writes about one's past and future (*daiva*). It is still found in many parts of India, where people have little books that were prepared at the time they were born, containing their birth charts, vargas, and predictions about their life. Lekha means a written document *and* it is also a classical name for devas. In Upaniṣad times, the devas names were written (yantras) and worshipped, therefore gods became synonymous with the written name/ yantra. The letters were also considered mātrikās (mother-goddesses) who manifested sounds and meaning and therefore conveyed reality and shared consciousness between people. In this way, the astrologer was able to communicate the will of the devas (destiny) to people.

Old school Western scholars sometimes say that Jyotiṣa as a Vedāṅga was done *only* to calculate when to do rituals (*yajña*). This is because the oldest astrological text, *Vedāṅga Jyotiṣam*, that has survived to the present is a text that says it is specifically for calendrical calculations (*kālavidhāna śāstra*) so that ritual may be done at the proper time.[2] It only teaches about the calendar and how to calculate it, that was its direct purpose. You don't write about the practical use of physics calculations if you are trying to make a short calculus text book that is easy to memorize. The Vedāṅga Jyotiṣam was written so poetically you can chant it like a morning prayer, and it is not too long, this is what allowed it to survive so long.

In the section on the Javādi Nakṣatra arrangement, the stars are arranged out of order and have only one syllable to denote them. Āsvayuja (Āsvini) is called *jau* (last syllable), while Chitrā is called *Chi* (first syllable). This strange system was used to denote when

2 Ṛṣi Lagadha says that the Vedas are created for ritual and ritual must be done at the right time. *Kālavidhāna śāstra* is the way to calculate the correct time. Therefore the one who knows Jyotiṣa is the one who knows ritual. (Vedāṅga Jyotiṣam I.3)

a fortnight began which part of the nakṣatra the Moon would be in. And the order was based upon the irregular motion during a five year yuga period. This is an extremely advanced notation to give something that was only the name of a month.

If there were no astrological meaning ascribed to those time periods then why should there be rituals done then, and for what purpose? In the Vedic culture, the Sun had deep meaning, the wheel had metaphorical meaning, and even the spoon had spiritual meaning. To think that huge expanses of the sky, advanced calculations of their moving lights, and their respective time periods only developed some meaning thousands of years later would be quite unlikely.

David Pingree, a famous scholar, believes that astrology as we know it was introduced into India around 190 A.D. through a single book called the Yavanajātaka. It is illogical to believe that one book in the 3rd century, with no printing presses, would have created enough astrologers for the Amarakośa to give eight names commonly used in literature in the 5th century, with the meanings that they have. Just because Pingree found a Greek text translated into Sanskrit from that time period does not give his theory logic. It is ignoring many facts of terminology found in the culture at that time, as well as astrological references made in stories previous to that time period.

The stars had meaning from the beginning, and the science of calculations wrapped itself around this. Yajña was done according to the astrological indications that affected the person, their life and the whole community. When we look at the definition of a Mauhūrtika as one who is *daiva-chintaka* then it is clear that ancient astrologers did more than just pick an auspicious moment. Jyotiṣa was a branch of the Vedas used for finding auspicious times as well as the entire range of predictions we are aware of today.

References

Aaboe, A., Britton, J.P., Henderson, J.A., Neugebauer, O., Sachs, A.J. *Saros Cycle Dates and Related Babylonian Astronomical Texts.*Transactions of the American Philosophical Society, Volume 81, Part 6, 1991.

Abhyankar, K.D. *Eclipse Period 3339 in Ṛgveda- In Support of R.N. Iyengar's Thesis.* Historical Notes, Indian Journal of History of Science, 41.3, p. 313-315, 2006.

Achar, B. N. Narahari. *A Note on The Five-Year Yuga of the Vedāṅga Jyotiṣa.* Electronic Journal of Vedic Studies, Vol.3 (1997), issue 4 (December), pp.21–28.

Achar, B.N. Narahari. *On the Meaning of AV XIX.53.3: Measurement of Time?*Electronic Journal of Vedic Studies,Vol. 4 (1998), issue 2 (December), http://www.ejvs.laurasianacademy.com.

Achar, B.N. Narahari. *Searching for Nakṣatras in the Ṛgveda.* Electronic Journal of Vedic Studies Vol. 6 (2000), issue 2 (December), http://www.ejvs.laurasianacademy.com.

Aiyangar, Pandit M. Duraiswami, and Venugopalacharya, Pandit T. ŚrīPāñcarātrarakṣā of ŚrīVedāntaDeśika. The Adyar Library and Research Centre, Madras, India, 1996.

Apte, Dr. P. P. (edited). *PauṣkaraSaṁhitā.* Rashtriya Sanskrit Vidyapeetha, Tirupati Series No.54, Tirupati, India, 1991.

Ashmand, J.M. (translator). *Claudius Ptolemy: Tetrabiblos.* Public Domain. Davis and Dickson, London, 1822.

Bannerji, Nimai. *Scaling Human Lives: Astro-Tantra-Yoga-Approach.* Maa Parameswari Publications, Cuttack, 2001.

Beck, Guy, L. *Sonic Theology: Hinduism and Sacred Sound.* MotilalBanarsidass Publishers, Delhi, 1993.

Bharatiya Vidya Bhavan's Swami Prakashananda Ayurveda Research Centre, Mumbai, 2003.

Bhatt, Dr. S. R. *The Philosophy of Pāñcarātra, AnAdvaitic Approach.* Ganesh and Company Private Ltd., Madras, India, 1968.

Chamberlain, Ph.D., David B. *The Fetal Senses: A Classical View*, Life Before Birth, www.birthpsychology.com, retrieval September 27, 2008

Chand, Devi, trans. *The Atharvaveda.* Munshiram Manoharlal Publishers Pvt Ltd, New Delhi, 2002.

Chattopadhya, Aparna. Studies in the Caraka Samhita. Banaras Hindu University, Varanasi, 1995

Chauhan, D. V. *Understanding Ṛgveda.* Bhandarkar Oriental Series No.20.Bhandarkar Oriental Research Institute, Poona, India, 1985.

Das , Gauranga. "Special Ascendants in Jyotish, Part 1". *Jyotish News.* Shri Jagannath Vedic Center, New Delhi, February 2001.

Das, Rahul Peter. *The Origin of the Life of a Human Being: Conception and the Female According to Ancient Indian Medical and Sexological Literature.* MotilalBanasidass Publishers, Delhi, 2003.

Dash, Vaidya Bhagwan and Kashyap, Vaidya Lalitesh. *Basic Principles of Āyurveda Based on the Āyurveda Saukhyaṁ of Toḍarānanda, TASS-2*. Concept Publishing Company, New Delhi, 2003.

Deshpande, Maitreyee. *The Concept of Time in Vedic Ritual*. New Bharatiya Book Corporation, Delhi, India, 2001, ISBN 81-87418-29-X.

DeVore, Nicholas. *Encyclopedia of Astrology*. Astrology Center of America, New York, 2005.

Dyczkowski, Mark S.G. *A Journey in the World of the Tantras*. Indica Books, Varanasi, India, 2004.

Dyczkowski, Mark. *Manthānabhairavatantram: Kumārikākhaṇḍaḥ*. Introduction, vol. 1, Indira Gandhi National Centre for the Arts, New Delhi, 2009.

Einstein, Albert. "What must be an essential feature of any future fundamental physics?" Letter to Max Born (March 1948); published in *Albert Einstein-Hedwig und Max Born* (1969) "Briefwechsel 1916-55".http://en.wikiquote.org/wiki/Albert_Einstein.

Fergusson, James. *Tree and Serpent Worship or Illustrations of Mythology and Art in India: From the Topes at Sanchi and Amravati*. Indian Museum, London, 1873. Reprint: Asian Educational Services, New Delhi, 2004.

Gaskin, Ina May. *Ina May's Guide to Childbirth*. Bantam Books, New York, New York, 2003.

Gaskin, Ina May. *Spiritual Midwifery (fourth edition)*. Book Publishing Company, Summertown, TN, 2002.

Gautam V, Dhingra MS, Gautam SP. FoetalDevelopment In-Utero: Modern Medical Knowledge or a Vedic Mystery? *The Internet Journal of Biological Anthropology*, 2007, Volume 1, Number 1.

Gupta, Sanjukta. *LakṣmīTantra, APāñcharātra Text*. MotilalBanarsidass Publishers, Delhi, 2003.

Hand, Rob. *Whole Sign Houses: The Oldest House System*, ARHAT Publications, 2000.

Harper, David. *A Brief History of the Calendar*.Kernow Plusfile Ltd., Cambridge, England, 2000.

Hawking, Stephan.*The Grand Design*.Bantam, New York, September, 2010.

Heinrisch Zimmer, *Myths and Symbols in Indian Art and Civilization*. Bollingen Series, Princeton University Press, 1972.

Hill, Stephan and Harrison, Peter.*Dhātu-Pāṭha: The Roots of Language (The foundations of the Indo-European verbal system)*. Munshiram Manoharlal Publishers Pvt. Ltd. New Delhi, 1991.

Hinze, Oscar Marcel. *Tantra Vidyā*. Motilal Banarsidass Publishers, Delhi, 1997.

Holden, James. *Ancient House Division*, Journal of Research of the American Federation of Astrologers 1 (1982), pgs. 19-28.

http://en.wikipedia.org/wiki/Dark_energy

http://en.wikipedia.org/wiki/Sarpa_Kavu

http://www.ibiblio.org/sripedia/cgi-bin/kbase/Pancaratra/Prapatti

http://www.mahabharataonline.com/translation/mahabharata_12c013.php

http://www.mahabharataonline.com/translation/mahabharata_12c020.php

Hu, Wanchung. *The Universal Frame Dragging Force (Spinity) and Maxwell-like Equations.* Post Doc Fellow, Academia Sinica, Taipei, Taiwan.

Hume, Robert Ernest. *The Thirteen Principal Upanishads.* Oxford University Press, 1921.

International Standard Bible Encyclopedia, ALMS; ALMSGIVING. http://bibleencyclopedia.com/alms.htm.

Iyengar, B.K.S. *Light on Yoga.* Schocken Books, New York, 1979.

Iyengar, R.N. *Connection Between Vedāṅga Jyotiṣa and other Vedic Literature.* Indian Journal of History of Science, 44.3, p.357-368, 2009.

Iyengar, R.N. *Dhruva the Ancient Indian Pole Star: Fixity, Rotation and Movement.* Raja Ramanna Fellow, Jain University, Jakkasandra.

Iyengar, R.N. *Eclipse Period Number 3339 In The Ṛgveda.* Indian Journal of Histroy and Science, 40.2, p.139-152, 2005.

Jaggi, O.P. *Indian Astronomy and Mathematics.* History of Science, Technology and Medicine in India, Volume 6. Atma Ram & Sons, Delhi, 1993.

Jennings, Hargrave.*Ophiolatreia: An Account of the Rites and Mysteries Connected with the Origin, Rise, and Development of Serpent Worship in Various Parts of the World, Enriched with Interesting Traditions, and a Full Description of the Celebrated Serpent Mounds and Temples, the Whole Forming an Exposition of One of the Phases of Phallic, or Sex Worship.* London, 1889.

Johnson, Willard. *Poetry and Specualtion of the Ṛg Veda.* ISBN 0-520-02560-1, University of California Press, Berkeley, 1980.

Jowett, Benjamin (translator). *Timaeus.* The Project Gutenberg EBook of Timaeus by Plato, www.gutenberg.org, [EBook #1572], September 15, 2008.

Kak, Subhash. *Astronomical code of Ṛgveda.* Aditya Prakashan, New Delhi, 1994.

Keith, A.B., Macdonell, A.A. *Vedic Index of Names and Subjects, Volume I.* Motilal Banarsidass Publishers Private Limited, Delhi 2007. ISBN 978-81-208-1332-8.

Krishnamacharya, Pandit V. (edited). *Ahirbudhnya-Saṁhitā of the Pāṇcarātrāgama* (vol I and II). The Adyar Library and Research Centre, Madras, India, 1986.

Krishnamacharya, Pandit V. (edited).*Lakṣmī Tantra, A Pāñcarātra Āgama.* The Adyar Library and Research Centre, Madras, India, 1959.

Krythe, M. R. *All About Months.* New York: Harper & Row, 1966.

Lad, Vasant. *Textbook of Ayurveda: Fundamental Principles.* The Ayurvedic Press, Albuquerque, New Mexico, 2002.

Lang, K. R. *Astrophysical Data: Planets and Stars.* New York: Springer-Verlag, p. 17, 1992.

Larsen, Visti. *Kāraka Kendrādi Graha Dasa: The Progress of the Soul.* Sri Jagannath Center, 2004.

Larsen, Visti. *Mūla Dasa- The Timing of Blessings and Curses.* Śrī Jagannath Center, London Conference, 2004.

Larsen, Visti. *Naisargika Daśā*: lecture 50. www.srigaruda.com.

Larsen, Visti. *Sri Lagna and Su-Dasa Calculation*, Śrī Jagannath Center.

Lecanuet and Schaal. *Sensory performances in the human fetus: a brief summary of research.* Intellectica, pp. 29-56, 2002/1, 34.

Letter to high school student Barbara Lee Wilson (7 January 1943), Einstein Archives 42-606. http://en.wikiquote.org/wiki/Albert_Einstein.

Matsubara, M. *Pāñcarātra Saṁhitās and Early Vaiṣṇava Theology*. Motilal Banarsidass Publishers, Delhi, 1994.

Miller, Barbara Stoler, trans. *The Hermit and the Love-Thief: Sanskrit Poems of Bhartrihari and Bilhaṇa.* Columbia University Press, New York, 1978.

Mishra, Dr. Suresh Chandra. *Vedanga Jyotisham: Akhilananda Bhashyopetam.* Ranjan Publications, New Delhi, 2005.

Mishra, Prof. Dr. Yogesh Chandra. *Padārtha Vijñāna: Basic Principles of Ayurveda.* Chaukambha Sanskrit Sansthan, Varanasi, 2009.

Monnier-Williams, M. *Sanskrit English Dictionary.* MunshiramManoharlal Publishers Pvt. Ltd., New Delhi, 2002.

Mukherji, Ramaranjan, editor, Thakur, Anantalal, editor, Bhattacharya, Sukumar, editor, Bhattacharya, Dipak, editor. *Traividyam: Vedic Studies In Memory of Durgamohan Bhattacharyya.* Subarnarekha, Kolkata, 2001.

Muller, Max, and Eggeling, Julius, *The Satapatha- Brahmana*, Part-V, Sacred Books of the East Vol. XLIV, XLIII, Low Price Publications, Delhi, 1996.

Narasimhacharyulu. *Padārtha Vijñāna.* Krishnadas Ayurveda Series 101, Chowkhambha Krshnadas Academy, Varanasi, 2004.

Neevel, Walter G. Jr. *Yāmuna'sVedānta and Pāñcarātra: Integrating the Classical and the Popular.* Harvard Dissertations in religion 10, Scholars Press for Harvard Theological Review, University of Montana, Missoula, Montana, 1977.

Neugebauer, O. and Van Hoesen, *H.B. Greek Horoscopes.*The American Philosphical Society, Independence Square, Philadelphia, 1959.

Nolle, Richard. *The Jupiter-Saturn Conjunction* (Geocentric Tropical Zodiac) 600 BCE to 2400 CE. www.astropro.com, 1998.

Pande, G. C. *Foundations of Indian Culture: Spiritual Vision and Symbolic Forms in Ancient India.* MotilalBanarsidass Publishers, Delhi, 1990.

Particle Physics and Astronomy Research Council.*The Metonic Cycle and the Saros,* Information Leaflet No. 5. Information Services Department of the Royal Greenwich Observatory. 1996.

Pillai, Dewan Bahadur L. D. Swamikannu. *Indian Chronology: A practical Guide to the Interpretation and Verification of Tithis, Nakshatras, Horoscopes and other Indian Time-Records B.C. 1 to A.D. 2000.* Reprint by Asian Edicational Services, New Delhi 1982.

Pingree, David. From *Astral Omens to Astrology From Babylon to Bīkāner*. Serie Orientale Roma LXXVII, Istituto Italiano Per L'Africa E L'Oriente, Roma, 1997.

Pingree, David. *The Yavanajātaka of Sphujidhvaja.*Volume II.Harvard University Press, Cambridge, Massachusetts, 1978.

Poddar, Sarajit. *Narayana Dasa*. SJC Singapore.

Poddar, Sarajit. *Natural Years of Fructification*. SJC Document.

Podder, Sarajit. *Aprakash Grahas, Upagrahas, and Pranapada*. Śrī Jagannath Center.

Podder, Sarajit. *Brahma & Maheswara in Ayur Jyotisha*. self-published PDF.

Podder, Sarajit.*Brahma Dasa*, self-published PDF.

Prabhakaran, Sanjay, *Venus Eclipse on 8 June 2004*. Self-published online PDF, 2004.

Radhakrishnan, S. *The Brahma Sūtra: The Philosophy of Spiritual Life*. Greenwoood Press Publishers, New York, 1968.

Ramakrishnan, S. General Editor. *Ayurvedicand Allopathic Medicine and Mental Health: Proceedings of Indo-US workshop on Traditional Medicine and Mental Health*. Bharatiya Vidya Bhavan's Swami Prakashananda Ayurveda Research Centre, Mumbai, 2003.

Raman, B.V. trans. *Prasna Marga*. Motilal Banarsidass Publishers, New Delhi, 1991.

Raman, S.K. Satya-*Jatakam of Sage Satyacharya: Treatise on Horoscopy based on the Principles of SatyaSaṁhita*. Ranjan Publications, New Delhi, 1979.

Rao, B. Suyanarain. *Varaha Mihira's Brihat Jataka*. Motilal Banarsidass Publishers Private Limited, Delhi, 2001.

Rao, Dr. Namburi Hanumantha. *Pañcabhūta Theory: A Study of the Pañcabhūtas at Molecular Level*. Chowkhamba Krishnadas Academy, Varanasi, 2003.

Rao, Dr. Pedaprolu Srinivasa. Manas: *Psychiatry of Ayurveda*. Chowkhamba Sanskrit Series Office, Varanasi, 2007.

Rao, Dr. Rallapalli Venkateswara. *The Concept of Time in Ancient India*. Bharatiya Kala Prakashan, New Delhi. 2003. ISBN 81-8090-032-0.

Rao, Narasimha. *Sudasa Calculation and Interpretation*. Lesson 15, Śrī Jagannath Vedic Center, 2001.

Rao, S.K. Ramachandra. *The Āgama Encyclopedia: Pāñcharātrāgama*. Volume IV, Sri Satguru Publications, Delhi, India, 2005.

Rao, Suryanarain B. *Varaha Mihira's Brihat Jataka*. Motilal Banarsidass Publishers, Delhi, 2005.

Rath, Sanjay, editor. *Varga Chakra*. "Kaulaka (Shastamsa)" by Goel, G.K. Vyankatesa Sharma Varga Workshop, Sagar Publications, New Delhi, 2002.

Rath, Sanjay. [SJVC] *Question on birth time*, sjvc@yahoogroups.com, 23 February, 2002.

Rath, Sanjay. *2004 Presidential Elections.* Lecturegiven in New York, 2004.

Rath, Sanjay. *Collected Papers in Vedic Astrology.*Volume I. Sagittarius Publications, New Delhi, 2006.

Rath, Sanjay. *Foundation of Vedic Astrology.* Presented in the SJC West Coast Conference, California, 2003.

Rath, Sanjay. *Horā Lagna.* Śrī Jagannath Center, Europe Conference, London, 8 August, 2004.

Rath, Sanjay. *Jaimini Maharishi's Upadesa Sutras.* Sagar Publications, New Delhi, 2002.

Rath, Sanjay. *Moola Dasa: Lagna Kendradi Graha Dasa.* Śri Jagannath Center, Lesson #10, 1999.

Rath, Sanjay. *Moola Dasa: Lagna Kendradi Graha Dasa.* Sri Jagannath Center, Handout, 2001.

Rath, Sanjay. *Naisargika Dasa.* Tenth International Symposium on Vedic Astrology, Sedona, AZ, November 16, 2003.

Rath, Sanjay. *Narayana Dasa.* Sagar Publications, New Delhi, India, 2001.

Rath, Sanjay. *Opening Lecture.*Vyasa Śri Jagannath Center, www.vyasasjc.org, 2005.

Rath, Sanjay. *The Hindu Calendar.* Jyotish News, Sri Jagannath Vedic Center, New Delhi, October 2001.

Rath, Sanjay. *Vedic Remedies for Curses.* Śrī Jagannath Center, Serbia Conference, 2004.

Rath, Sanjay. *Vedic Remedies in Astrology.* Sagar Publications, New Delhi, 2000.

Revel, A., Safran, A., Laufer, N., Lewin, A., Reubinov, B.E., and Simon, A. Human Reproduction, *Twin delivery following 12years of human embryo cryopreservation: Case report.*Vol. 19, No. 2, 328-329, February 2004.

Santhanam, R. *Essentials of Predictive Hindu Astrology.* Sagar Publications, New Delhi, 2003.

Santhanam, R. *Horasara by Prithuyasa Son of Varahamihira.* Ranjan Publications, New Delhi, 1995.

Santhanam, R. *Saravali of KalyanVarma.* Ranjan Publications, New Delhi, 2005.

Sareen, S.S. *JatakaDeshMarga.* Sagar Publications, New Delhi, 1992.

Sargeant, Winthrop. *The Bhagavad-Gītā.* State University of New York Press, Albany, 1984.

Sarma, Pandit K. Ramachandra (edited).*Pauṣkarāgama.* The Adyar Library and Research Centre. Madras, India, 1995.

Sastri, P.S. *UttaraKalamrita of Kalidasa.* Ranjan Publications, New Delhi, 2001.

Sastri, V. *VaidyanathaDixita'sJatakaParijata.* Vol.I, Ranjan Publications, New Delhi, 2004.

Schrader, F. Otto. *Introduction to the Pāñcarātra and the AhirbudhnyaSaṁhitā.* The Adyar Library and Research Centre, Madras, 1995.

Seidenberg, A. *The Origin of Mathematics.* Archive for History of Exact Sciences,Vol. 18, p.301-342, 1978.

Sewell, Robert, and Dikshit, Sankara Balakrishna. *The Indian Calendar.* Motilal Banarsidass Publishers, Delhi, 1996. ISBN 81-208-1207-1

Sharma, G.C. *BrihatParasaraHoraShastra.* Vol.I, Sagar Publications, New Delhi, 1995.

Sharma, P.V. *Suśruta-Saṁhitā.* Vol. II, Haridas Ayurveda Series, ChaukhambhaVisvabharati Oriental Publishers and Distributors, Varanasi, India, 2005.

Sharma, Priya Vrat, trans. *Essentials of Āyurveda: Ṣoḍaśāṅgahṛdayam.* Motilal Banarsidass Publishers Private Limited, Delhi, 1998.

Sharma, Prof. Rammurti. *Cosmology in the Vedas.* ISBN 81-7081-324-7 Dharam Hinduja International Centre of Indic Research, Nag Publishers, Delhi, India, 1995

Sharma, R.K. and Bhagwan Dash.*Caraka Saṁhitā.* Vol.II, Chowkhamba Sanskrit Series Office, Varanasi, 1998.

Sharma, R.K., Bhagawan Dash, trans. *Caraka Saṁhitā.* Chowkhamba Sanskrit Series Office, Varanasi, 2005.

Siddhantashastree, Rabindra Kumar. *VaiṣṇavismThrough the Ages.* MunshiramManoharlal Publishers Pvt. Ltd., New Delhi, 1985.

Sihna, Nandalal (translator). *The Samkhya Philosophy.* Munshiram Manoharlal Publishers, New Delhi, India, 2003.

Singh, Prof.Satya Prakash. *Life and Vision of Vedic Seers: 2 Dīrghatamas.* Standard Publishers, New Delhi, India, 2006.

Sivananda, Swami. *Mind- Its mysteries and Control.* The Divine Life Society, Shivanandanagar, 2001.

SJC West Coast Conference, Ukiah, 2002.

Sutton, Nicholas. *Religious Doctrines in the Mahābhārata.*Motilal Banarsidass Publishers, Delhi, 2000.

Tewari, P.V. *ĀyurvedīyaPrasūti-TantraEvaṁStrī-Roga.* ChaukambhaOrientalia, Varanasi, 1999.

Tewari, P.V. *Kāśyapa-Saṁhitā or VṛddhajīvakīyaTantra.*ChaukhambhaVisvabharati, Varanasi, 2002.

Thatte, D. G. *Suśruṭa-Saṁhitā.* Vol.III, Śārīrasthānam, Chaukambha Sanskrit Bhawan, Varanasi, 1994.

The Apocrypha. Oxford University Press, Inc., New York, NY. 2009.

The Holy Bible, English Standard Version (ESV).Crossway Bibles, a publishing ministry of Good News Publishers, 2001.

Thite, H.K. *Gunakar'sHoraMakarand.*Sagar Publications, New Delhi.

Usha, and Shashi, and Goel, G.K. *BrihatJataka of Varahamihira.* Sagar Publications, New Delhi,

2004.

Vahia, M.N. and Yadav, Nisha. *Origin and Growth of Astronomy in Indian Context*. Tata Institute of Fundamental Research, Centre for Basic Sciences, Mumbai, India, 2008.

Valiathan, M. S. *The Legacy of Caraka*. Orient Longman Private Limited, Hyderabad, 2007.

Varadachari, K. C. *Viśiṣṭādvaita and its Development*.Chakravarthy Publications, Tirupati, India, 1969.

Varadachari, V. and Tripathi, G.C. *Īśvarasaṁhitā:* Critically edited and translated in Five Volumes, Vol.I, Intoduction. Indira Gandhi National Centre For The Arts and MotilalBanarsidass Publishers PVT. LTD., Delhi, 2009.

Vatsyayan, Kapila, ed. *Concepts of Time: Ancient and Modern*. Indira Gandhi National Centre for the Arts, Sterling Publishers Private Limited, New Delhi, 1996.

Venkateswaran T. V.*Chinthamani Ragoonathachary and Secularisation of Time During the Late Nineteenth Century Madras Presidency*. Proceedings of epiSTEME 3, *P. 25-32*.Vigyan Prasar, New Delhi, India.

Wilson, H. H. and Bhāṣya of Sāyaṇācārya. *Ṛgveda Saṁhitā*. Parimal Publications, Delhi, 2001.

Wilson, H.H. *Śrī Viṣṇupurāṇam: Sanskrit Text and English Translation*. Parimal Publications, Delhi, 2002.

Witzel, Michael. *The Pleiades and the Bears viewed from Inside the Vedic Texts*. Journal of Vedic StudiesVol. 5 (1999), issue 2 (December).

www.babycenter.com, *Pregnancy Calendar*, retrieval September 27, 2008.

About the Author

Freedom Cole is a teacher of Vedic Astrology, Yoga and the Vedic Sciences. He teaches with the traditional usage of Sanskrit, meditation, mantra through modern technology. He teaches traditional Vedic Astrology in a practical way which is useful in the modern world.

Freedom was born into a family that practices yoga and has been teaching yoga and meditation since he was a teenager. He has studied with various teachers and is initiated by Paramhamsa Hariharananda Giri of Puri in the tradition of Kriya yoga. He has a BA in Psychology from the University of Massachusetts. He has studied Āyurveda with the New England Institute of Āyurvedic Medicine, the International Academy of Āyurveda and mentored with various doctors in India.

Freedom studied with various astrology teachers in the US and India until meeting Paramguru Pandit Sanjay Rath in 2001. He has lived for extended periods in India studying with his Jyotiṣa Guru in in Delhi, Bhubaneshwar, Puri and the Kamoan Himalayas. He was given the dikṣa of the sacred thread by his Sanskrit Guru Vāgīśa Śāstrī of Vārāṇasī and was given his Vaiṣṇava dikṣa by Baba Balia of Orissa.

Freedom is dedicated that people have access to true Vedic knowledge within a modern context. He focuses on using this knowledge to free the mind and give a universal perspective. His personal website is www.shrifreedom.org.

Educational classes that go along with Science of Light are available at www.ScienceOfLight.net.

Science of Light

17491984R00254

Made in the USA
Charleston, SC
13 February 2013